OPTIMIZED
LEARNING

180 MINI-LESSONS
THAT TRANSFORM TODAY'S STUDENTS INTO
CONFIDENT, CAPABLE & COLLABORATIVE,
SELF-DIRECTED LEARNERS

Created by **PAUL SOLARZ**
Author of *Learn Like a PIRATE*

Published by EduPioneers, an imprint of
Dave Burgess Consulting, Inc.

EduPioneers: www.PaulSolarz.com
DBC Inc.: www.DaveBurgessConsulting.com

Cover Design: Paul Solarz
Production: Paul Solarz
Proofreading: Paul Solarz

Library of Congress Control Number: 2024935207
Paperback ISBN: 978-1-956306-75-0

First printing: April 2024

OPTIMIZE THE WAY YOUR STUDENTS LEARN!

Congratulations on purchasing your guidebook to transforming your students into effective, efficient, collaborative learners who put forth strong effort, stay focused on tasks, get along with their peers, and are motivated to learn!

If this sounds too good to be true, give it a minute. Read through the Introduction chapter to discover WHY this collection of mini-lessons has been developed, HOW these mini-lessons can work collectively to empower students to become the strongest learners they can become, and HOW you can implement these skills into your classroom by following a simple, repeatable lesson format.

Since the structure of this book can be a little confusing at first, I've recorded a video that will help clarify the Introduction Chapter for you.

It would be most beneficial if you follow along in the book while I provide information. Pause the video whenever you want to write notes. You might even consider using sticky notes. Once you understand the information in this video, the rest is a cinch! Be patient with yourself, because your efforts will be rewarded!

Optimized Learning Introduction Video

bit.ly/43zp7Px

Since I am SURE that there are mistakes in this book and things that I've forgotten, I've included a QR Code and short link on the right that will take you to a Google Doc that will fill you in on any important notes that I have for you now that this book has been printed and distributed.

I won't waste your time on typos and minor editing mistakes, but rather include answers to important questions you have, confusing components that I can clarify or re-think, and ideas that you've given me for improving this process!

Part of being an OPTIMIZED LEARNER is being flexible and prepared for change, so I'm trying to model that for you here.

What big mistakes are in the book?

bit.ly/43r6u01

(All short links are Case Sensitive, which means capital letters & lower case letters matter.)

THE OPTIMIZED LEARNING TOP 10 LIST

Video
bit.ly/3PG1KhL

1 *Optimized Learning* will only work if you WANT to develop your students into self-directed learners and believe that the lessons within this book are part of the plan for doing this.

2 Encourage self-direction by stepping back from the front of the classroom and promoting collaborative work among students. If you're not thinking for them, they have to step up!

3 When students work collaboratively, partner them up randomly rather than giving them their choice of who they work with. This builds relationships among all students.

4 When students come to you with questions, ask them to first check in with their partner, then a different partnership, and only then you, unless it's a question that only you can answer.

5 Familiarize yourself with the mini-lessons in the book right away, so when your class needs a specific lesson, you can teach it as it is needed! Authentic purpose makes a big impact!

6 If your students only need an explanation of a microskill and don't need to do the activities, change the mini-lesson into a class discussion, and then assess whether that was effective.

7 Instead of skipping mini-lessons due to time, consider adapting the mini-lessons (i.e. combining similar ones, shortening longer ones, or turning some mini-lessons into class discussions).

8 Rather than skipping mini-lessons in the first several Instructional Spirals, consider completing all of them, but skip Instructional Spiral #7 (and maybe even #6) in its entirety.

9 If you've decided not to follow the suggested pacing in the Instructional Spirals and see that your students are confused, teach the mini-lessons in Instructional Spiral #1. They will help!

10 Students should complete the steps in the Student-Led Self-Improvement Process while working on Bulky Tasks, but not necessarily during lectures or simple or repetitive activities.

Credits

A.I. Editors
Poe ChatGPT 3.5-turbo
Google Gemini (& Bard)
Microsoft Bing Co-Pilot
MindPal.AI

Artwork
Google Gemini (& Bard)
Microsoft Bing CoPilot
Poe Playground v2.0
Pixabay.com
Creative Commons

Author
Paul Solarz

Short Links
bitly.com

QR Codes
qrcodegeneratorhub.com

Production Assistants
Ashley Pappas
Tyler Pappas

Editor
Sandra Solarz

Clarity Consultant
Amy Pappas

Production & Design Tool
Canva

Dedication

To all the teachers who are working tirelessly to make
a meaningful difference in the lives of their students.

Acknowledgements

This book took over five years to create. It was a labor of love that consumed most of my working hours, my attention, and my devotion. Because a project like this is usually created by a large publishing company with several specialists assigned to lesson design, image content, copy writing, editing & proofreading, layout & design, digital integration, and so on, it took me longer to complete than expected. I'd like to thank my family members for picking up a lot of my slack to help bring this project to the publishing stage. My mom, Sandra, spent hours editing the content at her dining room table. My niece, Ashley, created all of the QR codes and bitly short links and placed them into the final copy. My nephew, Tyler, assisted with graphic design elements on Canva that I could have never figured out. My sister, Amy, read through the confusing first chapter and helped me figure out how to make it a little easier to understand. And a shoutout to all of my friends and colleagues who spent time listening to my lesson ideas and providing me with feedback to help me transform my fledgling ideas into actual mini-lessons. I sincerely appreciate everyone's help and support!

Testimonials

During the final year and a half of writing this book, the mini-lessons within Optimized Learning *were tested in the 3rd, 4th and 5th grade classrooms of a virtual school in Virginia. Three members of the district provided testimonials:*

"...transformative impact on students' development as collaborative, goal-driven, and self-directed learners."
- Jennifer Thomason

The FLEx program, Hampton City Schools virtual K-6 program, enthusiastically embraced the resources and lessons within *Optimized Learning*. We recognized its transformative impact on students' development as collaborative, goal-driven, and self-directed learners. The program's innovative approach empowered students by providing a platform that encourages collaboration, allowing them to engage in meaningful discussions and peer-to-peer learning experiences. This collaborative aspect not only enriched the virtual classroom environment but also equipped students with essential teamwork and communication skills crucial for their future endeavors.

In addition, the lessons and materials served as a catalyst for cultivating goal-driven and self-directed learners. The program's adaptive features allow students to set and track their academic goals, fostering a sense of ownership and accountability for their learning journey. By tailoring resources to individual needs and learning preferences, students were encouraged to take an active role in their education, promoting a lifelong love for learning.

Jennifer Thomason, Coordinator of Innovation & Digital Learning, Hampton City Schools, Hampton, VA

"The slides did an excellent job of breaking down more challenging concepts for the younger students."
- Stacey Smithley

I utilized these lessons for a 100% virtual 5th grade class. This was used during our daily Morning Meeting to learn how to set goals through planning, self assessing, and reflection. The corresponding slides had clear visuals and descriptions that made it very straightforward for each student to follow along with each step. The slides did an excellent job of breaking down more challenging concepts for the younger students. For example, achievable and ambitious were broken down into a graphic utilizing "too easy," "Goldilocks Zone," and "too hard." These concepts are easy for elementary students to relate to.

As a teacher, I enjoyed the relatable examples that are included in the slides versus the teacher having to create their own. For example, when instructing students to set a basic goal, there is already a worksheet completed with "kid-friendly" text to model how they should complete their own goal setting worksheet. This leaves very little guess work on the part of the teacher and the students.

**Stacey Smithley, 5th grade teacher
Hampton City Schools, Hampton, VA**

"A program I wholeheartedly endorse."
- Candace Horsley

The program's unique approach actively engaged students, resulting in highly effective and enjoyable lessons. Their increased enthusiasm for the varied lesson formats demonstrated a positive response. Moreover, the program's adaptability made it effortless to teach and customize according to our specific grade level requirements.

The comprehensive lessons not only allowed students to express themselves but also equipped them with valuable skills for overcoming challenges at their age. With its real-world applications, the program brought lessons to life, fostering a more engaging and relatable learning experience.

As a fellow teacher, I highly recommend leveraging the program's adaptability to tailor lessons based on your students' specific needs and interests. Personally, I have witnessed the significant impact it has made on the dynamics within my virtual classroom, making it a program I wholeheartedly endorse.

**Candace Horsley, 5th Grade Teacher
Hampton City Schools, Hampton, VA**

Endorsements

I also reached out to some of my colleagues and educational heroes and asked for their opinion of the book. Here is what they had to say:

"Optimized Learning *can be a game-changer for you and your students.*"
- Stephanie Smith

Most teachers want to give students ownership of their learning, but the practicality of that can be daunting in a classroom of students whose levels of readiness and needs vary. To provide an environment built for students to truly own their learning, it is critical to engage students not just as learners of content but also as learners of themselves and the learning process.

Optimized Learning provides teachers with a roadmap to do just that. With usable, practical tools - lesson plans, templates, discussion questions, and more - *Optimized Learning* is the answer to the teacher question, "How can we do this?" when it comes to empowering learners to take the lead.

The Student-Led Self-Improvement Process (SLSI) engages students in the macro skills needed to build habits that will benefit them far beyond the classroom and school year, and Solarz has created and curated materials in a thoughtful way that allows room for teacher learning and reflection throughout the process. From thoughtful spots for teachers to annotate with sticky notes to editable materials designed to seamlessly be used digitally, Solarz models opportunities for teachers to take ownership of the book and to plan, reflect, assess, and set goals for their practice and student learning. Simply put, if you're a teacher and a learner *Optimized Learning* can be a game-changer for you and your students.

Stephanie Smith, 6th Grade Language Arts Teacher, Northbrook Junior High School, Northbrook, IL

Endorsements

"Paul's work here is inventing the future of education and encapsulates what we should be focused on in the area of student learning."
- Phil Collins

I have known Paul Solarz since he started his teaching career. I had the honor to be his first principal and to see the beginnings of the great insight he had into instructional practices. I was also lucky enough for one of my children to have Paul as a teacher. From both perspectives I had the chance to experience the early stages of the SLSI process before it even had the name.

What Paul has created here is a powerful tool for every teacher at every level in every subject. The lessons and activities guide teachers as they help their students develop true lifelong learning skills. He provides a systematic but flexible approach to foster learning dexterity with students. As students develop these skills they will be able to apply them to every learning opportunity in school and beyond.

The SLSI process will continue to help them in their careers as they are continuously challenged to learn and grow. Students who become proficient in this process will be successful professionals as they are faced with new challenges and opportunities. These are the skills that students will remember and use more than any specific piece of knowledge they gain within their school experience.

One of my favorite quotes is from Alan Kay who said "The best way to predict the future is to invent it." I believe that Paul's work here is inventing the future of education and encapsulates what we should be focused on in the area of student learning.

Phil Collins, Ed. D.,
Chief Customer Officer, Otus LLC

"Such a helpful resource! I kept going down rabbit holes with this book!"
- Mary Cay Ricci

In the acknowledgments, Paul stated that it has taken him over five years to create this resource, and after digging into Optimized Learning, I can see why. I kept going down rabbit holes with this book and resources! The amount of work put into this resource is mind-blowing! Paul has effectively identified and dug deep into vital tenets of a student-led self-improvement process. Kudos for developing such a helpful resource!

Optimized Learning provides a fresh way to guide students towards student-led learning through a focused approach on essential areas such as Planning, Metacognition, Synthesis, Reflection, Self-Assessment, Goal Setting, and Feedback. Through understanding these concepts, learners not only excel during their years in school but also develop the skills to take charge of their own learning pathway throughout their life.

Mary Cay Ricci,
Speaker and Author, Mindsets in the Classroom: Building a Growth Mindset Learning Community and Mindsets for Parents

"What Paul has created here should be mandatory in every teacher pre-service program worldwide. "
- Jon Corippo

Wow, what a masterpiece! Incredible, incredible, incredible. This has been said about several books, but what Paul Solarz has created here should be mandatory in every teacher pre-service program worldwide.

Optimized Learning truly delivers on its title, as this masterwork is a tour de force of pedagogy, mastering the paradox of the complexity of teaching while also being accessible in small bites. Anyone who seeks to be an optimal educator could literally open up any chapter of this book and raise their teaching potential immediately.

Jon Corippo,
Eduprotocol Field Guide Book 1 and 2 Author

"I can't wait to see this in every professional library."
- Michael Lubelfeld

In *Optimized Learning*, Paul Solarz has created scalable support for "metacognition" and "meta pedagogy" for students and teachers. Talk about engaging students!

The seven-step process, Planning, Metacognition, Synthesis, Reflection, Self-Assessment, Goal Setting, and Feedback will enhance ANY classroom and every student. Solarz lays out a teacher's guide for teaching. I can't wait to see this in every professional library. This is the "uber" study and student support system.

Michael Lubelfeld, Ed.D.
Superintendent and Author of *The Unfinished Teacher*

" ...the ULTIMATE resource to help teachers help students help themselves!"
- Rich Czyz

In *Optimized Learning*, Paul Solarz has created the ULTIMATE resource to help teachers help students help themselves! Drawing from his years of classroom experience and extensive research in education, Paul presents a groundbreaking approach that puts students in the driver's seat of their learning. With practical strategies and customizable lesson plans, this book equips teachers with the tools to cultivate students' intrinsic motivation and autonomy.

Optimized Learning provides a revolutionary blueprint for transforming education and unlocking the full potential of every learner. Join the movement and ignite a passion for lifelong learning in your classroom today!

Rich Czyz, School Principal and Author of *The Four O'Clock Faculty*, *The SECRET SAUCE*, and *ROGUE Leader*

Endorsements

"Optimized Learning... *is a blueprint for building a future where every student has the opportunity to fully matter.*"
- Angela Maiers

Optimized Learning isn't just a book—it's a manifesto for the future of education. With visionary insight, Paul Solarz invites educators to embark on a journey of transformation, where the focus shifts from imparting knowledge to nurturing the inherent potential within every student.

In Solarz's world, teaching isn't just about delivering lessons; it's about creating a culture of growth, where students are empowered to take ownership of their learning journey. His macro- and microskills aren't just strategies, they're keys to unlocking limitless possibilities, transcending boundaries of age, subject, and circumstance.

As educators, we understand and embrace student-centered teaching and learning, and now we have a treasured resource and guide that truly embodies the spirit of empowerment, offering students the tools and mindset to drive their own learning with purpose and agency.

Within the pages of *Optimized Learning* lies a call to action—a rallying cry for educators to embrace change, challenge convention, and empower students to become architects of their own learning destiny. It's more than just a book; it's a roadmap for revolution—a blueprint for building a future where every student has the opportunity to fully matter.

Angela Maiers,
Founder & CEO, Choose2Matter

"Optimized Learning *offers a comprehensive approach to improving the way students learn.*"
- Michael Albert

Optimized Learning by Paul Solarz offers a comprehensive approach to improving the way students learn. Within its pages, educators will find a rich array of learning strategies meticulously outlined in a mini-lesson format. Each strategy is accompanied by precise instructions, thoughtfully designed handouts, and visually engaging anchor charts.

What distinguishes this book is its meticulous structuring of lessons. Every strategy is presented with careful attention to detail, starting with essential questions that prompt critical thinking and guide instructional focus. Detailed overviews provide educators with a clear understanding of the strategy's purpose and implementation.

Additionally, practical teaching tips offer insights and suggestions for effectively delivering the lesson and supporting student learning. Furthermore, each lesson is designed with clear student-centered goals and outcomes in mind. By establishing these objectives, educators can track student progress, tailor instruction to individual needs, and foster a sense of achievement and growth among learners.

Michael Albert, Technology Integration Teacher
Plymouth South Elementary, Plymouth MA

"Optimized Learning *builds a bridge in the chasm between classroom frustration and self-driven, empowered learners.*"
- Matt Miller

Pedagogy best practice and cognitive science research have shown us the crucial skills that students need to succeed. But many of us haven't been exposed to them -- or just haven't known how to implement them. *Optimized Learning* builds a bridge in the chasm between classroom frustration and self-driven, empowered learners.

It's packed with well-organized tips and strategies. Not sure how to implement them? The classroom-tested mini-lessons get you started right away. This book is like an infusion of achievement vitamins, optimizing what already works in your classroom to level up learning.

Matt Miller, Educator, Author, and Speaker
Ditch That Textbook

"This is a MUST READ for all new teachers, and for teachers who want to teach in new ways!"
- Lori D. Bein

Wow! I could not put this book down! I have seen Paul Solarz's classroom myself, and I was always WOW'd at how self-directed and engaged his students were. They loved telling me what they were planning, reflecting on, and improving.

Now, Paul is sharing easy-to-follow lesson plans so that all teachers can guide their students to be empowered learners and leaders. This is a MUST READ for all new teachers, and for teachers who want to teach in new ways!

Lori D. Bein, Ed.D., Superintendent,
Arlington Heights School District 25

"...so many practical examples, strategies, and thoughtful options..."
- Bena Kallick

Paul Solarz has created a path for students to become more self-directed as they navigate the turbulence and complexity of new learning. This book does exactly what his theory suggests--boil it down to manageable steps that lead you through a "DIY" process that is transferable not only for school but for life.

There are so many practical examples, strategies, and thoughtful options that it is impossible to take it all in at once. And that speaks to the heart of this book--get started, try some of these ideas, see how it works, synthesize, reflect and set your goals for the next round. In other words, you too, can think like a pirate! I put a patch over my eye and I'm in!

Bena Kallick,
Co-Founder and Co-Director, Institute for Habits of Mind

Endorsements

"Don't miss out on this transformative resource! It's a game-changer for any educator... The lessons are a teacher's dream..."
- Melanie Kong

Get ready to dive into a powerhouse of a book! *Optimized Learning* is all about empowering students to take charge of their learning journey, setting them up for success in academics and beyond. By prioritizing student-directed learning, teaching becomes not just sustainable but invigorating. The result? A vibrant, joyful classroom where students support each other and tackle challenges head-on.

Optimized Learning supports student-led learning with a powerful, 7-step Student-Led Self-Improvement framework. The lessons are a teacher's dream, designed to be implemented with little preparation, yet easily adaptable by teachers to their own individual style. The thoughtfulness extends to the book's organization and design. With a personalized sticky note system and suggested lesson sequencing, it's the perfect toolkit for fostering lifelong learners.

Don't miss out on this transformative resource! It's a game-changer for any educator looking to make a real difference in their classroom.

Melanie Kong, Co-founder of Floop, Education Consultant, and STEM Teacher, Tesla STEM High School, Redmond, WA

"The ability to customize templates... is truly a transformative feature."
- Jocelyn M. Sanders

Optimized Learning is the perfect title for this book! Within its pages, Paul Solarz offers current and aspiring education practitioners an enduring scaffold system dedicated to the human side of change, growth, and development of students. The Macro and Micro skills outlined in his book will sustain their value across grade levels, subjects, and evolving educational landscapes. Solarz's Student-Led Self-Improvement Process (SLSI) presents individual and collaborative evaluative skills with intention and clarity.

Educators are always looking for ways to equip students with internal, viable skills that are transferable and measurable to encourage confidence, initiative, and self-efficacy in such a way that progress is the reward, not the final goal. *Optimized Learning* does all that and more, including all the necessary resources.

Transitioning from teaching in a physical classroom for 24 years to virtual instruction, I appreciate the inclusion of digital and printable options for handouts and instructional materials. The ability to customize templates according to the unique needs of students each year, without sacrificing any aspect of the curriculum, is truly a transformative feature. Finally, as an avid book annotator, thank you Paul for providing ample space on the pages for my sticky notes!

Jocelyn M. Sanders, G & G Education Services, Grades 2-8, Virtual Academic Support Specialist

"One of the most detailed tools that new and veteran teachers will use as their go-to resource."
- Scott Bedley

In a sea of education publications, this one rises to the top. Paul has crafted one of the most detailed tools that new and veteran teachers will use as their go to resource. In my 30 years in education this is the most comprehensive option for engaging learners in powerful teaching strategies. This is a must add!

Scott Bedley, 4th-Grade Teacher, Co-Founder Global School Play Day and California Teacher of the Year Finalist

"The holy grail of student-centered education."
- Alicia Ray

"Paul Solarz gave us *Learn Like A Pirate* which showed us what a student-centered classroom looks like in practice. Now he has given us the holy grail of student-centered education through scaffolding student independence and leadership in *Optimized Learning*!

I am blown away by the quality of each mini-lesson. The posters are perfection! The MicroSkills are truly impactful on our students' lives beyond any curricular content we could ever teach. These are the lessons that truly matter, and I am eager to use the templates in my own classroom!"

Alicia Ray, Educator, Speaker and Author of *Educational Eye Exam*

"Within these pages are the how-to's of transforming lives."
- Sandy King

As an instructional coach in a Title I school, I am beyond excited to share this amazing resource with my colleagues! Paul has thoughtfully and skillfully mapped the road for any teacher who desires to guide their students in becoming independent thinkers.

The resources are enough to make any educator giddy because they're beautiful, kid-friendly, based on research, and ready to use. Brand new or veteran educators can easily guide their students to set goals, have the highest expectations for themselves, confidently manage their time, and reach their highest aspirations. The skills that students will learn are life skills!

Every educator desires to make an impact- a difference. Within these pages are the how-to's of transforming lives. This is a true gift of love- a treasure trove for any "pirate." Thank you, Paul Solarz, for generously sharing your expertise with the world!

Sandy King, Instructional Coach and Winner of the Utah Educators Association Excellence in Teaching Award

Endorsements

"Solarz has created groundbreaking units that will lead to classrooms of truly independent, self-directed learners."
- Melissa Milner

In *Optimized Learning*, Paul Solarz provides a comprehensive road map for teachers, expanding on his ideas from his revolutionary book *Learn Like a Pirate*. Solarz has created groundbreaking units (each one centered around a "Macroskill") that will lead to classrooms of truly independent, self-directed learners. Each unit includes loads of lessons that take you through the journey, step by step, to students being in charge of their learning in that particular macroskill.

If you are thinking that there is no way you could get your kids to do this, check out how Paul has scaffolded the lessons. They are brilliantly designed and will guide all students to become more self-directed in a gentle, thoughtful way. Just like in *Learn Like a Pirate*, Paul aims to break his ideas down into manageable chunks for teachers and he gives great advice and tips along the way, as well as QR codes, posters, thumbnails of the student pages, and much more. After reading these lessons, I can't wait to start implementing *Optimized Learning* in my classroom.

Melissa Milner, Fourth Grade Teacher, Host of The Teacher As...Podcast

"The book is AMAZING! I already have a number of teacher friends that I would love to gift this to!"
- Amber Heffner

Transforming students into empowered, efficient, and collaborative learners is the cornerstone of educational success, and *Optimized Learning* is the ultimate guide to achieving this important goal. With clear insights and actionable strategies, Paul equips educators with practical tools they need to nurture a classroom culture where students take ownership of their learning journey.

Through the Student-Led Self-Improvement Process outlined in this book, educators discover how to create an environment where collaboration thrives, peer relationships flourish, and students are inspired to continuously strive for excellence.

If you're ready to empower your students to become resilient, focused, and enthusiastic learners, then *Optimized Learning* is an essential addition to your professional library. Get ready to witness the incredible transformation that occurs when students are given the tools and encouragement to take control of their educational journey.

Amber Heffner Former Educator, Executive Director, and Current Director of Customer Advocacy at ParentSquare

"Optimized Learning *is a comprehensive resource with the potential to transform teaching and learning in our classrooms.*"
- Jeffrey Zoul

Optimized Learning is a comprehensive resource with the potential to transform teaching and learning in our classrooms. Solarz provides educators with a step-by-step guide for helping students become self-directed learners by putting into practice seven essential learning process skills. The collection of mini-lessons designed to teach each of the seven skills includes everything a teacher will need to help students take control of their own learning and become better equipped to excel in the classroom and in society. I encourage schools and districts to use this resource intentionally; doing so will empower students to succeed in school and, more importantly, to succeed in life.

Jeffrey Zoul, Ed.D. Author of *Improving Your School One Week at a Time*

"Paul provides a very clear pathway for how teachers can guide their students to become [self-directed learners]."
- Todd Stanley

Paul Solarz has pulled off an amazing magic trick. Without ever using the term "executive functioning skills", he has managed to create mini-lessons that teach these very things. Planning, goal setting, focus, initiative, follow-through, and metacognition amongst others are all clearly laid out for teachers to intentionally teach to their students and for kids to learn on their own. This then leads to the "self-directed student". Like many terms in education, we throw this around but rarely know how to accomplish it. Paul provides a very clear pathway for how teachers can guide their students to become just this.

The best thing about *Optimized Learning* is that if you don't like one of the 180 lessons, you can either change it to suit your needs or merely skip it all together. Paul gives you options and tons and tons of resources.

Todd Stanley, Author of *Inquiry Learning in the Gifted Classroom* and *Promoting Rigor through Higher-Level Questioning*

"The benefits to students and teachers will be immediate and long lasting."
- Rusty May

As a school counselor, the thing that impressed me most about the *Optimized Learning* program was its laser focus on helping students learn how to learn while becoming more responsible for their educational journey. This program assists students in developing important life skills like self awareness, self reliance, resiliency and hard work while discovering their own unique learning style. Paul has found a way to combine an incredibly powerful learning tool with an equally powerful social emotional literacy/character education program and the benefits to students and teachers will be immediate and long lasting.

Rusty May, MS School Counseling, Creator of SchoolToolsTV.com

Endorsements

"Optimized Learning *is the perfect resource..."*
- Michael Olson

In my twenty years as an educator, I've experienced the profound impact of self-directed learning. Inspired by Paul's book *Learn Like a Pirate*, I've dedicated myself to fostering a student-centered classroom where students are empowered to take ownership of their learning.

Optimized Learning is the perfect resource that equips both my students and me with the resources to continue this approach. It offers easy-to-teach lessons and engaging resources that will help my students become successful, independent, lifelong learners. Thank you, Paul, for writing this book!

Michael Olson, 5th Grade Teacher
Folwell Elementary School, Rochester, MN

"...provides teachers with valuable insights for progress monitoring..."
- Mark Jackson

Optimized Learning offers a practical approach to tiered interventions that not only helps with data tabulation for necessary student interventions but also empowers students by giving them a voice in identifying areas where they need further assistance.

The book provides practical strategies for recognizing students' strengths and weaknesses in planning and learning, allowing them to take an active role in shaping their own learning experience. This student-friendly approach, which emphasizes student input in the design process and tailoring learning to their individual needs, not only benefits students but also provides teachers with valuable insights for progress monitoring and assessing student success on larger assignments. It is truly an asset for teachers who strive to create student-centered classrooms.

Mark Jackson, Humanities Coach
Great Oaks Charter School, Bridgeport, CT

"School and district leaders should invest in Optimized Learning!"
- Dr. Matthew Rhoads

Optimized Learning provides teachers with a plethora of lessons and resources to support student learning. Whether they are a beginner or veteran teacher, this set of lessons and resources can be implemented with ease saving teachers time for high impact learning. School and district leaders should also invest in *Optimized Learning* to support teachers in building out their curriculum and lessons as an ongoing resource!

Dr. Matthew Rhoads, EdTech Leader, University Adjunct,
Consultant, SDCUE Board Member, Podcaster, & 8x Author

"A work of HEART and then some. A labor of love that will change the way teachers teach those 'soft skills' for years to come. Self efficacy and regulation, here we come!"
- Barbara Gruener

If you've been looking to unlock self-sufficiency, self-confidence, and self-efficacy in your intermediate learners, then *Optimized Learning* by passionate educator Paul Solarz will be KEY in your classroom. Five years in the making, this work of heart will teach your scholars to own their learning and, in turn, optimize their classroom success.

With myriad mini-lessons, this manual will guide you step-by-step as you customize the units to meet the needs of each year's class family. Complete with essential questions and supported by editable slides, instructional posters and handouts, this treasure trove will serve to strengthen those success skills that every child needs to communicate and collaborate efficiently and effectively in today's world.

This comprehensive resource to equip our middle-grade leaders with agency and empower them to be the masters of their learning is one of those gifts you'll wish you'd have had when you first started teaching and that you will be grateful to have found now.

Barbara Gruener, Speaker, Educator, Coach and
Author of *Mr. Quigley's Keys* and *Birdie & Mipps*

"I know this will be so helpful for upper elementary teachers. It made me wish there was something similar for primary students."
- Christine Collins

Our ultimate goal as teachers is to empower our students to become self-reliant learners, much like parents guiding their children towards independence. *Optimized Learning* is a groundbreaking guide that explicitly outlines a structured approach to the essential skills required for fostering independent learning in students.

Through carefully crafted lessons and resources, this book clarifies the process of learning and self-improvement, making it accessible and achievable for students. By following the process outlined in *Optimized Learning*, educators can move beyond the role of merely teaching content, to using content as a springboard for developing students' ability to monitor and refine their own learning.

While content may evolve over time, the skill of learning how to learn will equip students with the tools they need to succeed in anything they need or want to learn in the future. I am so excited to use this invaluable teaching resource to set my students on a path towards lifelong success.

Christine Collins, Reading Specialist,
Euclid Elementary School, Mount Prospect, IL

Professional Development

Hire Paul Solarz* to provide your staff with professional development on *Optimized Learning* or dozens of other topics! Some recent topics Paul has provided PD on include:

- Creating a Student-Led Classroom
- Implementing Project-Based Learning
- Genius Hour (Passion Time)
- STEAM
- Social-Emotional Learning
- Mindfulness
- Improving Collaboration
- Going Grades-Free while focusing on Feedback
- Creating Lessons that Develop 21st Century Skills
- Using Student-Created Video for Assessment
- Making Learning Fun and Active
- Empowering Students to Make Responsible Decisions
- Improvement-Focused Learning (Plus, Growth Mindset!)
- Or have Paul tailor a program that meets your needs!
  Contact Paul at: OptimizedLearningBook@gmail.com

* In-Person rates and Remote rates are available.

Bulk Orders

Standard paperback copies of *Optimized Learning* are available in bulk and can be shipped directly to you from the printer.

- Purchase through DBC Consulting by emailing:
  wendy@daveburgessconsulting.com

Additional formats may be available upon request. These would be printed by an alternate printer. Inquire for more information.

- Hardbound
- Spiral-Bound
- Color
- Black-and-white
  - For pricing and availability, contact the author directly at: OptimizedLearningBook@gmail.com

Autographed, personalized copies are also available for gifts, keepsakes or professional development.

- For pricing and availability, contact the author directly at:
  OptimizedLearningBook@gmail.com

Optimized Learning: 180 mini-lessons that transform today's students into confident, capable & collaborative, self-directed learners

Learn Like a PIRATE

If you haven't already read *Learn Like a PIRATE*, my first book that was published in 2015, you ought to consider it now because it is an EXCELLENT companion to *Optimized Learning*. Here is what it says on the back of the book:

Collaboration. Empowerment. Student Leadership. These buzz words get a lot of press, but what do they really mean for today's students? Can students really handle the responsibility of leading the class? Can they actually learn what they need to if they're working together so often? Won't all this freedom cause chaos in the classroom? Not if you're teaching them to learn like PIRATES!

The P.I.R.A.T.E. acronym:
- Peer Collaboration builds community and supports teamwork and cooperation.
- Improvement-focused learning challenges students to constantly strive to be their best.
- Responsibility for daily tasks builds ownership in the classroom.
- Active learning turns boring lessons into fun and memorable experiences.
- Twenty-first century skills engage students now and prepare them for their futures.
- Empowerment allows students to become confident risk-takers who make bold decisions.

In *Learn Like a PIRATE*, teachers discover practical strategies for creating a student-led classroom in which students are inspired and empowered to take charge of their learning experience. You'll learn strategies for:
- Crafting active, relevant, and interesting lessons
- Creating opportunities for student leadership
- Providing effective and beneficial feedback
- Instilling confidence so students can take risks
- Increasing curiosity and passion for learning

Incorporate the techniques and strategies Paul Solarz uses in his student-led classroom and watch your students transform into confident, collaborative leaders!

Purchase on Amazon:

bit.ly/LearnLap

The paperback version of *Learn Like a PIRATE* is available at an extremely discounted rate on Amazon since it was published way back in 2015!

If you would prefer a hardcover, Kindle or Audio book, those versions are also available on Amazon.

Grab a copy today by scanning the QR Code above or visiting the short link URL.

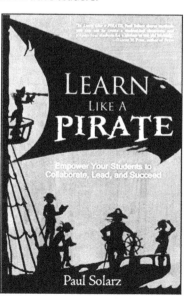

INTRODUCTION
Page 1

PLANNING
Page 32

METACOGNITION
Page 80

SYNTHESIS
Page 144

REFLECTION
Page 182

SELF-ASSESSMENT
Page 222

GOAL SETTING
Page 267

FEEDBACK
Page 336

INTRODUCTION

PLANNING

METACOGNITION

SYNTHESIS

REFLECTION

SELF-ASSESSMENT

GOAL SETTING

FEEDBACK

Personalized "Sticky Note" System

I have chosen to use this spot to represent:

I have chosen to use this spot to represent:

I have chosen to use this spot to represent:

I have chosen to use this spot to represent:

The pages on the left-side of the book have four spaces that bleed off the page for you to use to place sticky notes on according to a system that you create. Since everyone has different needs, nothing has been pre-determined.
- It is recommended that you use 1.5" x 2" or 2" x 2" sticky notes.

Some Ideas:

Keep track of the lessons you have completed. If you stick to a color coding system you don't even have to write anything on them (e.g. blue means DONE). Add the date to the sticky note if that can be of value in the future!

Done
Sept. 13

Keep track of how long each lesson took you to teach. As time goes on, you might find the lessons getting shorter as you become more efficient and the students help each other more!

This lesson took 20 minutes to complete.

Jot down curricular notes or lesson planning notes like components within a lesson to skip or add, ways to integrate lessons into the academic curriculum...

Combine this lesson with Reading Lesson 45.

Make note of Unit Plan changes for the following year, such as changing the order of lessons or moving a lesson from one Instructional Spiral to another.

Change the order next year. Do this before Lesson 719

Integration with Canva

The QR Codes and short links on each lesson plan page link to canva.com where you can completely personalize each slide for your class, but Canva actually offers you dozens more options too! Although everything on this page will change over time, here is a look at some integrations Canva currently offers teachers (for free) with an Educator account:

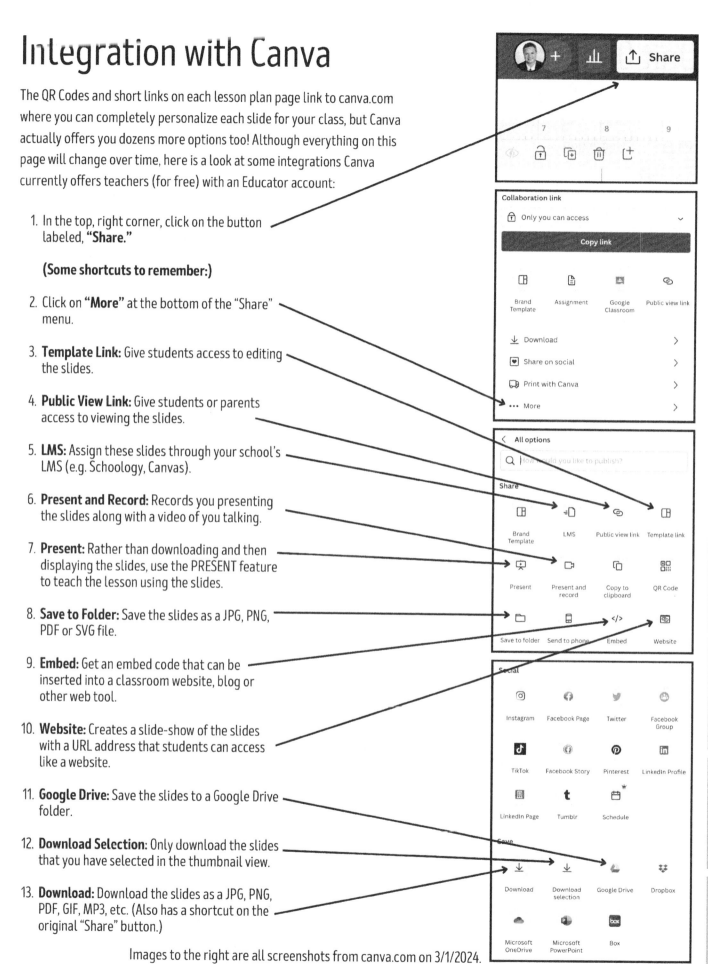

1. In the top, right corner, click on the button labeled, **"Share."**

   (Some shortcuts to remember:)

2. Click on **"More"** at the bottom of the "Share" menu.

3. **Template Link:** Give students access to editing the slides.

4. **Public View Link:** Give students or parents access to viewing the slides.

5. **LMS:** Assign these slides through your school's LMS (e.g. Schoology, Canvas).

6. **Present and Record:** Records you presenting the slides along with a video of you talking.

7. **Present:** Rather than downloading and then displaying the slides, use the PRESENT feature to teach the lesson using the slides.

8. **Save to Folder:** Save the slides as a JPG, PNG, PDF or SVG file.

9. **Embed:** Get an embed code that can be inserted into a classroom website, blog or other web tool.

10. **Website:** Creates a slide-show of the slides with a URL address that students can access like a website.

11. **Google Drive:** Save the slides to a Google Drive folder.

12. **Download Selection:** Only download the slides that you have selected in the thumbnail view.

13. **Download:** Download the slides as a JPG, PNG, PDF, GIF, MP3, etc. (Also has a shortcut on the original "Share" button.)

Images to the right are all screenshots from canva.com on 3/1/2024.

Unit 0 - Introduction
Table of Contents

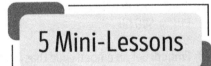

Teacher Support

Read through the following pages before teaching any mini-lessons. It provides the information you will need to understand:
1. Why this program is needed,
2. What all of the terms mean,
3. How to understand the lesson plans and support materials,
4. How to teach the mini-lessons from this program, and
5. How to plan the mini-lessons over the course of a school year.

Mini-Lessons

5 Mini-Lessons

INTRODUCTION
PLANNING
METACOGNITION
SYNTHESIS
REFLECTION
SELF-ASSESSMENT
GOAL SETTING
FEEDBACK

> "Self-regulated learning is the goal of schooling. It is that students will develop an internal dialogue to monitor, evaluate, and optimize their learning."
> — John Hattie

Imagine a classroom where self-driven, collaborative learners fill the space. Students who possess the ability to navigate their educational journey with confidence, purpose, and a clear sense of direction, equipped with the skills to conquer any task, big or small. Everywhere you turn, you see students wisely managing their time, completing tasks with accuracy, and handling setbacks and conflicts independently and with maturity.

These students possess a profound understanding of what needs to be done, how to do it, and the motivation to excel in their work. They aren't in a race to finish first, nor do they constantly rely on the teacher for directions. They don't waste time or veer off-task; instead, they have a clear grasp of expectations and possess the tools, drive, and determination to accomplish their work with excellence.

Creating such a classroom may seem like a distant dream, but I assure you, it is within your reach. Over the course of twenty years, I've dedicated myself to developing these essential skills within my students, and now I'm thrilled to share with you the individual microskills, invaluable lessons, and all the tips I can imagine in the hopes that you will embrace, adapt, expand, and improve upon them, approaching teaching from a slightly different perspective than traditional methods.

This approach centers on optimizing your students' learning abilities, transforming them into confident, collaborative, and self-directed learners who consistently exhibit high effort, a strong academic drive, and perform at peak performance in your classroom every single day.

The end result? A classroom brimming with lifelong learners who can think for themselves and transfer their knowledge and skills to new situations throughout their life—a combination of abilities that should be the ultimate goal of education.

As educators, we hold the power to nurture and cultivate these microskills within our students. It is our responsibility to proactively empower and prepare them for the challenges and expectations they will certainly encounter throughout their lives. By doing so, we equip them with the tools they need to thrive, both in and beyond the classroom.

Together, let us embark on this transformative journey, where we ignite the potential within each student and witness the incredible impact it has on their lives. Are you ready to join me in creating classrooms that foster independent, motivated, and accomplished learners? Then let's do this!

Let's start with some vocabulary terms that I refer to within the opening pages of this book and beyond. Some of these are educational jargon, while some others are simply words and phrases I created to suit my needs! :)

Macroskills - Macroskills refer to the seven main skills we'll focus on in this book: planning, metacognition, synthesis, reflection, self-assessment, goal setting & progress monitoring, and giving & seeking feedback. These seven immensely large skills encapsulate just about everything we need our students to be able to do independently (and with support from peers), so they can become competent, self-directed learners.

Microskills - These are the smaller building blocks, actions, and abilities that help students become proficient in each of the macroskills mentioned above. For example, we shouldn't assume that our students automatically know how to set goals and track progress. That's why this book contains a unit of goal-setting mini-lessons, where students learn specific microskills that ultimately guide them toward identifying areas for improvement, creating plans to address those areas, and collecting evidence that shows progress toward each goal!

Essential Questions - Each mini-lesson starts with a "guiding question" that focuses the lesson. Many essential questions are unanswerable, but students should be able to respond intelligently to an essential question by the end of the lesson because it describes the focus of the main idea of the lesson. I first learned about essential questions from Grant Wiggins who co-wrote *Understanding by Design* and was a huge mentor to me. He states that a question is essential when it:

- "causes genuine and relevant inquiry into the big ideas and core content;
- provokes deep thought, lively discussion, sustained inquiry, and new understanding as well as more questions;
- requires students to consider alternatives, weigh evidence, support their ideas, and justify their answers;
- stimulates vital, on-going rethinking of big ideas, assumptions, and prior lessons;
- sparks meaningful connections with prior learning and personal experiences;
- naturally recurs, creating opportunities for transfer to other situations and subjects."

Big Ideas - This term also comes from Grant Wiggins and Jay McTighe in *Understanding by Design*. Big Ideas are themes or main idea statements that attempt to collect all of the seemingly random bits of information being taught in a lesson and show how they all relate. I always stress to my students that understanding the Big Idea is crucial in every lesson. It's the main skill or concept they need to fully understand by the end of each lesson. If they don't truly understand the Big Idea, then I haven't done my job well enough. Wiggins shares this metaphor: "A good detective has some big ideas about motive to bring meaning to what might otherwise seem like odd, isolated, and unique little facts to the rest of us. The 'big idea' (whether it is 'Look for love triangles' or 'Follow the money') is thus quite practical: it helps distinguish clues from unimportant facts, and shows the way toward more facts - and a persuasive narrative."

Transfer Goals - One final homage to Grant Wiggins is how much he stressed the importance of "transfer." If we spend all of this time teaching students lessons and they don't know how to use the skills when it really matters, then we've done them a disservice. The ultimate goal of education is independent transfer to new situations. (Some lessons in school might focus in on skills that are building blocks for skills that transfer, but you get the idea.) Therefore, in each lesson, two tasks that students completed within the lesson have been identified and a "transfer goal" for each has been described: "The students will be able to... independently by the end of the lesson."

S.M.A.A.R.T.E.R. Goals - S.M.A.A.R.T.E.R. Goals, the *Optimized Learning* variation of S.M.A.R.T. Goals®¹, is a powerful eight-step process that helps students determine the value and feasibility of their goals. The acronym represents specific, measurable, achievable, ambitious, relevant, timely, everlasting, and rewarding objectives. By engaging in this process, students quickly identify if a goal is worth pursuing, saving valuable time. S.M.A.A.R.T.E.R. Goals involve creating a plan, tracking progress, and are designed to be accomplished over a longer timeframe than just a few days. For more information on S.M.A.A.R.T.E.R. Goals, see Lesson 6.04 on page 280, and read the first three pages of Chapter 6 on page 268.

Goal Bursts - Goal Bursts are like Mini-S.M.A.A.R.T.E.R. Goals and typically take a shorter amount of time to accomplish. These require a less formal plan, and progress monitoring is generally not expected. Students set these short-term goals to address important things that they just can't seem to do without setting their minds to it like remembering to share their thoughts when working collaboratively or getting into the habit of shutting down their computer before plugging it in. For more information on Goal Bursts, see Lesson 6.05 on page 282.

Bulky Tasks - The structure provided within this book works best with assignments and tasks that have some complexity to them OR take more time than average to complete. Therefore, a "bulky task" is an assignment that requires students to do more than the standard amount of work or thinking than ordinary assignments require. For more information on Bulky Tasks, see page 11.

Learning Cycles - A learning cycle is when your students are expected to use the seven steps in the SLSI Process on a "bulky task." The learning cycle begins when you start to explain the directions of the assignment and ends when each student has turned in their completed work and addressed all seven macroskills. For more info. on Learning Cycles, see pages 12-13.

Instructional Spirals - A set of lessons that teach students aspects of all seven macroskills in the SLSI Process at increasingly complex levels. The first Instructional Spiral introduces the basics of all seven macroskills and gets students using the process immediately, rather than waiting for all of the other lessons to be taught. It's a way to spiral through the macroskills, increasing their knowledge and skills over time. For more information on Instructional Spirals, see pages 14-21.

Although this is a lot to take in, the entire book follows the same structure, so once you understand the information within this Introduction chapter, you should be set for the rest of the book!

---

1. *S.M.A.R.T. Goals® is a registered trademark of Leadership Management® International, Inc.*

The Student-Led Self-Improvement Process

INTRODUCTION

PLANNING

METACOGNITION

SYNTHESIS

REFLECTION

SELF-ASSESSMENT

GOAL SETTING

FEEDBACK

The Student-Led Self-Improvement Process (SLSI) - The SLSI Process describes the cycle of seven steps that students will learn and use throughout this entire program. Students use the SLSI Process while completing independent or collaborative work that is not completely led by the teacher. Therefore, students will NOT use this process when listening to a lecture, participating in a class discussion, or other activities where the teacher is "on stage", directly addressing the class. Students will, however, use this process when working alone (e.g. to write a personal narrative or when brainstorming a list of tools they might choose to bring to Mars in the class simulation). They will also use this process when working collaboratively (e.g. when they've been partnered with a random peer by the teacher in order to design and engineer a tall, freestanding structure using the provided materials, or when they have a discussion with their partner about a book they're reading).

The Student-Led Self-Improvement Process (SLSI):

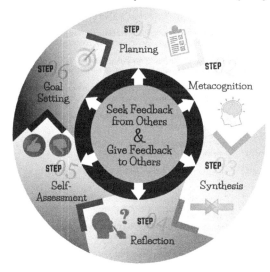

The SLSI Process guides students' thinking, prepares them for what to do next, helps them make informed decisions, and creates a routine for all of these types of learning tasks. The SLSI Process is not needed as much when the teacher is on stage, and in complete control of the class. During those times, the teacher will generally tell the students what to think and do, so student decision-making and problem-solving strategies are not generally needed then.

Students also won't need these steps very often when completing repetitive tasks they have already mastered, such as daily worksheets, or when handling brief and straightforward assignments, like exit tickets. Therefore, we say that students will use the SLSI Process on "Bulky Tasks" in which the teacher takes on a less direct role in guiding the learning process. For further details on "Bulky Tasks", please refer to page 10.

Here is a definition for each step in the SLSI Process, as it is used within this book. They are written with the students in mind:

Step 1 - Planning - Planning is what we do BEFORE we get to work. Planning starts as soon as your teacher begins teaching and finishes when you have a clear plan for how to use your work time. Some responsibilities are to: Know exactly WHAT you need to do and know HOW you're supposed to do it. Know what it is that your teacher is looking for and to what level of quality it needs to be done. Know how long it should take you to complete each component of the assignment or task, and know WHEN it is due. Have all of the materials you'll need for the assignment or task gathered ahead of time. And many more!

Step 2 - Metacognition - Metacognition is a person's awareness of their plan, progress, actions & inactions, interactions, effort, time, accuracy and flexibility WHILE working on a task, and their ability to make changes in those areas whenever necessary. Sometimes this is referred to as "Monitoring your Metacognition" in this book.

Step 3 - Synthesis - Synthesis is the act of organizing & combining accurate prior knowledge on a subject with accurate new information to form a new, deeper understanding. This is generally considered the purpose of learning and is done WHILE learning and AFTER learning!

Step 4 - Reflection - Reflection is the act of thinking about what just happened or what you did, what you learned during that experience, and what impact the experience had on you. Reflection helps us make sense of our experience, and store it for the long-term. This happens AFTER learning.

Step 5 - Self-Assessment - Self-assessment means taking a close look at your own learning to see how you're doing. You make judgments about your strengths & weaknesses, and you identify areas for improvement. This is different from Self-grading, which is when you give yourself a grade for your work or tests. This mostly happens AFTER learning.

Step 6 - Goal Setting (and Progress Monitoring) - Goal setting is the process of identifying relative weaknesses, writing a plan for improving those skills, working through the plan while monitoring progress, and revising the plan as needed. Goal Setting takes place during all three stages of learning (BEFORE, DURING and AFTER).

Step 7 - Feedback - Positive Feedback reinforces what we are doing and makes us feel good about our progress. Critical or Constructive Feedback helps us improve and grow. It tells us what we can be doing better, corrects misunderstandings, and refocuses us on what's most important. In *Optimized Learning*, feedback also includes asking others for help. Feedback is a process that needs to happen between students, not just from the teacher, and it takes place BEFORE, DURING and AFTER learning.

Table of Contents Components

Each unit begins with a Table of Contents, explaining important details about each lesson that you can use to identify which lessons your students might need right away.

Number of Lessons:
The number of lessons that each unit contains is listed in the top right-hand corner of the Table of Contents for each unit.

Page:
The page number that this lesson can be found on in this book.

Lesson:
The lesson number follows this format:
- Unit Number (dot)
- 2-digit Lesson Number

Example: Lesson 1.05 is the fifth lesson in Unit 1.

Essential Question:
The question that guides the purpose of each lesson. At the end of instruction, students should be able to explain their answer to this question.

MicroSkill:
Each unit is based on one of seven "MacroSkills" which are large, complex skills that need to be broken down into their component parts in order for students to learn how to excel at them. Each "MicroSkill" is one of those broken down pieces. Most lessons in this book focus on one or more MicroSkills (with a few exceptions for background knowledge lessons).

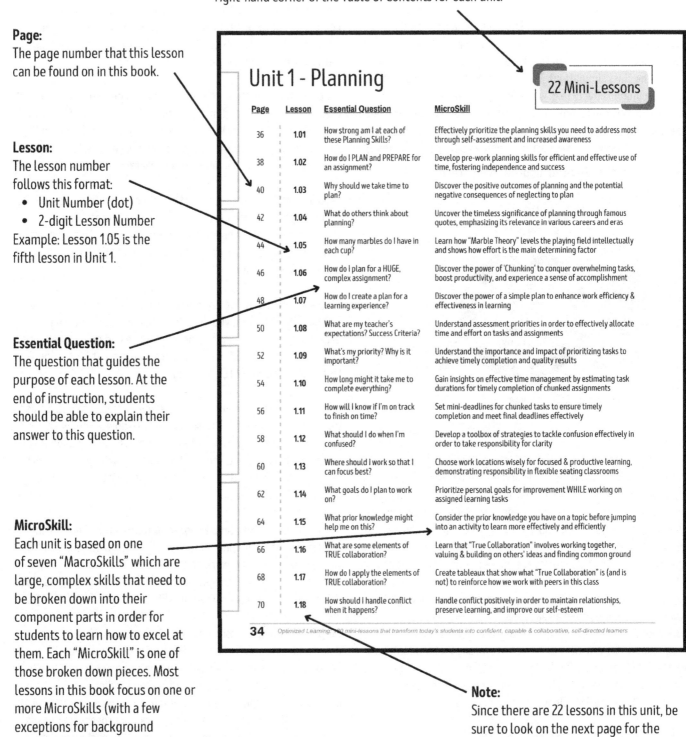

Unit 1 - Planning

22 Mini-Lessons

34 *Optimized Learning: 180 mini-lessons that transform today's students into confident, capable & collaborative, self-directed learners*

Note:
Since there are 22 lessons in this unit, be sure to look on the next page for the additional lessons.

Lesson Plan - Page One Components

INTRODUCTION

PLANNING

METACOGNITION

SYNTHESIS

REFLECTION

SELF-ASSESSMENT

GOAL SETTING

FEEDBACK

Lesson Overview:
What students will be doing during the lesson.

QR Code and Short Link:
Scan it with your phone or enter the short link into a browser to visit Canva where you can edit the Instructional Poster(s) and Student Handouts for this lesson.

Lesson Number:
The lesson number is inside of the SLSI diagram. This lesson is the seventh lesson in Unit 1.

MicroSkill (Title):
Each unit is based on one of seven "MacroSkills" which are large, complex skills that need to be broken down. Each "MicroSkill" is one of those broken down pieces.

Combine this lesson with Reading Lesson 45.

This lesson took 20 minutes to complete.

Done Use again next year.

Change the order next year. Do this before Lesson 7.19

1.07 — Discover the power of a simple plan to enhance work efficiency & effectiveness in learning

bit.ly/3RiwPbl

Big Idea:
What every student should understand by the end of the lesson (at a minimum)

Essential Question
How do I create a plan for a learning experience?

Big Idea
By focusing in on seven specific criteria, you can create a simple plan that will help you improve your efficiency and effectiveness while learning.

Lesson Overview
In this lesson, students learn about the seven steps that make up a good plan. (As the teacher, you might choose to add more or revise some that don't apply to your classroom.) Students begin to practice this skill by imagining themselves preparing to complete a complex task in class with a partner. They identify some of the specific things they ought to do prior to beginning to work (they don't need to use the steps taught on the Instructional Poster). Then, they turn those specific steps into generic steps that can be used in most learning experiences (e.g. SPECIFIC: "I need to research the reasons pioneers headed west." GENERIC: "Learn about my topic."). Finally, students take 10-15 minutes to write a formal plan for an academic lesson (see Teacher Tips for more information).

Teacher Tips
- The final Student Handout cannot be completed in isolation. Students need to complete it prior to beginning a separate academic learning experience. For example, teach the whole class a skill or concept, give them directions for completing a task, and then have them complete the final Student Handout prior to beginning the academic task. They will need 10-15 minutes at first, but should be able to write formal plans more quickly as they gain experience. (They do not always need to write a plan - eventually students should be asked to internalize the steps and do them in their heads prior to beginning to work.) The form is simply a scaffold that supports their growth.
- Having these seven steps posted somewhere in the classroom is a good reminder for students to PLAN before they start working. It will definitely help as you begin to withdraw support and expect them to do this independently.

Discussion/Reflection Questions
- Imagine a task you might be asked to complete in class. How will you plan for this upcoming learning experience?
- Why is it important to create a plan BEFORE beginning a learning experience? What could happen if we don't plan?
- Why do you think THESE seven steps were chosen to be the steps in the planning process? Why are they the most important?
- If you could add an 8th step to the planning process, what would it be? Why did you choose that one?
- Describe a time in the past when you wish you had known about these steps in the planning process? When would this have been useful to you? How might that situation have turned out differently if you had known about these steps?

Student Tasks ⟩ Transfer Goals

Student Tasks	Transfer Goals
Students learn about the seven steps that make up a good plan, and the elements of each step.	Students understand and value each step in the planning process and willingly dedicate some time to each.
Students practice and apply the seven steps in order to create a plan prior to beginning work on a fake task and a real task.	Students internalize the planning process and use the steps to prepare for other learning experiences.

48 — Optimized Learning: 180 mini-lessons that transform today's students into confident, capable & collaborative, self-directed learners

Essential Question:
The question that guides the purpose of each lesson. At the end of instruction, students should be able to explain their answer to this question.

Discussion / Reflection Questions:
Questions that can be used as Exit/Entrance Tickets, class discussions, reviews, etc. (If preferred, most questions can be answered AFTER instruction but BEFORE completing the Student Handouts.).

Sticky Note Tags:
Create your own system for sticky note tags to denote completed lessons, ones to skip next year, resources to add to a lesson, etc. There are four spots for sticky notes on each page. (Sticky notes not included.)

Teacher Tips:
Important notes that you should definitely read before teaching each lesson. They might include prerequisite lessons to teach prior to this one, ideas for combining lessons, important suggestions to get more out of each lesson, etc.

Student Tasks that lead to Transfer Goals:
The activities your students complete and what they should be able to do on their own after the lesson is complete.

Lesson Plan - Page Two Components

Teacher Directions for introducing the lesson to the class using the **Instructional Poster(s)** and for getting the students to complete the **Student Handouts.**

The number of Instructional Posters and Student Handouts that are available for this lesson are listed in the first bullet of both sections. (Not all of the materials MUST be used, but they all provide some sort of value to the lesson.) Most lessons have one Instructional Poster and two Student Handouts.

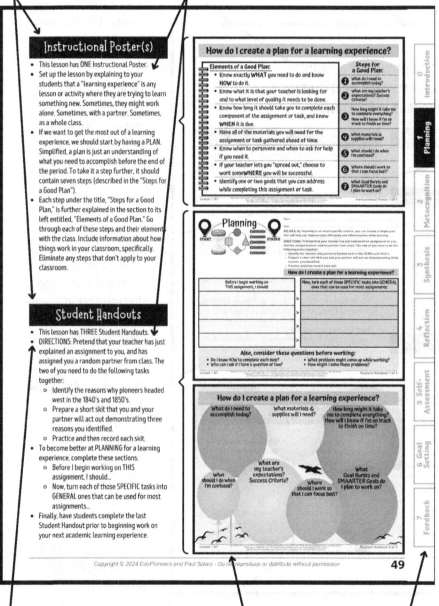

- This lesson has ONE Instructional Poster.
- Set up the lesson by explaining to your students that a "learning experience" is any lesson or activity where they are trying to learn something new. Sometimes, they might work alone. Sometimes, with a partner. Sometimes, as a whole class.
- If we want to get the most out of a learning experience, we should start by having a PLAN. Simplified, a plan is just an understanding of what you need to accomplish before the end of the period. To take it a step further, it should contain seven steps (described in the "Steps for a Good Plan").
- Each step under the title, "Steps for a Good Plan," is further explained in the section to its left entitled, "Elements of a Good Plan." Go through each of these steps and their elements with the class. Include information about how things work in your classroom, specifically. Eliminate any steps that don't apply to your classroom.

Student Handouts

- This lesson has THREE Student Handouts.
- DIRECTIONS: Pretend that your teacher has just explained an assignment to you, and has assigned you a random partner from class. The two of you need to do the following tasks together:
  o Identify the reasons why pioneers headed west in the 1840's and 1850's.
  o Prepare a short skit that you and your partner will act out demonstrating three reasons you identified.
  o Practice and then record each skit.
- To become better at PLANNING for a learning experience, complete these sections:
  o Before I begin working on THIS assignment, I should...
  o Now, turn each of those SPECIFIC tasks into GENERAL ones that can be used for most assignments...
- Finally, have students complete the last Student Handout prior to beginning work on your next academic learning experience.

- Not all of the lessons in this book will "speak to you," but hopefully you'll see those lessons as inspiration to create your own activities that work for your students in your classroom!

- Some of the MicroSkills in this book can be taught during a class discussion or classroom meeting and applied immediately during an activity. You may not feel the need to have your students complete the Student Handouts at all!

- Other lessons will need a bigger time commitment for students to improve and transfer the skill to new situations.

- If you don't want to create your own activities from scratch, consider modifying the activities provided in this book on Canva.com. Every Instructional Poster and Student Handout is unlocked so that you can change them to meet your needs!

- If you still don't think modifying the slides is the answer for you, ask your favorite Artificial Intelligence tool to create a fun, hands-on lesson for your grade level of students that focuses on the MicroSkill lesson you want to change!

Since the **Directions** on the thumbnail image are so small, they have been reprinted in this area for each Student Handout. If you are not aware of this, you will likely be confused when reading them in this section because they don't appear to connect with any of the other Teacher notes!

Thumbnails of the Instructional Poster(s) and the Student Handouts - (Use the Canva Assignments feature to assign these handouts to your students in color!).

The unit name and number "bleeds" off the side of the page so you can get your bearings in the book without even having to open it!

How do I teach each mini-lesson?
Here are three ideas you might consider

INTRODUCTION

PLANNING

METACOGNITION

SYNTHESIS

REFLECTION

SELF-ASSESSMENT

GOAL SETTING

FEEDBACK

Option 1 - (Paper Version - Highly Recommended)

Choose a time in your schedule when you can teach these mini-lessons with some flexibility on end time. Some lessons will last 15 minutes, while others will likely take longer. If you are forced to finish early because you've chosen to teach these right before lunch or right before a passing period, you will be more likely to rush through it. Create this routine:

- Start by projecting the Instructional Poster from the <u>previous</u> lesson in the classroom. Ask for a volunteer to remind everyone what the last lesson's Big Idea was. Be sure to clarify their answer if it doesn't capture the whole concept. Keep this short, but ensure that students understand and remember the purpose of the last lesson.
- Once everyone has settled in to the lesson, introduce the Instructional Poster for <u>this</u> lesson by projecting it in class. Use this time to follow the suggestions on the lesson plan and really create a class discussion on the topic. Encourage students to speak to the whole group, ask questions of the teacher, or turn and talk as you see fit.
- Once students understand the Big Idea for the new lesson, pass out the Student Handouts for this lesson (or if you've chosen to put them into a packet, have students take out the packet) and read through the directions together as a class if you have time, but create a routine where if the Instructional Poster takes longer than usual, students are required to read the directions themselves and follow them carefully.
    - Choose random partners with sticks or some other randomizer and have students work together collaboratively on the Student Handouts. Although they will be talking through each part of the Student Handout, they are not expected to write the same thing as their partner (although there will certainly be times when they end up doing so). Either way, both students are expected to complete a Student Handout (not just one for the partnership). This routine of working with a random partner will improve relationships as students learn how to work with everyone in class and not just their friends. (Keep an eye out for students who ignore the partnering rules, if you have any sneaky kiddos!)
    - Walk around to ensure students are completing their Student Handouts effectively. Remind students to be complete with their answers, yet efficient with their time. Give feedback to improve their work.
    - Decide what you want your students to do with the completed Student Handouts. I <u>don't</u> recommend turning them in, nor do I recommend that they get put away without feedback. Students need to know that you care about what they write and have high expectations, but a subjective grade on these will not necessarily improve effort. If you are vigilant about walking around and providing feedback, that should be enough.
    - You also need to decide what to do if students don't finish their work in the allotted class time. Is it homework? Is it okay to just move on? I believe that if the students worked hard during class and stayed focused, that it's okay if the work did not get finished, but if they finish a future assignment early, I would create the expectation that they go back and finish any incomplete Student Handouts.

Option 2 - (Electronic Version - Recommended)

Follow the same procedure as Option 1, but with the following modifications:

- Have students complete the Student Handouts on a device. Have students submit them to you when they are complete. Look them over and give feedback to help them improve.

Option 3 - (Shortened Version - Not Recommended)

This option should take half the time of Option 1 or 2 but may be less effective - Use only as needed! Follow the same procedure as Option 1, but with the following modifications:

- Skip the review slide.
- Instead of partnering students up, complete the Student Handouts together as a whole class. Have students complete the handouts during the class discussion, using information from the class discussion.
- Since you will be unable to circulate and provide feedback, have them turn in or submit their finished work just to ensure that they completed everything. Feedback shouldn't be necessary since the answers should all be similar.

Instructional Posters

Each lesson contains (at least) one Instructional Poster intended to kick off each lesson.

- Instructional Posters are created in COLOR and can serve as actual posters hung up in the classroom or simply as slides that are presented to the class.
- Each lesson is briefly introduced by the teacher using the Instructional Poster, and a short classroom discussion is encouraged to clarify meaning, activate background knowledge, and clear up misunderstandings.
- Each poster can be completely modified within Canva to meet the needs of your specific classroom.

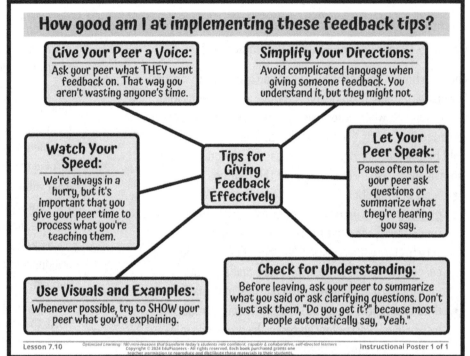

How good am I at implementing these feedback tips?

Give Your Peer a Voice:
Ask your peer what THEY want feedback on. That way you aren't wasting anyone's time.

Simplify Your Directions:
Avoid complicated language when giving someone feedback. You understand it, but they might not.

Watch Your Speed:
We're always in a hurry, but it's important that you give your peer time to process what you're teaching them.

Tips for Giving Feedback Effectively

Let Your Peer Speak:
Pause often to let your peer ask questions or summarize what they're hearing you say.

Use Visuals and Examples:
Whenever possible, try to SHOW your peer what you're explaining.

Check for Understanding:
Before leaving, ask your peer to summarize what you said or ask clarifying questions. Don't just ask them, "Do you get it?" because most people automatically say, "Yeah."

Sample Instructional Poster from Lesson 7.10

Instructional Posters are easily utilized in **virtual instruction** or provided to students as a resource through an **LMS**. They have been formatted horizontally for the purpose of **projecting in the classroom** or **viewing electronically on a device**. They are also set to the dimensions of 11" x 8.5" for **easy distribution on letter-size paper**.

How do I create a plan for a learning experience?

Elements of a Good Plan:

- Know exactly **WHAT** you need to do and know **HOW** to do it.
- Know what it is that your teacher is looking for and to what level of quality it needs to be done.
- Know how long it should take you to complete each component of the assignment or task, and know **WHEN** it is due.
- Have all of the materials you will need for the assignment or task gathered ahead of time.
- Know when to persevere and when to ask for help if you need it.
- If your teacher lets you "spread out," choose to work some**WHERE** you will be successful.
- Identify one or two goals that you can address while completing this assignment or task.

Steps for a Good Plan:

1. What do I need to accomplish today?
2. What are my teacher's expectations? Success Criteria?
3. How long might it take me to complete everything? How will I know if I'm on track to finish on time?
4. What materials & supplies will I need?
5. What should I do when I'm confused?
6. Where should I work so that I can focus best?
7. What Goal Bursts and SMAARTER Goals do I plan to work on?

Sample Instructional Poster from Lesson 1.07

Possible Procedure for teaching the Instructional Poster(s):

1. Project the image in the classroom for the students to see.
2. Refer to the Instructional Poster notes in the lesson plan.
3. Read the poster aloud, pausing to clarify meaning and to describe applications of the skill or procedure in your classroom.
4. Have students actively participate in a classroom discussion about the microskill taught on the poster.
5. Encourage questions from the students, and also pose questions to check for understanding.

Student Handouts - Page One Components

Each lesson includes a minimum of two Student Handouts (so you can copy them onto both sides of a piece of paper) intended to be completed with a random partner assigned by the teacher (but could also be done independently or as a whole class).

INTRODUCTION

PLANNING

METACOGNITION

SYNTHESIS

REFLECTION

SELF-ASSESSMENT

GOAL SETTING

FEEDBACK

Big Idea:
This is the most important concept that students need to understand by the end of the lesson.

Logo:
Each unit has a visual representation of the unit to help students remember the MAIN purpose of each lesson.

Important Note:
Student Handouts are not like traditional worksheets, but rather more like graphic organizers or templates that direct students' thinking.

Directions:
Directions are clearly explained in this location. If students don't read these directions, they almost assuredly won't be able to complete the activity correctly.

Essential Question (Title):
To remind students of the question they are trying to answer within this lesson.

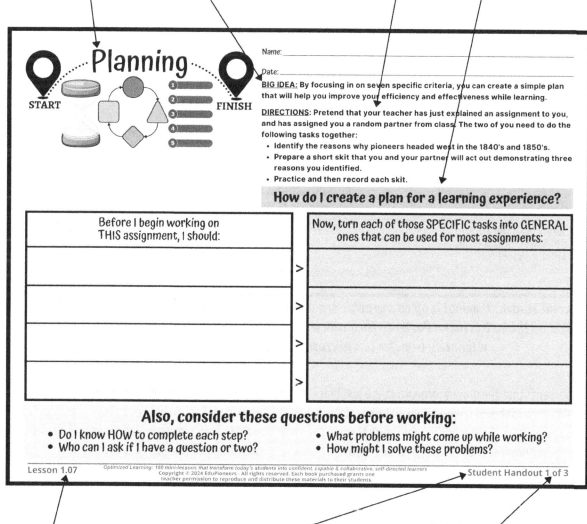

Unit and Lesson Number:
This slide happens to be from "Lesson 1.07" which means "Unit 1 - Lesson 7."

Slide Type:
Whether it's an "Instructional Poster," a "Student Handout" or one of the few "irregulars," the type of slide is described here.

Slide Number:
Each lesson has at least one Instructional Poster and two Student Handouts, but some have more. Here, you can see how many there are for this lesson and the suggested order for teaching them. Feel free to skip the ones you don't need!

Student Handouts - Page Two Components

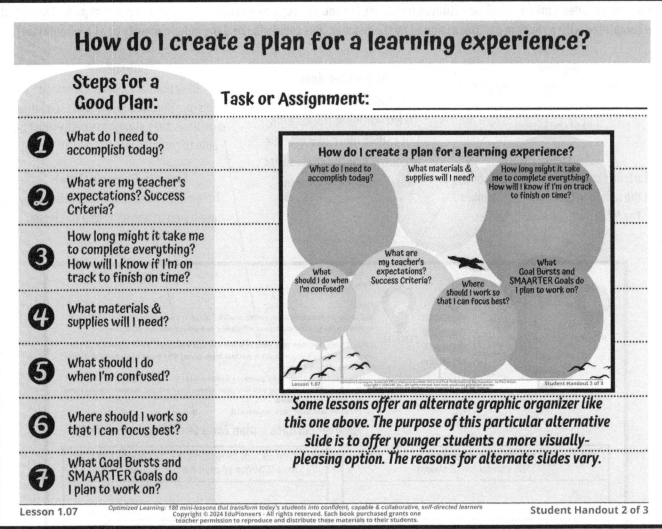

How do I create a plan for a learning experience?

Steps for a Good Plan:

Task or Assignment: _____

1. What do I need to accomplish today?

2. What are my teacher's expectations? Success Criteria?

3. How long might it take me to complete everything? How will I know if I'm on track to finish on time?

4. What materials & supplies will I need?

5. What should I do when I'm confused?

6. Where should I work so that I can focus best?

7. What Goal Bursts and SMAARTER Goals do I plan to work on?

How do I create a plan for a learning experience?

- What do I need to accomplish today?
- What materials & supplies will I need?
- How long might it take me to complete everything? How will I know if I'm on track to finish on time?
- What should I do when I'm confused?
- What are my teacher's expectations? Success Criteria?
- Where should I work so that I can focus best?
- What Goal Bursts and SMAARTER Goals do I plan to work on?

Lesson 1.07   Student Handout 3 of 3

Some lessons offer an alternate graphic organizer like this one above. The purpose of this particular alternative slide is to offer younger students a more visually-pleasing option. The reasons for alternate slides vary.

The second Student Handout is often a graphic organizer that helps students apply the microskill that was taught on the Instructional Poster to their own work. This step is necessary for students to be able to ultimately transfer this microskill to new situations in the future.

- Remind students that the graphic organizers are just like training wheels and should not be relied on forever (this is taught in Lesson 0.02). Their job is to internalize these processes (over time) so they ultimately don't need reminders or support.

- Before assigning a Student Handout, be sure that you, as the teacher, can complete the page without needing additional explanation. Some of these graphic organizers require you to connect to a current assignment in class and you might need to let them know which assignment that is. Whenever possible, let students know your Success Criteria for each handout.

- For this lesson, students are asked to USE the seven "Steps for a Good Plan" to plan out a task or assignment they are about to begin in class. Make sure that students have an assignment with which to apply this planning process!

- Many of these graphic organizers can be used with any subject, any teacher, on any day, so if you are teaching this skill in isolation, it can be applied later.

- A final note: many students will try to complete these graphic organizers with the least amount of effort possible. Don't allow that! Ask them to write more and to try their best! Nip careless work in the bud early and often, and you won't have to fight it all year long!

What is a Bulky Task?
An assignment that requires students to do more than the basics

Bulky Tasks - Even though we want our students to be self-directed learners ALL the time, the strategies in this book should be practiced with assignments and tasks that are more challenging and take longer to complete than just filling out a worksheet. If students practice these skills on simple activities with a small number of steps, they won't understand why the SLSI skills are important. The lessons in this book teach students how to learn without needing constant support. Students rarely need support to do basic work, but often need support completing challenging assignments, working collaboratively with classmates, or whenever they're asked to think in new or different ways. By practicing these nascent skills on "bulky tasks," students will discover their value and develop proper habits that help them become self-directed in all learning situations.

Project-Based Learning (PBL) is a great example of a bulky task! PBL often involves research or learning from the teacher, understanding the information, and doing something useful with it. This type of learning requires deep thinking and is generally not that easy to complete.

Although there is not a required list of components that make up a bulky task, there are several components that are often true. These are listed in the graphic above.

This is an example of a bulky task. They do not all have to be this many steps or this complex, but it shows that bulky tasks can contain components of more traditional assignments (e.g. reading, watching videos, answering comprehension questions), but they also need to have a thinking component that makes the assignment somewhat challenging to all students (in this case they created a model of a process).

But not all bulky tasks have to be project-based. If you have students who need a lot of help to succeed, the lessons in this book will guide them to success without your constant support.

If you're like most teachers, you probably have had to break down learning into small parts that you can teach one at a time, because that's all you felt your students could handle. A bulky task can simply be a combination of a few of these small parts into one assignment that may take a few periods for your students to complete!

For example, if today's lesson plan was to have students read an article and fill out a worksheet to show their understanding, and tomorrow you wanted them to work with a partner to compare information from the first article with another article using a Venn Diagram, you can combine these two lessons into one task that takes two days. Introduce all of the information on Day One, partner students up randomly to work together, and have your students work through a "Learning Cycle" together (which is explained on the next page)! This is a "Bulky Task."

INTRODUCTION

PLANNING

METACOGNITION

SYNTHESIS

REFLECTION

SELF-ASSESSMENT

GOAL SETTING

FEEDBACK

What is a Learning Cycle?

Any bulky task where you expect your students to apply the entire SLSI Process

Learning Cycle - A learning cycle is any bulky task where you expect your students to apply the entire SLSI Process. A learning cycle begins when you start to explain the directions of the assignment and ends when each student has submitted their completed work and considered all seven macroskills. The reason I say "considered" is because *what* you have students do during a learning cycle is up to you. You might have them complete a graphic organizer that shows their thinking for one or more steps in the SLSI Process (You are provided with packets that help you do this). You might have them simply think about each step and apply it. It will depend on your students, their experience with this program and the time you can afford to allot to this task.

If you'd rather not have to make this decision yourself, I provide you a suggested structure on pages 14-21 that will help you scaffold the process as you spiral through each round of instruction. To simplify things <u>for now</u>, let's say that a Learning Cycle is any bulky task where you expect your students to complete a "Learning Cycle Packet" along with it. **Want to see a sample Year-Long Plan for teaching Learning Cycles all year long? Visit: bit.ly/3TVYIZg**

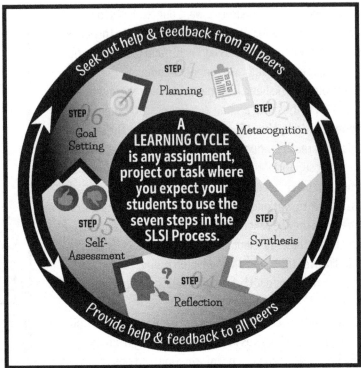

The definition of a Learning Cycle is provided in the center of the SLSI Process Chart. Note that Feedback is listed around the outside of the circle to represent that feedback occurs during all stages of learning.

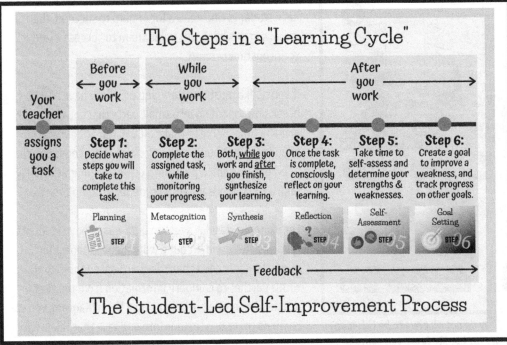

As taught to the students in Lesson 0.03, one full "Learning Cycle" is finished when students complete all seven steps in the Student-Led Self-Improvement Process (SLSI) for a bulky task. How you judge "completion" is completely up to you though, and if you'd rather not have to make that decision, simply follow the Instructional Spirals on pages 15-21, which guide you and your students toward success!

Lesson 0.03 teaches students what a "Learning Cycle" is and is a good place for you to start too! The materials in that lesson explains how the seven steps in the SLSI Process are divided into "Before you work," "While you work," and "After you work" groups so students are able to figure out when to apply each macroskill to their bulky task.

If you're interested in learning more about "Learning Cycles" from a student's perspective, see pages 26-27 and download the slides for the lesson.

Learning Cycle Packets

Eight or more graphic organizers that scaffold the SLSI Process for students while they work

All of the Learning Cycle Packet materials:

bit.ly/3vuutz7

Learning Cycle Packet - A Learning Cycle Packet is a collection of eight graphic organizers (and one direction sheet) that help students focus in on the essentials of each macroskill within the Student-Led Self-Improvement Process. ***This basic packet can be used throughout the entire program***, or you can add or swap out some organizers with new ones that become available as you teach each mini-lesson. There is one graphic organizer in the packet for each of the seven macroskills. Plus, there is one additional organizer to help students Progress Monitor one of their goals.

Students will complete one Learning Cycle Packet with each "bulky task" that you assign them, and students are expected to follow the directions correctly to work through the steps. These can be assigned as a packet or electronically. You can also modify any of these graphic organizers in order to suit your students' needs best. Alternate graphic organizers are available online for each of the **starred** lessons that are listed on pages 15-21.

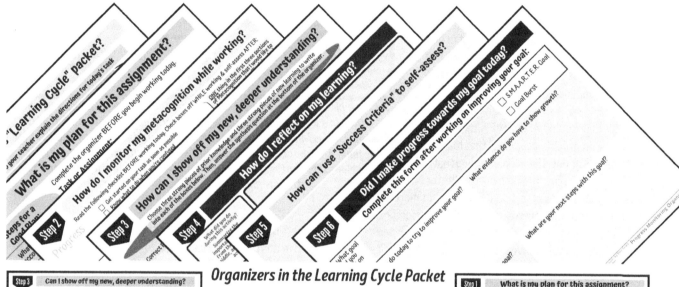

Organizers in the Learning Cycle Packet

As you teach mini-lessons, more advanced graphic organizers become available to add or replace existing ones in the Learning Cycle Packet. These optional organizers help students fine-tune their macroskill abilities.

Exemplars have been provided for all of the graphic organizers in the Learning Cycle Packet, and for many of the alternate graphic organizers that can be added as lessons are taught. Use them to give students an idea of what you are looking for in their efforts.

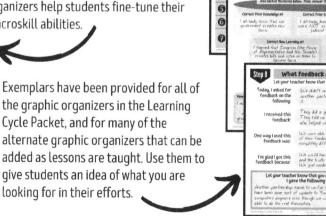

✱ IMPORTANT NOTE: In the Learning Cycle packet, you will find Goal Setting graphic organizers where students will be reporting on the goals they worked on during that specific bulky task. However, it is crucial to establish a separate system for students to keep their actual goal sheets apart from the Learning Cycle packets. For detailed instructions on how to implement this system, **please refer to page 270.**

Sidebar tabs: INTRODUCTION · PLANNING · METACOGNITION · SYNTHESIS · REFLECTION · SELF-ASSESSMENT · GOAL SETTING · FEEDBACK

What is an Instructional Spiral?

One of seven "rounds" of instruction that scaffolds each step in the SLSI Process

Instructional Spirals - Instead of dedicating a month to teaching PLANNING microskills followed by another month for METACOGNITION microskills and so on with each of the seven macroskills, *Optimized Learning* employs a spiraling approach that progressively develops all seven macroskills at the same time. During the first round of instruction, students gain a basic understanding of each macroskill, practice its application, and then delve deeper in subsequent rounds. This spiraling approach allows students to apply the SLSI Process throughout the year, rather than waiting until all of the lessons have been taught for each macroskill, ensuring steady and methodical improvement over time. Since students are not expected to master each macroskill before moving on, they can engage with the process at different levels and make progress toward independent transfer right away.

To align with this philosophy, all lessons in this book are divided into seven "Instructional Spirals" that teachers can choose to follow, or not. The initial Instructional Spirals focus on teaching foundational microskills for each macroskill, while later Instructional Spirals cover more supplemental, nuanced, and complex microskills. Therefore, in a given year, a teacher may choose to teach only the first few Instructional Spirals and still derive significant value from their efforts, as long as students continue to apply the learned skills throughout the year. In other years, teachers may opt to teach all seven Instructional Spirals. **Want to see a sample Year-Long Plan for teaching these Instructional Spirals? Visit: bit.ly/3TVYIZg**

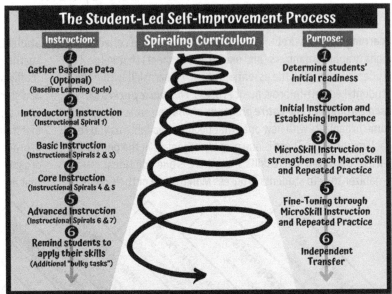

This graphic shows how the mini-lessons presented within **Optimized Learning** *"spiral" in a way that allows students to learn about all seven steps of the Student-Led Self-Improvement Process quickly, albeit at a surface level at the beginning. Each successive "Learning Cycle" revisits each macroskill and develops them further through mini-lessons that help students become stronger and stronger at the whole process.*

As teachers become more familiar with the microskill mini-lessons provided in this book, they can begin to customize the Instructional Spirals to cater to the specific needs of their students each year. Some of the ways this can be done include:

- skipping lessons that your students don't need,
- turning lessons into simple class discussions to save time by skipping the slides & handouts,
- modifying lessons to focus on aspects of a microskill that are more important for your class,
- combining similar lessons to avoid repetition or to save time, or
- delaying the teaching of a particular lesson in the school year to allow students to experience struggle and become more invested in the skill.

The most important aspect of implementing the mini-lessons is that teachers adapt them to work effectively for themselves and their students.

Finally, it is highly recommended that you read the first few pages of each of the remaining chapters before you teach any mini-lessons. This will help you understand the steps in the SLSI Process better, and therefore understand how to support your students better as they become more *Optimized Learners*.

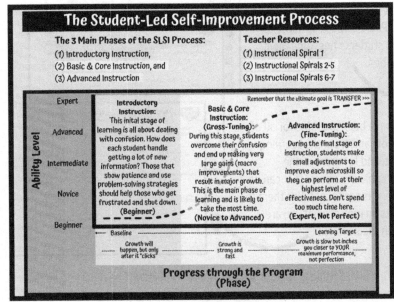

Expected Growth & Progress throughout the program

Instructional Spiral 1
Introducing the SLSI Process to your Class

All of the Materials for Instructional Spiral 1:
bit.ly/3tPolAA

Below, you will find a list of the 25 mini-lessons that should be taught during the first Instructional Spiral. You have been given a checkbox that you can use to check them off as you complete them. In addition, all of the graphic organizers that are found within the Learning Cycle packet are taught within these mini-lessons, so each of those lessons have been noted to the left of the checkboxes.

	1.	☐	Lesson 0.01	What is Student-Led Self-Improvement? Part 1 of 2
	2.	☐	Lesson 0.02	What is Student-Led Self-Improvement? Part 2 of 2
	3.	☐	Lesson 1.02	How do I PLAN and PREPARE for an assignment?
	4.	☐	Lesson 1.05	How many marbles do I have in each cup?
*	5.	☐	Lesson 1.07	How do I create a plan for a learning experience?
	6.	☐	Lesson 2.02	What is Metacognition?
*	7.	☐	Lesson 2.04	How can metacognition help me improve my work?
	8.	☐	Lesson 3.02	What does it mean to Synthesize?
	9.	☐	Lesson 3.03	What is Synthesis?
	10.	☐	Lesson 3.04	Why spend time Synthesizing?
*	11.	☐	Lesson 3.05	What are the steps in the Synthesis Process?
	12.	☐	Lesson 4.02	What is Reflection?
*	13.	☐	Lesson 4.04	How do I reflect on my learning?
	14.	☐	Lesson 5.02	What is Self-Assessment? What is Self-Grading?
	15.	☐	Lesson 5.05	How do I complete a Basic Self-Assessment?
*	16.	☐	Lesson 5.06	How can I use "Success Criteria" to self-assess?
*	17.	☐	Lesson 6.02	What is Goal Setting?
	18.	☐	Lesson 6.04	How do I write a S.M.A.A.R.T.E.R. Goal?
	19.	☐	Lesson 6.14	How can I authentically work on improving my goals?
*	20.	☐	Lesson 6.15	How can I monitor & assess progress on my goals?
	21.	☐	Lesson 6.31	What are Success Partners?
	22.	☐	Lesson 7.02	What is Positive Feedback? What is Critical Feedback?
	23.	☐	Lesson 7.18	How can a compliment help me give critical feedback?
*	24.	☐	Lesson 7.44	What feedback did I use? What did I give?
	25.	☐	Lesson 0.03	How do I complete a Learning Cycle packet?
	26.	☐		**Have students complete a "Learning Cycle Packet" WHILE they complete a "bulky task." Give feedback and discuss as a class before moving on.**

During the weeks you are teaching these mini-lessons, you might choose to have your students complete Learning Cycle Packets WHILE they complete some "bulky tasks" from your curriculum, in order to identify a baseline to determine growth. Since students will not have had much instruction in the SLSI Process, you can assess their readiness level on these skills by evaluating the quality of their work. Once you've taught most of the lessons in this spiral, you might still choose to have students complete Learning Cycle Packets, but I would no longer consider the results of their work "Baseline Data."

It is highly recommended that you teach all 25 lessons listed on the left. However, if you want to find ways to save a little time, one lesson has been un-bolded, which means that you can choose to skip that lesson without worrying that it will be a prerequisite for future lessons.

However, since the lessons in this book have been put into an order that is most meaningful for the students, it would be better to skip future lessons, than current lessons (i.e. If you have to skip lessons, skip the lessons in Instructional Spiral 7 rather than lessons in Instructional Spiral 1).

Each Instructional Spiral culminates with a packet of graphic organizers that allows students to apply the steps in the "Student-Led Self-Improvement Process" (SLSI) that they learned in the mini-lessons. So, once you have completed the mini-lessons from this Instructional Spiral, be sure to complete Step 26. (For more info, see pages 11-13.)

Although the mini-lessons are taught in isolation, the packet integrates all of the skills into a curricular lesson of your choice (a "bulky task") which is when students apply these skills in real-life learning scenarios.

INTRODUCTION
PLANNING
METACOGNITION
SYNTHESIS
REFLECTION
SELF-ASSESSMENT
GOAL SETTING
FEEDBACK

All of the Materials for Instructional Spiral 2:

Instructional Spiral 2

The Learning Cycle Packet stays the same from one Instructional Spiral to the next, but there are additional graphic organizers that you might choose to add to the packet (or swap in) - those lessons have been noted to the left of the checkboxes. If you want to use those graphic organizers, be sure not to skip these lessons!

It is highly recommended that you teach all 25 lessons listed on the right. However, if you want to find ways to save a little time, two lessons have been un-bolded, which means that you can choose to skip those lessons without worrying that they will be a prerequisite for future lessons.

However, since the lessons in this book have been put into an order that is most meaningful for the students, it would be better to skip future lessons, than current lessons.

Each Instructional Spiral culminates with a packet of graphic organizers that allows students to apply the steps in the "Student-Led Self-Improvement Process" (SLSI) that they learned in the mini-lessons. So, once you have completed the mini-lessons from this Instructional Spiral, be sure to complete Step 26. (For more info, see pgs. 11-13.)

Although the mini-lessons are taught in isolation, the packet integrates all of the skills into a curricular lesson of your choice (a "bulky task") which is when students apply these skills in real-life learning scenarios.

	☐	1.	Lesson 1.03	**Why should we take time to plan?**
*	☐	2.	Lesson 1.06	**How do I plan for a HUGE, complex assignment?**
	☐	3.	Lesson 1.08	**What are my teacher's expectations? Success Criteria?**
	☐	4.	Lesson 1.09	**What's my priority? Why is it important?**
	☐	5.	Lesson 1.10	**How long might it take me to complete everything?**
	☐	6.	Lesson 6.05	**How do I write a Goal Burst?**
*	☐	7.	Lesson 1.14	**What goals do I plan to work on?**
	☐	8.	Lesson 1.18	How should I handle conflict when it happens?
	☐	9.	Lesson 2.23	**How can I improve my awareness of time?**
	☐	10.	Lesson 2.28	**Shouldn't everything go according to my plan?**
	☐	11.	Lesson 2.29	**What do I do when things don't go according to my plan?**
*	☐	12.	Lesson 3.15	**How can I show off my new, deeper understanding?**
	☐	13.	Lesson 3.17	How will I know when I need to synthesize?
	☐	14.	Lesson 4.03	**Why should we spend time reflecting?**
*	☐	15.	Lesson 4.05	**What are the Four Dimensions of Reflection?**
	☐	16.	Lesson 5.03	**Why should we spend time on self-assessment?**
*	☐	17.	Lesson 5.09	**What can I do to self-assess WHILE I work?**
*	☐	18.	Lesson 5.11	**How can I use "I can" Statements to self-assess?**
	☐	19.	Lesson 6.03	**Why should we take time to set goals?**
	☐	20.	Lesson 6.12	**Do I have to write a PLAN for each of my goals?**
	☐	21.	Lesson 6.13	**How can I write PLANS that help me achieve my goals?**
	☐	22.	Lesson 7.03	**Why should we take time to give and ask for feedback?**
	☐	23.	Lesson 7.04	**How do you feel when people give you feedback?**
*	☐	24.	Lesson 7.19	**What are some formal strategies for giving feedback?**
	☐	25.	Lesson 7.31	**Why is it not enough to just tolerate others?**
	☐	26.		**Have students complete a "Learning Cycle Packet" WHILE they complete a "bulky task." Give feedback and discuss as a class before moving on.**

During the weeks you are teaching these lessons, you might choose to have your students complete a Learning Cycle Packet while they complete some "bulky tasks" from your curriculum. (Don't include any of the new graphic organizers that are taught in this Instructional Spiral until you get to Step 26 above, though.) The goal is to have students eventually begin to think about all seven macroskills in the SLSI Process whenever they are working in class without direct teacher support, and these additional experiences will help them transfer those skills. Having students complete Learning Cycle packets throughout instruction also helps students synthesize the information from each mini-lesson into a clearer understanding of how they can take ownership over their learning.

Instructional Spiral 3

The Learning Cycle Packet stays the same from one Instructional Spiral to the next, but there are additional graphic organizers that you might choose to add to the packet (or swap in) - those lessons have been noted below. If you want to use those graphic organizers, be sure not to skip these lessons!

All of the Materials for Instructional Spiral 3:

bit.ly/48reX57

	☐	1.	Lesson 1.16	**What are some elements of TRUE Collaboration?**
	☐	2.	Lesson 1.17	**How do I apply the elements of TRUE Collaboration?**
	☐	3.	Lesson 1.12	**What should I do when I'm confused? (Planning)**
	☐	4.	Lesson 2.06	**What should I do when I'm confused? (Metacognition)**
	☐	5.	Lesson 2.16	**How can I improve the way I work with others?**
	☐	6.	Lesson 2.25	How can reading directions carefully help me?
	☐	7.	Lesson 3.06	**Where can Prior Knowledge come from?**
*	☐	8.	Lesson 3.07	**How do I activate my Prior Knowledge?**
	☐	9.	Lesson 3.08	**How do I make sense of the new information I've collected?**
*	☐	10.	Lesson 4.09	**What is the Formal Reflection Process? Part 1 of 2**
*	☐	11.	Lesson 4.10	**What is the Formal Reflection Process? Part 2 of 2**
	☐	12.	Lesson 5.04	**How can I use Learning Targets to self-assess?**
*	☐	13.	Lesson 5.15	**What are some good questions to help me self-assess?**
*	☐	14.	Lesson 5.17	**How well am I doing on my work completion?**
	☐	15.	Lesson 6.06	**How do I write my goal so it is SPECIFIC?**
*	☐	16.	Lesson 6.07	**How do I MEASURE growth toward my goal?**
	☐	17.	Lesson 6.08	**Is this goal ACHIEVABLE? Is it AMBITIOUS enough?**
	☐	18.	Lesson 6.09	**Is this goal RELEVANT? Is it TIMELY?**
	☐	19.	Lesson 6.10	**Is this goal likely to be REWARDING? EVERLASTING?**
	☐	20.	Lesson 6.11	**What RESOURCES will I need to accomplish this goal?**
	☐	21.	Lesson 6.29	What impact do new and old skills have on my growth?
	☐	22.	Lesson 7.05	**How can I learn to appreciate critical feedback?**
	☐	23.	Lesson 7.14	**How can I make sure that my feedback is KIND?**
	☐	24.	Lesson 7.20	**How do I focus my feedback on the work, not the person?**
	☐	25.	Lesson 7.23	**When do I ask for help? When should I persevere?**
	☐	26.		**Have students complete a "Learning Cycle Packet" WHILE they complete a "bulky task." Give feedback and discuss as a class before moving on.**

During the weeks you are teaching these lessons, you might choose to have your students complete a Learning Cycle Packet while they complete some "bulky tasks" from your curriculum. (Don't include any of the new graphic organizers that are taught in this Instructional Spiral until you get to Step 26 above, though.) The goal is to have students eventually begin to think about all seven macroskills in the SLSI Process whenever they are working in class without direct teacher support, and these additional experiences will help them transfer those skills. Having students complete Learning Cycle packets throughout instruction also helps students synthesize the information from each mini-lesson into a clearer understanding of how they can take ownership over their learning.

It is highly recommended that you teach all 25 lessons listed on the left. However, if you want to find ways to save a little time, two lessons have been un-bolded, which means that you can choose to skip those lessons without worrying that they will be a prerequisite for future lessons.

However, since the lessons in this book have been put into an order that is most meaningful for the students, it would be better to skip future lessons, than current lessons.

Each Instructional Spiral culminates with a packet of graphic organizers that allows students to apply the steps in the "Student-Led Self-Improvement Process" (SLSI) that they learned in the mini-lessons. So, once you have completed the mini-lessons from this Instructional Spiral, be sure to complete Step 26. (For more info, see pages 11-13.)

INTRODUCTION
PLANNING
METACOGNITION
SYNTHESIS
REFLECTION
SELF-ASSESSMENT
GOAL SETTING
FEEDBACK

All of the Materials for Instructional Spiral 4:

bit.ly/3SeCuj9

The Learning Cycle Packet stays the same from one Instructional Spiral to the next, but there are additional graphic organizers that you might choose to add to the packet (or swap in) - those lessons have been noted below. If you want to use those graphic organizers, be sure not to skip these lessons!

It is highly recommended that you teach all 25 lessons listed on the right. However, if you want to find ways to save a little time, two lessons have been un-bolded, which means that you can choose to skip those lessons without worrying that they will be a prerequisite for future lessons.

However, since the lessons in this book have been put into an order that is most meaningful for the students, it would be better to skip future lessons, than current lessons.

Each Instructional Spiral culminates with a packet of graphic organizers where students apply the steps in the "Student-Led Self-Improvement Process" that they learned in the mini-lessons. So, once you have completed the mini-lessons from this Instructional Spiral, be sure to complete Step 26. (For more info, see pages 11-13.)

Although the mini-lessons are taught in isolation, the packet integrates all of the skills into a curricular lesson of your choice (a "bulky task") which is when students apply these skills in real-life learning scenarios.

	1.	Lesson 1.11	How will I know if I'm on track to finish on time?
	2.	Lesson 1.15	**What prior knowledge might help me on this?**
	3.	Lesson 1.20	**What distracts me and how can I overcome it?**
	4.	Lesson 2.05	**Why can it be SO HARD to get started?**
	5.	Lesson 2.08	**What do I do when I feel like giving up?**
	6.	Lesson 2.10	**I'm finished. What do I do now? (Metacognition)**
	7.	Lesson 2.19	**How can I develop a strong work ethic?**
	8.	Lesson 3.09	**How can I fill in the GAPS in my understanding?**
★	9.	Lesson 3.11	**How COMPLETE is my understanding of this information?**
★	10.	Lesson 4.06	**How can I improve my reflections with "Tell Me More?"**
★	11.	Lesson 4.13	How can I reflect with a partner?
	12.	Lesson 4.16	**How do I reflect on a mistake and accept it?**
	13.	Lesson 5.10	**How can I use checklists to self-assess?**
★	14.	Lesson 5.12	**How can I use rubrics to self-assess?**
★	15.	Lesson 5.13	**How can I use highlighting to self-assess?**
★	16.	Lesson 5.14	**How can I use exit tickets to self-assess?**
	17.	Lesson 5.18	**How well am I doing on the quality of my work?**
★	18.	Lesson 5.20	**What do I do when I finish an assignment early? (S.A.)**
★	19.	Lesson 6.19	**What do I do once I believe I've accomplished a goal?**
	20.	Lesson 7.11	**Why should I give feedback that is SPECIFIC?**
	21.	Lesson 7.12	**Why should I give feedback that is IMMEDIATE?**
	22.	Lesson 7.13	**Why should I give feedback that is PERSONALIZED?**
	23.	Lesson 7.34	**How can a Growth Mindset help me improve my skills?**
	24.	Lesson 7.36	**What do I do immediately after receiving feedback?**
	25.	Lesson 7.41	**How do I avoid repeating mistakes?**
	26.		**Have students complete a Learning Cycle Packet WHILE they complete a "bulky task." Give feedback and discuss as a class before moving on.**

During the weeks you are teaching these lessons, you might choose to have your students complete a Learning Cycle Packet while they complete some "bulky tasks" from your curriculum. (Don't include any of the new graphic organizers that are taught in this Instructional Spiral until you get to Step 26 above, though.) The goal is to have students eventually begin to think about all seven macroskills in the SLSI Process whenever they are working in class without direct teacher support, and these additional experiences will help them transfer those skills. Having students complete Learning Cycle packets throughout instruction also helps students synthesize the information from each mini-lesson into a clearer understanding of how they can take ownership over their learning.

Instructional Spiral 5

The Learning Cycle Packet stays the same from one Instructional Spiral to the next, but there are additional graphic organizers that you might choose to add to the packet (or swap in) - those lessons have been noted below. If you want to use those graphic organizers, be sure not to skip these lessons!

All of the Materials for Instructional Spiral 5:

bit.ly/3TQtR0t

✓	☐	1. Lesson 1.22	How much time should I dedicate to Planning?
	☐	2. Lesson 2.09	What do I do if I'm stuck in the Learning Pit?
	☐	3. Lesson 2.12	What if I keep getting distracted?
	☐	4. Lesson 2.13	How can I manage my impulsivity?
	☐	5. Lesson 2.24	How can I manage my time better?
*	☐	6. Lesson 3.12	How do I question what I've learned and think I know?
*	☐	7. Lesson 3.13	How do I clear up my misunderstandings?
*	☐	8. Lesson 4.08	What is a Yesterday, Today, Tomorrow Reflection?
*	☐	9. Lesson 4.15	How do I reflect Before, During and After working?
	☐	10. Lesson 4.17	How do I analyze and reflect on a grade?
	☐	11. Lesson 5.08	How accurate are my self-assessments?
*	☐	12. Lesson 6.16	How do I collect and organize my evidence of growth?
	☐	13. Lesson 6.20	What kinds of goals should I be working on?
	☐	14. Lesson 6.21	How do I come up with new goals to work on?
	☐	15. Lesson 6.22	Can I use self-assessment to create new goals?
	☐	16. Lesson 6.23	How do I prioritize which goals to focus on first?
*	☐	17. Lesson 6.24	Am I improving? What evidence supports that?
	☐	18. Lesson 6.27	What are some goal setting mistakes I should avoid?
*	☐	19. Lesson 6.30	How can I "Level Up"?
	☐	20. Lesson 7.06	How should I show appreciation for critical feedback?
	☐	21. Lesson 7.09	What are some tips for giving others feedback?
	☐	22. Lesson 7.10	How good am I at implementing these feedback tips?
	☐	23. Lesson 7.15	What factors should I consider when giving feedback?
	☐	24. Lesson 7.17	How do I make sure they understood my feedback?
	☐	25. Lesson 7.30	How do I get better at asking EVERYONE for feedback?
	☐	26.	**Have students complete a Learning Cycle Packet WHILE they complete a "bulky task." Give feedback and discuss as a class before moving on.**

During the weeks you are teaching these lessons, you might choose to have your students complete a Learning Cycle Packet while they complete some "bulky tasks" from your curriculum. (Don't include any of the new graphic organizers that are taught in this Instructional Spiral until you get to Step 26 above, though.) The goal is to have students eventually begin to think about all seven macroskills in the SLSI Process whenever they are working in class without direct teacher support, and these additional experiences will help them transfer those skills. Having students complete Learning Cycle packets throughout instruction also helps students synthesize the information from each mini-lesson into a clearer understanding of how they can take ownership over their learning.

It is highly recommended that you teach all 25 lessons listed on the left. However, if you want to find ways to save a little time, two lessons have been un-bolded, which means that you can choose to skip those lessons without worrying that they will be a prerequisite for future lessons.

However, since the lessons in this book have been put into an order that is most meaningful for the students, it would be better to skip future lessons, than current lessons.

Each Instructional Spiral culminates with a packet of graphic organizers that allows students to apply the steps in the "Student-Led Self-Improvement Process" (SLSI) that they learned in the mini-lessons. So, once you have completed the mini-lessons from this Instructional Spiral, be sure to complete Step 26. (For more information, see pages 11-13.)

Although the mini-lessons are taught in isolation, the packet integrates all of the skills into a curricular lesson of your choice (a "bulky task") which is when students apply these skills in real-life learning scenarios.

PLANNING

METACOGNITION

SYNTHESIS

REFLECTION

SELF-ASSESSMENT

GOAL SETTING

FEEDBACK

All of the Materials for Instructional Spiral 6:

bit.ly/4aPcraB

The Learning Cycle Packet stays the same from one Instructional Spiral to the next, but there are additional graphic organizers that you might choose to add to the packet (or swap in) - those lessons have been noted below. If you want to use those graphic organizers, be sure not to skip these lessons!

It is highly recommended that you teach all 25 lessons listed on the right. However, if you want to find ways to save a little time, four lessons have been un-bolded, which means that you can choose to skip those lessons without worrying that they will be a prerequisite for future lessons. However, since the lessons in this book have been put into an order that is most meaningful for the students, it would be better to skip future lessons, than current lessons.

Each Instructional Spiral culminates with a packet of graphic organizers where students apply the steps in the "Student-Led Self-Improvement Process" that they learned in the mini-lessons. So, once you have completed the mini-lessons from this Instructional Spiral, be sure to complete Step 26. (For more info, see pgs 11-13.)

Although the mini-lessons are taught in isolation, the packet integrates all of the skills into a curricular lesson of your choice (a "bulky task") which is when students apply these skills in real-life learning scenarios.

1. **Lesson 1.04**   **What do others think about planning?**
2. **Lesson 2.11**   **Why is "follow-through" so important?**
3. Lesson 2.15   How can I become more socially aware?
4. **Lesson 2.17**   **How can I become more empathetic?**
5. Lesson 2.18   How should I respond to verbal & non-verbal cues?
6. **Lesson 2.21**   **How can I develop intrinsic motivation?**
7. **Lesson 2.22**   **Am I trying too hard or not hard enough?**
8. **Lesson 2.26**   **How can I be responsible for several directions?**
   * 9. **Lesson 3.14**   **How do I keep an open mind while learning?**
   * 10. **Lesson 3.16**   **How can a KWHLCQ Chart explain my learning story?**
11. Lesson 4.18   How do I analyze and reflect on an incorrect answer?
   * 12. **Lesson 6.17**   **How can I use Check-In Stations to manage my time?**
   * 13. **Lesson 6.25**   **What do I need to do in order to reach my target?**
   * 14. **Lesson 6.26**   **How can I measure growth objectively & subjectively?**
15. **Lesson 7.07**   **What if I still can't handle getting critical feedback?**
16. **Lesson 7.21**   **How do I show tact when being asked for feedback?**
17. **Lesson 7.22**   **What are some final tips on giving feedback to others?**
18. Lesson 7.24   What are some good and bad times to ask for feedback?
19. **Lesson 7.25**   **What are some reasons why feedback might not be helpful?**
20. **Lesson 7.26**   **What should I do to get the most valuable feedback?**
21. **Lesson 7.27**   **What "level of feedback" do I need?**
22. **Lesson 7.28**   **How can I make it easy on others to give me feedback?**
23. **Lesson 7.29**   **How can I show a strong desire to seek out feedback?**
24. **Lesson 7.37**   **How do I respond to feedback I disagree with?**
25. **Lesson 7.40**   **How do I get the most out of the feedback I receive?**
26. **Have students complete a "Learning Cycle Packet" WHILE they complete a "bulky task." Give feedback and discuss as a class before moving on.**

During the weeks you are teaching these lessons, you might choose to have your students complete a Learning Cycle Packet while they complete some "bulky tasks" from your curriculum. (Don't include any of the new graphic organizers that are taught in this Instructional Spiral until you get to Step 26 above, though.) The goal is to have students eventually begin to think about all seven macroskills in the SLSI Process whenever they are working in class without direct teacher support, and these additional experiences will help them transfer those skills. Having students complete Learning Cycle packets throughout instruction also helps students synthesize the information from each mini-lesson into a clearer understanding of how they can take ownership over their learning.

Instructional Spiral 7
Transitioning to Independent Transfer

INTRODUCTION

PLANNING

METACOGNITION

SYNTHESIS

REFLECTION

SELF-ASSESSMENT

GOAL SETTING

FEEDBACK

All of the Materials for Instructional Spiral 7:

bit.ly/3vu1wCV

- [ ] 1. **Lesson 2.27** — **How can I improve my processing power?**
- [ ] 2. **Lesson 2.20** — **What do I do when my work isn't really motivating?**
- ★ [ ] 3. **Lesson 3.10** — **Can I find connections between pieces of my knowledge?**
- [ ] 4. **Lesson 4.07** — **How can I use a Wander Map to reflect on my learning journey?**
- [ ] 5. Lesson 4.11 — How does the amount of time I have affect my reflection?
- [ ] 6. Lesson 4.12 — What are some activities that are actually reflections?
- [ ] 7. Lesson 5.07 — How can others' work samples help me self-assess?
- [ ] 8. Lesson 5.16 — What can I learn by comparing my assessment to others?
- ★ [ ] 9. **Lesson 6.18** — **How can I use Check-In Stations to track my progress?**
- ★ [ ] 10. **Lesson 6.28** — **How much time might I need to achieve my goal?**
- [ ] 11. **Lesson 7.08** — **What are some other sources of feedback?**
- [ ] 12. **Lesson 7.16** — **How do I offer feedback if they didn't ask for it?**
- [ ] 13. **Lesson 7.32** — **How can rubrics and checklists guide my feedback?**
- [ ] 14. **Lesson 7.33** — **How can single-point rubrics help me with feedback?**
- [ ] 15. **Lesson 7.35** — **How does practice make permanent (not perfect)?**
- [ ] 16. **Lesson 7.39** — **What does it mean to "close my feedback loop?"**
- [ ] 17. **Lesson 7.42** — **How do I synthesize my feedback effectively?**
- ★ [ ] 18. **Lesson 7.43** — **How much can I grow if I seek out follow-up feedback?**
- [ ] 19. **Lesson 5.21** — **How much have I grown over the course of the year?**
- [ ] 20. **Lesson 0.05** — **How do I transition away from using the SLSI forms?**
- [ ] 21. **Have students complete a "Learning Cycle Packet" WHILE they complete a "bulky task." Give feedback and discuss as a class before moving on. Since this is the last Instructional Spiral, continue to assign "bulky tasks" but transition your students away from using the packets. (Posters and hints are fine, but eventually, students should do this independently.)**

See directions on the previous page. It is recommended that you teach all 20 lessons listed on the left. However, if you want to save a little time, four lessons have been un-bolded, which means that you can skip those lessons. Since this is the final Instructional Spiral, none of these lessons are prerequisites to future lessons.

Remind students that they need to transfer ALL of these skills to other classes now and in the future! That's the main goal of all of these mini-lessons!

During the weeks you are teaching these lessons, you might choose to have your students complete a Learning Cycle Packet while they complete some "bulky tasks" from your curriculum.

Optional Lessons - None of these are required

- If you choose to teach any of these lessons, they are best taught near the beginning of the year. Some are introductions to the macroskills (the lessons ending in *.01). Some create optional systems that you would use nearly everyday.

- I highly recommend:
  - Lesson 0.04, but you might want to teach this one after Instructional Spiral 2,
  - Lesson 2.03, before your students become experts at Metacognition, and
  - Lesson 4.14 or Lesson 5.19 (they're similar).

- [ ] 1. Lesson 0.04 — How do I show what I learned after a "Learning Cycle"?
- [ ] 2. Lesson 1.01 — How strong am I at each of these Planning Skills?
- [ ] 3. Lesson 1.13 — Where should I work so that I can focus best?
- [ ] 4. Lesson 1.19 — How can I organize myself better?
- [ ] 5. Lesson 1.21 — What should I do when I'm having a bad day?
- [ ] 6. Lesson 2.01 — How strong am I at each of these Metacognition Skills?
- [ ] 7. Lesson 2.03 — What is a Metacognition Check?
- [ ] 8. Lesson 2.07 — How can I organize my materials & workspace?
- [ ] 9. Lesson 2.14 — What if I don't meet behavior expectations?
- [ ] 10. Lesson 3.01 — How strong am I at each of these Synthesis Skills?
- [ ] 11. Lesson 4.01 — How strong am I at each of these Reflection Skills?
- [ ] 12. Lesson 4.14 — What are the Six A's of Reflecting on your day?
- [ ] 13. Lesson 5.01 — How strong am I at each of these Self-Assessment Skills?
- [ ] 14. Lesson 5.19 — How well did we do today as a whole class?
- [ ] 15. Lesson 6.01 — How strong am I at each of these Goal Setting Skills?
- [ ] 16. Lesson 7.01 — How strong am I at each of these Feedback Skills?
- [ ] 17. Lesson 7.38 — How can I keep track of all the feedback I receive?

bit.ly/3RjqBIe

Internalize the components of the SLSI Process, transforming from passive observers to active participants in learning

Essential Question

What is the Student-Led Self-Improvement Process (SLSI)?
Part 1 of 2

Big Idea

When we ultimately internalize and use the seven steps of the Student-Led Self-Improvement Process, we stop being passive observers during learning experiences, and instead become active participants in learning.

Lesson Overview

In this lesson, students learn about the Student-Led Self-Improvement Process (SLSI), which is the driving force behind all of the lessons in this book. In a very basic way, students learn about the seven components of the SLSI Process (Planning, Metacognition, Synthesis, Reflection, Self-Assessment, Goal Setting and Feedback). Before too much is taught, students have the opportunity to share their predictions for each macroskill and to close out the lesson, they infer what they might need to do during each macroskill on an assignment.

Discussion/Reflection Questions

- Why do you think we are taking time to learn the lessons within this program?
- Which of the seven steps do you feel most confident in right now? Which do you expect to grow the most in?
- How can you convince yourself that this program is going to be extremely valuable and helpful for you? What can you tell yourself right now to help you get on-board and start buying in to the lessons?

Teacher Tips

- This is the first lesson in the program and because it looks at the program from a MACRO point of view, very little of it will make sense to students right now. Ensure them that things will begin to make more sense as they complete lessons.
- Let students know that the Student-Led Self-Improvement Process is something that they will be expected to use whenever they work independently or with their peers. Although they won't need to complete Student Handouts forever, the handouts will help them grow their skills and eventually internalize the process so they can manage all of the steps independently.
- You as the teacher will get to decide how many of these lessons you will offer your students. The more lessons you teach, the stronger students should get at the given skill.
- Students need daily reminders to use what they've learned in previous lessons, so please be their reminder for as long as it makes sense to do so. Don't release responsibility too soon!
- Please come up with some sort of system for ensuring that students take the Student Handouts seriously, complete their work on time, and understand the concepts being taught in each lesson. I don't recommend grading them, but I do recommend providing feedback!
- For the second Student Handout, suggest a recent assignment you gave them that they can envision while completing this graphic organizer - something that they worked on without too much teacher support is best.

Student Tasks 〉 Transfer Goals

Student Tasks	Transfer Goals
Students learn about the Student-Led Self-Improvement Process.	Students value the process, despite not completely understanding it just yet.
Students learn about the seven components of the Student-Led Self-Improvement Process.	Students are prepared to learn more about each of the seven components of the SLSI Process.

Instructional Poster(s)

- This lesson has ONE Instructional Poster.
- The first Instructional Poster for this lesson shows students the "Student-Led Self-Improvement Process" cycle. It helps students understand the purpose of the program, even if it's just at a surface level for now.
- As with all of the Instructional Posters in this program, please display it for all students to see, read it aloud to the class, and then discuss it together.
- Before you teach Instructional Posters 2 and 3, have students complete the first half of the first Student Handout (they infer the meaning of each step).

Student Handouts

- This lesson has TWO Student Handouts.
- Every lesson comes with at least two Student Handouts. These are designed for the students to complete independently or with a randomly assigned partner, but all age groups will benefit from teacher guidance on them if you have the time. The DIRECTIONS for the Student Handouts will always appear here.
- SH1 DIRECTIONS: BEFORE your teacher uses the Instructional Poster to teach the following terms, do your best to predict what they mean and how you might use them in school. Write those predictions in the top boxes, labeled "My Prediction." Then, listen to your teacher explain each of the steps, and write a short summary of each into the bottom boxes labeled "Actual."
- SH2 DIRECTIONS: If you were asked to complete each of these steps while working on an assignment that your teacher gave you to complete in class with a randomly assigned partner, what would you do during each step? (You haven't really learned much about these steps yet, so you aren't expected to know exactly what to do, but we want to see how well you infer what you might need to do.) Just try your best!
- For the second Student Handout, suggest a recent assignment you gave them that they can envision while completing this graphic organizer - something that they worked on without too much teacher support is best.

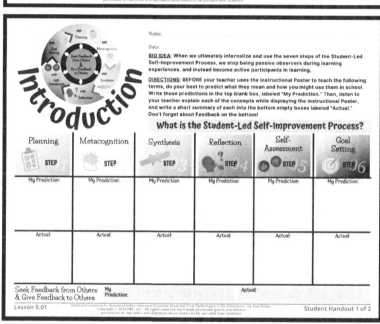

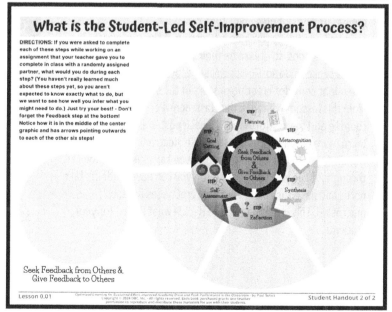

INTRODUCTION

PLANNING

METACOGNITION

SYNTHESIS

REFLECTION

SELF-ASSESSMENT

GOAL SETTING

FEEDBACK

bit.ly/3RbC5gD

Internalize the components of the SLSI Process, transforming from passive observers to active participants in learning

Essential Question

What is the Student-Led Self-Improvement Process (SLSI)?
Part 2 of 2

Big Idea

When we ultimately internalize and use the seven steps of the Student-Led Self-Improvement Process, we stop being passive observers during learning experiences, and instead become active participants in learning.

Lesson Overview

In this lesson, students continue to learn about the Student-Led Self-Improvement Process (SLSI), which is the driving force behind all of the lessons in this book. Students learn about the seven components of the SLSI Process (Planning, Metacognition, Synthesis, Reflection, Self-Assessment, Goal Setting and Feedback) through four Instructional Posters. Because this lesson has a lot of information all at once, students don't complete any activities during this lesson. The Student Handouts they receive are simply informative reminders of each macroskill.

Discussion / Reflection Questions

- Why do you think we are taking time to learn the lessons within this program?
- Which of the seven steps do you feel most confident in right now? Which do you expect to grow the most in?
- How can you convince yourself that this program is going to be extremely valuable and helpful for you? What can you tell yourself right now to help you get on-board and buying in to the lessons?

Teacher Tips

- This is the second lesson in the program and because it looks at the program from a MACRO point of view, students will continue to be a little confused about this whole process. Ensure them that things will begin to make more sense as they complete more and more lessons. They just need to have faith that it will get easier, and not give up or tune out!
- Students need daily reminders to use what they've learned in previous lessons, so please be their reminder for as long as it makes sense to do so. Don't release responsibility too soon!
- You might consider creating posters of the Student Handouts from this lesson to hang in the classroom. Perhaps you can leave room to add more information to each poster as your students learn more details. If you create these electronically (or modify what is given to you in this program) you can make additions all throughout the year! If you'd prefer, you can have students take notes and have their notes span several pages for each macroskill. This is all up to you to decide what is best for your students.

Student Tasks 〉 Transfer Goals

Student Tasks	Transfer Goals
Students learn about the Student-Led Self-Improvement Process.	Students value the process, despite not completely understanding it just yet.
Students learn about the seven components of the Student-Led Self-Improvement Process.	Students are prepared to learn more about each of the seven components of the SLSI Process.

Instructional Poster(s)

- This lesson has FOUR Instructional Posters.
- The first Instructional Poster for this lesson is called the "SLSI Cheat Sheet" because it summarizes all seven steps in the SLSI Process. This makes it an excellent poster to display in the classroom or a great choice to give to students to keep in a safe place.
- The purpose of this lesson is to review the Student-Led Self-Improvement Process, and to learn that the skills learned within the program need to be transferred to new situations in order to be useful. Therefore, three of the four Instructional Posters for today's lesson focus on how the graphic organizers in this program are similar to the training wheels on a bicycle. Training wheels support the child who is learning how to ride a bike, but they get taken off once the child is ready to try it on their own. That doesn't necessarily mean the child will be immediately successful - they may fall a few times, but it means that they are ready to try to transfer the skills independently. The graphic organizers must ultimately be taken away in order for students to transfer the skills of the Student-Led Self-Improvement Process to their life.

Student Handouts

- This lesson has TWO Student Handouts.
- Both sides of the Student Handout contain "bookmarks" that explain all seven steps in the SLSI Process. Although there is no expectation for students to use these as actual bookmarks, you may want them to keep this page handy as reference for when they need a reminder about a step.

What is the Student-Led Self-Improvement Process?

The SLSI "Cheat Sheet" Follow these seven steps whenever YOU are in charge of your learning! These steps will help you become a stronger, independent learner who is less reliant on teachers and other adults to think for them!

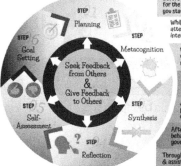

Before you begin to work independently or with others, you prepare or PLAN for the learning experience. What are all the things you need to do BEFORE you start to work? (You don't need to do this when your teacher is teaching.)

While you are working alone or with others, you monitor your behavior, attention, effort, time, quality & progress of work, actions & inactions, interactions with others, etc. You self-manage and self-correct, as needed.

While you are working alone or with others, you actively "process" what you are learning, combining it with prior knowledge to create a new, deeper understanding of the subject being learned.

Immediately after a learning experience, you think back on it and determine what you learned, what went well, and what was a struggle for you. You make sure that your new learning is stored for future use.

After reflecting, you determine what you did well and what you did poorly. You evaluate your behavior, effort, attention, etc. and determine if any changes need to be made in the future.

After self-assessing, you set goals to improve the knowledge, skills, or behaviors that you feel are relative weaknesses for you. You describe your plan for improvement and collect evidence to demonstrate growth.

Throughout the entire SLSI Process, you will ask others to give you feedback & assistance whenever you need it. You will also make time for others by providing them with meaningful feedback & assistance that helps them grow.

Transfer these skills to ALL learning experiences in life, like when you play a new video game, learn new skills on YouTube, or study for a test!

Lesson 0.02 — Instructional Poster 1 of 4

What is the Student-Led Self-Improvement Process?

The Ultimate Goal of the SLSI Process:

By the end of this program, the goal is for you to be an independent learner who knows what to do and how to do it when completing classwork and homework. On this page and the next are the seven steps briefly summarized as a reminder for you. The goal will be to do as many of the steps from these reminders and from the lessons you've learned from while independently working throughout life. This process will help you make the most of your learning time and become the best student you can be! Good luck on your learning journey!

PLANNING
Before beginning any task, independently or with peers:

- Make sure you have all of your materials and are working in a good place to learn.
- Know WHAT you need to do & WHEN it needs to be done by.
- Look through your materials so you know what you're about to learn.
- Think about what you really need to learn and what your teacher expects you to learn during this task.
- Make sure you have read and understood all of the directions before beginning.
- Make sure to work on specific, temporary goals that help you focus on what's most important or what you're currently struggling with.
- Before beginning a complex task (like studying for a test or completing a project), take time to break it down into smaller steps (chunks) so it's not too overwhelming.
- Before beginning a complex task, take time to estimate how long each step (chunk) will take so you meet your deadline(s).

META-COGNITION
Be aware of your:

Progress: Starting, Persisting and Finishing

Actions & Inactions: What you do & don't do

Interactions: Working with and around others

Effort: Your work ethic & pride in what you accomplish

Time: Using time wisely & meeting deadlines

Accuracy: Accomplishing your task correctly & completely

Flexibility: Making changes if needed

And be sure to:
- Focus on a SMAARTER Goal or a Goal Burst to work on
- Use Prior Knowledge, Skills & Strategies Effectively
- Integrate Feedback

SYNTHESIS
When learning new information:

- Always be ready to learn something new, so that you can process it and remember it in the future.
- Make connections with past experiences and prior knowledge to better understand what it is that you are learning.
- Question what you are learning and decide if it is more correct than what you already knew or less correct.
- When new information seems more accurate than your prior knowledge, use it to clear up misconceptions and misunderstandings.
- Combine what you learned today with what you already knew to create a deeper understanding that wasn't possible before today.

Lesson 0.02 — Student Handout 1 of 2

REFLECTION
After completing a task, think about your process and answer some of these questions:

- What did I do during today's activity?
- What skills or knowledge did I learn or improve today?
- What was hard for me? What did I do to overcome those challenges?
- What could I have done differently?
- What were the keys to my success?
- What was fun?
- What was boring?
- What should I get help on?
- Are there questions that I have that were never answered?
- How could I extend my learning further?

SELF-ASSESSMENT
After reflecting on your learning, take some time to assess how well you did:

- Did I try my best?
- Which goals did I improve today? Do I have evidence to add to my Goal Sheet?
- Could I have used my time better? How so?
- Did I work well collaboratively? How so?
- Was I organized and prepared? Examples?
- Did I learn from my mistakes and maintain a growth mindset?
- Did I seek feedback from others?
- Did I provide others with feedback?
- Did I meet or exceed the success criteria?
- Did I improve or show progress in any ways?

GOAL SETTING
After self-assessment, address any issues that you're struggling with by creating new goals...

S Specific
M Measurable
A Achievable
A Ambitious
R Relevant
T Timely
E Everlasting
R Rewarding
Goals!

AND Goal Bursts

...and monitoring progress on current goals:

FEEDBACK
Throughout every stage of learning, go to others for feedback and try to help others by providing feedback:

- Make sure that you understand "The Nuts & Bolts of Feedback"
- Be sure to "Seek Out Feedback From Others"
- Know how to "Make Sense of Feedback"
- Be sure that you are "Applying Feedback Effectively"
- Help your peers by "Giving Meaningful Feedback to Others"

Feedback is a POSITIVE thing that helps everyone improve. Never be embarrassed to get feedback!

Lesson 0.02 — Student Handout 2 of 2

Experience a "Learning Cycle" with a partner, completing the SLSI Process steps through graphic organizers

bit.ly/3uNrvVA

bit.ly/3uNrvVA

Essential Question

How do I complete a "Learning Cycle" packet?

Big Idea

A learning cycle is any task or assignment where you are expected to apply all of the steps in the Student-Led Self-Improvement Process. A learning cycle begins when your teacher explains the directions of the assignment and it ends when you've completed all seven steps in the SLSI Process and submitted (turned in) your completed work. Until you do this automatically, your teacher will assign a packet of graphic organizers for you to complete that guides you through all of the steps.

Lesson Overview

In this lesson, students learn about their role in the Student-Led Self-Improvement Process by completing an entire "Learning Cycle" while working on an academic assignment or task (preferably with a randomly assigned partner). They complete one graphic organizer for every step in the SLSI Process, plus one for creating a new goal for themselves. Although students haven't had much instruction in each of these steps in the process, they can infer much of what they need to know to be successful on the graphic organizers, assuming they read directions carefully and try their best. The instruction from the teacher focuses on teaching students what their Before, During, and After Learning responsibilities are.

Discussion/Reflection Questions

- Why do you think we are completing a "Learning Cycle" BEFORE we become confident about each step (macroskill)?
- What do you think you and your peers will have the most trouble with? What do you think will come most easily?
- How long do you think it will take you to complete both the academic assignment or task that your teacher gives you PLUS the graphic organizers in the packet?

Teacher Tips

- You need to read through the 11-page Teacher's Guide for this lesson before teaching. This will require extra prep time.
- A "Learning Cycle" is where you provide the students with directions for completing an academic task or assignment alone or with a partner(s) and they complete all of the steps of the Student-Led Self-Improvement Process WHILE completing the academic task or assignment (a bulky task).
- A Learning Cycle is nearly impossible to complete in one class period, so expect this to take some time, especially at first. However, the direct instruction component of this lesson, including the Student Handouts should only take the standard 15-20 minutes. Please make sure that you don't allow your students to get into the habit of rushing through the Learning Cycle packet once they begin their bulky task!
- If possible, allow students to focus more on the PROCESS of learning than the CONTENT of the lesson while completing these graphic organizers (at least during the first few Learning Cycles), because students can't really give 100% effort to both components. As students learn the SLSI Process over time, you can begin to ask them to dedicate more attention to the bulky task. Fortunately, students will transfer these learning process skills to new situations, and ultimately become stronger, more independent learners who get more out of their academic work.

Student Tasks 〉 Transfer Goals

Student Tasks	Transfer Goals
Students learn what the steps are in a complete "Learning Cycle."	Students know how the steps in the SLSI Process fit together and can better synthesize their learning during future lessons.
Students complete an entire "Learning Cycle," getting to experience all of the steps in the SLSI Process.	Students know what their role is when completing a "Learning Cycle" and become more independent learners.

Instructional Poster(s)

- This lesson has THREE Instructional Posters.
- The Instructional Posters for this lesson teach students the "Big Picture" for this program. It answers the question of "How do all of the steps in the SLSI Process fit together?" And it helps students know what to do along the way. Although students won't complete every component in a "Learning Cycle" every day, all year, this teaches them what a complete Learning Cycle looks like.

How do I complete a "Learning Cycle" packet?

Before you work (Preflection) **Step 1**

Do all of the Step 1 forms BEFORE you start working.

Step 1: Decide what steps you will take to complete this task.

Planning STEP

Teacher's Guide

- This lesson has 11 Teacher Instruction pages.
- This lesson is unique in that it comes with an 11-page Teacher's Guide to help you completely understand what is expected of your students, and what you will need to teach them in order to be successful!
- The Teacher's Guide breaks down each student step so you can scaffold their learning with front-end direct instruction and support them while they work.

Teacher Tasks during a Learning Cycle

1. Explain the assignment or task to students. Explain that they will also be completing a Learning Cycle today. Check for understanding. Assign random partners. Encourage collaboration, attention and effort. Provide extra time.

Support students by displaying Instructional Posters from this program or Anchor Charts that you've created to support each step.

2. **PLANNING**
3. Help students with the content for the assignment or task as much as you can. They may struggle more since they're balancing so many responsibilities.
4. **METACOGNITION**
5. **SYNTHESIS**
6. Help students transition from working on the assignment or task, to turning in their work, to completing the final three steps with strong effort.
7. **REFLECTION**
8. **SELF-ASSESSMENT**
9. **GOAL SETTING & PROGRESS MONITORING**

Observe and give FEEDBACK to students, but allow some mistakes to happen so students can reflect, self-assess and make goals to address them.

Student Handouts

- This lesson has TWO Student Handouts.
- Students will also need ONE Learning Cycle packet to complete while doing a "bulky task."
- DIRECTIONS: Complete the entire eight page packet BEFORE, DURING and AFTER working on an academic assignment or task given to you by your teacher. Ask questions of your peers and your teacher as needed. Although this is your first attempt at a "Learning Cycle," make it a good one! Show strong effort and try to infer what each graphic organizer is trying to get you to accomplish.
- Walk the students through the Student Handout to the right that helps students understand the steps they need to take in the SLSI Process. The rest of the packet contains the graphic organizers that walk students through the SLSI Process.

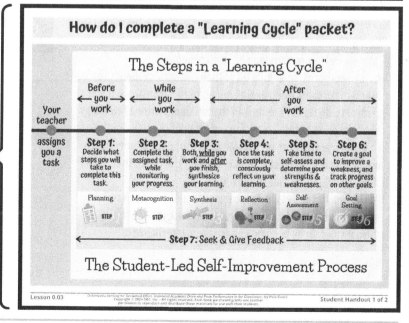

How do I complete a "Learning Cycle" packet?

The Steps in a "Learning Cycle"

Your teacher assigns you a task

| Before you work | While you work | After you work | | | |

Step 1: Decide what steps you will take to complete this task. — Planning STEP

Step 2: Complete the assigned task, while monitoring your progress. — Metacognition STEP

Step 3: Both, while you work and after you finish, synthesize your learning. — Synthesis STEP

Step 4: Once the task is complete, consciously reflect on your learning. — Reflection STEP

Step 5: Take time to self-assess and determine your strengths & weaknesses. — Self-Assessment STEP

Step 6: Create a goal to improve a weakness, and track progress on other goals. — Goal Setting STEP

Step 7: Seek & Give Feedback

The Student-Led Self-Improvement Process

0.04

Summarizing what was accomplished during the SLSI Process shows students the value of each step & solidifies learning

bit.ly/3RtBw3c

Essential Question

How do I show what I learned after a "Learning Cycle"?

Big Idea

The ultimate goal of the SLSI Process is to internalize the process so it can be used throughout life, whenever it makes sense to do so. Summarizing an entire Learning Cycle is a ton of work, but helps convert this experience into a lasting memory that can be utilized when needed. "We do not learn from experience. We learn from reflecting on experience." - John Dewey

Lesson Overview

In this lesson, students summarize what they accomplished throughout a complete Learning Cycle. They start by describing the assignment or task. Then, they describe how they planned, monitored their progress (metacognition), synthesized their learning to create a stronger, more complete understanding, reflected on my learning process, and self-assessed their relative strengths & weaknesses. They finish the summary by describing a goal they created to improve a weakness, and how they tracked progress on one of more of their previously created goals.

Discussion / Reflection Questions

- Why are we making you do this long writing assignment?
- What was one positive you discovered while completing this Learning Cycle? One negative?
- How often do you think you'll have to complete a summary like this one you did today? Because of that answer, how much effort should you put into it when you ARE asked to do one?

Teacher Tips

- The Student Handouts for this lesson will take students MUCH longer to complete than a typical mini-lesson. They are summarizing their thinking during each step in the SLSI Process.
- Ask students to put in strong effort on this LONG writing task, because they won't be asked to do very many assignments that are this time-consuming, there is actual value in completing the task well, and it can serve as an excellent piece of evidence of growth and understanding of these concepts.
- As an alternative to writing all of their answers, students can be asked to record a video explaining all of these answers. If you choose to do this, I recommend that students write a few notes to themselves before recording (which mimics think time), and that you ask students to "Tell Me More" for each answer so it's not just a surface-level summary without the detail that shows their actual process and discoveries.
- At the end of this lesson, try to encourage students to reflect on each step during a Learning Cycle independently, so these formal summaries become unnecessary. Internalize it!

Student Tasks 〉 Transfer Goals

Student Tasks	Transfer Goals
Students summarize what they accomplished during each step of the SLSI Process in a complete Learning Cycle.	Students know the value of each step in the SLSI Process and are willing to put in time and effort to do it well.
Students describe how the SLSI Process helped them grow as a learner and how well it helped them learn the academic skill or concept from the lesson.	Students see the cause and effect relationship between the steps in the SLSI Process and improved learning.

Instructional Poster(s)

- This lesson has TWO Instructional Posters.
- The Instructional Poster for this lesson walks students through a summary of each step in the Learning Cycle that they just completed in the prior lesson(s). It is written as a series of sentence starters that students can use or ignore (but they need to write in a way that fulfills the purpose of each sentence starter).
- EXEMPLAR: An additional Instructional Poster has been provided that shows how students should sound when completing theirs - It gives examples from their experience and delves deeply into some of those experiences in order to show growth or learning.

Student Handouts

- This lesson has TWO Student Handouts.
- DIRECTIONS: Answer the questions below as completely as you can. Remember to "Tell me more!" Your answers will be evidence that shows the level of your understanding.
- On the first Student Handout, students are asked to reflect on how the SLSI Process helped them learn the academic content better than without, and how it helped them grow as a learner, overall.
- DIRECTIONS: After you have completed one full "Learning Cycle," write out what you did during each step. This is a long assignment, but most of these lessons are not this long! :)
- On the second Student Handout, students are asked to write their responses to the sentence starters that were on the Instructional Poster, so leave that displayed for the students to utilize or give them a copy some other way. You may want them to have the exemplar as well - it's up to you!

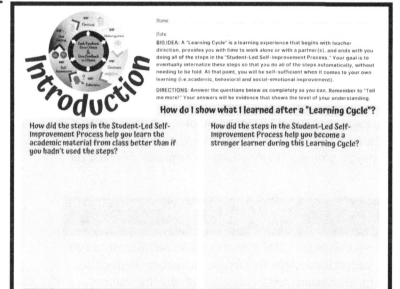

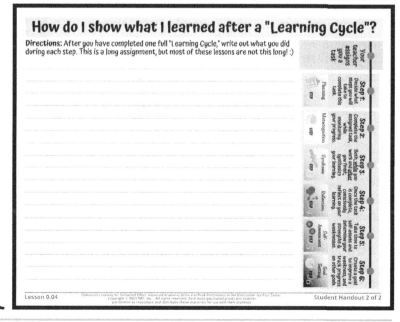

0.05

Transition away from a reliance on scaffolds to become proficient "Optimized Learners" who take ownership of the SLSI Process

bit.ly/47KR9Jk

Essential Question

How do I transition away from using the SLSI forms?

Big Idea

The ultimate goal of all learning is to independently be able to transfer it to real life situations. Therefore, it's important to learn how to use the Student-Led Self-Improvement Process without any graphic organizers or reminders from your teacher.

Lesson Overview

In this lesson, students are metaphorically taught to take the training wheels off of their bicycle and ride freely without support! They no longer should have to rely on the graphic organizers or posters from the program to guide their learning process. They should be truly "Optimized Learners" who know how to incorporate all of the strategies taught throughout these mini-lessons. This final mini-lesson is designed to formally announce the transition away from the scaffolds of "learning cycles" and teacher prompting, and toward the responsibility of independent, self-driven learning. Although it's not like snapping your fingers, students should be able to own this process with only a few gentle reminders every now and then.

Discussion / Reflection Questions

- How do you feel about the idea of transitioning from relying on graphic organizers to independent learning?
- What challenges do you anticipate encountering when trying to apply the strategies without reminders or prompts?
- How do you think becoming an "Optimized Learner" will benefit you in the long run?
- What steps can you take to ensure that you continue to use the strategies effectively without external support?
- How will you hold yourself accountable to consistently apply the strategies taught in this lesson, even when it's challenging?

Teacher Tips

- This mini-lesson will be shorter than most because there are no Student Handouts for the students to complete, and because the Instructional Posters will all be review for the students.
- After this lesson is taught, you need to decide if you will give your students ONE more learning cycle packet (with any of the optional or alternate pages), or if you will ask your students to apply all of the steps in the SLSI Process without the graphic organizers as training wheels. My suggestion is that if you have time for a few more learning cycles before the year is over, have students complete one more packet, but if you don't have many more learning cycles left, have them attempt it without the packet. Either way, please scaffold their transition from the packet to doing things mentally by providing verbal cues, reminders, etc.
- Keeping posters hanging in the room for this learning cycle is a good idea OR printing off copies of the Instructional Posters from this lesson to give to each student. These can act as the final scaffold in their attempt to internalize the entire process and complete each step independent of the teacher. Remember though that the goal will be to eventually have your students continue to complete the steps on their own without needing to have posters or handouts to refer to.

Student Tasks 〉 Transfer Goals

| Students learn that it is their responsibility to utilize the SLSI Process without reminders or support throughout their schooling (a.k.a. Transfer). | Students transfer the macro- and microskills from this program to future learning experiences on their own. |
| Students complete a "bulky assignment" to practice completing the steps in the SLSI Process without support (perhaps scaffolded over several assignments). | Students use their experience from this learning cycle to draw from as they complete future learning cycles without teacher support. |

Instructional Poster(s)

- This lesson has FOUR Instructional Posters.
- This lesson has ZERO Student Handouts, because the main purpose of the lesson is to transition AWAY from using the graphic organizers as reminders and guides.
- When you first teach this lesson, you should probably display each of the four Instructional Posters somewhere in the room for your students to refer to (or you can print them out for them to have with them). Eventually, students will need to transition away from even having the posters present. But this is likely the final step in the Student-Led Self-Improvement Process and shouldn't be done until students are likely to have some success moving away from all of the guides from the program.
- As the teacher, you will need to give lots of feedback at the beginning of this final process to help students transition from the handouts and the posters to independent transfer. But once your students begin to do this independently, they will likely have learned the macro and microskills from this program and you will not need to do much more other than provide gentle reminders over time!
- The fourth Student Handout contains Steps 6 and 7 which gives support for setting goals & monitoring progress toward those goals, and giving & receiving feedback throughout the learning experience.

Once you've had a chance to read *Optimized Learning*, I would sincerely appreciate your honest review and rating on Amazon.com!

Five star ratings on Amazon have a BIG impact on sales and can lead to more teachers getting this book in their hands! Positive Reviews help those who might be on the fence decide if this book is worth their hard-earned money, and if it might be something they will use in their classroom, school or district. Thanks in advance for your consideration!

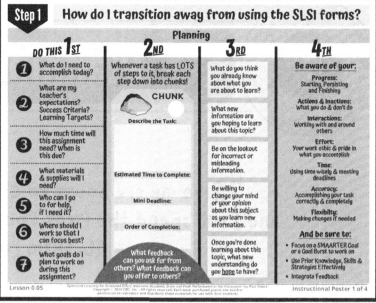

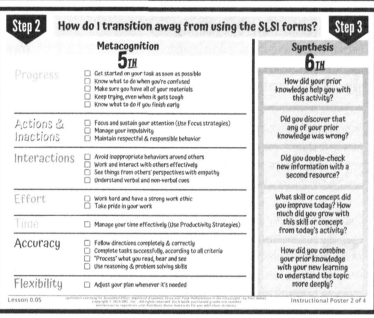

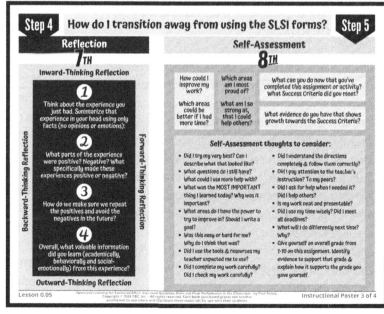

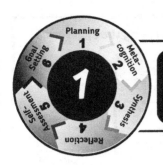

Download the Slides for this Unit:

bit.ly/47KVknL

Planning

> " Give me six hours to chop down a tree
> and I will spend the first four sharpening the axe. "
> — Abraham Lincoln

The first crucial macroskill that students need to develop in order to become successful, independent learners is "Planning". Planning is the process that "Optimized Learners" instinctively engage in BEFORE starting a task.

Imagine you're about to replace a broken toilet in your home for the first time. You know you need to buy a new toilet, but you lack knowledge about the other steps involved, and you don't have anyone available to ask for assistance.

Some people simply go to the store, purchase a new toilet, open the box, and attempt to figure it out on their own. This shows great initiative, but they soon realize they lack the necessary tools, background knowledge, and physical strength to install the toilet correctly. Their lack of planning leads to multiple trips to the store, numerous mistakes, wasted time, and frustration. These individuals are not optimized learners.

On the other hand, there are people who have developed planning microskills. They understand that installing a new toilet may present challenges, so they begin by watching a YouTube video tutorial on replacing a toilet independently. They make a list of the required tools and supplies, head to the store, gather all the necessary items in their cart, and consult a store employee to ensure they haven't overlooked anything. The store employee provides helpful suggestions and even demonstrates how to lift the toilet into place by oneself, making the installation process even easier. These individuals are considered optimized learners because they know how to efficiently tackle new problems, resulting in a finished product they can take pride in.

Our goal is to teach our students to emulate the latter approach. We want them to think before acting, understand the task at hand, and invest a little time upfront to save significant time and effort later on. Developing the skill of planning is the crucial first step toward achieving this.

Planning lays the foundation for students' success, as it refers to the deliberate process of organizing materials, breaking down tasks, estimating time requirements, anticipating potential issues, and more. It is the initial step that allows students to chart their course before undertaking independent or collaborative assignments, projects, or tasks where the teacher isn't providing step-by-step guidance. Through effective planning, students develop a complete understanding of the task, comprehend precisely what is expected of them, and skillfully manage their time to meet all deadlines.

When it comes to the skill of planning, there are several smaller skills, or microskills, that contribute to its successful execution. These microskills serve as the building blocks that empower students to plan and prepare effectively for their work. Each of the 22 mini-lessons within this unit focus on one or more of these microskills that support the macroskill of planning. Here are some examples (but not an exhaustive list):

Resource Gathering: Students should develop the ability to identify and gather the necessary resources for their assignments or tasks. This might be as simple as getting a worksheet from the teacher or as complex as signing in to multiple digital tools on their device. Effective resource gathering ensures that students have the necessary information and tools to complete their work and don't need to stop what they're doing to have to gather them later on.

Chunking: Breaking down large tasks into smaller, manageable steps is a crucial microskill in the Planning Stage. Students should be able to analyze the requirements of an assignment and identify the specific actions needed to complete it. This helps in organizing the work and creating a logical sequence of steps. In addition, identifying specific milestones or checkpoints helps students track their progress and stay on schedule.

Sequencing Tasks: Once tasks are broken down into smaller steps, students should arrange them in a logical order. Sequencing tasks ensures that prerequisite steps are completed before moving on to subsequent ones, maintaining a smooth workflow. Typically, teachers do this FOR their students, but it's important to provide opportunities for them to develop this skill themselves too!

Choosing where to work: In a flexible seating classroom (where students can work anywhere in the classroom), finding a suitable workspace that promotes focus and attention is another microskill that contributes to effective planning. Students should consider their own needs and be able to identify workspaces that are free from distractions, promote concentration, minimize interruptions, and provide the necessary tools and resources for their work.

Estimating Time: Estimating the time required for each step or subtask is an important microskill in planning. Students should be able to assess the complexity and scope of each portion of an assignment or task and allocate appropriate time for their completion. By estimating time properly before beginning their task, students are better able to identify when they are falling behind and avoid last-minute rushes.

Prioritizing: Students need to learn how to prioritize their tasks based on their importance, urgency, or deadline. This microskill involves understanding the relative significance of different steps or subtasks and making informed decisions about the order in which they should be tackled. Don't let your third grade students spend 30 minutes coloring the cover page of their reading packet when they should be devoting most of the time to answering the comprehension questions inside of the packet!

Anticipating Potential Problems: Identifying challenges that could come up during an assignment or task is a valuable micro-skill. Students should develop the ability to identify potential obstacles, such as technical issues, lack of resources, or difficult concepts, and use appropriate strategies to overcome them.

Preparing for Collaboration: Students are often assigned to work with a random partner. Unfortunately, instead of building off of each others' ideas, many students miss out on the valuable learning experience of true collaboration. Students should remind themselves to foster a positive and respectful working relationship with their partner by actively listening, valuing diverse perspectives, and promoting open communication throughout the collaborative process.

Knowing Success Criteria: Understanding how their work will be evaluated is a crucial microskill. Students should know the Success Criteria that will be used to assess their assignments, ensuring that their planning aligns with these criteria. This can be done by the teacher providing them with a rubric, checklist or explicit directions, or the students may need to infer these criteria based on the instruction that has been provided.

Selecting Goals: Within the "Student-Led Self-Improvement" Process, students create a multitude of personal goals based on their individual needs. In order to find the time to address all of these goals, many need to be tackled while completing other assignments in class. During the Planning Stage, students strategically select a goal or two that they can work on with their assigned task. For example, imagine a student wanting to be a better team player. They can use a partner activity as a chance to practice stepping back to encourage others to lead, building onto what others are saying, and supporting peers by asking them questions that lead them to correct answers.

Contingency Planning: Not everything always goes according to PLAN, so students should account for unexpected events or setbacks and find ways to be flexible and adaptable when these circumstances arise. Students need to be able to develop contingency plans to handle unforeseen circumstances, such as technical issues, schedule changes, or resource limitations.

Initially, students will find planning to be a time-consuming task, but it's important for them not to get discouraged. With practice, they will develop the ability to complete this step efficiently in about five minutes, ultimately saving much more time that would have otherwise been wasted. Lesson 1.22 focuses on this microskill, helping students understand that if planning becomes too time-consuming, it hinders academic progress rather than enhancing it.

By developing and honing these microskills, students become proficient planners, capable of effectively organizing their work, managing their time, and achieving their academic goals. As a result, they gain a clearer understanding of what they hope to accomplish by the end of an assignment and what knowledge and skills they need to acquire. Instead of merely following the teacher's directions or lacking direction altogether, students begin to take ownership of their learning and make intelligent decisions autonomously, without relying heavily on adult guidance. Abe Lincoln might even say that your students "won't need to spend all of their time and energy swinging a dull axe at a hard tree." And none of us can argue with Abe!

INTRODUCTION
PLANNING
METACOGNITION
SYNTHESIS
REFLECTION
SELF-ASSESSMENT
GOAL SETTING
FEEDBACK

Unit 1 - Planning

22 Mini-Lessons

Page	Lesson	Essential Question	MicroSkill
72	**1.19**	How can I organize myself better?	Boost productivity and enhance focus by de-cluttering, organizing your workspace & materials and staying organized
74	**1.20**	What distracts me and how can I overcome it?	Create a plan to manage distractions, improve your focus and increase your productivity while working
76	**1.21**	What should I do when I'm having a bad day?	Be aware of your emotional state to help reduce conflict, receive support, and prevent unnecessarily challenging days
78	**1.22**	How much time should I dedicate to PLANNING?	Although planning is extremely important, it needs to be done quickly so it doesn't impact learning time

INTRODUCTION

PLANNING

METACOGNITION

SYNTHESIS

REFLECTION

SELF-ASSESSMENT

GOAL SETTING

FEEDBACK

Students with well-developed PLANNING MicroSkills...

Stay organized by keeping their workspace and materials tidy

Gather all necessary supplies before starting work

Minimize distractions and stay focused on the task at hand

Create a plan or schedule for completing work

Break down complex assignments into smaller chunks

Estimate the time needed for each task or assignment

Prioritize tasks based on importance, difficulty or upcoming deadlines

Use a planner or digital tool to organize & track assignments and set reminders for important deadlines

Use time management techniques, such as setting timers or using a schedule

Accurately use provided to-do lists or checklists to ensure progress and completion of tasks

Anticipate potential obstacles and plan for contingencies

Revise plans as needed to stay on track

Reflect on their planning process and make adjustments for improvement

Students with poorly-developed PLANNING MicroSkills...

Have a disorganized workspace and struggle to find necessary materials

Need to make multiple trips to get supplies

Easily get distracted and lose focus

Start working without a plan

Attempt to tackle complex assignments all at once

Underestimate or overestimate the time needed

Work on tasks randomly without prioritizing, leave important tasks until the last minute, and spend excessive time on less important tasks

Miss deadlines, neglect to allocate enough time to accomplish certain tasks, and forget to turn in completed work

Waste time and get easily distracted

Fail to use class time wisely, end up completing much less than expected, neglect to complete certain tasks

Get easily overwhelmed by unexpected challenges

Fail to adjust plans when falling behind schedule and stick to initial plans even if they are not effective

Fail to evaluate their planning strategies and repeat the same mistakes over and over

bit.ly/3uAa0Ig

Evaluate PLANNING MicroSkills to take pride in relative strengths and to set personalized goals for areas of weakness

Essential Question

How strong am I at each of these PLANNING Skills?

Big Idea

By evaluating our current level of achievement on the MicroSkills that will be taught in this unit, we gain a clearer understanding of our individual strengths and weaknesses. Additionally, by synthesizing each MicroSkill, we develop a stronger understanding of the MacroSkill that this unit focuses on, which is PLANNING.

Lesson Overview

In this lesson, students evaluate their perceived ability for each of the identified PLANNING skills. These skills have been chosen from the lessons that follow in this unit. Although students are choosing a somewhat arbitrary number from 1-10, the self-assessment process requires them to: (1) understand what the skill means, (2) determine their perceived ability for the skill, and (3) sort each skill into areas of weakness or strength (or in-between) so that they help others improve at the skill (for scores 7-10) or make the skill into a goal that they try to achieve (for scores 1-4). If a student scores a 5 or 6, they are asked to reassess themselves after the unit to determine if they would benefit from making it a goal or not.

Discussion/Reflection Questions

- Which planning skills did you feel you were strongest at? Provide some evidence to support your self-assessment.
- Which planning skills did you feel you were weakest at? Explain why you feel that this is true.
- If you could set a goal to improve ONE of these skills, which one would you choose? Why did you choose that one? How do you plan to improve this skill? What will you do?

Teacher Tips

- On the Student Handouts, it tells students to "highlight all the numbers up through your score." The reason I didn't just have them circle the number is so they can see "how full" their grade band is if they choose a high number, and "how empty" their grade band is if they choose a low number. If you don't think it's too important for your students, feel free to let them just circle their number.
- When doing a self-assessment like this, I like to teach my students about the importance of being honest with themselves. I remind them that self-assessment in our classroom don't affect your grades or the way I see them. Self-assessments help us focus in on what matters to us, rather than focusing in on everything and not spending enough time on the skills that we need to improve most. No one is a 10 on all of these skills and no one is a 1 on all of them, but there's a good chance that each of us is a 10 and a 1 on at least one skill in this self-assessment!

Student Tasks ⟩ Transfer Goals

Student Tasks	Transfer Goals
Students assess themselves on various planning skills using a scale from 1 to 10.	Students are more aware of their strengths AND the areas in which they need to grow.
Students are asked several reflection questions that require them to explain their self-assessments and to set a goal for one skill.	Students understand that having weaknesses is normal and that they should be improved through goal setting.

Instructional Poster(s)

- This lesson has ONE Instructional Poster.
- A variation of this Instructional Poster is used with the first lesson of each unit. It shows students how to use the 1-10 scale for assessing their current level of ability with each skill. Numbers 1-4 mean that they know they need to improve at this skill (and maybe create a goal for the skill), and numbers 7-10 mean they believe that they are capable of helping others improve this skill. (4-5 means they will reassess at the end of the unit - which will be up to you or the student to remember to do. It's not a lesson.)
- Tell students that the real value in this activity is discovering their <u>relative</u> strengths and weaknesses, so giving yourself a 10 for each skill is wasting everyone's time, as is repeating any other number. Finding the variation in each skill is the key, so give yourself scores of 1, 2, and 3 and give scores of 8, 9, and 10 as well!
- If your students really struggle with assigning numerical values, consider having them rank order each microskill from weakest to strongest. It takes more time, but gets at what's most important the best!

Student Handouts

- This lesson has TWO Student Handouts.
- Depending on when you choose to teach this lesson, the following bullets may or may not make much sense.
  - If your students have not yet learned how to make S.M.A.A.R.T.E.R. Goals or Goal Bursts, let students know that they can just make the skill a personal goal to improve, but nothing needs to be written out (unless they want a reminder to actually do it). Obviously, the more seriously they take things, the more likely they'll improve!
  - If your students have learned about S.M.A.A.R.T.E.R. Goals or Goal Bursts, have them follow the directions on the Student Handout.
- DIRECTIONS: Look at the Planning MicroSkills in each box below and on the following page(s). Determine a rating from 1-10 for yourself on each, and then circle it. For your lowest MicroSkill(s), create a S.M.A.A.R.T.E.R. Goal to address each weakness.

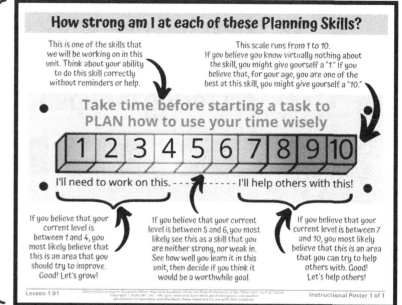

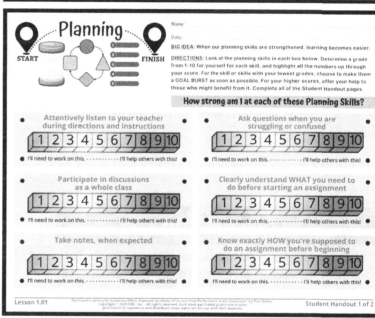

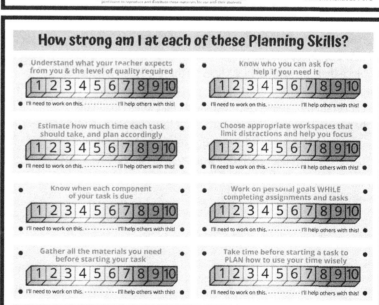

INTRODUCTION

PLANNING

METACOGNITION

SYNTHESIS

REFLECTION

SELF-ASSESSMENT

GOAL SETTING

FEEDBACK

bit.ly/46x0h2Q

Develop pre-work planning skills for efficient and effective use of time, fostering independence and success

Essential Question

How do I PLAN and PREPARE for an assignment?

Big Idea

"Planning" is what we do BEFORE we get to work. It involves gathering materials, having a plan for learning, and several other components that prepare us for an efficient and effective use of our time.

Lesson Overview

In this lesson, students learn WHAT planning is. They understand that being prepared to accomplish an assigned task can lead to us using our time efficiently and accomplishing our goals effectively. The overarching goal of ALL of the lessons in this book is to improve independence and decision-making skills in each of our students. Today's students are far too reliant on others to make decisions for them and remind them of what to do. Building independence in students in school should lead to more confident and successful adults.

Discussion / Reflection Questions

- Imagine that your writing teacher has just assigned you a random partner and you are given the next 30 minutes to revise each others' papers. How might you PLAN to accomplish this task? What would you do BEFORE working?
- Imagine that your social studies teacher has just assigned you a random partner and you are given the next 45 minutes to learn about the Vikings and create a 30-second commercial trying to recruit others to go with them on their journeys. How might you PLAN to accomplish this task? What would you do BEFORE working?
- What repetitive (daily or weekly) assignment or task in this classroom do you think would be improved the most from PLANNING?

Teacher Tips

- A lot of components of planning are mentioned on the Student Handouts and students will likely not remember them all, but if they process each component, they are likely to have a stronger understanding of what needs to be done during the Planning Stage. Therefore, you may want to go through this page with the class (if you had planned to let them complete the Student Handouts independently).
- Since there are a lot of blank lines on the last Student Handout page, you may want to give some direction as to your expectations. I always tell my students that when I made the handout, I thought long and hard about how many lines students would need to answer each question to my expectations, and therefore most lines should be written on to explain your answers and to "tell me more" (which is a lesson that comes up later in the book: Lesson 4.06).

Student Tasks 〉 Transfer Goals

Students learn that planning is the first step in becoming a more independent learner, and that being unprepared to learn can lead to bad consequences.	Students become more independent by integrating planning skills into their learning.
Students learn that there are several components of planning, and that each of these components can help us be more efficient and effective when learning.	Students apply the skills of planning in their everyday lives at school and away from school.

INTRODUCTION

PLANNING

METACOGNITION

SYNTHESIS

REFLECTION

SELF-ASSESSMENT

GOAL SETTING

FEEDBACK

Instructional Poster(s)

- This lesson has ONE Instructional Poster.
- This poster attempts to explain to students that the "Planning Stage" is when we take time to understand WHAT it is that we are about to do in class, what SUPPLIES we need to get it done, and how much TIME we have to accomplish everything. (There will be more components introduced in future lessons, but these are the basics for now.)
- Planning begins when the teacher starts the lesson (usually with some direct instruction, but not always) and ends when you have a plan (formal or informal) for accomplishing the assigned task.
- Planning is the first step in becoming independent learners who don't rely on their teacher or other adults to think for them and tell them what to do and when to do it. Our goal is to become capable of independent decision-making.

Student Handouts

- This lesson has TWO Student Handouts.
- DIRECTIONS: Read through the ideas below. They explain many of the things you should do BEFORE beginning to work. Then, complete the three columns on the next page.
  - How does a coach and his or her team PLAN for an upcoming game? (You choose the sport or activity.)
  - What does a bride and groom have to do to PLAN out their perfect wedding?
  - What does a YouTuber need to PLAN before they start recording an episode?
- You may choose to help your students get started by discussing a possible answer or two (scaffold).

How do I PLAN and PREPARE for an assignment?

"Planning" is what we do BEFORE we get to work.
- Has your teacher ever given the class directions and then said, "All right! Let's get to work!" and you had NO IDEA what you were supposed to do? Planning helps us ensure that never happens!
- Have you ever gotten to work only to realize that you didn't get all of the supplies you needed? So, you get back up, go get supplies, and now you're behind everyone else. Planning helps us organize ourselves and our materials.
- Have you ever gotten to work, but then realized that you are almost out of time and you haven't even gotten to the most important part yet? Planning helps us manage our time properly.

Planning starts as soon as your teacher begins teaching and finishes when you have a clear plan for how to use your work time. You need to be successful without needing extra guidance from your teacher.

Lesson 1.02   Optimized Learning for Sustained Effort, Improved Academic Drive and Peak Performance in the Classroom - by Paul Solarz   Instructional Poster 1 of 1

Planning
START   FINISH

Name:
Date:
BIG IDEA: "Planning" is what we do BEFORE we get to work. It involves gathering materials, having a plan for learning, and several other components that prepare us for an efficient and effective use of our time.

DIRECTIONS: Read through the ideas below. They explain many of the things you should do BEFORE beginning to work. Then, complete the three columns on the next page.

How do I PLAN and PREPARE for an assignment?

FIRST...

As your teacher begins the lesson, your responsibilities are to:
- Listen to your teacher
- Participate in discussions
- Take notes, if expected
- Ask questions, as needed
- And anything else that shows you are actively processing what your teacher is explaining.
- WHAT ELSE?

SECOND...

Once your teacher has "released" you to start working on your own or with a partner, your responsibilities are to:
- Know exactly WHAT you need to do and know HOW you're supposed to do it.
- Know what it is that your teacher is looking for and to what level of quality it needs to be done.
- Know how long it should take you to complete each component of the assignment or task, and know WHEN it is due.
- Have all of the materials you'll need for the assignment or task gathered ahead of time.
- Know who you can ask for help if you need it.
- If your teacher lets you "spread out," choose to work someWHERE you will be successful.
- Identify one or two goals that you can address while completing this assignment or task.
- WHAT ELSE?

Lesson 1.02   Optimized Learning for Sustained Effort, Improved Academic Drive and Peak Performance in the Classroom - by Paul Solarz   Student Handout 1 of 2

How do I PLAN and PREPARE for an assignment?

How does a coach and his or her team PLAN for an upcoming game? (You choose the sport or activity.)	What does a bride and groom have to do to PLAN out their perfect wedding?	What does a YouTuber need to PLAN before they start recording an episode?

Lesson 1.02   Optimized Learning for Sustained Effort, Improved Academic Drive and Peak Performance in the Classroom - by Paul Solarz   Student Handout 2 of 2

bit.ly/47vxrRL

Discover the positive outcomes of planning and the potential negative consequences of neglecting to plan

Essential Question

Why should we take time to plan?

Big Idea

Although our plans often change as things come up, MAKING a plan can have numerous positive consequences. Alternatively, neglecting to make a plan can result in several negative consequences.

Lesson Overview

In this lesson, students learn about the planning and preparation that a chef needs to go through in order to be successful. This is used as an analogy for the importance of planning before beginning a learning task or assignment. Students learn that good things often happen when we plan (like finishing on time and accomplishing our goals), and that bad things often happen when we neglect to plan (like forgetting an important ingredient or burning our food while chopping onions). There are several benefits of planning, so students are asked to rank order each benefit and then explain why they chose their first choice. This requires understanding, analysis, and evaluation in order to do successfully.

Discussion/Reflection Questions

- Let's say it took the chef 20 minutes to prepare her mise en place. Is this wasted time? Would she have saved time by preparing the ingredients as they cooked? Explain.
- Let's say you jump right in to a task that your math teacher has assigned you. You spread out in the classroom and get right to work on the problems only to discover that you don't have a pencil. You go back to your seat and get one. Now you realize you need your calculator, so you go back, etc. Describe how planning could save you time in this situation.
- Create a real or fictional children's story about a time when someone neglected to plan or prepare for an activity, and the consequences ended up being negative (but appropriate for school). Explain what the character should have done instead.

Teacher Tips

- This lesson does not provide much content about chefs to teach the students, so if you feel your students don't have the necessary background information to understand what a chef does, use one or more of the resources on this Google Doc to help: bit.ly/CHEFINFO
- It might be a good idea to discuss the following question in order to ensure students understand this concept completely:
  - What other professions can you think of where planning is a vital skill? (The answer should be that MOST professions require planning to be successful.)
- Have a short discussion about these and have students point out the benefits of planning and the consequences of not planning for each.

Student Tasks 〉 Transfer Goals

Student Tasks	Transfer Goals
Students discover the importance of planning and preparing before beginning to cook for chefs.	Students realize the value of planning and preparing before beginning learning tasks.
Students analyze seven positive outcomes of planning and determine their importance by ranking them.	Students agree that the small amount of time spent planning often leads to valuable outcomes.

INTRODUCTION

PLANNING

METACOGNITION

SYNTHESIS

REFLECTION

SELF-ASSESSMENT

GOAL SETTING

FEEDBACK

Instructional Poster(s)

- This lesson has ONE Instructional Poster.
- Students are led to discover the importance of PLANNING by learning about how a chef plans her recipes and prepares her ingredients before beginning to cook. Through critical thinking, students discover a number of things that can go wrong for a chef who doesn't properly plan and prepare before cooking the meal.
- Once the chef analogy has been played out, it's time to make the connection to learning. Students are asked to brainstorm some things that they should do prior to beginning a task or assignment in class. This will lead to understanding the seven steps in the "Planning Process" that is taught in Lesson 1.06.
- This lesson does not provide much content about chefs to teach the students, so if you feel your students don't have the necessary background information to understand what a chef does, use one or more of the resources on this Google Doc to help: bit.ly/CHEFINFO

Student Handouts

- This lesson has TWO Student Handouts.
- DIRECTIONS: Below, brainstorm several ways that PLANNING can have positive results and several ways that neglecting to plan can lead to negative consequences. Then, follow the directions on the next page.
- DIRECTIONS: Take a little time to decide which of the following "Benefits of Planning" might benefit YOU the most. Write a "1" in the white circle of the one that you connect strongest with and continue until all seven have been numbered. Explain your number 1 choice. Why do you connect most strongly with it?
- The first page asks students to explain the value of planning, while the second page asks students to prioritize different aspects of planning. Evaluation is a higher-level thinking skill that requires deep understanding to do well. Therefore, students are asked to EXPLAIN their #1 answer to ensure they didn't select an answer at random.

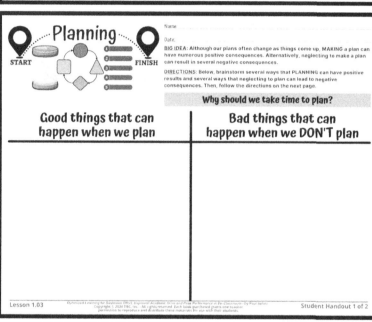

bit.ly/3t51Ib2

Uncover the timeless value of planning through famous quotes, emphasizing its relevance in various careers and eras

Essential Question

What do others think about planning?

Big Idea

By exploring and interpreting famous quotes about planning, we discover just how important this skill is across all careers and time periods.

Lesson Overview

In this lesson, students read 11 quotes about PLANNING from relatively famous individuals. Each quote attempts to teach students about the value of planning, but also tries to be realistic in that planning doesn't automatically lead to success. Hopefully, students will connect with at least one or two individuals who they look up to and buy-in to the idea of planning before getting to work.

Discussion/Reflection Questions

- What is one quote that really made you think? What did you learn from that quote in relation to PLANNING?
- What is one quote that you think you could successfully argue AGAINST? Explain your argument.
- Create your own quote about PLANNING. Your quote could teach us a new idea about planning, or it could reinforce an idea in one of the quotes from the lesson. If your teacher allows it, consider using artificial intelligence to invent a good quote about the importance of planning <u>that you can explain</u>.

Teacher Tips

- I highly recommend that you explain some of the more complicated quotes to your students. I would save 3-5 quotes for students to work collaboratively with an assigned random partner to interpret and write onto the Student Handouts.
- Assigned random partnerships may take away choice from students, but they effectively improve relationships between all students and ensure inclusion. I highly recommend implementing random partnerships for all short-term collaborative work. However, if students are expected to remain in partnerships for an extended period, I recommend creating partnerships privately ahead of time. This allows for consideration of student traits that will complement each other, enabling both partners to be successful on the assignment or task.

Student Tasks 〉 Transfer Goals

Student Tasks	Transfer Goals
Students read and interpret quotes about PLANNING from relatively famous people.	Students understand the value of PLANNING and begin to prioritize it in their lives.
Students discuss or write about ways that planning is valuable.	Students connect success, achievement and accomplishment with planning and modifying your plan.

INTRODUCTION

PLANNING

METACOGNITION

SYNTHESIS

REFLECTION

SELF-ASSESSMENT

GOAL SETTING

FEEDBACK

Instructional Poster(s)

- This lesson has ONE Instructional Poster.
- Read through the 11 quotes on the Instructional Poster. Discuss each to ensure that students can extract some meaning from each. Try to connect each quote to the skill of PLANNING.
- If you have the time, use the 3-step model from teachdifferent.com for analyzing a quote:
  - State your claim (What do you think the quote means?)
  - State a counter-claim (How might you successfully dispute the quote?)
  - Create an Essential Question that students can try to answer.
- A short and quick example: For the Yogi Berra quote on the Instructional Poster:
  - You're not likely to meet your goals if you don't have a plan.
  - You can't plan for everything, and yet you can still have success.
  - Is planning essential?

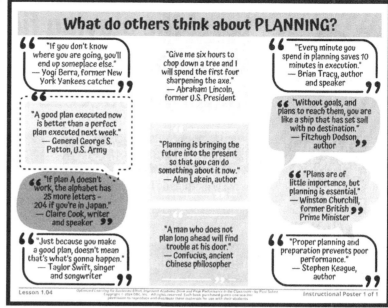

Student Handouts

- This lesson has TWO Student Handouts.
- DIRECTIONS: Read each famous quote on the left. Then, write a two or more sentence interpretation of the quote in your own words on the right. Feel free to get help from an adult or older sibling, since several of these can be tough!
- Feel free to let students write in the interpretations of these quotes during the class discussion. The goal is NOT to have a perfect paper, but to listen to the discussion, participate when possible, and learn about the importance of planning in order to meet and accomplish goals.
- Circulate to ensure students are writing SOMETHING that is appropriate and about planning, but try not to evaluate too much.

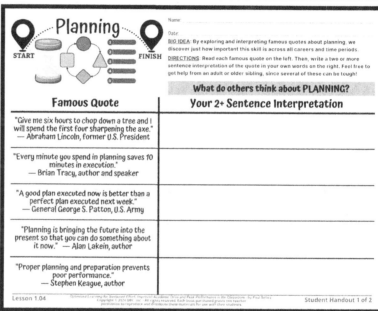

bit.ly/3uHBk71

Level the playing field intellectually and show how effort is a more important factor for success with "Marble Theory"

Essential Question

How many marbles do I have in each cup?

Big Idea

We are all born with the ability to learn and improve over time. It just takes effort, attention to detail, and feedback to go from our Personal Point A to our Personal Point B. Although everyone is different from one another, we all have the capacity for growth and the potential to do amazing things. See that potential in yourself AND in your peers. Understand that anyone in the classroom can help you and you can help anyone.

Lesson Overview

In this lesson, students learn that "Marble Theory" is a belief that we are ALL born with exactly one billion marbles in our brain all sitting in a bowl (metaphorically). A small amount of these marbles are already allocated into small cups that represent very specific skills that we have a predisposition to (a natural ability). The rest don't get allocated into cups until we gain ability in each skill. The harder we try and the more we practice, the more marbles move into the cups and the better we get at a skill. Students with a growth mindset know that effort and dedication lead to improvement. Students who think they are done learning (a fixed mindset) have a defeatist attitude and lack the determination to allocate their marbles.

Discussion/Reflection Questions

- Summarize "Marble Theory" for me.
- Sean (age 13) teases his younger brother Devon (age 8) for constantly swinging and missing the ball in baseball. Sean can hit it nearly every time it's pitched to him. What do you say to each boy to help them understand what's happening?
- Jenna (age 12) and Millie (age 12) sign up for the same gymnastics class. Jenna has been doing gymnastics for five years, but Millie is just beginning. Millie is embarrassed by how "bad" she is. What do you say to Millie?
- Think about everyone in this classroom. Privately, come up with ways you can help each student and ways that each student can help you. If you struggle for ideas, get to know them better - everyone in this classroom has talents and abilities!

Teacher Tips

- Marble Theory resources can be found at: bit.ly/MARBLETHEORY
- Cup labels should not be general like "reading" or "math," but specific like "Use context clues to determine a word's meaning" or "Know which operation to use in a word problem." (Young children may require it to be less specific.) Instructional Poster 4 helps to clarify this point.
- One of the main goals of this lesson is to get students to see each other as equals. The hierarchy of intelligence that exists in classrooms as young as kindergarten needs to be disassembled so students feel comfortable asking each other for help or offering help to others. This won't work if students see themselves as smarter than others or dumber than others.
- When I teach this lesson, I hand out Dixie cups and marbles to students. I ask them to mentally label one cup that they see as relatively full (a strength of theirs) and one cup that they see as relatively empty (a weakness of theirs). We share some as a group. I point out that intelligence as we know it is flawed. People who are "gifted" at soccer aren't less intelligent than people who are "gifted" at math, they just allocated their marbles differently. Schools just value math marbles more than they value soccer marbles, but calling them smarter is not a fair assessment. "Who decides what makes a person smart!?"

Student Tasks > Transfer Goals

Student Tasks	Transfer Goals
Students participate in a class meeting where Marble Theory is explained and examples are provided.	Students see ALL peers as equals. Hierarchy of intelligence is gone. Everyone is on an equal playing field.
Students assess themselves on various specific skills in order to determine relative strengths and weaknesses.	Students have a new understanding of intelligence that is not directly tied into grades or awards.

INTRODUCTION

PLANNING

METACOGNITION

SYNTHESIS

REFLECTION

SELF-ASSESSMENT

GOAL SETTING

FEEDBACK

Instructional Poster(s)

- This lesson has FOUR Instructional Posters.
- You might want to look through the resources on this Google Doc before you teach this lesson: bit.ly/MARBLETHEORY
- There are several additional Teacher pages within the slides for this lesson. It includes a possible script you can use to teach Marble Theory. Be sure to check these out!
- There is an additional Instructional Poster for this lesson. It shows six elements to a successful pitch in baseball. A pitcher would need to gain marbles in all six areas in order to become a more competent pitcher, not just one or two. This shows how specific each cup is, with regard to microskills.
- Although we all start out with few or no marbles in each skill cup, we can allocate marbles by learning, practicing, and trying hard to improve. It just takes time and effort.
- On the bottom of the Instructional Poster, choose a VERY SPECIFIC skill to use as an example of improving over time (allocating marbles over time). Repeat several times.
- What happens when your cup is full? Well, we all know that kid who is the best basketball player on the court, but he's only 9 years old and wouldn't be able to play in the NBA yet. Therefore, as he adds more marbles to his basketball skills cups, the cups continue to grow and allow for more marbles to be contained.

Student Handouts

- This lesson has THREE Student Handouts.
- For the first few pages, students assess themselves on various skills by assigning themselves a score of 1-10. Low scores should result in becoming a personal goal, while high scores should lead to an awareness to help others.
- The final page asks students to identify very specific skills of their choosing to self-assess.
- An additional page of blank cups has been provided if you would either like to have students label them themselves OR if you would like to label them with skills from your own classroom.

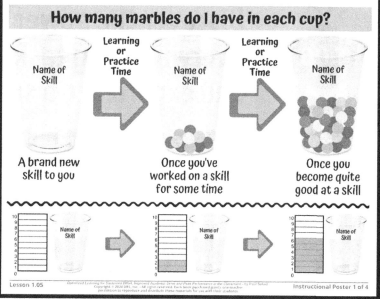

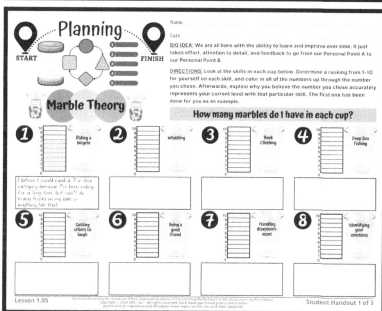

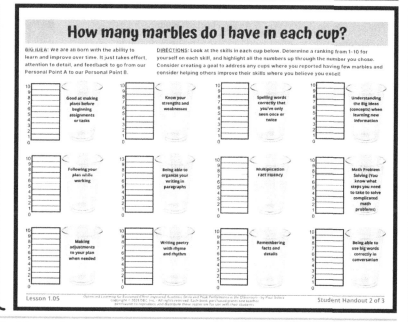

bit.ly/3t2o9gO

Discover the power of 'Chunking' to conquer overwhelming tasks, boost productivity, and experience a sense of accomplishment

Essential Question

How do I plan for a HUGE, complex assignment?

Big Idea

Large, complex tasks can be overwhelming, intimidating, and stressful to complete. They can even cause us to avoid them altogether, miss deadlines and lower our grade. Breaking these complex tasks into smaller, more manageable "chunks" can make even the most challenging projects seem doable!

Lesson Overview

In this lesson, students learn that becoming overwhelmed shouldn't stop us from accomplishing our goals, but it should lead us to using a strategy called, "Chunking." Chunking is when we take a large, overwhelming or complicated assignment or project and break it down into manageable pieces (called chunks). We put those pieces in order of how we want to accomplish them, and then focus only on the first chunk. This small piece of the large task feels doable. We focus on that task until it is done, and only then to do we move on to the next chunk. Every time we complete a chunk, we feel a sense of accomplishment, and a weight gently lifts off our backs.

Discussion/Reflection Questions

- Becoming overwhelmed is a natural emotion, but it doesn't have to take control over us. If we have a plan for dealing with things that overwhelm us, we can get through it. Outside of school projects and assignments, what else has overwhelmed you in the past? How did you get through it (or how did you struggle with it)? Now that you've learned one strategy for dealing with being overwhelmed, can you think of a way you could have handled it differently that would have been more successful?

- In the future, you will certainly be given MANY overwhelming tasks to complete (whether it be in school, at home, or at work). How do you plan to handle these overwhelming tasks? What specifically will you do to tackle them?

Teacher Tips

- Chunking Resources Google Doc: bit.ly/CHUNKING
- I always taught this skill prior to beginning a LARGE project that my students completed in class. I set it up with chunks already established, mini-deadlines assigned, and weekly check-ins to ensure students stayed on track. I created a checklist with all of the chunks on it, and students checked off each task as they completed them, and stored them for the final deadline (another challenging skill for students). I shared with them the idea of chunking and setting mini-deadlines and told them that they would be doing this themselves for the next project.
- For the next project, I gave them another copy of the chunks, mini-deadlines, and checklist that I created for the first project, and I had them use that as an exemplar for creating a new set of chunks, mini-deadlines, and a checklist for this new project. This took time, but was well-worth it because parents were beyond impressed by their child's new abilities, and students became so confident and rarely shared that they felt overwhelmed again. This is a very valuable skill that will be transferred many times over.

Student Tasks ⟩ Transfer Goals

Student Tasks	Transfer Goals
Students learn to break down huge, complex tasks into small, more manageable chunks in order to avoid becoming overwhelmed.	Students break down large tasks into more manageable chunks, rather than focus on its challenges.
Students apply this skill to an assignment in class, by breaking it down, determining its order and setting mini-deadlines.	Students successfully complete overwhelming tasks on-time, with confidence and a plan.

Instructional Poster(s)

- This lesson has ONE Instructional Poster.
- More chunking resources at: bit.ly/CHUNKING
- Use the metaphor of a large, complex assignment or project being like a HUGE boulder. If you need to move that boulder (complete that assignment), it might be more manageable to break it down into smaller pieces, rather than try to move the entire boulder all at once!
- Analogy: A large chapter book that has dozens of chapters, might make readers feel as though they can read the whole thing because they take it one chapter at a time. Each time they reach the end of a chapter, they feel a sense of accomplishment. Large projects and assignments can be broken down into "chapters" as well, and students will feel progress as they accomplish each component.
- The key steps of "Chunking" are (1) Knowing when the assignment is due, (2) Splitting it into appropriate-sized chunks to handle, (3) Estimating the time it should take to complete each chunk, and (4) Completing the chunks in an order that makes sense.

Student Handouts

- This lesson has TWO Student Handouts.
- DIRECTIONS: Use this organizer to break down a complex task from class into manageable chunks.
- Ideally, you would complete one of these together as a class for a fictional overwhelming task (like building a treehouse), but it can also be done as a short teacher demonstration or you can show an exemplar for students to use.
- The most important part is making sure to ask students to complete this organizer for an upcoming project, and then apply it to future large tasks without prompting.

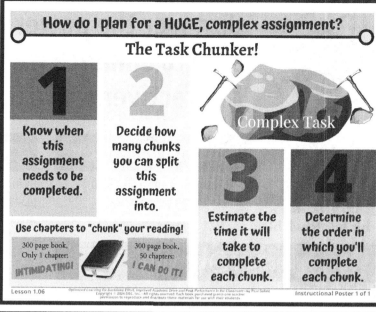

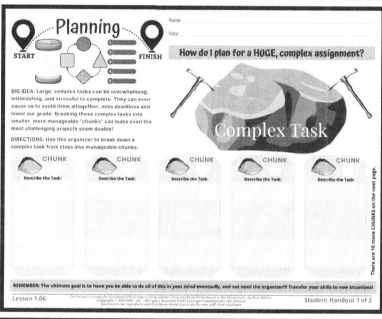

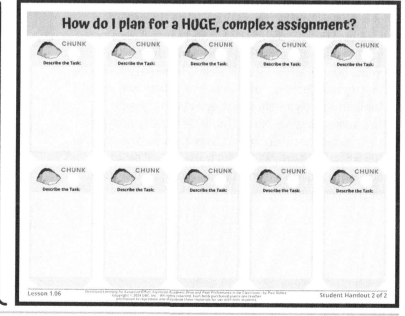

INTRODUCTION

PLANNING

METACOGNITION

SYNTHESIS

REFLECTION

SELF-ASSESSMENT

GOAL SETTING

FEEDBACK

bit.ly/3RiwPbl

Discover the power of a simple plan to enhance work efficiency & effectiveness in learning

Essential Question

How do I create a plan for a learning experience?

Big Idea

By focusing in on seven specific criteria, you can create a simple plan that will help you improve your efficiency and effectiveness while learning.

Lesson Overview

In this lesson, students learn about the seven steps that make up a good plan. (As the teacher, you might choose to add more or revise some that don't apply to your classroom.) Students begin to practice this skill by imagining themselves preparing to complete a complex task in class with a partner. They identify some of the specific things they ought to do prior to beginning to work (they don't need to use the steps taught on the Instructional Poster). Then, they turn those specific steps into generic steps that can be used in most learning experiences (e.g. SPECIFIC: "I need to research the reasons pioneers headed west." GENERIC: "Learn about my topic."). Finally, students take 10-15 minutes to write a formal plan for an academic lesson (see Teacher Tips for more information).

Teacher Tips

- The final Student Handout cannot be completed in isolation. Students need to complete it prior to beginning a separate academic learning experience. For example, teach the whole class a skill or concept, give them directions for completing a task, and then have them complete the final Student Handout prior to beginning the academic task. They will need 10-15 minutes at first, but should be able to write formal plans more quickly as they gain experience. (They do not always need to write a plan - eventually students should be asked to internalize the steps and do them in their heads prior to beginning to work.) The form is simply a scaffold that supports their growth.
- This is one of the core lessons of PLANNING. Having these seven steps posted somewhere in the classroom is a good reminder for students to PLAN before they start working. It will definitely help as you begin to withdraw support and expect them to do this independently.

Discussion/Reflection Questions

- Imagine a task you might be asked to complete in class. How will you plan for this upcoming learning experience?
- Why is it important to create a plan BEFORE beginning a learning experience? What could happen if we don't plan?
- Why do you think THESE seven steps were chosen to be the steps in the planning process? Why are they the most important?
- If you could add an 8th step to the planning process, what would it be? Why did you choose that one?
- Describe a time in the past when you wish you had known about these steps in the planning process? When would this have been useful to you? How might that situation have turned out differently if you had known about these steps?

Student Tasks 〉 Transfer Goals

Student Tasks	Transfer Goals
Students learn about the seven steps that make up a good plan, and the elements of each step.	Students understand and value each step in the planning process and willingly dedicate some time to each.
Students practice and apply the seven steps in order to create a plan prior to beginning work on a fake task and a real task.	Students internalize the planning process and use the steps to prepare for other learning experiences.

INTRODUCTION

PLANNING

METACOGNITION

SYNTHESIS

REFLECTION

SELF-ASSESSMENT

GOAL SETTING

FEEDBACK

Instructional Poster(s)

- This lesson has ONE Instructional Poster.
- Set up the lesson by explaining to your students that a "learning experience" is any lesson or activity where they are trying to learn something new. Sometimes, they might work alone. Sometimes, with a partner. Sometimes, as a whole class.
- If we want to get the most out of a learning experience, we should start by having a PLAN. Simplified, a plan is just an understanding of what you need to accomplish before the end of the period. To take it a step further, it should contain seven steps (described in the "Steps for a Good Plan").
- Each step under the title, "Steps for a Good Plan," is further explained in the section to its left entitled, "Elements of a Good Plan." Go through each of these steps and their elements with the class. Include information about how things work in your classroom, specifically. Eliminate any steps that don't apply to your classroom.

Student Handouts

- This lesson has THREE Student Handouts.
- DIRECTIONS: Pretend that your teacher has just explained an assignment to you, and has assigned you a random partner from class. The two of you need to do the following tasks together:
  - Identify the reasons why pioneers headed west in the 1840's and 1850's.
  - Prepare a short skit that you and your partner will act out demonstrating three reasons you identified.
  - Practice and then record each skit.
- To become better at PLANNING for a learning experience, complete these sections:
  - Before I begin working on THIS assignment, I should...
  - Now, turn each of those SPECIFIC tasks into GENERAL ones that can be used for most assignments...
- Finally, have students complete the last Student Handout prior to beginning work on your next academic learning experience. There are two versions of this second Student Handout - the one to the right is for younger students and the alternative one (not pictured) would be for older students.

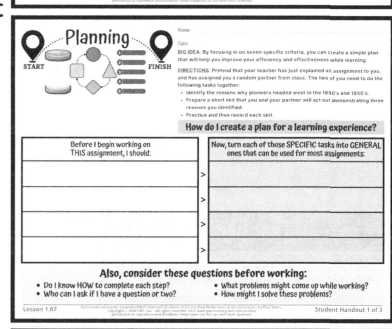

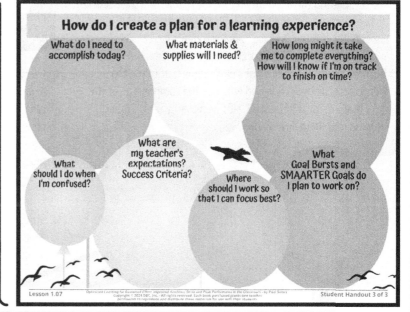

bit.ly/3uzbUcd

Understand assessment priorities in order to effectively allocate time and effort on tasks and assignments

Essential Question

What are my teacher's expectations? Success Criteria?

Big Idea

Knowing WHAT your teacher is assessing you on can help you focus on what's most important while completing your tasks or assignments. If your art teacher gives you an assignment and you create the most beautiful black & white pencil sketch, but he needs to see how you combine colors, you've failed the task.

Lesson Overview

In this lesson, students learn to focus in on what's MOST important to their teacher. In my experience, students sometimes give equal time to each aspect of a task or even spend MORE time on the less important components (e.g. drawing a beautiful cover page for a booklet). This lesson challenges students to learn the skills they will be assessed on so they can allocate their time and attention to what's most important to their teacher.

Discussion/Reflection Questions

- Why is it important that students know WHAT they are being assessed on?
- What can be done when it's unclear what skills your teacher is planning to assess you on?
- In the past, how have you mis-allocated your time and effort during a project or assignment? If you can't think of an example, make one up to show that you understand this skill.

Teacher Tips

- For this lesson, you need to attach it to a content area task where students are asked to complete some work independently or with a partner. Through this activity, they will describe the skill they are being assessed on, and write a plan for completing the assignment in a way that allows their teacher to see their growth and improvement in the desired skill area.
- Essentially, this lesson tries to help students improve their time management and prioritization skills. It asks students to become hyper-aware of what's most important to the teacher so they can focus their time and effort on the components of the task that are most important, NOT necessarily what's most engaging to them or most fun.

Student Tasks ⟩ Transfer Goals

Based on their teacher's expectations, students create a simple plan for completing their work on time and focused on what's most important.

Students understand the connection between classwork and evidence of growth and improvement.

Students learn to know what skills they are being assessed on BEFORE beginning to work.

Students put their time and effort into the things that matter most in school and in life.

INTRODUCTION

PLANNING

METACOGNITION

SYNTHESIS

REFLECTION

SELF-ASSESSMENT

GOAL SETTING

FEEDBACK

Instructional Poster(s)

- This lesson has TWO Instructional Poster.
- One of the most important steps a teacher might forget is ensuring that their students know what they're being assessed on. Sometimes, it can be obvious to the students (e.g. I just taught them how to use long division, now they are practicing dozens of problems). But sometimes, it's not as clear (e.g. I just taught my class how to add adverbs to improve a writing piece, but I'm assessing students on that skill AND all the others we learned in this unit). If it's not automatically known by ALL students, take the time to explain how students will be assessed, so they can focus their time and attention to that skill.
- Teach your students to ASK how they're being assessed. It may seem annoying at first, but imagine if you were being evaluated by your administrator on completely random criteria and ended up failing your review!
- The additional Instructional Handout is an exemplar that shows the students how they should complete the second Student Handout.

Student Handouts

- This lesson has TWO Student Handouts.
- DIRECTIONS: The following organizer can help you identify your teacher's expectations for this assignment AND make a plan for meeting those expectations.
- Have students complete this organizer at the end of instruction, before beginning independent or partner practice. Make sure you know the criteria through which you will be assessing each student.
- If you're not sure that your students will read the second Student Handout on their own, you might want to read it to them. It shows four examples of plans students might make based on their teacher's expectations.

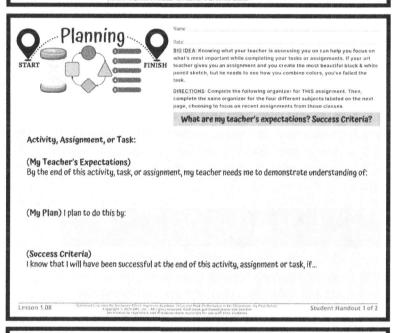

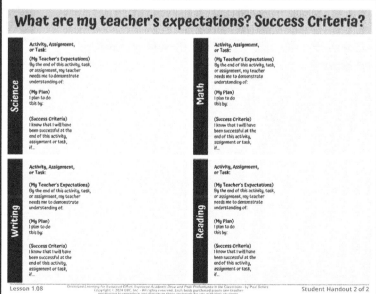

bit.ly/49RMA17

Understand the importance and impact of prioritizing tasks to achieve timely completion and quality results

Essential Question

What's my priority?
Why is it important?

Big Idea

The order we complete our chunks in matters. If we choose to do the least important chunk first, and we take a large amount of time on it, we haven't left ourselves with enough time to spend on the tasks that matter most.

Lesson Overview

In this lesson, students learn that there are many ways that we can prioritize our tasks in order to complete them on-time with high quality. The goal is to ensure that we think through the consequences of choosing to work on one task over another. Students think about one To Do List that has already been prioritized based on importance. Then, they attempt to prioritize the chores they need to complete before they would be allowed to go out to the carnival with friends. Students consider time factors, distractions, and even multi-tasking in order to create a plan that will allow them to have fun with friends! This activity helps students see the value in planning - a little time spent up front can pay off in the end.

Discussion/Reflection Questions

- Why does the order that we complete tasks in matter?
- What might happen if we run out of time and still have one task to complete? What if it was the most complicated task or the most important task?
- What if we spent all of our time struggling to complete one task, and didn't consider getting help on it so we could quickly move on to another task?
- When we start to run out of time, we begin to hustle through our work. Other than poor grades, what negative consequences can come from doing that?

Teacher Tips

- Any real-life connections you can share with the class?
- When I wrote this lesson, I thought about how my students all wanted to do a drawing task first, but when they finished with that, they all needed to do a computer task and we only had 10 computers in the classroom. They needed to understand that shared equipment needed to be scheduled so that it was always being used and no one was ever waiting to use it. Can you think of an example like that to share with the students from your classroom?

Student Tasks ⟩ Transfer Goals

Student Tasks	Transfer Goals
Students brainstorm ways we can prioritize tasks (e.g. by importance, due dates, complexity, logical order, etc.)	Students are aware of multiple reasons for prioritizing tasks and apply it to new situations.
Students prioritize several tasks in a fictional scenario in order to try to hang out with friends at a carnival.	Students apply the skills from their experience on this activity to similar circumstances in their daily life.

Instructional Poster(s)

- This lesson has ONE Instructional Poster.
- Discuss the many ways students might prioritize their "chunks" (or tasks) when there are several to do. Sorting based on importance, due dates, complexity, logical order, etc. are common ways to prioritize tasks, but there are many more. Help students understand that the end result needs to be high quality work completed on-time.
- If you have any activities that you've given your students in recent weeks where you can model this process with, do so now. The stronger the examples, the more likely they are to understand and internalize this process.

Student Handouts

- This lesson has FOUR Student Handouts.
- DIRECTIONS: Read the next page FIRST. Then, complete the chart below.
- A fictional example is offered to students on the second Student Handout. They want to go to the carnival with friends, but have to finish their chores first. Students are asked to identify all of the tasks, estimate the time it should take to complete each task, and then prioritize them in order to complete them all before the carnival. Because some of these tasks require that other tasks be done first, it can be tricky to do everything before they run out of time! Allow students to discover this, but ensure that they don't settle on skipping the carnival! Help them if they need it.
- Students fill out the chart on the first Student Handout with their final plan. The goal is to understand that several factors go into prioritizing tasks, but ultimately, we finish on-time with high quality work.
- The two additional pages are the Chunking organizers from Lesson 1.06 but with an additional section for prioritizing chunks.

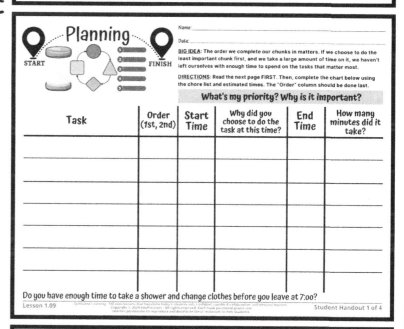

INTRODUCTION

PLANNING

METACOGNITION

SYNTHESIS

REFLECTION

SELF-ASSESSMENT

GOAL SETTING

FEEDBACK

bit.ly/3sJN5K9

Gain insights on effective time management by estimating task durations for timely completion of chunked assignments

Essential Question

How long might it take me to complete everything?

Big Idea

Once you've broken down your complex tasks into manageable chunks, it's time to estimate how long each chunk should take you. These estimates don't have to be perfect, but they should give you an idea of how long it will take you to complete all of the chunks, and can help you manage your time effectively.

Lesson Overview

In this lesson, students work on improving their time management skills. Students should have recently "chunked" a large project or task into smaller pieces. Now, students will estimate the time it takes to complete each of those chunks. The goal of this lesson is to learn to plan our time wisely and finish before any deadlines. As students discover that they are falling behind their schedule, they need to immediately revise their estimates and plan in additional work time in order to finish on-time.

Discussion/Reflection Questions

- Why is it important to estimate the time it might take us to complete each "chunk" of a task or project?
- Once we've estimated the times for each chunk, why might it be a good idea to schedule our work time for completing each chunk before the deadline?
- What should we do if we discover that we are falling behind, according to our schedule?

Teacher Tips

- This lesson should either be taught immediately after students have chunked a large project or task, so they can use those chunks to estimate times. Or, this mini-lesson can be another opportunity for students to practice chunking, along with the newer microskill of estimating the time each chunk should take to complete.
- The more you can expand this lesson, the better. For example, students should be able to make wise decisions based on several if-then scenarios:
  - If you estimated Task 1 to take 30 minutes, and you are still not done with it at the end of a 60 minute period, what should you do immediately?
  - If you estimated that Task 3 would take you two hours, but you are still working on it after three hours, what should you do immediately?
  - If you estimated the entire project to take six periods, and you are now done with it and still have three periods to go, what should you do immediately?

Student Tasks 〉 Transfer Goals

Student Tasks	Transfer Goals
Students estimate the time it should take them to complete familiar and unfamiliar activities.	Students become stronger at estimating times to complete tasks in and out of school.
Students estimate the time it should take them to complete a large project that has been chunked for them.	Students use the sample chunks as an exemplar for future chunking and become better at breaking a large task down to small pieces.

Instructional Poster(s)

- This lesson has ONE Instructional Poster.
- Once students have learned how to break large, intimidating tasks down into smaller chunks, it's time to learn how to estimate the time it might take to complete each chunk. Often, students see four chunks and assume it will take them four equal amounts of time to do each, but as we know that is rarely the case. If chunks 1-3 take 30 minutes each, and we only have one more 30 minute period to complete the 4th chunk, we better hope it doesn't take longer than that to finish! Estimating the time each chunk should take should cut down on running out of time if we learn to do it correctly.

Student Handouts

- This lesson has FOUR Student Handouts.
- DIRECTIONS: Follow the directions in the column headers below to complete the chart.
- Students are first asked to brainstorm three tasks that they are GOOD at estimating the time it takes to complete and three tasks that might be a CHALLENGE to estimate. Students are then asked to estimate the time it might take to complete each task.
- On the second Student Handout, they are given a sample project that has already been chunked into four parts. Students are asked to estimate how long it will likely take them to complete each chunk.
- The next lesson (Lesson 1.11) acts as an extension to this one. It asks students how they could plan out each of these tasks on a calendar, so they can try to meet any deadlines that might be assigned.
- The two additional pages are the Chunking organizers from Lesson 1.06 but with an additional section for estimating the time it will take to complete each chunk.

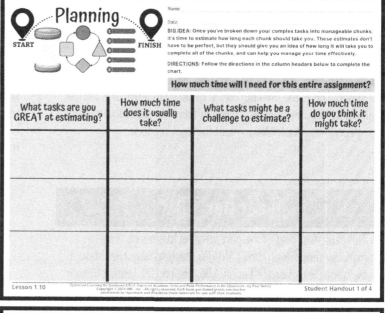

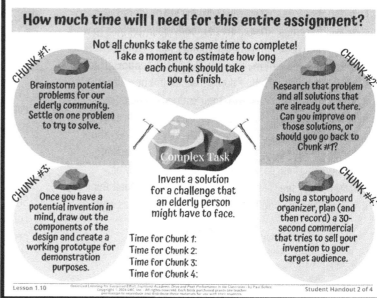

INTRODUCTION
PLANNING
METACOGNITION
SYNTHESIS
REFLECTION
SELF-ASSESSMENT
GOAL SETTING
FEEDBACK

bit.ly/47RxwPf

Set mini-deadlines for chunked tasks to ensure timely completion and meet final deadlines effectively

Essential Question

How will I know if I'm on track to finish on time?

Big Idea

Once we know how long each chunk should take us, it's important to set Mini-Deadlines for each chunk. Make sure you complete each chunk by your own Mini-Deadline, and you won't end up missing the final due date!

Lesson Overview

In this lesson, students put several microskills together by chunking a large task, setting mini-deadlines for each chunk, and estimating the time each chunk should take to complete. Students plan out each chunk on a calendar, taking into account class periods available to work on this task, days off school, etc. As they progress through their calendar, they determine if they are ahead of schedule, behind schedule, or on-schedule, and make adjustments as needed. This is the final hurdle for getting students to plan their time wisely in order to dedicate enough time to each component of a large project or task AND to meet the final deadline.

Discussion/Reflection Questions

- Why is it important to plan out our time when completing a large, complex project or task, rather than just wing it?
- What are some negative consequences of missing deadlines in school and out?
- Explain how the skill(s) taught in this lesson will prevent you from:
  - Stressing out the night before a due date because you just realized you weren't even close to being finished,
  - Prevents your parents from having to make excuses for why you're not done on time, or
  - Prevents you from faking sick to miss school, etc.

Teacher Tips

- This is the last part of a 4-part series of lessons on time-management during the PLANNING stage. Ideally, they should be taught in this order: Lesson 1.06, Lesson 1.09, Lesson 1.10 and then Lesson 1.11 (this lesson). If you are following the Instructional Spirals, this order has been followed.
- I used these tasks successfully with my 5th graders, but every class is different, so make sure to modify these lessons to work with your age group, in your community. More support at first might be needed, but make sure to withdraw support gradually so students can internalize it and transfer it it new situations.
- Keeping students honest with their estimates and mini-deadlines is required to strengthen this skill within each student. Whenever possible, talk with the whole class about monitoring their progress on their calendars and making adjustments as necessary. Check in with each student individually to see that they are keeping up with their mini-deadlines and making the necessary adjustments as well.

Student Tasks 〉 Transfer Goals

Student Tasks	Transfer Goals
Students consider various possibilities of finishing early, falling behind, and being on-track in order to determine next steps.	Students know what to do when they are falling behind, and they do it without adult support.
Students estimate times for completing chunks of a large project and plan out each step on a calendar in order to meet the due date.	Students meet deadlines and avoid procrastination.

INTRODUCTION

PLANNING

METACOGNITION

SYNTHESIS

REFLECTION

SELF-ASSESSMENT

GOAL SETTING

FEEDBACK

Instructional Poster(s)

- This lesson has ONE Instructional Poster.
- Once students have become better at breaking down large, complex projects into small chunks AND learned to estimate the time it should take them to complete each chunk, it's time to set mini-deadlines to ensure everything is done on time.
- The bottom of this Instructional Poster contains a sample calendar with mini-deadlines that could have been created by the teacher or by each student. What matters is that students are estimating times somewhat accurately, meeting their mini-deadlines (or making adjustments), and not feeling overwhelmed.

Student Handouts

- This lesson has FOUR Student Handouts.
- DIRECTIONS: Start on the next page, which is a sample COMPLEX TASK (a project). It has already been broken up into chunks, but it's your job to estimate how long each chunk should take you to complete. Then, set Mini-Deadlines on the calendar below for each chunk. They do not have to be completed in order.
- In order to help my students get stronger at this skill, I used projects like the one on the Student Handout. It contained SEVERAL components and had a FINAL due date established.
- I had them create mini-deadlines for each component (usually clusters of components), and I checked in with them on each Friday to see if they were meeting their deadlines. If they weren't, I asked them what they should do to ensure they finish the whole project on time, and students always came up with a plan to make it happen. Sometimes they stayed in for lunch recess OR came into school early OR they occasionally even gave themselves a personal "Give Me Five" which meant they couldn't talk with anyone until they finished what they were working on!
- Finally, I realize that this is not my finest project! It is old-fashioned, allows for little creativity & all the explorers were men! I'd like to believe I would do better now!
- The two additional pages are the Chunking organizers from Lesson 1.06 but with a section to write a mini-deadline on each chunk.

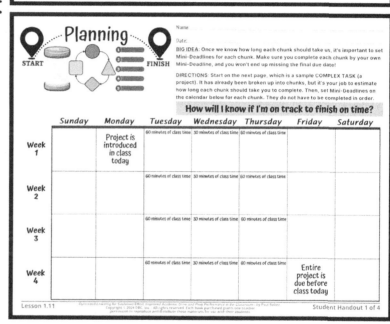

57

bit.ly/3sSuJGN

Develop a toolbox of strategies to tackle confusion effectively in order to take responsibility for clarity

Essential Question

What should I do when I'm confused?

Big Idea

When we are confused, it's really important that we do something about it. Build your "toolbox" of strategies that you can use when you're confused, and learn to choose the best one for each situation.

Lesson Overview

In this lesson, students learn that it is THEIR responsibility, not the teacher's responsibility, to identify when they are confused and use a strategy for clearing up their confusion. They brainstorm possible strategies for clearing up confusions and consider some that are given. Students read through some scenarios and choose the best strategy to use in each scenario. This lesson focuses on having a PLAN for handling confusion, while Lesson 2.06 in the Metacognition chapter focuses on identifying when one is confused and implementing a strategy to overcome the confusion. Both lessons are valuable and have unique aspects to them.

Discussion/Reflection Questions

- Why is it important to have multiple strategies for clearing up our confusion?
- Do you think that the most innovative and successful people in our world become so completely on their own, or do you think they learn from others and use resources successfully to learn what they need to know. How can we apply our answer to this question to us as students?
- How can YOU help to eliminate the embarrassment of asking others for help in your classroom? How can you demonstrate that asking for help is an important step in the learning process?

Teacher Tips

- In our classroom, ALL of my students are in charge of helping ALL of my other students. Likewise, ALL of my students are responsible for asking each other for help when they need it. I am always walking around the classroom observing and giving feedback, so I'm aware of which students need help and ask for it, as well as which students require others to offer their help. Confusion (& understanding) can be described on a continuum starting at helplessness and improving toward resourcefulness and independence. I need to know which of my students are staying helpless, and I need to quickly move them up on that spectrum.
- When you require that your students help each other in the classroom, the pros definitely outweigh the cons. Traditionally, teachers have avoided student collaboration so they could more accurately assess each student. Then, teachers avoided collaboration so the more able children weren't being the teacher to the less able children all the time. Due to creating a collaborative classroom, I am BETTER able to assess each of my students since I have more time to observe and thanks to the Marble Theory Lesson (Lesson 1.05), every student in our classroom helps others and every student asks for help in our classroom. Everyone gets an opportunity to teach others!

Student Tasks 〉 Transfer Goals

Student Tasks	Transfer Goals
Students brainstorm strategies to use when being confused in class.	Students no longer remain helpless. They know what to do when confused.
Students are given several strategies to use when confused and are asked to list pros and cons of each, as well as to choose one strategy to use given a specific scenario.	Students have a large selection of "tools" to use when confused, and know what is allowed & encouraged, and how to use each tool successfully.

Instructional Poster(s)

- This lesson has ONE Instructional Poster.
- During the brainstorm activity, students should come up with:
  - Being confused
  - Being distracted
  - Being tired
  - Being too busy
  - Forgetting deadlines
- Go through each item on their brainstorm list. As you read through the "perfect world" scenarios on the right, see if it resonates with your students, but make sure they know reality isn't usually a perfect world!
- Before beginning this assignment, make sure you've looked through the Student Handouts to see if they match your classroom or school policy. If not, make adjustments, if needed.

Student Handouts

- This lesson has TWO Student Handouts.
- DIRECTIONS: Pretend you are confused about something in your work. Look at the following strategies and decide what the pros and cons are of each. On the next page, choose a possible strategy for each problem listed.
- I have included eight strategies to use when you are confused that are somewhat universal. Can you (the teacher) or the students come up with more? The more options, the better.
- Make sure that when students choose a "Strategy" for each "Problem" on the Student Handout, they can defend their choice by explaining why it's a good way to handle the problem.

INTRODUCTION

PLANNING

METACOGNITION

SYNTHESIS

REFLECTION

SELF-ASSESSMENT

GOAL SETTING

FEEDBACK

What should I do when I'm confused?

Let's brainstorm reasons why we have trouble completing our work (i.e. What causes you to miss deadlines or have to finish classwork at home?):

-
-
-
-
-
-

Let's focus on a BIG ONE: Not knowing HOW to do the assignment or task (being confused, doing things incorrectly, not knowing what to do next, etc.).

In a perfect world:
- You would understand everything immediately without confusion.
- Your teacher would teach you each skill perfectly, explain all directions clearly, and you'd remember everything whenever you needed it.
- You could transfer your thoughts quickly, accurately and easily to paper (without difficulty spelling, reading, or doing mental math).
- You wouldn't be distracted by people around you, noises and off-topic thoughts.
- You would be comfortable asking for help from your teacher and peers without embarrassment.

However, the reality is that many of these things slow us down and prevent us from completing our work on time and free from silly mistakes. We just need to learn strategies to make LEARNING easier for us!

Lesson 1.12 — Optimized Learning for Sustained Effort, Improved Academic Drive and Peak Performance in the Classroom - by Paul Solarz — Copyright © 2024 GBC, Inc. - All rights reserved. Each book purchased grants one teacher permission to reproduce and distribute these materials for use with their students. — Instructional Poster 1 of 1

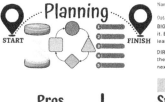

Planning
START FINISH

Name:

Date:

BIG IDEA: When we are confused, it's really important that we do something about it. Build your "toolbox" of strategies that you can use when you're confused, and learn to choose the best one for each situation.

DIRECTIONS: Pretend you are confused about something in your work. Look at the following strategies and decide what the pros and cons are of each. On the next page, choose a possible strategy for each problem listed.

What should I do when I'm confused?

Pros	Strategy	Cons
	Ask the teacher for help	
	Ask a peer for help	
	Ask someone at home for help	
	Look it up in a resource (book, online, etc.)	
	Look back at your notes or the board	
	Compare your work with someone else's	
	Re-read for understanding	
	Analyze your work to discover your mistakes	
	Your idea:	

Lesson 1.12 — Optimized Learning for Sustained Effort, Improved Academic Drive and Peak Performance in the Classroom - by Paul Solarz — Copyright © 2024 GBC, Inc. - All rights reserved. Each book purchased grants one teacher permission to reproduce and distribute these materials for use with their students. — Student Handout 1 of 2

What should I do when I'm confused?

Problem	Strategy	Hopeful Solution
I don't understand the directions for this assignment		If I understand the directions properly, I should have an easier time completing the assignment correctly.
I don't understand HOW to do the work on this assignment.		If I can get some re-teaching or some support while working, I'll be able to complete this task successfully.
I've forgotten HOW to do something that I need to work on right now.		If someone can remind me of what I've forgotten, I should be able to be successful from that point onward.
I understand HOW to do the assignment, but there are parts that still confuse me.		If someone can help me whenever I get stuck, that should allow me to complete the assignment and improve my skills at the same time.
I think I know HOW to do this assignment, but I seem to be getting several problems wrong.		If someone can show me where I'm making small mistakes, then I will likely have an easier time finding success!

Lesson 1.12 — Optimized Learning for Sustained Effort, Improved Academic Drive and Peak Performance in the Classroom - by Paul Solarz — Copyright © 2024 GBC, Inc. - All rights reserved. Each book purchased grants one teacher permission to reproduce and distribute these materials for use with their students. — Student Handout 2 of 2

bit.ly/47R7fkd

Choose work locations wisely for focused and productive learning, demonstrating responsibility in flexible seating classrooms

Essential Question

Where should I work so that I can focus best?

Big Idea

When we are allowed to spread out in our classroom to work, it's important that we choose our locations carefully and responsibly. Our teacher needs to know that we are going to be focused and productive wherever we work.

Lesson Overview

(If you do not have a flexible seating classroom, feel free to skip this lesson.) In this lesson, students think about the best and worst places in the classroom to work (assuming they are allowed to spread out.) Encouraging students to choose the best spots for their needs empowers them and reminds them not to choose areas where they might end up getting distracted or in trouble. If working with a partner AND the partner's needs are different than their own, students should rock, paper, scissors to determine the spot (or use one of the other conflict management strategies learned in class).

Discussion/Reflection Questions

- Why is it worthwhile to spend time thinking about places in the classroom that are GOOD for us to work and places that are NOT?
- Is it true that some locations in the classroom or some seating options in the classroom can be good for some students, yet distracting for others? Explain.
- When teachers give you any kind of choice, they expect that you will choose wisely. If a student repeatedly makes bad choices, what should your teacher do?

Teacher Tips

- Skip this lesson if you don't allow students to spread out to do their work.
- If you use the Student Handouts, you will need to replace the second handout with a map of your classroom. Consider if students can spread out beyond your classroom as well when creating a map for them to use. I also recommend adding any special seating options (e.g. standing desks, bouncy chairs, rolling chairs, etc.).
- Continue this conversation throughout the year. My students often discovered things like:
  - "I can work behind the file cabinets alone, but when I'm with others, I get off-task."
  - "The bouncy chair works great for a lot of kids, but it doesn't work for me."
  - Whenever I sit in a spot where I can look out the window, I get so distracted by the birds and squirrels."

Student Tasks 〉 Transfer Goals

Student Tasks	Transfer Goals
Students think about all the areas in the classroom where they've worked before and decide which have been good and which have been bad.	Students choose to work in locations in the classroom that lead to positive results, solid focus, and efficient work.
Students learn that being given choices is a privilege, not a right. Making wise decisions leads to more choice, but choosing poorly could result in loss of choice.	Students become better decision-makers, basing their choices on results and consequences, rather than urges and impulses.

INTRODUCTION

PLANNING

METACOGNITION

SYNTHESIS

REFLECTION

SELF-ASSESSMENT

GOAL SETTING

FEEDBACK

Instructional Poster(s)

- This lesson has ONE Instructional Poster.
- This Instructional Poster contains possible thoughts students might have when thinking about locations in the classroom that work well for them and locations that might not work well for them.
- Discuss each of them to see which ones students agree with and which ones they might see differently.
- Try to add more bullets to the list through a classroom discussion. The more you can brainstorm with the class, the more they'll be able to add to their maps on the Student Handout.
- If you have extra time, walk students through the first page of the Student Handout so they actually take the time to answer each question and consider them for the next page.

Student Handouts

- This lesson has TWO Student Handouts.
- DIRECTIONS: The directions are explained in detail below (on the Student Handout).
- Students should answer the questions on the first Student Handout in their heads (or by writing on the paper if you prefer).
- Feel free to simplify the directions for labeling the map (possibly with colored pencils or markers). The goal is to encourage students to make thoughtful decisions and have some evidence of those decisions for them to refer to if they struggle to maintain their focus when working around the room.

Where should I work so that I can focus best?

When I work alone, I...

- ...probably shouldn't sit near my closest friends, because I might be tempted to be off-task with them.
- ...need to face AWAY from the windows because I enjoy watching everything outside.
- ...like to be comfortable and my chair is NOT comfortable. I would prefer to sit on the floor or stand while working.
- ...would benefit from having someone closeby to ask questions, because I'm not very likely to get up to ask someone!

When I work with others, I...

- ...need to have some space between my group and the other groups so I don't listen in to their ideas or want to add things to their conversations.
- ...prefer to look directly at my partners rather than sit next to them, so I'd like a place where we can sit across from each other.
- ...I like to have my own space to write and not feel crammed in with my partners.
- ...don't enjoy working out in the hallway, because my partners aren't usually on-task as much.

Lesson 1.13   Optimized Learning for Sustained Effort, Improved Academic Drive and Peak Performance in the Classroom - by Paul Solarz   Instructional Poster 1 of 1

Planning

START   FINISH

Name:

Date:

BIG IDEA: When we are allowed to spread out in our classroom to work, it's important that we choose our locations carefully and responsibly. Our teacher needs to know that we are going to be focused and productive wherever we work.

DIRECTIONS: The directions are explained in detail below.

Where should I work so that I can focus best?

Sometimes, in our class, you will spend time **WORKING ALONE**. Think about what you need when you work alone.
- Do you need quiet?
- Do you need comfort?
- Do you need access to peers to ask questions or get reassurance?
- Do you need to avoid distractions like the windows or the clock?

Where in the classroom do you think would be the three BEST locations for you to work? Be ready to explain why!
- On the classroom map, label the Best Location: BL1a
- Label the 2nd Best Location: BL2a
- Label the 3rd Best Location: BL3a

Where might the three WORST locations be?
- On the classroom map, label the Worst Location: WL1a
- Label the 2nd Worst Location: WL2a
- Label the 3rd Worst Location: WL3a

Sometimes, in our class, you will spend time **WORKING WITH OTHERS**. Think about what you need when you work with others.
- Do you need space?
- Do you need comfort?
- Do you need to be close to the teacher?
- Do you need to avoid distractions like the windows or the clock?

Where in the classroom do you think would be the three BEST locations for you to work? Be ready to explain why! And keep in mind that others need to be able to sit next to you!
- On the classroom map, label the Best Location: BL1b
- Label the 2nd Best Location: BL2b
- Label the 3rd Best Location: BL3b

Where might the three WORST locations be?
- On the classroom map, label the Worst Location: WL1b
- Label the 2nd Worst Location: WL2b
- Label the 3rd Worst Location: WL3b

Lesson 1.13   Optimized Learning for Sustained Effort, Improved Academic Drive and Peak Performance in the Classroom - by Paul Solarz   Student Handout 1 of 2

Where should I work so that I can focus best?

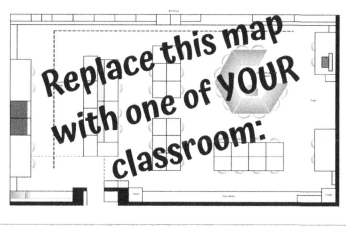

Lesson 1.13   Optimized Learning for Sustained Effort, Improved Academic Drive and Peak Performance in the Classroom - by Paul Solarz   Student Handout 2 of 2

bit.ly/3RhYtpV

Prioritize personal goals for improvement while working on assigned learning tasks

Essential Question

What goals do I plan to work on?

Big Idea

Most of the goals that we set for ourselves need to be practiced WHILE we are working on some learning task. Therefore, we need to identify the goal or goals that we want to improve BEFORE working on a task so we can address it.

Lesson Overview

In this lesson, students simply choose a goal or two to address WHILE they work on an academic assignment given by the teacher. For example, in science, students have been directed to measure the angles and lengths of the shadows made by the sun's position in the sky against their homemade sundials. Although a student might be working on ten or more goals, they choose one that states, "I need to improve my time-on-task when working with a partner." Therefore, they will try their best to accomplish the academic goals of the science lesson AND the S.M.A.A.R.T.E.R. Goal of being more focused and efficient with their time.

Discussion/Reflection Questions

- Usually, multi-tasking is a bad thing, because we steal attention from one task in order to focus on another, causing the quality of both tasks to suffer. However, achieving our goals HAS to be an exception to that rule. Can you explain why? Why would it be harder to improve most of our goals on their own, instead of WHILE WORKING?
- Why is it extremely important that we are organized with our goals when it comes to working on them during an academic lesson?
- How can you get better at writing important goals and choosing the best goals for each academic task? What would you suggest students do to improve?

Teacher Tips

- PREREQUISITE: Lesson 6.04. (S.M.A.A.R.T.E.R. Goals)
- PREREQUISITE: Lesson 6.05. (Goal Bursts)
- This lesson needs to happen concurrently with an academic lesson of any sort. Students will be choosing a goal of theirs to try to improve WHILE working on the academic lesson.
- This lesson should be the beginning of a routine that students continue independently the rest of the year, where they work on their goals DURING academic lessons. You will need to remind them of this step for several weeks before they will do it on their own, but it will be worth it. Students will be more attentive to their academic work AND accomplishing goals that affect them today and into the future!

Student Tasks 〉 Transfer Goals

Student Tasks	Transfer Goals
Students write short- and long-term goals that they believe they need to improve.	Students accurately identify areas where they struggle and need to improve.
Students choose goals to work on WHILE completing academic work in class based on importance or opportunity.	Students address their own deficits without the need of adults, and actively work on their goals independently.

Instructional Poster(s)

- This lesson has ONE Instructional Poster.
- This Instructional Poster reminds students of the two types of goals we set for ourselves in our classroom. S.M.A.A.R.T.E.R. Goals are typically bigger, more long-term goals that have a larger impact on us academically. Goal Bursts are immediate, short-term goals that often fix a small problem or get you into a better habit.
- As you go through this poster, make sure that students understand that THEY are the ones who need to identify a goal or two to work on WHILE they are working on academic work in class. They likely won't have any other time to address those goals.

Student Handouts

- This lesson has THREE Student Handouts.
- DIRECTIONS: Identify one or two Goal Bursts and/or S.M.A.A.R.T.E.R. Goals that you should work on DURING today's task. You need to ensure that you complete your assigned task to your highest ability, WHILE also addressing 1-2 of these goals.
- Students describe the goal or the problem on the first Student Handout, and explain why they chose that particular goal to work on on the second Student Handout.
- The third Student Handout is a combination of the first two Student Handouts and is only to be used in a Learning Cycle packet as an additional graphic organizer.

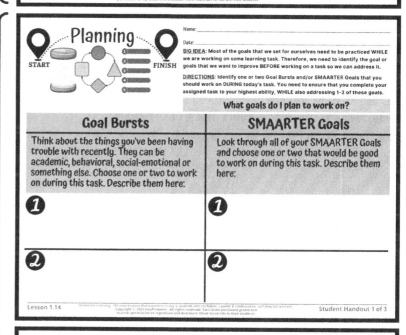

INTRODUCTION

PLANNING

METACOGNITION

SYNTHESIS

REFLECTION

SELF-ASSESSMENT

GOAL SETTING

FEEDBACK

bit.ly/4807dq4

Consider the prior knowledge you have on a topic before jumping into an activity to learn more effectively and efficiently

Essential Question

What prior knowledge might help me on this?

Big Idea

Jumping right into an unfamiliar task can lead to failure, but planning it out using background knowledge and critical thinking can improve our odds of success! We shouldn't fear failure, but if we have some tricks that we can use to improve our odds of success, we need to use them!

Lesson Overview

In this lesson, students learn about the value of thinking about their prior knowledge of a subject before diving deep into learning about it. Accurate prior knowledge can help students understand what they are learning better, but inaccurate prior knowledge can cause problems if students don't keep an open mind to new learning (and possibly check its accuracy through a quick online search). To apply this skill, students are entered into a (fake) chicken soup cooking contest where they need to use ONLY their prior knowledge (no resources) to list out the ingredients their soup will contain, the tools they will need to make it, and the methods they will use to cook it.

Discussion/Reflection Questions

- Why should we take time to consider what we already know about a subject before beginning to learn more about it? What benefits come from doing that?
- What should we do when our prior knowledge is different from what we are learning in a lesson? (Inaccurate prior knowledge and inaccurate new learning can really hurt your understanding of a subject.)
- The chicken soup cooking contest was a bit like a POP QUIZ (you weren't allowed to study for it & didn't know it was coming). What should you do when you find yourself in a situation where you don't have all the information you need? How can you still make it a positive, learning experience?

Teacher Tips

- It might not be a bad idea to have a simple chicken soup recipe nearby for your own knowledge. Don't show the students though (until the end)!
- Since the Student Handout portion is a brainstorming activity, don't allow students to collaborate or talk (if they complete this in class). If they do it at home, ask them NOT to ask anyone for help or use any other resources. We are having students explore their own prior knowledge to see what they already know about a subject (not using resources to learn about a subject).
- Feel free to extend this lesson past the idea of accessing prior knowledge. Extension ideas:
  - Even when you believe you have ALL the background knowledge you need, you can still learn more (e.g. Undercook your noodles because they will continue to cook until the soup cools down).
  - When you don't have enough prior knowledge to be successful, what are some things you can do?

Student Tasks 〉 Transfer Goals

Students learn that accessing your prior knowledge before beginning to learn more about a subject can help make learning easier and longer-lasting.	Students access their prior knowledge before learning new information on the subject.
Students brainstorm ingredients, tools, techniques, and steps for making homemade chicken noodle soup.	Students successfully access their prior knowledge on any subject that they hope to explore further.

INTRODUCTION

PLANNING

METACOGNITION

SYNTHESIS

REFLECTION

SELF-ASSESSMENT

GOAL SETTING

FEEDBACK

Instructional Poster(s)

- This lesson has ONE Instructional Poster.
- Before beginning an assignment or task in class, students should think about their prior knowledge on the subject. If I'm about to learn about the Boston Tea Party, I might want to think about what I've already learned about that time period earlier in the unit so I can make connections and see cause and effect relationships. When we use accurate prior knowledge WHILE learning new information, we understand it more deeply and improve our retention.
- Four steps students should consider:
  - Access your prior knowledge on the subject (What do you already know?)
  - What specific pieces of that prior knowledge might be helpful for today's learning?
  - HOW might those pieces be useful during today's learning?
  - Beware of incorrect prior knowledge! New information that conflicts with our prior knowledge might be ignored or assumed wrong if we don't keep an open mind.

Student Handouts

- This lesson has TWO Student Handouts.
- DIRECTIONS: Read about the pretend Cooking Contest below. Imagine jumping right in versus using the planning sheet on the next page. Then, plan your soup!
- In this activity, students summon their prior knowledge of chicken noodle soup and pretend to enter a cooking contest to make some! Sadly, the lesson ends before we get to try any of these soups, but hopefully students will have remembered most of the important ingredients and figured out a successful (safe) way to cook everything and make it taste good!

What prior knowledge might help me on this?

1 - Access Prior Knowledge
When you're about to begin an assignment, it's a good idea to think about what you already know about the topic. This is called, "accessing your prior knowledge."

2 - What specifics might help me?
For example, if you're beginning a new history unit on the Revolutionary War, think about the specifics that you already know about people like George Washington, events like the Boston Tea Party, and other important ideas like the Declaration of Independence.

3 - How might I be able to use this old information today?
FACTUAL information on this time period could help you understand NEW information that you're about to learn. The same is true in a subject like math where new SKILLS build on old ones.

4 - Beware False Knowledge
But, be careful! Prior knowledge that is incorrect can lead you down the wrong path! Don't always trust what you THINK you know! Be willing to listen to others' perspectives and find evidence that supports your prior knowledge.

Lesson 1.15 — Instructional Poster 1 of 1

Planning

START — FINISH

Name:
Date:

BIG IDEA: Jumping right into an unfamiliar task can lead to failure, but planning it out using background knowledge and critical thinking can improve our odds of success! We shouldn't fear failure, but if we have some tricks that we can use to improve our odds of success, we need to use them!

DIRECTIONS: Read about the pretend Cooking Contest below. Imagine jumping right in versus using the planning sheet on the next page. Then, plan your soup!

Congratulations!
You have just been selected to participate in a (pretend) cooking contest! If you create the best-tasting Chicken Noodle Soup, you'll win $25,000! Here are the rules:

1. You must use Pasta Perfect's Macaroni noodles in your soup because we are the sponsor of this contest!
2. Other than the noodles, everything needs to be made from scratch (which means that you can't buy anything that is pre-made like a box of chicken stock or a can of soup!).
3. You can't get any help from people or any other resources like recipe books or the internet.
4. You will be given four hours (pretend) to create your soup using ONLY the ingredients you ask for BEFORE starting, and all the kitchen equipment you want to use.

What prior knowledge might help me on this?

Well this is pretty awesome! All you need to do is create the best tasting Chicken Noodle Soup and you get to walk away with $25,000! It's possible that you've never made soup from scratch before, but that's okay - you have lots of BACKGROUND KNOWLEDGE that should help you do pretty well!

What prior knowledge might help you win this contest?
-
-
-

Lesson 1.15 — Student Handout 1 of 2

What prior knowledge might help me on this?

Ingredients that I've had in chicken noodle soup in the past:	Herbs, spices & seasonings that might make my soup taste good:	Kitchen equipment I think I need to prepare the soup:

Here are the first few steps I plan to take to begin making my soup:

Lesson 1.15 — Student Handout 2 of 2

bit.ly/47uqgcr

Learn that "True Collaboration" involves working together, valuing & building on others' ideas and finding common ground

Essential Question

What are some elements of TRUE Collaboration?

Big Idea

Collaboration is often misunderstood. TRUE COLLABORATION means working WITH (not nearby) others to solve problems, accomplish tasks, and learn new topics or skills! True collaboration means that each partner VALUES each others' ideas, and WANTS to discuss their learning while building on each others' thoughts, politely disagreeing and making compromises.

Lesson Overview

In this lesson, students try to identify the elements of TRUE collaboration by looking at several photos that show students collaborating on tasks and assignments, and through brainstorming. Since collaboration is a more complex skill than just "working together," students need to learn some of the differences. After doing some reflection, students should choose one or more elements of TRUE collaboration to try to improve during a regular academic lesson where they get to work with another student in class.

Discussion/Reflection Questions

- Why do you think I keep using the term TRUE collaboration instead of just collaboration?
- In what ways are TRUE collaboration different from just working with a partner?
- Why has collaboration become one of the most important skills, according to businesses today? Isn't it easy to work with someone else? What makes it so challenging?

Teacher Tips

- I recommend following these steps for the lesson:
  1. Teach Instructional Poster (have students take notes)
  2. Have students complete Student Handout page 1
  3. Have students complete a collaborative learning experience of any sort (assignment, experiment, project, task) where they will apply at least one element of True Collaboration from their Student Handout while they work with a partner
  4. Have students complete Student Handout page 2 using their notes from the Instructional Poster
- If you are able to do so, collect all the ideas the students brainstorm and create a poster of "Elements of True Collaboration."

Student Tasks 〉 Transfer Goals

Student Tasks	Transfer Goals
Students identify the elements of TRUE collaboration.	Students apply the elements of TRUE collaboration whenever they work with others.
Students identify one element of TRUE collaboration to try to improve during a partner activity.	Students become TRUE collaborators who know how to combine ideas, build off ideas, and handle conflict.

Instructional Poster(s)

- This lesson has ONE Instructional Poster.
- On this Instructional Poster, there are 9 photos of students collaborating. But what are they doing specifically that tells you they are collaborating? (Students can complete page two of the Student Handout during this discussion OR have them take notes to do it later. Just don't let them look at page one of the Student Handout until the end of the conversation.)
  - What can you SEE in each photo?
  - How do you think they are talking with each other?
  - What do you think students are thinking about?
  - What are students NOT doing?
  - How do you KNOW that they are engaged and involved in their work?
  - Encourage inferences. What COULD be happening in each photo and WHY do you think that?
  - How do you think these students get along with each other? How do they feel about each other?
- How could we translate these "Traits of True Collaboration" to our classroom setting?

Student Handouts

- This lesson has TWO Student Handouts.
- DIRECTIONS: Read all three boxes below and follow the directions in each box.
- DIRECTIONS: Look at the photos on the first page of this lesson. Try to identify ONE aspect of TRUE COLLABORATION in each photo. You will have to imagine what they are doing and you might have to PRETEND that they are thinking something or saying something. You get to decide, but try to find at least SIX characteristics of TRUE COLLABORATION in the photos and write them down in the chart below.

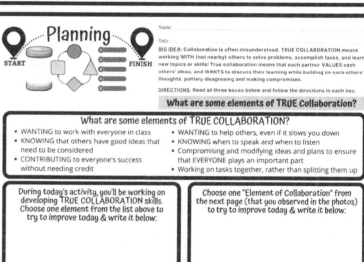

bit.ly/47Usv8P

Create tableaux that show what "True Collaboration" is and is not to reinforce how we work with peers in this class

Essential Question

How do I apply the elements of TRUE Collaboration?

Lesson Overview

In this lesson, students apply what they learned about TRUE collaboration in the last lesson by creating photo tableaux (posed, still photos) that exaggerate one non-example of collaboration. Then, they "fix" that non-example to create a new tableau where everyone is collaborating successfully. (I highly recommend taking photos of each to put side-by-side for students to see throughout the year.)

Big Idea

Collaboration is often misunderstood. TRUE COLLABORATION means working WITH (not nearby) others to solve problems, accomplish tasks, and learn new topics or skills! True collaboration means that each partner VALUES each others' ideas, and WANTS to discuss their learning while building on each others' thoughts, politely disagreeing and making compromises.

Discussion/Reflection Questions

- Why did we spend time creating tableaux that showed non-examples of TRUE collaboration? Why not just focus on correct examples? Why can it be helpful to see non-examples of something?
- What are some elements of TRUE collaboration that you learned during this lesson and the last that you didn't necessarily realize before, or that become clearer now?
- If you could explain TRUE collaboration to a kindergartner, what would you say to them in order to get them to become better at collaborating?

Teacher Tips

- You will need to put students into partnerships or small groups for this activity. As with all partnerships, I HIGHLY recommend choosing groups randomly so students can have practice working with everyone in the room. I think groups of three might be ideal for this.
- If you leave the "element" of TRUE collaboration open for each partnership or small group to choose, they will all likely want to choose things like hitting each other, or ignoring each other. These don't really help teach the elements of TRUE collaboration that most student lack. I recommend having a checklist of some sort (I use a Google Sheet and project it in class) and having partnerships or small groups choose one or two to focus on. Maybe, after being approved by you, they can do others that weren't on the list if they can avoid distracting others.
- You can be the one who takes photos of each tableau, or have the students ask a group nearby to do so (it's good practice for collaboration!).

Student Tasks ⟩ Transfer Goals

Students collaborate with peers to create tableaux that show examples and non-examples of TRUE collaboration.	Students identify when they are collaborating & when they are not and make adjustments as needed.
Students describe how they would collaborate with a random partner if they were given various scenarios.	Students anticipate opportunities to collaborate and apply the elements of TRUE collaboration to their task.

INTRODUCTION

PLANNING

METACOGNITION

SYNTHESIS

REFLECTION

SELF-ASSESSMENT

GOAL SETTING

FEEDBACK

Instructional Poster(s)

- This lesson has ONE Instructional Poster.
- Today's Instructional Poster is really just a set of directions for today's activity. Students will be working together as a partnership or small group to create posed, still images called tableaux. These tableaux will be designed to show the right way and the wrong way to collaborate using the elements of TRUE collaboration that we brainstormed in the previous lesson.
- Once students have signed up for an element or two, they work together to come up with a plan for creating their tableaux - they need to use their collaboration skills to do this. When they have a plan, they can pose in a non-example of the element (and take a photo), and then an example of the element (and take a photo). At the end of the lesson, you should have dozens of photos showing what to do and not do while collaborating!

Student Handouts

- This lesson has TWO Student Handouts.
- DIRECTIONS: For each row below, place a check mark in the correct column.
  - This is a simple check for understanding. Be sure to go over this with the students at some point so they know if they are correct or not, and so they can become clearer on what collaboration is and isn't.
- DIRECTIONS: Imagine your teacher assigning you each of the tasks below. How would you collaborate if you were assigned a random partner for this assignment? What would you do? Each assignment should offer you some new ways to collaborate, so don't waste too much time repeating what you've already written.
  - Ask students to come up with something new for each question.

How do I apply the elements of TRUE Collaboration?

1 Create a Tableau (posed photograph) showing what COLLABORATION is NOT:

2 Then, try to "fix" your tableau so it shows how TRUE COLLABORATION should look:

3 Finally, describe the "Before" and "After" tableaux

In the first tableau, the students are... and... and... and...
In the second tableau, the students are... and... and... and...
This is better because... and... and... and...

Lesson 1.17   Instructional Poster 1 of 1

Planning
START   FINISH

Name:
Date:
BIG IDEA: Collaboration is often misunderstood. TRUE COLLABORATION means working WITH (not nearby) others to solve problems, accomplish tasks, and learn new topics or skills! True collaboration means that each partner VALUES each others' ideas, and WANTS to discuss their learning while building on each others' thoughts, politely disagreeing and making compromises.

DIRECTIONS: For each row below, place a check mark in the correct column.

How do I apply the elements of TRUE Collaboration?

COLLABORATION means working together with others to create something that you couldn't create on your own. It's combining the knowledge, expertise, wisdom, and skills of EVERYONE in the group.

Examples of Collaboration or NOT?	Collaboration	Not Collaboration
Divide up the work and each complete one part.		
Bounce ideas off of each other until you both come up with something that might work.		
Work separately, but compare what you each created individually before turning it in.		
Your partner takes the lead and does most of the work. You accept what your partner creates.		
You communicate with your partner, but occasionally disagree with each other. Eventually, you settle on a solution and work together to get it done.		

Lesson 1.17   Student Handout 1 of 2

How do I apply the elements of TRUE Collaboration?

DIRECTIONS: Imagine your teacher assigning you each of the tasks below. How would you collaborate if you were assigned a random partner for this assignment? What would you do? Each assignment should offer you some new ways to collaborate, so don't waste too much time repeating what you've already written.

Assignment	How would you collaborate if you were assigned a random partner for this assignment?
25 word problems in math.	
You are given 30 minutes to learn everything you can about the Revolutionary War	
Over the course of one week, create a 5 minute podcast arguing both sides of a debate topic that you know nothing about.	

Lesson 1.17   Student Handout 2 of 2

bit.ly/46yVjT1

Handle conflict positively in order to maintain relationships, preserve learning, and improve our self-esteem

Essential Question

How should I handle conflict when it happens?

Big Idea

We can't avoid conflict forever. It's bound to catch up with us eventually! But conflict is only BAD when we let it hurt relationships, take away from our learning, or lower our self-esteem. It's how we handle our conflict that really matters!

Lesson Overview

In this lesson, students learn three strategies for handling conflict with their peers. Conflict is bound to happen and shouldn't be discouraged - these are great opportunities for settling differences positively and making amends for our mistakes. When conflict occurs, students should choose one of the three strategies taught in class to use to solve the problem in the moment. No one should be upset by the outcome - they need to accept it move on. Because emotions can be high when collaborating, students should be reminded of respectful, kind behavior OR apologizing and making it up to the person they overreacted to.

Discussion/Reflection Questions

- Why is it important to learn how to manage conflict ourselves, rather than relying on adults to jump in?
- In what ways can disagreement lead to something positive?
- What are some ways we can disagree with our peers that shows respect and maintains relationships without needing conflict management strategies?

Teacher Tips

- These strategies could be displayed somewhere in the classroom for the students to see.
- Whenever you see conflict happening, PAUSE and observe them, if they begin to use a strategy PRAISE them for it. If not, point to the sign in the room, or gently remind them to use their strategies from this lesson. Stay with them until they are successful and can move past the conflict.
- When you praise your students for successfully handling challenges, students will learn that it's not vital to AVOID disagreement, but it is vital to get through it and repair the relationship. My students bickered like brothers and sisters, but I knew that was because they were comfortable with each other and cared about each other.
- If students are ever willing, have them show the class the situation they just solved using a conflict management strategy, but stop doing so after a few examples so it doesn't become a time-waster and attention-getter.

Student Tasks 〉 Transfer Goals

Student Tasks	Transfer Goals
Students learn three strategies for handling conflict on their own, without needing an adult to intervene.	Students use the three strategies when working with their peers in or out of school, without the need for reminders.
Students act out various scenarios and then use the conflict management strategies to resolve the problem.	Students work hard to maintain relationships in and out of school, by choosing their words and actions carefully.

INTRODUCTION

PLANNING

METACOGNITION

SYNTHESIS

REFLECTION

SELF-ASSESSMENT

GOAL SETTING

FEEDBACK

Instructional Poster(s)

- This lesson has ONE Instructional Poster.
- This is such a simple lesson that really pays off if referred to throughout the year! Students are bound to get into conflict with other, ESPECIALLY if you have them working collaboratively everyday. But that's a great thing, because they can practice managing conflict, just like everyone has to do to maintain relationships outside of school! Although the three strategies taught in this lesson might not be easily used outside of class, students learn that conflict is okay, but leaving it unsettled or holding a grudge is not.
- Introduce the three strategies to the class. Tell them that Rock-Paper-Scissors is the most commonly used strategy (best out of one, unless a tie). But that the other two strategies are very valuable and should be practiced often.
- Since students have an act-it-out next, make the instruction short, but assign students a partner and give clear directions on the next activity.

Student Handouts

- This lesson has TWO Student Handouts.
- DIRECTIONS: Using each of the three strategies from the Instructional Poster, act out each scene and reflect on them below. On the next page, create two of your own scenarios for each strategy.
- Students need to reflect on their act-it-out to say how well the strategy worked in each scenario and what they might do differently next time.
- Finally, students create six new scenarios (two for each strategy). These just need to be described on the second Student Handout, not acted out.

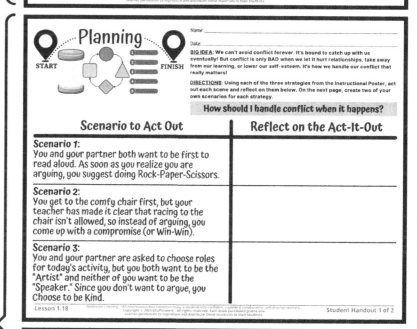

1.19

Boost productivity and enhance focus by de-cluttering, organizing your workspace & materials and staying organized

bit.ly/3TOCfK1

Essential Question

How can I organize myself better?

Big Idea

Being surrounded by a mound of papers can be overwhelming and distracting. Organizing our work and de-cluttering can help us get started quicker, focus better, and feel better about our work ethic.

Lesson Overview

In this lesson, students learn tips and strategies for organizing their schoolwork more effectively. They think about ways they can store their papers and books so they are easily found, create routines for turning in homework, etc. All of these tasks can be directed by you and modified to meet the needs of your students at your school. The goal is to help students improve their organizational skills through systems and routines.

Discussion/Reflection Questions

- Why is it important to be organized?
- What are some natural consequences of not being organized? What can happen that will cause you grief if you are not organized?
- How would you help a younger sibling who is struggling to keep their schoolwork organized in school and at home?
- What aspect of organization would like more help or support with? What might you be able to help others with?

Teacher Tips

- Be prepared to teach any of the organizational systems that your school or grade level want instituted (if applicable), like assignment notebooks, zipper binders, etc.
- Younger students may benefit from having the same system in place as their peers so the teacher and parents can assist them each day until they are ready to take on more responsibility for the system. Older students might benefit from having choice and flexibility, with the knowledge that if their system doesn't end up working after an acceptable period of time, the teacher may need to choose a different one for them and assist them with implementing it.
- If you have the time to go over the Student Handout before or after students complete it, it may be worth the time. The tips and strategies on the second page of the Student Handout are ideas that can be implemented in most classrooms with the support of the teacher.

Student Tasks 〉 Transfer Goals

Student Tasks	Transfer Goals
Students learn the importance of de-cluttering and getting organized.	Students prioritize staying organized and de-cluttered and have an easier time finding the things they need.
Students read through several tips for staying organized and assess themselves on each tip.	Students improve their ability on each tip and use these ideas for staying organized in school and out.

INTRODUCTION

PLANNING

METACOGNITION

SYNTHESIS

REFLECTION

SELF-ASSESSMENT

GOAL SETTING

FEEDBACK

Instructional Poster(s)

- This lesson has ONE Instructional Poster.
- The goal of this Instructional Poster is to teach students the best ways that they can organize themselves at school and de-clutter. Feel free to add or revise the ideas on the poster to suit the needs of your students.
- If you are teaching this lesson at a time when students' desks or lockers are messy, use this time to clean them out, BUT WITH A PLAN! Brainstorm with your students things that need to be done and write them down for all to refer to when cleaning. I tell my students you can throw anything out from any subjects or chapters that we've finished in class (had the test or final assessment & moved on to a new unit). If you give grades, students should take home graded papers, for example. If there is no organizational strategy, require one now. The specific strategy itself isn't what matters - just that they have a strategy for organization!

Student Handouts

- This lesson has TWO Student Handouts.
- DIRECTIONS: Read and complete all of the directions below. Add some of your own "Tips for Staying Organized" on the next page.
- In this activity, students are asked to clean out their desks or lockers, but are given some direction to help them do it effectively. Feel free to add further support as needed.
- Students are then tasked with creating an organizational system for themselves. This can be a whole-class organizational system if you teach it and structure it (great for younger students), or students can choose their own, assuming they have been exposed to several good ideas that might work for them.

How can I organize myself better?

Ever wonder why your parents are always wanting you to clean your bedroom? Or why your teacher wants you to keep a clean desk or locker?

It's NOT just to torment you and make you have to work as much as they have to work! It's because organization and neatness generally leads to saved time and prevents lost assignments!

If we are constantly surrounded by CLUTTER and DISORGANIZATION, it can be hard to manage all of our materials in a timely manner.

So, try to find time in your busy schedule to de-clutter and organize yourself. Then, create a system that maintains that order so you don't have to constantly be cleaning up after yourself!

1. De-clutter and organize your materials in your desk or locker.

2. Throw away things you no longer need (e.g. if you've already moved on to a new topic in that class, you probably don't need that old work anymore - unless you forgot to turn it in!).

3. Create an organizational system that works for YOU. Some students like using folders. While some students like having a Zipper Binder. Still, some students never find a system that works for them. Don't be one of them! Let's create a system that works for YOU!

4. Maintain your system over time. Make any necessary changes to it so that it keeps working well for you. If it stops working, ditch this system, but be sure to create a new one!

Lesson 1.19 — Instructional Poster 1 of 1

Planning

START — FINISH

Name:

Date:

BIG IDEA: Being surrounded by a mound of papers can be overwhelming and distracting. Organizing our work and de-cluttering can help us get started quicker, focus better, and feel better about our work ethic.

DIRECTIONS: Read and complete all of the directions below. Add some of your own "Tips for Staying Organized" on the next page.

Complete the following FOUR steps:

1. De-clutter and organize your materials in your desk or locker.

2. Throw away things you no longer need (e.g. if you've already moved on to a new topic in that class, you probably don't need that old work anymore - unless you forgot to turn it in!).

3. Create an organizational system that works for YOU. Some students like using folders. While some students like having a Zipper Binder. Still, some students never find a system that works for them. Don't be one of them! Let's create a system that works for YOU!

4. Maintain your system over time. Make any necessary changes to it so that it keeps working well for you. If it stops working, ditch this system, but be sure to create a new one!

How can I organize myself better?

Look at the "Tips for Staying Organized" on the next page. Highlight or circle any of the tips that you've already learned AND have used.

Which 2-3 tips on the list do you think you are REALLY good at?	Which 2-3 tips on the list do you think you need to try to improve?

Lesson 1.19 — Student Handout 1 of 2

How can I organize myself better?

- Create checklists
- Label folders or binders to make them easier to sort through
- Bring the right materials to class
- Develop routines
- Set rules for yourself
- Write everything down
- Create mini-deadlines
- Work on one task at a time; don't multitask
- Use a planner
- De-clutter at the end of each week
- Put sticky notes on your bedroom door to help you remember things
- Do five minutes of daily planning each day
- Once a week, review the upcoming events in your planner/calendar

- If a task takes two minutes or less to do, do it immediately
- Break down big tasks into smaller tasks
- Use a stopwatch or timer

- Keep a list of the questions you have about the class material and ask your questions as often as possible
- Every school night, pack your backpack for the following day
- Wake up a little bit earlier each morning so you don't have to rush

Add some of your own:

- •
- •
- •
- •

Tips for Staying Organized

- Double-check that you've completed all the homework that's due the next day
- Before you start work, eliminate all distractions

Many of these ideas came from: https://www.daniel-wong.com/2017/04/10/students-get-organized-for-school/

Lesson 1.19 — Student Handout 2 of 2

1.20

Create a plan to manage distractions, improve your focus and increase your productivity while working

bit.ly/3Ri2Hha

bit.ly/3Ri2Hha

Essential Question

What distracts me and how can I overcome it?

Big Idea

No matter how great of a student you are, you are bound to be distracted by SOMETHING when you work. The best solution is to learn to "tune it out" but the reality is that distractions can truly slow us down when working!

Lesson Overview

In this lesson, students identify the things that distract them when they work in school. They write these distractions down and then describe how they will overcome the distraction. Those distractions that are within our control can be dealt with directly by us. We can advocate for eliminating those distractions that are within our circle of influence, but need to find other ways to overcome them if we're not successful eliminating them. Some distractions are completely out of our control and influence - these are the ones we need to learn how to deal with successfully without making excuses or allowing them to overpower us.

Discussion/Reflection Questions

- Why did we spend time learning about distractions that are within our circle of control? Circle of influence? Outside of those circles?
- What can we do about distractions that are within our circle of control? Circle of influence? Outside of those circles?
- One of the best strategies that my students used when it came to distractions was learning to "tune it out." This isn't always possible for everyone and every distraction, but it worked well for most! What are some distractions in your classroom that you can just tune out?

Teacher Tips

- Think about any distractions that are common to your classroom and possible solutions for overcoming that distraction. For example, our classroom had no temperature control for an entire year. We all learned to wear layers to school and take layers off when warm and put them on when cold. What might be specific to your classroom?
- If you are a teacher who often lets the class work with the lights off or with music playing, ask them if that can be distracting at all. If so, can students use noise-cancelling headphones or sit in a part of the room where there is better light? How can those distractions be overcome? Can you encourage your students to advocate for certain changes or accomodations?

Student Tasks ⟩ Transfer Goals

Student Tasks	Transfer Goals
Students think about all the possible distractions in their classroom and identify the ones that affect them the most.	Students are aware of distractions in their life and find ways to deal with them instead of allowing them to steal our attention.
Students describe ways to avoid, prevent, or overcome distractions in the classroom so they remain on-task better.	Students use strategies for dealing with distractions, rather than allow them to be an excuse for low-quality work.

Instructional Poster(s)

- This lesson has ONE Instructional Poster.
- Spend a little time talking about distractions. What distracts you in class? How about at home? Which distractions do we have some control over? Which distractions are out of our control? What can we do about each distraction? What about those that we can't control?
- Explain that we have full power over things that are within our "circle of control." Examples might include who you choose to sit next to, what type of chair you choose to sit on, etc.
- We have some power over things that are within our "circle of influence," but we won't always be able to get our way with these. Examples include the temperature in the room (if it can be changed), wearing headphones to silence annoying noises, etc.
- In the outer circle, we have no control and no influence over it. These we just need to accept and find ways to deal with it.

Student Handouts

- This lesson has TWO Student Handouts.
- DIRECTIONS: Think about things that distract you when you work. List as many of them on the next page as you can and complete the chart for each.
- The first Student Handout gives students ideas for what might distract them in the classroom. They need to read through these and come up with some ideas of their own (if any apply) to complete the chart on the next page. If they truly don't get distracted easily, then great! They shouldn't be expected to write much, but should be expected to stay on task 99% of the time throughout the year! :)
- Remind students never to name names (or hint around) when being critical of them.

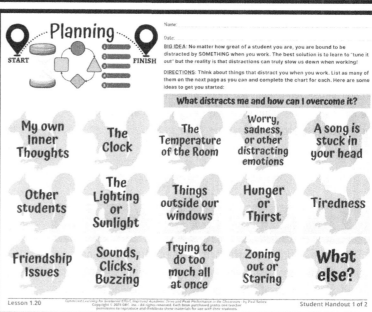

INTRODUCTION

PLANNING

METACOGNITION

SYNTHESIS

REFLECTION

SELF-ASSESSMENT

GOAL SETTING

FEEDBACK

bit.ly/49XkDVA

Be aware of your emotional state to help reduce conflict, receive support, and prevent unnecessarily challenging days

Essential Question

What should I do when I'm having a bad day?

Big Idea

Being aware of your emotional state can prevent conflict, invite others to help you get through the day, and prepare others that you might not have your best patience and understanding today.

Lesson Overview

In this lesson, students learn the importance of identifying your mood before others discover it. Once we know if we are in a bad mood, we can do something about it. The techniques in this lesson are kept simple (five steps), but teachers are encouraged to modify this lesson to include other strategies that are useful for your age group. No matter what mood students are in, it is not an excuse for bad behavior. Students need to work harder on days when they are on edge, but teachers and their peers might also help support students on these tougher days.

Discussion/Reflection Questions

- Why is it important to be aware of our mood when we enter class? Tell me more...
- What can we do on days when we are having a bad day to improve our mood?
- How can we help others who are having a bad day that doesn't encourage them to use a bad mood to get out of work?

Teacher Tips

- There is an additional Instructional Poster called, "Calming Down Techniques" that can act as a poster or a handout to help students learn specific strategies to use when having a bad day. Depending on your grade level, this may or may not be helpful, but hopefully it will at least inspire you to modify it for your students.
- Do your best to help students understand when their classmate is having a bad day. Remind them that we all have bad days and that sometimes we can't control everything. Try not to allow a student who is having a bad day to lose friends or have students talk behind their back. Everyone in the classroom is part of our team and we support them in good times and in bad!

Student Tasks 〉 Transfer Goals

Student Tasks	Transfer Goals
Students learn what to do when they walk into a classroom and are having a bad day.	Students know that a bad mood doesn't give them the right to make life difficult for others.
Students act out the five steps of handling a bad day.	Students use the five steps of handling a bad day whenever they find themselves in that position.

INTRODUCTION

PLANNING

METACOGNITION

SYNTHESIS

REFLECTION

SELF-ASSESSMENT

GOAL SETTING

FEEDBACK

Instructional Poster(s)

- This lesson has TWO Instructional Posters.
- Since every classroom is different, you should definitely decide what it is that you would like your students to do if they know they are having a bad day. In my 5th grade classroom, I asked my students to give me a heads up in the morning when they came into class if they knew they were having a rough start to their day. Whenever they let me know, I made a point of making a big (private) deal out of it and offering to talk with them during the first chance we had. Honestly, most kids just needed some attention, but rarely did any of those kids end up having a bad day behaviorally! The few exceptions were the ones who didn't respond well to the attention I gave them and didn't want to talk about it. I needed to get their mind off of their troubles in a different way, but again - they rarely had any conflict throughout the day. Most of the time, they were just sullen.
- The second Instructional Poster is a list of ten "Calming Down Strategies" that have been modified from: https://quotesgram.com/anger-quotes-for-teens/

Student Handouts

- This lesson has TWO Student Handouts.
- DIRECTIONS: Read the following chart below. Imagine yourself in each situation and what that might look like to others. Then, on the next page, prepare an act-it-out for each scenario and perform them with or without a partner. Record them if you're allowed!
- The main goal of this activity is to increase students' awareness of their mood, and to help them make an effort to improve it. The first Student Handout teaches students five steps to handling a bad day and gives extra information about each step.
- The second Student Handout asks students to PLAN out an act-it-out on the paper for each step, and then act it out & record it if you allow that.

What should I do when I'm having a bad day?

I want to give you a head's up that I'm in a really bad mood for some reason, and I don't want to act out.

We ALL have bad days!

I'm so glad you brought it to my attention! What's going on?

- What are some misbehaviors you (or someone else) may have experienced when having a bad day?
- Why would it be beneficial to talk about your problems with your teacher BEFORE getting into trouble for a misbehavior?
- What can you do if your teacher doesn't have time right away to talk?

Lesson 1.21 — Instructional Poster 1 of 2

Planning

START — FINISH

Name:

Date:

BIG IDEA: Being aware of your emotional state can prevent conflict, invite others to help you get through the day, and prepare others that you might not have your best patience and understanding today.

DIRECTIONS: Read the following chart below. Imagine yourself in each situation and what that might look like to others. Then, on the next page, prepare an act-it-out for each scenario and perform them with or without a partner. Record them if you're allowed!

We ALL have bad days!   What should I do when I'm having a bad day?

The secret to handling those bad days is:	How might you do this?
1. Being aware of when you're having a bad day before others find out.	If you feel easily frustrated or bothered by everyone around you, you might be having a bad day!
2. Controlling your actions, reactions and behaviors.	Every time you feel like yelling, hitting, or showing your frustration in another way, STOP & use a calming down technique.
3. Tuning out thoughts or impulses that aren't positive.	Whenever you think negative thoughts like how annoying your brother is or how much you want to throw your pencil, STOP & use a calming down technique.
4. Letting others know that you're having a bad day and that you don't want to get into trouble or make others upset.	Get comfortable letting the adults around you know when you're having a bad day. They might be able to help you get through it better!
5. Talking with someone you trust and continuing to learn strategies for dealing with bad days.	If you can talk with your parents or another adult (especially a counselor or therapist), they might be able to give you great ideas for dealing with these emotions! Give it a try!

Lesson 1.21 — Student Handout 1 of 2

What should I do when I'm having a bad day?

Perform an Act-It-Out showing all of the "Secrets" to handling a bad day. Start by planning out your actions and dialogue.

We ALL have bad days!

The secret to handling those bad days is:

1. Being aware of when you're having a bad day before others find out.

2. Controlling your actions, reactions and behaviors.

3. Tuning out thoughts or impulses that aren't positive.

4. Letting others know that you're having a bad day and that you don't want to get into trouble or make others upset.

5. Talking with someone you trust and continuing to learn strategies for dealing with bad days.

Lesson 1.21 — Student Handout 2 of 2

bit.ly/3T2AFrk

Although planning is extremely important, it needs to be done quickly so it doesn't impact learning time

Essential Question

How much time should I dedicate to PLANNING?

Big Idea

Planning needs to be done quickly and efficiently for it to be worth the time spent on it. Planning should NOT take so long that it prevents us from putting sufficient time and effort into our learning.

Lesson Overview

In this lesson, students look at a unique timeline that shows how planning could take WAY longer than it should if not completed efficiently. Then, students look at each step in "The Planning Process" and discover that they all need to be done quickly and efficiently. Finally, students answer each question in "The Planning Process" on paper (which adds additional time that won't be needed once the students have internalized the skill).

Discussion/Reflection Questions

- Why is it important that we complete the Planning stage quickly and efficiently? What could happen if we didn't?
- What do we do if there are questions that we don't know the answer to in "The Planning Process?"
- How do you plan to TRANSFER this skill to other situations in school and out? Decide right now when you plan to try this independently.

Teacher Tips

- Start by pointing out how "Timeline 1" allows too much time in the Planning stage. There isn't enough time for students to get their work done. (Although it will take extra time at first & will get quicker as students do it over time.) Next, look over the steps in "The Planning Process" and think if you have addressed each step or not (you may have to remind some students of these steps again). Finally, have a common assignment in mind for students who can't think of one.
- This lesson is the last lesson in this unit, and it is a culmination of most of the lessons from this unit (including some you may have skipped). If you've skipped some lessons in this unit, look over this lesson and see if you need to provide any instruction on the steps in the Planning Process so students can complete the Student Handouts correctly (and implement the Planning Step correctly in their everyday work). Students need to have a "Common Assignment" in mind for this lesson (e.g. weekly spelling activities, partner math practice, etc).

Student Tasks 〉 Transfer Goals

Student Tasks	Transfer Goals
Students observe a timeline to discover how quickly our class time gets used up during the Planning stage if we're not careful.	Students use their class time efficiently and understand the value of each minute of class.
Students analyze "The Planning Process" and learn that each step needs to be completely quickly and efficiently in our heads.	Students understand the value of "The Planning Process" and seek to use it independently in all learning situations.

INTRODUCTION

PLANNING

METACOGNITION

SYNTHESIS

REFLECTION

SELF-ASSESSMENT

GOAL SETTING

FEEDBACK

Instructional Poster(s)

- This lesson has ONE Instructional Poster.
- The Instructional Poster for this lesson shows students how planning could take WAY longer than it should if not completed efficiently. A unique timeline is used to visually explain how if students spend too much time planning, they won't have enough time to get their work done. This whole unit stressed the importance of Planning, but this stage in the SLSI Process needs to be done quickly and efficiently. That won't happen immediately, but with practice, students should find the sweet spot between racing through Planning and obsessing about each component.
- Make sure that students understand that not every lesson will follow a timeline structured like this with Teacher Instruction, then Planning, etc., but they need to understand how to transfer this concept to all other lesson formats.
- The additional Instructional Poster is a set of ten Calming Down Strategies that you can go over with your class if you think it is appropriate at your grade level.

Student Handouts

- This lesson has TWO Student Handouts.
- DIRECTIONS: Read the sample Planning Organizer below. Try to understand the purpose of the term "Fast" in each column. Try to imagine yourself completing each step quickly and moving on to the next one. Finally, answer the questions on the next page using an activity or assignment you do often or have done recently.
- The first Student Handout breaks down the components in the Planning Stage and states that each component should be completed "FAST" and provides a short explanation of the step.
- The second Student Handout asks students to answer each question in the Planning step in writing for a current assignment (which will take a long time and should not be used too often, since the goal is to complete this step quickly, but accurately. This handout helps provide evidence that it is being done accurately by each student..

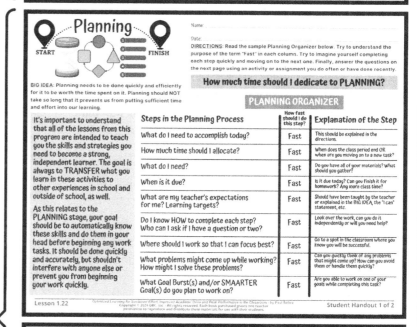

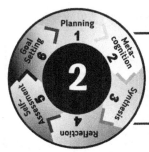

Download the Slides for this Unit:

bit.ly/48Lm7Rr

Metacognition

"A perfect dish isn't just ingredients, it's the dance of the chef, the awareness of every stir, every season. That's Metacognition on a plate."
— Google Bard's invented quote

In order to become successful, independent learners, students must develop the crucial macroskill of monitoring their metacognition while working. "Metacognition" refers to the awareness and understanding of one's own thinking processes. Further, it is "the use of reflective awareness to make timely adjustments to behaviors that support a goal-directed process," according to improvewithmetacognition.com. No matter how you define it, monitoring our metacognition during tasks is essential for optimizing the learning process.

Imagine that you are a student back in middle school (uh oh - nightmares!). You are working with a partner on a collaborative assignment, making excellent progress and getting along just fine. Your teacher is circulating, helping partnerships that need it and observing everyone's learning.

You pause to look around the room to see how your progress compares with others. Here's what you see:

- *One partnership is still on step one of the assignment, which is the least important step and should have the least amount of time dedicated to it.*
- *Another partnership is having a conversation that is completely off-topic, but they don't even realize it because they've asked the teacher for their opinion!*
- *A different partnership is already finished, but they completely missed several required steps. Maybe they have no idea, or maybe they don't care. You can't tell.*
- *And yet another partnership looks so confused, but doesn't seem to be doing anything about it. You decide to go over there and offer them some help.*

No one is using their metacognitive strategies like you are! They're all unaware of their lack of progress, poor attention, low effort, inaccurate work and ineffective prioritizing!

Their lack of metacognitive awareness is likely to lead to incomplete work, frustration with collaborative activities, poor results and a general dislike of the class and school.

Whereas, you and your partner have taken steps to remove distractions, prioritize your responsibilities, discuss confusions, and seek out assistance when needed. You are monitoring your progress by keeping an eye on the clock to ensure that you complete all of your work before the deadline and spend more time on the parts that matter than the parts that aren't as important. You are an optimized learner because you've learned about the importance of metacognition and have incorporated into your work ethic.

When students possess the ability to use metacognition while working, they gain a valuable tool for self-regulation and continuous improvement. Metacognitive skills enable students to monitor their own learning process, identify areas of strength and areas that require further attention, and adjust their strategies accordingly. This self-regulatory aspect empowers students to take ownership of their learning, become more self-directed, and make meaningful progress toward their goals. By actively engaging in metacognition, students develop a growth mindset, embrace challenges, and view setbacks as opportunities for learning and improvement.

Metacognitive awareness empowers students to adapt, modify, and refine their thinking strategies. It encourages them to become more flexible and open-minded in their approach to solving problems that come up. By being aware of their own cognitive processes, students recognize when their current methods aren't working, prompting them to explore other strategies that may lead to better results. This metacognitive flexibility allows them to think critically, consider different perspectives, and approach challenges with creative and novel ideas, ultimately improving their problem-solving ability.

Being metacognitive requires students to reflect on their understanding, evaluate their progress, and make adjustments to improve their performance. By engaging in metacognitive monitoring, students identify areas where they need additional support, seek out resources or assistance, and make informed decisions about their learning process, thereby becoming "optimized learners."

The lessons within this chapter focus on important microskills that contribute to effective metacognitive monitoring. Here are some examples (but not an exhaustive list):

Progress: Students should be aware of their progress throughout a task, from start to finish. Are you close to finishing? Does it look like you're going to need extra time to complete your work? Should you wrap up this step in order to move on to the next step? Students should track their progress, mentally check off completed tasks, and always be aware of "where" they are at in relation to the end of the assignment. By monitoring their progress, students identify areas where they may need to put in more effort or adjust their strategies to improve their performance.

Actions & Inactions: Students need to be mindful of their behaviors and choices. They should be able to see their actions and inactions as if watching in a mirror, making adjustments as necessary to improve their learning outcomes. Students are not always able to prevent misbehaviors and withdrawn actions, but they should be able to recognize them and immediately flip the switch to making better decisions. By being aware of what they are doing and not doing, students make immediate changes that get them back on track.

Interactions: Students should consider how they work with and around others. This includes being aware of verbal and non-verbal cues, understanding others' perspectives, and effectively collaborating with peers. Are they including everyone in their group? Are they contributing to others' ideas? Are they using social awareness? By monitoring their interactions, students develop strong relationships, enhance their communication skills, and create a collaborative classroom community.

Effort: Students should demonstrate a strong work ethic and take pride in their efforts. They should commit to putting in the necessary work to accomplish their tasks successfully. When students are aware of their level of effort in the work they are completing, they are better able to make adjustments that can lead to better results. Additionally, some students struggle with

perfectionism and need to be able to see when they are putting forth too much effort that is leading to negative emotions or an inefficient use of time. By monitoring their effort, students stay motivated, persevere through challenges, and achieve their academic goals.

Time: Students should manage their time effectively, using focus and productivity strategies to make the most of their time. They should be mindful of using their time wisely, meeting deadlines, and making adjustments to their plans when needed. For younger students, this starts with learning how to tell time, so they can own this skill without needing a countdown timer or the teacher's guidance. Older students need to be able to say to themselves, "I have 30 more minutes in class to complete the last three sections, so I should try not to go over 10 minutes each section." By monitoring their time, students prioritize tasks, avoid procrastination, and maintain a balanced workload.

Accuracy: Students should strive to complete tasks correctly and thoroughly. They should follow directions accurately, meet all success criteria, objectives and standards, and use reasoning and problem-solving skills to ensure accuracy in their work. By monitoring their accuracy, students identify areas where they may need to review, seek clarification or ask for more intense support, leading to improved learning outcomes.

Flexibility: Students should be flexible in their approach to tasks. This includes making changes when needed, integrating feedback, and using prior knowledge, skills, and strategies effectively. Students should refer back to their plan while working, while maintaining an awareness that plans must be flexible and change when new complexities arise. By monitoring their flexibility, students adapt to different situations, think critically, and find innovative solutions to challenges.

By cultivating these metacognitive microskills, students learn the essential tools to become active, self-directed learners. They develop a deep understanding of their own thinking processes and gain the ability to regulate their learning effectively. Armed with metacognitive awareness, students know how to identify when things aren't going well, adjust their strategies, seek out necessary support, and make informed decisions to optimize their learning experiences.

Ultimately, by honing these metacognitive microskills, students develop into confident, capable, and collaborative self-directed learners who navigate the complexities of academic challenges with a clear purpose. No longer do they rely on adults to think and make decisions for them. Spoon-feeding is not needed, nor is it wanted. These students are optimized learners who know what to do and how to handle situations when things don't go as planned.

INTRODUCTION
PLANNING
METACOGNITION
SYNTHESIS
REFLECTION
SELF-ASSESSMENT
GOAL SETTING
FEEDBACK

Silent Day - The Ultimate Test of Metacognition

An entire day near the end of the year when I can't speak all day & the kids run it all!

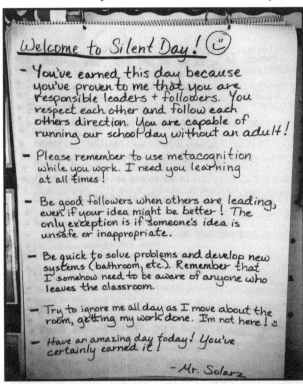

Welcome to Silent Day! ☺

- You've earned this day because you've proven to me that you are responsible leaders + followers. You respect each other and follow each others direction. You are capable of running our school day without an adult!

- Please remember to use metacognition while you work. I need you learning at all times!

- Be good followers when others are leading, even if your idea might be better! The only exception is if someone's idea is unsafe or inappropriate.

- Be quick to solve problems and develop new systems (bathroom, etc.). Remember that I somehow need to be aware of anyone who leaves the classroom.

- Try to ignore me all day as I move about the room, getting my work done. I'm not here! ☺

- Have an amazing day today! You've certainly earned it!

— Mr. Solarz

G O

Goal:
Do your own metacognition checks (especially for Silent Day)

A Remind Others L

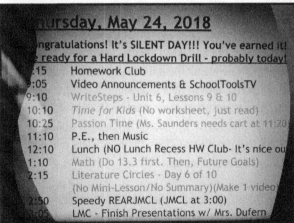

Thursday, May 24, 2018

Congratulations! It's SILENT DAY!!! You've earned it!
Be ready for a Hard Lockdown Drill - probably today!

8:15	Homework Club
9:05	Video Announcements & SchoolToolsTV
9:10	WriteSteps - Unit 6, Lessons 9 & 10
10:10	Time for Kids (No worksheet, just read)
10:25	Passion Time (Ms. Saunders needs cart at 11:20
11:10	P.E., then Music
12:10	Lunch (NO Lunch Recess HW Club- It's nice ou
1:10	Math (Do 13.3 first. Then, Future Goals)
2:15	Literature Circles - Day 6 of 10
	(No Mini-Lesson/No Summary)(Make 1 video
2:50	Speedy REARJMCL (JMCL at 3:00)
3:05	LMC - Finish Presentations w/ Mrs. Dufern

Student Directions, Sub plans that the students read aloud & follow and our Math Teacher's Guide, Me (I can't speak all day), Students write our daily whole-class goal on a white board, The schedule for the day is always posted so students can lead transitions, The students created a system that kept me informed about who was out of the classroom, The students all starting an activity, Me at the end of the day.

For more information on Silent Day, visit: bit.ly/SILENTDAY

Bathroom:

Girl	Boy
Isabella	Mikey

Other:
Melanie ELL

Unit 2 - Metacognition

29 Mini-Lessons

INTRODUCTION

PLANNING

METACOGNITION

SYNTHESIS

REFLECTION

SELF-ASSESSMENT

GOAL SETTING

FEEDBACK

Have you made changes to any slides?

If you've made changes to any of the slides from Optimized Learning and think that other educators might enjoy having access to them, please submit them here, and they will be uploaded to the Google Drive so everyone can access them!

The QR Code and short link on the right will take you to a Google Form that will allow you to submit a link to a template that you create for your modified slide(s). The directions for creating a template are on the form and are very easy to do, so please don't think that this is outside your comfort zone!

If you have any notes for teachers (e.g. reasons for making the change, the grade level each slide has been created for, etc.), please include that in the provided sections on the Google Form.

Thanks so much for making this a valuable tool for other educators!

bit.ly/492T23Y

Students with well-developed METACOGNITION MicroSkills...	Students with poorly-developed METACOGNITION MicroSkills...
Monitor their own understanding and progress	Lack self-awareness of their own understanding and progress
Recognize when they are confused about their learning	Fail to realize when they are confused and continue without seeking clarification
Use strategies to make sense of their learning when confused	Lack strategies to address confusion and continue doing things incorrectly
Recognize when they need help and seek assistance	Hesitate to ask for help or support when needed
Seek feedback from teachers and peers to improve their learning	Avoid seeking feedback and miss opportunities for improvement
Regulate their learning through self-questioning and self-monitoring	Lack metacognitive strategies to regulate their learning effectively
Regulate their emotions and manage stress	Struggle to regulate their emotions and become easily overwhelmed
Adapt their learning strategies based on feedback and assessment results	Resist adapting their learning strategies and persist with ineffective approaches
Take responsibility for their own learning and actively participate in the learning process	Exhibit a passive approach to learning and rely on others for guidance
Monitor their own level of engagement and motivation in learning tasks	Lack awareness of their own level of engagement and motivation
Monitor their own progress toward learning goals	Lack self-monitoring of progress and goal attainment
Show persistence and resilience in the face of challenges	Give up easily when faced with challenges or setbacks
Adapt their learning strategies based on their strengths and weaknesses	Use the same learning strategies regardless of their effectiveness
Seek out additional resources or materials to enhance their learning	Rely solely on provided materials without seeking additional resources
Accomplish S.M.A.A.R.T.E.R. Goals and Goal Bursts while they work on academic tasks	Struggle to focus both on academic work and the goals that they've set for themselves
Cite evidence that supports their metacognitive awareness	Make claims with regard to metacognition that they can't support with evidence
Make adjustments as soon as they realize things are not going as hoped	Resist making adjustments when they are needed

INTRODUCTION

PLANNING

METACOGNITION

SYNTHESIS

REFLECTION

SELF-ASSESSMENT

GOAL SETTING

FEEDBACK

bit.ly/3Ns6k23

Evaluate METACOGNITION MicroSkills to take pride in relative strengths and to set personalized goals for areas of weakness

Essential Question

How strong am I at each of these METACOGNITION Skills?

Big Idea

By evaluating our current level of achievement on the MicroSkills that will be taught in this unit, we gain a clearer understanding of our individual strengths and weaknesses. Additionally, by synthesizing each MicroSkill, we develop a stronger understanding of the MacroSkill that this unit focuses on, which is METACOGNITION.

Lesson Overview

In this lesson, students evaluate their perceived ability for each of the identified METACOGNITIVE skills. These skills have been chosen from the lessons that follow in this unit. Although students are choosing a somewhat arbitrary number from 1-10, the self-assessment process requires them to (1) understand what the skill means, (2) determine their perceived ability for the skill, and (3) sort each skill into areas of weakness or strength (or in-between) so that they help others improve at the skill (for scores 7-10) or make the skill into a goal that they try to achieve (for scores 1-4). If a student scores a 5 or 6, they are asked to reassess themselves after the unit to determine if they would benefit from making it a goal or not.

Discussion/Reflection Questions

- Which metacognitive skills did you feel you were strongest at? Provide some evidence to support your self-assessment.
- Which metacognitive skills did you feel you were weakest at? Explain why you feel that this is true.
- If you could set a goal to improve ONE of these skills, which one would you choose? Why did you choose that one? How do you plan to improve this skill? What will you do?

Teacher Tips

- On the Student Handouts, it tells students to "highlight all the numbers up through your score." The reason I didn't just have them circle the number is so they can see "how full" their grade band is if they choose a high number, and "how empty" their grade band is if they choose a low number. If you don't think it's too important for your students, feel free to let them just circle their number.
- When doing a self-assessment like this, I like to teach my students about the importance of being honest with themselves. I remind them that self-assessment in our classroom don't affect your grades or the way I see them. Self-assessments help us focus in on what matters to us, rather than focusing in on everything and not spending enough time on the skills that we need to improve most. No one is a 10 on all of these skills and no one is a 1 on all of them, but there's a good chance that each of us is a 10 and a 1 on at least one skill in this self-assessment!

Student Tasks 〉 Transfer Goals

Student Tasks	Transfer Goals
Students assess themselves on various metacognitive skills using a scale from 1 to 10.	Students become more self-aware of their abilities and areas in which they need to grow.
Students are asked several reflection questions that require them to explain their self-assessments and to set a goal for one skill.	Students understand that having weaknesses is normal and that they should be improved through goal-setting.

Instructional Poster(s)

- This lesson has ONE Instructional Poster.
- A variation of this Instructional Poster is used with the first lesson of each unit. It shows students how to use the 1-10 scale for assessing their current level of ability with each skill. Numbers 1-4 mean that they know they need to improve at this skill (and maybe create a goal for the skill), and numbers 7-10 mean they believe that they are capable of helping others improve this skill. (4-5 means they will reassess at the end of the unit - which will be up to you or the student to remember to do. It's not a lesson.)
- Tell students that the real value in this activity is discovering their relative strengths and weaknesses, so giving yourself a 10 for each skill is wasting everyone's time, as is repeating any other number. Finding the variation in each skill is the key, so give yourself scores of 1, 2, and 3 and give scores of 8, 9, and 10 as well!

Student Handouts

- This lesson has FOUR Student Handouts.
- DIRECTIONS: Look at the Metacognition MicroSkills in each box below and on the following page(s). Determine a rating from 1-10 for yourself on each, and then circle it. For your lowest MicroSkill(s), create a S.M.A.A.R.T.E.R. Goal to address each weakness.
- If you have not taught the lesson on Goal Bursts, let students know that they can just make the skill a personal goal to improve, but nothing needs to be written out (unless they want a reminder to actually do it). Obviously, the more seriously they take things, the more likely they'll improve!

How strong am I at each of these Metacognitive Skills?

This is one of the skills that we will be working on in this unit. Think about your ability to do this skill correctly without reminders or help.

This scale runs from 1 to 10. If you believe you know virtually nothing about the skill, you might give yourself a "1." If you believe that, for your age, you are one of the best at this skill, you might give yourself a "10."

Develop a strong work ethic so that effort is always high without reminders

1 2 3 4 5 6 7 8 9 10

I'll need to work on this. - - - - - - - - - - I'll help others with this!

If you believe that your current level is between 1 and 4, you most likely believe that this is an area that you should try to improve. Good! Let's grow!

If you believe that your current level is between 5 and 6, you most likely believe that you are neither strong, nor weak in. See how well you learn it in this unit, then decide if you think it would be a worthwhile goal.

If you believe that your current level is between 7 and 10, you most likely believe that this is an area that you can try to help others with. Good! Let's help others!

Metacognition

Name:

Date:

BIG IDEA: When our metacognitive skills are strengthened, learning becomes easier.

DIRECTIONS: Look at the metacognitive skills in each box below. Determine a grade from 1-10 for yourself for each skill, and highlight all the numbers up through your score. For the skill or skills with your lowest grades, choose to make them a GOAL BURST as soon as possible. For your higher scores, offer your help to those who might benefit from it. Continue on the next few pages.

How strong am I at each of these Metacognitive Skills?

Jump right in & get started on a task (after making a plan)
1 2 3 4 5 6 7 8 9 10
I'll need to work on this. - - - - - I'll help others with this!

Accept that small failures, asking for help, and persisting are all part of learning
1 2 3 4 5 6 7 8 9 10
I'll need to work on this. - - - - - I'll help others with this!

Know when to persevere and when to ask for help
1 2 3 4 5 6 7 8 9 10
I'll need to work on this. - - - - - I'll help others with this!

Know which strategies to use when you're frustrated and confused
1 2 3 4 5 6 7 8 9 10
I'll need to work on this. - - - - - I'll help others with this!

Organize and manage your materials and information
1 2 3 4 5 6 7 8 9 10
I'll need to work on this. - - - - - I'll help others with this!

Know what to do when you're done with an assignment or task
1 2 3 4 5 6 7 8 9 10
I'll need to work on this. - - - - - I'll help others with this!

How strong am I at each of these Metacognitive Skills?

Deal with distractions in order to stay focused
1 2 3 4 5 6 7 8 9 10
I'll need to work on this. - - - - - I'll help others with this!

Work with ALL peers in a positive way
1 2 3 4 5 6 7 8 9 10
I'll need to work on this. - - - - - I'll help others with this!

Manage your impulsivity
1 2 3 4 5 6 7 8 9 10
I'll need to work on this. - - - - - I'll help others with this!

Empathize with others to understand & respect their opinion or point of view
1 2 3 4 5 6 7 8 9 10
I'll need to work on this. - - - - - I'll help others with this!

Reflect on poor behavior choices in order to make better choices in the future
1 2 3 4 5 6 7 8 9 10
I'll need to work on this. - - - - - I'll help others with this!

Interpret & respond appropriately to verbal and non-verbal cues
1 2 3 4 5 6 7 8 9 10
I'll need to work on this. - - - - - I'll help others with this!

Develop social awareness to improve relationships, empathy and behavior
1 2 3 4 5 6 7 8 9 10
I'll need to work on this. - - - - - I'll help others with this!

Develop a strong work ethic so that effort is always high without reminders
1 2 3 4 5 6 7 8 9 10
I'll need to work on this. - - - - - I'll help others with this!

INTRODUCTION
PLANNING
METACOGNITION
SYNTHESIS
REFLECTION
SELF-ASSESSMENT
GOAL SETTING
FEEDBACK

bit.ly/40WRUfN

Unlock the power of metacognition to navigate tasks with awareness, adaptability, and personal growth

Essential Question

What is Metacognition?

Big Idea

Metacognition is a person's awareness of their plan, progress, actions & inactions, interactions, effort, time, accuracy and flexibility while working on a task.

Lesson Overview

In this lesson, students learn what metacognition means as it relates to the lessons in this book. They discover that it has MANY components, but that all of the components basically revolve around being aware of everything going on around you, inside your head, and between others while you work AND being able to improve any of those areas where you may not be meeting expectations. This lesson teaches students the importance of applying feedback and prior knowledge or abilities to their work today and into the future. Students also learn that it is during the metacognition stage that they need to work on goals that they've set for themselves in order to improve those skills and achieve those goals.

Discussion/Reflection Questions

- We discussed seven different components of metacognition while looking at the Instructional Poster. The definition of metacognition is your awareness of these components while working on a task. Give an example of when you think you should focus on these metacognitive components.
- How are "Interactions" different from "Actions & Inactions"?
- What do you think "Progress" and "Flexibility" mean when it comes to metacognition?
- Do you think we have control over these elements?

Teacher Tips

- You might want to give students the Student Handout for the Instructional Poster mini-lesson, but you need to tell them not to look on the front side because it will give away some of the inferences that they will need to make during the lesson. Students can then use the back of the Student Handout to write their inferences as they try to predict what each metacognitive component means.
- Students could also put a final explanation or set of examples on the same chart mentioned above if they draw a line down the middle before starting.
- On the first page of the Student Handout is a list of the components of metacognition and a basic explanation or example of each. This would make a good sticker for notebooks or desks, or even a bookmark.

Student Tasks 〉 Transfer Goals

Student Tasks	Transfer Goals
Students learn the definition of metacognition and understand when they need to monitor it.	Students monitor each of the components of metacognition whenever they work in school and ultimately through life.
Students learn to apply three additional tasks while monitoring their metacognition (goals, feedback, prior learning).	Students apply what they've learned to new situations, which reinforces it within each student.

INTRODUCTION

PLANNING

METACOGNITION

SYNTHESIS

REFLECTION

SELF-ASSESSMENT

GOAL SETTING

FEEDBACK

Instructional Poster(s)

- This lesson has ONE Instructional Poster.
- Metacognition has a lot of different definitions. For the purposes of this book, the definition of metacognition is "a person's awareness of their progress, actions & inactions, interactions, effort, time, accuracy and flexibility while working on a task."
- Rather than explaining each of these components to your students right away, give them some time to predict what they mean. Either partner them up to come up with explanations and examples of each component of metacognition, or provide some time to answer the questions on the poster before giving them the answers.
- Each of these seven components of metacognition will be taught throughout this unit.

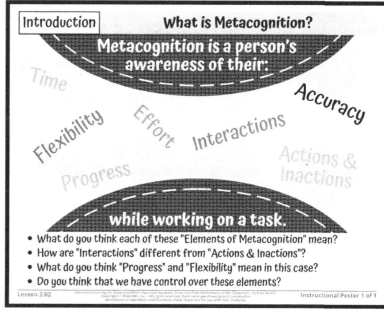

Student Handouts

- This lesson has TWO Student Handouts.
- DIRECTIONS: Read the information below and to the right. Then, on the next page, write your own definition or explanation of each component of metacognition in each row.
- The bottom three boxes on the first Student Handout add three more components to our definition of metacognition: "While working, make sure that we (1) work on any goals that we've set for ourselves (S.M.A.A.R.T.E.R. Goals or Goal Bursts), (2) use prior knowledge, skills, and strategies that we've already learned effectively (which means to apply our prior skills to new experiences), and (3) integrate all of the feedback we've been given into our work (which means to transfer all of the feedback we've received to new experiences).
- Students can use the second Student Handout to write their predicted explanation of each component and/or a more thorough, correct one.

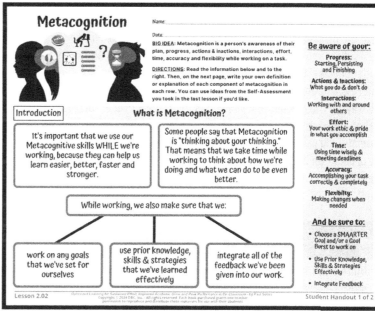

bit.ly/47z1h7Q

Self-assess your focus, effort, and progress during independent work for growth and improved performance

2.03

Essential Question

What is a Metacognition Check?

Lesson Overview

In this lesson, students learn to evaluate their current success or struggle while working in the classroom. For example, students are spread out, reading an article with a partner. They need to discuss all of the main ideas together before going on to the next section of the reading. The teacher calls out, "Metacognition Check!" and every student in class thinks about their current level of focus, effort, progress, etc. and gives a thumbs up, thumbs down, or thumbs sideways to the teacher that shows their perceived level of success at that moment. If some of your students aren't likely to reflect honestly, you can let them know that a lot of metacognition checks are brought on by one or more students' behavior & you hope that they know when it's them who is not performing at their highest level!

Teacher Tips

- Quite often, students change their self-assessment after a few more seconds of reflection. That's a GREAT thing. It means they've identified more evidence that brings them up or down on the rating scale. It's not important that YOU know what they identified, but it is important that you encourage changes to their self-assessment whenever it's based on new evidence that entered their minds.
- If you know that a student or two are currently off-task or otherwise misbehaving, call a whole class "Metacognition Check" and be sure to make polite eye contact with those students who should be giving themselves less than a thumbs up! If they did give themselves a thumbs up, be sure to talk to them about it once everyone is back to work. You might want to ask them for evidence that supports their claim. If students consistently overrate or underrate themselves, give them feedback that helps them self-assess better!
- If students seem confused by the subjectiveness of this self-assessment, feel free to brainstorm certain behaviors or actions that can be associated with thumbs up, thumbs down, and thumbs sideways.

Big Idea

Becoming metacognitive takes time and awareness. In order to help you become stronger at using metacognition while you work, your teacher will occasionally ask you to self-assess your current metacognitive abilities. You will need to learn to ask yourself that question several times each time you are working without direct teacher support so you can become stronger at metacognition.

Discussion/Reflection Questions

- Do you think "Metacognition Checks" will help you and others improve their metacognitive skills & awareness? Why or why not?
- What exactly are you assessing yourself on during a "Metacognition Check"? (Answer: All of the components of metacognition listed on the first Student Handout on the right side.)
- How will you be able to transfer "Metacognition Checks" to other classes and into the future? You won't likely have a teacher who calls them out in class!

Student Tasks 〉 Transfer Goals

Student Tasks	Transfer Goals
Students improve and refine their metacognitive skills through "Metacognition Check" reflection.	Students are successful at assessing their metacognitive skills while working in class, and can provide evidence to support their claim.
Students participate in regular "Metacognition Checks" posed by the teacher publicly AND each student privately.	Students check their metacognition naturally, and make adjustments when necessary while working on schoolwork and throughout life.

Instructional Poster(s)

- This lesson has ONE Instructional Poster.
- Metacognition Checks are called by the teacher whenever they observe that some students aren't using their metacognitive skills while working in class. They announce, "Metacognition Check!" and all of the students raise their hand and give a thumbs up, down, or sideways based on the Instructional Poster. This is for the teacher to understand how the majority of students are doing, not to grade or call out individual students. However, you expect them to answer accurately after they reflect honestly about their focus, effort, progress, etc. while working. They need to know when they are not using their strategies (taught in this book) and when they are.
- When the off-task student who inspired the metacognition check self-assesses honestly, give them a wink or a nod in appreciation. When they aren't honest (or are just wrong) be sure to privately let them know what you saw.
- In our classroom, I would start my shout-out with an "interrupter" - We used the phrase "Give me five! Give me five!" and then I would say "Metacognition Check!" - That interrupter helped students transition from their work to evaluating themselves and reporting out.

Student Handouts

- This lesson has TWO Student Handouts.
- DIRECTIONS: Read this page and the next. Answer the questions on the next page.
- The first page of the Student Handout teaches students what they need to do during a "Metacognition Check" and reinforces its benefits.
- The second Student Handout asks students to identify actions or behaviors that support a thumbs up, thumbs down, or thumbs sideways grade. (Evidence to support their claim)
- Consider having a short class discussion: "Although these self-assessments are somewhat public, there's no need to feel embarrassed or uncomfortable. We're evaluating ourselves on a skill, not our level of intelligence.
- After every "Metacognition Check" students are expected to make all necessary changes to ensure that the next "Metacognition Check" is better if it wasn't already a thumbs up.

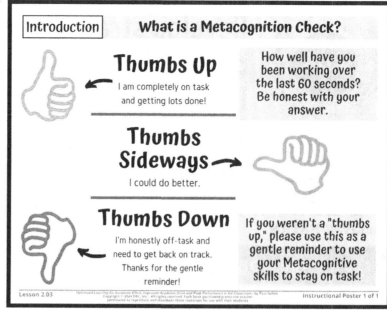

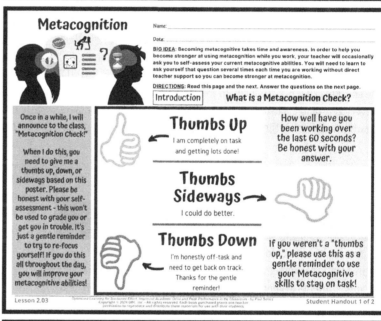

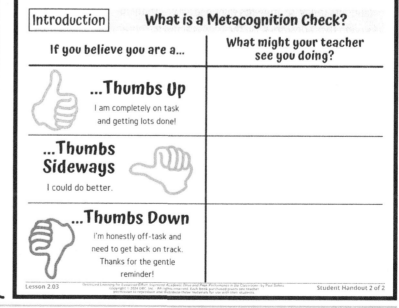

INTRODUCTION

PLANNING

METACOGNITION

SYNTHESIS

REFLECTION

SELF-ASSESSMENT

GOAL SETTING

FEEDBACK

Develop strategies for focus and productivity that lead to self-directed improvement and optimal outcomes

bit.ly/47E81RR

bit.ly/47E81RR

Essential Question

How can metacognition help me improve my work?

Big Idea

Metacognition goes beyond recognizing when you're struggling with a skill or when you're successful with it. You also need to be able to improve "on the spot." Learning some helpful strategies for focusing and productivity will help you make those improvements, without relying on others to direct you.

Lesson Overview

In this lesson, students are taught what they can do in order to be metacognitive. They are given specific questions to reflect on while working that will ensure that they are on the right track. If they decide that they are not on track, a suggestion is given to help them improve. In addition, students are introduced to two Strategy Posters that will help them improve their FOCUS and PRODUCTIVITY. The checklist that is introduced to the students in this lesson is used in every Learning Cycle packet throughout the year for students to use while monitoring their metacognition.

Discussion/Reflection Questions

- While you are first learning to be metacognitive, your teacher or your peers might need to remind you to check your metacognition quite often. But ultimately, you need to do this on your own without reminders. Why do you suppose that is?
- How often should you check your metacognition during a task in class?
- Is there any way that you can ensure that you ask yourself these questions when you need it most?
- What might happen to people who never learn how to monitor their metacognition?

Teacher Tips

- You might want to look through the ideas on each of the Instructional Posters and decide if you agree with them all for your students in your classroom. I suggest adding your own and removing any that don't work for your students. Students will need to use these Instructional Posters for their Student Handouts today, so students will need access to them.
- Leaving these posters up in the room should encourage students to use these strategies often. Consider posting them or reviewing them occasionally until students are successful with these strategies without support.

Student Tasks 〉 Transfer Goals

Student Tasks	Transfer Goals
Students learn to ask themselves specific questions that check on their level of success while working.	Students independently identify aspects of a task that determine its success or failure, and they monitor their progress toward these.
Students learn strategies for improving their FOCUS and PRODUCTIVITY.	Students use these strategies in future classes and in real-world applications.

Instructional Poster(s)

- This lesson has FOUR Instructional Posters.
- Poster #1 is a checklist of behaviors that students should try to be able to do (or avoid) during every learning experience. If they are able to check off each item on the list, they will have monitored their metacognition extremely well and will likely have more success on the assignment or task than if they couldn't check off each item. For this reason, please discourage students from checking items off that they didn't really do. This is not meant to score them - it is a way to let themselves know how well they monitored their metacognition, and any missed checkmarks can be reflected on to see if there were any consequences of not checking off those items.
- Poster #2 teaches students what they should be asking themselves while working. If they ask these four questions (and any additional ones that you suggest to them or they come up with on their own), they will be much more aware of their level of success while working. The four main questions focus students' attention on their preparedness for the task, their level of focus and production, and finally their time management skills.
- Poster #3 gives students ideas for being more FOCUSED while working.
- Poster #4 gives students ideas for being more PRODUCTIVE while working.

Student Handouts

- This lesson has TWO Student Handouts.
- DIRECTIONS: Add six new strategies to each poster below. If you and your peers can't think of six for each, choose some from the Instructional Poster that you believe you should try to improve. Then, fill in the four gray ovals on the next page.
- On the first Student Handout, if students have any trouble coming up with new ideas to put into each of the blank sections, you can allow them to choose a few from the poster in class that they truly plan to use within the next week or two.
- On the second Student Handout, parts of the poster have been removed and students are asked to fill in the ovals with the correct answer (it can be in their own words or copied directly from the poster in class - your call).

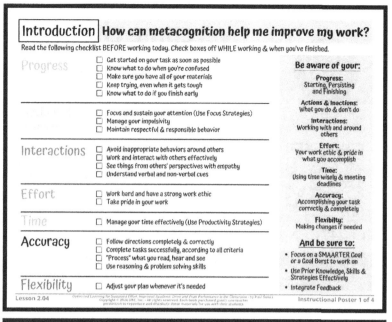

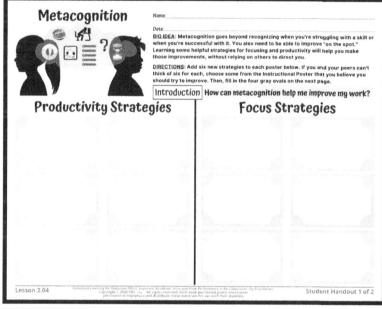

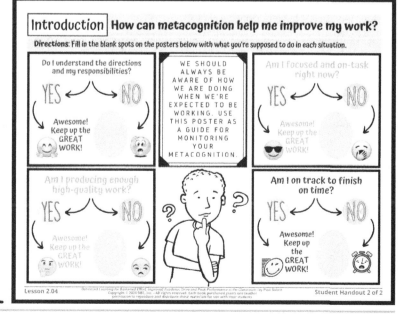

INTRODUCTION

PLANNING

METACOGNITION

SYNTHESIS

REFLECTION

SELF-ASSESSMENT

GOAL SETTING

FEEDBACK

bit.ly/47BEN68

Overcome challenges and confidently begin tasks, unlocking greater efficiency and minimizing confusion or overwhelm

Essential Question

Why can it be SO HARD to get started?

Big Idea

Getting started on a task can be a challenge for many people. Maybe the task is overwhelming. Maybe it's confusing. Maybe you just have something on your mind. Use strategies that make "Getting Started" easier and you're sure to find more success.

Lesson Overview

In this lesson, students think about the factors that make "getting started on a task" difficult. They also learn several strategies that can help them look past their obstacles and jump right in to working. It is believed that if students are more confident at starting a task, they will be more efficient with their time and will be less likely to behave poorly due to confusion or being overwhelmed.

Discussion/Reflection Questions

- Why can it sometimes be difficult to begin a new task? What reasons have prevented you from getting started on a chore or an assignment right away?
- What do you plan to do the next time you find yourself struggling to begin a task? Obviously, it will depend on the task but do your best to answer this question (possibly use an example or two).
- How will you remind yourself to use these strategies in the coming days? Do you have an idea of how you can keep these strategies nearby?

Teacher Tips

- Be sure to explain to students that although this lesson encourages them to "start a task right away," that it doesn't mean to skip steps in the PLANNING stage or to begin without completely understanding the directions and teacher expectations. It simply means that once they do those things, they need to get to work right away.
- Ask your students to add reasons why they are sometimes unable to begin an assignment that might not be focused on in this lesson. Also see if they have any strategies that have worked for them.
- The Student Handouts will likely need teacher support for directions and follow-through (transfer).

Student Tasks 〉 Transfer Goals

| Students learn several reasons why it can be challenging to get started on a task. | Students recognize when they are struggling to begin a task and this awareness leads them to using a strategy. |
| Students learn several strategies for overcoming the difficulty of getting started on a task. | Students no longer struggle to get started on a task. |

Instructional Poster(s)

- This lesson has ONE Instructional Poster.
- This lesson is all about getting started on a task, even when it's overwhelming, boring, confusing, etc. Discuss each box on the poster with the class and see if any of these tips can help them be more efficient with time both at home and in the classroom.
- See if you and your students can come up with any more ideas that could have been a box on this Instructional Poster.

Why can it be SO HARD to get started?

Progress

Are you overwhelmed by the amount of work you need to do? Break down large tasks into "chunks." If the chunk you plan to work on is still too big, break it down into mini-chunks.

Do you know WHY you are doing this task? If not, learn the value of doing this task. If you get why it's important, you might be more willing to put effort in. If it's not important, remember to "fake it 'til you make it!"

Are you just not that interested in doing this work? Then create motivators that encourage you to complete the task. What small reward can you give yourself for finishing your work? Keep others in mind!

Do you completely understand WHAT to do and HOW to do it? If not, you might be hesitant to start out of fear of making a mistake or confusion. Ask for help, re-read directions, or take a risk & start anyway!

Are you working some place that is ALWAYS dedicated to work? Don't work where you play, sleep or look at your phone. Create a spot that is only for work. Here, you won't associate off-task behaviors with this area.

Are you getting frustrated or mad at yourself for struggling to get started? When we let our emotions take over, it gets extremely difficult to transition into work. Think positively & use positive self-talk.

Do you feel distracted? Some people can tune out distractions, but others need to minimize them until they learn to tune them out. Turn off electronics, avoid windows to stare out of, and minimize noise.

Are you competitive? If so, challenge yourself to finish the first few steps in a short timeframe. If competition motivates you, this should help you start right away & accomplish a small chunk immediately!

Student Handouts

- This lesson has TWO Student Handouts.
- DIRECTIONS: Read through the strategies for "Getting Started" below. Rank them by writing a "1" in front of the task you believe will be most helpful, then a "2" etc. Then, on the next page, follow the directions in the box to discover how hard it can be to transition to new tasks and begin right away!
- Student Handout #1: Encourage students to write themselves a note or sticky that reminds them to use these strategies and place it somewhere they will see it when they are working (spiral notebook, binder, desk, etc.).
- Student Handout #2: Go over the directions with the class if you think it might be hard for your students to understand. Them, make sure that they reflect on the process at the end, because the activity isn't as valuable without reflecting on each transition.

Metacognition

Name: _____

Date: _____

BIG IDEA: Getting started on a task can be a challenge for many people. Maybe the task is overwhelming. Maybe it's confusing. Maybe you just have something on your mind. Use strategies that make "Getting Started" easier and you're sure to find more success.

DIRECTIONS: Read through the strategies for "Getting Started" below. Rank them by writing a "1" in front of the task you believe will be most helpful, then a "2" etc. Then, on the next page, follow the directions in each column to imagine various scenarios that help you feel how hard it can be to transition to new tasks right away!

Progress · Why can it be SO HARD to get started?

_____ Make sure you've broken down large tasks into "chunks."

_____ Create motivators that encourage you to complete the task.

_____ Create a spot that is dedicated to only doing work.

_____ Turn off electronics, avoid windows to stare out of, and minimize noise, even if they're not usually a problem for you.

_____ Learn the reason for doing this task & its value, or "fake it 'til you make it!"

_____ Think positively & use positive self-talk.

_____ Challenge yourself to finish the first few steps in a short timeframe.

_____ If you're not sure how to start, ask for help, re-read directions, or take a risk & start anyway!

Based on your rankings, use one of your first few choices RIGHT AWAY so you practice it and make it a habit! These strategies can be used ALL THE TIME! At least, until you build up skills like ignoring distractions and being intrinsically motivated to work hard, no matter the task.

Why can it be SO HARD to get started?

Progress

Your Situation	What should you do to get started?	Why is it SO HARD to start this?
You promised a parent that you would MAKE a gift for their birthday this year. Their birthday is tomorrow.		
All the kids on your block are outside. You can hear them having a great time, but you can't leave the house until your room is clean.		
A huge project is due tomorrow and you haven't even started on it yet even though you know exactly what you need to do. It's going to take about 3 hours to complete.		
The math page that you struggled on in class is the only homework you still have to do, but you don't know how to do it.		
You are furious with your brother. Since the two of you were arguing, you're both forced to stay in your rooms until dinner. You COULD do your homework, but you are SO MAD!		

bit.ly/3uDKJNt

Develop resilience and resourcefulness to maximize learning through perseverance and seeking help strategically

Essential Question

What should I do when I'm confused?

Big Idea

There are times in life when we should just keep trying at something. We just need to persevere until we figure it out. But there are also times when we should realize that we need someone's help (or the help of a resource).

Lesson Overview

In this lesson, students learn that there are times in class when you are expected to persevere through a problem and times when you are expected to ask for help. Obviously, this will look different in everyone's classroom, so you can tailor this lesson to fit your situation. In our classroom, the focus was on building strong interpersonal skills between all students, so most times, students were expected to go to a peer for help for nearly everything. Whenever they would come to me for a simple question, I would politely ask them to check with a peer first, because they probably know the answer and would enjoy helping you. This allowed me to work with the neediest students and kept students from wasting time waiting for me to help them.

Discussion/Reflection Questions

- Why might it be appropriate for a teacher to expect their students to struggle on a task without seeking help? In what situations might that be reasonable?
- What would you do if you saw a peer struggling on a task that they should be asking for help on? Why would you do that?
- How can you help others become more confident asking you for help when they are struggling? How can you become more confident asking others for help when you are struggling?

Teacher Tips

- If you can, try to teach your students to err on the side of asking their peers for help if they don't know what to do. Then, when they ask their peers for help at the wrong time, politely give feedback that clarifies what they should do. (In our 4th grade classroom, students were getting so good at this that when they had their first math test of the year, one of my students called out, "Give me five! Give me five!" during the test to ask the whole class a question! It turned out to be completely acceptable too - it was a direction question that everyone needed clarification on!)
- Students need to know that it is almost never acceptable to struggle for longer than a certain amount of time. Back when I gave homework, I learned of stories of students struggling for hours to complete an assignment that they truly didn't understand. Please make sure your students know that there is a time limit to persevering on most school tasks. I told them that no matter what, they should not exceed 50 minutes of homework on any night.
- There is a similar lesson in the Planning chapter (Lesson 1.12), but it is more focused on having a plan for being confused. If you are following the Instructional Spirals, these two lessons are taught back-to-back.

Student Tasks 〉 Transfer Goals

Student Tasks	Transfer Goals
Students learn how to use the Teachback Process to determine where their confusion lies.	Students are aware of when they are confused and know how to clear up their misunderstandings.
Students learn when it is appropriate to persevere and struggle on their own and when it's appropriate to ask for help.	Students ask questions of their peers and teacher when appropriate, and persevere when necessary.

INTRODUCTION

PLANNING

METACOGNITION

SYNTHESIS

REFLECTION

SELF-ASSESSMENT

GOAL SETTING

FEEDBACK

Instructional Poster(s)

- This lesson has ONE Instructional Poster.
- This Instructional Poster is a little different from the earlier ones. It is a strategy students can use to find out WHERE their confusion lies. They use the Teachback Process to explain to a peer what they think they understand about what they're supposed to do, and the peer fills in the gaps or clarifies the misunderstandings for the student. It's a great first step when being confused about a task or assignment and can be handled without teacher support.
- If a student is still confused after using the Teachback Process or after asking a peer for help, it might be a conceptual misunderstanding, not a simple misunderstanding of directions, for example. Now they will need to learn from the Student Handouts to determine if they should continue to struggle (because it's meant to be challenging) or if they should go to others for more specific help.

Student Handouts

- This lesson has TWO Student Handouts.
- DIRECTIONS: Read through the situations below. Add at least one additional situation to each section. Then, complete the next page by describing what you should do in each situation and why. Finally, try to use "Teachback" sometime in the next week or two.
- Student Handout #1 teaches students that there are some times when it is appropriate to struggle without asking others for help (e.g. trying to solve a challenge problem, taking a test, etc.), and there are times when you need to ask someone for help (sometimes you ask a peer & sometimes you ask your teacher). In our classroom, students were always encouraged to ask a peer or two BEFORE asking the teacher. This helped build relationships between students, made them all feel more independent, and allowed the teacher to focus on bigger challenges or to observe and assess. I highly recommend creating a similar classroom culture so your students can also become more collaborative and self-sufficient.

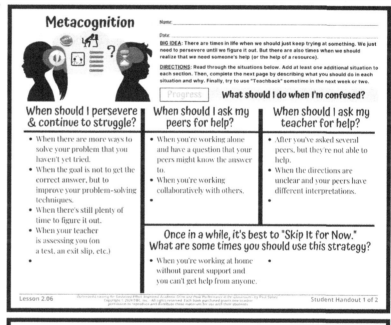

bit.ly/47XKyeh

Enhance productivity and success through optimized organization of materials, workspace, and learning

Essential Question

How can I organize my materials & workspace?

Lesson Overview

In this lesson, students learn how to organize their materials, their workspace, and their learning in class. "Materials" encompasses everything they need to be responsible for and not lose. "Workspace" refers to their desk or table's surface that they will be working on during a learning task. "Their Learning" refers to where they will store their incomplete work, where they will write notes so they can refer to them in the near future, etc. Since this sort of topic varies from grade to grade, you will probably need to tailor this lesson to fit your situation.

Big Idea

Organization of our materials requires us to: (1) Know what we need, (2) Know where to find them, and (3) Know where to place them while working. Organizing the information we learn while working might involve (1) Storing that information into our long-term memory, (2) Taking quality notes, or (3) Completing an activity that uses it.

Discussion/Reflection Questions

- Why is it important to learn how to stay organized?
- What is your plan for keeping your classwork (and homework if you have it) organized so it doesn't get lost AND so it gets turned in on time?
- What organizational tips can you share with others that have worked for you in the past?

Teacher Tips

- Consider doing the Instructional Poster AND the Student Handouts together as a class (unless your students already know how to answer the questions without your assistance).
- This would be a good lesson to complete early in the school year when you are teaching students daily routines and procedures that they need to practice regularly, but it is considered an optional lesson, so it doesn't appear in any of the Instructional Spirals.

Student Tasks 〉 Transfer Goals

Student Tasks	Transfer Goals
Students learn ways that they can organize their materials and their workspace in class.	Students use those organizational techniques in the classroom and throughout life, when applicable.
Students predict or infer WHEN they will likely use various organizational strategies to organize their learning in class.	Students anticipate when they need to use each organizational strategy in class and don't need to be told by others.

INTRODUCTION

PLANNING

METACOGNITION

SYNTHESIS

REFLECTION

SELF-ASSESSMENT

GOAL SETTING

FEEDBACK

Instructional Poster(s)

- This lesson has ONE Instructional Poster.
- The goal of this lesson is to help your students organize their materials and their workspace and that will of course vary from grade to grade and setup to setup. In my 5th grade classroom, I would focus on how we organize our desks, our folders, and our borrowed materials (e.g. laptops, arts & crafts supplies, etc.). The image in the Instructional Poster is a sample work space that can inspire a discussion, but you will need to tailor the actual information to your situation.

Student Handouts

- This lesson has TWO Student Handouts.
- DIRECTIONS: This is your work space for this task. Draw ALL the materials that you need for this task, and label everything, including WHERE you will be organizing the information that you learn today. Then, complete the task on the next page.
- On the first Student Handout, students are asked to draw their work space. Its intention is to draw the desk or table surface where students will be working for this specific lesson you are connecting it with, but you can modify it to relate to the inside of desks or lockers, or something else.
- Student Handout #2: In addition to organizing our materials, it's important to learn how to organize our "learning." Where do we write notes down? Where should I put incomplete work that I would like to finish tomorrow? When will I use these techniques in THIS classroom?
- Students will likely need your assistance completing this handout if they don't know the answers to these questions. I would choose to do these Student Handouts together as a class.

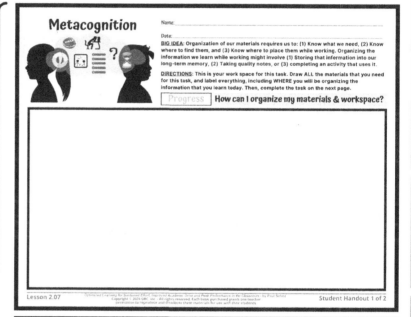

Progress | How can I organize my materials & workspace?

Sample Work Space:

My glasses

Directions from the teacher

My Science Notebook, where I'll be organizing all of my information today.

Laptop

Pencil

Calculator

Lesson 2.07 — Instructional Poster 1 of 1

Metacognition

Name:

Date:

BIG IDEA: Organization of our materials requires us to: (1) Know what we need, (2) Know where to find them, and (3) Know where to place them while working. Organizing the information we learn while working might involve (1) Storing that information into our long-term memory, (2) Taking quality notes, or (3) completing an activity that uses it.

DIRECTIONS: This is your work space for this task. Draw ALL the materials that you need for this task, and label everything, including WHERE you will be organizing the information that you learn today. Then, complete the task on the next page.

Progress | How can I organize my materials & workspace?

Lesson 2.07 — Student Handout 1 of 2

Progress | How can I organize my materials & workspace?

Method for "Organizing" your Learning	An example of WHEN you might use this method in your classroom
Taking notes with pencil and paper	
Memorizing the information for future use	
Learning something and immediately using the information with a peer	
Making note cards that you will study from in the near future	
Using a web tool to store your information or practice its meaning	
Learning something and immediately using the information on an assignment or project	

Lesson 2.07 — Student Handout 2 of 2

bit.ly/47WmCrp

Accept that small failures, asking for help, and persisting are all important parts of the learning process

Essential Question

What do I do when I feel like giving up?

Big Idea

Success is not always easy. To become successful often takes lots of hard work, struggles or failures along the way, and a little help from those who know what they're doing!

Lesson Overview

In this lesson, students learn about the value of persisting despite setbacks. Very few skills can be mastered immediately. Most require practice, patience, tinkering, effort, etc. Sometimes, we need to ask others for help. Sometimes, it's just a matter of analyzing what we're doing wrong and making an effort to fix it. Students need to learn that setbacks and failures are perfectly acceptable steps in the learning process. However, they also need to learn that setback and failures require increased effort or a change in strategy so that improvements are seen. I don't expect mastery from my students, but I do expect improvement.

Discussion/Reflection Questions

- Why do some people react negatively when they fail if failure is such an important part of the learning process?
- What can you do to handle setbacks and failures with understanding and a desire to improve? Imagine getting an "F" on a social studies test. What can you tell yourself that will help you handle the moment AND improve in the future?
- How do we know when it's time to STOP persisting? Isn't there a point when we HAVE to give up? Use examples, if necessary.

Teacher Tips

- This lesson is a great opportunity to review Growth Mindset. I like to discuss how a newborn baby has very few skills that they've mastered. Perhaps they're great at crying or sleeping or drinking from a bottle, but they can't tie their shoes, read a book or drive a car, YET. If you've taught the Marble Theory lesson, remind students how we usually start with zero marbles in our cup for each skill. Newborns begin to add marbles to their skills cups as they improve. Same with children and adults! Babies are great at observing their surroundings, listening, trying things, grabbing things, etc. If you try to interpret what they're doing, you might even be able to "see" them learning! They are putting forth effort. They are relying on those around them to serve as a model from them. They learn from your reactions and tone of voice, and they learn from experience: "Well, now he knows not to do THAT again!"
- This lesson is similar to Lesson 2.09, which is taught in Instructional Spiral 5. This lesson focuses on persistence and asking for help, while Lesson 2.09 introduces a few other ideas and has a few more steps. Feel free to teach one or the other. Or feel free to combine them into one lesson.

Student Tasks ⟩ Transfer Goals

Student Tasks	Transfer Goals
Students learn how a PERSISTENCE CHART helps us visualize the learning process.	Students ask others for help, persist when things are hard, and don't get frustrated along the way, because we rarely succeed immediately!
Students create their own PERSISTENCE CHART to show the path that their learning took for a specific skill.	Students know that new skills require effort and time, so they embrace the learning process and maintain their confidence.

Instructional Poster(s)

- This lesson has ONE Instructional Poster.
- The Instructional Poster tries to show students that the path from TRYING to SUCCEEDING often has many detours in between. This particular path shows a student who:
  - 1 - Tries
  - 2 - Fails
  - 3 - Tries again
  - 4 - Fails again
  - 5 - Asks someone for help
  - 6 - Tries again
  - 7 - Improves, but not there yet
  - 8 - Asks for a little more help
  - 9 - Tries again
  - 10 - SUCCEEDS!
- This could represent someone trying to successfully twirl a hoola-hoop OR it could be someone trying to get a math problem correct. A Persistence Chart helps students see that there is rarely a direct path to success, but that success can come to those who put in the effort and ask for help when needed.

Student Handouts

- This lesson has TWO Student Handouts.
- DIRECTIONS: Using the diagram on the previous page, describe the path I took while learning to ski on the bunny slope (Hah!). (My learning path follows the numbers in order.) Then, on the next page, fill out a Persistence Chart for one of your own skills.
- On the first Student Handout, students interpret the Instructional Poster and make sense of it.
- Once they completely understand how the "Persistence Chart" works, they will be able to create their own chart on the second Student Handout. Students should choose a skill that they didn't pick up immediately, so it demonstrates that persistence was used to become successful.

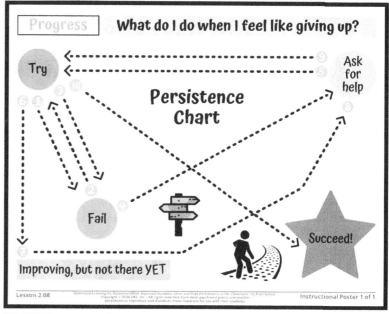

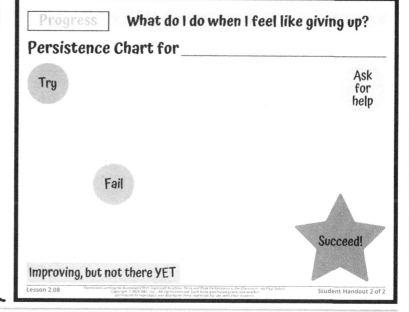

bit.ly/3T2HUiV

Discover the power of perseverance by navigating The Learning Pit with grit, help from others and strong effort

Essential Question

What do I do if I'm stuck in The Learning Pit?

Big Idea

Sometimes we struggle with new learning. It can often sneak up on us when we least expect it. For example, you might think a task is going to be easy, but then you run into problems and realize you don't know how to solve it on your own! Fortunately, there are things that can be done to help you "dig yourself out" of The Learning Pit!

Lesson Overview

In this lesson, students learn about the emotions that can come with new learning. They connect their own thoughts with a fictional character who falls into a pit and has to climb out. It shows how confidence can start strong, but can waver when you experience struggles or setbacks. But it also shows the importance of believing in yourself and using all your strategies and resources to achieve your goal. "The Learning Pit" has been used with permission from Challenging Learning and James Nottingham.

Discussion/Reflection Questions

- Why is a "pit" a good metaphor for struggle and helplessness? What other visual representations might also work to teach this concept?
- What should you do when you are feeling defeated, confused, lost, frustrated, and ready to quit? How can you overcome those emotions?
- Describe a time when you felt like you were in "The Learning Pit." Were you able to climb out or did you give up and just stay in the pit? Describe what happened.

Teacher Tips

- Even if it's mostly made up, share a personal learning story with your class that follows some of the steps in the process on the Instructional Poster. Let students know that not every learning experience follows the same pattern, but that some of the steps are similar for some learning experiences. It's just important to use your strategies and resources to ensure that you don't get stuck in the pit!
- The main goals of this lesson are to encourage persistence and perseverance, but also to ensure that students recognize when they are feeling helpless or ready to quit. That's when they need to say, "Okay. This isn't as easy as I thought it was, but I can still do it!" And they need to find a way to become successful, even if it means asking for help, or starting over...
- "The Learning Pit" has been used with permission from Challenging Learning and James Nottingham.

Student Tasks 〉 Transfer Goals

Student Tasks	Transfer Goals
Students learn a metaphor for struggle, confusion and frustration and are reminded of ways they can overcome those emotions.	Students recognize when they are "stuck in the Learning Pit" and know how to climb out of it.
Students learn that a "defeatist attitude" is not acceptable in our classroom, and that they need to find ways to overcome challenges.	Students give up on things less frequently because they understand that it's up to them to overcome challenges.

Instructional Poster(s)

- This lesson has ONE Instructional Poster.
- "The Learning Pit" is a metaphor, developed by James Nottingham, that helps students visualize what they should do when feeling like they're stuck for good. It shows several steps that lead to being at the bottom of the pit, and it also shows several steps for getting out of the pit. I've taken that metaphor and tied it into the ideas in this book.
- Walk students through the Instructional Poster and help them understand the metaphor. See if they have anything they would add to the image. Make sure that they understand each step, especially the ones for climbing out of the pit. You might want to use the exemplars (Student Handouts 3 and 4) as notes for yourself to explain the Instructional Poster. I just don't recommend showing the students the exemplar until they are able to complete the Student Handouts on their own or with a partner.
- "The Learning Pit" has been used with permission from Challenging Learning and James Nottingham.

Student Handouts

- This lesson has FOUR Student Handouts.
- DIRECTIONS: Look at "The Learning Pit" diagram to the right. You are represented by the character falling into the pit and then climbing out. This is a metaphor for how the learning process can occasionally go. On the next page, explain each step of "The Learning Pit" in your own words. Then, answer the following question:
- Students will use Student Handout #1 to fill out Student Handout #2.
- Once that's complete, students need to answer the question on Student Handout #1 that asks, "What is the purpose of 'The Learning Pit'? What is it trying to teach us?"
- The third and fourth Student Handouts are an exemplar that you can use on your own when giving directions (don't show the students the exemplar before they get a chance to write their own answers in). But feel free to use it to talk through the metaphor when introducing the Instructional Poster!

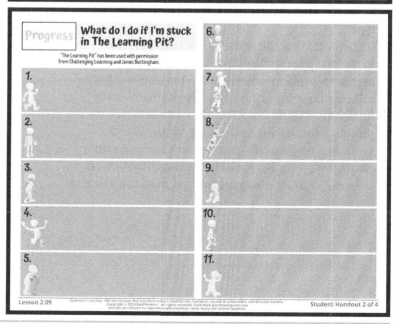

Effectively manage your time and actions when finishing tasks, ensuring care, quality, and completeness

bit.ly/3T2Jrpf

Essential Question

I'm finished. What do I do now?

Lesson Overview

In this lesson, students learn what they should and should not do when they finish a task in class. This will vary for each classroom (and sometimes each assignment), but the idea is to create a routine that students can follow while in your class. Many ideas are provided as a starting point, but teachers will tailor the lesson to their own expectations. Preventing students from becoming "Fast Finishers" so they can draw or so they can read their favorite book is important to instill the values of care, quality, and completeness. If an assignment meets all of your expectations and is completed much earlier than other students, your routine should provide opportunities for students to explore enrichment or acceleration options.

Teacher Tips

- Whenever possible, avoid allowing students to decide when they have completed an assignment on their own. Build in a simple teacher-check before letting them go on to other activities. If enrichment or acceleration options are more enticing than the main assignment, students are more likely to rush to get to them.
- Discover additional differentiation strategies that you can use for students who complete their work earlier than their peers, but also try to teach students how they can become better collaborators who help "bring their peers to the top of the mountain" with them. In our classroom, we believe that "No one should stand atop the mountain alone - we should help everyone reach the summit together!" Imagine the immense growth that can happen across the board when students know how to help each other improve and grow, and actually want to help!

Big Idea

Sometimes, you may finish an assignment before others. As long as you took your time, paid attention to directions, avoided careless mistakes, and produced something that you're proud of, it's okay to finish early. If you didn't do all those things, you are not actually done! Know what to do once you've finished your work so you don't need to distract the teacher (who may be helping those who haven't finished yet).

Discussion / Reflection Questions

- Why can it be both a good thing and a bad thing for students to finish an assignment quickly?
- What can be done to help ALL students see the value in producing quality work with care and effort?
- How can students in our classroom learn to use their class time wisely? What can they do when they finish their work so they are not just wasting time?

Student Tasks 〉 Transfer Goals

Student Tasks	Transfer Goals
Students learn to ask themselves 6+ questions when they believe they've finished a task BEFORE deciding they are done.	Students have an increased awareness of effort, focus, care, and direction-following on assigned tasks in life.
Students learn what to do and what not to do when they finish an assignment or task in class to the best of their abilities.	Students understand the value of time. They see that wasted time takes opportunities for learning away from us.

Instructional Poster(s)

- This lesson has ONE Instructional Poster.
- Fast Finishers can be a challenge, not just keeping them busy, but also encouraging them to produce work they are proud of and eliminating careless mistakes. This lesson is your opportunity to focus in on the actions you'd like your students to complete BEFORE deciding that they are finished AND the options they have to choose from when they do complete their work satisfactorily. This may vary from assignment to assignment, but having a routine in place will improve work quality and classroom independence.

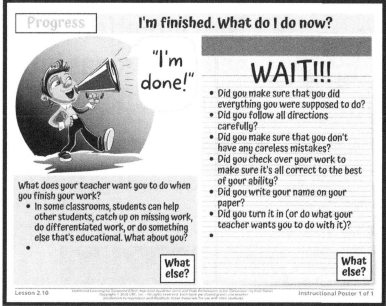

Student Handouts

- This lesson has TWO Student Handouts.
- DIRECTIONS: Explain why you shouldn't do the following things if you finish your work early. Then, complete the next page according to the directions.
- By focusing in on some of the WRONG decisions some students make when they finish a task early, you can help students acknowledge that those behaviors are not acceptable in your classroom. This should prevent these actions from happening, but if they don't - be sure to reference this assignment to remind them.
- DIRECTIONS: You believe that you have just completed a test or assignment in class. Complete the checklist below to see if you are truly finished. Then, write all of the things your teacher expects you to do when you finish on the note on the right.
- You can try to have your students internalize this checklist when completing tasks in class, you can post it as a poster in the room, or you can print out a checklist that they actually fill out. Either way, students need to become responsible for their actions once they've finished a task.

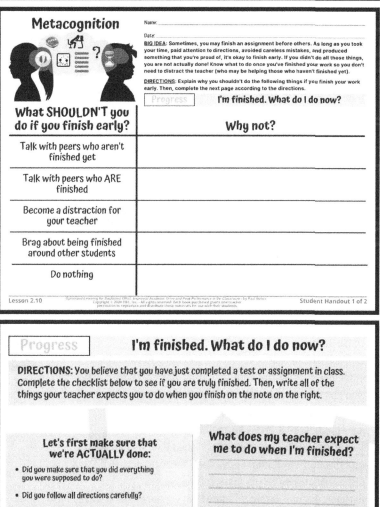

INTRODUCTION

PLANNING

METACOGNITION

SYNTHESIS

REFLECTION

SELF-ASSESSMENT

GOAL SETTING

FEEDBACK

bit.ly/3GllZe9

Turn intentions into accomplishments and good ideas into concrete victories using the power of "follow-through"

Essential Question

Why is "follow-through" so important?

Big Idea

It's not enough to DO your homework - you also need to turn it in! It's not enough to SAY you'll clean your room - you have to actually clean it! Follow-through matters, so finish what you start and do what you say you're going to do.

Lesson Overview

In this lesson, students learn about the importance of follow-through. It's not enough to say you are going to do something - it needs to get done! In school, students begin several tasks and assignments every day, but many students struggle to complete each assignment or turn it in. This lesson is designed to help students see that irresponsibility has consequences. Students consider several scenarios and decide what might happen if they don't follow-through on the task.

Discussion / Reflection Questions

- Why is "follow-through" important enough to be a topic of a lesson?
- What examples can you think of where students don't "follow-through" successfully in school?
- How would you help students who struggle with follow-through in your classroom? What advice can you give them?

Teacher Tips

- In our classroom, there are some tasks and assignments that students are NOT required to finish if we run out of time or if I decide to move along. It's important to clarify to your students if this is the case in your classroom. Otherwise, it may cause confusion or indifference if it looks like it's not being followed consistently.
- Give students a chance to "follow-through" on something immediately after this mini-lesson. Maybe start a task that they won't be able to complete, and have them complete it at home for homework. (If you are a no-homework classroom like I was, just tell them that this is an application of today's lesson). Tomorrow, check that everyone finished their homework and talk through why it might have been hard for some to do so & discuss what they can do in the future.
- Perhaps, discuss "biting off more than we can chew." It's easy for us to over-commit, so it's important that we learn our limits and learn how to say no sometimes.

Student Tasks 〉 Transfer Goals

Students learn that there are consequences when we don't "follow-through" with our promises or our plans.	Students avoid negative consequences by following through on the things they begin.
Students learn that initial consequences can result in further consequences if we're not careful.	Students see the MANY cause and effect relationships of inaction & lack of follow-through and avoid those experiences.

Instructional Poster(s)

- This lesson has ONE Instructional Poster.
- Discuss the situation described on the Instructional Poster. Point out the importance of following through on your plans. Irresponsibility affects others, as well as yourself.
- Make the connection between the situation described on the Instructional Poster and our everyday experiences. We start activities or assignments in each of our subjects or classes and we need to make sure they all get completed. How do we ensure that everything gets done? Assignment notebooks, online calendars, routines for homework, using our class time wisely, etc.

Student Handouts

- This lesson has TWO Student Handouts.
- DIRECTIONS: Read through the table below & on the next page. Fill in the blanks with appropriate answers that might be true for you or others. The last one has been left blank for you to come up with your own scenario.
- The focus on these student handouts is that our irresponsibility has consequences, but regardless of the consequences, we need to improve our responsibility and follow-through. That should start in class with guidance from the teacher, but students gradually taking on the responsibility themselves.
- Ensure that students' answers are serious and reasonable. Some answers may vary. Some answers can be extended past the first consequence to multiple consequences that really have negative affects on the student.

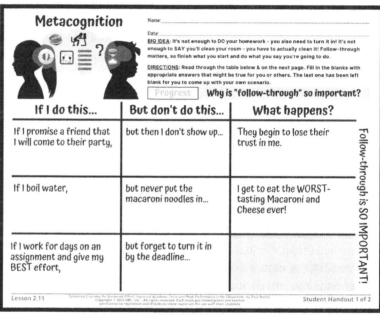

bit.ly/3uxyOk1

Unlock the secrets of staying on track by learning to tune out distractions while tuning into your goals

Essential Question

What if I keep getting distracted?

Big Idea

Some of us are able to tune out distractions and some of us struggle to do so. Some days we're better at it than other days. If you learn to use a few simple strategies, you can have more distraction-free days, and fewer distraction-filled days!

Lesson Overview

In this lesson, students consider six tips for staying focused in class. Using these tips, or ones brainstormed in class, students make simple plans for dealing with common distractions. For example, if I am often cold or hot in class, I will bring several layers of clothes to school so I can add or subtract layers, as needed. Teachers can remind students of their goals for handling common distractions whenever it appears necessary, and students can even track their progress toward meeting each goal if it is deemed important enough.

Discussion/Reflection Questions

- Why is it beneficial to have a plan for dealing with common distractions in class?
- Which distraction do you think you will be able to eliminate or reduce first, due to the plan that you wrote? Why do you think that?
- What advice would you give others who are feeling distracted in class? How could you help them eliminate or reduce distractions?

Teacher Tips

- You might consider including the Instructional Poster from Lesson 2.04 that deals with FOCUS Strategies for this lesson.
- Spending some time discussing the tips as a whole class on the Instructional Poster should lead to stronger plans being written by the students.
- Having students work together with a randomly selected partner should prevent students from getting "stuck." Encourage them to bounce ideas off of each other and help each other clearly express their plans.
- On the student handout, if some students claim they have no distractions, encourage them to think deeper.
  - When have they struggled in class?
  - Which environments are less enjoyable for them?
- If they still struggle to brainstorm distractions, encourage others to share some of theirs or offer up suggestions yourself (assuming that you've seen them be distracted in the past).
- Not everyone gets distracted all that easily, so feel free to turn it into a "How do you prevent distractions?" activity for these students.

Student Tasks 〉 Transfer Goals

Student Tasks	Transfer Goals
Students will read and discuss six tips for staying focused during distractions.	Students will apply these six tips to future experiences in order to reduce or eliminate distractions.
Students will write a plan for addressing six distractions that are common to them.	Students will put their plans into action immediately and reduce or eliminate many common distractions.

Instructional Poster(s)

- This lesson has ONE Instructional Poster.
- Discuss the "Tips for Staying Focused" on the Instructional Poster with the class. During each tip, discuss how each student may choose to apply each tip. Make sure that students have plans for implementation, otherwise this may be "tuned out."
- Tip 1 is one of the core qualities of "metacognition." Without this ability, the other tips are very difficult to implement.
- Tips 2 and 3 are covered in THIS lesson in the Student Handouts.
- Tip 4 is addressed during this lesson and was addressed during Lesson 2.04 on the poster entitled, "Focus Strategies."
- Tips 5 and 6 require reflection by each student. If possible, provide some time & support in class for this.

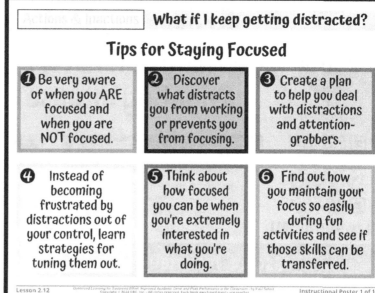

Student Handouts

- This lesson has TWO Student Handouts.
- DIRECTIONS: Read the sample answer below. Then, brainstorm six or more things that often distract you while you work and write a plan for dealing with each distraction.
- Although this activity require students to come up with their own plans for handling distractions, it should be encouraged to get ideas from peers or from the teacher. Students are much more likely to follow a plan that they put into place than a plan given to them by someone else. Students may just need ideas, materials, permission, etc. from the teacher to bring these plans into action.

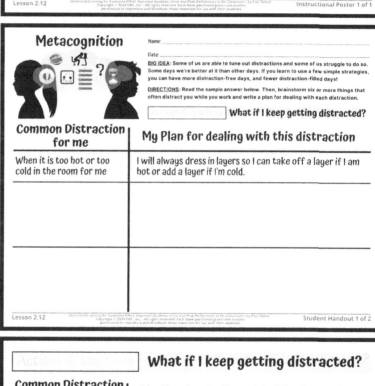

INTRODUCTION

PLANNING

METACOGNITION

SYNTHESIS

REFLECTION

SELF-ASSESSMENT

GOAL SETTING

FEEDBACK

bit.ly/46wmSMJ

Discover some powerful strategies for turning inner storms into sunshine and navigating intense emotions with grace

Essential Question

How can I manage my impulsivity?

Big Idea

It's in our nature to react to things in our environment, so acting impulsively is natural. However, in order for society to run smoothly, people need to try to react in positive, appropriate ways.

Lesson Overview

In this lesson, students read a few tips for managing impulsivity, discuss some Calm-Down Strategies to use when they are worked up, analyze their emotions during times of frustration, analyze one episode where they acted impulsively, and finally brainstorm possible solutions for handling impulsive behavior in the future. The goals of the lesson are to increase awareness of impulsive behaviors, discover how taking the time to think through an emotion or action is beneficial, and implement some strategies that reduce impulsivity (which allows more time to think).

Discussion/Reflection Questions

- Why can impulsive behavior be a bad thing?
- What do you plan to do in order to reduce impulsive behavior in the future?
- How can we help others slow down and think through their actions BEFORE they react? How can we help them reduce their impulsivity?

Teacher Tips

- There are six total pages for this lesson, so you may want to allow extra time to complete it, or pick and choose the pages that you want to use with your class.
- Younger students might need assistance throughout most of this lesson, while older students may be able to complete the Student Handouts independently.
- The Student Handout entitled, "Describing one of my impulses" would make an excellent permanent addition to your classroom for students to complete when they acted impulsively in class. This can be a "Think Sheet" or a "Recovery form," but either way, it asks a student to reflect on their impulsive behavior and try to find a way to think before acting next time.

Student Tasks 〉 Transfer Goals

Student Tasks	Transfer Goals
Students will read and discuss six tips for managing their impulsivity.	Students will apply these six tips to future experiences in order to reduce impulsive behavior.
Students analyze and reflect on ONE impulsive event from their recent past.	Students will take time to reflect on impulsive events in the future in order to reduce them.

Instructional Poster(s)

- This lesson has FOUR Instructional Posters.
- Start by making sure that your students understand what "Impulsivity" means. (Acting before thinking.)
- Read through the "Tips for Managing Impulsivity" Instructional Poster.
- There are three additional posters available for this lesson. If you choose to use them, it's recommended that you take time to present them to the class, so they are used by the students successfully.
  - "Calm-Down Strategies"
  - "Let's figure out WHY you felt this way"
  - "Tips for Managing Impulsivity Flow Chart"

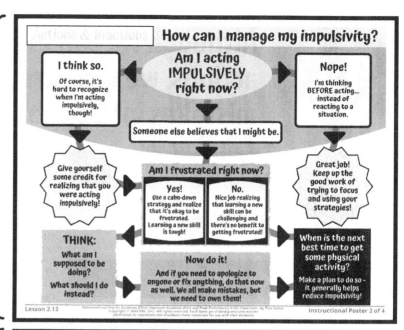

Student Handouts

- This lesson has TWO Student Handouts.
- DIRECTIONS: Complete the second page first. Then, come back to complete the first page.
- "Describing One of My Impulses:" This form can act as a "Behavior Recovery" Sheet after a student has acted out impulsively and caused a distraction in the classroom. Or it can be used simply as a reflection sheet for students to review their thoughts, feelings, and actions after acting impulsively in a more minor context. For the purposes of this lesson, students need to choose a recent event where they may have acted impulsively, even if it was very minor.
- "What makes you act impulsively?" Some students will be able to complete this sheet independently, whereas others might need support. Depending on the age of your students, you may wish to have them complete this with partners, as a whole class, with a parent or other adult, or independently.

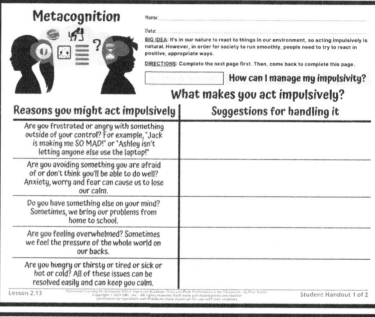

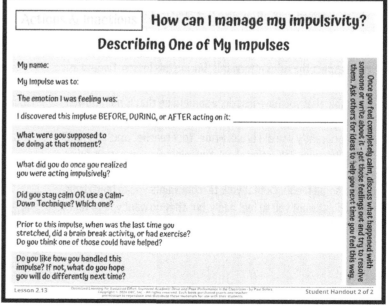

bit.ly/3sUstPj

Although we can't hit rewind on our actions, we can turn behavioral mistakes into opportunities for growth

Essential Question

What if I don't meet behavior expectations?

Big Idea

Most people have a distorted view of what it means to "get into trouble." The reality is that behaving appropriately is a SKILL just like most of the other things you're learning about in this program. Sometimes, we just need to add more marbles to our "Behave appropriately" cup in order to avoid "getting into trouble."

Lesson Overview

In this lesson, students learn how to complete a "Behavior Reflection" sheet. This sheet is a type of "Think Sheet" where the student is asked to reflect on a poor choice or behavioral mistake they made in class. It is during this lesson where the teacher tried to help their students understand that behavioral mistakes are just like academic mistakes: they earn feedback and sometimes consequences (not necessarily punishment). Students learn to accept the fact that they are likely to make behavioral mistakes in class, and that they will need to reflect on each mistake using a "Behavior Reflection," and then try to avoid making the same mistake again in the future. This helps to create a classroom community that sees mistakes as opportunities to grow and improve, and that no one is perfect.

Discussion/Reflection Questions

- Which teacher would you prefer & why:
  a. a teacher that controls students by giving serious consequences for misbehavior, OR
  b. a teacher that wants to help their students learn how to control their own behavior by providing feedback and requiring reflection?

- Which teacher do you think will help you be more in control of your behavior in the long run? Why?
  a. a teacher that controls students by giving serious consequences for misbehavior, OR
  b. a teacher that wants to help their students learn how to control their own behavior by providing feedback and requiring reflection?

- How does marble theory work with behavior? Describe the cups that might represent behavior skills and describe how marbles can be added to each cup over time if you receive helpful feedback and practice behaving properly.

Teacher Tips

- I always taught this lesson during the first week of class. I let my students know that I expected to have to use the Behavior Reflection sheets more often during the first couple months of class, and much less often after that. And that was because students will still be learning the rules and expectations of our classroom during the first couple months, but then understand and respect the rules afterwards. During this lesson, I would ask my students:
- "Imagine that you have just done something that is not allowed in our classroom. You probably didn't mean to break any rules, but apparently you did break a rule. Your teacher asks you to fill out a Behavior Reflection sheet. You might feel embarrassed or upset, but what I'd like you to feel is that you have just been given some feedback that your teacher wants you to learn from. They don't want you to feel badly, but they do want you to take it seriously and avoid making the same mistake again."

Student Tasks 〉 Transfer Goals

Student Tasks	Transfer Goals
Students complete a "Behavior Reflection" for a pretend misbehavior.	Students can complete "Behavior Reflection" sheets independently when needed.
Students answer the questions on the "Behavior Reflection" sheet to the best of their ability.	Students internalize the reflection questions and learn to avoid making the same mistakes again and again.

INTRODUCTION

PLANNING

METACOGNITION

SYNTHESIS

REFLECTION

SELF-ASSESSMENT

GOAL SETTING

FEEDBACK

Instructional Poster(s)

- This lesson has ONE Instructional Poster.
- This Instructional Poster is a Step-by-Step explanation of how to complete the Behavior Reflection sheet. You only need to complete this lesson if you plan on using the Behavior Reflection sheet in your classroom when students need to complete a "Think Sheet." In my classroom, students would complete one of these whenever they did something wrong three times in one day, or if they did something that didn't deserve a warning (excessive bad behavior). The use of this sheet was rare, but being consistent with it was essential.

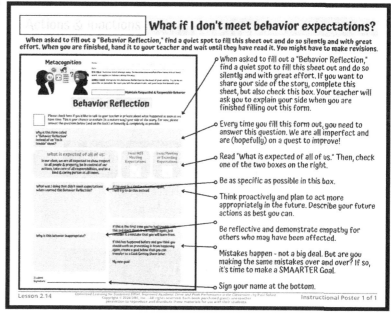

Student Handouts

- This lesson has TWO Student Handouts.
- DIRECTIONS: Complete this Behavior Reflection to the best of your ability. Try to be as specific as possible. Be sure you tell the whole truth, not just facts that benefit you.
- You, as the teacher, should provide your students with a pretend reason for needing to fill out this Behavior Reflection. It should be something relatively minor, but often a problem in your classroom (e.g. someone who talks when they shouldn't, gets into arguments with peers, mis-uses technology, etc.).
- Students complete the form as if they have just been given feedback from the teacher that their behavior was not wanted in the classroom. They are asked to accept the feedback and reflect on each question that is asked of them. This has historically been an emotional task and very upsetting to both the student and the teacher. However, in this classroom, it is just another form of feedback that we need to learn from. Encourage your students to see it as a learning experience, not a punishment.

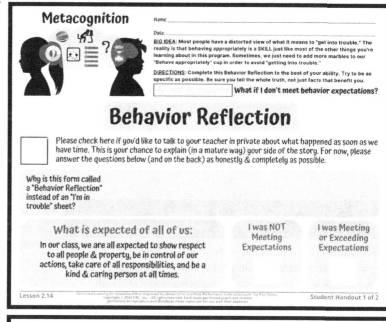

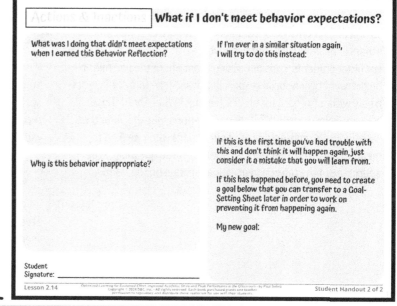

bit.ly/47OyETG

Discover how our words & actions impact others so we can navigate the world with grace & avoid unintentional hurt

Essential Question

How can I become more Socially Aware?

Big Idea

Avoid inappropriate behaviors in public or around others (e.g. volume control, body movements, talking about others, facial expressions (e.g. gasping, staring, gaping), etc.).

Lesson Overview

In this lesson, students students learn about social awareness and the importance of considering others' feelings when reacting to situations that happen in life. They learn to try to control their volume, body movements, facial expressions, and other reactions that are common amongst youngsters, but not as common amongst adults. Students try to empathize with those who may be affected when someone responds in a hurtful way (even unintentionally), and make efforts to avoid hurting others by their words or actions.

Discussion/Reflection Questions

- Why should we worry about our behavior in society? Shouldn't everyone just be allowed to be themselves at all times?
- What subtle things can you do when you are with others who are behaving without social awareness?
- How did you learn how to behave in society when you were younger? Who taught you what you know and how did they teach you these things?
- Does our intention matter? Should we care about the consequences of our actions when we didn't mean to hurt the other person?
- What about folks who say, "I was just kidding!" but no one thought it was a joke? What about folks who say, "You're just over-sensitive!" even though they were the normal amount of sensitive?

Teacher Tips

- Although this lesson sounds better for students in the lower grades, it's important to address the concept with older students as well. Perhaps taking it into the realm of "Playful Teasing vs. Hurtful Teasing" or for even older students "Gossip and Spreading Misinformation about others." All students benefit from a reminder that our actions and words can have a strong impact on others. Our goal is to be sure that we impact others in positive ways, not negative.
- For older students, consider asking them where the line might be drawn between social responsibility and free will - Can we act freely without regard for others' feelings? What about those who are "over-sensitive"? Does our intention matter? Should we care about the consequences of our actions when we didn't mean to hurt the other person? Some of these questions are addressed in the reflection questions section on the right.

Student Tasks ⟩ Transfer Goals

Student Tasks	Transfer Goals
Students learn about Social Awareness through a discussion with the teacher.	Students apply a stronger understanding of the importance of behaviors in public.
Students consider various scenarios where someone wasn't very socially aware.	Students empathize with others and avoid making choices that may impact them in negative ways.

INTRODUCTION

PLANNING

METACOGNITION

SYNTHESIS

REFLECTION

SELF-ASSESSMENT

GOAL SETTING

FEEDBACK

Instructional Poster(s)

- This lesson has ONE Instructional Poster.
- This lesson's Instructional Poster focuses on "Social Awareness" and gives students the background knowledge they will need in order to complete this lesson successfully.
- Walk students through each question and check for understanding.
- Students should understand that this lesson is not an attempt to change them or to force them to comply with social customs and rules, but rather to be aware of actions, behaviors, and words that may cause conflict.

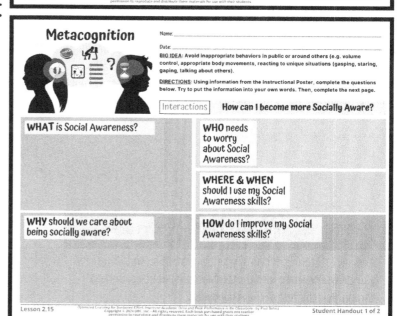

Interactions — **How can I become more Socially Aware?**

WHAT is Social Awareness?

Social Awareness is the ability to:
- understand situations that involve others,
- feel empathy for others,
- know what to do and how to react to others, and
- know how to behave around others.

WHO needs to worry about Social Awareness?

Everyone! When people don't develop their social awareness skills, they struggle to get along with each other!

WHERE & WHEN should I use my Social Awareness skills?

Everywhere & all the time, because even if our family members and closest friends understand us, occasionally neglecting social awareness skills can reinforce behaviors we don't want to repeat.

WHY should we care about being socially aware?

Social awareness:
- allows people to get along with each other,
- helps build relationships,
- prevents misunderstandings & false judgments, and
- maintains happiness in society.

HOW do I improve my Social Awareness skills?

I can help you with that!

Lesson 1.15 — Instructional Poster 1 of 1

Student Handouts

- This lesson has TWO Student Handouts.
- DIRECTIONS: Using information from the Instructional Poster, complete the questions below. Try to put the information into your own words. Then, complete the next page.
- The first Student Handout asks students to put each answer from the Instructional Poster into their own words. This can be done WHILE you present the Instructional Poster to the class or afterwards - your call.
- The second Student Handout has three "long-answer" questions. The first question focuses on awareness of differences, appropriate reactions, and age-appropriate responses. The second question focuses on how our behaviors affect others' feelings and that we have a responsibility to consider others' feelings as we grow up. The final question asks students to brainstorm any personal situations that they've experienced where someone struggled with social awareness. You may want to remind them not to use names if these end up being shared with others.

Metacognition

Name: _____

Date: _____

BIG IDEA: Avoid inappropriate behaviors in public or around others (e.g. volume control, appropriate body movements, reacting to unique situations (gasping, staring, gaping, talking about others).

DIRECTIONS: Using information from the Instructional Poster, complete the questions below. Try to put the information into your own words. Then, complete the next page.

Interactions — **How can I become more Socially Aware?**

WHAT is Social Awareness?

WHO needs to worry about Social Awareness?

WHERE & WHEN should I use my Social Awareness skills?

WHY should we care about being socially aware?

HOW do I improve my Social Awareness skills?

Lesson 2.15 — Student Handout 1 of 2

Interactions — **How can I become more Socially Aware?**

My mom had a stroke a few years ago and has to get around using a walker or a wheelchair. Sometimes, when we're out in public, young children point and stare at my mom or ask their parents loudly, "Why is that lady in a wheelchair?" We know they aren't TRYING to be mean or rude, but is it appropriate for them to do that? Can children be taught to react in some other way? What can we teach them?

Why should people learn not to point and stare at others who might look or act differently than we do? What about asking questions loudly - in the moment?

What other situations have you experienced where someone was behaving in a way that is not acceptable in public or around others? If you were a parent or loved one, what might you teach them to do instead?

Lesson 2.15 — Student Handout 2 of 2

bit.ly/3QYPb0E

Respectfully handle disagreements with Conflict Management Strategies that turn differences into shared victories

Essential Question

How can I improve the way I work with others?

Big Idea

Work and interact with others effectively (e.g. handle conflict successfully, accept opposing viewpoints, de-escalate tense situations, choose your words carefully, etc.).

Lesson Overview

In this lesson, students reflect on their own abilities when it comes to collaborating with their peers. They try to take responsibility for their actions and words, and try to improve moving forward. Students learn several strategies that might be helpful for handling conflict successfully and de-escalating tense situations. Finally, students decide how they would handle various scenarios that could come up while working with others in class.

Discussion / Reflection Questions

- Why is it so easy to notice when someone else is to blame for causing conflict, but so hard to admit when we are to blame?
- What is one thing you would like to improve when it comes to working with your peers? Think deeply! Consider making this a goal of yours for the immediate future.
- Are the rules different for different people? For example, can you be sarcastic to a close friend, but not to someone you don't know that well? Describe how the rules of behavior can sometimes differ and why that is.

Teacher Tips

- Add any strategies or tips of your own to this lesson. Whatever you choose to share with the students should be reinforced throughout the rest of the school year.
- Consider walking your students through a scenario that you make up before they attempt to work on the Student Handouts. Scaffold their learning so you end up with answers that are detailed, empathetic, and result in stronger interpersonal relationships between students.

Student Tasks 〉 Transfer Goals

| Students reflect on ways that they might be part of the problem when it comes to conflict while working with peers. | Students know that they may be responsible for causing certain problems with others and that awareness helps them address it. |
| Students consider various scenarios where disagreement could happen and share what they would say or do to prevent conflict. | Students apply their newly discovered de-escalation strategies as needed when working with others. |

Instructional Poster(s)

- This lesson has ONE Instructional Poster.
- This lesson builds on the last lesson (Lesson 2.15) with regard to "Social Awareness." However, we might choose to call this lesson "Collaborative Awareness" as we are trying to improve our awareness of the way we are when working with our peers.
- Go through the four main points on the Instructional Poster with the class. Adjust each message to fit the age level of your students. Try to tailor it to your students' needs without calling anyone out for past behavior.

Student Handouts

- This lesson has TWO Student Handouts.
- DIRECTIONS: For each situation below and on the next page, decide what you would say or do in that scenario and explain why you would say or do that. Remember to "tell me more!"
- Both Student Handouts ask students to consider various scenarios. Students are asked what they would say or do in those scenarios AND give a reason why. Encourage deep thinking and creative solutions, but ask students not to just write the first thing that comes into their heads - they should try to write the best answer they can think of for each situation.
- Remind students that the ultimate goal of each situation is to build strong relationships with everyone in class WHILE following the rules of the school, classroom, and assignment.

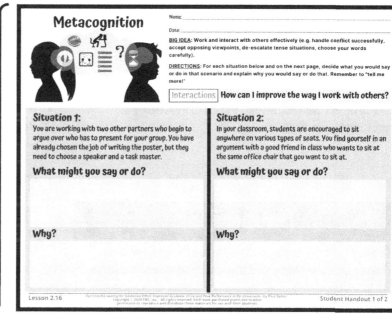

INTRODUCTION
PLANNING
METACOGNITION
SYNTHESIS
REFLECTION
SELF-ASSESSMENT
GOAL SETTING
FEEDBACK

Unmask the secrets of empathy, building bridges of understanding and treating others with the kindness they deserve

bit.ly/3N4yb8i

Essential Question

How can I become more empathetic?

Lesson Overview

In this lesson, students try to think about others' feelings in different situations. They learn to ask themselves questions like:

- "How might they be feeling right now?"
- "How would I feel in the same situation?"
- "What would I want others to do for me if I were in this situation?"

Through empathy, students are more likely to avoid being the source of others' pain and are more likely to treat each other with respect and kindness.

Teacher Tips

- Obviously, empathy cannot be mastered through one short lesson, so it's recommended that you try to expand this lesson to include:
  - Class Discussions,
  - Additional Situations,
  - Real-Life Connections, and
  - Personal Stories.
- Students have most likely been taught this subject before in the past, but we all know that that doesn't guarantee the skill will be transferred to real life situations without repeated instruction. Take the time to point this out to the students if necessary. Let them know you realize that this subject gets mentioned a lot, but that it wouldn't need to be mentioned as often if everyone found ways to be more empathetic in life, and think about others' feelings more often.

Big Idea

Empathy is the remarkable ability to understand and share the emotions of others. By embracing empathy, we are able to identify times when our peers may not be comfortable, might not understand what's going on, or might be having a bad day. Empathy allows us to "step into others' shoes" and imagine what it feels like to be them in that moment. Once we understand how others feel, we can better support them and interact with them.

Discussion/Reflection Questions

- Why is important that we continue to learn about empathy year after year? Why can't we skip this lesson?
- What is one thing that you wish others were more empathetic about in your circle of friends or family? What do you wish they were more accepting of, or what do you wish they knew about their actions or words?
- How is it possible to feel what others are feeling when we have never felt the exact same way as the other person? How can we encourage others to "walk in others' shoes" even if their experiences are different?

Student Tasks ⟩ Transfer Goals

Student Tasks	Transfer Goals
Students learn about ways they can be more empathetic.	Students show empathy in new situations where they haven't before done so.
Students ask themselves different questions that seek to improve their empathy in various situations.	Students ask those same questions when they find themselves in similar situations in their life, leading to increased empathy

INTRODUCTION
PLANNING
METACOGNITION
SYNTHESIS
REFLECTION
SELF-ASSESSMENT
GOAL SETTING
FEEDBACK

Instructional Poster(s)

- This lesson has ONE Instructional Poster.
- Empathy means "the ability to understand and share the feelings of another." Our goal for our students should be helping them learn to understand how others are feeling in all situations.
  - If we can teach each of our students to think internally, "How does it make this person feel when I..." then we can avoid being the cause of negative feelings for others.
  - If we are merely an observer (not the cause of the negative feelings), then we can learn to think to ourselves, "How would I feel if I were in this situation?" and "What do I wish someone would do or say to help me?"
- Share the notes above with your students and read through the Instructional Poster together being sure to explain your interpretation of each section.

Student Handouts

- This lesson has TWO Student Handouts.
- DIRECTIONS: Read through Situation 1 below. Then, complete the same questions for Situation 2 on the next page.
- If you have time, read through "Situation 1" with the class. Otherwise, make sure your students do so independently (or collaboratively) before completing "Situation 2."
- If your students have historically answered any questions facetiously, be sure to tell them to answer "Situation 2" with the idea that "your friend" likes candy bars and wanted that candy bar that Ben ate. If you don't you might have some answering that they don't like candy bars anyway, etc.

Interactions | **How can I become more empathetic?**

Understand & accept others' beliefs, behaviors, feelings, intentions, thoughts, and what they say.

Not everyone was raised the same way you were. Maybe they never learned the "right way" to behave. Have patience with them.	Not everyone has the same control over their emotions and behaviors that you have. Don't make life harder on them by arguing or staring or correcting them. Just accept them and be kind.	If you know the person and can politely correct them, great! If not, don't. Just accept them for who they are today. You never know where they are in the learning process.

You don't have to AGREE with everyone, but you DO have to allow everyone to have their own opinion.

Whenever possible, find common ground. What is one thing you both agree on? Focus on that.	"I respect your opinion, but I politely disagree" is what my students say when we are debating, so we also use it in our daily interactions!	If there continues to be disagreement and it doesn't look like the other side is accepting YOUR opinion, just "Agree to Disagree" (POLITELY).

Lesson 2.17 · Optimized Learning for Sustained Effort, Improved Academic Drive and Peak Performance in the Classroom - by Paul Solarz · Copyright © 2024 DBC, Inc. - All rights reserved. Each book purchased grants one teacher permission to reproduce and distribute these materials for use with their students · Instructional Poster 1 of 1

Metacognition

Name: _____
Date: _____

BIG IDEA: Empathy is the remarkable ability to understand and share the emotions of others. By embracing empathy, we are able to identify times when our peers may not be comfortable, might not understand what's going on, or might be having a bad day. Empathy allows us to "step into others' shoes" and imagine what it feels like to be them in that moment. Once we understand how others feel, we can better support them and interact with them.

DIRECTIONS: Read through Situation 1 below. Then, complete the same questions for Situation 2 on the next page.

Situation 1: [Interactions] How can I become more empathetic?

You and your friend decided to hang out at their house after school. When you got there, your friend's mom was crying. She said she had to put down their family dog, because it was really sick.

How might your friend be feeling?
I imagine my friend is shocked & feeling REALLY sad!

Have you ever felt that way? When?
Yes, I have lost pets and family members over the years and some were extremely shocking, but all were sad.

How should you react? (How do you wish others would've reacted in your situation?)
I need to try to "read" my friend's body language and facial expressions to determine if I should keep my distance or try to console them. Sometimes, we need a hug and sometimes we need some space. When you give them the wrong support, they might not handle it well.

Lesson 2.17 · Optimized Learning for Sustained Effort, Improved Academic Drive and Peak Performance in the Classroom - by Paul Solarz · Copyright © 2024 DBC, Inc. - All rights reserved. Each book purchased grants one teacher permission to reproduce and distribute these materials for use with their students · Student Handout 1 of 2

Interactions | **How can I become more empathetic?**

Situation 2:
Your teacher hid 10 candy bars around the classroom and said anyone who can find them can have them. Everyone searched and after nine were found, most people had given up. Your friend spotted the last candy bar and whispered to you, "There it is!" Ben overheard us, grabbed it & ate it in a blink of an eye, not sharing any with your friend.

How might your friend be feeling?

Have you ever felt that way? When?

How should you react? (How do you wish others would've reacted in your situation?)

Lesson 2.17 · Optimized Learning for Sustained Effort, Improved Academic Drive and Peak Performance in the Classroom - by Paul Solarz · Copyright © 2024 DBC, Inc. - All rights reserved. Each book purchased grants one teacher permission to reproduce and distribute these materials for use with their students · Student Handout 2 of 2

bit.ly/3SX3TI3

Explore the power of verbal & non-verbal cues to build stronger relationships and avoid unspoken misunderstandings

2.18

Essential Question

How should I respond to verbal and non-verbal cues?

Big Idea

Understand & respond appropriately to verbal and non-verbal cues (e.g. facial expressions, body language, personal space, gestures, volume, pitch, tone, talking speed, sarcasm, eye contact, posture, body movements).

Lesson Overview

In this lesson, students learn that it's not always WHAT we say that's important, but HOW we say it. Similarly, our words don't always mean what we think they mean! In this lesson, students try to interpret verbal and non-verbal cues to get to the truth of a conversation. Students then try to determine how they should respond. Sometimes, we need to give others some space. Sometimes, we need to dig deeper to find out what's really wrong with someone. Improving our skills at interpreting verbal and non-verbal cues will help in understanding how we've made others feel and can also teach us to be more aware of how we look when feeling certain emotions.

Discussion / Reflection Questions

- Why do some people SAY one thing but MEAN another? Have you ever done that? When?
- What are some additional cues that we can use to interpret others' true emotions or intentions that weren't mentioned in the Instructional Poster? Think about conversations or situations you have been in for ideas.
- How will you work at improving your interpretation of verbal and non-verbal cues over the next few weeks? How can you improve your responses to those cues? What specifically can you do to get better?

Teacher Tips

- This can be a very challenging lesson, despite its relatively simple concept. Be sure you let students know that verbal and non-verbal cues are clues to helping us understand what others may be thinking, but it's not foolproof. Sometimes, our mind can be elsewhere in a conversation and it looks like they're mad at us, when they really aren't. Sometimes, people are joking or being sarcastic, but we think they are begin mean. It takes effort and experience to learn to interpret verbal and non-verbal cues correctly, and even then, mistakes are bound to happen.
- Be sure to point out any verbal and non-verbal cues that you see in the classroom over the next few days, and ask the students to do the same (if they can handle doing so with respect). Make sure your students are okay with this. I just ask my students before I make any public announcements and they usually agree to it.

Student Tasks 〉 Transfer Goals

Student Tasks	Transfer Goals
Students learn about several verbal and non-verbal cues people use when in conversations.	Students internalize the cues, become more aware of their use of them, and work to match the cues to the actual emotion.
Students reflect on how they might respond to different verbal and non-verbal cues.	Students improve their communication skills with others by correctly interpreting verbal and non-verbal cues.

INTRODUCTION

PLANNING

METACOGNITION

SYNTHESIS

REFLECTION

SELF-ASSESSMENT

GOAL SETTING

FEEDBACK

Instructional Poster(s)

- This lesson has ONE Instructional Poster.
- Sometimes, it's not WHAT you say, but HOW you say it!
- Sometimes, people say they're not mad, but are obviously fuming at you!
- Sometimes, we learn more about how a person feels by watching their non-verbal cues and listening carefully to their verbal cues than by just trusting the words they say.
- Go through the following verbal and non-verbal cues on the Instructional Poster with the class. Ask students to demonstrate some, or show some yourself. Act out times when someone may SAY something, but MEAN something different. Let students know that the words people use are not always as trustworthy as the way they say them.

Student Handouts

- This lesson has TWO Student Handouts.
- DIRECTIONS: Using the verbal and non-verbal cues below, interpret what is happening and describe how you would respond. On the next page, you are given the "Interpretation" and need to describe some verbal and non-verbal cues that might have led to that interpretation, and describe how you should respond.
- Reading and understanding verbal and non-verbal cues is not an exact science. There are definitely times when we over-read a situation or interpret cues incorrectly. Always give the other person an opportunity to explain themselves, rather than trust your instincts, but understand that sometimes, emotions cause us to leave out parts of our truth.
- Students need to interpret three situations on the first page, and explain one acceptable way to respond. On the second page, things are switched up a bit.

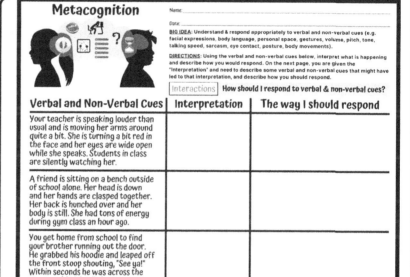

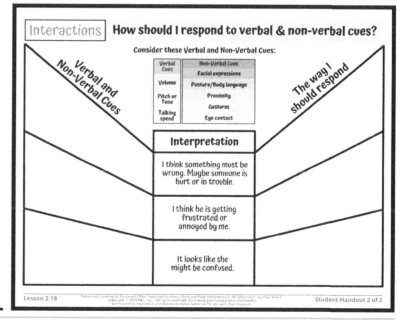

121

Unlock the secrets of a strong work ethic, leaving laziness in the dust and paving your way to personal victory

bit.ly/3N2tfk0

bit.ly/3N2tfk0

Essential Question

How can I develop a strong work ethic?

Big Idea

Your work ethic can have a HUGE impact on the path your life takes. People who develop a strong work ethic, where hard work comes easily, are able to CREATE their own path. People who avoid hard work and rarely put in much effort often have to take the path that is offered to them. Be a trailblazer and develop a strong work ethic!

Lesson Overview

In this lesson, students learn about several ways we can show strong effort at school. As a class, students brainstorm additional examples of showing effort (possibly specific to your classroom), and also describe the opposite of each behavior so they know what NOT to do. Later, students evaluate themselves on each behavior and determine where they are weakest and strongest. If time allows, students can collect evidence to support their claims.

Discussion/Reflection Questions

- What are at least three additional "Signs you are giving your best effort" that weren't listed on the instructional poster? (It's okay if they came up in a class discussion or activity.)
- What are some examples of occupations (jobs) where you wouldn't want to have someone with a poor work ethic or low effort working for you? Why?
- On today's student handout, you identified three areas of effort that you wanted to improve. How will you ensure that you improve in those three areas? What specifically will you do to become stronger in those areas?

Teacher Tips

- Do your best to tailor this lesson to specific ways students can show strong effort in YOUR classroom, but be careful not to just make it about academic effort. Include behavior, social-emotional interactions, attention, etc.
- Remind students that everyone's effort might look different based on their own personal strengths and weaknesses
- For the "Three areas of effort that I would like to improve" section, consider having students write S.M.A.A.R.T.E.R. Goals to address these specific areas of effort. Since effort is tied into everything we do, these goals might be more important than many others they might consider creating.
- If your students ever struggle to evaluate themselves honestly and correctly, ask them to provide evidence to support their claims. Searching for actual evidence requires students to think critically about a behavior and even if they can't come up with specific examples, they are more likely to be able to transfer the skill after deep reflection.

Student Tasks 〉 Transfer Goals

Student Tasks	Transfer Goals
Students discuss various ways they can show strong effort and work ethic.	Students demonstrate strong effort and work ethic in new ways not thought of before.
Students evaluate ways they are strong and weak at showing good effort and work ethic.	Students improve their effort in at least three specific areas, leading to an improved overall work ethic.

Instructional Poster(s)

- This lesson has ONE Instructional Poster.
- Read through the boxes on the Instructional Poster with your class. Let students know that you need to see examples of these behaviors in order to believe that their effort is high, and on the flip side, you DON'T want to see the opposite behaviors (which you might want to brainstorm together, so it's clear what to avoid).
- I consistently include "fake it 'til you make it" because some students honestly have to start at that point - not everyone cares about everything that we care about. But if they "pretend" that they are hard workers, they may actually become hard workers!
- Brainstorm MORE examples together.

Student Handouts

- This lesson has TWO Student Handouts.
- DIRECTIONS: Complete the next page first. Then, come back to complete this page.
- DIRECTIONS: Choose three of these "Signs that you are giving YOUR BEST effort" that you feel you are good at. (Write a 1, 2, and 3 on the lines). Then, choose three that you think you need to improve at, and write a 10, 11, 12 on those lines. Feel free to fill in the middle numbers (optional).
- Remind students that they should be able to think of examples of each area of effort that they believe they are strong at. In addition, they should not be able to think of many examples where they behaved in the opposite way.
- One possible modification on the first side would be to have students write evidence into both columns (the second column would likely need to be done over time).

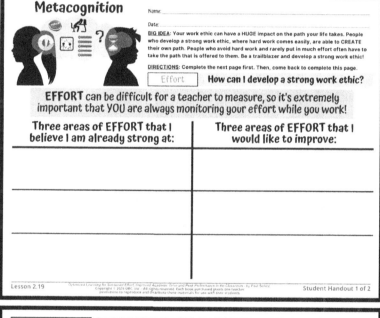

INTRODUCTION

PLANNING

METACOGNITION

SYNTHESIS

REFLECTION

SELF-ASSESSMENT

GOAL SETTING

FEEDBACK

bit.ly/49YEhRs

Learn how to "Fake it 'til you make it" so you can turn drudgery into triumph and unlock pride in even the dullest tasks

Essential Question

What do I do when my work isn't really motivating?

Big Idea

Not everything we do is fun and motivational. Sometimes, we have to just accept that we HAVE to do something that we don't want to do. It's part of life. One way to motivate yourself to work on something you don't enjoy is to "fake it 'til you make it!"

Lesson Overview

In this lesson, students consider the many tasks, activities, and assignments they are asked to complete at home or in school that are boring, tedious, or just plain work! You as the teacher acknowledge that there are many things we do that just isn't fun or rewarding, but that still need to be done AND need to be done well. This lesson helps students identify these activities and provides them a strategy (fake it 'til you make it) for accomplishing these tasks successfully and proudly.

Discussion/Reflection Questions

- In your mind, switch places with the person asking you to complete a mundane or time-consuming task that you don't enjoy. Why are they asking you to do that task? Why does it need to be done well? How would you feel if they responded to their request like you did or gave as little effort as you did?
- On your Student Handout, look at the four tasks where you believe that you should have put forth better effort. What would you do differently to improve each assignment or activity if you could do it over again? If your answer is, "I'll fake it 'til I make it," then describe HOW you will do that.

Teacher Tips

- If you have a moment, I would recommend brainstorming a few mundane tasks that your students have had to do in the past couple weeks where their effort is important because if it's not done well or correctly, it could lead to problems or mistakes. Some examples include routine tasks like turning in assignments, checking in for attendance, etc. Some school work might include simple worksheets or note-taking.
- Ask students to brainstorm things that they are asked to do at home to help out around the house or assist their family members. Help them process WHY most tasks are important, and WHY a parent can't do ALL of them themselves! If you're asked to do some chores or drive your sister to her friend's house, this is something that you should do WITHOUT complaint because SOMEONE has to do it and everyone needs to pitch in! These things need to be done well, so if a student doesn't know how to do it well, they need to ask or try their hardest, rather than just "phone it in."

Student Tasks 〉 Transfer Goals

Student Tasks	Transfer Goals
Students reflect on recent events where their effort on a mundane or time-consuming task was lackluster.	Students put forth better effort on mundane or time-consuming tasks, and learn to find pride in their hard
Students consider various mundane or time-consuming scenarios, and make a plan for how to approach each with a strong effort and pride their in work.	Students recognize when they are about to complete a mundane or time-consuming task, and begin to "fake it 'til they make it."

INTRODUCTION

PLANNING

METACOGNITION

SYNTHESIS

REFLECTION

SELF-ASSESSMENT

GOAL SETTING

FEEDBACK

Instructional Poster(s)

- This lesson has ONE Instructional Poster.
- Read through the four statements on the Instructional Poster with the class. Feel free to add or replace some with your own examples. The key here is to teach students to work hard, even when there is no prize and it's not motivational or fun.
- If you don't love the "Fake it 'til you make it" concept, replace this lesson with your own version that helps motivate students through boring or tedious assignments, which they are sure to get eventually, even with the most thoughtful teachers!
- Try to help students understand that "phoning it in" on these assignments will accomplish the "DONE" part, but not the "High Quality" part. Not everything we do in life (or at work) is fun and motivating, so we have to learn how to put strong effort in, even when it's hard to do so.

Student Handouts

- This lesson has TWO Student Handouts.
- DIRECTIONS: Read each column header on this page and the next. The directions are built into each column header. Remember to "tell me more!"
- On this Student Handout, students are recalling four assignments or activities that they put in a lot of effort into and ended up with something they were very proud of, and four that they should have done a better job with.
- The back side of the Student Handout asks students how they might be able to put forth great effort and produce quality results when put into various scenarios. Will they be able to fill in each box with great effort? Or will they phone it in? Ask them and see if they're able to include additional details with each of their answers!

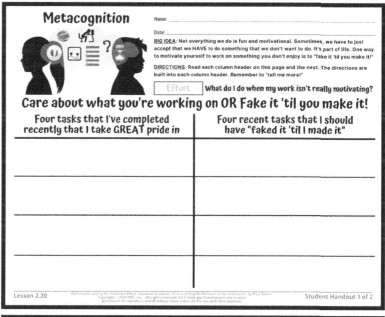

bit.ly/410mkxq

Tackle assignments with passion while leaving rewards in the dust through the power of intrinsic motivation

Essential Question

How can I develop intrinsic motivation?

Lesson Overview

In this lesson, students are given a somewhat boring or mundane task to complete in class (teachers need to determine the task ahead of time), and are asked to reflect on their feelings toward completing that task. Using information from the Instructional Poster, students try to build in intrinsic motivators to help them improve their effort without the need for rewards, grades, or prizes. Then, they analyze how some extrinsic motivators can lower intrinsic motivation and they suggest ways they could put forth strong effort without the need for those extrinsic motivators.

Teacher Tips

- Have a specific task in mind before teaching this lesson! A small packet of work or some worksheets would probably work just fine. Use your judgment based on what you teach and the grade level of your students.
- This lesson provides a great opportunity for class discussion on the topic of motivation. Students know and enjoy talking about the ways adults coerce them to do various things. They want to talk about bribes, punishments, blackmail, and idle threats! They also enjoy thinking about the things they do without being told or asked. Point out how intrinsic motivation is the key to putting forth the best effort over time. Yes - we can motivate children through extrinsic rewards or consequences, but eventually those motivators become less and less powerful over time. Doing things because you want to do them and you see their value can have a lasting effect that no prize could ever have.

Big Idea

Intrinsic motivation means that you are able to work hard at something without needing a prize or reward. You don't fear consequences or need praise, you just do it. Think about how hard you might work to solve a video game or a complete a piece of art. Usually, intrinsic motivation is what drives you to do your best on these. Extrinsic motivation means you rely on a reward or prize to do your best (winning a contest for example), or you want to avoid negative consequences (like getting grounded if you don't clean your room). But you wouldn't try hard otherwise.

Discussion/Reflection Questions

- What's the value in working hard because you know you should, rather than to avoid consequences or to try to win a prize?
- What is something that you enjoy doing that most others don't (specific chores, errands, worksheets, reports, etc.)? Why do you like it? Why don't others?
- How could you help others improve their intrinsic motivation on tasks that they don't enjoy?

Student Tasks 〉 Transfer Goals

Student Tasks	Transfer Goals
Students learn tips for increasing their intrinsic motivation toward completing boring tasks.	Students put forth strong effort in work that is normally not motivating on its own.
Students replace extrinsic motivators that may have bad, long-term affects with intrinsic motivators in several scenarios.	Students work hard for their own personal reasons instead of relying on grades or payment as motivation.

Instructional Poster(s)

- This lesson has ONE Instructional Poster.
- On the Instructional Poster, I've listed six ways students can improve their intrinsic motivation for a specific task in class. Go over each with the class and make sure they understand what each suggestion means. See if anyone can add to the list (How else can we improve our intrinsic motivation when we have to do tasks in school or in life that aren't motivating on their own?)
- Discuss how prizes can be motivating for some students (if they believe they have a chance of winning one), but that this is called extrinsic motivation - you would only be working hard in the hopes of winning a prize, not because you see value in task itself. What are some other extrinsic motivators in school and at home?

Student Handouts

- This lesson has TWO Student Handouts.
- DIRECTIONS: Your teacher has just given you a task to complete. Fill out the form below describing how you feel about having to do this task. Then, complete the task your teacher assigned you. Finally, complete the next page by thinking about how the extrinsic motivator in the first column can actually do harm over time. Then, describe how intrinsic motivation can help you find long-term success.
- Prior to getting the Student Handout, you need to assign them a task or assignment to complete. It doesn't matter what it is, but it probably shouldn't be overly motivating on its own. Students will reflect on how they feel about having to complete the task and come up with ideas for motivating themselves to try hard.
- Then, students will brainstorm potential negative consequences of extrinsic motivators and replace them with intrinsic motivators.

Effort — How can I develop intrinsic motivation?

Tips for Increasing your Intrinsic Motivation
(Caring about things without needing a prize or reward)

Mood:
How are you feeling right now? It's hard to put your best effort into something when you're crabby, sad, or frustrated. Do what you can to be HAPPY!

How can you beat your previous best?
Competition often helps increase motivation, but shouldn't come at the expense of helping others around you. Compete against YOUR previous best!

Readiness to Learn:
On a scale of 1-10, how "ready to learn" are you right now? What made you choose that number? How do we get that number up to a 10?

Pretend that others will see this!
If you believe that your work will be seen by your classmates, your parents, or other people who's opinion you care about, you are more likely to work hard.

Predicted Success:
How well do you think you will do on this task? Why? If you feel like you'll be successful, it's a lot easier to put in your best effort. But if you feel like you're going to do poorly, effort is often LOW.

Commitment:
Believe in the importance of hard work. In order to be successful in life, you will need to work hard at something. It might be something you love, but it might not. Commit to trying your best at everything!

Metacognition

Name: _____
Date: _____

BIG IDEA: Intrinsic motivation means that you are able to work hard at something without needing a prize or reward. You don't fear consequences or need praise, you just do it. Think about how hard you might work to solve a video game or a complete a piece of art. Usually, intrinsic motivation is what drives you to do your best on these. Extrinsic motivation means you rely on a reward or prize to do your best (winning a contest for example), or you want to avoid negative consequences (like getting grounded if you don't clean your room). But you wouldn't try hard otherwise.

DIRECTIONS: Your teacher has just given you a task to complete. Fill out the form below describing how you feel about having to do this task. Then, complete the task your teacher assigned you. Finally, complete the next page by thinking about how the extrinsic motivator in the first column can actually do harm over time. Then, describe how intrinsic motivation can help you find long-term success.

Task:

Effort — How can I develop intrinsic motivation?

Mood: How are you feeling right now?

Predicted Success: How well do you think you will do on this task? Why?

Readiness to Learn: On a scale of 1-10, how "excited to learn" are you right now? What made you choose that number?

How can you do even better?

How can you get that number up to a 10? What can YOU do to increase your motivation to do well?

Commitment: Write one sentence below that shows your commitment to working hard at this task, no matter what:

Effort — How can I develop intrinsic motivation?

Develop intrinsic motivation so you do things for the right reasons.

Extrinsic Motivation	Possible Negative Consequence of Extrinsic Motivator	Replace it with Intrinsic Motivation
You study hard for your math test because you don't want to fail it.	If grades motivate you to work hard, will you work hard when grades AREN'T there? Think about work around the house as an adult, being a parent, or working for a company.	Although math isn't my favorite subject AND I have no interest in getting a job that requires a lot of math, I do want to learn as much as I can, because learning ANYTHING will help me grow & improve.
If you fail your math test your parents will ground you.		
If you get straight A's on your report card, your parents will give you $100.		
If you get home after curfew, your curfew will be an hour earlier for 3 months.		
If you stay up past midnight on the weekends, your parents will make your weeknight bedtime an hour earlier.		

bit.ly/411RswD

Ditch the pressure and discover the sweet spot where balanced effort unlocks excellence without the burnout

2.22

Essential Question

Am I trying too hard or not hard enough?

Big Idea

It's very important that we always try our best. It doesn't really make any sense to give less than our best effort! However, some people think that they can try even HARDER than their best, but that's impossible! Learn that our best is our best, and we can't give any more than that. And yes, some of our work won't be perfect!

Lesson Overview

In this lesson, students visualize the Effort Continuum in order to see that low effort AND overly high effort can both lead to poor consequences. Low effort is fairly understandable, but unrealistically high effort is often overlooked. We can only give the best that we can, but sometimes we (or others in our life) have unrealistically high expectations of us that we can't yet meet. Aspiring to perfection is okay, but NOT when it leads to negative consequences like stress, inappropriate amounts of time dedicated to the work, frustration when it isn't exactly right, etc. Talk these points out with students so they see that both apathy AND perfection should be avoided, but that effort in "The Goldilock's Zone" is all we can and should deliver.

Discussion/Reflection Questions

- Today's Student Handout contains questions that can be used as an exit slip or class discussion. I wouldn't recommend including any additional questions for this lesson. But, if you'd like to ask students for a short reflection on today's lesson, I recommend that you keep it open-ended and non-specific. For example:
  - Now that you know your teacher's expectations about effort...
    - What would you do differently?
    - How might you change moving forward?
    - What surprised you during this lesson?
    - What goal might you set for yourself for the future?

Teacher Tips

- Most students don't realize that they have perfectionistic tendencies. They've either LEARNED to keep working until their final product is perfect or they have an INNATE need to achieve perfection in order to earn appreciation or pride. Schools need to break students of this self-defeating pattern of impossible expectations and disappointing outcomes. We can do that by explaining our true intentions when we ask students to put forth their best effort, stay focused on the task at hand, avoid distractions, have pride in your work, etc.
- One important note about perfection: We can all TRY for perfection to some degree, but when it forces us to have unrealistic expectations, spend more time than necessary, and feel disappointed when things don't end up perfect, we have a perfectionism problem! Shooting for "our best effort" often achieves the same results WITHOUT the stress!

Student Tasks 〉 Transfer Goals

Students analyze the "Effort Continuum" to see where their effort level should be.	Students give the appropriate amount of effort in all of their work (not apethetic, not overly perfectionistic).
Students answer several questions digging in to their understanding of perfectionism and apathy.	Students use this awareness to adjust their effort levels when they discover they are outside of the "Goldilock's Zone."

Instructional Poster(s)

- This lesson has ONE Instructional Poster.
- The Instructional Poster for this lesson tries to help students visualize the importance of trying their hardest, BUT not trying so hard that they aim for perfection. "The Goldilocks Zone" represents a person's attempt to try hard (up to a 10 out of 10 on effort). Our best effort is a 10, and aiming for anything more is impossible to reach & only leads to frustration and disappointment.
- Most of the time, teachers focus on ensuring that students avoid being apathetic & giving LOW effort, but this lesson hones in on the importance of avoiding perfectionism (impossibly HIGH effort), which is just as prevalent in many classrooms today.

Student Handouts

- This lesson has TWO Student Handouts.
- DIRECTIONS: Read the poster on the left. Then, complete each question in the boxes on this page and the next. Some sentence starters have been provided to help you.
- The sentence starters on the first Student Handout are an attempt to GUIDE students toward the main idea of this lesson: that trying harder than our best is impossible and being perfect is unsustainable.
- The questions on the second Student Handout continue to dig into each student's comprehension of the lesson's Big Idea, without sentence starters. Use this sheet to assess how well each student has grasped the concepts taught in the lesson and give individual feedback to those who don't seem to understand the core concepts. I recommend reading through these questions BEFORE teaching the lesson to ensure you address most of them together as a class.

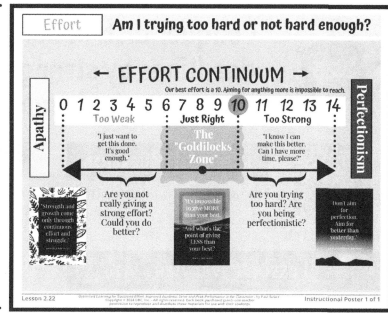

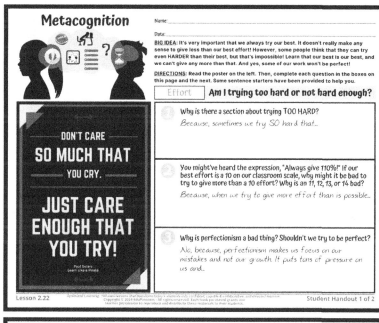

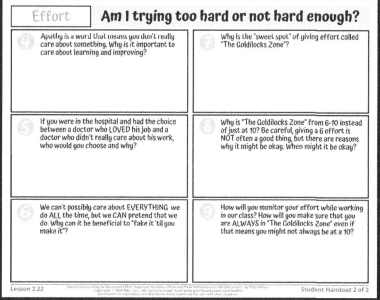

INTRODUCTION

PLANNING

METACOGNITION

SYNTHESIS

REFLECTION

SELF-ASSESSMENT

GOAL SETTING

FEEDBACK

129

2.23

Conquer distractions and meet deadlines by strengthening your awareness and understanding of time

bit.ly/47vl1ch

Essential Question

How can I improve my awareness of time?

Big Idea

Knowing what time it is at all times (and how much time is left to complete a task) is vital for meeting deadlines and expectations. Don't "let time get away from you."

Lesson Overview

In this lesson, students learn about the importance of time awareness. Through a fictional scenario, students discover that a simple one-class period assignment can have a long list of potential barriers to success. These barriers to success can be overcome, but it will take awareness, practice, patience, and understanding in order to do it successfully. (The next lesson will focus more on MANAGING time - this lesson helps improve AWARENESS of time.)

Discussion/Reflection Questions

- Why is it important to be aware of time when working toward a deadline? (I need at least three sentences for this answer, so be sure to "tell me more!")
- What sometimes happens when we're not aware of time? (I need at least three sentences for this answer, so be sure to "tell me more!")
- What should we do if we planned SO well that we ended up finishing long before the deadline? What would my teacher want me to do with this extra time?

Teacher Tips

- This would be a good time to have the students discuss past experiences where time has been a challenge to them.
  - What distractions or problems have come up recently that has led to you not finishing a task on time?
  - What did you do to overcome those distractions or problems? Or what COULD you have done to overcome them?
  - What are potential distractions or problems that may come up in the near future? How might we overcome those?
- I would show a clip of the show "Wipeout" or something similar and use it as a metaphor for students completing a task without direct teacher influence. Contestants are trying to get through an obstacle course to reach the finish line, but they are constantly bombarded by flying objects, swinging bars, and potential pitfalls. Distractions and problems that come up while we work are similar!

Student Tasks ⟩ Transfer Goals

Student Tasks	Transfer Goals
Students analyze quotes about the awareness of time, and its importance.	Student use these building blocks to improve their ability to manage time in the next lesson.
Students reflect on a fictional scenario to discover that meeting a deadline involves dealing with many barriers to success!	Students stop making excuses for missing deadlines and start finding solutions to meet those deadlines.

Instructional Poster(s)

- This lesson has ONE Instructional Poster.
- Discuss each quote with the class. How do they interpret each quote? Let them know that it's okay to get something out a quote that isn't what the author intended. (That helps students attempt to interpret each quote without fear of failure.)
- Actual definition of EFFICIENCY:
  - The act of working in a well-organized and competent way that conserves time and effort.
- Actual definition of EFFECTIVENESS:
  - The degree to which something is successful in producing a desired result; Your level of success.
- How can we extend each quote past its intended purpose?
- How can we connect each quote to our classroom or school? Home? Future?
- What additional tips about "our awareness of time" can we add to this mix? (They don't have to be quotes.)

Student Handouts

- This lesson has TWO Student Handouts.
- DIRECTIONS: The following timeline shows the steps you took to complete an assignment with an assigned partner. Answer the questions on the next page using this information to help you. Each event has been numbered in the order they happened.
- The first Student Handout shows a timeline of events that COULD take place during a task students completed in class. Having an awareness of time allows them to recover from each setback or distraction, make adjustments to their plan for finishing on time, and ultimately meet the deadline. Without time awareness, students use each blip on the timeline as an excuse for not being able to meet expectations.
- On the second Student Handout, students analyze each event from the timeline and make decisions that lead to success finishing on time and with strong effort.
- There is a third Student Handout, but it is not meant to be give to the students - It is an Answer Key for the second Student Handout.

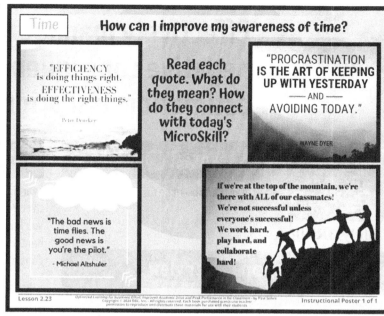

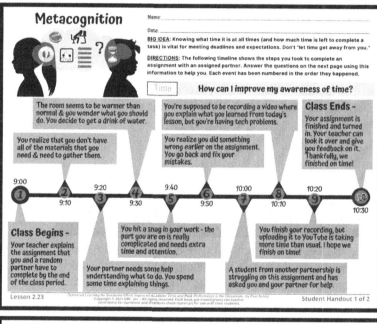

INTRODUCTION

PLANNING

METACOGNITION

SYNTHESIS

REFLECTION

SELF-ASSESSMENT

GOAL SETTING

FEEDBACK

bit.ly/3Ric00A

Effectively manage your time to avoid negative consequences by improving estimation and prioritization skills

Essential Question

How can I manage my time better?

Big Idea

Learning how to estimate how much time certain tasks should take to complete them will help ensure that you can do everything that you hope to do. When we underestimate the time things take (or neglect to estimate them at all), we often end up with a negative consequence that we'd rather not have.

Lesson Overview

In this lesson, students reflect on their actions when asked to do specific tasks within an understood timeline. For example, a parent may ask their child to clean their room, but the child does not do so immediately and often "forgets" causing frustration by the parent. In this lesson, students explore several fictional scenarios where they might naturally avoid getting to work immediately, but realize that it's important to stop what they're doing and transition to the request made by their parent or teacher (or boss, etc.).

Discussion/Reflection Questions

- Why is it important to start a task immediately when asked?
- What can you do to ensure that you respond respectfully to those who ask you to complete a task right away?
- What tips can you provide students who aren't very good at managing their time while working in class? What could you say to them that might help them meet deadlines and use their time wisely?

Teacher Tips

- If your students are old enough, have them estimate the amount of time it would likely take them to complete each of the tasks described on the Student Handouts. Compare this amount of time to the time their parent (or teacher) dedicates to their own needs, as well as their children's (or students') needs. Although adults may do similar tasks more quickly due to past experience, they have MANY more responsibilities that are rarely considered by youngsters.
- Discuss that one of the hardest things about doing a task immediately is simply transitioning from one thing to another. Transitions require us to accept that we need to stop doing whatever it was that we were doing and begin doing something else (that likely is not more enjoyable). Even if we are somewhat bored, it can be challenging to successfully transition without frustration. Rather than expect adults to give lots of warning (which CAN be done as a scaffold, if needed), students should try to learn to expect interruptions to their free time, and accept it because it's part of life for everyone.

Student Tasks 〉 Transfer Goals

Student Tasks	Transfer Goals
Students reflect on their immediacy when it comes to completing tasks they are asked to do.	Students stop procrastinating and immediately attempt to complete tasks asked of them.
Students explain correct and incorrect actions to take when asked to complete a task.	Students notice when they are avoiding work or procrastinating and immediately switch gears.

Instructional Poster(s)

- This lesson has ONE Instructional Poster.
- The Instructional Poster clarifies the importance of putting in enough time to do something well, but not so much time that the goal becomes perfection.
- On the right half of the poster, start reading from the bottom, moving upwards as you progress along the timeline. The main point here is to ensure that students understand that it's better to do everything correctly and on-time than to have to redo it or work past the deadline and deal with the consequences that follow.

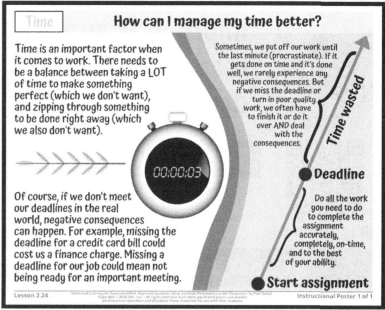

Student Handouts

- This lesson has TWO Student Handouts.
- DIRECTIONS: Read the scenario below between a mother and her daughter. Answer the questions in your mind or with a peer. Then, complete the next page.
- On the first Student Handout, we read a fictional scenario between a daughter and her mother. Putting off things that aren't fun like cleaning your room often ends up being forgotten, leading to frustrated parents. One tip is to do things immediately when you're told. That way, we show respect toward our parents and become more responsible in the long run.
- The second Student Handout shows the Cause & Effect relationship between being asked to do a task and missing its deadline. Having students come up with the possible consequences of their actions will better instill the value of time management and immediacy in accomplishing their tasks.

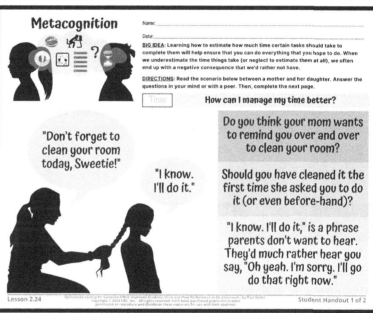

INTRODUCTION

PLANNING

METACOGNITION

SYNTHESIS

REFLECTION

SELF-ASSESSMENT

GOAL SETTING

FEEDBACK

bit.ly/3RhF605

Improve accuracy & time management by reading directions carefully and breaking down tasks into manageable steps

Essential Question

How can reading directions carefully help me?

Big Idea

Multiple step directions cause people trouble quite often! You might read all the directions, and then do everything you remember but it's so easy to forget one or two parts. That's why it's important to chunk the directions into smaller tasks and check them off as you complete them.

Lesson Overview

In this lesson, students learn a strategy for breaking down complex directions into simple steps that they can follow. Too often, students miss a direction or complete some of the steps of a direction but not all of the steps. This lesson focuses in on analyzing the directions and breaking them down into actionable steps and additional information using two color highlighters. Regardless of whether you choose to ask your students to use this method in the future, it's a valuable lesson in noticing just how many steps may be involved in some sets of directions.

Discussion/Reflection Questions

- Why should you have to learn about following directions at your age? Isn't that a skill that only young children need to learn?
- What is one additional tip you would give students who are having trouble completing every single step of a complex direction?
- How might you use or modify the strategy taught in this lesson in the future? What will you do the next time you read complex directions?

Teacher Tips

- Make sure that each student has two different color highlighters before distributing the Student Handouts.
- The Student Handouts are a bit confusing at first glance, so you might want to review the directions before expecting them to be completed individually (ironic, huh?). Even though this IS a lesson on following directions carefully, we want our students to improve their skills at this, rather than be assessed on their skills at this on the Student Handouts, so helping them get started is completely understandable!
- It would be great if you could plan to have a few assignments ready in the near future where students are expected to read and follow complex directions. As you assign these, I recommend giving immediate feedback to students on their progress at this skill. Re-teach if necessary.

Student Tasks 〉 Transfer Goals

Student Tasks	Transfer Goals
Students learn several tips about complex directions (directions with more than one step).	Students put those tips to good use as they try to complete multiple step directions.
Students are taught a strategy for breaking down complex directions into manageable chunks.	Students implement their version of this strategy in the future to ensure that each step is followed correctly.

Instructional Poster(s)

- This lesson has ONE Instructional Poster.
- This Instructional Poster can be a bit overwhelming at first, so consider covering part of it and exposing it as you go. The box on the left side of the page lets students know some important tips about reading directions: (1) contain several steps, (2) in order or not, (3) may contain info that's not needed, (4) important details, etc.
- The rest of the Instructional Poster contains an example of complex directions that require great attention in order to complete correctly.
- You can teach your students to break down directions into "actionable steps," and "additional details." Point out how the steps were followed on the example.

Student Handouts

- This lesson has TWO Student Handouts.
- DIRECTIONS: Place check marks next to the steps or details that were completed correctly and completely on the notepad on the right. Write an "X" next to the steps that have not been done correctly or completely. Then, fix or complete those steps.
- On the first Student Handout, students are asked to follow directions that have already been broken down for them (but not categorized).
- On the second Student Handout, students are asked to follow directions that are not yet broken down. Both pages use a checklist system for ensuring that everything gets done. If you see students needing to use a system like this, encourage its future use. If not, explain to them that this lesson just highlights the importance of analyzing complex directions carefully.
- An Answer Key has been provided for Student Handout 2 (in the slides).

Accuracy — How can reading directions carefully help me?

Directions are a lot like multiple step word problems in math. They often contain several steps. Sometimes they are written in order, but not always. Sometimes they have information that's not needed. Sometimes they have lots of details that you need to pay attention to! Read directions carefully to do them correctly.

Directions: On the left side of your paper, write a list of five different single-digit numbers vertically. Next, put those five numbers in order from greatest to least in a column on the right side of the page. Finally, add up all of the numbers and write your answer in the middle of your paper inside of a sun that you have drawn.

In this example, yellow highlighting represents the steps you have to complete.

The green highlighting represents important details to consider when completing each task.

What's left are the transition words (e.g. Next, Finally, etc.).

Don't forget your name!

Lesson 2.25 — Instructional Poster 1 of 1

Metacognition

Name: _____
Date: _____

BIG IDEA: A lot of times, we can just look at a worksheet and know exactly how to complete it. We don't need the directions at all. But sometimes, the directions ask us to do something different, and if we don't read them we end up doing everything wrong. Reading directions carefully EVERY time is a habit that we should all try to develop.

DIRECTIONS: Place check marks next to the steps or details that were completed correctly and completely on the notepad on the right. Write an "X" next to the steps that have not been done correctly or completely. Then, fix or complete those steps.

Accuracy — How can reading directions carefully help me?

Directions: On the left side of your paper, write a list of five different single-digit numbers vertically. Next, put those five numbers in order from greatest to least in a column on the right side of the page. Finally, add up all of the numbers and write your answer in the middle of your paper inside of a sun that you have drawn.

The directions have been broken down into manageable chunks that help you see each step and all of the details clearly. On the next page, you will get to do this step yourself.

- On the left side of your paper,
- write a list
- of five different
- single-digit numbers
- vertically.
- Next, put those five numbers in order
- from greatest to least
- in a column on the right side of the page.
- Finally, add up all of the numbers and
- write your answer in the middle of your paper
- inside of a sun that you have drawn.

Paul Solarz

5	3
8	5
3	5
10	8
5	+ 10
	31

Lesson 2.25 — Student Handout 1 of 2

Accuracy — How can reading directions carefully help me?

Directions: Break down the directions below like I did for you on the previous page. Some have been started for you. You get no help on the last three! Then, follow the directions using the notepad at the right.

Directions: At the bottom of this notepad, write down five colors from left to right (horizontally in a row). Next, re-write those colors in alphabetical order in a column (vertically) on the left side of the page. Finally, circle two of those colors and write on the right side of your paper what color they would make if they were equally blended together.

- At the bottom
- write
- from
- re-write
- in
- in
- on
-
-
-

Did you remember to write your name? Did you check off all of the boxes? These are all important steps that YOU need to remember on your own!

Lesson 2.25 — Student Handout 2 of 2

bit.ly/3Rgj91B

Develop the habit of reading ALL directions carefully before starting to avoid mistakes and unnecessary effort

2.26

Planning 1
Goal Setting 6
Meta-cognition 2
Synthesis 3
Reflection 4
Self-Assessment 5

Essential Question

How can I be responsible for several directions?

Big Idea

A lot of times, we can just look at a worksheet and know exactly how to complete it. We don't need the directions at all. But sometimes, the directions ask us to do something different, and if we don't read all of the direction carefully BEFORE beginning, we end up doing everything wrong. Reading directions carefully EVERY time is a habit that we should all try to develop.

Lesson Overview

In this lesson, students are told that they are just taking the last lesson further. That is, developing a successful strategy for handling multiple step directions. However, what is really going on is that they are about to learn about the importance of reading the directions carefully before beginning in order to avoid making mistakes that require a great deal of effort to fix! In this lesson, students who read the directions carefully will know to write or draw each task that is asked of them in a DIFFERENT color. Those who don't read that direction ahead of time will do the activity in one color and have to explain how they fixed the problem at the end of the lesson.

Discussion/Reflection Questions

- Why is it important to read through ALL of the directions carefully BEFORE assuming that you know what to do and just diving right in?
- How could this activity have been even HARDER to fix? What direction could have been used that would have made all of your work completely useless, so you had to do it all over?
- How could the experience from this lesson help you improve your direction-reading skills in your future? What might you now do differently or better?

Teacher Tips

- This lesson should be completed after the prior lesson (they work well together, and although they appear to be similar lessons, they actually focus on fairly different skills).
- Don't share anything from this lesson plan with the students prior to them completing the Student Handouts. Lots of spoilers are found in these pages!
- There are two additional pages that go with this lesson.
- The final Student Handout works well as a classroom discussion. If you have the time, go over that page together as a class, along with the Class Discussion questions (Exit Slip questions).
- There are lots of great activities that are similar to this one, but many involve embarrassing behaviors that allow other students to see who does it correctly and who doesn't. If you choose to add another activity to this lesson, I recommend trying to avoid ones requiring humiliating actions.

Student Tasks ⟩ Transfer Goals

Student Tasks	Transfer Goals
Students review the strategy taught from the last lesson for chunking complex directions.	Students strengthen their skills with this strategy and are more likely to use it on their own.
Students discover the importance of reading ALL directions carefully BEFORE beginning an assignment.	Students stop assuming that they automatically know what to do on an assignment, and spend a little extra time reading directions carefully.

Instructional Poster(s)

- This lesson has ONE Instructional Poster.
- The Instructional Poster for this lesson continues what was taught in the prior lesson and further develops the strategy of breaking down a multiple step direction into smaller chunks.
- Make sure that students understand that it is very common for students to THINK they are done with a task, only to lose points or have the assignment returned because one or more parts were not completed (due to not completing each step of a complex set of directions).
- Breaking these complex directions down into small chunks that can be checked off as they are completed can help ensure that nothing is missed and everything is completed.

Student Handouts

- This lesson has TWO Student Handouts.
- DIRECTIONS: Read all of the multiple step directions on the left of this page. Then, complete the directions using the box below. Be sure to complete the task successfully, according to all criteria. Finally, complete the reflection on the next page.
- On the first Student Handout, students are asked to READ all of the directions BEFORE doing any of the tasks. Since most students "see direction, do direction," many are likely to do everything wrong, which should be allowed to happen so students can learn from their mistake. The final direction explains that each bulleted task needs to be done in a different color! Don't help them understand this step AND don't allow others to ruin it for everyone else (this would be best in a silent classroom or as homework).
- On the second handout, students reflect on the experience and share how they handled their mistakes if they had any.

INTRODUCTION

PLANNING

METACOGNITION

SYNTHESIS

REFLECTION

SELF-ASSESSMENT

GOAL SETTING

FEEDBACK

Accuracy — How can I be responsible for several directions?

What do you do when you have a long list of tasks to complete on an assignment?

Thoughts?

Have you ever forgotten a step or two?

Of course! No one's perfect!

One Possible Solution:
1. Turn the steps into a checklist.
2. Chunk them with a highlighter.
3. Check off each chunk as you complete it!

Example:
Your task for today is to take out a piece of paper and fold it in half hamburger style. There are four panels to write on. On one inside panel, write "Fruit" as a title and on the other inside panel, write "Cereal" as a title. On the two outer panels, write "Granola Bar" on one panel and "Chips" on the other outer panel. All of these titles should be written at the top of the panel, looking at each panel vertically (pretending it's how you'd write on a normal piece of paper.)

Does it matter if you forget a step or two, or is it okay to just do the first step and move on?

Yes, it matters otherwise it wouldn't be on there!

☑ Your task for today is to take out a piece of paper and fold it ☑ in half hamburger style. There are four panels to write on. On
☑ one inside panel, write "Fruit" as a title and on the other inside ☑ panel, write "Cereal" as a title.
☑ On the two outer panels, write "Granola Bar" on one panel and ☑ "Chips" on the other outer panel.
☑ All of these titles should be written at the top of the panel, looking at each panel vertically (pretending it's how you'd write on a normal piece of paper.)

Metacognition

Name: _____

Date: _____

BIG IDEA: Multiple step directions cause people trouble quite often! You might read all the directions, and then do everything you remember but it's so easy to forget one or two parts. That's why it's important to chunk the directions into smaller tasks and check them off as you complete them.

DIRECTIONS: Read all of the multiple step directions on the left of this page. Then, complete the directions using the box below. Be sure to complete the task successfully, according to all criteria. Finally, complete the reflection on the next page.

Accuracy — How can I be responsible for several directions?

Draw the following objects in the space to the right:
- a square,
- a stick figure,
- a simple house,
- the number that comes after 14,
- the month that comes before May,
- the missing letter from ARIZ __ NA,
- and a flower
using a different color for each object above.

Accuracy — How can I be responsible for several directions?

Reflect on these questions. If you're doing this in class, discuss your answers with the whole group or a partner.

Our goal for this lesson was to:
- ☐ Complete (Finish)
- ☐ the task successfully (correctly),
- ☐ according to all criteria (according to all directions and requirements).

Were you successful in all three ways on your first try?

- Did you FINISH the task?

- Did you do it all CORRECTLY?

- Did you follow all directions and requirements (CRITERIA)?

Or, did you discover that you made a mistake and had to revise or start over?

- Did you notice that you had to draw each object using a different color? It wasn't mentioned until the end (which is TOTALLY unfair, right?!), but it was part of the directions (which you should always read ahead of time, before beginning any tasks so you know all of what you're supposed to do).

- How did you fix your mistake? Did you just draw over your work with a different color, making sure that it covered the original color? Did you start over so you could turn in something that you would be proud of? Are you proud of your final product?

2.27

Dive into powerful processing strategies to master the art of turning new knowledge into lasting power

bit.ly/3RetESZ

Essential Question

How can I improve my processing power?

Big Idea

When we're learning new information, it's important that we "process" everything that we read, hear and see. There are many ways that we can show our teacher that we are actively processing information.

Lesson Overview

In this lesson, students are reminded of the importance of "processing" new information when they are in the act of learning. It does them no good to zone out during lectures or allow others around them to do the thinking for them when working collaboratively - they need to be "present." Students learn a four-step strategy that should help them "process" new learning: (1) Collect new information or learn a new skill, (2) Make sense of that information or skill, (3) Store that new information or skill permanently for future use, and (4) Transfer the new information or skill to new situations independently.

Discussion/Reflection Questions

- What are the four steps that you were taught today that help you process information or skills so that you can transfer them to new situations successfully?
- Why should we measure "actual learning" by whether or not you are able to TRANSFER the skill or information to a new situation INDEPENDENTLY? Why shouldn't you just need to know it for a test and then never need it again?
- What can you do if you realize that you are not processing something while learning in school? How will you recognize it and what will you do about it?

Teacher Tips

- Don't forget to use the second Instructional Poster.
- Discussing this topic as a class, using examples and stories, would help students understand its true meaning and apply it to their learning. Share some stories of your own where you were successful and unsuccessful "processing" new skills or information. Also share if you were successful "transferring" the skill or information to a new experience. Make up some fictional scenarios to show how not processing information could be troublesome (e.g. repelling down a mountain, etc.).
- The Student Handouts attempt to find out if the students are able to "process" the directions correctly and apply what they read to completing each sheet correctly. Provide minimal support to them during this activity and ask them not to ask others for too much help, as students should apply the four steps strategy to these tasks.

Student Tasks 〉 Transfer Goals

Students learn four steps that will help them process new information or skills successfully, ending with transfer.	Students improve their ability to process new information or skills and find success transferring it to new situations.
Students learn ways that show they are TRYING to process new learning and ways that show they were SUCCESSFUL at it.	Students use this improved awareness and list of identifiable behaviors to improve their processing effort and success.

Instructional Poster(s)

- This lesson has TWO Instructional Posters.
- On the first Instructional Poster, students learn the concept of "processing" or "making sense of new learning and storing it for later use." They also learn that the fourth step of learning new skills and information is to be able to TRANSFER it to new situations independently in the future without reminders or re-teaching. This poster is complicated, so check for understanding often & provide examples if possible to further help them understand.
- The second Instructional Poster highlights some examples of "ways that show you are trying to process new information" and "ways that show you were successful at processing new information." These are just examples, so supplement them with examples from your classroom to help it become clearer.

Student Handouts

- This lesson has TWO Student Handouts.
- DIRECTIONS: Answer the questions on this page and the next. Whenever you see a half-circle, draw an arrow from the center dot to the section you feel represents your ability on the dial.
- Students may want to begin this task without reading the directions carefully. Remind them of the importance of "processing" the directions and using the four steps in the Processing Strategy. Don't help them too much!
- FYI - Students should first describe what kind of reader they are. They don't need to circle a letter! They need to use those choices to help them put into words their self-assessment as a reader. Next, they need to answer if they "picture a story while reading" or "just try to get through the reading." There are obviously other possibilities too - they need to write their answer in the available space. Finally, they need to draw in their arrows where they believe they belong, based on the directions and their self-assessment.
- The second Student Handout is the same, but it focuses in on LISTENING skills, rather than reading skills.

Instructional Poster 1 of 2

Accuracy How can I improve my processing power?

"Process" what you read, hear and see

If we are successful at processing new information, then we are able to:
1. collect new information,
2. make sense of it,
3. store it for later, and then
4. use it correctly whenever it's needed in the future.

The ENTIRE PURPOSE of learning something new is so that you can do something with it later on. If you learn to ride a bike, it does you NO GOOD unless you get to eventually ride a bike! This is called TRANSFER. Transfer is using a new skill or new information correctly whenever it's needed in the future without being reminded or re-taught in the moment.

Collecting new information might include:
- Listening to what your teacher says
- Reading
- Watching a video or demonstration
- Experiencing something new

Making sense of new information might include:
- Comprehending what you read
- Hearing what is being said and connecting it to what you already know
- Asking questions until it makes sense

Storing new information for later might include:
- Filing away new information in a way that you can access it again when it's needed
- Memorizing details, conversions, facts, or vocabulary
- Reflecting on new learning through writing, video recording, or discussion

Lesson 2.27

Student Handout 1 of 2

Metacognition

Name:

Date:

BIG IDEA: When we're learning new information, it's important that we "process" everything that we read, hear and see. There are many ways that we can show our teacher that we are actively processing information.

DIRECTIONS: Answer the questions on this page and the next. Whenever you see a half-circle, draw an arrow from the center dot to the section you feel represents your ability on the dial.

Accuracy How can I improve my processing power?

What kind of READER are you?
a. A speed reader who doesn't really process what you're reading but finishes reading quickly?
b. A slow reader who needs to sound out lots of words and doesn't understand as much as you should?
c. Not fast or slow, but what you read is easily understood and remembered?
d. Something else? Describe it here:

Do you picture a story as you are reading it, or do you just try to get through the reading?

Medium Reader — Fast Reader / Slow Reader

Average Understanding — Strong Understanding / Weak Understanding

Lesson 2.27

Student Handout 2 of 2

Accuracy How can I improve my processing power?

What kind of LISTENER are you when someone is reading to you, teaching you information, or giving you directions?
a. I have no trouble understanding what they're saying and rarely ever miss any details.
b. I have to concentrate really hard in order to understand everything that is said, but usually have no trouble remembering everything.
c. I find myself thinking about other things pretty quickly and often miss parts or forget things that were said.
d. Something else? Describe it here:

Describe how you can improve your ability to understand and remember what you read and hear in school:

Do you remember details better when you have a visual to look at while you're listening? Explain what you mean:

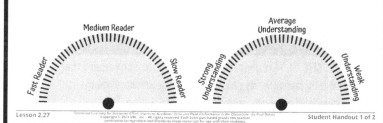

Understands what you hear easily / Struggles to understand what you hear

Remembers what you hear easily / Struggles to remember what you hear

Lesson 2.27

INTRODUCTION

PLANNING

METACOGNITION

SYNTHESIS

REFLECTION

SELF-ASSESSMENT

GOAL SETTING

FEEDBACK

bit.ly/47StLcp

Manage unexpected situations calmly using the power of flexibility, because not all plans go according to plan

Essential Question

Shouldn't everything go according to my plan?

Big Idea

Plans are very important, but they rarely work out EXACTLY like you expected. Prepare to make changes to your plans, and don't get upset.

Lesson Overview

In this lesson, students learn that planning is very important, but that plans rarely go the way we think they will. We need to be flexible when things change, and we need to adapt in order to be successful. Students also analyze a plan they recently created and completed to discover how things changed from the original plan, and how they adjusted to make things work.

Discussion/Reflection Questions

- Why is it important to identify things that are "within our control" and things that are "out of our control"? What is the benefit of classifying things into those two categories?
- What should we do when our plans aren't going the way we thought they'd go? How can we still find success?
- How can we teach ourselves to stop using excuses as reasons we aren't successful? Just because things happen that are outside of our control doesn't mean we will automatically fail to complete our goals.

Teacher Tips

- PREREQUISITE: The Student Handouts for this lesson require that the students have already created a plan for accomplishing something, and have gotten to the end of that plan. They will analyze how the plan worked out and recall things that did not go exactly as planned.
- I recommend teaching students about their "Circle of Control" during this lesson. We can only control so many things in life. When it comes to everything else, we need to roll with the punches and adjust as necessary.
- The true purpose of this lesson is to help students understand that, even the best laid plans don't always work out. But that doesn't mean that we stop planning! It just means that we need to anticipate bumps in the road, and make adjustments as needed.

Student Tasks 〉 Transfer Goals

Student Tasks	Transfer Goals
Students learn that plans rarely go exactly as we thought they'd go. We need to expect and accept this.	Students "expect the unexpected" and adjust their plans when things go differently than anticipated.
Students learn to anticipate and prevent roadblocks to their plan before they happen & adjust and adapt when needed.	Students stop using excuses for not achieving their goals. Ultimately, it's still our own responsibility no matter what.

Optimized Learning: 180 mini-lessons that transform today's students into confident, capable & collaborative, self-directed learners

Instructional Poster(s)

- This lesson has TWO Instructional Posters.
- The top two images on the first Instructional Poster help to explain that plans are very linear - they try to take us from Point A to Point B using the most direct route possible. Unfortunately, the road to Point B is often met with challenges, distractions, struggles, and twists. We need to "Expect it and Accept it."
- The rest of the poster focuses in on three quotes about PLANNING. You could have the students interpret the quotes themselves, or you could discuss their meaning. Either way, students should learn from each quote's message.
- The second Instructional Poster shows students a sample plan and the actual results that followed. It refers to experiences within our control and outside of our control. We need to be able to adapt to both successfully.

Student Handouts

- This lesson has TWO Student Handouts.
- DIRECTIONS: You've just completed a task where you created a plan and tried to follow that plan. Describe your initial plan below. Then, explain what actually happened (which is often at least slightly different). On the next page, categorize the changes to your plan as things that were within your control or not and explain one way you could have prevented each change to your plan, and what you actually did in to find success.
- Point out to students that things that are truly out of our control, generally cannot be prevented (there may be exceptions). So, becoming frustrated by those challenges does us no good. Let's focus on the things that are within our control.

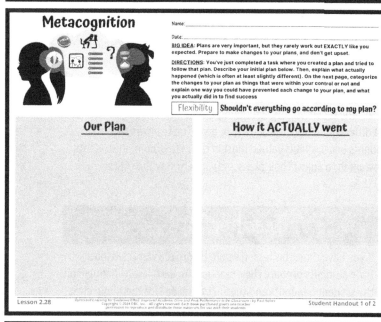

INTRODUCTION
PLANNING
METACOGNITION
SYNTHESIS
REFLECTION
SELF-ASSESSMENT
GOAL SETTING
FEEDBACK

bit.ly/47DsiqU

Unlock the power of flexibility to help you navigate unexpected situations with calm and confidence

Essential Question

What do I do when things don't go according to plan?

Big Idea

Sometimes, things happen (that are out of your control) that force you to change your plan. This can be VERY frustrating, but the quicker you learn to handle it, the happier you'll be! It's a part of life that we all need to deal with.

Lesson Overview

In this lesson, students contemplate various scenarios that can easily frustrate and challenge even the most flexible of students. BUT, they need to consider how they would accept that it happened and how they would respond to it in a flexible and calm manner. Students learn that sometimes (maybe even most of the time), it's best to be flexible and adaptable, rather than rigid when it comes to our own plans. We might need to fall a little behind in order to help a peer who is completely struggling, and then we will try to catch up at a different point in the activity or task. The teachers will let students know what is valued most in their classroom, so students know when to adjust their plans and when to stay the course!

Discussion/Reflection Questions

- Why is it important to show flexibility and calmness when dealing with a "Plan Changer"? Why shouldn't we just allow our natural emotions to play out?
- Have you ever overreacted to anything before? What was the situation and how did you overreact? What do you wish you would have done instead?
- How can we teach kindergartners this concept? It can be hard for youngsters to be flexible because they can't think that far ahead (anticipate the overreaction and prevent it from happening). Any ideas?

Teacher Tips

- If you have time, this lesson would be great as an act-it-out. Have students prepare their reactions to each "Plan Changer" on the student handouts and then act them out for the whole class, or on video to post online for others to see. In my experience, having the students act out each scene creates stronger memories and makes the Big Idea of the lesson more permanent. After all, the true goal of all of these lessons is transfer, and that will be easier for students to accomplish if it becomes meaningful to them.
- Students probably have many more examples of "Plan Changers" than are listed on the Student Handouts. Ask them for experiences they've recently had to deal with and how they handled each. Even if they handled it poorly, ask them what they wish they would have done instead! This can be a class discussion, small group chats, or acted out!

Student Tasks 〉 Transfer Goals

Student Tasks	Transfer Goals
Students learn that there are times to be flexible, adjust plans & try something different, and times to stay the course.	Students make wise decisions when needing to choose between following their plan or adapting to something that has come up.
Students learn to be flexible and calm when "Plan Changers" enter their lives.	Students no longer overreact to disruptions or allow them to consume their time and effort.

INTRODUCTION

PLANNING

METACOGNITION

SYNTHESIS

REFLECTION

SELF-ASSESSMENT

GOAL SETTING

FEEDBACK

Instructional Poster(s)

- This lesson has ONE Instructional Poster.
- This Instructional Poster has eight "inner dialogues" that students might think at some point in school. Discuss each of these thoughts as a class and make sure that students understand that there are times to be flexible, and times to stick with the plan. But it's important to know your values, beliefs, goals, and needs before making each decision. In our classroom, helping others is prioritized over finishing on time (provided it was necessary to help the peer). You may have different values in your classroom. Help your students understand these values and they will ultimately learn to prioritize those above their own.

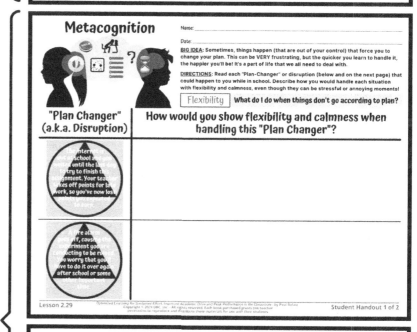

Student Handouts

- This lesson has TWO Student Handouts.
- DIRECTIONS: Read each "Plan-Changer" or disruption (below and on the next page) that could happen to you while in school. Describe how you would handle each situation with flexibility and calmness, even though they can be stressful or annoying moments!
- These are "role plays" that can be acted out, explained on video, or just written out. Students might come up with several possible solutions to dealing with each "Plan Changer" but the end goal is to remain calm, show flexibility, and accomplish goals (while keeping classroom priorities in mind).
- Consider having the students share some "Plan Changers" that have actually happened recently, and have them share how they handled each.

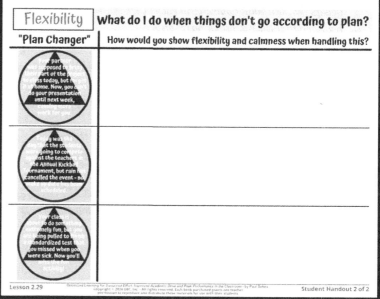

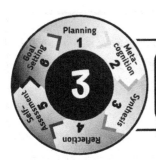

Synthesis

3

> **"Like the blending of colors on an artist's palette, the purposeful combination of new learning and our prior knowledge creates a richer, more vibrant canvas of understanding."**
> **— ChatGPT's invented quote**

The third macroskill students need to develop in order to become successful, optimized learners is "Synthesis." Synthesis happens when we combine accurate prior knowledge with accurate new information, in order to create a deeper, more correct understanding. Consider the following scenario:

You've partnered your students up randomly and assigned them the task of reading a few articles on fossil fuels and alternative energy sources for powering the country. Their objective is to engage in thoughtful discussions, share their perspectives, and complete a corresponding worksheet. You observe the following:

- *One partnership demonstrates excellent turn-taking skills while reading each paragraph. However, they are close to finishing all three articles without engaging in any discussions or completing their worksheets.*
- *Another partnership fully embraces the discussion aspect of the assignment and is diving deeply into their political beliefs that are polar opposites of each other, both believing that their information is correct.*
- *One partnership lacks background knowledge that is vital to understanding the readings and doesn't know how to use context clues to figure it out. Despite their efforts, they are not making progress in terms of acquiring knowledge or comprehension.*
- *One final partnership exclaims, "Ohhh! Now I get how that works!" and engages in a conversation where they share surprises and correct misconceptions. These students actively process the information, integrate it with their prior knowledge, and develop a stronger understanding of the material. In the perfect environment, every partnership would be saying "Ohhh!" and "But I thought..." and "Let's look this up to see if it's true." These students are synthesizers!*

Synthesis is the process of combining existing knowledge with new information to form a more complete and well-rounded perspective. When explaining synthesis to students, I often emphasize that it encapsulates the essence of learning itself. In school, we bring with us a mix of correct and incorrect background knowledge, as well as a vast array of skills and unfamiliar subject matter. It is through our lessons and experiences that we acquire new skills and gather accurate information, which lays the groundwork for future learning. Through synthesis, students make connections between different concepts, recognize patterns, and develop a more nuanced understanding of a given topic.

Synthesis occurs when students actively engage with information, process it, critically analyze it, and make connections between different ideas. It requires students to go beyond surface-level comprehension and delve into the complexities of a subject. By synthesizing information, students can develop a more holistic view and identify relationships between concepts that may not be immediately apparent.

To facilitate synthesis, teachers can provide students with various activities and tasks that encourage them to combine and organize their knowledge. These activities may include completing synthesis organizers, writing synthesis paragraphs, or engaging in discussions that require students to integrate multiple perspectives.

In our classroom, I would often say, "Be sure to 'process' what you read!" in order to get my students to focus while they read instead of mindlessly saying the words without thinking about them.

Additionally, in order to make my students' synthesis visible to myself and others, I would encourage them to say, "Ohhhh!" to express their "Aha Moments" causing other students to want that same experience. Sometimes, students would ask each other what they discovered, and although they didn't have the Aha Moment themselves, they were able to see the value of the information that their peer learned and incorporate it into their own understanding of the topic.

Synthesis plays a vital role in students' academic growth and development. It enables them to move beyond rote memorization and passive learning, fostering critical thinking and analytical skills. By synthesizing information, students make connections between different topics, apply their knowledge to real world situations, and develop a deeper understanding of complex ideas.

Furthermore, synthesis allows students to make their thinking visible, both for themselves and others, facilitating effective communication and collaboration. By synthesizing information, students are better able to articulate their thoughts and explain complex ideas, enhancing their ability to express themselves clearly and concisely.

Students are taught to follow four main steps when synthesizing information:

1. **Activate Prior Knowledge:** This step involves recalling and accessing existing knowledge on a subject before learning new information. By activating prior knowledge, students are better able to make connections between what they already know and the new information they are about to learn. This step helps build a foundation for understanding and provides a framework for integrating new knowledge.

2. **Collect New Information and Make Sense of It:** In this step, students gather accurate and reliable new information related to the subject they are studying. They analyze and interpret this new information to understand its meaning and relevance. The focus is on comprehending the new information and identifying key concepts or ideas.

3. **Question What You've Learned and Clear Up Misunderstandings:** Students critically evaluate their prior knowledge and the new information they have collected. They identify any misconceptions or incorrect understandings and seek to correct them by finding evidence from reliable sources. This step promotes critical thinking and helps students refine their understanding.

4. **Organize and Combine All Accurate Knowledge to Form a New Deeper Understanding:** Students integrate their prior knowledge with the new information they have collected, organizing it in a way that allows them to see connections, patterns, and relationships. Through this process, they

develop a more comprehensive and nuanced understanding of the subject.

These steps in the synthesis process guide students in actively engaging with information, critically analyzing it, and creating a deeper understanding by combining prior knowledge with new information. By following these steps, students enhance their critical thinking skills, make connections between different concepts, and develop a more comprehensive understanding of the subject. There are also several strategies that can help students synthesize their understanding. Some of which are explained below:

Analyzing Relationships:
- Identifying Parts and Wholes: Breaking down complex systems into smaller components and understanding their interactions.
- Identifying Sequences and Timelines: Grasping the order and timing of events or processes
- Identifying Underlying Principles and Theories: Seeking out the fundamental rules or laws governing a subject.

Making Comparisons and Contrasts:
- Good old-fashioned Compare and Contrast: Identifying similarities and differences between two or more things.
- Analogies and Metaphors: Drawing explicit connections between seemingly unrelated concepts to gain understanding.
- Identifying Trends and Patterns: Recognizing recurring themes or sequences within information.

Problem-Solving and Taking Action:
- Identifying Problems and Solutions: Analyzing situations, pinpointing challenges, and evaluating potential solutions.
- Making Inferences and Predictions: Using existing information to draw conclusions and anticipate future outcomes.
- Creative Problem-Solving: Generating new and original ideas to address challenges.

Organizing and Building Knowledge:
- Classifying and Categorizing: Organizing information into groups based on shared characteristics or themes.
- Mapping and Diagramming: Visualizing relationships and connections between concepts using graphic representations.
- Summarizing and Paraphrasing: Condensing key points of information into your own words to ensure understanding.

Through these, and many other strategies, students become able to dig deeper into their learning, and ultimately become a more effective and efficient, optimized learner.

INTRODUCTION
PLANNING
METACOGNITION
SYNTHESIS
REFLECTION
SELF-ASSESSMENT
GOAL SETTING
FEEDBACK

Unit 3 - Synthesis

17 Mini-Lessons

Students with well-developed SYNTHESIS MicroSkills...	Students with poorly-developed SYNTHESIS MicroSkills...
Identify incorrect prior knowledge and replace it with accurate information	Allow incorrect prior knowledge to remain uncorrected
Recognize conflicting information and distinguish between correct and incorrect information	Struggle to distinguish between correct and incorrect information
Combine accurate prior knowledge with new information to form a deeper understanding	Fail to integrate prior knowledge with new information effectively
Seek out additional sources of information to support or refute prior knowledge	Rely solely on limited sources of information without seeking alternative perspectives
Use critical thinking skills to evaluate the credibility and reliability of sources	Accept information from unreliable sources without critical evaluation
Apply synthesized knowledge to real-life situations or scenarios	Struggle to apply synthesized knowledge to practical contexts
Communicate their synthesized understanding effectively through verbal or written means	Struggle to articulate their synthesized understanding clearly
Actively engage in discussions or debates to refine their synthesis through collaboration	Avoid participating in discussions or debates that challenge their existing synthesis
Continuously update and refine their synthesis as new information becomes available	Maintain a static synthesis without incorporating new information
Synthesize information from diverse disciplines or subject areas to gain a holistic understanding	View information in isolation without considering its broader context
Identify gaps or inconsistencies in their understanding and seek to fill those gaps	Overlook gaps or inconsistencies and maintain an incomplete understanding
Seek feedback and input from others to enhance their synthesis and consider different perspectives	Avoid seeking feedback or input and rely solely on their own viewpoint
Recognize patterns and connections between different pieces of information or concepts	Fail to identify patterns or connections and view information as isolated facts
Organize information in a logical and coherent manner	Present information in a disorganized, disjointed manner

INTRODUCTION

PLANNING

METACOGNITION

SYNTHESIS

REFLECTION

SELF-ASSESSMENT

GOAL SETTING

FEEDBACK

bit.ly/46wqkXH

Evaluate SYNTHESIS MicroSkills to take pride in relative strengths and to set personalized goals for areas of weakness

Essential Question

How strong am I at each of these SYNTHESIS Skills?

Big Idea

By evaluating our current level of achievement on the MicroSkills that will be taught in this unit, we gain a clearer understanding of our individual strengths and weaknesses. Additionally, by synthesizing each MicroSkill, we develop a stronger understanding of the MacroSkill that this unit focuses on, which is SYNTHESIS.

Lesson Overview

In this lesson, students evaluate their perceived ability for each of the identified SYNTHESIS skills. These skills have been chosen from the lessons that follow in this unit. Although students are choosing a somewhat arbitrary number from 1-10, the self-assessment process requires them to (1) understand what the skill means, (2) determine their perceived ability for the skill, and (3) sort each skill into areas of weakness or strength (or in-between) so that they help others improve at the skill (for scores 7-10) or make the skill into a goal that they try to achieve (for scores 1-4). If a student scores a 5 or 6, they are asked to reassess themselves after the unit to determine if they would benefit from making it a goal or not.

Discussion / Reflection Questions

- Which synthesis skills did you feel you were strongest at? Provide some evidence to support your self-assessment.
- Which synthesis skills did you feel you were weakest at? Explain why you feel that this is true.
- If you could set a goal to improve ONE of these skills, which one would you choose? Why did you choose that one? How do you plan to improve this skill? What will you do?

Teacher Tips

- On the Student Handouts, it tells students to "highlight all the numbers up through your score." The reason I didn't just have them circle the number is so they can see "how full" their grade band is if they choose a high number, and "how empty" their grade band is if they choose a low number. If you don't think it's too important for your students, feel free to let them just circle their number.
- When doing a self-assessment like this, I like to teach my students about the importance of being honest with themselves. I remind them that self-assessment in our classroom don't affect your grades or the way I see them. Self-assessments help us focus in on what matters to us, rather than focusing in on everything and not spending enough time on the skills that we need to improve most. No one is a 10 on all of these skills and no one is a 1 on all of them, but there's a good chance that each of us is a 10 and a 1 on at least one skill in this self-assessment!

Student Tasks ⟩ Transfer Goals

Students assess themselves on various synthesis skills using a scale from 1 to 10.	Students become more self-aware of their abilities and areas in which they need to grow.
Students are asked several reflection questions that require them to explain their self-assessments and to set a goal for one skill.	Students understand that having weaknesses is normal and that they should be improved through goal-setting.

Instructional Poster(s)

- This lesson has ONE Instructional Poster.
- A variation of this Instructional Poster is used with the first lesson of each unit. It shows students how to use the 1-10 scale for assessing their current level of ability with each skill. Numbers 1-4 mean that they know they need to improve at this skill (and maybe create a goal for the skill), and numbers 7-10 mean they believe that they are capable of helping others improve this skill. (4-5 means they will reassess at the end of the unit - which will be up to you or the student to remember to do. It's not a lesson.)
- Tell students that the real value in this activity is discovering their relative strengths and weaknesses, so giving yourself a 10 for each skill is wasting everyone's time, as is repeating any other number. Finding the variation in each skill is the key, so give yourself scores of 1, 2, and 3 and give scores of 8, 9, and 10 as well!

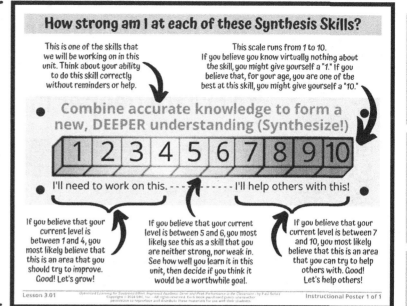

Student Handouts

- This lesson has FOUR Student Handouts.
- DIRECTIONS: Look at the Synthesis MicroSkills in each box below and on the following page(s). Determine a rating from 1-10 for yourself on each, and then circle it. For your lowest MicroSkill(s), create a S.M.A.A.R.T.E.R. Goal to address each weakness.
- If you have not taught the lesson on Goal Bursts, let students know that they can just make the skill a personal goal to improve, but nothing needs to be written out (unless they want a reminder to actually do it). Obviously, the more seriously they take things, the more likely they'll improve!

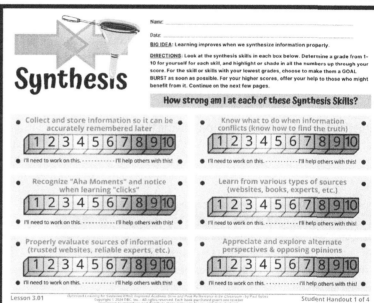

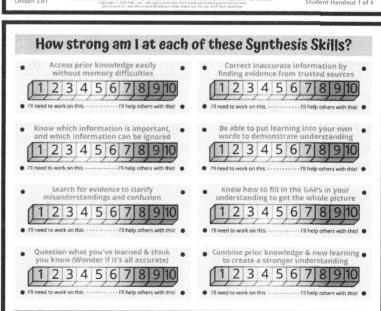

INTRODUCTION

PLANNING

METACOGNITION

SYNTHESIS

REFLECTION

SELF-ASSESSMENT

GOAL SETTING

FEEDBACK

3.02

Discover the power of synthesis by combining old and new knowledge to create deeper meaning

bit.ly/3uEyVuj

Essential Question

What does it mean to synthesize?

Big Idea

To SYNTHESIZE means to organize & combine accurate prior knowledge on a subject with accurate new knowledge to form a new, DEEPER understanding.

Lesson Overview

In this lesson, students learn the definition of synthesis and analyze a metaphorical image that shows how synthesis is like water pouring through a strainer into a large bowl. New learning and Prior knowledge gets poured, incorrect and inaccurate information gets strained out and what's left is a combination of all of the correct information about a subject. Then, students discover several examples of synthesis in action using examples from reading, writing, social studies, and math. After learning a bit about synthesis, students are then asked to explain in their own words what it means to "Synthesize."

Discussion/Reflection Questions

- Why do we include "Prior Knowledge" in our definition of synthesis?
- What do the strainers represent in the image on the Instructional Poster?
- What is one example of something you've recently synthesized? It can be simple or complex.

Teacher Tips

- If you can share any examples of synthesis that the students might have experienced in your class recently, that could help them understand the concept more clearly.
- I like to have my students explain answers on video, so if you're up for having your students try to answer the essay style question on the Student Handout on video, please do so! My rules have always been: (1) One take only - if they mess up or get interrupted, it's okay - they just need to correct themselves and continue on, (2) No silly stuff before, during, or after recording, (3) Make sure the video answers the question completely. I would probably add that students should provide an example of synthesis in action in their life to the video, to ensure that they are connecting it to life experiences.

Student Tasks 〉 Transfer Goals

Student Tasks	Transfer Goals
Students learn the definition of synthesis, as it relates to learning.	Students utilize this definition throughout the unit and understand that it often is a conscious act that they need to complete.
Students discover that learning information or skills permanently can't happen without first synthesizing it.	Students make stronger efforts to synthesize new learning throughout life in order to make it more permanent.

INTRODUCTION

PLANNING

METACOGNITION

SYNTHESIS

REFLECTION

SELF-ASSESSMENT

GOAL SETTING

FEEDBACK

Instructional Poster(s)

- This lesson has ONE Instructional Poster.
- The image on this Instructional Poster continues throughout the entire unit. It tries to show that "Synthesized Learning" is Prior Knowledge with the incorrect information strained out added to New Learning with the incorrect information strained out combined to make a new, deeper understanding.
- The definition of synthesis used in this book is to organize & combine all accurate knowledge on a subject to form a new, deeper understanding. Obviously, there are other definitions of "synthesis," so if you feel like you would prefer to use a variation of this definition, please modify the slides to remain consistent.

Student Handouts

- This lesson has TWO Student Handouts.
- DIRECTIONS: Read through the four examples of synthesis on the next page. Then, synthesize everything you've learned so far about SYNTHESIS by explaining what it means to "Synthesize" (in the lines below). Feel free to use the image below to help you organize your thoughts, but put your definition in your own words.
- The second Student Handout gives four examples of synthesis in different subjects. These examples, plus the information provided during the class discussion on the Instructional Poster should give students enough information to form an early understanding of synthesis.
- There is nothing that students need to do on the second Student Handout, other than read it.

bit.ly/47xCdOE

Create a unified understanding from diverse pieces of information through the power of synthesis

Essential Question

What is Synthesis?

Big Idea

SYNTHESIS is the act of combining & organizing all accurate knowledge on a subject to form a new, DEEPER understanding.

Lesson Overview

In this lesson, students use a "Synthesis Organizer" to visually combine accurate prior knowledge and accurate new information to explain their new, deeper understanding of a specific topic. The lesson starts with the teacher completing an organizer with the students watching (Instructional Poster). The Gradual Release of Responsibility method is used to empower students to complete an organizer independently on the Student Handout. The lesson ends with the students applying their synthesized information to purchasing an appropriate gift for a fictional friend.

Discussion/Reflection Questions

- How does the Synthesis Organizer help you create an accurate synthesis about a topic?
- Why is it important that you eventually learn how to synthesize WITHOUT using the Synthesis Organizer?
- How will you know when it's time to synthesize information in real life? Will you be able to realize that you're synthesizing for a real purpose in real life?

Teacher Tips

- A prerequisite lesson is 3.02.
- The graphic organizer used in this lesson is like "Training Wheels" on a bike. It should be used as students are learning to synthesize information, but it's important that students don't use it forever, nor rely upon it in order to synthesize information once they understand how to synthesize at a high level. Teaching students to internalize this process is the key to successful transfer!
- For the topic on the first Student Handout, it's a great opportunity to choose an upcoming unit that students will be learning about. It is a great replacement for a KWL Chart since students need to list four things they think they already know about the topic, then add four things that you teach them, and combine all of that to describe their new, deeper understanding of the topic.

Student Tasks 〉 Transfer Goals

Student Tasks	Transfer Goals
Students work with their teacher to complete a Synthesis Organizer together.	Students are able to complete Synthesis Organizers independently on different topics.
Students complete a fictional task of buying a present for a friend after synthesizing information about her likes and dislikes.	Students are able to synthesize information naturally, without needing a graphic organizer.

Instructional Poster(s)

- This lesson has ONE Instructional Poster.
- This lesson's Instructional Poster is a "Gradual Release of Responsibility Activity." You choose the topic and follow this process to complete the organizer together as a class:
  - 1 - I do. You watch.
  - 2 - I do. You help.
  - 3 - You do. I help.
  - 4 - You do. I watch.
- An example might be to complete a Synthesis Organizer on "Current Trends" that are appropriate for school.
- Complete the organizer using the Gradual Release of Responsibility steps above, but focus on what YOU already know (whether correct or not) and then learn new things from your students. Synthesize your learning by explaining your new, deeper understanding of current trends.

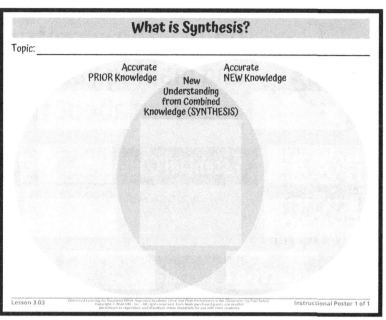

Student Handouts

- This lesson has TWO Student Handouts.
- DIRECTIONS: Using a topic of your own choosing or one that your teacher has chosen, complete the following "Venn Diagram" to show how you combined accurate prior knowledge with accurate new knowledge to synthesize your understanding.
- On the first Student Handout, have students complete the same organizer using a DIFFERENT topic. It can be something you're learning in class, something happening in the world, or allow your students to choose a topic that interests them. This practice will be foundational for the rest of the unit.
- On the second Student Handout, the students will need to combine fictional prior knowledge and fictional new information that is provided to them in order to synthesize it and APPLY it to a specific scenario.

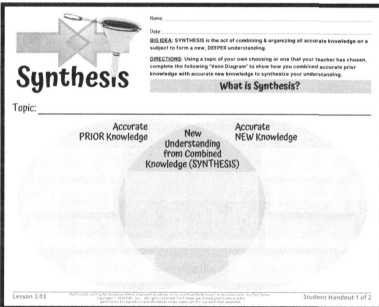

INTRODUCTION

PLANNING

METACOGNITION

SYNTHESIS

REFLECTION

SELF-ASSESSMENT

GOAL SETTING

FEEDBACK

bit.ly/47qfYdj

3.04

Unlock the secrets of connecting the dots and making your knowledge truly click as you learn about the benefits of synthesis

Essential Question

Why spend time Synthesizing?

Big Idea

Learning to synthesize information correctly is vital to a deeper, more accurate understanding of a topic.

Lesson Overview

In this lesson, students explore a fictional scenario where synthesis is required in order to be successful: creating a YouTube channel and gaining followers by promoting videos on Twitter. (They won't actually be doing this - it's fictional.) This scenario should help students see how a personal interest (like creating a successful YouTube channel) may require combining prior knowledge with new information in order to create a new, stronger understanding (synthesis). They also complete a Funnel Organizer to show synthesis of a topic, and they answer two essay questions that lead them to understanding, "why we spend time synthesizing."

Discussion/Reflection Questions

- Why might it be hard to create a successful YouTube channel without taking some time to learn HOW successful channels are made? Could you just rely on your prior knowledge? (If so, is that because you have an advanced understanding of the topic already?)
- Now that you're becoming stronger at synthesizing, what tips might you give others to help them with this skill?
- What personal interest topic would you like to learn more about, synthesize with your prior knowledge, and put to use (like we did with the YouTube example)?

Teacher Tips

- There are TWO Instructional Posters for this lesson.
- If you don't think your students will appreciate the topic on the Instructional Posters due to their age or any other reason, try to use the format of the posters to modify it using a different example.
- You will need to have a topic in mind for the first Student Handout - it would work well with a current events article or some other non-fiction short reading. Just remember to have students write their prior knowledge about the topic BEFORE they begin reading the article (like you would do with a KWL Chart).

Student Tasks 〉 Transfer Goals

Students explore a complex example of synthesizing for a purpose.	Students see the value of synthesis as it connects to their personal interests.
Students describe the value of synthesis through two essay questions.	Students synthesize information independently, because they see its value and understand its purpose.

Instructional Poster(s)

- This lesson has TWO Instructional Posters.
- The first Instructional Poster takes students through the synthesis process of learning to create their own YouTube Channel.
- The second Instructional Poster focuses on gaining Twitter followers so they can promote their YouTube channel to gain more subscribers. (If this is not of interest to your age group, modify the idea to make it work for your group.)
- Make sure that students know what the brackets in the Instructional Poster mean. Brackets are used in many upcoming slides.
- When you read through these Instructional Posters with the class, please be sure to point out how each step that is being done is a conscious effort to synthesize information in order to accomplish a goal of some sort. In this case, it's to try to create a YouTube Channel where they have lots of subscribers.

Student Handouts

- This lesson has TWO Student Handouts.
- DIRECTIONS: Using a topic of your own choosing or one that your teacher has chosen, complete the following "Funnel Organizer" to show how you combined accurate prior knowledge with accurate new knowledge to synthesize your understanding.
- On the first Student Handout, students complete a new Synthesis Organizer called a Funnel Organizer. It asks for three bits of prior knowledge, two pieces of new information, and a paragraph explaining their new, deeper understanding of the topic. You need to choose the topic or have them choose one if they know how to make that choice successfully. It would work well with a short article or current event news story, among other things.
- On the second Student Handout, students answer two essay questions. In order to get high quality answers, you may want to explain these two questions before students get to work on them, but use your best judgment for your group. This page attempts to have students answer the Essential Question of the lesson.

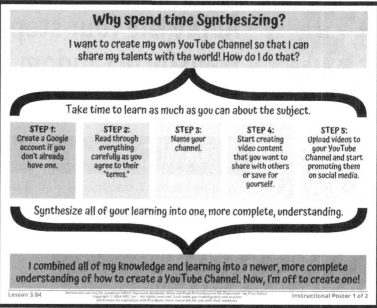

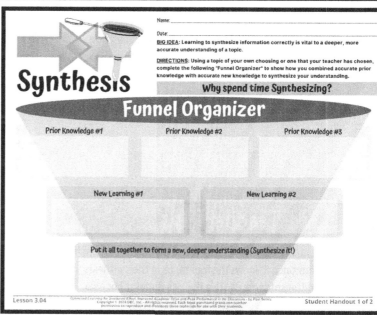

bit.ly/4a0s5iQ

Apply the four steps of synthesis to transform random bits of information into deeper, stronger understanding

Essential Question

What are the steps in the Synthesis Process?

Big Idea

There are four basic steps required to synthesize learning. When we learn how to follow these steps correctly, we are able to form a stronger, more complete understanding of a topic.

Lesson Overview

In this lesson, students learn the four step process for synthesizing information that we refer to throughout the rest of this unit. This lesson has students synthesize another topic of the teacher or student's choosing and offers four useful tips for synthesizing. Although this is a fairly simple, quick and straight-forward lesson, it does provide a solid foundation for the lessons that follow.

Discussion/Reflection Questions

- What are the four steps in the Synthesis Process?
- Are you expected to use organizers for the rest of your life whenever you need to synthesize information, or are you supposed to eventually be able to do it in your head?
- What will you do to try to synthesize information WITHOUT having to use an organizer in the coming weeks?

Teacher Tips

- The Instructional Poster would make a good poster to hang in the classroom since it shows the four steps in the synthesis process, and the students can use the visual metaphor as a reminder to synthesize their learning
- The second Student Handout can be used as a form that students fill out when learning new information about a subject or unit in class. Similarly, the organizers from the previous lessons can also be used. Find out which organizer is most useful to your students and offer that to students if they need it until they can synthesize independently.
- You may want to go over the first Student Handout with the students if you don't think they will read it on their own OR if you think it may be too difficult for them to understand on their own. It is not vital information, however, so it may be a good opportunity to see what your students can do without your support as well.

Student Tasks ⟩ Transfer Goals

Student Tasks	Transfer Goals
Students learn the four steps of the Synthesis Process.	Students use these four steps in the upcoming lessons in this unit.
Students complete a "4 Steps of Synthesis Organizer."	Students apply these four steps when synthesizing information independently, without teacher support.

Instructional Poster(s)

- This lesson has ONE Instructional Poster.
- The Instructional Poster for this lesson focuses on the FOUR steps in the Synthesis Process. These four steps will be referred to throughout the rest of this unit.
- The four steps are expressed visually in the image on the right (which first appeared in Lesson 3.2). It's a metaphor for synthesis that shows water pouring from pots into a large bowl, after passing through strainers.
- Another way of saying these four steps is through the four questions in the bottom, right box on the page.

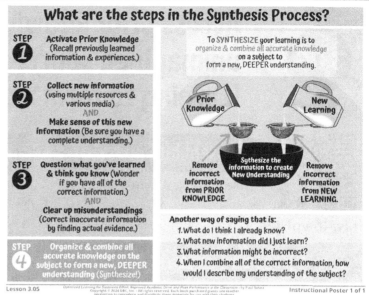

Student Handouts

- This lesson has TWO Student Handouts.
- DIRECTIONS: Read through the Synthesizing tips below. Then, using a topic of your own choosing or one that your teacher has chosen, complete the following "4 Steps of Synthesis Organizer" to show your thinking.
- On the first Student Handout, students read four tips for synthesizing.
- On the second Student Handout, students complete a "4 Steps of Synthesis Organizer" on a subject of the teacher's choice or student's choice. It is similar to a KWL Chart in that it asks students what they think they already know about a topic, what they're hoping to learn, and what they actually learned. It then asks students to be on the lookout for incorrect information and to find the correct replacements. Finally, it asks students to describe their current understanding of the subject (a written synthesis of the information they learned). The boxes are relatively small, so the students' answers will likely be short for this task.

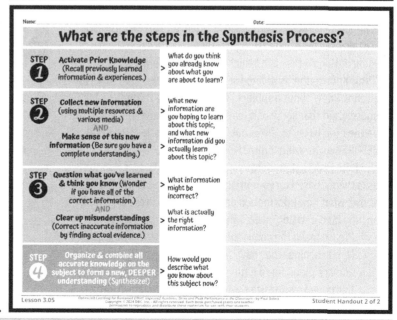

3.06

Access prior knowledge from previously unimagined sources and blend it with new learning to form a deeper understanding

bit.ly/46wpUk5

Essential Question

Where can Prior Knowledge come from?

Big Idea

It's important to recall prior knowledge before beginning to learn new information about a subject, because it helps you link the old with the new, and ultimately, synthesize it all into a new, deeper understanding.

Lesson Overview

In this lesson, students learn that we "collect" knowledge from multiple sources over time. Each of those sources are synthesized to form what we call our "Background Knowledge." So that students don't think that all of our background knowledge comes from school lessons, it's important to identify other sources information can come from. These sources include experiences we've had, lessons learned in school and at home, things that we've read, videos that we've watched, things people have told us, and lots more! Not all of this information is accurate, however, so we need to be willing to allow new information to replace incorrect prior knowledge when it's clear that we've had the wrong information in the past.

Discussion/Reflection Questions

- Why is it important to know that information is learned from different sources?
- What is one source of information that you never realized was actually a source of information? If none, name one that might be a surprise to others.
- How can you encourage others to learn information from sources outside of their comfort zone?

Teacher Tips

- On today's Student Handout, students will be imagining that they are about to purchase a big cost item. Depending on the age of your students, this can be anything from a gaming system to a car! The key is that they have SOME knowledge about their item, but don't know EVERYTHING about it. You may want to brainstorm some items that your students might be interested in saving for prior to teaching this lesson (to provide them with some options if they can't think of anything themselves).
- "Prior Knowledge" is defined as: "Everything that you THINK you already know about a subject." Make sure that students understand that some of it may be incorrect, however, and it will be their job to try to "filter out" the incorrect prior knowledge BEFORE synthesizing it into their new learning.
- The final task that students complete on the Student Handouts asks them: "Based on your prior knowledge that you listed above, what new information do you still need in order to make an informed decision on your purchase? Describe that here:"
  - Please make the connection between Prior Knowledge and New Learning. They have activated their prior knowledge and are planning to gather the new information that will help them synthesize the information to make an informed decision.

Student Tasks 〉 Transfer Goals

Student Tasks	Transfer Goals
Students learn that their background knowledge comes from multiple sources.	Students realize that we don't just learn in school, but all throughout life, and use this understanding to synthesize information from other sources.
Students list where each piece of background knowledge came from about an upcoming purchase they hope to make.	When students synthesize information in the future, they will consider ALL sources of information, not just the obvious ones.

INTRODUCTION

PLANNING

METACOGNITION

SYNTHESIS

REFLECTION

SELF-ASSESSMENT

GOAL SETTING

FEEDBACK

Instructional Poster(s)

- This lesson has ONE Instructional Poster.
- This lesson's Instructional Poster identifies five sources that Prior Knowledge can come from. It asks students to come up with more. If you brainstorm these as a class, be sure to write down what the students (and teacher) come up with so they can refer to the list of resources when needed.
- Many additional sources of Prior Knowledge may be specific to your classroom situation (textbook, experts, reference materials, etc.). Be sure to think through those, as well as materials that may be more universal.

Student Handouts

- This lesson has TWO Student Handouts.
- DIRECTIONS: Imagine that you are about to make a BIG purchase of some sort. Maybe it's a new game system or maybe a used car! Choose something that you know a little bit about, but not everything. Then, answer the questions on this page and the next.
- You may want to spend a few minutes as a class brainstorming ideas for small, medium and large purchases. Students should select something that they know a little about, but not everything.
- You may want to offer a few sample subjects for your students to focus on for these two pages in case they can't come up with something on their own.
- If students can't think of an example of Prior Knowledge for each category, allow students to "invent" something that would be possible. This way, students have the experience of brainstorming ideas for each category for future experiences.
- The final box can be a general paragraph describing information still needed, or a bulleted list.

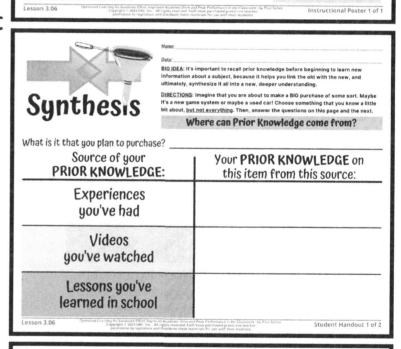

bit.ly/3N1deuI

Dig deep into your memory to activate prior knowledge and past experiences to spark connections with new learning

3.07

Essential Question

How do I activate my Prior Knowledge?

Big Idea

In order to SYNTHESIZE new learning, we need to first activate our prior knowledge, which means recalling what we already know about a subject that we are beginning to learn. Some ways that we can activate our prior knowledge include thinking about what we think we already know, recalling any ideas that we've heard about but never experienced, and remembering the experiences that we've had with it.

Lesson Overview

In this lesson, students consider additional ways of activating background knowledge outside of "What do you think you already know about..." The types of organizer you choose to use with your students depends on their grade level, what kind of background knowledge they are activating, and how much time you can provide for this portion of an activity. For this lesson, you will choose one organizer to go with the Instructional Poster and the first Student Handout. You may choose to use the other organizers immediately, or down the line.

Discussion/Reflection Questions

- Why is it valuable to take time to activate your prior knowledge before learning new information on a subject?
- What method works best for you to activate your prior knowledge? Do you prefer to be asked questions that focus your thinking? Brainstorm all you know about a subject? etc.
- If you don't access your prior knowledge before beginning to learn about a tough subject, what might happen?

Teacher Tips

- Think of some examples that you can share with your students about when you did and did not activate prior knowledge before learning new information. These can be real or made up. The idea is to help your students understand that activating prior knowledge helps make connections between prior knowledge and new learning. These connections help create new understanding (synthesis) as well as improve retention of information.
- You can do this lesson with just the Instructional Poster and the first Student Handout. It's not required to include a second Student Handout if you don't see the need for it. Additionally, since there are multiple organizers you can choose from for the second Student Handout, you may wish to return to this lesson whenever you want your students to activate prior knowledge formally (on paper) instead of informally (in their heads).
- If you do choose to use a second Student Handout with this lesson, you will need to select an academic lesson to connect it to (or help your students select one that will work).

Student Tasks 〉 Transfer Goals

| Students learn what it means to activate their prior knowledge. | Students see the value of activating prior knowledge and attempt to do so before new learning. |
| Students practice activating their prior knowledge before learning new information on a topic. | Students independently activate prior knowledge before learning new information. |

Instructional Poster(s)

- This lesson has ONE Instructional Poster.
- Read through the dialogue on the Instructional Poster for this lesson. It demonstrates the basic idea behind "Activating Prior Knowledge."
- Explain to students that when we take the time to activate our prior knowledge before learning new information, we make stronger connections between old and new information. These connections make our learning more understandable and longer lasting. It also increases our awareness of when we are confused or need more information in order to get a complete understanding.

Student Handouts

- This lesson has <u>SEVEN</u> Student Handouts. You do NOT need to use all seven! Activating Prior Knowledge can happen in many different ways, so several graphic organizers have been provided so you can choose which one(s) you'd like to use with your students. Here are the types:
  - Concept Map,
  - Anticipatory Guide,
  - KWM Chart,
  - Brainstorm List,
  - Hot Potato, and
  - some simplified graphic organizers that can be used in almost any situation.
- DIRECTIONS: Complete the organizer or activity on the next page first, Then, add items to each of the boxes below to activate your prior knowledge for the current assignment or unit you're working on in class.
- The first Student Handout is a type of organizer that has no name. It could be called a "KHE Organizer" because it asks: "What do you think you <u>K</u>now already?" "What have you <u>H</u>eard about, but aren't sure about?" and "What <u>E</u>xperiences have you had?"
- The example shown for the second Student Handout is a KWM Chart (What do I think I already <u>K</u>now? What do I <u>W</u>ant to learn? What are some common <u>M</u>isconceptions people might have about this topic?).
- Feel free to select the graphic organizer(s) that best align with the activity you are integrating. Choose the ones that best meet your needs.

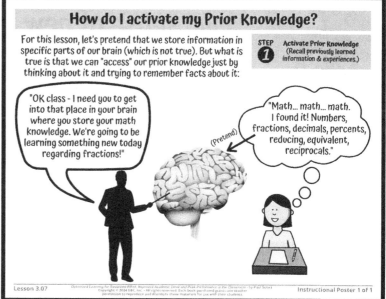

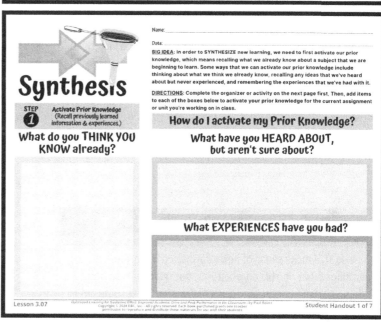

bit.ly/3N0325x

Make sense of new information through critical thinking and analysis, unlocking the secrets of true understanding

Essential Question

How do I make sense of the new information I've collected?

Big Idea

There are lots of ways we can make sense of new information and lots of strategies we can use to improve learning.

Lesson Overview

In this lesson, students move on from Step 1 - "Prior Knowledge" and move into Step 2 - "New Learning." The actual act of collecting new information is NOT a lesson in this unit, because that is what students do all day, every day and would be too large to include in this curriculum. However, making sense of the new information students have just collected IS addressed in this unit, and the future lessons continue to help students with the rest of the learning process.

Discussion/Reflection Questions

- Why is it important that we slow ourselves down WHILE learning new information? Why should we think about our prior knowledge on a subject WHILE we learn?
- What tips did you connect most strongly with? What tips would you add to the lesson?
- How would you help a student who feels overwhelmed in class when learning a new subject? What advice would you give them?

Teacher Tips

- How do YOU make sense of new information when you are learning? What do YOU do when you zone out while reading? When you don't understand a word? When you feel confused or overwhelmed? What do you do when you are learning from a master at her craft and you have no idea what she's talking about? When a salesman is bombarding you with details you don't understand? When you go to the closing on your newly purchased home and you're signing papers you have no idea about? These are the kinds of tips your students need to learn. They need to know how they are supposed to feel, what they're supposed to say, and how they're supposed to learn what they need to learn. You are the lesson! Not these student handouts!

Student Tasks 〉 Transfer Goals

Student Tasks	Transfer Goals
Students learn tips for making sense of new information before, during, and after learning.	Students use each of the tips in class over time in order to make sense of new information.
Students explain, in their own words, WHY each tip that is provided can help us make sense of new information.	Students understand the value of each tip provided and independently utilize each tip as needed.

INTRODUCTION

PLANNING

METACOGNITION

SYNTHESIS

REFLECTION

SELF-ASSESSMENT

GOAL SETTING

FEEDBACK

Instructional Poster(s)

- This lesson has TWO Instructional Posters.
- The Instructional Posters (there are two) for this lesson provide students with tips for making sense of new information. It's not enough for students to "go through the motions" of learning without being cognizant of their metacognition and level of understanding. These posters provide helpful tips and encourage a healthy conversation on the students' role before, during, and after learning. I encourage you to lead that conversation and add your own tips as you think of them. Remind students of the importance of "processing" what they read or listen to, ask questions when they don't understand, and take notes when the amount of information exceeds what they can hold in their short-term memory.

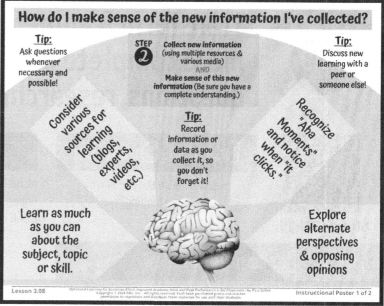

Student Handouts

- This lesson has TWO Student Handouts.
- DIRECTIONS: For every strategy listed below and on the next page, explain WHY it can help us make sense of the new information we collect. If you really aren't sure, describe your plan for using it in the coming weeks.
- This lesson's Student Handouts are more time-consuming than most others. Students are asked to explain WHY each tip helps us make sense of new information we are learning. If your students need you to cut it down some, please do so. You could definitely go over a few together as a class and not require students to write the answers in, or you could copy the sheets with some answers complete already. One example has already been provided.
- Some answers may not be obvious for your students. You may wish to chat about these before having the students complete the assignment independently.

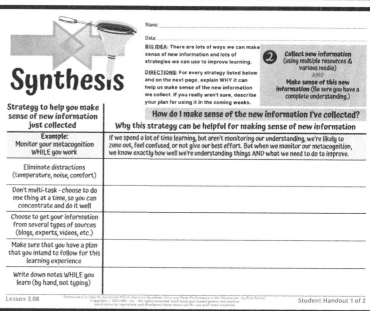

bit.ly/47Usj9r

3.09 Transform fragmented knowledge into a more complete understanding by asking questions, researching, and inferring

Essential Question

How can I fill in the GAPS in my understanding?.

Big Idea

Although we will never know everything about a subject, it's important to fill in the gaps in our understanding so that we have as much information as possible.

Lesson Overview

In this lesson, students dive further into understanding the new information that they are learning, but instead of focusing on comprehension of that new information, they now identify which bits of information they might be missing in order to have a more complete picture? Are there other sides to the story? Do we understand each step in the process? etc. Students focus on three main strategies to fill in those gaps: (1) Research it, (2) Ask an expert, and (3) Make an inference.

Discussion/Reflection Questions

- Why is it important to try to fill in the gaps in our understanding?
- Describe an experience where you just accepted the fact that you didn't understand something. You didn't ask anyone, didn't look it up, and didn't even make an inference - you just accepted that you didn't understand it. Did it have a negative consequence, or did it work out because it wasn't vital?
- What should we do when we're in a situation where EVERYTHING is confusing? What has worked in the past?

Teacher Tips

- Once again, personal stories and connections are worthwhile here. What have you done to fill in the gaps in your understanding? Who have you gone to in order to understand something better? What resources do you use when you are confused? Share these things with your students - they need to know that even intelligent adults have gaps in their understanding that need to be filled.
- The method(s) we use in order to "fill our gaps in understanding" depends on the type of learning we are doing. If students wanted to know the percentage of students at their school who own at least one pet, this would require a survey or questionnaire. If they wanted to know which seed grows tallest in the dark, they would need to experiment. Point this out to the students, so they understand that: (1) not everything is researchable, (2) not everything is already known, (3) there aren't experts for every question (YET), etc.

Student Tasks 〉 Transfer Goals

Student Tasks	Transfer Goals
Students learn to recognize when they have gaps in their understanding so they can be "filled."	Students use this awareness to pause and take a moment to fill in the gaps in their understanding.
Students learn three (and possibly more) strategies for filling in the gaps in their understanding.	Students use these strategies independently when needed to fill the gaps in their understanding.

Instructional Poster(s)

- This lesson has ONE Instructional Poster.
- For this lesson's Instructional Poster, students learn the purpose of filling in the gaps in our understanding, and learn three strategies for doing so: (1) Research it, (2) Ask an expert, and (3) Make an inference.
- Encourage students to brainstorm other ways to fill in their gaps in understanding (e.g. experimenting, surveying, polling). Develop these ideas further if they apply well to their situation. If you have any additional strategies, share those too.
- The key here is ensuring that your students know that it is their responsibility to identify gaps in their understanding and do what is needed to fill those gaps independently. NOT to expect adults to do it for them.

Student Handouts

- This lesson has TWO Student Handouts.
- DIRECTIONS: Answer each question on this page and the next as completely as possible.
- On the first Student Handout, students are asked to answer an essay-type question. If your students are too young for the question (about looking information up online), feel free to modify the question to suit your needs.
- On the second Student Handout, there are two more essay-style questions, focusing on asking an expert questions and making an inference to fill the gaps. Please let your students know that an expert is really anyone who knows more about a topic than we do ourselves. And we make inferences to fill gaps whenever the information is NOT vital or NOT easily obtainable. But inferences are unconfirmed, so they need to be noted in presentations or essays.

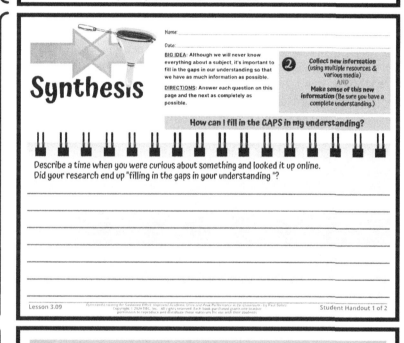

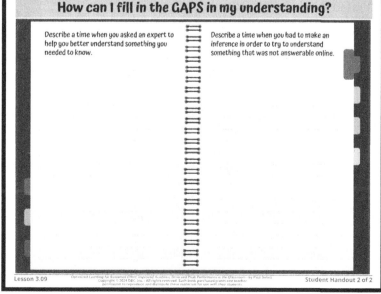

INTRODUCTION

PLANNING

METACOGNITION

SYNTHESIS

REFLECTION

SELF-ASSESSMENT

GOAL SETTING

FEEDBACK

bit.ly/47ziNsq

Make connections between pieces of information to strengthen your understanding of each part, as well as the whole

Essential Question

Can I find connections between pieces of my knowledge?

Big Idea

When we discover connections within information, we're able to synthesize it to create a clearer understanding.

Lesson Overview

In this lesson, students learn the importance of making connections between pieces of information. How do they relate? How does what I already know fit in with what I am learning today? These connections strengthen our understanding of old and new information as they are tied together and patterns start to form. Although this lesson included eight total Student Handouts, none of them are prerequisites for future lessons and can be skipped, or just one set of two can be chosen. Students focus on four sample strategies in this lesson to make connections between information: (1) Cause & Effect, (2) Problem-Solution, (3) Classification, and (4) Compare & Contrast.

Discussion/Reflection Questions

- Why is it beneficial to find connections between information? (Provide at least two sentences for this answer, please.)
- Using one of the four ways to connect information from this lesson, share a connection that hasn't already been discussed that connects new learning with other new learning OR with prior knowledge.
- How will you train yourself to FIND these connections in your learning? Your teacher won't point them out to you, so you need to do it independently to experience the benefits.

Teacher Tips

- For this lesson, you will need to choose an academic lesson to connect the Student Handout to. You need a lesson where students are learning information that can be connected in some way. The four choices include: Cause and Effect, Problem-Solution, Compare-Contrast, and Classification.
- This lesson includes four strategies for finding connections between information, but there are more that are not included.
  - One strategy you could focus on during this lesson might include Sequencing:
    - How do all of the pieces of my knowledge on this subject fit onto a timeline?
    - What happened first, second, third...?
    - In what order did the events take place?
  - Another strategy you could focus on during this lesson might include Making Personal Connections:
    - How does the information you are currently learning connect with a past experience of yours?
    - What does this concept or fact make you think of?
    - How can you empathize with this person or group of people? What experience might you have to compare it with?

Student Tasks 〉 Transfer Goals

Student Tasks	Transfer Goals
Students learn about the value of connecting pieces of information in meaningful ways and how to make those connections while learning.	Students identify connections in the information they are learning, independently.
Students practice making connections with each of the four sample strategies provided in this lesson.	Students use the connections that they've identified in their learning to make stronger meaning.

INTRODUCTION
PLANNING
METACOGNITION
SYNTHESIS
REFLECTION
SELF-ASSESSMENT
GOAL SETTING
FEEDBACK

Instructional Poster(s)

- This lesson has ONE Instructional Poster.
- On this Instructional Poster, students learn that there are many ways to connect pieces of knowledge, and that these connections can lead to a deeper understanding of what they're learning about. As you go over the four sample ways to connect information with the class, be sure to give any examples that you can think of that might apply.
- Although students are NOT likely to completely understand how connections help them synthesize information based on this Instructional Poster alone, the supporting Student Handouts should help them see the benefits.

Student Handouts

- This lesson has **EIGHT** Student Handouts. You do NOT need to use all eight! Finding connections between pieces of information can be done in many different ways, so several graphic organizers have been provided so you can choose which one(s) you'd like to use with your students. Here are the four types:
  - Cause and Effect Organizer,
  - Problem-Solution Organizer,
  - Compare-Contrast Organizer, and a
  - Classification Organizer.
- The first Student Handout and second Student Handout need to match, so be sure to choose the correct pairs.
- DIRECTIONS: Read the explanation in the box below. Then, read the example to see if you understand. Finally, complete the activity on the next page using information that you need to synthesize in class.
- The Student Handout shown here is Cause & Effect, but there are also three others that support the other three examples of connection from the Instructional Poster. A simple example is provided on the first Student Handout and a graphic organizer is provided on the second Student Handout.
- It would be very valuable if you could assign each of the Student Handouts to the class when they are about to learn something that allows them to fill it out immediately. If not, you can also find picture story books that have the element in them, or current events, etc.

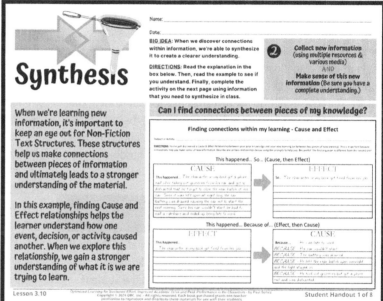

bit.ly/3sTFOrc

Move from "I understand" to "I can explain" by clearly articulating your synthesis in your own words

3.11

Essential Question

How COMPLETE is my understanding of this information?

Big Idea

A synthesis of information can only be considered complete when it can be put into your own words successfully.

Lesson Overview

In this lesson, students learn a simple structure for describing their synthesis of a topic. They learn to write or verbally explain, "Before today's activity... After today's activity... Now that I've combined all of my knowledge..." or some variation of those sentence starters. The idea is to consider what was known before today's activity, what was learned during today's activity, and how your knowledge or understanding has improved in some way because of today's activity. You have the flexibility to modify that format to meet the needs of your group of students. This is considered the last "hurdle" when trying to decide if you have a strong understanding of a topic or not. The prior two lessons describe the first two hurdles.

Discussion/Reflection Questions

- Why is a "Synthesis Summary" a good way to assess how well you've synthesized your new learning with your prior knowledge?
- Consider a skill that you are really good at (maybe a sport, hobby, activity or video game). How might you describe your synthesis of that skill when you were just beginning?
- If someone did not learn anything new from an activity, what would their "Synthesis Summary" include in it? Do we have to learn something new in order to synthesize information?

Teacher Tips

- This lesson needs to be completed immediately after students learn about a topic in which they had some background knowledge, but not much. My example topic on the Student Handouts is "Dreams." Students might read an article, watch an educational show, listen to a lecture, or complete research on a topic of their own choosing. You decide what works for your students and what makes sense for your class.
- Make sure that students read through the entire example on Student Handout #1. If you don't believe they will do so, please read it aloud to the class and discuss the format, so students can create a "Synthesis Summary" using a similar format, or one that you describe to them.
- If writing isn't easy for your students, consider allowing them to do this assignment as a video recording or one-on-one with others. The "Synthesis Summary" model is easily modified to work in different formats.

Student Tasks ⟩ Transfer Goals

Student Tasks	Transfer Goals
Students learn that they are not done learning about a topic until they can describe their synthesis of that topic.	Students use this new awareness to keep working if they don't understand a topic completely.
Students learn how to write a "Synthesis Summary" to describe how their understanding of a topic has improved.	Students use the structure of the "Synthesis Summary" to mentally determine their new level of understanding on a topic.

INTRODUCTION

PLANNING

METACOGNITION

SYNTHESIS

REFLECTION

SELF-ASSESSMENT

GOAL SETTING

FEEDBACK

Instructional Poster(s)

- This lesson has ONE Instructional Poster.
- The Instructional Poster for this lesson shows three ways that we can make our understanding of information more complete. The prior two lessons focused in on finding connections or relationships between parts of your knowledge and filling in the gaps in our understanding. This lesson adds a third component that focuses in on being able to EXPLAIN your new, deeper understanding. If a student can't explain it, they might have gaps or misunderstandings in their knowledge.
- Obviously, our learning is NEVER "complete," but are there any other ways we can determine if we have a relatively "complete" understanding of a topic, rather than a skewed or impartial understanding? If so, add them to the class discussion.

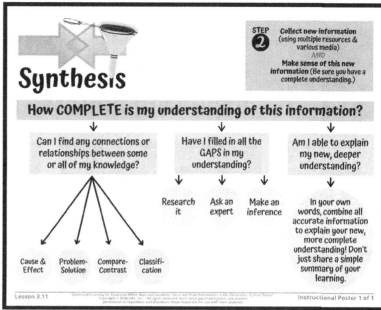

Student Handouts

- This lesson has THREE Student Handouts.
- DIRECTIONS: Read the tips below. Implement as many of those tips as you can while learning new information. Transfer those strategies to new situations in the future, so that these strategies become a vital part of how you learn.
- The first Student Handout gives an example of a student putting their new learning into their own words. It provides a simple structure for what they will need to do on the next Student Handout. I recommend:
  - Before today's activity...
  - After today's activity...
  - Now that I've combined all of my knowledge...
- On the second page, students need to write their own Synthesis Summary based on something they just learned in your class.
- The third Student Handout is an exemplar of the second Student Handout.

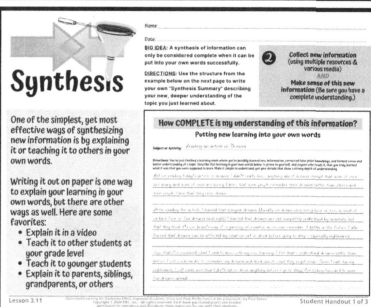

Become a critical inquirer by challenging assumptions, questioning information, exploring doubts, and finding the truth

3.12

bit.ly/411nt7Z

Essential Question

How do I question what I've learned & think I know?

Big Idea

Not everything you read about, learn about, or get told about is correct, so it's important that you question what you've learned and what you think you know.

Lesson Overview

In this lesson, students learn to question what they believe they already know and what they are learning. They are provided five questions they can ask themselves that will help them discover concepts or ideas that they never really doubted before. They explore these doubts, as well as contradictions, disagreements among experts, false assumptions, and confusions to try to find the truth. They do this by locating two or more trusted sources that verify what they now believe to be true. The goal is to improve our students' Media Literacy skills and develop more discriminating learners.

Discussion/Reflection Questions

- Why is it important to doubt the truth of new information if it doesn't sound convincing or if experts disagree?
- What can you do when you try to find evidence to support a claim, but little to no evidence exists?
- How will you make sure to keep an open mind when learning new information so you don't let your prior knowledge (which may be incorrect) dominate over new information (which may be correct)?

Teacher Tips

- This lesson needs to be completed immediately after students learn about a topic in which they had some background knowledge. If you can choose a topic where they might have incorrect prior knowledge, that would be excellent. You could also provide students with incorrect information that is believable to see if they doubt it and try to find evidence that supports or refutes it. The "The Pacific Northwest tree octopus" comes to mind as a potential topic.
- Most students will automatically trust their prior knowledge over new learning despite finding evidence that refutes that fact. You need to explain this to the class and help them keep an open mind while learning, trust facts found from reputable sources, and be willing to look at something in a new way.
- Students will likely need access to technology for this lesson in order to find trusted sources to confirm or deny claims.

Student Tasks 〉 Transfer Goals

Student Tasks	Transfer Goals
Students learn to question what they think they know and what they are learning about.	Students become discriminating learners who don't blindly believe everything people tell them.
Students locate evidence to support claims that they believe in order to ensure their accuracy.	Students don't accept false claims - they search for evidence to confirm or deny the truth of an issue.

Instructional Poster(s)

- This lesson has ONE Instructional Poster.
- In this Instructional Poster, students learn how to question what they know and are learning. Media Literacy is such an important skill these days considering the amount of false information that exists in our world. Teaching students to question what they think they know and what they are learning about will lead them to become more discriminating learners.
- I've provided five questions that students should get into the habit of asking themselves while they learn new information. Can you think of any others to add to the list?
- Whenever students recognizes a contradiction, false assumption, confusion, or disagreement, they need to find EVIDENCE to support their understanding (preferably two or more trusted sources). Despite all of these efforts, students still might not find the truth & need to understand that this is today's reality. We need to develop & use keen judgment to determine fact vs. fiction.

Student Handouts

- This lesson has TWO Student Handouts.
- DIRECTIONS: Do your best to answer as many questions below as you can based on today's learning (not all are required). Then, complete the next page.
- The first Student Handout gives students an opportunity to answer four of the five questions from the Instructional Poster on paper about a topic they just learned about in your class.
- The second Student Handout gives students practice finding two trusted sources to prove or disprove facts while learning. Try not to skip this activity - It's very beneficial!

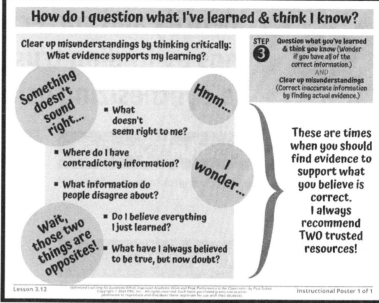

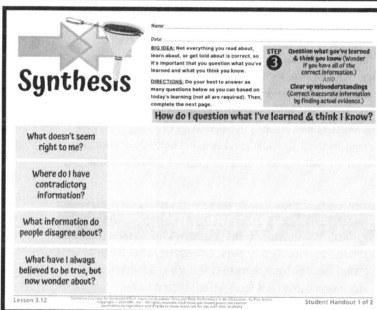

INTRODUCTION

PLANNING

METACOGNITION

SYNTHESIS

REFLECTION

SELF-ASSESSMENT

GOAL SETTING

FEEDBACK

bit.ly/3T0z4Ci

Identify and correct your misunderstandings by finding trustworthy evidence and re-synthesizing using correct facts

Essential Question

How do I clear up my misunderstandings?

Big Idea

One goal of synthesis is to discover & eliminate incorrect prior knowledge and replace it with correct information based on evidence from reliable sources.

Lesson Overview

In this lesson, students learn a simple process for identifying misunderstandings and working toward correcting those misunderstandings. First, students question what they think they know, believe, or are learning. (This was taught last lesson.). Then, identify the misunderstanding. Use a strategy to correct it (i.e. research it, ask an expert, or make an inference). And finally, synthesize the new, correct information with everything else they believe to be true. Students then practice identifying misunderstandings in their prior knowledge of a subject they are learning in school, by finding evidence that supports or disproves their prior knowledge and citing the source of the information.

Discussion/Reflection Questions

- Why should we take the time to clear up our misunderstandings?
- What negative consequences could happen if we don't clear up our misunderstandings in areas that are important like purchasing a new car, operating on a patient, or getting a new job?
- How will you ensure that you discover your misconceptions before they become a problem? What actions will you take?

Teacher Tips

- This lesson works best if taught immediately after the prior lesson, "How do I question what I've learned & think I know?"
- This lesson doesn't just focus on "misunderstandings" but it also helps students correct "false understandings" or incorrect information. Rather than focus on the semantics, this book chooses to call them all "misunderstandings."
- Connect this lesson with something students are learning about in class or personal research projects.

Student Tasks 〉 Transfer Goals

Student Tasks	Transfer Goals
Students learn four basic steps for identifying misconceptions in our prior knowledge and correcting those.	Students use the four steps to clear up misunderstandings in important, real life situations.
Students find evidence to support or disprove prior knowledge and cite sources for this evidence.	Students rely on evidence more than hearsay or hunches when making important decisions in life.

INTRODUCTION

PLANNING

METACOGNITION

SYNTHESIS

REFLECTION

SELF-ASSESSMENT

GOAL SETTING

FEEDBACK

Instructional Poster(s)

- This lesson has ONE Instructional Poster.
- Use this Instructional Poster to discuss with your students that SOME of the things we believe to be true are actually NOT true, and some of the things we read or learn about are also NOT true. It's up to US to identify our misunderstandings and correct them.
- Students should follow these steps to clear up misunderstandings:
  a. Question what you think you know, believe, or are learning. (This was taught last lesson.)
  b. Identify the misunderstanding.
  c. Use a strategy to correct it (i.e. research it, ask an expert, or make an inference).
  d. Synthesize the new, correct information with everything else you believe to be true.

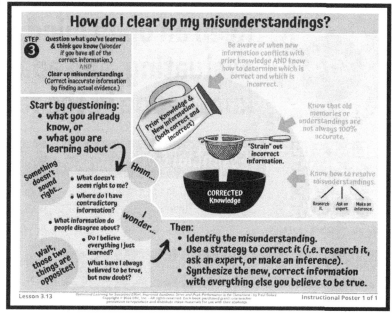

Student Handouts

- This lesson has TWO Student Handouts.
- DIRECTIONS: Brainstorm three things you thought you knew about the topic you're studying in class (at least one should be a misunderstanding). Enter those in each Prior Knowledge box on this page and the next. Then, fill in the remaining boxes based on what the headers ask for.
- On this lesson's Student Handout, students are asked to identify three pieces of prior knowledge about the subject they are learning about in class (with at least one that is incorrect in some way). They need to find evidence that, proves or disproved each piece of prior knowledge, and informally cite their source. Feel free to modify the directions to meet the needs of your students.

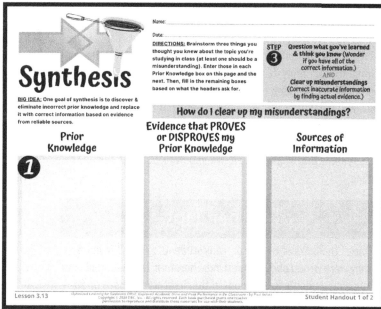

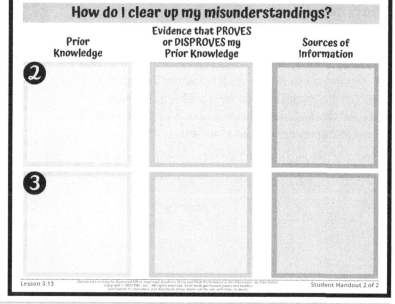

bit.ly/3SXUG2n

Keep an open mind by challenging, re-evaluating, and adapting your prior knowledge in the face of new evidence

Essential Question

How do I keep an open mind while learning?

Big Idea

Sometimes, we are so confident in our background knowledge that we ignore all new information that contradicts what we think we know. Prior knowledge can be hard to replace because it requires admitting that we had it wrong before, but keeping an open mind while learning allows us to fix incorrect prior knowledge and learn new information.

Lesson Overview

In this lesson, students learn ways to keep an open mind while learning. This is similar to the prior lessons in that students should allow new information that has evidence to replace old, prior knowledge that lacks evidence if it seems plausible. Students look for bits of information in their learning that make them: (1) change their mind completely, (2) question what they thought they knew, (3) made them wonder if they need more information, (4) confirm what they already knew, and (5) feel stronger about their level of understanding. The goal of the lesson is to try to help students realize that prior knowledge can be hard to replace because it requires admitting that we had it wrong before, but that it needs to be done.

Discussion / Reflection Questions

- Why is it hard for some people to keep an open mind while learning? What is it that makes them disagree with new (sometimes contradicting) information?
- What are the benefits of keeping an open mind while learning? Why should we allow ourselves to learn different perspectives & new (sometimes contradicting) information?
- What potential drawbacks are there to keeping an open mind while learning? How can keeping on open mind while learning actually cause us trouble?

Teacher Tips

- One of the hardest things for many students to admit is when they were wrong about something. Therefore, I recommend only allowing students to circle one of the first three options on the first Student Handout (don't allow the last two). The first three options involve some level of changing what they believe to be true in their minds, whereas the last two options reinforce prior knowledge. As it stands, the directions printed on the page allows students to choose any of the five options.
- You may need to clarify the middle option on the Instructional Poster for your students. "...made me wonder if I needed more information" means that you have conflicting information
- Students are encouraged to use their own "sentence starter" if none of the provided ones work for them.

Student Tasks 〉 Transfer Goals

Student Tasks	Transfer Goals
Students learn to identify portions of a lesson that proves or disproves their prior knowledge.	Students notice when new information confirms or contradicts prior knowledge and use that evidence to clarify their understanding.
Students learn to describe how new evidence changes their thinking about a topic or idea.	Students use their evidence to create a new, more accurate understanding of information.

INTRODUCTION

PLANNING

METACOGNITION

SYNTHESIS

REFLECTION

SELF-ASSESSMENT

GOAL SETTING

FEEDBACK

Instructional Poster(s)

- This lesson has TWO Instructional Posters.
- Use the first Instructional Poster to help students keep an open mind while learning. The prior lessons taught students to "doubt" what they already know and are currently learning in order to find evidence that supports each claim. This lesson asks students to consider new information that may disprove prior knowledge or might even conflict with something they are currently learning (there are often two or more sides for each issue!).
- Students are asked to be aware of supporting information and conflicting information while learning something in class. Based on that information, students need to THINK or FEEL something about its impact on their understanding of the topic.
- Read through the example at the bottom of the Instructional Poster to show students how their reflection might sound once it's completed.
- On the second Instructional Poster, students learn nine tips for keeping an open mind while they learn. They will receive nine MORE tips on the third Student Handout.

Student Handouts

- This lesson has TWO Student Handouts.
- DIRECTIONS: Start at the top of this page and circle one of the five choices that best matches your experience. Then, circle the reflection prompt directly below your first circle and continue writing it in the lined space below.
- In a perfect world, students would identify one of EACH of the five possible sentence starters on the first Student Handout, but that would be difficult to do, so students are asked to find one and explain it well.
- On the second Student Handout, they are given nine more tips for keeping an open mind while they learn. These can be assigned to be read, or read aloud as a class and discussed.

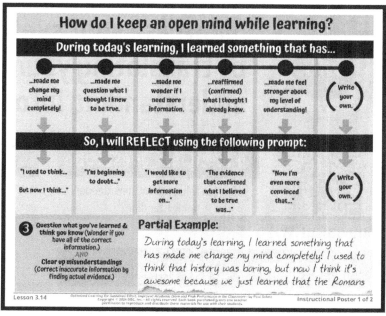

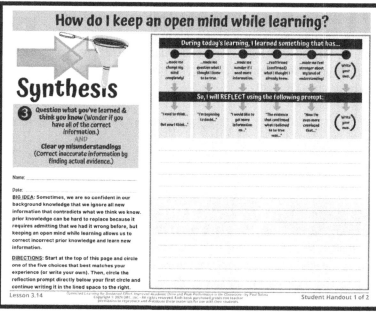

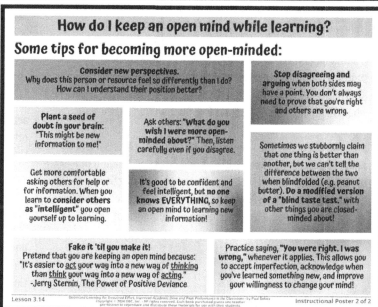

bit.ly/3GkKWrj

Showcase your synthesis for all to see by translating your inner understanding into a tangible product

Essential Question

How can I show off my new, deeper understanding?

Big Idea

Making our thinking visible for ourself and others is important when we synthesize information, and there are many unique ways we can display our new understanding tangibly.

Lesson Overview

In this lesson, students discover myriad ways they can display their thinking visibly for themself and others. It's one thing to synthesize information in our heads, but it's another to be able to understand that new thinking deeply enough to be able to explain it or show it to others. This lesson includes four possible routes that teachers can use to get their students to display their thinking - choose your favorite or share them all!

Discussion/Reflection Questions

- Why should we take the time to make our thinking "visible" for ourself and others? What benefits can YOU get from doing this? What benefits can our teacher get from us doing this?
- What are some additional ways you'd like to use to show off your new, deeper understanding?
- Your teacher won't always ask you to complete a product or take a test to check your understanding of a topic, so how will YOU make sure that your teacher sees that you have synthesized information and have a deeper understanding?

Teacher Tips

- Definitely look at each of the eight Student Handouts prior to teaching this lesson. You might want to use one set of strategies or several. If you want to use several, decide how many class periods you'll need and the order you choose to teach them.
- Each of these activities require a curricular connection - they should be used as a way for students to demonstrate their new understanding of a topic that they've recently learned about. A traditional test is ONE way that students can show their synthesis of information, but these lessons offer several alternatives that may provide similar information to the teacher, while being more enjoyable and less stress-inducing for your students.
- Don't forget about the value of having students record a video or audio describing their synthesis or new understanding of a topic. Our rule was ONE TAKE no matter what distractions happened or errors were made - students just needed to correct and move on. No time limit was given so students got really deep!

Student Tasks ⟩ Transfer Goals

Student Tasks	Transfer Goals
Students complete one or more synthesis activities that show others their new, deeper thinking.	Students gain a stronger awareness of how their understanding of a topic improves over time & uses this awareness to continually learn & improve.
In order to complete these activities, students must understand how their thinking has changed over time.	Students use their heightened awareness of their synthesis to recognize how their learning activities are helping them improve their understanding.

Instructional Poster(s)

- This lesson has ONE Instructional Poster.
- The Instructional Poster for this lesson reminds students of our metaphor for synthesis (pouring water through a sieve into a bowl) and reminds them what each step of the metaphor stands for. It also reviews the definition of synthesis, as described in this book. The reason there is no new information in this image is because students will be learning between one and four graphic organizers in their Student Handouts (Teacher's choice).
- It's recommended to review this Instructional Poster with the class, but also show students how you might fill out the graphic organizer(s) for the lesson.

Student Handouts

- This lesson has <u>EIGHT</u> Student Handouts. You do NOT need to use all eight! Showing off our new, deeper understanding can be done in many different ways, so several graphic organizers have been provided so you can choose which one(s) you'd like to use with your students. Here are the four types:
  - A Sunrise Organizer (as seen on the right),
  - An Evidence of Synthesis Chart (which takes students through the four identified steps of synthesis, as explained in this book),
  - A list of 38 possible Synthesis Products that students can create to show their thinking, and
  - A list of 11 Synthesis Question Stems that can help students put their thinking into words.
- The first and second Student Handouts need to match, so be sure to choose the correct pairs.
- DIRECTIONS: In the graphic organizer on the next page, write four bits of prior knowledge in the boxes on the left, four bits of new information in the boxes on the right, and then summarize your synthesis of your learning in the shape in the center of the page. An example has been provided for you below.
- It would be very valuable if you could assign each of the Student Handouts to the class when they are about to learn something that allows them to fill it out immediately. If not, you can also find picture story books that have the element in them, or current events, etc.

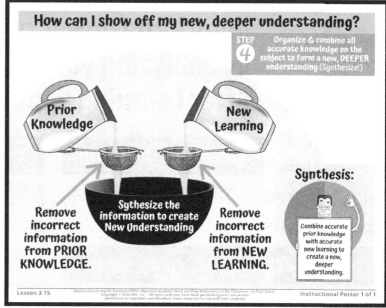

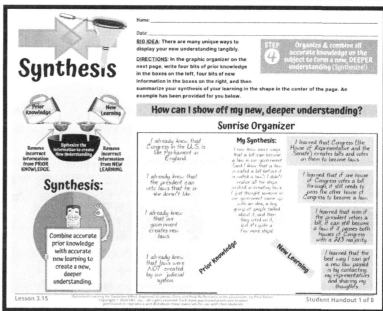

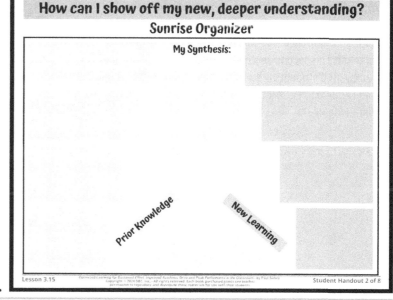

bit.ly/3GqlnVG

Unlock the power of the KWHLCQ Chart by analyzing your Before, During and After Learning Experiences

Essential Question

How can a KWHLCQ Chart explain my Learning Story?

Big Idea

A KWHLCQ Chart helps you track your Learning Story by including notes from BEFORE you started learning, DURING the learning, and even AFTER the learning has ended.

Lesson Overview

In this lesson, students complete a KWHLCQ Chart before, during, and after learning about a topic in class. This works well with an independent research project that the student has little background knowledge on. Prior to learning about the topic, students share what they believe they already know about the topic, what they hope to learn, and how they plan to learn it (if the teacher requires a specific resource, this step loses its effectiveness). As they learn, students should be thinking about how their prior knowledge is either confirmed or disputed by their new learning. And after learning, students describe what they learned, what wrong information was corrected, and any new questions they have about the topic.

Discussion/Reflection Questions

- The first three questions in the KWHLCQ Chart focused on "Before Learning" strategies like recalling prior knowledge, setting a purpose for learning, and having a plan. The second three letters focused on "After Learning" strategies like evaluating and summarizing new learning, correcting false information, and extending your learning. Describe what you were doing WHILE you were learning. In order to successfully complete this KWHLCQ Chart, you had to do several things WHILE you learned new information today. Reflect on the experience and describe what you did.

Teacher Tips

- Have a curricular lesson in mind to connect with this lesson.
- If possible, let students choose HOW they plan to learn about the topic (maybe research, experimenting, surveying, observing, etc.). Try not to provide hints to guide them at first, but definitely point out good ideas before the end of the lesson.
- Within each section of the organizer, encourage your students to "Tell Me More." In our classroom, that means writing at least one additional sentence after the first (usually more generic) sentence. This second sentence is where the real information is usually at! If students are writing ideas using bullets, it might mean adding one sub-bullet to each idea and then having fewer overall ideas.

Student Tasks 〉 Transfer Goals

Student Tasks	Transfer Goals
Students practiced "Before Learning" strategies like recalling prior information, setting a purpose for learning, and having a plan.	Students recall prior knowledge, set a purpose for learning, and create a plan prior to learning information in other areas of their life.
Students practiced "After Learning" strategies like evaluating & summarizing new learning, correcting false information, and extending their learning.	Students evaluate & summarize new learning, correct false information, and extend their learning in other areas of their life.

Instructional Poster(s)

- This lesson has ONE Instructional Poster.
- This lesson's Instructional Poster is considered an "exemplar" for filling out a KWHLCQ Chart. It contains multiple bulleted thoughts in each section, providing the teacher or others with valuable information that explains the student's learning story. This is not the ONLY way to complete the chart - students can write a paragraph inside each section, a few sentences, younger students might draw pictures and attempt some words. etc.
- The synthesis paragraph at the end shares personal insights into the students' learning story and describes their new, deeper understanding.

Student Handouts

- This lesson has THREE Student Handouts.
- DIRECTIONS: Complete the three columns below BEFORE you begin learning today (K-W-H). Then, when you're finished learning about that subject, complete the three columns on the next page (L-C-Q) and write a short synthesis paragraph.
- These Student Handouts allow students to explain their learning story on a topic they've studied in class. The key with any organizer in this book that asks students to write a sentence or more to answer a question is having a complete answer. Please encourage your students to "Tell Me More." In our classroom, that means writing at least one additional sentence after the first (usually more generic) sentence. This second sentence is where the real information is usually at!
- The one additional handout is the same as the first two Student Handouts, but it puts all six sections of the KWHLCQ Chart onto one page. You should just choose to use the one-page version OR the two-page version.

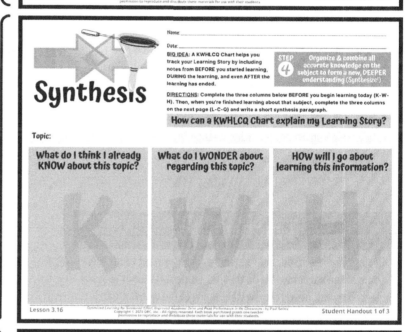

3.17

Synthesis is all around us - Recognize the call of synthesis "signal words" to unlock the true purpose of our teachers' tasks

Essential Question

How will I know when I need to Synthesize?

bit.ly/40XPugG

Lesson Overview

In this lesson, students realize that many of the assignments or tasks that their teachers have them complete are actually synthesis-type tasks. We are always synthesizing information as we learn, so it only makes sense that teachers need to know how well that synthesis is coming along for each student. Students learn to identify certain verbs that a teacher uses in assignments and tasks in class as synthesis "signal words." When they hear or read these verbs being used by their teacher, they should begin to understand that they are being asked to synthesize their learning.

Big Idea

When your teacher uses certain verbs in a specific way, they can be an indicator that you are about to synthesize your learning. However, synthesis should be happening all the time. Constantly be on the lookout for new information, contradictory information, arguments that support the opposite side of what you believe, etc. Your goal should always be to improve your understanding!

Discussion/Reflection Questions

- Come up with two more words to add to the list on the first Student Handout that would lead a student to share or explain their synthesis of a topic.
- Using one of the words you came up with, create a pretend assignment or task that asks students to synthesize information (just like you did in the Student Handout).
- Why can it be helpful to recognize these words as "synthesis words" when your teacher uses them? What might it do in your brain when you recognize them?

Teacher Tips

- In classrooms with younger students, you may want to go over some of the harder words on the first Student Handout with the class. They will need to know what many of the words mean in order to complete the assignment independently.
- You might want to encourage students to think about recent assignments that they've completed and try to see if any of the words on the first Student Handout work within that context. This would make it more real for them and possibly make the Big Idea of the lesson more permanent.
- If you can share any assignments or tasks that you've had your students complete in the past few weeks that use any of these verbs in a manner that requires synthesis, please share them with the class. These connections will further solidify the Big Idea within each student.

Student Tasks 〉 Transfer Goals

| Students discover that we are always synthesizing. | Students have an increased awareness of how often they synthesize information, leading to stronger metacognition. |
| Students learn to associate certain verbs as signal words for an assignment or task that requires synthesis. | Students associate the verbs their teacher uses in assignments and tasks with the need for them to synthesize information. |

Instructional Poster(s)

- This lesson has ONE Instructional Poster.
- This Instructional Poster tries to show students that we are always synthesizing new information with our prior knowledge (when we have prior knowledge!). It uses mushrooms as an example. Read through the three pieces of prior knowledge on the left of the brain and the three pieces of new learning to the right of the brain. Then, read the synthesis paragraph below the brain (it's a fairly weak example if you'd like to point that out to your students - I would expect better!). Finally, there is a "teaser" at the bottom of the poster that leads into the Student Handout activity.
- The answer to the question, "How will I know when I need to Synthesize?" is that we always should be synthesizing - creating new, deeper understanding.

Student Handouts

- This lesson has TWO Student Handouts.
- DIRECTIONS: Choose one verb from each column below to create a pretend assignment or task that asks students to synthesize information. Write your answers on the next page (there is an example to help). Be careful, these verbs can be used in many ways - many of which are NOT asking you to synthesize. So be sure to use each verb correctly in a synthesis activity
- The verbs listed on the first Student Handout each can be a signal word for an upcoming synthesis activity. Students choose one word from each column to create an assignment or task that uses that word in a way that encourages synthesis in some form. An example has been provided on the second Student Handout. Be sure that students know they can use any form of the word (past tense, future, etc.) as long as it keeps the meaning of the word intact.

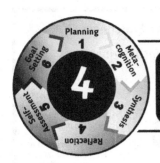

Planning
1
Goal Setting 6
Meta-cognition 2
Synthesis 3
Reflection 4
Self-Assessment 5
4

Reflection

> " We do not learn from experience.
> We learn from reflecting on experience. "
> — John Dewey

The fourth step in the Student-Led Self-Improvement Process is Reflection. Reflection refers to the process of students recalling WHAT they did during a learning experience, WHAT they learned, WHAT went well and WHAT went poorly. This purposeful act helps students gain a deeper understanding of their learning, retain the information better, and synthesize it with prior knowledge.

Reflection involves looking back on the experience and considering the positives and negatives, along with the reasons for them. It involves making a conscious decision about whether you would approach things differently next time. This seemingly simple yet powerful practice unlocks a world of self-directed learning, improves intrinsic motivation, and prepares our students for lifelong improvement.

Reflection can be one of the most challenging skills to do on our own, not because it's overly complex or difficult, but because when we finish learning, we usually want to move on to something else quickly instead of spending more time thinking about what we've learned! It is this instinct that we need to teach our students to fight off.

Reflection is a powerful tool that helps students solidify their learning and build deeper understanding. When they actively think about what they've learned, they strengthen the connections in their brains, making the information easier to remember and use later. This goes beyond simply memorizing facts. Reflection encourages students to explore the underlying principles and complexities of the material. They examine the details, consider how it applies to real-world situations, and piece together a complete picture.

Through reflection, students engage in a deeper level of understanding, which allows them to revisit the synthesis step and make connections between ideas once again. By doing so, they can see how different pieces of knowledge fit together and relate to each other, ultimately building a broader and more comprehensive understanding of the topic. Reflection serves as a bridge that spans the gap between isolated facts and a holistic view of the subject. It prompts students to actively analyze information, draw well-founded conclusions, and integrate fragmented knowledge into a cohesive whole. In this way, reflection supports their ability to develop a more cohesive and meaningful grasp of the subject matter.

Consider this fictional scenario:

The students in this classroom just completed a challenging math assignment, and most students were spending a few minutes reflecting on the experience. However, you observed a few students who neglected to reflect on their learning experiences. As a result, each of these students encountered a negative consequence of their inaction.

Zach, eager to move on quickly, failed to reflect on the assignment. Consequently, when a similar problem appeared on the upcoming test, he struggled to recall the necessary formulas and concepts. The lack of reflection led to limited retention, hindering Zach's performance.

Molly, being satisfied with her initial understanding, did not engage in reflection. As a result, she had a superficial grasp of the subject matter. When the teacher introduced a more complex topic that built upon the previous assignment, Molly found herself struggling to connect the dots, realizing she had missed crucial details by not reflecting.

Chris, oblivious to their areas of weakness, neglected reflection altogether. Consequently, they missed out on identifying their misconceptions and addressing them. Chris continued to make the same mistakes repeatedly, resulting in frustration and a lack of progress.

Reflection empowers students to take ownership of their learning and become active participants in the learning process, not just passive recipients of information. Reflection improves retention, so when students neglect to reflect, they run the risk of forgetting important information that they would have otherwise remembered had they reflected.

John Dewey recognized the transformative power of reflection in the learning process. Dewey believed that genuine learning occurs through active engagement with experiences and subsequent reflection upon them. He emphasized that reflection should not be a passive or isolated act but an integral part of the entire learning cycle.

According to Dewey, reflection allows students to connect their experiences with prior knowledge, enabling them to construct meaning and develop a more comprehensive understanding (Synthesis). He advocated for reflection as a means to bridge theory and practice, emphasizing that students should actively engage in thoughtful analysis and interpretation of their experiences to make sense of the world around them.

Reflection isn't just an afterthought; it's a powerful mental tool that strengthens learning through specific cognitive processes:

- Reflecting involves actively recalling information, bringing it back into the forefront of our mind. This retrieval process strengthens the neural connections associated with the information, making it more likely to be stored in long-term memory.
- When we reflect, we subconsciously search for connections between different pieces of information, identifying patterns and relationships we may have missed initially. This deeper understanding allows us to see the bigger picture and integrate various knowledge fragments into a cohesive whole.
- Reflection activates our self-awareness about our own learning process. By examining our understanding, identifying knowledge gaps, and evaluating our learning strategies, we can adjust our approach to maximize future learning effectiveness.
- As we reflect, we naturally explore different perspectives and angles. This mental agility enhances our problem-solving skills, creativity, and adaptability, allowing us to tackle challenges and learn from diverse viewpoints.

In essence, reflection is more than just reviewing; it's a mental workout that strengthens memory, deepens understanding, and hones our learning skills. By dedicating time to reflect after learning experiences, we're actively shaping our brain to become a more efficient and adaptable learning machine.

Although Reflection and Self-Assessment have similar qualities and overlapping concepts, each macroskill has been isolated in the SLSI Process in order to ensure that the proper attention is given to each. Doing one without the other is not likely to result in the same level of improvement as doing both macroskills would.

The lessons within this chapter focus on important microskills that contribute to effective reflection. Here are some examples:

Basic Reflection: Learn how to complete a Basic Reflection by describing WHAT you did and explaining WHAT you learned.

Tailored Reflection: Add a few additional parts that fit your learning experience to make the reflection process more beneficial: Students do this by answering questions like:
- What was easy for you? Challenging? Surprising?
- What was fun for you? Not very enjoyable?
- What did you find interesting? What do you wonder about?
- How will you learn more about the subject on your own?
- What skills did you improve while working on this task?

Formal Reflection: Emotionally connect to your learning experience by identifying what went well and what went poorly, and explaining why each experience happened and what you hope to do about it in the future (e.g. continue it, avoid it, etc.).

Four Dimensions of Reflection: When we think of "reflecting," we usually think about a backward-looking reflection. It's about looking at what happened, why it happened, and deciding if it was good or bad, successful or unsuccessful. Here are three additional dimensions of reflection that we should consider:
- Forward: Based on today's experience, what's to come in our near and distant future?
- Inward: What thoughts & emotions do we have about today's experience?
- Outward: What might others have to say about this experience?

Reflection is a powerful tool that deepens our understanding and solidifies our learning. By actively thinking about what we've learned, we strengthen the connections in our brains and make information easier to remember and use later. Reflection, however, goes beyond just memorization; it allows us to understand the intricate details of the material, helping us synthesize a complete picture. Reflection works together with synthesis to help us identify misconceptions, address weaknesses, and take ownership of our learning. It's a vital part of the SLSI Process that helps students optimize their learning. So, let's teach our students to embrace the power of reflection and make it an integral part of their learning journey!

INTRODUCTION
PLANNING
METACOGNITION
SYNTHESIS
REFLECTION
SELF-ASSESSMENT
GOAL SETTING
FEEDBACK

Unit 4 - Reflection

Students with well-developed REFLECTION MicroSkills...	Students with poorly-developed REFLECTION MicroSkills...
Understand the importance of reflection in the learning process	Neglect the practice of reflection and move on to other tasks
Take the time to think about what they did during a learning experience	Fail to reflect on their actions or experiences
Consider what they learned from the learning experience	Neglect to identify key takeaways or insights
Recognize the value of reflecting on mistakes and learning from them	Avoid reflecting on mistakes and miss opportunities for growth
Recognize the impact of the learning experience on their personal growth	Fail to connect the learning experience to their own development
Consider the impact of their actions on others and take responsibility for their behavior	Fail to acknowledge the impact of their actions and avoid taking responsibility
Apply insights from reflection to future learning experiences	Repeat the same mistakes without learning from past experiences
Engage in self-reflection to enhance self-awareness of personal strengths and weaknesses	Lack self-awareness and fail to recognize their strengths and weaknesses
Take responsibility for their own learning and growth	Exhibit a passive approach to learning and rely on external factors
Analyze their learning strategies and adjust them based on their reflection	Use the same learning strategies without reflection or adjustment
Consider the influence of external factors on their learning and adapt accordingly	Blame external factors without reflecting on their own actions or efforts
Engage in deep reflection to uncover underlying assumptions and biases	Maintain surface-level reflection without exploring underlying assumptions
Set goals for future learning based on their reflection and self-assessment.	Lack direction and fail to set goals for improvement based on their learning experiences.
Take time to think deeply about what they've learned and its significance.	Quickly move on to the next task without thoughtful consideration of their learning.
Use reflection as a tool for growth and continuous learning.	View reflection as a waste of time or unnecessary in the learning process.

INTRODUCTION

PLANNING

METACOGNITION

SYNTHESIS

REFLECTION

SELF-ASSESSMENT

GOAL SETTING

FEEDBACK

bit.ly/49Yr22R

Evaluate REFLECTION MicroSkills to take pride in relative strengths and to set personalized goals for areas of weakness

Essential Question

How strong am I at each of these REFLECTION skills?

Big Idea

By evaluating our current level of achievement on the MicroSkills that will be taught in this unit, we gain a clearer understanding of our individual strengths and weaknesses. Additionally, by synthesizing each MicroSkill, we develop a stronger understanding of the MacroSkill that this unit focuses on, which is REFELCTION.

Lesson Overview

In this lesson, students evaluate their perceived ability for each of the identified REFLECTION skills. These skills have been chosen from the lessons that follow in this unit. Although students are choosing a somewhat arbitrary number from 1-10, the self-assessment process requires them to (1) understand what the skill means, (2) determine their perceived ability for the skill, and (3) sort each skill into areas of weakness or strength (or in-between) so that they help others improve at the skill (for scores 7-10) or make the skill into a goal that they try to achieve (for scores 1-4). If a student scores a 5 or 6, they are asked to reassess themselves after the unit to determine if they would benefit from making it a goal or not.

Discussion/Reflection Questions

- Which reflection skills did you feel you were strongest at? Provide some evidence to support your self-assessment.
- Which reflection skills did you feel you were weakest at? Explain why you feel that this is true.
- If you could set a goal to improve ONE of these skills, which one would you choose? Why did you choose that one? How do you plan to improve this skill? What will you do?

Teacher Tips

- On the Student Handouts, it tells students to "highlight all the numbers up through your score." The reason I didn't just have them circle the number is so they can see "how full" their grade band is if they choose a high number, and "how empty" their grade band is if they choose a low number. If you don't think it's too important for your students, feel free to let them just circle their number.
- When doing a self-assessment like this, I like to teach my students about the importance of being honest with themselves. I remind them that self-assessment in our classroom don't affect your grades or the way I see them. Self-assessments help us focus in on what matters to us, rather than focusing in on everything and not spending enough time on the skills that we need to improve most. No one is a 10 on all of these skills and no one is a 1 on all of them, but there's a good chance that each of us is a 10 and a 1 on at least one skill in this self-assessment!

Student Tasks 〉 Transfer Goals

Student Tasks	Transfer Goals
Students assess themselves on various reflection skills using a scale from 1 to 10.	Students become more self-aware of their abilities and areas in which they need to grow.
Students are asked several reflection questions that require them to explain their self-assessments and to set a goal for one skill.	Students understand that having weaknesses is normal and that they should be improved through goal-setting.

Instructional Poster(s)

- This lesson has ONE Instructional Poster.
- A variation of this Instructional Poster is used with the first lesson of each unit. It shows students how to use the 1-10 scale for assessing their current level of ability with each skill. Numbers 1-4 mean that they know they need to improve at this skill (and maybe create a goal for the skill), and numbers 7-10 mean they believe that they are capable of helping others improve this skill. (4-5 means they will reassess at the end of the unit - which will be up to you or the student to remember to do. It's not a lesson.)
- Tell students that the real value in this activity is discovering their relative strengths and weaknesses, so giving yourself a 10 for each skill is wasting everyone's time, as is repeating any other number. Finding the variation in each skill is the key, so give yourself scores of 1, 2, and 3 and give scores of 8, 9, and 10 as well

Student Handouts

- This lesson has TWO Student Handouts.
- DIRECTIONS: Look at the Reflection MicroSkills in each box below and on the following page(s). Determine a rating from 1-10 for yourself on each, and then circle it. For your lowest MicroSkill(s), create a S.M.A.A.R.T.E.R. Goal to address each weakness.
- If you have not taught the lesson on Goal Bursts, let students know that they can just make the skill a personal goal to improve, but nothing needs to be written out (unless they want a reminder to actually do it). Obviously, the more seriously they take things, the more likely they'll improve!

INTRODUCTION

PLANNING

METACOGNITION

SYNTHESIS

REFLECTION

SELF-ASSESSMENT

GOAL SETTING

FEEDBACK

How strong am I at each of these Reflection Skills?

This is one of the skills that we will be working on in this unit. Think about your ability to do this skill correctly without reminders or help.

This scale runs from 1 to 10. If you believe you know virtually nothing about the skill, you might give yourself a "1." If you believe that, for your age, you are one of the best at this skill, you might give yourself a "10."

Be willing and able to take time to think about a learning experience

1 2 3 4 5 6 7 8 9 10

I'll need to work on this. - - - - I'll help others with this!

If you believe that your current level is between 1 and 4, you most likely believe that this is an area that you should try to improve. Good! Let's grow!

If you believe that your current level is between 5 and 6, you most likely see this as a skill that you are neither strong, nor weak in. See how well you learn it in this unit, then decide if you think it would be a worthwhile goal.

If you believe that your current level is between 7 and 10, you most likely believe that this is an area that you can try to help others with. Good! Let's help others!

Lesson 4.01 — Instructional Poster 1 of 1

Reflection

Name: _____
Date: _____

BIG IDEA: Learning becomes more permanent when we take time to reflect after a learning experience.

DIRECTIONS: Look at the reflection skills in each box below. Determine a grade from 1-10 for yourself for each skill, and highlight all the numbers up through your score. For the skill or skills with your lowest grades, choose to make them a GOAL BURST as soon as possible. For your higher scores, offer your help to those who might benefit from it. Continue on the next few pages.

How strong am I at each of these Reflection Skills?

Be willing and able to take time to think about a learning experience
1 2 3 4 5 6 7 8 9 10
I'll need to work on this. - - - - I'll help others with this!

Be aware of your learning styles, strengths, weaknesses & personal interests.
1 2 3 4 5 6 7 8 9 10
I'll need to work on this. - - - - I'll help others with this!

Make sense of a learning experience to store it in long-term memory
1 2 3 4 5 6 7 8 9 10
I'll need to work on this. - - - - I'll help others with this!

Understand the "why" and "how" of learning to make learning permanent
1 2 3 4 5 6 7 8 9 10
I'll need to work on this. - - - - I'll help others with this!

Make improvements for the future by understanding the mistakes you've made
1 2 3 4 5 6 7 8 9 10
I'll need to work on this. - - - - I'll help others with this!

Be able to identify what you know & don't know about a topic
1 2 3 4 5 6 7 8 9 10
I'll need to work on this. - - - - I'll help others with this!

Lesson 4.01 — Student Handout 1 of 2

How strong am I at each of these Reflection Skills?

Be able to anticipate what is coming next in learning - what's the next level?
1 2 3 4 5 6 7 8 9 10
I'll need to work on this. - - - - I'll help others with this!

Be able to describe the valuable parts of what you learned during a task
1 2 3 4 5 6 7 8 9 10
I'll need to work on this. - - - - I'll help others with this!

Allow mistakes & setbacks to BUILD your self-esteem rather than knock it down
1 2 3 4 5 6 7 8 9 10
I'll need to work on this. - - - - I'll help others with this!

Be able to look forward, backward, inward and outward when reflecting
1 2 3 4 5 6 7 8 9 10
I'll need to work on this. - - - - I'll help others with this!

Be able to identify tasks that were easy and hard, boring and fun.
1 2 3 4 5 6 7 8 9 10
I'll need to work on this. - - - - I'll help others with this!

Complete thorough reflections no matter the amount of time given
1 2 3 4 5 6 7 8 9 10
I'll need to work on this. - - - - I'll help others with this!

Be able to identify tasks that you need help with & those you want more challenge
1 2 3 4 5 6 7 8 9 10
I'll need to work on this. - - - - I'll help others with this!

When reflecting with others, be able to stay focused and produce quality work
1 2 3 4 5 6 7 8 9 10
I'll need to work on this. - - - - I'll help others with this!

Lesson 4.01 — Student Handout 2 of 2

bit.ly/3uC9yt1

Unlock the power of reflection to turn momentary learning experiences into long-lasting treasures of knowledge

Essential Question

What is reflection?

Big Idea

Reflection is the act of thinking about what just happened or what you did, what you learned during that experience, and what impact the experience had on you. Reflection helps us make sense of our experience, and store it for the long-term.

Lesson Overview

In this lesson, students learn the definition of reflection and discuss aspects of reflection that the teachers chooses to focus on. After learning a bit about reflection, they are asked to consider how the act of reflection is similar to looking into a mirror. They're encouraged to go beyond the obvious and state deeper similarities. Finally, students end the lesson by reflecting on this lesson using the following reflection process:

- What just happened? What did you just do?
- What did you learn from this experience?
- What impact did this experience have on you?

Discussion/Reflection Questions

- What is reflection?
- How is reflection like looking in a mirror? (Only share the best one that you came up with or a new one you didn't already write.)
- When should you take time to reflect on your learning?

Teacher Tips

- This lesson takes slightly less time than most lessons.
- You may want to decide just how deep into reflection you plan on going with your class this year. Not so much regarding how many lessons you plan to teach, but how often you plan to have your students reflect after classwork. In a perfect world, we would give our students 5-10 minutes to reflect on their learning after EVERY learning experience. Unfortunately, we don't always have the time. In Lesson 4.11, I suggest ways students can reflect with as little as one minute. If you think you can dedicate one or more minutes toward the end of most lessons for reflection, then this chapter will really help your students make the most of their reflection time! If you won't be able to provide time very often, then this chapter will teach students what to do if they have time on their own to reflect.

Student Tasks ⟩ Transfer Goals

Student Tasks	Transfer Goals
Students learn the definition of reflection.	Students use this definition to reflect independently throughout life.
Students compare reflection to looking in a mirror.	Students have a deeper understanding of what it means to reflect and is able to get more out of reflection because of it.

Instructional Poster(s)

- This lesson has ONE Instructional Poster.
- The goal of this Instructional Poster is to promote a discussion on reflection. What is it? What is it not? Why is it valuable? When will we use it?
- Spend some time explaining the value of reflection:
  - Improves retention of information
  - Helps students get the most out of the lesson or activity
  - Brings closure to the lesson or activity, helping students transition to whatever is next
  - Allows students time to make the learning personal - connecting it to experiences in their own life.
  - etc.
- Ask students about times where they didn't reflect and ended up forgetting information and times when they did reflect and had better retention.

Student Handouts

- This lesson has TWO Student Handouts.
- DIRECTIONS: Answer the questions below. Try to come up with as many ways that reflection is similar to looking in a mirror. Then, on the next page, reflect on today's reflection lesson, and fill out each of the sticky notes using the image provided as your guide.
- Encourage students to try to explain as many ways that reflecting is like looking into a mirror. At minimum, students should try to fill in all of the lines so they get past the obvious answers and get into the deeper thinking answers.
- On the second Student Handout, students should match the numbers from the image at the top of the page with the numbers on each sticky note, writing a response for each of the respective prompts.

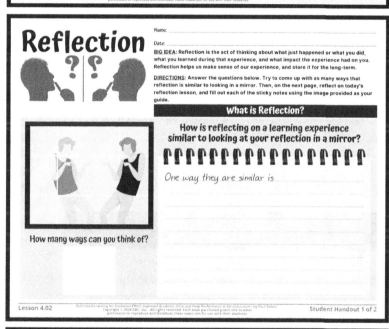

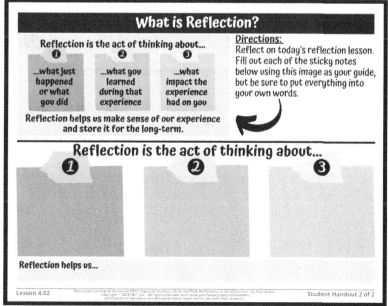

INTRODUCTION

PLANNING

METACOGNITION

SYNTHESIS

REFLECTION

SELF-ASSESSMENT

GOAL SETTING

FEEDBACK

bit.ly/3Rm4diC

Observe how the power of reflection weathers the storms of forgetfulness, and makes learning stronger and more resilient

Essential Question

Why should we spend time reflecting?

Big Idea

Reflecting on our learning has numerous benefits. Some benefits include:

- long-term retention of information,
- a clearer understanding of how things work and why they are so, and
- building our self-esteem when we acknowledge our strengths and learning gains.

Lesson Overview

In this lesson, students learn to discover the value of reflection and discuss several examples of reflection in action. After learning a bit about reflection, they are asked to predict what might happen to a student who didn't reflect after a certain experience, and explain their thinking behind their reasons. Students end the lesson by reading nine reasons why reflection is important. They are asked to evaluate those reasons and choose three that are the most important to them and defend their reasons for selecting each.

Discussion/Reflection Questions

- Why is it worth taking a couple minutes of class time after learning new information to consciously reflect on your learning? How can teachers be convinced that it is time well-spent?
- What is one positive result you would like to experience if you start reflecting after each lesson? Explain.
- If your teacher said that you have the next three minutes to silently reflect on your learning (at the end of a lesson), how would you spend that time? What would you think about or do? How would you make sure you didn't waste that time?

Teacher Tips

- Before reading the reasons why reflection is beneficial provided to you on the Instructional Poster and the second Student Handout, try to brainstorm some reasons on your own. If you have some that are not included in the lesson, be sure to share them with your students!
- If you can think of a time where reflecting on an experience helped you in some way, this lesson would provide a good opportunity for you to share it.
- If you can create additional fictional scenarios where reflection would be beneficial for the character, talk through them before letting your students work on the Student Handouts. (See the first Student Handout for examples.)

Student Tasks 〉 Transfer Goals

Student Tasks	Transfer Goals
Students learn about the many benefits of reflection.	Students take time to reflect on their learning in order to reap the benefits that reflection offers.
Students predict potential problems that could happen if reflection doesn't take place in various scenarios.	Students proactively reflect in order to avoid problems that could result after learning something new.

Instructional Poster(s)

- This lesson has ONE Instructional Poster.
- The Instructional Poster for today's lesson has eight boxes that each share one reason why Reflection is beneficial. Read through these together as a class and discuss what each means. Allow students to add their ideas to the discussion as they have them - encourage quick stories of reflection (or fictional scenarios) that led to something positive.

Student Handouts

- This lesson has TWO Student Handouts.
- DIRECTIONS: Read each scenario on the left, then write what negative consequence(s) might occur if you don't take time to reflect in the middle column. Finally, explain why you think that may be true in the column on the right.
- Feel free to do one of these together as a class and then allow the students to finish the other two independently or with a partner. If your students are younger, you may wish to do them all together as a class, but you could also provide your students time to complete them independently and then go through their answers together afterwards, providing constructive feedback.
- DIRECTIONS: Read through the nine boxes below. Each box contains a reason why reflecting is beneficial. Evaluate which three reasons would be the most important for YOU. Maybe it addresses an area where you are weak or inexperienced. Write a 1, 2, and 3 in the three circles that describe the most important benefits to you. Then explain why you made each decision in the space on the right.
- Make sure that students don't just choose three easy choices to explain. Encourage them to self-assess and choose the ones they NEED most!

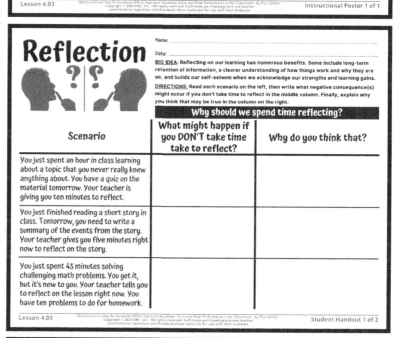

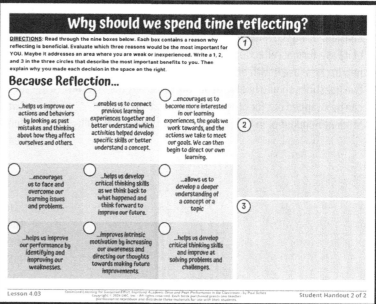

bit.ly/3sXq3Q4

4.04

Watch your understanding deepen as you think back on what you did and learned, while completing a simple reflection

Essential Question

How do I reflect on my learning?

Big Idea

Reflection doesn't need to be overly complex. Sometimes, a simple reflection can still be extremely valuable. When each step is considered carefully and honestly, our learning becomes more permanent.

Lesson Overview

In this lesson, students learn that a basic reflection includes thinking about what you DID during a lesson, task, activity, or assignment and what you learned. Sometimes, a reflection can include additional components that focus on the lesson's difficulty, enjoyment, future plans, etc. These additional components should be considered based on the type of activity that the student is reflecting on.

Discussion/Reflection Questions

- Other than: (1) What did you do? and (2) What did you learn, why might it be a good idea to include a few additional questions when you reflect on your learning?
- When should you choose to include: (1) What was easy for you? and (2) What was hard for you? as reflection questions?
- When should you choose to include: (1) What did you enjoy? and (2) What didn't you enjoy? as reflection questions?
- What other questions might you consider reflecting on after a learning experience?

Teacher Tips

- The Student Handouts for this lesson require students to complete a content-related activity, task or assignment in class BEFORE working on them. Any task that allows students to reflect on their learning and be able to evaluate how things went will work. If it's collaborative in some way, that's even better!
- Consider using the final Student Handout (or a modified version of it) as a formal reflection tool after students learn something new in class (use it with other lessons in the future). The first two questions should likely remain the same, but the last two can be swapped out for others that are listed on the first Student Handout or in future Reflection lessons in this unit.

Student Tasks 〉 Transfer Goals

Student Tasks	Transfer Goals
Students learn a basic, two-question method for reflecting on their learning.	Students independently reflect on their learning whenever they complete an experience, without the need for support.
Students learn to extend the reflection process by including additional questions that relate to their learning experience.	Students reflect more deeply when they notice that certain lessons provide excellent context for certain extension questions.

Instructional Poster(s)

- This lesson has ONE Instructional Poster.
- The Instructional Poster for this lesson attempts to give students a basic definition and understanding of what is expected of them when they are asked to "reflect" on their learning. A good basic reflection should include a description of what they did during the lesson AND what they learned. A partial example is provided; students are encouraged to imagine what might also be included.
- Once the basic level of reflection is understood and valued by the students, additional components can be added depending on the type of activity or learning experience. Sometimes you, the teacher, need to choose these additional options and sometimes students should be allowed to choose.

How do I reflect on my learning?

When your teacher asks you to "Reflect on today's learning" that can mean many things. Basically, your teacher wants you to:

- Describe WHAT you did, and
- Explain WHAT you learned.

Reflection

During today's lesson, we learned about how energy forms transfer in toys and electronics. For example, the radio converts electrical energy (or chemical energy if it uses batteries) into sound energy (and heat as a byproduct). No energy is created nor...

BUT, a more complete Reflection includes a few additional parts. Although you don't have to include ALL of these parts, it is a good idea to include some of them if they fit your learning experience:

- Explain what was easy for you,
- Explain what was challenging for you,
- Explain what was fun for you,
- Explain what was not very enjoyable for you,
- Explain what you found interesting,
- Explain what you still wonder about,
- Explain how you plan to learn more about the subject on your own,
- Explain what was surprising to you,
- Explain what prior knowledge was reinforced through this experience,
- Explain the skills you improved while working on this task, etc.

Student Handouts

- This lesson has TWO Student Handouts.
- DIRECTIONS: Evaluate the following optional components of a reflection. Write a "1" on the line next to the component you look forward to completing the most, all the way down to writing an "11" next to the one you really don't look forward to completing. Use the next page to complete a 4-step reflection on an activity from class.
- In an effort to get your students to internalize each of the eleven reflection "add-ons," they are asked to evaluate the options using a ranking system. They then are asked to explain their ranking in order to prevent random answers.
- On the final Student Handout, students reflect on their learning of a lesson from class with the two basic components of a reflection AND two additional reflection components. Remind students to "Tell Me More" with each answer!

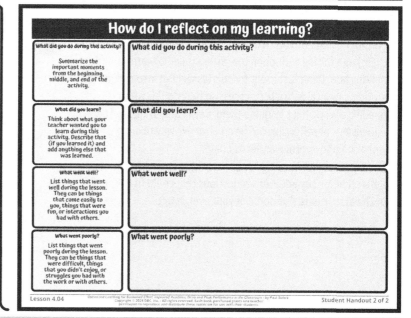

Sidebar tabs: INTRODUCTION, PLANNING, METACOGNITION, SYNTHESIS, REFLECTION, SELF-ASSESSMENT, GOAL SETTING, FEEDBACK

bit.ly/3T0H6Lu

Analyze your learning experience from four different angles to connect the dots and refine your understanding

Essential Question

What are the Four Dimensions of Reflection?

Big Idea

When we use all four domains of reflection to deeply analyze our learning experiences, we solidify our learning and improve future experiences.

Lesson Overview

In this lesson, students learn about the four dimensions of reflection: backward, forward, inward and outward. While most reflection focuses only on backward-thinking, there is great value in reflecting in other ways too. For example, forward-thinking reflection involves contemplating on what you wish turned out better and how you could make that happen next time, or what others around you did that you'd like to try sometime soon. Inward-thinking reflection involves personal emotions and self-assessment of the work. And outward-thinking reflection imagines what others (including their teacher, parents, or peers, for example) would think of their effort, work quality, and overall learning.

Discussion/Reflection Questions

- Why should we make sure that our reflections don't just focus on the past? Why should we reflect on forward-thinking, inward-thinking, and outward-thinking perspectives as well?
- What is one question that you would add to one of the four dimensions of reflection that wasn't on the Student Handout?
- How will you "transfer" this skill (of reflecting in all four dimensions after a learning experience) to future assignments without your teacher needing to assign you a formal reflection? How will you take on this responsibility yourself?

Teacher Tips

- The Student Handouts for this lesson require students to complete a content-related activity, task or assignment in class BEFORE working on them. Any task that allows students to reflect on their learning and be able to evaluate how things went will work. If it's collaborative in some way, that's even better!
- Consider using both Student Handouts (or a modified version of them) as a formal reflection tool after students learn something new in class. Don't just use it for this lesson! But also encourage students to internalize the process so they do this without needing a worksheet to guide them. Reflecting using the four dimensions of reflection can be an effective way to increase retention and improve understanding.
- See if your students can think of any additional "Dimensions of Reflection" or any additional questions that could fit within any of the dimensions. Add some of your own as well.

Student Tasks 〉 Transfer Goals

Student Tasks	Transfer Goals
Students learn that reflection doesn't just have to be backward-thinking (focusing on what happened).	Students naturally think about the past when they reflect, but now they think of reflection in several new ways,
Students learn about three other dimensions of reflection: forward-, inward- and outward-thinking.	Students go past simple backward-thinking reflection by looking to the future, within themselves and by considering others' possible opinions.

INTRODUCTION

PLANNING

METACOGNITION

SYNTHESIS

REFLECTION

SELF-ASSESSMENT

GOAL SETTING

FEEDBACK

Instructional Poster(s)

- This lesson has TWO Instructional Posters.
- The first Instructional Poster for this lesson attempts to describe four different ways of looking at "reflection." Most of us understand how reflection looks BACKWARD at what we just did or accomplished, but there is a strong benefit to looking FORWARD, INWARD and OUTWARD as well. Each of the dimensions are explained in detail on the first Instructional Poster.
- The second Instructional Poster is set up the same way, but instead of having descriptions of each dimension, it provides the class with sample reflection questions that relate to each dimension. This helps students understand each dimension better, and provides examples that they can use independently.

What are the Four Dimensions of Reflection?

Backward-Looking

Backward-Looking Reflection:
When we think of "reflecting," we usually think about a backward-looking reflection. It's about looking at what happened, why it happened, and deciding if it was good or bad, successful or unsuccessful. Looking to our past is very valuable to learn from, but it's already happened, so we can't dwell on it!

Forward-Looking Reflection:
Forward-looking reflection is all about the future and what's to come. We use what's happened in the past to help us determine what should happen in the future. Too often, people make mistakes, but don't reflect on those mistakes. This often leads to repeating mistakes that could have been prevented.

Forward-Looking

--- Definitions ---

Credit: Whitfield Career Academy adapted from High Tech High - found on Edutopia: learningrenaissance.files.wordpress.com/2015/05/edutopia-stw-replicatingpbl-reflection-questions.pdf

Inward-Looking

Inward-Looking Reflection:
Inward-looking reflection allows us to consider our thoughts, feelings, and emotions about an experience (we try to avoid those in backward & forward thinking reflections). It can allow you to evaluate how well you did and if you need to set goals for improvement. It also helps you learn about yourself.

Outward-Looking Reflection:
When we take time to look outward, we remove ourself from the situation and think about what happened from someone else's perspective like a teacher or a peer. We might also compare ourself to others, but we must acknowledge that we all have different strengths and weaknesses!

Outward-Looking

Lesson 4.05 · Optimized Learning for Sustained Effort, Improved Academic Drive and Peak Performance in the Classroom - by Paul Solarz · Copyright © 2024 DBC, Inc. - All rights reserved. Each book purchased grants one teacher permission to reproduce and distribute these materials for use with their students. · Instructional Poster 1 of 2

Student Handouts

- This lesson has TWO Student Handouts.
- DIRECTIONS: Choose one question from each section to answer regarding a learning experience you recently had. Highlight or circle the question that you are answering.
- In order to complete today's Student Handouts, students need to have just completed a learning experience in class. They will use the sample reflection questions from the second Instructional Poster (and the Student Handouts) to reflect using the four dimensions of reflection.

Reflection ⁇

Name: _____

Date: _____

BIG IDEA: When we use all four domains of reflection to deeply analyze our learning experiences, we solidify our learning and improve future experiences.

DIRECTIONS: Choose one question from each section to answer regarding a learning experience you recently had. Highlight or circle the question that you are answering.

What are the Four Dimensions of Reflection?

Credit: Whitfield Career Academy adapted from High Tech High - found on Edutopia: learningrenaissance.files.wordpress.com/2015/05/edutopia-stw-replicatingpbl-reflection-questions.pdf

Backward-Looking
- How much did you know about this topic before you started? How much did you learn today?
- Have you done similar tasks in the past, or was this completely new to you?
- How have you improved at this kind of work? Where should you still improve?
- What problems did you encounter while working? How did you solve them?

Forward-Looking
- What would you change if you had a chance to do this piece over again?
- What's one thing you saw in your classmates' work or process that you would like to try in the future?
- What's one goal you would like to set for yourself for next time?
- What things might you want more help with?
- What things could you help others with next time?

Lesson 4.05 · Optimized Learning for Sustained Effort, Improved Academic Drive and Peak Performance in the Classroom - by Paul Solarz · Copyright © 2024 DBC, Inc. - All rights reserved. Each book purchased grants one teacher permission to reproduce and distribute these materials for use with their students. · Student Handout 1 of 2

What are the Four Dimensions of Reflection?

Credit: Whitfield Career Academy adapted from High Tech High - found on Edutopia: learningrenaissance.files.wordpress.com/2015/05/edutopia-stw-replicatingpbl-reflection-questions.pdf

Inward-Looking
- How do you feel about this piece of work? What do you like? Dislike? Why?
- What did you enjoy today? Why?
- What was frustrating today? Why?
- What were your goals, standards, requirements, or expectations for this piece of work? Did you meet them all?
- What did you learn about yourself today? Did you surprise yourself at all?

Outward-Looking
- How did you do things similarly to various peers today? Differently?
- What thoughts might you expect your teacher to have about this piece?
- What grade would you give it? Why?
- What specifically would you like people to notice when they look at your work?
- What might others learn about you when watching you work today?

Lesson 4.05 · Optimized Learning for Sustained Effort, Improved Academic Drive and Peak Performance in the Classroom - by Paul Solarz · Copyright © 2024 DBC, Inc. - All rights reserved. Each book purchased grants one teacher permission to reproduce and distribute these materials for use with their students. · Student Handout 2 of 2

bit.ly/3Ro7v4Y

Get to the heart of your understanding by elaborating on your initial reflections to go deeper than you thought you could

Essential Question

How can I improve my reflections with "Tell Me More"?

Big Idea

When we push ourselves to tell just a little bit more, we get to the heart of our answer. Therefore, whenever there is a reflection question that we know we are connecting with, we need to take the time to elaborate and explain it more.

Lesson Overview

In this lesson, students learn and practice a simple technique that helps them get to the crux of their reflection. So often, students' answers to long-answer style questions are short and sweet. Many students like to say the least possible, while still getting credit for it being done! This method requires students to elaborate further on their answer in order to hone in on the details and the nitty-gritty. All it asks students to do is to write an additional sentence that further explains the first sentence(s) that they wrote for their reflection. But, the results that come from these additional sentences are gold! Make sure they understand that you are not asking for additional answers, but more detailed answers that are clear to their reader.

Discussion/Reflection Questions

- Have you ever asked for help from someone or wanted to get information from someone who would only give you short, simple answers? (Use your imagination, if you've never had this kind of experience.) How did it make you feel? Did you come away with the information or answer that you wanted, or were you honestly hoping for a little more detail?
- Why do you think your teacher wants you to "Tell Me More"? What's the purpose or value of this strategy?
- How can these "more detailed reflections" help you? (Think about WHY we reflect to help you answer this question.)

Teacher Tips

- The Student Handouts for this lesson require students to complete a content-related activity, task or assignment in class BEFORE working on them. Any task that allows students to reflect on their learning and be able to evaluate how things went will work. If it's collaborative in some way, that's even better!
- This lesson uses the questions that students learned in Lesson 4.05, so they have been included in the slides that you will download - They are still labeled "Lesson 4.05", so it may look like it is a mistake, but it's not.
- Consider using the second Student Handout (or a modified version of it) as a formal reflection tool after students learn something new in class. (Don't just use it for this lesson!) But also encourage students to internalize the process so they do this without needing a worksheet to guide them.
- The "Tell Me More" method can be used to get your students to expand any essay-style or long answer style response.
- Students sometimes think that "Tell Me More" means give me MORE answers to the question, but that's NOT what it means. It means to elaborate on the answer that you DID give, by explaining it FURTHER.

Student Tasks ⟩ Transfer Goals

Student Tasks	Transfer Goals
Students discover that although a short, simple answer often satisfies requirements, more detail is preferred & beneficial.	Students provide deeper, more detailed answers in situations that benefit from the extra detail.
Students use a simple strategy for deeper reflection that asks them to add additional sentences to their written reflections.	Students apply the strategy to all aspects of thought - wondering, "How can I dig deeper?"

Instructional Poster(s)

- This lesson has ONE Instructional Poster, but also includes the TWO Instructional Posters from Lesson 4.05 for use with today's Student Handouts (see Teacher Tips).
- The Instructional Poster for today's lesson serves to help students understand that their goal is to expand their reflections to be more complete than they've typically shared. The "Tell Me More" strategy is brutally simple -- it just means to write another sentence or two that explains their previous point more deeply. BUT, there is magic in these additional sentences! These sentences contain the true nuggets that teachers want to read (and that will be most meaningful to the student as they process what they've done and learned during the lesson or activity).

Student Handouts

- This lesson has TWO Student Handouts.
- If you plan to use the Student Handouts, please display or hand out the Instructional Posters from Lesson 4.05 which are included in this unit. Students will need to select a question from one of the posters for their first Student Handout. Try not to let them choose a question that's on the second Student Handout.
- DIRECTIONS: Choose a reflection question from the previous activity or one of your own. Write that question in the first box below. Answer that question as well as you can, but then push yourself to dig just a little bit deeper by "Telling Me More."
- I would recommend having the students READ the six questions on the second Student Handout before beginning on the first in order to prevent them from choosing the same question. If this is not possible, have students cross out the repeated question and write in an alternate one.
- On the first Student Handout, students learn the format: (1) Answer question, (2) Tell me more. (Simple, right!?) :)
- On the second Student Handout, students apply the format to six questions that have been selected for them to use to reflect. Feel free to swap some questions for others if these don't work as well with the lesson from class!

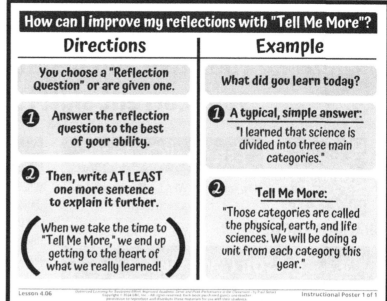

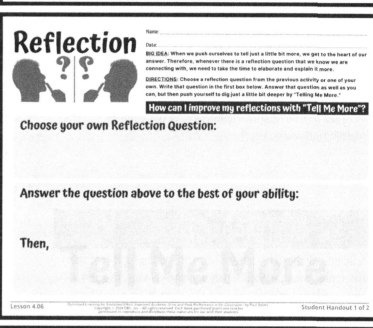

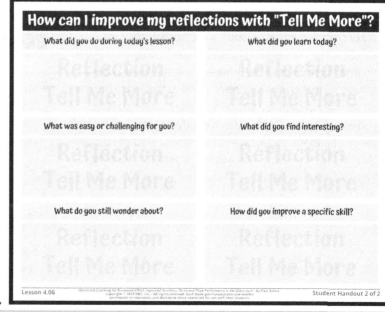

INTRODUCTION

PLANNING

METACOGNITION

SYNTHESIS

REFLECTION

SELF-ASSESSMENT

GOAL SETTING

FEEDBACK

bit.ly/3QYxAGb

Reflect on each learning experience (positive and negative) that have shaped your current skill level or understanding

4.07

Essential Question

How can I use a Wander Map to reflect on my learning journey?

Big Idea

When we identify how far we've come with regard to a skill or understanding, the better we feel about the things we might still not understand. Quite often, people feel dumb when they don't understand things. But the reality is, you understand quite a bit and don't always realize it! Let's strengthen our self-esteem!

Lesson Overview

In this lesson, students reflect on the journey that they've taken to get to where they are today in a particular skill or topic. Growth and improvement often requires a series of learning experiences (and practice, setbacks, feedback, etc.) in order to get to a point where you feel that you've become stronger. This lesson provides the time that students need to identify those learning experiences or specific skills or facts that helped them get to this point in their learning journey. But learning doesn't end at this point. Where does the learning journey go next?

Discussion/Reflection Questions

- Why is it important that we don't have an "end" on our Wander Map?
- If we had LONG lines between cities on our Wander Map and SHORT lines between cities. What might they represent metaphorically? Think about a LONG road trip versus a SHORT road trip.
- How might this lesson have helped students who occasionally feel dumb when they don't know something or are confused? How can YOU use this concept to prevent yourself from feeling dumb when you struggle with something?

Teacher Tips

- Students will need to come up with ONE skill or topic that they have come a long way with. They don't need to be an expert, but they need to have worked at this skill or topic for a long time, improving along the way. If you think your students will struggle to come up with a topic for this, ask them to come prepared with this ahead of time.
- Try to have students avoid skills or topics where they just practiced the same exact thing 1,000 times in order to improve (like getting a yo-yo to "Walk the Dog"). It's better to choose something that involved different activities that led to their growth (like becoming a strong gymnast or soccer player).
- This lesson has ten steps. Ten is an arbitrary number, so feel free to cut it down some if that would benefit your students OR have them double it or triple it for a deeper dive into a skill or topic!

Student Tasks 〉 Transfer Goals

Students use a Wander Map to discover how far they have come with regard to a skill or topic.	Students put struggle into perspective - sometimes learning comes easily & sometimes it's tough!
Students imagine the steps that were involved in a famous person's journey toward their expertise.	Students understand that becoming an expert at something takes hard work & perseverance no matter who you are!

Instructional Poster(s)

- This lesson has ONE Instructional Poster.
- The Instructional Poster for this lesson shows students what a "Wander Map" is. (Don't Google it - I made it up.) :)
- A Wander Map attempts to show learning as a journey. You start somewhere and end up somewhere with lots of stops along the way! A map is one way to show that journey.
- Be sure to discuss the comments and questions typed onto the Wander Map with the class and ensure that the students understand the metaphor before moving on.

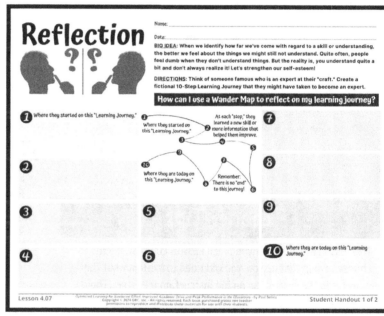

Student Handouts

- This lesson has TWO Student Handouts.
- DIRECTIONS: Think of someone famous who is an expert at their "craft." Create a fictional 10-Step Learning Journey that they might have taken to become an expert.
- This first Student Handout can go well with a historical figure that you are studying in class or a fictional character from a book you are reading. OR, feel free to just let the students choose someone "famous" to pretend and imagine what their journey toward expertise may have looked like - it's all to be made up if students don't really know what the process was!
- DIRECTIONS: Choose a skill or understanding that you consider yourself strong at. Think about where you started with this skill or understanding. Describe how little you knew. Then, try to identify & write the small pieces you learned on your way to today.
- On the second Student Handout, students apply the activity to their own life. They choose ONE skill to map out. Some of it can be made up if needed.

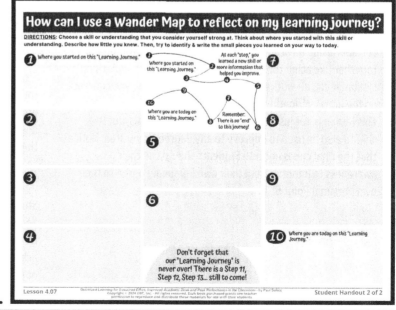

bit.ly/3RlIGqj

Connect the dots from "what I knew" to "what I learned" to "what's next" on your path to deeper understanding

4.08

Essential Question

What is a Yesterday, Today, Tomorrow Reflection?

Big Idea

When we are learning something relatively new to us or trying to meet a long-term goal, it can be helpful to look at what we knew to begin with, what we learned during our first few learning experiences, and make a plan for further learning in the future.

Lesson Overview

In this lesson, students think about the connection between synthesis, reflection, and goal setting through a "Yesterday, Today, Tomorrow Reflection." Through this activity, students consider a long-term goal that they have by reflecting on the prior knowledge they had related to this skill or topic prior to today's learning, what they just learned about in class today, and what they still need to learn about in the near future in order to achieve their goal.

Discussion/Reflection Questions

- Why is it helpful to think about "what comes next" in our learning journey when we're trying to meet a long-term goal of ours? Tell me more.
- What are some ways that you might use this strategy in your non-school life? How can you apply it to your personal goals?
- You recently learned about the importance of being more specific through the "Tell Me More" strategy, but the Student Handout didn't give you enough space to do so. How can you make sure that that doesn't stop you from "Telling Me More" at other times?

Teacher Tips

- This lesson works best if you teach Lesson 1.05 first. If you choose to skip that lesson, you will need to explain what the marbles in the cups mean on the Instructional Poster. (They represent the amount of knowledge or skill we have in a specific area - more marbles equals more knowledge or skill.)
- In addition, this lesson works best if your students have a long-term goal that they can consider for this exercise. If they don't, consider using an academic goal that everyone is working on together like acing the current unit test in math or something similar. If you all work on the same long-term goal, you can work on the activity together as well!
- This lesson is not just for achieving long-term goals, but it should also be used to improve to any degree in any area. Notice that the final cup is not full! Students should use their awareness to improve from their own Personal Point A to their own Personal Point B!

Student Tasks 〉 Transfer Goals

Student Tasks	Transfer Goals
Students learn to look to the past and present in order to decide what needs to be addressed in the future to meet a goal.	Students achieve their goals by being aware of HOW they need to improve in order to find success.
Students apply the Yesterday, Today, Tomorrow Reflection strategy to achieving a long-term goal or improving in any area.	Students internalize the strategy and use it to focus their improvement efforts on the areas that need the most attention.

INTRODUCTION

PLANNING

METACOGNITION

SYNTHESIS

REFLECTION

SELF-ASSESSMENT

GOAL SETTING

FEEDBACK

Instructional Poster(s)

- This lesson has ONE Instructional Poster.
- Use the Instructional Poster to help your students see how they can meet their long-term goals by combining (synthesizing) their prior knowledge with their new learning AND future learning. If it's a long-term goal, it won't be accomplished "today." So it's important to look at what needs to be done "tomorrow" to get to where you want to be.
- Yesterday and Tomorrow are in quotes on the Instructional Poster because students need to understand that it simply means "the past" and "the future." Today is not in quotes because it truly stands for today, but can be thought of as "the present" if that helps students in some way!
- Notice that the bottom of the Instructional Poster has overlays that show which step in the "Yesterday, Today, Tomorrow Reflection Process" relates to each step in the "Synthesis Process."

Student Handouts

- This lesson has TWO Student Handouts.
- DIRECTIONS: Choose a skill or topic that you would like to GROW. Make sure you know SOMETHING about it (but you don't need to know a lot). Decide what you will learn about today (or complete the New Learning section AFTER you learn about it today). Skip the Future Learning section and decide what you WANT to know or be able to do at the end of your learning process. Then, go back and explain what you will need to learn or practice in order to get your desired result.
- Make sure that students see that the steps are NOT in order on purpose on the first Student Handout.
- DIRECTIONS: Choose a topic you have just begun to learn about in school, and then answer the questions below.
- The second student handout doesn't allow for much space to write. That's just because this is a simple exercise to understand the process, but let students know that the process should be internalized more deeply in order to reap the most benefit.

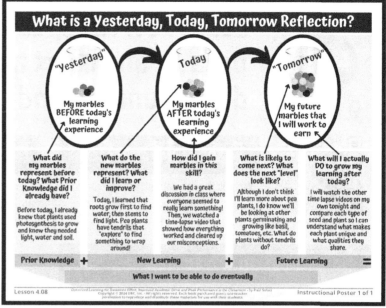

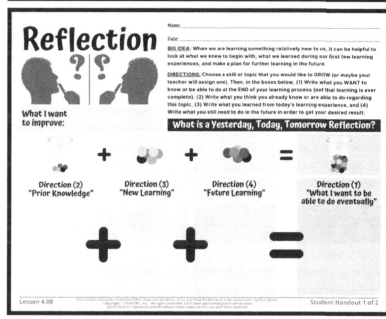

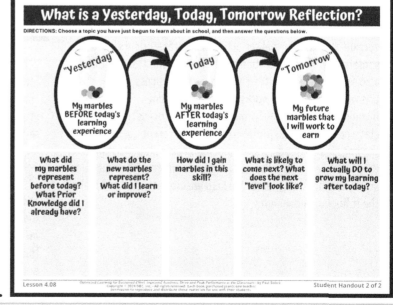

bit.ly/3QYc18B

Learn how to repeat the good, avoid the pitfalls, and chart a course for even deeper understanding for future success

Essential Question

What is the Formal Reflection Process?
(Mini-Lesson 1 of 2)

Big Idea

When we are learning something relatively new to us, it can be helpful to look at what we knew to begin with, what we learned during our first few learning experiences, and make a plan for further learning in the future.

Lesson Overview

In this lesson, students are taught a formal reflection procedure that they can use whenever they need a structured plan for reflecting. It begins with a summary of the experience, focusing strictly on the facts. Next is an exploration of the positive and negative events or situations the student experienced, along with an analysis of the reasons why the events or situations happened, and what can be done in the future to repeat the positive experiences and avoid the negative experiences. The procedure ends with a statement of what was learned academically, behaviorally, social-emotionally, etc. If preferred, this lesson can be combined with the next lesson, but teaching them as two separate lessons is recommended.

Discussion/Reflection Questions

- Why are you asked to "analyze the reasons for the positive (and negative) experiences"? Shouldn't it be enough that you list them? Why should you also analyze their causes?
- What is the purpose of having you write a "plan for the future" as it relates to the positive and negative experiences? Is it just a needless extra step, or is there some benefit?
- How do you plan to internalize this process so that your teacher doesn't need to make you write or record your reflection after each lesson? How will you make this a natural part of learning, rather than something extra?

Teacher Tips

- The Student Handouts for this lesson require students to complete a content-related activity, task or assignment in class BEFORE working on them. Any task that allows students to reflect on their learning and be able to evaluate how things went will work. If it's collaborative in some way, that's even better!
- Consider using the second Student Handout (or a modified version of it) as a formal reflection tool after students learn something new in class. (Don't just use it for this lesson!) But also encourage students to internalize the process so they do this without needing a worksheet to guide them.
- If you choose to have a "Formal Reflection Process" in your classroom, but would prefer to focus on different questions than the ones in this lesson, feel free to modify the slides to make them work for your group. This version is an attempt to dial in to students emotional memory to help ensure retention and make the reflection meaningful.

Student Tasks 〉 Transfer Goals

Student Tasks	Transfer Goals
Students learn "The Formal Reflection Process" as one means of reflecting on learning.	Students utilize this procedure for formal written reflections, but also internalize the steps and use them independently.
Student write reflections that focus strictly on the facts in some areas and their opinions (or emotions) in another.	Students keep fact and opinion separate in their minds as they reflect on learning experiences, ensuring that each is dealt with differently.

Instructional Poster(s)

- This lesson has ONE Instructional Poster.
- Today's Instructional Poster explains "The Formal Reflection Process." This is to be used when students need to formally write a reflection of an experience, but not when they are just asked to reflect internally.
- There are eight steps to the Formal Reflection Process. First, students summarize the experience using only facts. Then, they get to share the positives and negatives (opinions) along with the reasons for them and their plan for the future. Finally, students describe what was learned during the experience.

Student Handouts

- This lesson has TWO Student Handouts.
- DIRECTIONS: Read through the tips on how to summarize a learning experience below. Then, answer the question on the right hand side of the page as completely as you can.
- The first Student Handout provides additional tips to the students and asks a question that was answered on the Instructional Poster.
- DIRECTIONS: Complete the Formal Reflection Process for any learning experience you have in school. Try to be specific and detailed!
- The second Student Handout is the form for "The Formal Reflection Process" that students need to complete for a task that they recently completed (from earlier today is best). This form can be used often to formally reflect on important learning experiences, but the goal should always be to have the students complete these steps in their minds when they are NOT asked to complete a written one.

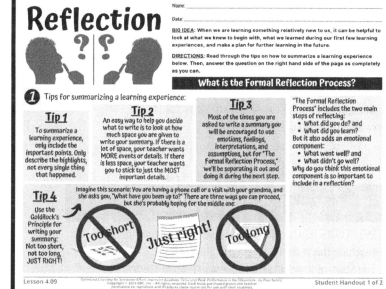

bit.ly/47S2y9U

4.10 Personalize and amplify your reflection to unlock deeper understanding and richer insights

Essential Question

What is the Formal Reflection Process?
(Mini-Lesson 2 of 2)

Big Idea

When we are learning something relatively new to us, it can be helpful to look at what we knew to begin with, what we learned during our first few learning experiences, and make a plan for further learning in the future.

Lesson Overview

In this lesson, students deepen their understanding of "The Formal Reflection Process" by discovering variations on the steps without changing the purpose of each step. Students still summarize the activity and their learning, while also connecting to their emotions. Students are provided several ways that they can interpret each step in the process that might not have been thought of originally. If preferred, this lesson can be combined with the previous lesson and taught all at once, but separating them into two lessons is recommended in order to prevent students from being overwhelmed by all of the the details.

Discussion/Reflection Questions

- Name one thing you learned today. Why was it important?
- How will you use what you learned in this lesson to make your formal reflections even better than they've been?
- If you had to add one more step to "The Formal Reflection Process," what would it be? Why did you choose this?

Teacher Tips

- PREREQUISITE: Teaching Lesson 4.09 is a prerequisite to teaching this lesson.
- The Student Handouts for this lesson require students to complete a content-related activity, task or assignment in class BEFORE working on them. Any task that allows students to reflect on their learning and be able to evaluate how things went will work. If it's collaborative in some way, that's even better!
- This is the same reflection process as the students completed during the last lesson. However, students are given several ideas for how they can interpret each section and it should result in deeper, more meaningful reflections. Students have also been given more space to write, so they can be expected to "Tell Me More" with their answers.
- Since the Student Handouts in this lesson expect a lot of effort on the students' part, please provide them enough time to do their best, and try not to assign this version too often.

Student Tasks 〉 Transfer Goals

Student Tasks	Transfer Goals
Students are provided several questions that help them see each step in "The Formal Reflection Process" a little bit differently.	Students see reflection as a process that changes to fit the situation, not a standard one-size-fits-all framework.
Students utilize those additional questions to reflect in a deeper, more authentic manner.	Because of its authenticity, students internalize & adopt "The Formal Reflection Process" leading to improved retention of information.

INTRODUCTION

PLANNING

METACOGNITION

SYNTHESIS

REFLECTION

SELF-ASSESSMENT

GOAL SETTING

FEEDBACK

Instructional Poster(s)

- This lesson has TWO Instructional Posters.
- There are two Instructional Posters for today's lesson. The first is a clarification of the last lesson, as well as an expansion of the ideas. Since students should know how to complete "The Formal Reflection Process" from the last lesson, this poster provides additional details that should improve the quality of their reflections. Go through the possible questions in each section in order to help students see the various ways they can reflect.
- The second Instructional Poster is "The Formal Reflection Process" by itself without the explanations from the last lesson. Time shouldn't need to be spent on it again today, but you may want to display it for students to be able to refer to.

Student Handouts

- This lesson has TWO Student Handouts.
- DIRECTIONS: Choose a topic you have just begun to learn about in school, and answer the questions below. Since this is a formal reflection, try to be as complete as possible with your answers. Be sure to "Tell Me More!"
- The two Student Handouts for this lesson are similar to the prior lesson's second Student Handout. It asks students to write out their answers to "The Formal Reflection Process." Students are given a little more space for this task and are asked to "Tell Me More." They should need additional time to complete everything with a high level of quality. They should be encouraged to use the additional questions taught on today's Instructional Poster when completing today's handout.

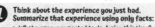

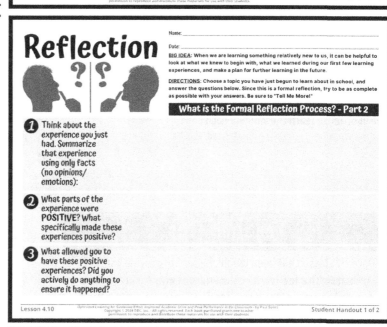

bit.ly/3GiWb3w

Don't wait for permission to reflect, use those spare minutes to think about your learning and make it more permanent

Essential Question

How does the amount of time I have affect my reflection?

Big Idea

After most lessons, we don't have a lot of time to reflect, but that doesn't mean we shouldn't try! Even if we have just one or two minutes, we can silently describe our learning experience and plan to transfer that learning to new experiences in the future! The more time we have, the more detailed our reflection should become.

Lesson Overview

In this lesson, students learn that the more time that their teacher gives them to reflect on their learning, the more detailed their reflection should be. Students also learn that many teachers will not actually provide them with classtime to reflect on learning, so it will be up to them to remember to take a moment after a learning experience to reflect on some basic information. Students are asked to complete several different types of reflections over a period of time in order to learn the value of each.

Discussion/Reflection Questions

- Why does the amount of time provided to you for reflection matter?
- What is expected of you now that you've been taught how to reflect after learning experiences?
- How will you decide if you are successful at remembering to reflect on your own over the next few weeks? What will you do to self-assess on this skill?

Teacher Tips

- Once this lesson has been taught, be sure to provide your students with a few learning experiences where you ask them to complete a reflection afterwards. Try to give students between 1-2 minutes, 3-5 minutes, 6-10 minutes, and more than 10 minutes for four different reflections. Provide them with a copy of "The Formal Reflection Process" and perhaps a simple reminder of the informal reflection questions discussed in this lesson.
- Students will need to be scaffolded in order to internalize this skill and transfer it to new situations on their own. So for the next few weeks, if you can remind them to reflect after each significant learning experience, that will eventually help them remember on their own to do so. You will just need to transition from reminding them after each experience to asking them about their reflections after the reflection time is over. At that point you can remind them that they should be reflecting on their own without reminders.

Student Tasks 〉 Transfer Goals

Student Tasks	Transfer Goals
Students reflect quickly in their heads after a learning experience to prepare for days when their teacher doesn't provide them with reflection time.	Students automatically reflect on each learning experience after it is completed whether prompted by the teacher or not..
Students explore scenarios in the classroom where they are given varying amounts of time in class to reflect.	Students choose appropriate reflection activities to complete after learning experiences that are based on the amount of time they are given.

Instructional Poster(s)

- This lesson has TWO Instructional Posters.
- The first Instructional Poster sets the purpose for the lesson: to help students transfer the skill of Reflection to future learning experiences without requiring the teacher's help. It also provides suggestions for the type of reflections that might work depending on the time allotted for reflection.
- The second Instructional Poster goes more in depth on what students are expected to do in their reflection based on the amount of time they are given to reflect.

Student Handouts

- This lesson has TWO Student Handouts.
- DIRECTIONS: This lesson describes several types of reflections, based on the amount of time each should take. With your teacher's guidance or on your own, complete each reflection below for four different learning experiences. Place check marks in each box when they are done. On the next page, answer each question on the lines provided.
- The first Student Handout lists four basic reflections based on the time given to reflect and is to be used a checklist for students. Their goal is to try to do a reflection from each of the four main timeframes for reflecting.
- The second Student Handout gives students four sample learning experiences and asks the students what kind of reflection they believe would be the most appropriate.
- Students are asked to write their answers on the notebook paper lines provided.

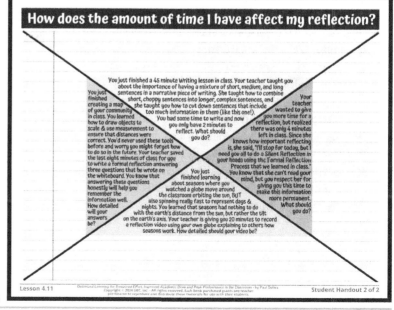

How does the amount of time I have affect my reflection?

The ultimate goal of these lessons is to get you, the student, to do these skills on your own, without a teacher asking you to do so. Obviously, you have to want to do them, you have to know how to do them, and have to have time to do them.

Since you will not always have a teacher who provides you with time in class to reflect (or any of the other skills in this program), it becomes your responsibility to learn how and when to do them independently.

Learning Task	Time available for reflection	Possible Reflection Styles
You just listened to a lecture on the Ancient Greeks. You took notes and have a worksheet for homework.	None	Since class just ended and your teacher didn't give any time for reflection, it's up to you to take a moment to review what you learned. Just think about the first part of the lesson, then middle and the end. Then transition.
It's the middle of your Writer's Workshop class period, and your teacher just finished a mini lesson on commas.	1-2 minutes	You'll have to re-focus on your writing soon, but you decide to reflect on the commas lesson. If you have a partner, ask them clarifying questions about what you think you learned & encourage your partner to do the same.
Your class just watched a video on Photosynthesis and your teacher said you will have a quiz on it tomorrow.	3-5 minutes	Your teacher has given you 3-5 minutes at the end of the period to reflect on the video and discuss it with a partner. You decide to use the "The Formal Reflection Process" as a way to discuss what you learned.
You learned about sales prices in math and used some recent ads from the newspaper to do percent problems (50% off!).	6-10 minutes	Your teacher has asked you to take the next 6-10 minutes to write a reflection of today's activity. You write down what you did during today's activity, what you learned, and how you hope to use your learning in the future.
After two months of preparation, your class just finished the Science Fair! Your project was on DNA.	10+ minutes	Your teacher has given you 10-20 minutes to formally reflect on the whole Science Fair process independently. You decide to use the "The Formal Reflection Process" as a way to organize your thoughts in writing.

Reflection

Name: _____ **Date:** _____

BIG IDEA: After most lessons, we don't have a lot of time to reflect, but that doesn't mean we shouldn't try! Even if we have just one or two minutes, we can silently describe our learning experience and plan to transfer that learning to new experiences in the future! The more time we have, the more detailed our reflection should become.

DIRECTIONS: This lesson describes several types of reflections, based on the amount of time each should take. With your teacher's guidance or on your own, complete each reflection below for four different learning experiences. Place check marks in each box when they are done. On the next page, answer each question on the lines provided.

How does the amount of time I have affect my reflection?

Good for a simple activity or an introductory activity

1-2 minutes — 1. What did you do? 2. What did you learn? 3. How you plan to transfer it to a new situation in the future? — Silently in your head or out loud with a partner, describe your learning experience, what you learned, and how you plan to transfer it to a new situation in the future.

3-5 minutes — Complete "The Formal Reflection Process" in your head silently, or out loud with a partner. You don't need to write anything down, but complete all of the steps in the process! — **Good for reading, writing or spelling strategies**

Good for a new math, science or social studies concept

6-10 minutes — 1. What did you do? 2. What did you learn? 3. A new plan to transfer it to a new situation in the future? — Describe your learning experience, and how you plan to transfer it to a new situation in the future on paper or on video. Answer any additional reflection questions from your teacher, as well.

Over 10 minutes — Complete "The Formal Reflection Process" on paper or on video. Be sure to complete all of the steps and "Tell Me More" so we dig deeply into each component of your reflection! — **Good for the end of a project or the end of a unit**

How does the amount of time I have affect my reflection?

You just finished a 45 minute Writing lesson in class. Your teacher taught you about the importance of having a mixture of short, medium, and long sentences in a narrative piece of writing. She taught you how to combine short, choppy sentences into longer, complex sentences, and she taught you how to cut down sentences that include too much information in them (like this one!). You had some time to write and now you only have 2 minutes to reflect. What should you do?

You just finished creating a map of your community in class. You learned how to draw objects to scale & use measurement to ensure that distances were correct. You'd never used these tools before and worry you might forget how to do so in the future. Your teacher saved the last eight minutes of class for you to write a formal reflection answering three questions that he wrote on the whiteboard. You know that answering these questions honestly will help you remember the information well. How detailed will your answers be?

Your teacher wanted to give you more time for a reflection, but realized there was only 4 minutes left in class. Since she knows how important reflecting is, she said, "I'll stop for today, but I need you all to do a Silent Reflection in your heads using the Formal Reflection Process that we learned in class." You know that she can't read your mind, but you respect her for giving you this time to make this information more permanent. What should you do?

You just finished learning about seasons where you watched a globe move around the classroom orbiting the sun, BUT also spinning really fast to represent days & nights. You learned that seasons had nothing to do with the earth's distance from the sun, but rather the tilt on the earth's axis. Your teacher is giving you 20 minutes to record a reflection video using your own globe explaining to others how seasons work. How detailed should your video be?

bit.ly/40ZiAwd

Discover how seemingly ordinary class activities are actually reflections, helping you make your learning more permanent

Essential Question

What are some activities that are actually reflections?

Big Idea

Sometimes, you are doing a reflection activity in class and you don't even realize it! Your teacher might not call it reflection, but that's its main purpose! It is during these times that you may feel like you are getting the same benefits from the activity as you would have gotten from reflecting!

Lesson Overview

In this lesson, students make a connection between certain class activities and more formal reflection activities. A large number of class activities are assigned so that students can apply what they just learned in a lesson in class. These activities, and many more, not only serve as a means of transferring the newly acquired skill to a new situation, but also serve as a tool for reflection. If students can internalize how these activities help us reflect on our learning, they will better understand what is happening inside their brain as they convert short-term into long-term memory. In addition, when students participate in activities like these, they don't have to do as much reflecting on their own, since reflection already occurred during the lesson.

Discussion/Reflection Questions

- Why don't we have to spend as much time reflecting on our own after a class activity that had reflection built in?
- What impact does reflection have on our long-term memory of a newly-learned skill or concept from class?
- How can a class activity (like the ones from today's lesson) take the place of a formal reflection? How can it achieve the same purpose?

Teacher Tips

- A tableau vivant is a posed "photograph" of a scene where the characters in the photograph (your students) pose doing something specific for their individual persona.
  - Wikipedia: A tableau vivant, French for "living picture", is a static scene containing one or more actors or models. They are stationary and silent, usually in costume, and carefully posed, with props and/or scenery. It thus combines aspects of theatre and the visual arts.
  - Tate.org.uk: Tableau is used to describe a painting or photograph in which characters are arranged for picturesque or dramatic effect and appear absorbed and completely unaware of the existence of the viewer.
- Have a few ideas of some activities you have done in class where the students "basically" ended up reflecting on their learning. Perhaps it was through an application activity or a 15-minute project. Either way, you didn't consider it a reflection activity originally, but can see how it acted as one now.

Student Tasks > Transfer Goals

Student Tasks	Transfer Goals
Students learn that many class activities can serve as a means of reflecting, instead of doing a formal reflection on their own.	Students only formally reflect when they haven't already done so in class, which helps them see the benefits of their time better.
Students describe how certain class activities act as reflection activities, in addition to their original purpose.	Students value the act of reflection more and integrate it into their everyday life, because they see how reflection is all around them.

Instructional Poster(s)

- This lesson has TWO Instructional Posters.
- Read through a list of class activities that act as reflections, but are disguised as classwork. Then, brainstorm four more as a class!
- Directions for the second Instructional Poster: Time to think creatively and work together as a class! The following Classroom Reflection Activities are all pretty fun to complete, but not every reflection activity goes well with every lesson! Think back to all of the lessons you've done in school this year and last. Which lesson would fit best with each of the following activities? You might not be able to come up with an answer for each, but try your best!
- Identify the activities from your classroom that might also be reflection activities.

Student Handouts

- This lesson has TWO Student Handouts.
- DIRECTIONS: Write a "1" next to your favorite activity, a "2" next to your second favorite, etc. Be sure to put a number next to all 12 options! Answer the two questions in the gray boxes. Finally, complete the next page by drawing a line connecting the activity with how it helps us to reflect and explain the final two on your own.
- If some students haven't already discovered the connection between each activity and how it helps us reflect, this final task will help. Students match the activity to how it helps us reflect and then have to write two of their own at the end. Feel free to swap out activities if you don't think they apply or if you have more personalized ones in your class.

What are some activities that are actually reflections?

Sometimes, you are doing a reflection activity in class and you don't even realize it! Your teacher might not call it reflection, but that's its main purpose!

It is during these times that you may feel like you are getting the same benefits from the activity as you would have gotten from reflecting!

- Participating in a class discussion
- Conducting and participating in an interview with a peer
- Answering reflection questions from a list of choices
- Collecting & describing work samples for a portfolio
- Writing about your learning experience in a journal
- Completing an exit slip
- Role playing with others to demonstrate a process
- Photographing a tableau vivant you create with explanations
- Summarizing your learning on a fictional newscast
- Creating a photo album of your learning with captions
- Creating a slideshow with photos, videos & descriptions
- Recording yourself explaining your learning on a video blog

What else?

Lesson 4.12 — Instructional Poster 1 of 2

Reflection

Name:
Date:

BIG IDEA: Sometimes, you are doing a reflection activity in class and you don't even realize it! Your teacher might not call it reflection, but that's its main purpose! It is during these times that you may feel like you are getting the same benefits from the activity as you would have gotten from reflecting!

DIRECTIONS: Write a "1" next to your favorite activity, a "2" next to your second favorite, etc. Be sure to put a number next to all 12 options! Answer the two questions in the gray boxes. Finally, complete the next page by drawing a line connecting the activity with how it helps us to reflect and explain the final two on your own.

What are some activities that are actually reflections?

- Conducting and participating in an interview with a peer
- Answering reflection questions from a list of choices
- Collecting & describing work samples for a portfolio
- Writing about your learning experience in a journal
- Participating in a class discussion
- Completing an exit slip

Describe your reasons for your **#1** choice:

Describe your reasons for your **#12** choice:

- Role playing with others to demonstrate a process
- Photographing a tableau vivant you create with explanations
- Summarizing your learning on a fictional newscast
- Creating a photo album of your learning with captions
- Creating a slideshow with photos, videos & descriptions
- Recording yourself explaining your learning on a video blog

Lesson 4.12 — Student Handout 1 of 2

What are some activities that are actually reflections?

Activity	How it helps us reflect
Participating in a class discussion	In order to participate, you need to think back to what you learned and put it into words to share.
Conducting and participating in an interview with a peer	
Answering reflection questions from a list of choices	Your teacher might ask you to find evidence that shows growth or mastery of a skill or understanding and you reflect as you think about each activity.
Collecting & describing work samples for a portfolio	
Writing about your learning experience in a journal	To come up with things to say, you need to first reflect on what you did before you can put it into words.
Completing an exit slip	
Role playing with others to demonstrate a process	Since you need to remain still in some sort of position for this activity, you first need to reflect on what the characters or historical figures might have been doing.
Photographing tableaux that you create with explanations	
Summarizing your learning on a fictional newscast	
Creating a photo album of your learning with captions	
Creating a slideshow with photos, videos & descriptions	
Recording yourself explaining your learning on a video blog	

Lesson 4.12 — Student Handout 2 of 2

INTRODUCTION
PLANNING
METACOGNITION
SYNTHESIS
REFLECTION
SELF-ASSESSMENT
GOAL SETTING
FEEDBACK

bit.ly/47xmrTD

Reflect with a partner to gain new perspectives and broaden your understanding of your learning journey

Essential Question

How can I reflect with a partner?

Big Idea

For many of us, reflection is made stronger when it includes others in the process. When we're open to sharing our thoughts and concerns and hearing what others have to say about them, we can maximize our learning potential. After all, two brains are better than one! By occasionally reflecting with a random, assigned partner, we can begin to understand how our learning varies from other people's learning styles.

Lesson Overview

In this lesson, students learn how to reflect on a learning experience with a partner. They learn about the benefits of reflecting with others, their responsibilities while reflecting with others, and an informal and formal guide for reflecting with a partner. Students sign a contract stating that they agree to be responsible for several tasks that are designed to make the most of their reflection time. They also get to experience the "Formal Reflection Process" with a partner AND the "Informal Reflection Process" with a partner.

Discussion/Reflection Questions

- Why do we need to sign a contract stating that we will be responsible for several tasks during all partner reflections?
- What are some differences between the "Informal Reflection Process" and the "Formal Reflection Process"? What are some similarities?
- How will you step up and demonstrate leadership skills next time you get to reflect with a partner? How will you step back and encourage your partner to do the same?

Teacher Tips

- Try to provide students with at least two opportunities to reflect with a randomly-assigned partner on an activity or task from class so they can complete the "Informal Reflection Process" with a partner AND the "Formal Reflection Process" (the Student Handouts).
- Decide if you want to add or revise any questions on either reflection process. Then, consider modeling a partner reflection for the class where two students discuss the informal questions and another partnership discusses the formal questions AND writes their answers down. Provide students with suggestions and feedback for making each discussion as meaningful and reflective as possible.

Student Tasks 〉 Transfer Goals

Student Tasks	Transfer Goals
Students read about the benefits of reflecting with others.	Students reflect with partners when given the chance because they see its value.
Students read about their responsibilities while reflecting with others and sign a contract agreeing to try to follow them.	Students take partner reflection seriously and get the most out of each experience.

INTRODUCTION

PLANNING

METACOGNITION

SYNTHESIS

REFLECTION

SELF-ASSESSMENT

GOAL SETTING

FEEDBACK

Instructional Poster(s)

- This lesson has ONE Instructional Poster.
- The Instructional Poster for this lesson is a web that describes the benefits of reflecting with others. It contains five ideas, but asks you and your students to brainstorm more on your own. Even if you or the students can't come up with many more benefits, hopefully the deep thought and discussion will be worthwhile.

Student Handouts

- This lesson has TWO Student Handouts.
- DIRECTIONS: It is extremely important that we learn how to accomplish tasks WITH others, rather than separate from them. However, the more we interact with each other, the more comfortable we get, and possibly the more we might get off-task! Remind yourself of your responsibilities while working with a partner, and then sign the contract. Then, look over the Informal Reflection Process and Formal Reflection Process we will use in class this year (below and on the next page). Complete both as soon as possible.
- The first Student Handout asks students to read through their responsibilities while reflecting with a partner, and then sign the contract stating that they agree to try their best to follow those responsibilities.
- In addition, the "Informal Reflection Process" is described on this page. Students are asked to practice this informal process with a partner some time soon. They don't need to write anything down, just have a conversation about the three questions listed (and any others you or they want to add).
- The second Student Handout is the "Formal Reflection Process" modified for partners. Students need to complete one of these soon as well.

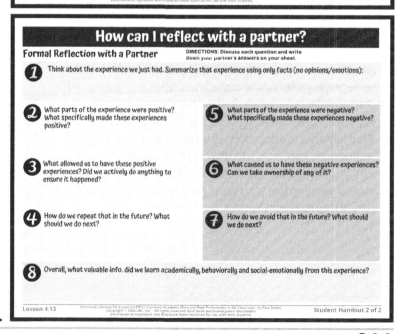

4.14

Own your successes, forgive yourself for any missteps, and revel in those lightbulb moments with the Six A's of Reflection

bit.ly/47Ora3P

Essential Question

What are the Six A's of Reflecting on your day?

Big Idea

Taking time at the end of our school day to reflect can be valuable for many reasons. One way to do that is to have a few dedicated areas in which to reflect each day. By using the 6 A's of Reflection, you are certain to reflect on at least one valuable experience every day.

Lesson Overview

In this lesson, students learn a reflection routine they can use each day to reflect on their day in school. It provides students with six reflection prompts they can choose between that gets them to think back on their day. The "Six A's" include: Acknowledging what you did well today, Apologizing to yourself or others for something you wish you could do over, "Aha" means identifying something important that was learned today, Assessing yourself and describing what you could have done better and how you will try to improve, Appreciating someone in class that helped you, and Admiring someone who impressed you by doing something kind or selfless.

Discussion/Reflection Questions

- Why is it beneficial to reflect on our day in school?
- Which "A" do you think you will have the easiest time answering? Which "A" do you think you will have the hardest time answering? Why?
- How will you ensure that you consider ALL of the A's each day, rather than just focus in on the same one day after day?

Teacher Tips

- I suggest providing a certain amount of time (~5 minutes) for students to complete this activity each day at the end of the day. Students should try to complete as many of the "Six A's" as they can in the given time. If your students won't get as much out of doing this every day, do it every other day or 1-2 times each week.
- Provide time at the end to share the public apologies, appreciations and admirations of others. Remind students that some people prefer private appreciation rather than public, and that some things are better done in private than in front of everyone (e.g. embarrassing situations involving others, etc.).
- You might want to ask students to try to get at least one in each section every week or two. You may say they shouldn't repeat a section more than once per week, etc. You may also want to add some of your own (or the students' own) "A" ideas or remove some if they don't work for you.

Student Tasks 〉 Transfer Goals

Student Tasks	Transfer Goals
Students learn six reflection prompts that help them reflect on their day in school.	Students internalize these six types of reflections and make them a part of their everyday routine.
Students share some of their reflections publicly in order to praise others for what they've done.	Students feel good when praising their peers for doing good things for others and eventually want to do those things for others too!

Instructional Poster(s)

- This lesson has ONE Instructional Poster.
- The Instructional Poster explains the Six A's of reflecting on your day: Acknowledge what you did well today, Apologize to yourself or others for something you wish you could do over, Aha means something important that was learned today, Assess yourself and describe what you could have done better and how you will try to improve, Appreciate someone in class that helped you, and Admire someone who impressed you by doing something kind or selfless.
- You can decide how many of the six A's your students complete each day, or you can decide how much time to allow students to do as many as possible.

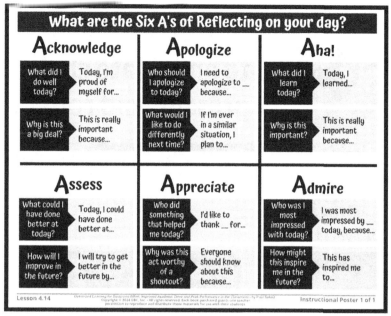

Student Handouts

- This lesson has TWO Student Handouts.
- DIRECTIONS: At the end of each school day, choose one "A" to focus on for the day. Complete the sentence starter in both boxes and try to mix it up each day - try not to repeat an "A" until the next week. If your reflection involves others, consider sharing it with them if your teacher doesn't have a formal routine for doing so.
- Today's student handouts are a reproducible form (front and back) that students can complete each day, every other day, or less occasionally. For today's lesson, have students complete all six sections, even though it is most likely that they will not usually complete all six.
- Remind students to follow the sentence starters in each box. If you'd like to encourage creative thinking, have students ask you if they can modify a sentence starter to make it work for a different application that also involves reflecting on important aspects of their day!

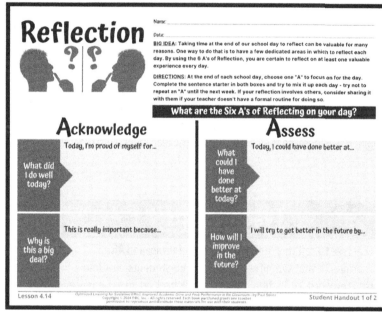

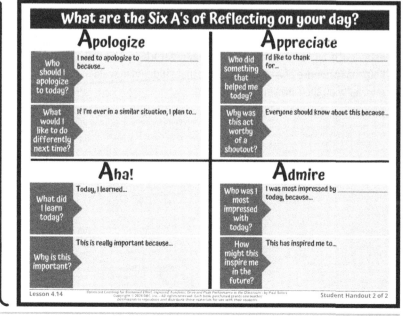

bit.ly/411p2mn

Utilize "Preflection" and "Intraflection" to anticipate challenges, adapt to the present, and reflect on experiences

Essential Question

How do I reflect Before, During and After working?

Big Idea

When we take time to Preflect, we can anticipate problems & be ready to handle them proactively. We can address our concerns and prepare for things we don't enjoy. Preflecting also assists us in reflecting once the learning experience is over because we made certain predictions and addressed certain goals before we started.

Lesson Overview

In this lesson, students learn to apply the concept of "reflection" to thinking about an experience BEFORE it happens and WHILE it is happening, in addition to the more traditional reflecting AFTER an experience happens. We use two new words: Preflection and Intraflection to help solidify this concept. By thinking about an experience before it happens, students can better prepare for the unexpected, anticipate potential issues, and avoid mistakes that they can predict. By thinking about an experience while it is happening, students become conscious of the Preflections they imagined and increase their awareness of the learning taking place.

Discussion/Reflection Questions

- Why were the words "Preflection" and "Intraflection" created for this lesson? Why didn't we just call it all "Reflection"?
- When in the recent past do you wish you had used this routine (reflecting before, during, and after a learning experience)
- How might this routine have helped you?
- When will you use this on your own in the near future? Why are you choosing this activity? Is it in school or out of school?

Teacher Tips

- Feel free to call this "Reflecting Before, During, and After Learning" if that simplifies things for your students. Just know that the word "reflection" means to look back on an experience. These two newly invented words attempt to avoid confusion with the "re-" prefix.
- Once students have completed this lesson, remember to ask your students to "Preflect" before beginning a learning experience, and to "Intraflect" while they are working. This will help make it more of a routine or habit that students may do internally on their own in the future.

Student Tasks 〉 Transfer Goals

| Students learn how to "reflect" before, during, and after a learning experience. | Students use this thinking routine before, during and after learning experiences in class. |
| Students practice this routine using a fictional example of an Olympic athlete. | Students apply this routine to activities outside of the classroom. |

Instructional Poster(s)

- This lesson has ONE Instructional Poster.
- This Instructional Poster teaches two new words (they are made-up words):
  - Reflection: (re- means "again" or "back," and -flect means "bend.") When light "bends back" off a mirror, we see our reflection. When we look back at our recent history, we review "back" to everything that happened.
  - Preflection: (pre- means "before.") This invented word is an attempt to try to imagine what an experience might be like "before" you begin.
  - Intraflection: (intra- means "within.") This invented word is an attempt to describe what is actually happening and compare it to your "Preflections."

Student Handouts

- This lesson has THREE Student Handouts.
- DIRECTIONS: Read all of the sentence starters and explanations of Preflection, Intraflection, and Reflection on this handout and the previous page. Then, answer the question at the bottom as completely as you can. Finally, complete the next page.
- The first Student Handout helps guide students while "Preflecting," "Intraflecting," and "Reflecting" using sentence starters and guiding questions. Have students use these you have them do this activity again in the future.
- The second Student Handout guides students through a fictional scenario where they pretend to be an Olympic athlete who uses the Preflection, Intraflection, and Reflection strategy before participating in their event. An Olympic high diver is given as an example.
- The third Student Handout is optional and is just a blank chart with the three columns on it for students to use with an assignment of your choice or their choice.

INTRODUCTION
PLANNING
METACOGNITION
SYNTHESIS
REFLECTION
SELF-ASSESSMENT
GOAL SETTING
FEEDBACK

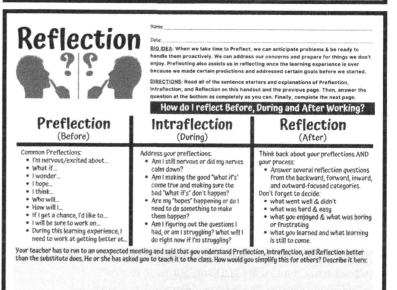

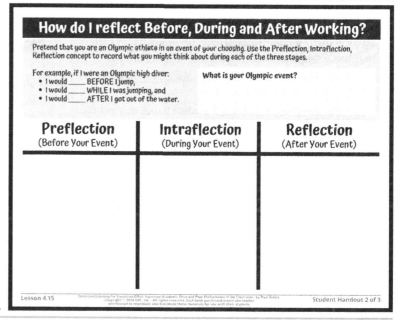

bit.ly/47VcfUK

Use the "Redo" superpower to reflect on past actions, envision better choices, and learn from them without regret

4.16

Essential Question

How do I reflect on a mistake and accept it?

Big Idea

We all make mistakes. Some of us don't care at all when we make mistakes. That's not great because our mistakes might affect others in negative ways or cause us to have negative consequences. But some people care too much! They cry or get angry when they make a mistake. That's not ideal either. We need to accept the fact that we all make mistakes and try to prevent the same mistakes from happening in the future.

Lesson Overview

In this lesson, students imagine that they have a superpower where they can go back in time and change what they did during an event. We call this the power of "Redo." After the students reflect on their past and consider what they would like to change, they describe how they would change their behavior and imagine how things might turn out differently. Finally, students are left with the fact that we don't have the power of Redo in real life, so we need to make our actions count and then accept how things turn out afterwards. When we make a mistake, we need to apologize, make amends, and try not to repeat that mistake. And most importantly, we need to get over it and move on.

Discussion/Reflection Questions

- Why is it important that we accept our mistakes and try to move on from them, rather than have regrets and wish we could turn back time?
- What is one way you can make an amends for a mistake that you made in the past? (An amends is "to do something to correct a mistake that one has made or a bad situation that one has caused.")
- Imagine that your best friend is extremely upset with themself over the way they treated a mutual friend. How could you talk them through the process of moving on?

Teacher Tips

- "Don't care so much that you cry, Just care enough that you try," was an actual quote that I said to my 5th grade students accidentally one day. One of my students liked it so much that she created a poster for our classroom with that quote on it! I always wanted my students to work hard and care about their work, but sometimes some students would put more pressure on them than I wanted, causing them to cry when they believed they had disappointed me. Be aware of the pressure you inadvertently place on your students. Make sure they care just the right amount. No more, no less! :)
- If you like the setup of the second Student Handout, you might consider using it when students make mistakes with their behavior. Instead of traditional consequences, you might find that many students do well with a reflection sheet like the one in this lesson. Just be sure to go over it with the student before the end of class so you can be sure they took it seriously and will indeed try to learn from their mistake.

Student Tasks ⟩ Transfer Goals

Student Tasks	Transfer Goals
Students use their imaginary "Redo" superpower to change a mistake they made in the past.	Students become more reflective on their actions and develop deeper empathy toward others.
Students learn a method for forgiving themself and moving on from a mistake they made or an action they wish they could change, but can't.	Students acknowledge the mistakes they make, apologize, make amends, try not to repeat the same mistake again & ultimately move on without remorse.

Instructional Poster(s)

- This lesson has ONE Instructional Poster.
- The Instructional Poster discusses the idea of having the superpower of being able to "redo" past experiences in order to never make mistakes! Although this superpower would be amazingly awesome, we all need to learn how to handle mistakes in a positive way, while still reflecting on them so we can make amends or prevent future recurrences.
- By using this "superpower," we can reflect on an experience that we regret, and imagine how we would redo things if we were given another chance!
- You may wish to point out at this time that we DON'T actually have this superpower, so we will need to learn steps we can take to accept our mistakes and move on from them.

Student Handouts

- This lesson has TWO Student Handouts.
- DIRECTIONS: Follow the directions below and on the next page to reflect on a mistake you recently made and learn to accept it. If your teacher is asking you to complete this activity due to a mistake you JUST made, think carefully about what you write so it is clear to your teacher that you WILL make an amends and move on from it successfully.
- For the first Student Handout, students circle statements that are correct & cross out statements that are incorrect. Answers: O, O, X, O, X, O, O, X, X.
- On the second Student Handout, students reflect on a mistake they made recently. (Avoid encouraging students to have regrets. If they don't have any regrets, they are living life mindfully!) They will describe their mistake and then use the steps that are provided in order to move on.

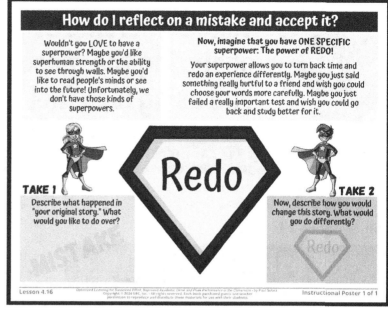

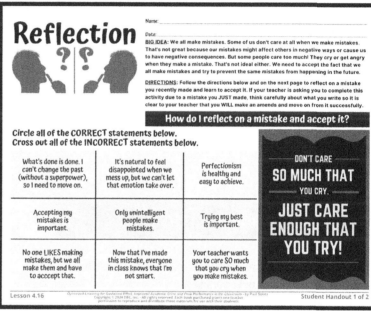

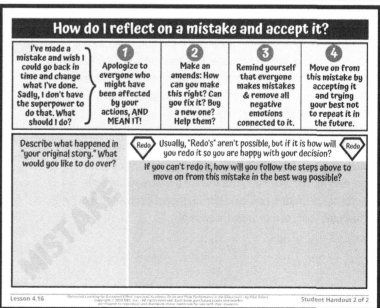

INTRODUCTION

PLANNING

METACOGNITION

SYNTHESIS

REFLECTION

SELF-ASSESSMENT

GOAL SETTING

FEEDBACK

217

bit.ly/4abeV2T

Take ownership of your learning by analyzing the reasons behind a low grade, and using it to fuel future improvement

Essential Question

How do I analyze and reflect on a grade?

Lesson Overview

In this lesson, students learn how to analyze and reflect on a grade they received that is lower than the student expected or had hoped for. It teaches them what to do when retakes are available , but also stresses the importance of being prepared in the first place. As students complete the organizer regarding the grade they received, they identify areas of their work that could have been better, thereby leading to the grade they received. Students make a plan for avoiding similar mistakes in the future and are encouraged to make a S.M.A.A.R.T.E.R. Goal or a Goal Burst if the student feels it could help.

Teacher Tips

- Asking students to highlight their errors can help them see which mistakes they made and how those mistakes could have led to a lower-than-expected grade.
- Requiring students to create a Goal Burst or S.M.A.A.R.T.E.R. Goal after completing this lesson would be a great way to show students how all of the steps in the Student-Led Self-Improvement Process are connected. If you hope to have your students complete this organizer independently in the future, be sure to let them know that, normally, they get to decide if they are going to make a goal or not (so they don't avoid this organizer in order to avoid extra work).
- If your students are older, you may want to have them analyze their mistakes more deeply in order to fully understand how their grade reflects their achievement. Depending on your grading format, you may want to have them calculate their percentage grade by dividing the number of wrong answers by the number of correct ones, for example.

Big Idea

Getting a grade that is lower than you hoped or expected can sometimes result in negative emotions. Some people get sad, angry or defensive. Some people try to blame others or use excuses to take the blame off of themselves. Taking time to analyze WHY you got the grade that you did can actually result in valuable learning that can be applied in future situations.

Discussion/Reflection Questions

- Why are there times in life that you deserve a second chance? Why are there times in life that you shouldn't get a second chance? Don't focus on providing examples. Try to explain WHY different situations deserve different expectations.
- What questions might you change, add or remove from the Student Handouts to make it more useful for you and your classmates? Why?
- How will you independently use the questions from the Student Handout in the future, without being prompted? How will you respond logically to a low grade or constructive feedback, instead of reactively?

Student Tasks ⟩ Transfer Goals

Student Tasks	Transfer Goals
Students learn that there are times when a retake or revision opportunity make sense, and times when they don't.	Students don't expect everyone to give them second chances, and are prepared the first time.
Students learn how to identify WHY they earned the grade that they earned through analysis and reflection.	Students don't reactively complain about a low grade. Instead, they analyze & reflect on what they did to earn a lower-than-expected grade.

Instructional Poster(s)

- This lesson has ONE Instructional Poster.
- The Instructional Poster for this lesson focuses on the importance of being prepared BEFORE beginning an assignment or assessment so you don't experience any negative surprises.
- Since there are times in life when a re-take or a chance to revise is possible, students need to accept low grades or constructive feedback and use it to improve the quality of their work or paint a more accurate picture of their level of achievement.
- Finally, students need to learn from negative academic experiences (e.g. poor grades, harsh feedback, etc.) and improve their work in the present and the future, but not dwell on the past.

Student Handouts

- This lesson has TWO Student Handouts.
- DIRECTIONS: Follow the directions below and on the next page to analyze and reflect on the grade you just earned. Take responsibility for the grade regardless of any excuses that come to mind.
- The Student Handout is a two page graphic organizer for students to analyze and reflect on a grade they received that was lower than they had hoped or expected. By going through the questions, students take more ownership of their present results and create a plan for future improvement.
- If desired, feel free to modify the questions to more appropriately suit your students' needs.

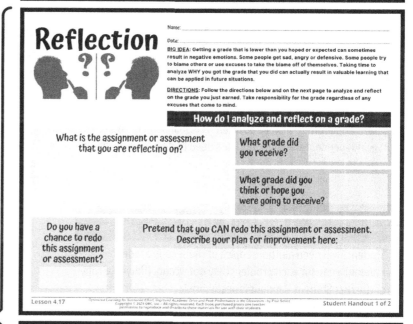

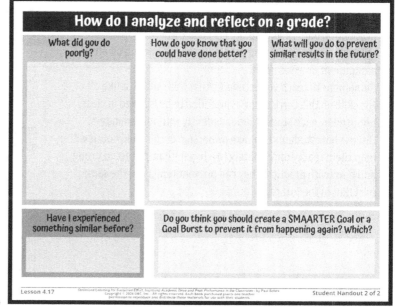

INTRODUCTION
PLANNING
METACOGNITION
SYNTHESIS
REFLECTION
SELF-ASSESSMENT
GOAL SETTING
FEEDBACK

Become a mistake detective by digging deep to uncover the "why" behind wrong answers to prevent similar mistakes later

bit.ly/40X4M5v

Essential Question

How do I analyze and reflect on an incorrect answer?

Big Idea

By taking the time to analyze WHY you are making the mistakes that you are making, you'll be able to discover patterns that can be corrected. If you are making lots of careless mistakes, you might consider making a goal to eliminate those so your teacher can discover what you actually know! Find out the SOURCE of your mistakes so you can fix it and continue to grow.

Lesson Overview

In this lesson, students take what was learned in the prior lesson and dig deeper into analyzing and reflecting on each wrong answer. They learn to see WHY they got an answer wrong. For example, did they rush? Were they distracted? Did they misread a direction? Did they forget to carry the two? When students learn to identify WHY they got a problem wrong, they are more likely to make the appropriate improvements in the future. Once they understand why they got the problem wrong, they can make a plan for the future so they don't repeat that mistake as often. The goal of all of this is, of course, independent transfer. Students need to do a form of this on their own in the future in order to reap the most benefits.

Discussion/Reflection Questions

- Why is it important to know the specific reasons why you got a problem wrong?
- How can knowing the specific reasons why you got a problem wrong also help your self-esteem or self-image academically?
- What is the most common mistake you made on a recent assignment or assessment? How will you try to avoid repeating that mistake in the future?

Teacher Tips

- Students will need multiple copies of the second Student Handout - one for each problem they got wrong. (Only one copy of the first Student Handout is necessary.)
- This lesson should be taught DURING or AFTER Lesson 4.18 in order to be most effective.
- Consider making a poster out of the reasons why students get a problem wrong. Then, display this poster whenever your students are analyzing the problems they got wrong on an assignment or assessment.
- Remember to teach your students that this skill (just like all of the skills in this curriculum) is intended to be learned in class, but used by each student independently without reminders. Discuss how students can take ownership of this skill, how it will help them react appropriately to a lower-than-expected grade, and how (with practice) they can prevent repeating the same mistakes in the future.

Student Tasks 〉 Transfer Goals

Student Tasks	Transfer Goals
Students learn that there are many reasons why a student might get a problem wrong on an assignment or assessment.	Students no longer assume they get wrong answers because they are dumb. Instead, they can explain the real reason why they got each wrong answer.
Students make a personalized plan to address the types of mistakes they are making for future experiences.	Students improve more quickly in areas of weakness because they address the specific mistakes directly.

Instructional Poster(s)

- This lesson has ONE Instructional Poster.
- The Instructional Poster for this lesson tries to identify some of the more common answers to, "Why did I get that problem wrong?" Although these responses could work for any subject or grade, many of them seem to fit a math test most accurately in my opinion. Encourage your students to brainstorm more reasons that could be added to the list and perhaps posted somewhere in the room when students are analyzing their summative assessments after they've been graded.
- The second column focuses on preventing the same mistake from happening again, although you should remind students that no one expects perfection - just progress toward future improvement.

Student Handouts

- This lesson has TWO Student Handouts.
- DIRECTIONS: Follow the directions below and on the next page to analyze and reflect on ONE specific problem that you got wrong. Add extra sheets to analyze additional problems. Try to discover any patterns so you can correct them in the future.
- This Student Handout is set up similarly to the Student Handout in the previous lesson. It asks students to look at the specific problems they got wrong on an assessment or assignment, identify WHY they got it wrong, and describe what they will do in the future to prevent a repeated mistake.
- The first Student Handout only needs to be completed once per assignment or assessment, but students should use multiple copies of the second Student Handout to analyze each problem that they got wrong.

INTRODUCTION

PLANNING

METACOGNITION

SYNTHESIS

REFLECTION

SELF-ASSESSMENT

GOAL SETTING

FEEDBACK

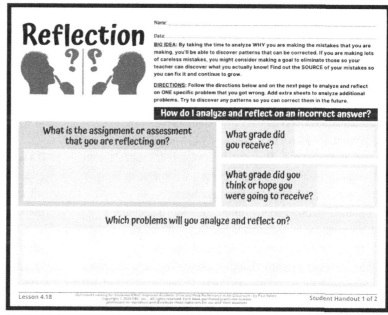

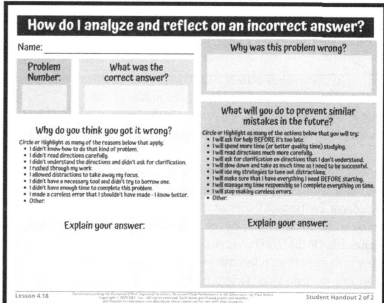

Self-Assessment

Download the Slides for this Unit:

bit.ly/48oKnsT

"*Self-assessment is the bridge that connects self-awareness with progress. Embrace it and witness the transformation that unfolds.*"
— ChatGPT's invented quote

Think back to a time when you completed a learning activity. Did you take any time to look back on that experience in order to determine what worked well and what could have been improved? This process of self-assessment, the act of critically examining your learning journey to identify strengths and weaknesses, is a cornerstone of becoming an optimized learner.

When students reflect on a recently completed activity or assignment, they have the opportunity to evaluate their decisions, actions, and processes. They can determine which aspects went well and which ones may require minor adjustments or even significant changes. Here are three examples:

1. Reflecting on a negative interaction with a peer and determining that you could have acted differently might lead to an immediate repair of that relationship.
2. Students may realize that they didn't allocate their time appropriately in relation to the task's importance and make a plan to manage their time more effectively in the future.
3. Students might reconsider taking the easy way out on an assignment and decide that challenging themselves could have resulted in a more meaningful experience.

Regardless of the nature of these reflections, they all involve an evaluative component that helps students consciously decide whether they would make the same choices in the future or if they would opt for changes if given another opportunity.

Reflection and self-assessment are definitely intertwined. What sets self-assessment apart from reflection is the evaluative component. Even though Reflection and Self-Assessment have similar qualities and overlapping concepts, each macroskill has been isolated in the SLSI Process in order to ensure that the proper attention is given to each. Doing one without the other is not likely to result in the same level of improvement as doing both macroskills would.

Once students have reflected on a learning experience, they can use those reflections to determine what went well and what could have gone better, which skills they should work on improving, and which skills they might be able to help others with. They also identify what knowledge and information they didn't know before the learning experience but need to know moving forward. These evaluative reflections will ultimately lead to the next step in the SLSI Process: "Goal Setting."

If a student didn't know certain information during the learning experience and worries that they might not be able to remember it without studying, they might create a Goal Burst to study that material that night or shortly before an assessment. If a student didn't know how to perform a skill that is important (e.g., subtracting numbers with varying numbers of decimals), then they might decide to create a S.M.A.A.R.T.E.R. Goal that directs their attention to learning that skill over time. These next steps are explained in detail in the next unit.

Without self-assessment, students are unable to identify areas in which they struggle and lack the necessary self-direction to address those deficiencies. However, through formal self-assessment in which students actively participate, they can dedicate time and attention to these areas, allowing them to address their struggles without relying solely on the teacher to discover the struggle and make time to both point it out and re-teach it.

Students can be trained to do this on their own, just like adults do. The reason most students do not already engage in this practice is due to several factors: (1) they have never been asked to do so, (2) there is often a lack of available time, (3) students may not always be aware of their own deficiencies, (4) students may have a distorted perception of their skill level and knowledge, and (5) students may lack knowledge about how to address their deficiencies. The SLSI Process effectively addresses all of these concerns, empowering students to take responsibility for their own improvement.

In addition to the value of self-improvement, students also benefit from utilizing self-assessment strategies to discover areas in which they excel or meet expectations. They can take pride in reflecting on experiences where they made wise decisions, interacted positively with peers, or demonstrated significant growth. Teachers rarely have the opportunity to praise these actions enough to help students develop self-confidence and pride in their work. However, when students engage in self-assessment themselves, they learn to recognize their accomplishments and witness their growth over time, regardless of their starting point.

NOTE: Self-assessment, as envisioned in this book, is an opportunity for students to identify how well they think they know and understand information, their ability to perform skills, and other subjective gradations based on clear expectations. It is important to note that self-assessment does not ask students to grade themselves, nor am I recommending that self-assessment be linked to their overall grades in any way (although that is becoming a more common practice these days). Instead, self-assessment allows students to reflect on their progress and identify areas where they are finding success and areas where they are struggling. This process will help them focus their efforts in the right areas, set goals appropriately, and become stronger managers of their learning.

The lessons within this chapter focus on important microskills that contribute to effective self-assessment. Here are some examples (but not an exhaustive list):

Self-Assessment vs. Self-Grading: This is an important distinction that students must learn up front in order to improve their knowledge and skills in ALL areas of their learning, not just on assignments and evaluations. We are focusing on Self-Assessment within the SLSI Process, not necessarily Self-Grading. The difference between the two is taught in Lesson 5.02.

Aiming for the "Learning Target": Self-Assessment is determining how close one is to "hitting" their Learning Target. Students learn to think of "Learning Targets" just like targets in archery. When we shoot an arrow, we are aiming for a target. Same with learning! When we do work in class, we're doing it to eventually hit the target (maybe even a bullseye!).

Using "Success Criteria" to Self-Assess: Success Criteria are the things students need to do correctly and at a high level in order to be successful on that assignment. Sometimes, the teacher will

provide these criteria, but most of the time, students will need to infer what they are.

Completing a Basic Self-Assessment: The most basic self-assessment requires students to answer four questions:
- What could I do better? (How could I improve this work?)
- What am I most proud of? (What could I help others on?)
- What were the highlights of this experience?
- What were some challenges I faced during this experience?

Self-Assessment WHILE working: Students are taught to periodically think about their current progress and accuracy WHILE they are working. They determine if they should: (1) Stop and get help, (2) Use caution and check in with someone, or (3) Keep going. (This microskill also fits within Metacognition.)

Using Self-Assessment Tools: Checklists and rubrics are not just for grading! Students learn how to use them as self-assessment tools both WHILE they work and AFTER they've finished working.

Supporting Self-Assessments with Evidence: Students are taught to use strategies like "I can..." Statements and highlighting to show evidence of fixed errors, completed directions and growth.

Using exit tickets to self-assess: Exit tickets are more than a tool to check for understanding. They can also offer students an opportunity to share their self-assessment with their teacher.

Assessing an entire school day or class period: Taking time as a class to have students evaluate how they did holistically can lead to amazing results! My students did this every day and managed to address each of our whole-class struggles over time.

Self-assessment plays a crucial role in developing optimizing learners. When students engage in self-assessment, they reflect on their learning journeys, identify strengths and weaknesses, and make conscious decisions about how they would approach similar situations in the future. By actively participating in self-assessment, students address areas of struggle without relying solely on the teacher's guidance, leading to academic, social and behavioral self-improvement. Furthermore, self-assessment allows students to recognize and celebrate their accomplishments, fostering self-confidence and pride in their work.

The microskills taught in this chapter provide valuable tools for effective self-assessment, enabling students to become skilled self-assessors who can navigate their learning journeys with confidence. By developing these skills, students enhance their ability to manage their learning effectively and become lifelong learners committed to continuous improvement.

INTRODUCTION
PLANNING
METACOGNITION
SYNTHESIS
REFLECTION
SELF-ASSESSMENT
GOAL SETTING
FEEDBACK

Unit 5 - Self-Assessment

21 Mini-Lessons

Students with well-developed SELF-ASSESSMENT MicroSkills...	Students with poorly-developed SELF-ASSESSMENT MicroSkills...
Recognize the importance of self-reflection in the learning process	Neglect self-reflection and fail to recognize its value
Reflect on their own strengths and weaknesses	Lack awareness of their own strengths and weaknesses
Accurately identify areas where they need to make improvements	Struggle to identify areas where they need to improve
Seek feedback from others to gain different perspectives	Avoid seeking feedback and miss opportunities for growth
Take responsibility for their own learning and growth	Exhibit a passive approach and rely on external factors
Regularly monitor their progress and adjust their strategies	Neglect to monitor their progress and continue with ineffective strategies
Apply insights from self-assessment to improve their performance	Disregard self-assessment insights and repeat the same mistakes
Actively seek resources and support to address areas of weakness	Fail to seek resources or support to address areas of weakness
Embrace challenges as opportunities for learning and improvement	Avoid challenges and stick to their comfort zone
Identify areas of strength and leverage them to maximize their learning	Overlook their strengths and fail to utilize them effectively
Use self-assessment as a tool for self-improvement in and out of school	Neglect to transfer self-assessment skills to other aspects of their life
Understand that accepting challenges and taking risks may result in critical self-assessments	Avoid taking risks and embracing challenges due to negative self-assessment concerns

INTRODUCTION

PLANNING

METACOGNITION

SYNTHESIS

REFLECTION

SELF-ASSESSMENT

GOAL SETTING

FEEDBACK

225

bit.ly/47BKPUk

Evaluate SELF-ASSESSMENT MicroSkills to take pride in relative strengths and to set personalized goals for areas of weakness

Essential Question

How strong am I at each of these SELF-ASSESSMENT Skills?

Big Idea

By evaluating our current level of achievement on the MicroSkills that will be taught in this unit, we gain a clearer understanding of our individual strengths and weaknesses. Additionally, by synthesizing each MicroSkill, we develop a stronger understanding of the MacroSkill that this unit focuses on, which is SELF-ASSESSMENT.

Lesson Overview

In this lesson, students evaluate their perceived ability for each of the identified SELF-ASSESSMENT skills. These skills have been chosen from the lessons that follow in this unit. Although students are choosing a somewhat arbitrary number from 1-10, the self-assessment process requires them to (1) understand what the skill means, (2) determine their perceived ability for the skill, and (3) sort each skill into areas of weakness or strength (or in-between) so that they help others improve at the skill (for scores 7-10) or make the skill into a goal that they try to achieve (for scores 1-4). If a student scores a 5 or 6, they are asked to reassess themselves after the unit to determine if they would benefit from making it a goal or not.

Discussion / Reflection Questions

- Which self-assessment skills did you feel you were strongest at? Provide some evidence to support your self-assessment.
- Which self-assessment skills did you feel you were weakest at? Explain why you feel that this is true.
- If you could set a goal to improve ONE of these skills, which one would you choose? Why did you choose that one? How do you plan to improve this skill? What will you do?

Teacher Tips

- On the Student Handouts, it tells students to "highlight all the numbers up through your score." The reason I didn't just have them circle the number is so they can see "how full" their grade band is if they choose a high number, and "how empty" their grade band is if they choose a low number. If you don't think it's too important for your students, feel free to let them just circle their number.
- When doing a self-assessment like this, I like to teach my students about the importance of being honest with themselves. I remind them that self-assessment in our classroom don't affect your grades or the way I see them. Self-assessments help us focus in on what matters to us, rather than focusing in on everything and not spending enough time on the skills that we need to improve most. No one is a 10 on all of these skills and no one is a 1 on all of them, but there's a good chance that each of us is a 10 and a 1 on at least one skill in this self-assessment!

Student Tasks ⟩ Transfer Goals

Student Tasks	Transfer Goals
Students assess themselves on various self-assessment skills using a scale from 1 to 10.	Students become more self-aware of their abilities and areas in which they need to grow.
Students are asked several self-assessment questions that require them to explain their self-assessments and to set a goal for one skill.	Students understand that having weaknesses is normal and that they should be improved through goal-setting.

Instructional Poster(s)

- This lesson has ONE Instructional Poster.
- A variation of this Instructional Poster is used with the first lesson of each unit. It shows students how to use the 1-10 scale for assessing their current level of ability with each skill. Numbers 1-4 mean that they know they need to improve at this skill (and maybe create a goal for the skill), and numbers 7-10 mean they believe that they are capable of helping others improve this skill. (4-5 means they will reassess at the end of the unit - which will be up to you or the student to remember to do. It's not a lesson.)
- Tell students that the real value in this activity is discovering their relative strengths and weaknesses, so giving yourself a 10 for each skill is wasting everyone's time, as is repeating any other number. Finding the variation in each skill is the key, so give yourself scores of 1, 2, and 3 and give scores of 8, 9, and 10 as well!

Student Handouts

- This lesson has FOUR Student Handouts.
- DIRECTIONS: Look at the Self-Assessment MicroSkills in each box below and on the following page(s). Determine a rating from 1-10 for yourself on each, and then circle it. For your lowest MicroSkill(s), create a S.M.A.A.R.T.E.R. Goal to address each weakness.
- If you have not taught the lesson on S.M.A.A.R.T.E.R. Goals, let students know that they can just make the skill a personal goal to improve, but nothing needs to be written out (unless they want a reminder to actually do it). Obviously, the more seriously they take things, the more likely they'll improve!

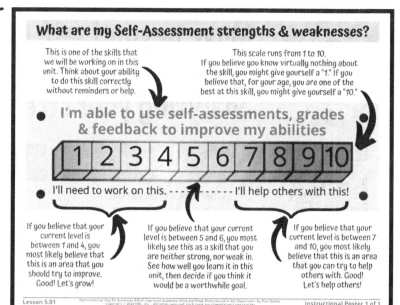

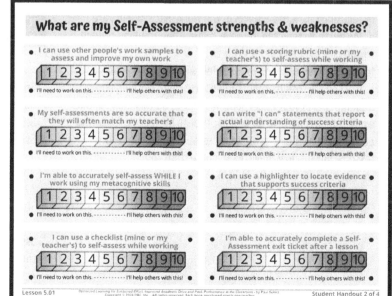

Move beyond self-grading and dive into the rich realm of self-assessment, analyzing your strengths & weaknesses

5.02

bit.ly/47xo7wp

Essential Question

What is Self-Assessment?
What is Self-Grading?

Big Idea

Many people mistakenly confuse Self-Assessment and Self-Grading. They think marking their paper RIGHT or WRONG is self-assessment, but it's not. Self-Assessment is much deeper and much more open to interpretation than that.

Lesson Overview

In this lesson, students learn that "Self-Assessment" and "Self-Grading" are two distinctly different things, and that they may be confusing the two. The main purpose of Self-Grading is to mark things right or wrong and to assign a score of some sort to the assignment. We instead prefer to focus on Self-Assessment which attempts to analyze all the aspects of what we've done during a task, assignment or activity and decide what we could have done better, and what we excelled at. This is the main purpose of Self-Assessment in this program.

Discussion/Reflection Questions

- Why do we need to know the difference between Self-Grading and Self-Assessment?
- What is the difference between Self-Grading and Self-Assessment?
- During the Self-Assessment stage, how do we direct our attention away from thinking about what is right and what is wrong on an assignment, and instead focus on what we can do better or what we can feel proud of and help others with?

Teacher Tips

- Self-Assessment can actually be harder for teachers to adjust to than students. Most of us grew up with no self-grading OR self-assessment, but if we had either, it was likely some form of self-grading (probably to help the teacher save time)! So it's important that YOU become very comfortable with this concept of focusing on all the aspects of the work that students are doing and how they can improve, rather than thinking right vs. wrong or 3 out of 4 points, etc.
- It would be valuable for your students if you could point out a few of the microskills that students use while working on assignments in your classroom. In order to do this, think about what students need to do well in order to be successful during each aspect of their work. Examples will be given in future lessons, but for now they should come from you.

Student Tasks ⟩ Transfer Goals

Student Tasks	Transfer Goals
Students learn the difference between Self-Assessment and Self-Grading.	Students separate the two skills and use them each when appropriate.
Students discover several examples of self-assessment that help them see what Self-Assessment truly is.	Students regularly self-assess all the microskills they use both during and after learning experiences.

Instructional Poster(s)

- This lesson has ONE Instructional Poster.
- On today's Instructional Poster, read through the Self-Grading section first. Tell the students that this is NOT actually what we will be doing much of while "Self-Assessing," because Self-Grading is different. Then, read the Self-Assessment section. Explain that this is what we will be spending most of our time doing during "Self-Assessment." Finally, read the "Both" section and say that we WILL be doing this during Self-Assessment because its main focus is on self-identification of strengths and weaknesses, not on a grade.
- Read the bottom notes. Discuss.

Student Handouts

- This lesson has THREE Student Handouts.
- DIRECTIONS: Read through the following definitions of Self-Assessment. They are not easy to understand, but they provide three different views of the concept. Please make sure that a teacher is willing to help you understand them, no matter your age! At the bottom of the page, write your own definition of Self-Assessment that synthesizes the elements of each definition that you resonate with & add your own thoughts!
- DIRECTIONS: Complete the following VENN DIAGRAM by deciding how self-assessment is valuable, how self-grading is valuable, and the ways in which they are similarly valuable. I've started it for you - just add a few more to show that you understand. Write small, please!
- ADDITIONAL PAGE - Directions: Brainstorm all of the tasks/assignments you've completed in the past few weeks in school. Which ones have right and wrong answers? Those go in the "Self-Grading" column. Which ones can be improved through hard work and attention to detail? Those go in the "Self-Assessment" column. If they have aspects of both, they go in the middle column.

What is Self-Assessment? What is Self-Grading?

Self-Assessment

Self-assessment means taking a close look at your own learning to see how you're doing. You make judgments about your strengths, weaknesses, and you identify areas for improvement. Examples:
- Reflecting on your level of understanding in different subjects and explaining why you feel confident or uncertain.
- Identifying areas where you need to put in extra effort or seek additional resources to improve your skills.
- Evaluating if your study habits and strategies are effective in helping you learn and retain information.
- Assessing your ability to work collaboratively and identifying areas where you can improve your teamwork skills.
- Determining if you have met the learning objectives or goals set for a specific project or assignment.
- Usually works best with tasks & assignments that can be improved through hard work & attention to detail, and often leads to further improvement.

Both

Both self-assessment and self-grading help you become more aware of your learning and take ownership of it. They give you a chance to see how you're doing and encourage you to make changes to get even better. By using self-assessment and self-grading, you become more in control of your learning journey and can make great strides in improving your skills and knowledge.

Both Self-Assessment and Self-Grading:
- Give you feedback on how well you've done.
- Provide you with benefits if you reflect thoughtfully on the results of your work.
- Provide the teacher with evaluative language and evidence that can be used for grading purposes.
- Require the use of evaluation criteria, learning targets, or clear & specific expectations to be meaningful & helpful.
- Take time to learn how to do correctly and ultimately apply the information gained from them to new situations.

Self-Grading

Self-grading is when you give yourself a grade for your work or tests. But this isn't just guessing or picking a grade randomly. You use specific criteria or guidelines to decide how well you did. Self-grading focuses specifically on evaluating the quality or level of achievement in your work. Examples:
- Assigning yourself a number or letter grade based on a rubric provided by the teacher for a project or assignment.
- Assessing the quality of your artwork by assigning it a score based on criteria like creativity, technique, and composition.
- Awarding yourself points based on the completion and accuracy of a problem, using an answer key for reference.
- Evaluating your presentation skills by rating yourself on criteria such as poise, delivery, and audience engagement.
- Usually works best with tasks & assignments that have right and wrong answers, with little room for interpretation, and you usually end up with a score of some sort.

Although self-assessment AND self-grading can be valuable, MOST of the examples in this chapter and this book focus on Self-Assessment. To minimize confusion, the term self-grading won't be used after this lesson.

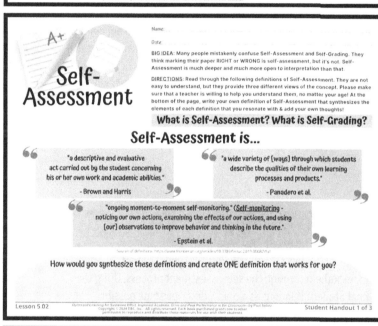

Name:

Date:

BIG IDEA: Many people mistakenly confuse Self-Assessment and Self-Grading. They think marking their paper RIGHT or WRONG is self-assessment, but it's not. Self-Assessment is much deeper and much more open to interpretation than that.

DIRECTIONS: Read through the following definitions of Self-Assessment. They are not easy to understand, but they provide three different views of the concept. Please make sure that a teacher is willing to help you understand them, no matter your age! At the bottom of the page, write your own definition of Self-Assessment that synthesizes the elements of each definition that you resonate with & add your own thoughts!

What is Self-Assessment? What is Self-Grading?

Self-Assessment is...

"a descriptive and evaluative act carried out by the student concerning his or her own work and academic abilities."
- Brown and Harris

"a wide variety of [ways] through which students describe the qualities of their own learning processes and products."
- Panadero et al.

"ongoing moment-to-moment self-monitoring." (Self-monitoring - noticing our own actions, examining the effects of our actions, and using [our] observations to improve behavior and thinking in the future."
- Epstein et al.

How would you synthesize these definitions and create ONE definition that works for you?

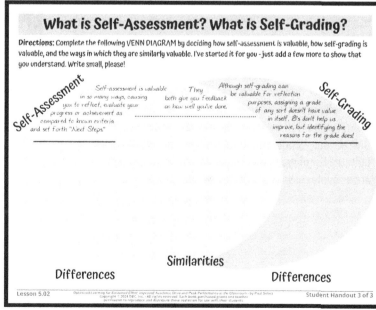

What is Self-Assessment? What is Self-Grading?

Directions: Complete the following VENN DIAGRAM by deciding how self-assessment is valuable, how self-grading is valuable, and the ways in which they are similarly valuable. I've started it for you - just add a few more to show that you understand. Write small, please!

Self-Assessment

Self-assessment is valuable in so many ways, causing you to reflect, evaluate your progress or achievement as compared to known criteria and set forth "Next Steps"

They both give you feedback on how well you've done.

Self-Grading

Although self-grading can be valuable for reflection purposes, assigning a grade of any sort doesn't have value in itself. B's don't help us improve, but identifying the reasons for the grade does!

Differences   Similarities   Differences

bit.ly/46D2XMn

Illuminate areas for celebration and growth through self-assessment, allowing you to take control of your learning

Essential Question

Why should we spend time on Self-Assessment?

Lesson Overview

In this lesson, students learn about the many benefits of taking time to self-assess such as identifying relative strengths and weaknesses, increasing self-monitoring behaviors, and becoming more independent learning, among others. They're given several benefits of self-assessment are asked to explain why or how each can be beneficial. Finally, students examine a self-assessment exemplar and describe how the process of self-assessment can benefit their learning.

Big Idea

Self-assessment is an important skill because when we know what we need improvement on, we can focus our attention in that area. When we know what we're having success with, we can help others in that area. When we don't know our relative strengths and weaknesses, we rely on others to help us grow, and our goal in this program is to become strong, independent learners.

Discussion/Reflection Questions

- Why is self-assessment worth our time?
- What can we learn about ourselves or our learning through self-assessment that we typically wouldn't learn if we didn't self-assess?
- How would you explain self-assessment to a younger student now that you learned about diving deeper or "Tell me more?"

Teacher Tips

- Brainstorm a few recent activities that your students completed to walk them through the self-assessment process. Using the final Student Handout as a guide, describe some possible answers students might have come up with for the questions provided (i.e. How could I improve this work? etc.). Ask students to share their self-assessments using your examples as a guide. It's important to go BEYOND the surface level self-assessment and dig deeper. When I do this with my students I just keep repeating, "Tell me more..." or "Why?" or "How?" until it seems as though we've gotten to the heart of their answer. Keep in mind that "Tell me more..." doesn't mean "Tell me additional things." It should mean "Tell me more about what you just said. Elaborate. Dive deeper." Students naturally believe that you want a long bulleted list of reasons or thoughts, but what is most beneficial are a couple reasons that have been described deeply.

Student Tasks 〉 Transfer Goals

Student Tasks	Transfer Goals
Students read about the benefits of Self-Assessment and brainstorm some more themselves.	Students understand the value of Self-Assessment when they are asked to do so in class and will likely continue the practice independently.
Students examine a Self-Assessment exemplar and identify the benefits of completing one themselves.	Students dig deeper when Self-Assessing to get at the heart of what really matters, instead of being content with a generic good or bad.

INTRODUCTION
PLANNING
METACOGNITION
SYNTHESIS
REFLECTION
SELF-ASSESSMENT
GOAL SETTING
FEEDBACK

Instructional Poster(s)

- This lesson has ONE Instructional Poster.
- You will need to come up with at least two more benefits as a class (while teaching the Instructional Poster) for the Student Handouts later in the lesson.
- Share as many additional benefits of Self-Assessment as you can, so students understand its value.

Student Handouts

- This lesson has TWO Student Handouts.
- DIRECTIONS: Fill in the two blanks below with the answers you came up with as a class. Then explain why or how each of the eight points show the value of Self-Assessment.
- DIRECTIONS: Self-Assessment can be done WHILE you are working or AFTER you finish working. In this program, we call Self-Assessment WHILE working "Metacognition," so we reserve the term "Self-Assessment" for AFTER you finish working. Pretend that you have just finished an assignment in class. You completed the following Self-Assessment explaining your beliefs. In the blanks, describe why that analysis is useful and a valuable use of your class time. Explain how you can use that self-assessment to improve in the future.
- If you are completing the Student Handouts as a whole class, focus in on what might have been learned by writing answers to the Self-Assessment questions on the left. Have students write what was learned in the column on the right.
- Build the expectation that students need to dive deeper with their answers. "Tell me more" is a great prompt for elaboration. (See "Teacher Tips" section for more.)

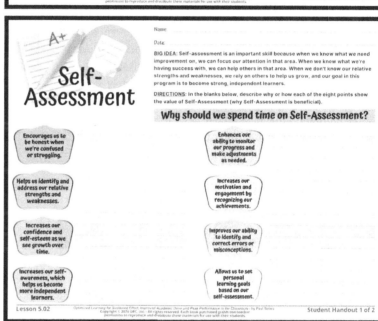

5.04

Accurately assess your progress and chart your course to success using "Learning Targets" as your bullseye

bit.ly/3SVHuem

Essential Question

How can I use Learning Targets to Self-Assess?

Lesson Overview

In this lesson, students learn to focus on a "Learning Target" in order to help them make a more accurate Self-Assessment. After all, it's hard to know how well you're doing without knowing where you're trying to go! At first, it's expected that teachers will provide learning targets for the students since the teacher likely has a better idea of the path they're on together, but ultimately, students should be able to write their own learning targets as they become more comfortable. Although the point system doesn't really matter in the long run (it's not a grading system), students learn that the greater the scale (e.g. five levels instead of three), the more intricate the self-assessment.

Teacher Tips

- This lesson focuses on a basic topic (Learning Targets), but it will get more complex over the course of this unit. If you have older students who don't need this lesson on its own, feel free to combine the concept of Learning Targets into a future lesson and either skip this one or complete it quickly together as a class.
- The scale of 1-2-3 or 1-2-3-4-5 will be expounded upon in the final lesson of this unit (Lesson 5.25) and then even more so in the next unit (Goal Setting) Lessons 6.15-6.17.

Big Idea

By self-assessing "with the end in mind" we try to describe exactly where we need to get to (our Learning Target), so there's no confusion about our final goal. Then, we decide how close we are to our end point and we use that location to determine how much work we need to do in order to find success.

Discussion/Reflection Questions

- What is a Learning Target?
- Why is it important to have a Learning Target when Self-Assessing?
- When your teacher doesn't provide you with a Learning Target, how can you come up with one yourself?

Student Tasks 〉 Transfer Goals

Student Tasks	Transfer Goals
Students learn what a "Learning Target" is.	Students understand that learning is a journey that requires many steps to complete.
Students assess themselves while using a Learning Target as their guide.	Students are stronger self-assessors because they use Learning Targets from which to judge their distance.

Instructional Poster(s)

- This lesson has ONE Instructional Poster.
- Use this Instructional Poster to help students understand the concept of a Learning Target. This term will come up regularly in future lessons. Learning Targets are endpoints that we hope to reach while learning. They don't have to represent mastery or perfection, but they should represent the level at which students are trying to attain within the current learning cycle (current unit, grade level, etc.).
- Really focus in on the questions students should ask themselves in each section. This is the self-assessment component. Try to distinguish this from a score or a grade and simply focus on the idea that you may be close to your Learning Target, far from it, somewhere in between, etc.

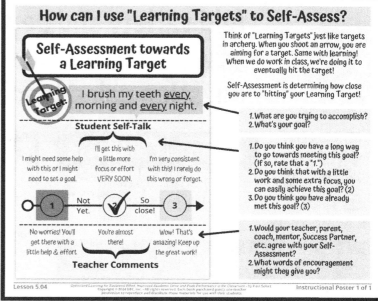

Student Handouts

- This lesson has TWO Student Handouts.
- DIRECTIONS: Use the example below to complete the four "Learning Target Self-Assessments" on the next page. Choose four skills that you know have a specific end point (they can be academic or not), and then decide what level you think you currently find yourself. (1-2-3 is a basic level, 1-2-3-4-5 requires a little more thought.)
- On this lesson's Student Handout, the "Teacher Comments" section has been removed (it was a scaffolding structure). Now they need to internalize those thoughts while determining a self-assessment level.
- Notice how the levels increase in scope (from three 3 to 5) once they reach the bottom of the second Student Handout. Help students understand they will need to create their own systems as they become more independent learners and the more levels they have, the more detailed their self-assessment can be.

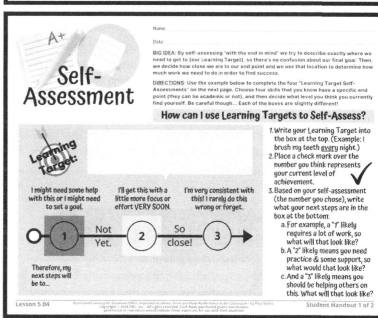

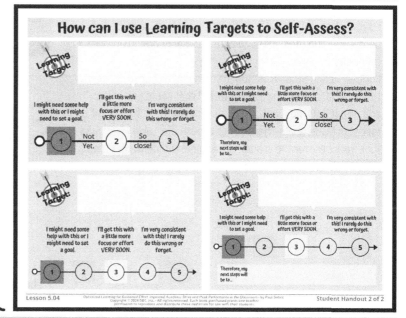

bit.ly/3RioYeW

Add variety and depth to your self-assessment process with alternative question pairs, leading to richer insights

Essential Question

How do I complete a
Basic Self-Assessment?

Big Idea

The basic components of a self-assessment include identifying what is weak and what is strong within your work. If there are several examples for either category, it's important to identify the most important or most relevant strengths & weaknesses.

Lesson Overview

In this lesson, students look at a basic self-assessment exemplar that shows them ways they can assess themselves that they might not have thought of yet, such as "What would I want to add if I had more time?" or "What would I do to improve the quality if I had more time?" When it comes to elements that students are proud of, they might want to consider what others would consider strong, and sharing some examples that support their claims. Students then complete a basic self-assessment that asks our standard questions, "What could I do better?" and "What am I most proud of?" But they also learn how they can change those questions up with other word pairs that guide the self-assessment process.

Discussion / Reflection Questions

- Why might your teacher allow you to choose your own self-assessment questions to answer after a learning experience?
- What is one thing you learned about self-assessment from today's Instructional Poster?
- How should you choose what to focus on in your self-assessment since there are probably several ways you could have improved and several things you did well?

Teacher Tips

- Students need to complete a self-assessment on a learning experience for this lesson, so you will need to have students work on an academic assignment or task before they can complete today's Student Handout.
- The first Student Handout can be confusing to younger students, so you might want to walk students through an example or two before sending them off to complete it independently or with a randomly-assigned partner.
- For the second Student Handout, you need to choose between the traditional self-assessment with "What could I do better?" and "What am I most proud of?" already listed, or if you want to give your students the freedom to choose their own word pairs that work best for the academic task or assignment that they are assessing themselves on.

Student Tasks 〉 Transfer Goals

Student Tasks	Transfer Goals
Students examine a well-written Self-Assessment to identify ways they can improve their self-assessments.	Students understand the components of a well-written self-assessment and use those components when writing their own.
Students complete a self-assessment for an academic assignment or task they just completed in class.	Students use the experience from today's self-assessment to continue to improve future self-assessments.

INTRODUCTION

PLANNING

METACOGNITION

SYNTHESIS

REFLECTION

SELF-ASSESSMENT

GOAL SETTING

FEEDBACK

Instructional Poster(s)

- This lesson has ONE Instructional Poster.
- In this Instructional Poster, students look at a self-assessment of a book review, where the reviewer was told to include specific quotes from the book to support their claims. Our two standard self-assessment questions are asked (What could I do better? and What am I most proud of?). This Instructional Poster acts as an exemplar that shows students how to self-assess at a high level. Discuss each part of the exemplar in general terms so that students learn the importance of digging deeper and finding specific examples that support their claims.

Student Handouts

- This lesson has THREE Student Handouts.
- DIRECTIONS: Read through the pairs of words and phrases below. Try to imagine you have been given an assignment to use each pair to assess yourself on a recent task or skill. How might your answers vary based on the set of words you are given? Are there any subtle differences between the words that might only work for certain situations?
- The first Student Handout tries to show students other ways to think about Self-Reflection beyond our two standard self-assessment questions: "What could I do better?" and "What am I most proud of?" If you complete this page as a whole group, consider brainstorming examples of lessons where some of these Self-Assessment "pairs" might have worked well.
- Teacher's Choice for the second Student Handout: (1) Our basic self-assessment with the questions: "What could I do better?" & "What am I most proud of?" OR (2) One that has blanks for students to write their own self-assessment questions based on the previous Student Handout.

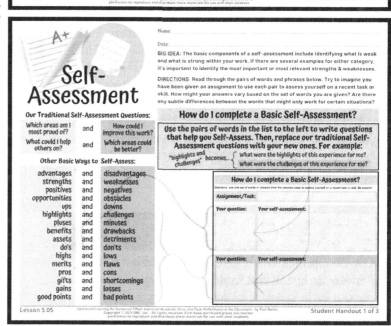

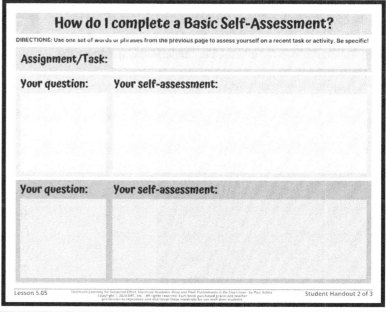

bit.ly/3RiCM9k

Use "Success Criteria" to guide your learning journey - You may have to craft your own when they are not provided

5.06

Essential Question

How can I use "Success Criteria" to self-assess?

Lesson Overview

In this lesson, students learn that "Success Criteria" are the things they need to do correctly, and at a high level, in order to be successful on a particular assignment. Sometimes, teachers will provide these for students, but most of the time, students will have to figure these out on their own in order to be successful with the assignment. As a class, students brainstorm Success Criteria for an assignment that asks them to create a new "better" book cover for a book they've recently read. Examples are provided to discuss. Next, students write three Success Criteria for three separate assignments. Finally, students assess themselves on one Success Criterion using the provided graphic organizer.

Teacher Tips

- Consider replacing some of the examples on the Instructional Poster or the first Student Handout with assignments from your class - it will be easier for you and the students to identify meaningful Success Criteria.
- Consider using the second Student Handout multiple times in the coming days for different assignments. The idea of "Success Criteria" is a major concept throughout this unit and beyond, so the more students can improve their understanding of them, the better they will be.

Big Idea

Sometimes, your teacher will give you "Success Criteria" for an assignment or task, BUT most of the time they won't. When they DO, use it as a clear guide for "where you are headed" with your learning. When they DON'T, use it as an opportunity to decide "where you need to end up." Identifying success criteria on your own will help you focus on what really matters AND help you determine importance in the real world.

Discussion/Reflection Questions

- Why are "Success Criteria" SO important when it comes to self-assessment and in order to try to do our best on our work?
- What tips could you give others for coming up with Success Criteria for a given assignment?
- What should you do when you can't figure out the Success Criteria for a specific assignment? Shouldn't you know what it is that you need to do on an assignment to be successful?

Student Tasks ⟩ Transfer Goals

Student Tasks	Transfer Goals
Students identify Success Criteria for three sample assignments.	Students no longer rely on their teacher to provide all of the Success Criteria because they now can identify them on their own.
Students use one Success Criterion to assess themselves on that aspect of a given assignment.	Students know that it is their job to meet and possibly exceed expectations for each Success Criteria for a given assignment.

Instructional Poster(s)

- This lesson has ONE Instructional Poster.
- The Instructional Poster for this lesson teaches students what "Success Criteria" are and how students can create their own Success Criteria for an assignment or task.
- Students think about what the Success Criteria might be for a task that asks them to create a better book cover for a book they just read in class. Since there are no Success Criteria provided, students think about what makes a book cover good. Four Success Criteria are offered as suggestions and a sample book cover is provided. It would be best to use a book that your students are familiar with for this lesson, if you can.

Student Handouts

- This lesson has TWO Student Handouts.
- DIRECTIONS: Your teacher has NOT provided you with Success Criteria for these assignments, and you want to do well and improve your skills. Brainstorm three strong "Success Criteria" for each assignment below. Then, complete the next page with PRETEND information from ONE of these assignments or REAL information from an assignment your teacher suggests.
- The first Student Handout provides students with three sample assignments for which they need to brainstorm three Success Criteria each.
- The second Student Handout asks students to use ONE of those Success Criteria from ONE of those assignments to write PRETEND answers to each question. As the teacher, you have the opportunity to choose a real assignment from class and a Success Criterion that you would prefer your students answer with REAL answers if you'd prefer.

INTRODUCTION
PLANNING
METACOGNITION
SYNTHESIS
REFLECTION
SELF-ASSESSMENT
GOAL SETTING
FEEDBACK

How can I use "Success Criteria" to self-assess?

Success Criteria are the things you need to do correctly & at a high level in order to be successful on that assignment.

Sometimes, your teacher will give you "Success Criteria" for an assignment or task, BUT most of the time they won't. When they DO, use it as a clear guide for "where you are headed" with your learning. When they DON'T, use it as an opportunity to decide "where you need to end up." By that I mean...

ASSIGNMENT: Design a better book cover for the book we just read in class.

Since there are no specific "Success Criteria" included in the assignment, I need to figure out what they are myself. I COULD ask my teacher for what he or she is looking for, but it would be better if I could figure them out myself!

Brainstorm some Success Criteria:
- A "better book cover" should catch the eye of potential readers.
- It should include some elements from the plot of the book, but it shouldn't give away any spoilers.
- It might include some characters or settings.
- It should evoke the mood of the book.
- It should have professional-looking design elements with no errors.

What else?

Wynthrope Castle
By: Paul Solarz

Lesson 5.06 · Instructional Poster 1 of 1

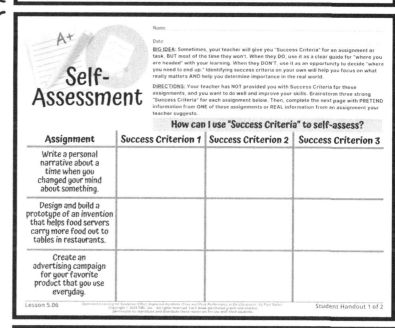

Self-Assessment

Name:

Date:

BIG IDEA: Sometimes, your teacher will give you "Success Criteria" for an assignment or task, BUT most of the time they won't. When they DO, use it as a clear guide for "where you are headed" with your learning. When they DON'T, use it as an opportunity to decide "where you need to end up." Identifying success criteria on your own will help you focus on what really matters AND help you determine importance in the real world.

DIRECTIONS: Your teacher has NOT provided you with Success Criteria for these assignments, and you want to do well and improve your skills. Brainstorm three strong "Success Criteria" for each assignment below. Then, complete the next page with PRETEND information from ONE of these assignments or REAL information from an assignment your teacher suggests.

How can I use "Success Criteria" to self-assess?

Assignment	Success Criterion 1	Success Criterion 2	Success Criterion 3
Write a personal narrative about a time when you changed your mind about something.			
Design and build a prototype of an invention that helps food servers carry more food out to tables in restaurants.			
Create an advertising campaign for your favorite product that you use everyday.			

Lesson 5.06 · Student Handout 1 of 2

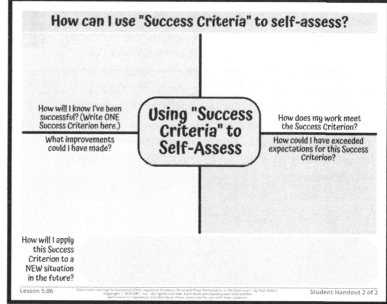

How can I use "Success Criteria" to self-assess?

Using "Success Criteria" to Self-Assess

How will I know I've been successful? (Write ONE Success Criterion here.)

What improvements could I have made?

How does my work meet the Success Criterion?

How could I have exceeded expectations for this Success Criterion?

How will I apply this Success Criterion to a NEW situation in the future?

Lesson 5.06 · Student Handout 2 of 2

bit.ly/3N48DIk

Analyze others' work to sharpen your own assessment skills and gain valuable insights for self-improvement

Essential Question

How can others' work samples help me self-assess?

Big Idea

Sometimes it's difficult to notice everything strong and weak within our own work, but we can improve our self-assessment skills by identifying the varying degrees of success on others' work. We can do this with anonymous work samples.

Lesson Overview

In this lesson, students practice assessing an exemplar or non-exemplar for an academic lesson they are working on in class. By identifying the strengths and weaknesses of work samples, they are better able to determine how their work compares. Once they learn the best ways to assess someone else's work, they begin to think of their own work in a similar way. By initially removing themselves from the assessment process, students are better able to see the best ways to identify strengths and weaknesses within a final product. They can then transfer the ideas learned to the more personal (and usually more challenging) self-assessment process.

Discussion/Reflection Questions

- Why can it be helpful to start by assessing others' work before we attempt to assess our own work?
- How can you use the second Student Handout from today's lesson as a self-assessment tool in order to improve your work? Use a lesson from class as an example to answer this question.
- Exemplars are nearly perfect examples of a completed assignment, but Non-Exemplars are clearly NOT meeting certain success criteria. How can we improve our self-assessment skills by analyzing others' non-exemplars?

Teacher Tips

- This lesson works best if you have an exemplar or non-exemplar from a recent assignment or task that the students completed in class. Don't use an actual student sample from this school year, because it will likely embarrass the student regardless of if they did well or did poorly. Feel free to use a prior year's student work sample if you remove the name, or create one yourself.
- The final Student Handout is purposely generic so it can be used for Self-Assessments or assessing someone else's work. Feel free to modify it to make it more specific for your use in class, or make it even less specific by removing the "Success Criteria" heading to allow students to write in a different characteristic for which they can provide evidence.
- Students may want to use a form of the bulleted questions on the Instructional Poster as "Success Criteria" for them to assess and cite evidence.

Student Tasks 〉 Transfer Goals

Student Tasks	Transfer Goals
Students cite evidence of Success Criteria within others' work samples and their own.	Students are more accurate at self-assessment because they understand the importance of citing evidence.
Students use exemplars and non-exemplars to assess Success Criteria.	Students can tell the difference between meeting the Success Criteria and not meeting them.

Instructional Poster(s)

- This lesson has ONE Instructional Poster.
- The lesson has ONE page of Teacher Directions.
- The Instructional Poster for this lesson teaches students how to assess someone else's work in a similar way that they would self-assess their own work. Although they can't assess other students' effort or process, they can assess their product based on the success criteria provided for the assignment or based on standard self-assessment questions.
- This lesson works best if you have an exemplar or non-exemplar from a recent assignment or task that the students completed in class. Don't use an actual student sample from this school year, because it will likely embarrass the student regardless of if they did well or did poorly. Feel free to use a prior year's student work sample if you remove the name.

Student Handouts

- This lesson has TWO Student Handouts.
- DIRECTIONS: Take some time to look at a few work samples that your teacher provides you. During this time, try to evaluate whether the success criteria for this assignment have been met and try to answer some of the "Assessment Questions" listed below. Then, complete the table on the next page. Write the Success Criteria in the first column, circle whether the Success Criteria was met or not and provide evidence.
- There is a Teacher Handout that provides directions for leading a lesson using work samples (exemplars or otherwise). Be sure to check it out if you'd like any ideas!
- The first Student Handout contains the sample assessment questions that appeared on the Instructional Poster, so students can use them on the second Student Handout.
- The second Student Handout is an assessment form that students can use when assessing an exemplar or non-exemplar from class.

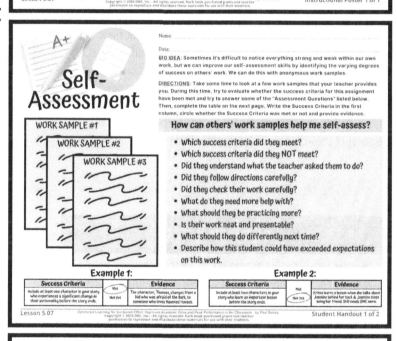

INTRODUCTION

PLANNING

METACOGNITION

SYNTHESIS

REFLECTION

SELF-ASSESSMENT

GOAL SETTING

FEEDBACK

bit.ly/3uG0gMQ

Analyze discrepancies between your self-assessment and your teacher's to improve understanding of Success Criteria

Essential Question

How accurate are my self-assessments?

Lesson Overview

In this lesson, students compare their self-assessment of an assignment or test to their teacher's (or another assessor like a peer or parent, for example). As they identify ways that they differed from their assessor, they describe why the differences exist. It may be subjective interpretation or a misunderstanding on someone's part. It may also be that the Success Criteria needs to be more clearly explained. Either way, students see that assessment of the content of an assignment or test may vary from person to person, but the act of assessing is still valuable as its own skill.

Teacher Tips

- In order for students to complete this lesson, they will need an assignment (or preferably several) that has feedback written on it. It can be subjective OR objective feedback, but students should be able to define the Success Criteria for the areas in which they struggled (or you would need to provide it for them).
- If there is just a little extra time available, this lesson can be extended a bit by analyzing the wording of the Success Criteria and deciding if it can be revised so it more clearly states what students need to do in order to be successful. On the Instructional Poster, for example, the first row describes how the student got full credit for a multiplication problem that they accidentally got right, but did their work wrong. The Success Criteria is not clear on whether a student is successful simply by getting the answer right, or if they also needed to do the work correctly. Either way is fine, but clarity in the Success Criteria will lead to stronger self-assessments and more focused improvement by the students.

Big Idea

Not everyone is great at self-assessing. Sometimes, we think we did better on a task, assignment or assessment than our teacher believes. Sometimes, we think we got away with something when the teacher didn't mark it wrong! Either way, we should compare the reasons for why we have differing opinions to determine how we can be more successful in the future.

Discussion/Reflection Questions

- How is it possible for one person to think that someone did a fantastic job on one Success Criterion, while another person thinks the exact opposite?
- Why is it important to be on the same page with your teacher when it comes to Success Criteria? Why do you need to have a strong understanding of what your teacher is looking for?
- What might happen if you and your teacher disagree on SEVERAL aspects of an assignment or test due to a misunderstanding of the Success Criteria? What if you think you did well on an assignment, but your teacher disagrees?

Student Tasks 〉 Transfer Goals

Student Tasks	Transfer Goals
Students compare their own self-assessments to those of their teacher's or another assessor's.	Students know that assessment is subjective and that closing the gap requires clearer Success Criteria.
Students analyze and describe why they believe their self-assessment differs from a peer's or teacher's assessment.	Students develop a deeper understanding of the Success Criteria of life, not just academic applications.

Instructional Poster(s)

- This lesson has ONE Instructional Poster.
- The Instructional Poster for this lesson helps students see that our self-assessments may differ from our teacher's assessment of the same assignment for many reasons. Sometimes, our teacher gives us more credit than we deserve and other times we give ourselves more credit than we deserve. The key is figuring out WHY the two assessments differ. We can do that by analyzing the Success Criteria and the reasons for each mistake that we made.

Student Handouts

- This lesson has TWO Student Handouts.
- DIRECTIONS: Brainstorm FIVE skills (or Success Criteria) that you politely disagree with your assessor (teacher, parent, peer, etc.) on. You may think you are better at the skill or worse, it doesn't matter, but you do need to identify why there is a difference in opinion from the two of you! (This won't have any negative affect on you or your grade). An example has been provided.
- The second Student Handout is simply a continuation of the first. On these Student Handouts, students are asked to choose five differences of opinion between themselves and another assessor, and try to explain why the differences exist. This may have to be done across several assignments if one assignment doesn't offer five opportunities for comparison.
- The Instructional Poster should remain visible for the students while they complete the Student Handouts for this lesson. They can use the examples to help them come up with their own answers. The ultimate goal of this assignment is to see how subjective assessment can be, even with Success Criteria spelled out, and that our assessment differences can actually inspire more accurate Success Criteria.

How accurate are my self-assessments?

Not everyone is great at self-assessing. Sometimes, we think we did better on a task, assignment or assessment than our teacher believes. Sometimes, we think we got away with something when the teacher didn't mark it wrong! Either way, we should compare the reasons for why we have differing opinions to determine how we can be more successful in the future.

Success Criteria are the things you need to do correctly & at a high level in order to be successful on that assignment.

Skill or Success Criterion	My Self-Assessment	My Teacher's Assessment	Why our assessments are different
Solve each multiplication problem correctly.	I struggled with this. I think I need some help with long multiplication.	10 out of 10 points	My teacher gave me full credit on this problem, but I got the answer right by mistake. I completely multiplied wrong!
Write topic sentences that introduce the focus of the paragraph.	I think I met all of my teacher's expectations, but I want to get better.	Exceeds Expectations	I don't think that I do a very good job at writing effective topic sentences, but I think for my age and grade level, it probably does exceed expectations.
Interpret what the remainder represents in division problems.	I think I'm doing very well.	My teacher thinks I'm struggling with this a bit.	I think I do a good job of interpreting remainders, but I seem to make a lot of careless mistakes, leading to incorrect answers. If I fix my careless mistakes, my teacher will likely agree with me.
Identify the Author's Purpose in various writing pieces.	Not Yet	Met	I can categorize the Author's Purpose into the three categories we focused on in class, but outside of those three, I'm not very good at it.

Instructional Poster 1 of 1

Self-Assessment

Name:

Date:

BIG IDEA: Not everyone is great at self-assessing. Sometimes, we think we did better on a task than our teacher believes. Sometimes, we think we got away with something when the teacher didn't mark it wrong! Either way, we should compare the reasons why we have differing opinions to determine how we can be more successful in the future.

DIRECTIONS: Read the example below. Then, brainstorm FOUR skills (or Success Criteria) that you politely disagree with your assessor (teacher, parent, peer, etc.) on. You may think you are better at the skill or worse, it doesn't matter, but you do need to identify why there is a difference in opinion from the two of you and you need to explain it all in each box below and on the next page! (This won't negatively affect your grade).

How accurate are my self-assessments?

Skill or Success Criterion	My Self-Assessment	My Assessor's Assessment	Why our assessments are different
EXAMPLE: My parents wanted my room to be "spotless" before I could hang out with my friends.	I cleaned my room for an hour and everything was put away. I believed my room was clean.	My dad said the garbage needed to be emptied, my snake's cage cleaned and my schoolwork put in folders.	We each had different ideas of what a clean bedroom looks like. I will add these new things to my internal checklist when I clean my room (trash, snake, school work.).

Student Handout 1 of 2

How accurate are my self-assessments?

Skill or Success Criterion	My Self-Assessment	My Teacher's Assessment	Why our assessments are different

Student Handout 2 of 2

bit.ly/3N4E31k

Become a self-assessment mastermind, developing the critical skill of monitoring your own understanding as you work

5.09

Essential Question

What can I do to self-assess WHILE I work?

Big Idea

Being aware of our level of understanding straddles the line of metacognition and self-assessment. It's one of the most important skills when it comes to learning. Students will become stronger at this skill if they know they can ask their peers for help, but only if a safe, collaborative classroom environment is in place.

Lesson Overview

In this lesson, students practice monitoring their understanding while they work on an academic assignment. Every five minutes (or a different amount of time), students will decide if they are understanding what they're doing (green), not entirely confident (yellow), or confused (red), and will write WHY they felt that way and WHAT they are doing about it. Although this is highly structured and unsustainable in real life, it is a great way to begin to self-assess WHILE they work. Teachers should choose an academic assignment for this lesson that has components that are both easy and challenging, so student get to fill in all three colors at some point.

Discussion/Reflection Questions

- Why did we self-assess so many times during today's lesson!? It probably made it hard to focus on your work and get everything done, right!?
- What did you learn today about yourself while self-assessing? Are you usually aware of when you struggle? Are you usually aware of when to slow down and check in with others? Are you usually aware of when you can make yourself available to help others?
- How will you apply the concept from this lesson (self-assessing WHILE you work) to assignments in the near future? How will you make sure you self-assess while you work?

Teacher Tips

- This lesson needs to be taught with an academic assignment that students will need to complete independently in class or with a partner. They will need to monitor their understanding on the student handouts today, while they work.
- A good strategy to use with this lesson is to have students use colored pencils/pens to work. When students use their green pencils, give them space and time to work, but start thinking about how you can enrich their learning or accelerate their progress. They are also allowed to help anyone who is on red or yellow, but should not be required to do so on a regular basis. (However, it does build self-esteem and confidence when allowed to help others.) For those using a yellow pencil, they often just need time to keep practicing - look over their shoulder and give feedback if necessary. Otherwise, leave them alone to work. Those on red should get your immediate attention. You can look for students on green and see if they are indeed correct with their work - if so, you can ask them to help OR you can help those on red yourself. I believe that when there are a majority of red pencils in the classroom, it's time to reteach. When there's about a fourth of the classroom on red, enlist help from your greens, and when there's only a few reds, help them yourself or pull them into a small group for reteaching.

Student Tasks 〉 Transfer Goals

Student Tasks	Transfer Goals
Students formally assess their understanding in ten increments while working on an academic assignment.	Students' awareness of their progress is improved and struggle or confusion is normalized so others can attempt to help them.
Students support their self-assessments with evidence and explain what they did about it when they were confused or less confident.	Students have an increased awareness of their level of understanding while working & are empowered to do something about it.

Instructional Poster(s)

- This lesson has THREE Instructional Posters.
- The Instructional Poster for this lesson uses a stoplight as a metaphor. Stoplights are a simple way for many students to understand self-assessment, as they can relate it to the real world. Red means stop - I don't get it! Green means go - I got this! And yellow means to slow down to solidify understanding. If you'd like to modify this concept for older students, change the stoplight into colored phone cases or red, yellow, and green pencils that students should write with. Get creative!
- The third Instructional Poster is an EXEMPLAR for the second Student Handout. Don't forget to project this Exemplar and explain the directions for the lesson. Students will complete the Student Handout while working on an academic assignment today.

Student Handouts

- This lesson has TWO Student Handouts.
- DIRECTIONS: Read everything below. Then, using a red, yellow, and green marker, complete the following page WHILE you work on the task given to you by your teacher. Red represents moments where you're confused, yellow means you're getting stronger, but not an expert yet, and green means you can teach others the skill.
- REMEMBER: These lessons are meant to scaffold a skill that students need to eventually internalize. Therefore, although the first Student Handout teaches them how to divide the number of minutes available in a class period, that doesn't mean they would be expected to do that all the time! It's just another skill that can be useful in life. Same with coloring in the circles and filling out the second Student Handout - this is not something students should do forever! It's just a way to help students self-assess while they work.

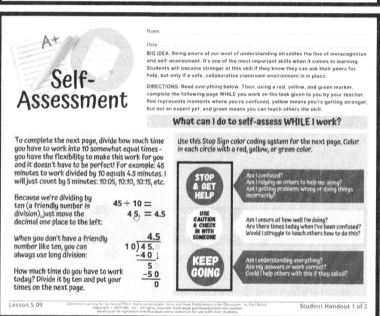

bit.ly/3GmNCoA

Ensure you meet not just quantity but also excellence in your work by assessing each task individually using a checklist

Essential Question

How can I use checklists to self-assess?

Big Idea

When we use a checklist to self-assess, we make sure that we have completed each task on the list AND we make sure that it is done with high quality. If there are boxes left unchecked, we know that we are NOT done yet and need to continue working. When all of the boxes have been checked, we can consider ourselves done.

Lesson Overview

In this lesson, students learn the value of checklists when it comes to self-assessment. Checklists help students (and teachers) make sure they completed everything required on an assignment or task. If any checklist items remain blank, students know that they are not yet done with the assignment. In addition, each checklist item can be individually assessed by students in order to determine their overall success, or lack there of.

Discussion/Reflection Questions

- Why did we have two sets of Student Handouts for this lesson today? What did you learn from each set?
- What COULD happen if we miss a step on a checklist? Think about a task like driving a car or fixing a computer.
- How can checklists be used to self-assess, other than helping you decide if you are done or not?

Teacher Tips

- It is helpful (but not required) to combine this lesson with an academic lesson that includes a checklist that students need to complete before they can consider themselves finished.
- In addition to using checklists to determine if students are done or not, please teach them that each checklist item can be examined during a self-assessment. Students can learn to ask themselves questions like: "Did I do this one completely? Did I put in strong effort on it? Should I have added more or revised it?" etc. This lesson leads into rubrics very well, since each checklist item get analyzed and assessed on a rubric.
- Be very aware of the two sets of Student Handouts for this lesson before teaching it. You don't want to ruin the "trick" for the students - they need to internalize the idea that direction-following is important!

Student Tasks 〉 Transfer Goals

Student Tasks	Transfer Goals
Students learn that skipping a checklist item can result in lots of wasted time.	Students don't check items off of a checklist unless they truly complete them!
Students learn how to use a checklist to help them assess their work.	Students use checklists to self-assess each checklist item, rather than assessing their work holitically.

Instructional Poster(s)

- This lesson has ONE Instructional Poster.
- The Instructional Poster for this lesson describes what the purpose of a checklist is. If you have any that you use on a regular basis, please consider sharing them with the class. Explain how you use the checklist and when you consider being "done" with everything. Then, share how checklists are often used in academic settings, so they understand that they are NOT done with an assignment until ALL of the checklist items have been checked off!

Student Handouts

- This lesson has FOUR Student Handouts.
- DIRECTIONS: Read through each of the following tasks before checking any of them off. Be ready to gather some simple supplies for many of the directions below. Go ahead and complete the checklist. This is a two-page assignment.
- This first two Student Handouts are really a decoy - it asks students to read ALL directions before checking off anything and the last direction states that it was a trick. As soon as everyone realizes the trick, move on to the real Student Handouts!
- DIRECTIONS: Choose a task that takes between 5 and 8 steps to do properly (like making a peanut butter & jelly sandwich). Write the directions in the order you'd recommend doing those tasks. Ask someone to follow these directions carefully without making any assumptions about what you meant to write. This is definitely harder than you think!!!
- The real Student Handout asks students to break down a task into 5-8 steps that others can do that requires every step to be checked off in order for it to be successful by the end (like making a PB&J sandwich).

How can I use checklists to self-assess?

A checklist is a list of tasks that you need to accomplish to be successful. YOU can create checklists, or your teacher might create one for you.

Checklist

When we use a checklist to self-assess, we make sure that we have completed each task on the list AND we make sure that it is done with high quality. If there are boxes left unchecked, we know that we are NOT done yet and need to continue working. When all of the boxes have been checked, we can consider ourselves done.

Name:

Date:

BIG IDEA: When we use a checklist to self-assess, we make sure that we have completed each task on the list AND we make sure that it is done with high quality. If there are boxes left unchecked, we know that we are NOT done yet and need to continue working. When all of the boxes have been checked, we can consider ourselves done.

DIRECTIONS: Read through each of the following tasks before checking any of them off. Be ready to gather some simple supplies for many of the directions below. Go ahead and complete the checklist. This is a two-page assignment.

Self-Assessment

How can I use checklists to self-assess?

Check off when Complete

- [ ] Always read the directions carefully before beginning any assignment.
- [ ] Take a piece of paper and try to fold it in half five times. Can you do it?
- [ ] Using another piece of paper and markers, what color is created when you draw a thick line with a light blue marker, then a light green marker over that line, and finally, a light yellow marker over that line?

How can I use checklists to self-assess?

Check off when Complete

- [ ] Go online and find a synonym of the word "effusive." Write that synonym here. ---->
- [ ] Find a wall that you can safely lean on. Face the wall about three feet away and spread your legs out to a shoulder's distance apart. Bend at the waist (but not at the knees) and carefully rest your head against the wall (you can use your hands to safely get into position). Now, without using your arms, moving your feet or bending your knees, try to stand up straight. Can you do it? This is a test of center-of-gravity.
- [ ] Instead of doing any of these activities, write "I read the directions" at the top of this page and make sure your name is on the other side. Don't check any of the boxes, except this one. This was a trick to try to teach others to read directions. You have the rest of the time for yourself, but don't allow anyone to know the trick.

INTRODUCTION
PLANNING
METACOGNITION
SYNTHESIS
REFLECTION
SELF-ASSESSMENT
GOAL SETTING
FEEDBACK

245

bit.ly/47qilwJ

Pair "I can" statements with powerful evidence from your work to provide proof of meeting each Success Criteria

5.11

Essential Question

How can I use "I can" Statements to self-assess?

Big Idea

When we can put our Success Criteria into "I can" statements, we are telling others that we feel we have met our Learning Target for this skill. "I can" statements can be powerful ways of self-assessing when paired with evidence collecting.

Lesson Overview

In this lesson, students learn how to use "I can..." statements to make self-assessment claims. These claims might suggest completion of tasks, quality of work, or level of accomplishment, for example. Each "I can..." statement is supported with evidence from their work that they believe shows their claim is true. These "I can..." statements can be provided by the teacher, or the students can be asked to come up with them on their own. This technique can be used to self-assess a task or assignment, or it can be used to self-assess an entire unit or marking period.

Discussion/Reflection Questions

- Why are we asked to include evidence with each of our "I can..." statements?
- What do we do when we DON'T believe that we've met a specific Success Criterion?
- How can we make sure we come back to our incomplete "I can..." statements once we have evidence that shows we've met them?

Teacher Tips

- The students need an academic assignment that they can complete before doing today's Student Handouts. It should be something they can identify the Success Criteria for, or you should provide the Success Criteria to them so they can use it to make appropriate "I can..." statements that help them self-assess their work.
- A refresher about Growth Mindset would go well during this lesson, so students understand that they shouldn't worry if they are not yet successful at a specific Success Criterion. They simply acknowledge the "I can..." statement that they are working toward, and write, "Not Yet" for the evidence that supports their claim. The key is teaching each student to make sure they come back to the graphic organizer once they feel they've met the Success Criterion and add that evidence.
- The second Instructional Poster is a list of Success Criteria that student can track with a spot to indicate once evidence has been gathered that supports the claim that it's been met.

Student Tasks 〉 Transfer Goals

Students write "I can..." statements when they believe a specific Success Criterion has been met.	Students see how self-assessment relates directly to their accomplishments.
Students provide evidence to support their claims of meeting each individual Success Criterion.	Students no longer make claims that can't be supported with evidence, making their self-assessments more accurate.

INTRODUCTION
PLANNING
METACOGNITION
SYNTHESIS
REFLECTION
SELF-ASSESSMENT
GOAL SETTING
FEEDBACK

Instructional Poster(s)

- This lesson has TWO Instructional Posters.
- This lesson has ONE page of Teacher Directions.
- The Instructional Poster for this lesson shows students how they can use "I can..." statements to determine if they were successful or not on an assignment at a completion level. Each completion level statement can be further broken down into "I can..." statements that assess quality of work and level of accomplishment if needed. All statements are backed up with evidence to support their claims.
- Student Directions and Success Criteria have been provided to help students come up with appropriate "I can..." statements for the assignment. This particular assignment focuses more on completion of various tasks, while other assignments may focus more on quality and level of accomplishment.

Student Handouts

- This lesson has TWO Student Handouts.
- DIRECTIONS: After you complete an assignment in class, use your directions and success criteria to make three "I can" statements that weren't true before this assignment. These need to be skills that your teacher is hoping for and can use for assessment purposes. Then, describe or attach any evidence that proves your claim.
- A Teacher Handout has been provided to help plan an academic lesson that supports this skill lesson.
- The Student Handouts for today's lesson ask students to identify three Success Criteria for an assignment they recently completed. (The teacher can provide them or the students can infer them from the directions or what was taught in class). If they believe that they met each Success Criterion, they write an "I can..." statement that states their belief, and provide evidence to support each claim. If they don't believe they've met a Success Criterion yet, they write the "I can..." statement, and the words, "Not Yet" in the evidence section.

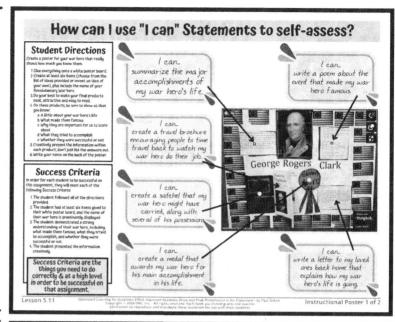

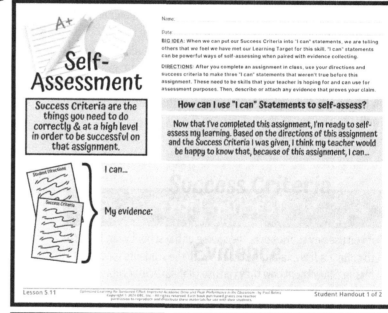

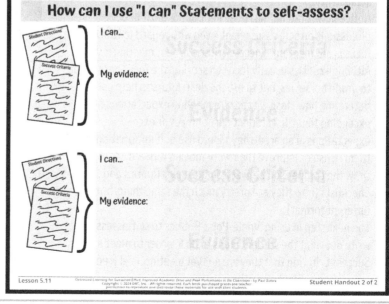

bit.ly/46AcYtE

While various types of rubrics aid in self-assessment, discover the distinct advantages of Single-Point Rubrics

Essential Question

How can I use rubrics to self-assess?

Big Idea

Single Point Rubrics can really help us focus in on what's most important during a self-assessment. Starting with the Success Criterion in the center column, we can list all of our attempts at meeting our goal and any plans we make for future attempts in the left column. In the right column, we can record when we've met our goal, an explanation of how it was done, and any evidence of exceeding the goal as well.

Lesson Overview

In this lesson, students learn about three types of rubrics and how they can be used for self-assessment. They then focus in on Single-Point Rubrics, and use them to self-assess a recent assignment. Single-Point Rubrics use a "MET" and "NOT YET" system of assessment that aligns well with growth mindset. Students track all of their attempts to meet a Success Criterion, and record evidence when they believe that they've finally met it. If they believe that they have exceeded expectations in any way, they can explain that as well.

Discussion/Reflection Questions

- Why do single-point rubrics work so well with a growth mindset?
- What will you do if you have some Success Criteria that you haven't yet met and the class is moving on to a new unit of study?
- How will you let your teacher know that you believe you have exceeded expectations for a Success Criterion? Where will you write it? What will you write?

Teacher Tips

- If you use any rubrics over the course of the school year, be sure to collect a few examples to share with the students for this lesson. Show them how they can use that particular rubric as a self-assessment guide. Discuss the subjectivity of it all, but explain how including evidence takes away some of the subjectivity.
- Notice how "grading" has been kept out of most of our discussions on self-assessment, even with regard to rubrics. The focus is on "meeting" Success Criteria or "not meeting it yet."
- Although rubrics usually focus on scoring, the focus here is not to grade ourselves, but to use the descriptors to help us determine how close we came to meeting expectations or exceeding them. If a student did not meet or exceed expectations in an area, they should use that information to help them revise or improve their work moving forward.
- Draw the comparison between Single-Point Rubrics and Checklists (how they are pretty much the same thing, but in a different format).
- The next step in using Single-Point Rubrics to self-assess is to write out what the student plans to do in order to meet a Success Criterion that they are not yet meeting. Feel free to encourage student to do this.

Student Tasks 〉 Transfer Goals

Students learn about three types of rubrics and how they can be used for self-assessment.	Students use rubrics as a guide WHILE they work, not just as a scoring tool when they get their grade on an assignment.
Students use a Single-Point Rubric to self-assess a recent assignment.	Students see learning as a process that often includes many attempts before succeeding.

Instructional Poster(s)

- This lesson has FIVE Instructional Posters (but it's really like two Instructional Posters).
- The first Instructional Poster for this lesson explains three different types of rubrics that might be used in a school setting. You might choose to show them an example of each from your curriculum if you use each type, because the definitions are not easy to understand without a visual. However, this lesson will focus in on Single-Point Rubrics and provides examples for the students to look at.
- The four additional Instructional Posters show the process of filling out a Single-Point Rubric, step-by-step. It explains how to list evidence toward meeting Success Criteria (before you believe that you've MET the criteria), and how to explain how you believe you may have EXCEEDED expectations.

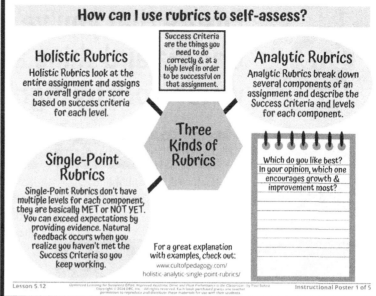

Student Handouts

- This lesson has TWO Student Handouts.
- DIRECTIONS: Complete & attach this Single-Point Rubric to any assignment you choose. Read each column heading carefully & be as clear as you can! Exemplars on back!
- The Student Handouts for this lesson provide students with room to assess themselves on two Success Criteria (just add more pages to address additional Success Criteria). Exemplars have been included for students to use as a guide while completing their own.
- Remind students that Single-Point Rubrics focus on "MET" and "NOT YET" as the two categories of self-assessment, but encourages students to explain how they may have exceeded expectations in the column on the right.

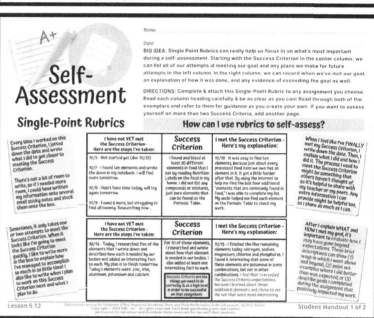

bit.ly/40Wrv1D

Ensure that you've tackled all Success Criteria and shine a light on your best & worst work by highlighting the evidence

5.13

Essential Question

How can I use highlighting to self-assess?

Big Idea

Highlighting our work is an amazingly useful tool for self-assessment. It can be used to find best and worst examples of our work, easiest and hardest, most confident and least confident. It can also be used to provide evidence of completion.

Lesson Overview

In this lesson, students learn about the ways they can use highlighters to self-assess their work. It can be used simply to identify completion of Success Criteria, or it can be used to have students find their highest quality examples and lowest quality examples. Highlighting not only helps students with self-assessment, but it also helps teachers assess student work too!

Discussion/Reflection Questions

- Why is it beneficial for you to highlight areas of strength and areas of weakness in your work?
- What will you do if you discover that it's hard for you to decide between areas of strength and weakness on a specific assignment? (Everything looks good to you OR everything needs work!)
- How could you use five different color highlighters to self-assess? For what purpose might you use each color?

Teacher Tips

- For this lesson, students will need at least one completed assignment or assessment that they can self-assess using highlighters. They will also need a few different color highlighters to do this work (or it can be done on devices using the highlighting tools available online).
- If you can show them the process of highlighting strongest examples and weakest examples on an assignment from earlier in the year, they will benefit from the time spent.

Student Tasks 〉 Transfer Goals

Student Tasks	Transfer Goals
Students learn to highlight evidence that supports their claims of meeting Success Criteria.	Students independently use highlighters to ensure they've completed everything before submitting it to their teacher.
Students learn to use highlighters to identify strong examples and weak examples within their work.	Students use highlighters to identify areas of their work they'd like to improve before submitting it to their teacher.

INTRODUCTION

PLANNING

METACOGNITION

SYNTHESIS

REFLECTION

SELF-ASSESSMENT

GOAL SETTING

FEEDBACK

Instructional Poster(s)

- This lesson has ONE Instructional Poster.
- The Instructional Poster for this lesson describes two ways that students can use highlighters to help them self-assess. One focuses on quality and the other focuses on completion. Discuss past assignments from class where highlighting could have been used.
- Let students know that they can decide which colors represent which qualities - they just need to specify how they are being used in a key of some sort.

How can I use highlighting to self-assess?

Highlighting areas of strength and weakness in a written assignment is a GREAT way to self-assess!

Highlighting evidence of completion of tasks on a checklist or rubric is a GREAT way to determine if you've completed everything AND gives you another chance to decide if it meets the Success Criteria or not.

For example:
Highlight your highest quality cursive "y" in yellow and highlight your lowest quality cursive "y" in pink:

For example:
In this piece of poetry, be sure to meet the following minimum requirements (highlighter color):
- At least ONE example of a metaphor (green)
- At least ONE example of a simile (orange)
- At least ONE example of personification (pink)
- At least ONE example of onomatopoeia (yellow)

Success Criteria are the things you need to do correctly & at a high level in order to be successful on that assignment.

Lesson 5.13   Optimized Learning for Sustained Effort, Improved Academic Drive and Peak Performance in the Classroom - by Paul Solarz   Instructional Poster 1 of 1

Student Handouts

- This lesson has THREE Student Handouts..
- DIRECTIONS: Using an assignment that your teacher gave you or one of your own, complete the following self-assessment. You will need a yellow and blue highlighter. Then, complete the following page.
- The first Student Handout is to be used with an assignment that students have recently completed in class where they can highlight high quality examples and examples that still need more work - this could work with a quiz or test, or a first draft of a writing piece. It also asks for one question they would like their teacher to answer about their work, so be sure to read these so you can provide that feedback. This page can be used throughout the year on other assignments as well.
- The second Student Handout contains two questions that gets students to think deeply about why highlighting in each situation is a valuable use of time.

A+

Self-Assessment

Name:

Date:

BIG IDEA: Highlighting our work is an amazingly useful tool for self-assessment. It can be used to find best and worst examples of our work, easiest and hardest, most confident and least confident. It can also be used to provide evidence of completion.

DIRECTIONS: Using an assignment that your teacher gave you or one of your own, complete the following self-assessment. You will need four different colored highlighters. Then, complete the following page.

How can I use highlighting to self-assess?

Go back through your work and highlight your BEST WORK in yellow. Why do you consider this your best work?

Go back through your work and highlight your SECOND BEST WORK in orange. Why do you consider this your second best work?

Go back through your work and highlight one area that NEEDS IMPROVEMENT in blue. Why does it need improvement?

Go back through your work and highlight one more area that NEEDS IMPROVEMENT in green. Why does it need improvement?

Lesson 5.13   Optimized Learning for Sustained Effort, Improved Academic Drive and Peak Performance in the Classroom - by Paul Solarz   Student Handout 1 of 3

How can I use highlighting to self-assess?

You just finished an assignment where you had to write a paragraph using the ten words from your weekly vocabulary list. You are expected to use each word correctly and clearly in order to get credit for it. Words that are not used correctly are marked wrong. Your teacher lets you highlight two words you're most confident about in blue and two words you're least confident about in red. She won't grade the red words. How is this an example of Self-Assessment? Why is this a valuable use of your time?

You just finished a challenging math worksheet where every problem was hard, but not impossible. You think you did well but you aren't completely sure and it's not something you can check on a calculator. Your teacher says, "I'm only grading one problem on each student's paper and that will be your grade - 0% or 100%."

Fortunately, YOU get to highlight the one problem you want graded. How is this an example of Self-Assessment? Why is this a valuable use of your time?

Lesson 5.13   Optimized Learning for Sustained Effort, Improved Academic Drive and Peak Performance in the Classroom - by Paul Solarz   Student Handout 2 of 3

bit.ly/46CQcS3

Elevate exit tickets from teacher feedback tools to powerful self-assessment weapons that drive personal improvement

5.14

Essential Question

How can I use exit tickets to self-assess?

Lesson Overview

In this lesson, students learn about exit tickets and how they lend themselves to being excellent self-assessment tools. They examine different versions of exit slips to see the wide variety of them, and look at an exemplar that shows how students should complete an exit slip so that it encourages self-assessment. Exit slips are just one way of combining student reflection, self-assessment and checking for understanding. It can also be done using entrance slips, quizzes, surveys, Google forms, etc. The key is finding something that you can use regularly so students get in the habit of self-assessing regularly.

Teacher Tips

- The best way to ensure students self-assess regularly is to make it a habit. One way to do that is by assigning exit slips or something similar on a regular basis. The front of the exit slip can remain the same each day, but the question on the back should vary based on the subject and the concept that was learned in class. Because it can be difficult to anticipate the best question to include on the back prior to teaching the lesson, I suggest writing one on the board each day and having the students copy it onto the exit slip themselves.
- Consider creating additional exemplars for some of the other emojis that can represent realistic answers that students might write for various lessons and concepts. The more detailed and explicit your exemplars are, the more likely students will also write detailed and explicit answers.

Big Idea

Exit tickets are often used by teachers to assess how well the class understood the lesson, but they are also extremely valuable for self-assessment! In addition to one or two academic questions, your teacher might ask you how well you think you understood the lesson or task and have you explain your answer. You might also be asked what you will do to understand the skill better or how you might challenge yourself further.

Discussion/Reflection Questions

- Why is it important to take time to thoroughly explain to your teacher how you are feeling about a concept or skill that you are struggling with in class?
- What is one emoji that is missing from the exit slip that you wish was on there? What emotion isn't represented by the eight emojis that might be needed sometime? (Only describe real answers to this question.)
- How would you handle it as a teacher if a student thought they completely understood a concept in class, but got all of the problems wrong on the exit slip?

Student Tasks 〉 Transfer Goals

Student Tasks	Transfer Goals
Students learn about exit tickets and how they lend themselves to being excellent self-assessment tools.	Students use their exit slip to do the self-assessment step in the SLSI Process when they are provided.
Students complete an exit slip after an academic lesson in class and share their self-assessment of the concept or skill learned.	Students complete future exit slips completely and to the best of their ability.

Instructional Poster(s)

- This lesson has FOUR Instructional Posters.
- The four Instructional Posters for this lesson take a look at various types of Exit Slips (self-assessments, checking for understanding, reflections, etc.), and then focuses in on one that combines several types together.
- The second Instructional Poster helps students put into words how they are feeling about today's learning. It is assumed that most of the time, students will be feeling indifferent or confident, but on those days when they didn't really understand everything, it's valuable to have them share that with the teacher so individual support, small group re-teaching, or another whole group lesson can be scheduled and completed in order to meet the needs of your students.

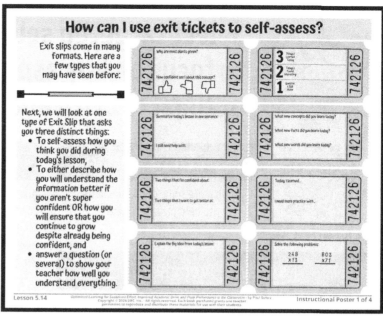

Student Handouts

- This lesson has FOUR Student Handouts.
- DIRECTIONS: Explain what you think each emoji means to YOU. How might you use each emoji? When was the last time you FELT the same as that emoji? Make this into your own personal Emoji Glossary for Exit Tickets!
- Emojis seem to work well with all age groups, so the first Student Handout asks students to create their own personal "Glossary" that explains what each emoji means to them, so they can use them to report how they feel about their learning each day.
- DIRECTIONS: Fill out the exit ticket below. Circle one of the emojis and then explain what you mean by it. Then, circle one of the reflection questions and answer it. Finally, use the back of this exit ticket to answer the question(s) that your teacher gave you.
- The second Student Handout is an actual Exit Ticket that should be filled out after an academic task or assignment. Try to plan this lesson to correlate with an assignment in class that would benefit from an Exit Slip like this one. Feel free to use this format in the future, or design your own that incorporates self-assessment by each student.

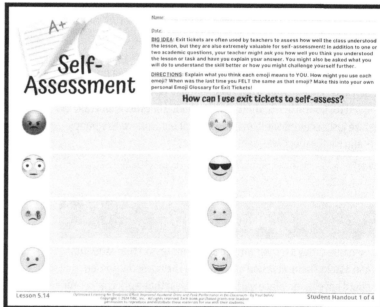

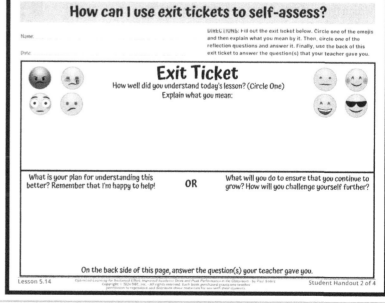

5.15

Select targeted self-assessment questions to focus on key aspects of your learning for optimal growth and improvement

bit.ly/3uHW3Ic

Essential Question

What are some good questions to help me self-assess?

Big Idea

Answering generic self-reflection questions is a quick and easy way to assess your progress, work ethic, achievement and more. Choosing questions WISELY from the following list (or your own) can make self-assessment an extremely valuable part of the learning process!

Lesson Overview

In this lesson, students discover a large selection of self-assessment questions that they can ask themselves instead of the traditional, "What did I do well?" and "What did I do poorly?" Self-assessment is deeper than quality of work and can involve an analysis of effort, growth, importance, difficulty, attention, decision-making, neatness, use of resources, etc. The true goal of the self-assessment step is not to complete a task that our teacher assigned us, but rather to think deeply about what was important in what we just accomplished, what aspects of our work we are happy with, and what aspects we want to improve.

Discussion/Reflection Questions

- Why do we need any self-assessment questions outside of the traditional, "What did I do well?" and "What did I do poorly?"
- What is one additional self-assessment question you would add to the Instructional Poster or Student Handouts for this lesson? It can be one you came up with, or one discussed in class, but make sure it gets you to assess your work or process!
- How is self-assessment different from reflection?

Teacher Tips

- Combine today's lesson with an academic lesson that students can assess themselves on afterwards. (The academic lesson could have taken place earlier in the day if that works better for your schedule.)
- While teaching today's lesson, spend some time choosing the wrong types of self-assessment questions to show students why those are not valuable or appropriate to choose for that situation. Then, show them how other questions are more appropriate to dig into what really matters.
- If you or your students can brainstorm any additional generic self-assessment questions that can be added to the Instructional Poster and Student Handouts, please do! Just be sure they are self-assessment questions, not reflection questions or something else. It's important to keep the concept of self-assessment clear with the students.

Student Tasks 〉 Transfer Goals

Students discover that there are dozens more self-assessment questions they can ask themselves than our standard two.	Students begin to assess themselves in several new ways during and after learning.
Students choose five questions to assess themselves on for a recently completed assignment or task.	Students consider a variety of questions whenever they assess their work in class and out of it.

INTRODUCTION

PLANNING

METACOGNITION

SYNTHESIS

REFLECTION

SELF-ASSESSMENT

GOAL SETTING

FEEDBACK

Instructional Poster(s)

- This lesson has ONE Instructional Poster.
- This lesson has ONE page of Teacher Tips.
- The Instructional Poster for this lesson teaches students that self-assessment doesn't always have to be "What did I do well?" and "What did I do poorly?" There are several other questions we can ask ourselves, depending on our purpose and the task we just completed. The goal here is to teach the student to choose a self-assessment that FITS their situation best, not just choose one that can be answered quickly and easily.
- Answering generic self-reflection questions is a quick and easy way to get students to assess their progress, work ethic, achievement and more without much prep work. Rather than give students complete autonomy to choose any question (they'll often choose the quickest & easiest to answer), give them choices between types of questions or assign specific questions based on the assignment & purpose.

Student Handouts

- This lesson has TWO Student Handouts.
- DIRECTIONS: Choose a bullet from the list on the right to answer in a box on the left. Draw a line connecting the dots so your teacher knows which question you are answering. For any Yes/No question (or anything else with a short answer), be sure to add evidence/additional detail to support your answer. Each box should have multiple sentences inside. Some bullets have multiple questions - please answer them all!
- The Student Handouts for this lesson allow students to choose appropriate self-assessment questions for the academic lesson they just completed in class. Once they've chosen a question for each box, they answer each to the best of their abilities.

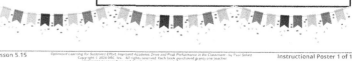

What are some good questions to help me self-assess?

Answering generic self-reflection questions is a quick and easy way to assess your progress, work ethic, achievement and more. Choosing questions WISELY from the following list (or your own) can make self-assessment an extremely valuable part of the learning process!

> **Success Criteria are the things you need to do correctly & at a high level in order to be successful on that assignment.**

- Which success criteria did I meet? Which didn't I meet?
- Did I try my very best? Can I describe what that looked like?
- What questions do I still have? What could I use more help with?
- What was the MOST IMPORTANT thing I learned today? Why was it important?
- What areas do I have the power to try to improve in? Should I write a goal?
- Was this easy or hard for me? Why do I think that was?
- Did I use the tools & resources my teacher expected me to use?
- Did I complete my work carefully? Did I check my work carefully?
- Did I understand the directions completely & follow them correctly?
- Did I pay attention to the teacher's instruction? To my peers?
- Did I actively participate and collaborate well with my peers?
- Did I ask for help when I needed it? Did I help others?
- Did I make connections between what I learned today and my prior knowledge
- Is my work neat and presentable?
- Did I use my time wisely? Did I meet all deadlines?
- What will I do differently next time? Why?

Lesson 5.15 — Instructional Poster 1 of 1

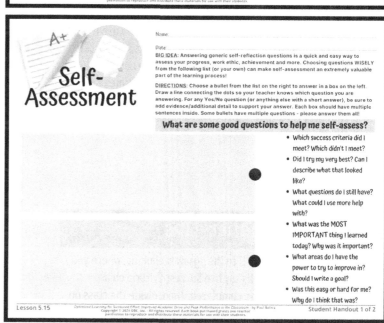

Name:

Date:

BIG IDEA: Answering generic self-reflection questions is a quick and easy way to assess your progress, work ethic, achievement and more. Choosing questions WISELY from the following list (or your own) can make self-assessment an extremely valuable part of the learning process!

DIRECTIONS: Choose a bullet from the list on the right to answer in a box on the left. Draw a line connecting the dots so your teacher knows which question you are answering. For any Yes/No question (or anything else with a short answer), be sure to add evidence/additional detail to support your answer. Each box should have multiple sentences inside. Some bullets have multiple questions - please answer them all!

What are some good questions to help me self-assess?

- Which success criteria did I meet? Which didn't I meet?
- Did I try my very best? Can I describe what that looked like?
- What questions do I still have? What could I use more help with?
- What was the MOST IMPORTANT thing I learned today? Why was it important?
- What areas do I have the power to try to improve in? Should I write a goal?
- Was this easy or hard for me? Why do I think that was?

Lesson 5.15 — Student Handout 1 of 2

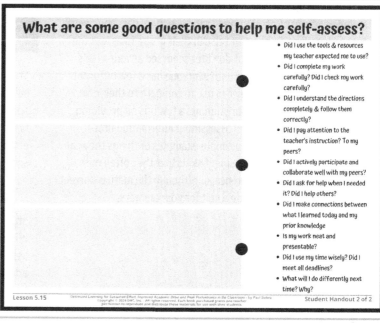

What are some good questions to help me self-assess?

- Did I use the tools & resources my teacher expected me to use?
- Did I complete my work carefully? Did I check my work carefully?
- Did I understand the directions completely & follow them correctly?
- Did I pay attention to the teacher's instruction? To my peers?
- Did I actively participate and collaborate well with my peers?
- Did I ask for help when I needed it? Did I help others?
- Did I make connections between what I learned today and my prior knowledge
- Is my work neat and presentable?
- Did I use my time wisely? Did I meet all deadlines?
- What will I do differently next time? Why?

Lesson 5.15 — Student Handout 2 of 2

bit.ly/3T2k7Q7

5.16 Overcome self-assessment "blind spots" through peer collaboration to uncover otherwise hidden areas for improvement

Essential Question

What can I learn by comparing my assessment to someone else's?

Lesson Overview

In this lesson, students compare their self-assessment of one Success Criterion to the assessment of the same Success Criterion by someone else (e.g. a peer, parent, teacher, etc.). They use the two assessments as a means of identifying any blindspots in their self-assessment abilities (e.g. Some of us are too hard on ourselves, sometimes we miss errors that we always make, sometimes we repeat a misconception or misunderstanding over and over). Once students discover their blindspots, they can make an effort to address them.

Big Idea

One of the toughest aspects of self-assessment is stepping away from our work and seeing it through others' eyes. To us, everything might make sense, but to someone else it might need more explanation. When we compare our own self-assessments to the assessments of others, we gain that perspective that we truly need.

Discussion/Reflection Questions

- Why is it that OUR self-assessments can be different from other people's assessments of the same work? Assuming we are both focused on the same Success Criterion, aren't we both looking at the same thing?
- What is one "blindspot" that you discovered about yourself when it comes to self-assessment? (A blindspot is something you always miss, but others may have no trouble finding.)
- How can we fix blindspots, so we begin to notice them more often?

Teacher Tips

- This lesson lends itself well to the jigsaw technique, where you provide students with let's say five Success Criteria on an assignment that everyone completed. Then, divide the class up into five groups and assign each group one of the Success Criteria. Have everyone begin by assessing their own work on the assigned Success Criterion, and then have them pass their work around the circle to someone else in their group to assess the same Success Criterion (but don't let them see anyone else's assessment). Keep rotating until everyone has a few different peer assessments that they can use to compare to their own. (You may have to teach your students a few tips on providing their peers with meaningful assessment information first.)
- Provide the students with a couple examples of things they can learn about their self-assessment skills like: they often miss where commas go in a sentence, or although the math is correct, you always forget to include a unit for your answers.

Student Tasks ⟩ Transfer Goals

Student Tasks	Transfer Goals
Students compare their self-assessment of a specific Success Criterion to someone else's assessment of the same work.	Students have new perspectives on assessing work and integrate these new ideas into their own self-assessments.
Students identify blindspots in their self-assessments and try to address them.	Students are more accurate with their self-assessments, leading to stronger improvement acadmically.

Instructional Poster(s)

- This lesson has ONE Instructional Poster.
- The Instructional Poster for this lesson introduces students to the idea of having a peer, a parent or a teacher assess their work in order to give meaningful feedback to help them improve their work.
- In this lesson, students will be asking someone else to look over their assignment and assess them on one specific Success Criterion that they specify ahead of time. They then compare their self-assessment to the assessment of the other person to try to identify any variations. Based on these variations, students can improve their self-assessment skills or strengthen their confidence in them.

Student Handouts

- This lesson has TWO Student Handouts.
- DIRECTIONS: Complete this page and attach it to a completed assignment that you consider a great example of you meeting or exceeding one or more Success Criteria. You can have a peer or the teacher give you feedback on it, but if it is a great example, be sure your teacher gets to see it so they can add it to their evidence of success!
- The first Student Handout asks students to identify one Success Criterion that they would like someone else to assess themselves on, so they can compare it to their own self-assessment.
- The second Student Handout guides students through the comparison phase by asking them what their self-assessment is, how it differs from the other person's assessment, and what can be learned from the difference.

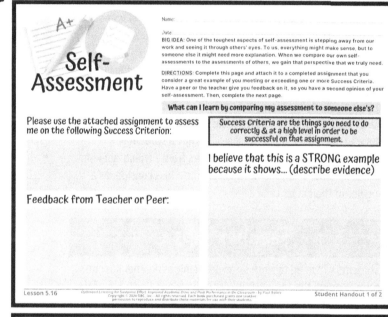

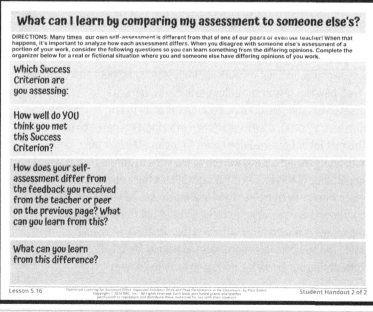

bit.ly/3uBluvb

Use self-assessment techniques while you work to plan, prioritize, and efficiently complete assignments on time

Essential Question

How well am I doing on my work completion?

Big Idea

Managing our time can be a real challenge sometimes. If we get caught up in something fun, we may lost track of time. If we are confused, we may struggle for a while which costs us time. By bringing it to our attention, we have a better chance of meeting our deadlines and completing our work.

Lesson Overview

In this lesson, students assess their work completion on an assignment in class. They try to measure whether they completed everything that they wanted to accomplish during the class period or to which degree they managed to do so. The purpose of this lesson is to increase student awareness of how they use and manage their time in class, and how well they meet deadlines. On the flip side, there are some exceptions to the rule of using class time to completely focus on your work. In a collaborative classroom, students are expected to devote some of their work time to helping others who need their support. Likewise, when a student is struggling, rather than just get the answers from a friend, seeking help to learn HOW to do the work takes time and is considered a strong use of their class time.

Discussion/Reflection Questions

- Why is this lesson about self-assessment, not self-grading? Weren't there numbers on the target?
- What is one acceptable reason for NOT completing all the work you hoped to complete in class? What might be worth your time MORE than finishing your work?
- If you end up missing a deadline, what will you do immediately to try to meet your teacher's expectations? How will you try to finish everything immediately?

Teacher Tips

- Students will need to work on an academic assignment in class prior to doing this lesson. It is best if they don't finish ALL of the components of the assignment, because then they can assess their progress without having to default to "100% complete." A great activity might be a story that they are writing that should take a few more writing periods to complete, or a project that they are working on over the next couple weeks.
- As you and your students work on this lesson, you should all "feel" how this lesson straddles the line between self-assessment and self-grading because the archery target has numbers associated with each concentric ring. I hesitated to use this metaphor because I don't want to confuse the two, but ultimately thought it was worthwhile to include. The key importance of this lesson is having students think about how much work they completed and how much they have left to still do. The archery target helps make it visual, but the thinking and awareness is what really matters. In this situation, we're just using the numbers like coordinates to help us identify the correct ring our arrow hit, not trying to assign grades.

Student Tasks 〉 Transfer Goals

Students learn to use an archery target to describe how close they came to a bullseye on their work accomplishment.

Students have an improved sense of time, use their time in class more wisely, and meet more deadlines.

Students analyze how they could have used their work time better, keeping in mind the importance of helping their peers.

Students are able to allocate some of their work time to helping others, yet still manage to finish their own work.

Instructional Poster(s)

- This lesson has ONE Instructional Poster.
- The Instructional Poster for this lesson helps students visualize and quantify how much work they have completed and how much work still is yet to be done. The idea of "work completion" is very basic: you are either done or you are not done. If you are not done, how much more do you need to do and when will you do it?
- Just like an archer aiming for the bullseye, we generally try to finish all of our work by the deadline, but sometimes we miss slightly and sometimes we miss a whole bunch! We need to hone our skills so that we hit more bullseyes, and try to limit the misses. Hopefully, students can use this lesson to improve their work completion and meet more deadlines.

Student Handouts

- This lesson has TWO Student Handouts.
- This lesson has ONE Examplar.
- DIRECTIONS: You just reached a deadline in class and your teacher wants to see how you would assess your progress on the assignment that is due. Read everything on this page and the next and answer each question completely and honestly.
- The first Student Handout asks students to self-assess their completion based on the Archery Target descriptors. The students can use the numbers to help explain where they hit the target, since not everyone will be using the color version of these handouts. Students will likely think of these numbers as "grades" due to being brought up in a graded school environment. Please remind them that there is a difference between self-assessment and self-grading. In this situation, we're just using the numbers like coordinates, not trying to assign grades.
- The second Student Handout asks students to answer four questions reflecting on the assignment they just finished working on.

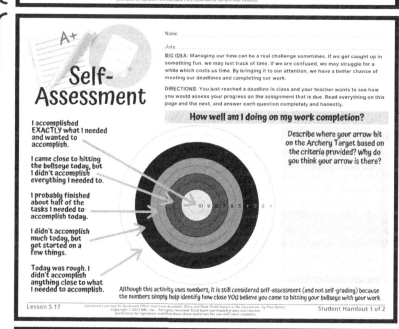

How well am I doing on my work completion?

You just reached a deadline. It might have been the end of class, the last day to complete an assignment, or a deadline you made for yourself. Did you accomplish what you hoped to accomplish? Did you meet ALL of your goals?

- I accomplished EXACTLY what I needed and wanted to accomplish.
- I came close to hitting the bullseye today, but I didn't accomplish everything I needed to.
- I probably finished about half of the tasks I needed to accomplish today.
- I didn't accomplish much today, but got started on a few things.
- Today was rough. I didn't accomplish anything close to what I needed to accomplish.

Lesson 5.17 · Instructional Poster 1 of 1

Self-Assessment

BIG IDEA: Managing our time can be a real challenge sometimes. If we get caught up in something fun, we may lost track of time. If we are confused, we may struggle for a while which costs us time. By bringing it to our attention, we have a better chance of meeting our deadlines and completing our work.

DIRECTIONS: You just reached a deadline in class and your teacher wants to see how you would assess your progress on the assignment that is due. Read everything on this page and the next, and answer each question completely and honestly.

How well am I doing on my work completion?

Describe where your arrow hit on the Archery Target based on the criteria provided? Why do you think your arrow is there?

Although this activity uses numbers, it is still considered self-assessment (and not self-grading) because the numbers simply help identify how close YOU believe you came to hitting your bullseye with your work.

Lesson 5.17 · Student Handout 1 of 2

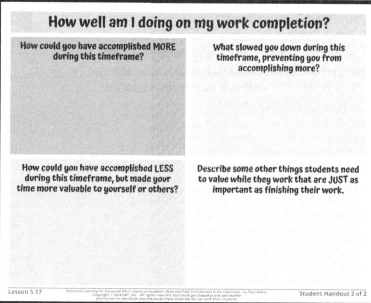

How well am I doing on my work completion?

How could you have accomplished MORE during this timeframe?	What slowed you down during this timeframe, preventing you from accomplishing more?
How could you have accomplished LESS during this timeframe, but made your time more valuable to yourself or others?	Describe some other things students need to value while they work that are JUST as important as finishing their work.

Lesson 5.17 · Student Handout 2 of 2

259

bit.ly/3Rm2gSY

Achieve and surpass expectations for each Success Criterion by actively assessing the quality of your work in real-time

Essential Question

How well am I doing on the quality of my work?

Big Idea

When we know our Success Criteria, we can collect evidence toward meeting expectations in order to monitor our work quality.

Lesson Overview

In this lesson, students do a basic self-assessment of their work quality for several Success Criteria. Their first job is to determine if they are "Above Water" or "Below Water" (a.k.a. meeting expectations or not yet meeting expectations). If they are above water, they are also asked if they are exceeding expectations or still at the standard "meets" level. The way this is set up, students want to be above water, so that's the first motivator. For those who can do that without much difficulty, the next motivator is to exceed expectations by doing "better than what was asked of me." Finally, students cite evidence that supports each claim, and consider how they might be able to transfer one Success Criteria to a new situation in the future.

Discussion/Reflection Questions

- Why are you always being asked to include evidence to support your claims?
- What does the water level represent in this metaphor (You are either above or below water - what does that mean)?
- How will you transfer or apply one of these Success Criteria to a new situation in the future?

Teacher Tips

- For this lesson, students need an assignment that they can self-assess that has multiple Success Criteria. You can provide students with the Success Criteria or have them identify them (depending on your students grade level, age, ability, or readiness). For younger students, you are encouraged to also share the delineation between meets and exceeds expectations, so they are better able to successfully self-assess.
- The concept of this lesson is similar to using a checklist or a Single-Point Rubric, because the student either falls into the "MET" or "NOT YET" section. You may want to draw the comparison with your students.

Student Tasks 〉 Transfer Goals

Student Tasks	Transfer Goals
Students assess themselves on various Success Criteria as either above water or below water.	Students know when they're meeting expectations & when they're not, and make an effort to get above water for all Success Criteria.
Students determine if any of their above water Success Criteria might be exceeding expectations or just meeting them.	Students know that there is value in exceeding expectations and make attempts to do so.

Instructional Poster(s)

- This lesson has ONE Instructional Poster.
- The Instructional Poster for this lesson asks students determine how well they are doing on the quality of their work. The metaphor used is "Above Water" or "Below Water" to signify passable and not passable. Since we should never aim for the bare minimum, there is room to be stronger than "passable" that we call "Better than what was asked of me." The key distinction that students need to make though is between Level 1 and Level 2. By adding additional gradations, it would really only confuse students and wouldn't bring much more value.
- Each level has been assigned one of the stoplight colors (red, yellow, or green) so that students can use the color codes on the Student Handouts.

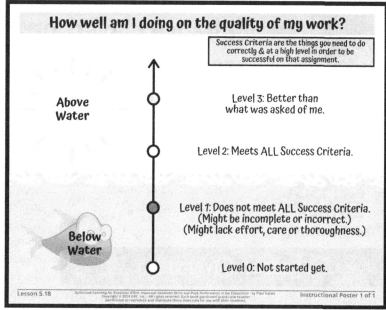

Student Handouts

- This lesson has TWO Student Handouts.
- DIRECTIONS: In the first column, write each Success Criterion you are self-assessing. In the middle column, color in the circle with the color from the Above/Below Water Chart (or write the Level Number inside). Finally, describe the evidence that supports your assessment in the final column.
- The Student Handouts for today's lesson have the students cite evidence that supports their self-assessment of each Success Criterion that they are reporting on. In addition, students will color in the circle with the color from the Above/Below Water Chart (or write the Level Number inside).
- Students are also asked how they will transfer or apply one of the Success Criteria to a new situation in the future - always focused on transfer!
- This Student Handout can be used again and again until students have internalized the skill.

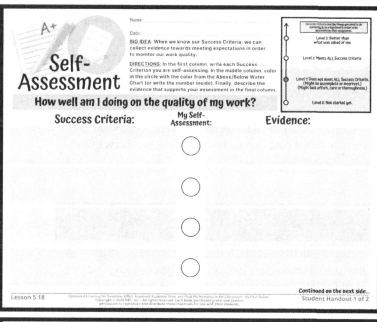

INTRODUCTION

PLANNING

METACOGNITION

SYNTHESIS

REFLECTION

SELF-ASSESSMENT

GOAL SETTING

FEEDBACK

5.19

Enhance classroom progress by evaluating areas for improvement and celebrating shared victories at the end of each day

bit.ly/3Rll6tJ

Big Idea

Dedicating ten minutes each day to reflecting on the good and not so good aspects of our day reaps benefits beyond imagination. When we take time to evaluate our own behavior, effort, shared skills, and that of the collective class, we identify where we need to improve and we feel pride where we've made progress. If we identify the most important ways we are struggling in class and create goals to improve those areas, we are more likely to find immediate and long-term success.

Lesson Overview

In this lesson, students learn a daily routine that we call REARJMCL (but you can call whatever you'd like). REARJMCL is done during the final 10-15 minutes of a school day and is completely led by the students. Its purpose is for students to write their homework down into assignment notebooks, remind each other of important events & due dates, and to evaluate our day as a whole class (the main purpose of THIS lesson). If you're not interested in doing the entire routine, please consider incorporating the "Evaluate" step into your daily end-of-the-day routine. The self-assessment and whole group assessment that is done during these ten minutes is incredible and leads to so much improvement!

Discussion/Reflection Questions

- Why should we NOT name names when evaluating our day? Why should we keep things anonymous and try to help everyone improve?
- What goal do you think is the most important one for your class to try to improve today?
- How well do you think you would do as Evaluator? Do you think you could politely keep everyone's attention for the whole ten minutes each day? Do you think you could coax important goals out of your peers?

Teacher Tips

- Included with this lesson is a Teacher Packet of information on how to lead whole-class evaluation and goal setting (which we call REARJMCL - an acronym for our end-of-the-day routine). We spend the last 15 minutes everyday, evaluating our day and setting a goal for the next day (often based on the challenges we had today).
- The best Evaluators are students who are well-respected by their peers, are confident in front of the whole group, want to do a good job, and take feedback from the teacher well (I gave a lot of feedback when they didn't have everyone's attention or when the students were just going through the motions instead of truly reflecting, etc.). I usually kept an Evaluator in the position for 1-2 months so they could get good at the job. Then, I had them train their successor. Not everyone would get a chance to do the job (they had to apply for it and meet certain criteria (e.g. couldn't be a patrol guard because they would have to leave early, etc.).

Student Tasks 〉 Transfer Goals

Student Tasks	Transfer Goals
Students learn twelve tips for brainstorming whole class goals that can lead to valuable change.	Students use their skills for evaluating themselves as a member of the class to create goals that lead to real change.
Students brainstorm potential whole class goals for their class based on current needs.	Students use this experience to brainstorm new goals each day that address current struggles that the class is having collectively.

Instructional Poster(s)

- This lesson has ONE Instructional Poster.
- This lesson has 14 pages of Teacher Directions.
- The Instructional Poster for this lesson runs through 12 tips for brainstorming whole class goals that are beneficial for the well-being of the entire class and worth the students' time and effort to work on improving.
- Even though it can be hard to come up with a new goal every single day of the school year, there are honestly an endless supply of ideas the students can access when they need inspiration. Here are 12 ideas that have helped us in the past. Also, be sure to look at the photographs of the Whole Class Goal Charts we created over the years for more ideas (in the 14-page Teacher Packet).

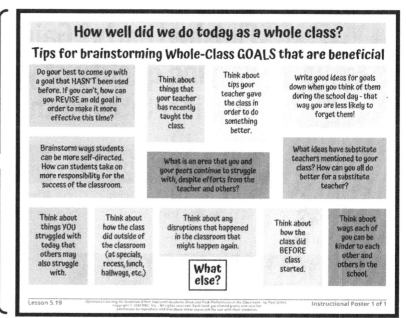

Student Handouts

- This lesson has TWO Student Handouts.
- DIRECTIONS: Describe the responsibilities of the Evaluator and the responsibilities of everyone else below. Then on the next page, brainstorm some whole-class goals for your class to improve.
- The first Student Handout asks students to explain what their responsibilities are if they ARE the Evaluator and if they are not.
- The second Student Handout provides students with six boxes to write their own suggestions for whole-class goals based on the struggles they see the class having (or for other reasons).

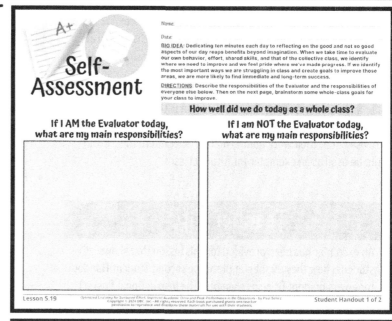

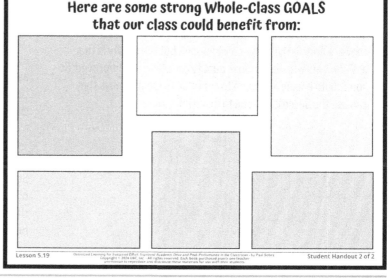

INTRODUCTION

PLANNING

METACOGNITION

SYNTHESIS

REFLECTION

SELF-ASSESSMENT

GOAL SETTING

FEEDBACK

bit.ly/47xnbYV

Finished early? Gain insight into the varying quality of your work by assessing how it relates to the Success Criteria

Essential Question

What do I do when I finish an assignment early?

Big Idea

Whenever an assignment can be done better or worse, more complete or less complete, there is no real reason to think you are done early. You can always go back and identify how you can improve your work according to the Success Criteria.

Lesson Overview

In this lesson, students learn how to identify "Levels of Achievement" for a skill by envisioning how their work would look if they did things better or worse than they really did them. This is great for helping students decide what to do when they finish an assignment early. To start, students pretend their assignment is currently at a Level 3 (out of 5). They identify things they might have done poorly or with little detail. Then, they brainstorm ways they could improve the quality of their work, things they could add to make it more complete, and ways they could add, remove, change or revise to get their work quality up to a level where their work could be used as an exemplar for future classes.

Discussion/Reflection Questions

- Why does this lesson ask you to pretend that all of your assignments are always at Level 3 (out of 5) when thinking about "Levels of Achievement"?
- What did you learn from the exemplar from this lesson about progressing to Level 4 and Level 5? What did you learn about Levels 1 and 2?
- How will you ensure that you maintain an improvement-focused attitude and mindset whenever self-assessing your work?

Teacher Tips

- An exemplar has been provided for this lesson that shows students how they might complete the second Student Handout for an assignment (it also resembles the Instructional Poster).
- This concept only works with tasks and assignments that can have variation in quality. It will not work with worksheets that have only one correct answer, for example. For that type of assignment, you should really just suggest that they look over their work and determine if they finished everything completely.
- Students will naturally believe that they are at a Level 5 when they are finished with their assignment, but the reality is that assignments with variation in quality can always be improved. So you should encourage them to continue to identify ways they can use the Success Criteria to make improvements.

Student Tasks ⟩ Transfer Goals

Student Tasks	Transfer Goals
Students envision aspects of their assignment that they completed BETTER than they could have.	Students never settle for the minimum and can identify ways they have exceeded minimum standards.
Students envision aspects of their assignment that they could have completed better than they did.	Students know what they need to do to exceed standards and just have to be motivated enough to attempt to do so.

INTRODUCTION

PLANNING

METACOGNITION

SYNTHESIS

REFLECTION

SELF-ASSESSMENT

GOAL SETTING

FEEDBACK

Instructional Poster(s)

- This lesson has THREE Instructional Posters.
- The first Instructional Poster for this lesson teaches students about the concept of continual growth and improvement. No matter how good we believe our assignment is today, it could always be improved tomorrow if we identify ways we can tweak it to improve it.
- To understand this concept, students need to ALWAYS think of themselves at Level 3 (out of 5) whenever they think they are done with an assignment. If there is no time left to work on it, Level 3 will have to do. But if there is still time to improve their work, they need to identify what they need to do to get up to Level 4 and even Level 5 if possible. The key is understanding that we are never "done" early, unless there's something more worth our time than the current assignment. (Fast Finishers).
- The second and third Instructional Posters are an exemplar for the second Student Handout. You should show this ahead of time so the students have an example to use before filling out their own.

Student Handouts

- This lesson has TWO Student Handouts.
- DIRECTIONS: Follow the directions in the boxes below. Then, on the next page, describe the "Levels of Achievement" for an assignment you have finished early.
- The first Student Handout asks students to identify their teacher's expectations and Success Criteria on an assignment they are currently completing. By having students do this, they discover the specific ways they can improve their work to "take it up a notch" from Level 3 to Level 4, for example.
- The second Student Handout might look a little confusing, so an exemplar has been provided to help you and the students see how to fill one out properly. It has been split up over two slides and are described in the Instructional Posters section above.

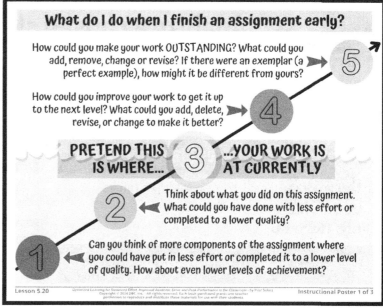

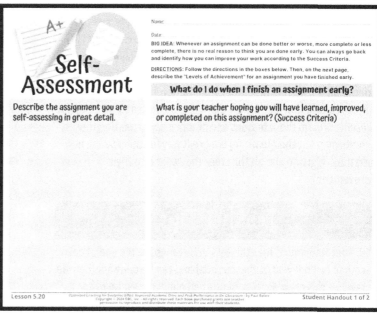

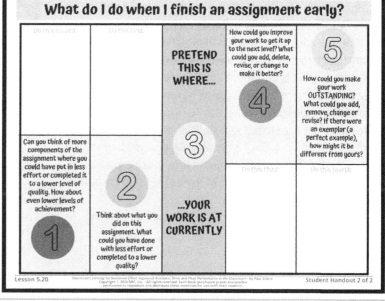

bit.ly/46xSvFL

Analyze a chosen skill, trace each step from start to today, and solidify your understanding of your learning journey

Essential Question

How much have I grown over the course of the year?

Big Idea

It can be difficult to identify growth and improvement when you're immersed in school every day, so taking time at the end of a unit, semester, or year to reflect and look back at the learning experiences that helped you grow can be really valuable.

Lesson Overview

In this lesson, students do one final self-assessment for the year (or for the term that is ending). They brainstorm as many skills that they've developed through lessons and practice in class, and ultimately choose one to map out the steps that were involved in going from their Personal Point A to their Personal Point B (from their baseline to their current level of achievement). If they understand the marble metaphor from Lesson 1.05, they also complete a task that shows how they added marbles to their cup for that skill through those lessons and practice opportunities. Having students map out their learning is a great way for them to see how much they've grown and all the steps that went into their improvement.

Discussion/Reflection Questions

- Why is it beneficial for us to spend time describing how ONE of our skills was developed over the course of the year? What did we all hopefully learn from this self-assessment?
- What were some of the factors that led you to choose the skill that you chose to use for the graphic organizer?
- How would you plan to continue to develop your abilities with this skill that you identified? What might some of the Learning Experiences look like?

Teacher Tips

- It is recommended that this lesson be taught at the end of each course (school year, semester, etc.) and can be done at all grade levels if this program is being spread out over several grades.
- If students can't come up with skill ideas on their own, be prepared to offer them some ideas. You may even choose to complete one together in class to show them how it is done.
- The Learning Experiences on the Instructional Poster and Student Handout branch off of a line that goes from their baseline (1) to their current level of achievement (6). If you can discuss how this is similar to a timeline, they might have an easier time seeing how each Learning Experience was a point in time that helped them grow.
- You will likely need to tell your students what they should write into Box 1 and Box 6. Box 1 is their baseline - where they started the year. Box 6 is where their current level of achievement is. They will need to describe both of those in words to the best of their ability.
- Challenge students to identify more than the four Learning Experiences, if applicable.

Student Tasks 〉 Transfer Goals

Student Tasks	Transfer Goals
Students brainstorm a list of skills that they improved over the course of the year (or grading term).	Students can distinguish between skills, concepts and facts, and can identify and evaluate the most important ones.
Students chose one skill and identified at least four Learning Experiences that led to them improving over time.	Students know the complexity that is involved in improving a skill and value all of the time and experiences necessary to improve.

Instructional Poster(s)

- This lesson has ONE Instructional Poster.
- The Instructional Poster for this lesson walks students through the Student Handouts for the final lesson in the Self-Assessment unit.
- As you go through the Instructional Poster, have your students write their skills onto the first Student Handout, and follow the additional directions provided.
- Next, they choose ONE of the skills that they've developed over the course of the year (or term) and recall the Learning Experiences that led them toward growth. Students describe this process on the second Student Handout.
- If you taught your students about Marble Theory (Lesson 1.05), have them follow a similar process with the additional Student Handout for another skill they made improvement on this year or term.

Student Handouts

- This lesson has THREE Student Handouts.
- DIRECTIONS: Follow the directions in the boxes below and on the next page. Your goal is to identify how you've grown and improved over time, and acknowledge the learning experiences that went into your improvement. Remember to focus in on ONE skill only.
- Students complete the first Student Handout while the teacher goes over the Instructional Poster with the class. Once they've completed the first Student Handout with teacher support, they go on to the second Student Handout and complete it independently (or preferably with a randomly assigned partner who is working on their own skill).
- If students know about Marble Theory (Lesson 1.05), there is one additional Student Handout to complete. It asks them to consider a specific skill that they learned this year and has them fill in the number of marbles they started with and the number of marbles in their cup today.

INTRODUCTION

PLANNING

METACOGNITION

SYNTHESIS

REFLECTION

SELF-ASSESSMENT

GOAL SETTING

FEEDBACK

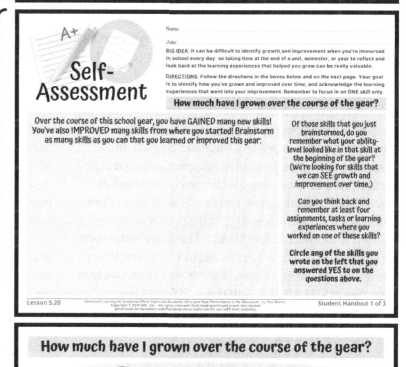

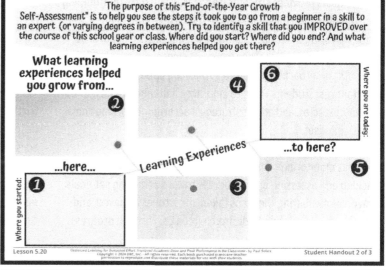

Goal Setting

"We can't become what we need to be
by remaining what we are."
— Oprah Winfrey

In this chapter, we explore valuable lessons to help students of all ages develop essential skills in goal setting and progress monitoring. These skills empower students as independent thinkers and problem solvers, allowing them to address weaknesses proactively. Engaging in the goal setting process sets students on a lifelong journey of self-improvement, constantly refining their skills as they gain experience.

Goal setting involves identifying specific objectives or targets that students aim to accomplish. These goals can be short-term or long-term, academic or personal, encompassing areas such as academic performance, personal development, extra-curricular pursuits, or career aspirations. Effective goal setting requires creating goals that are specific, measurable, achievable, relevant, and time-bound (S.M.A.R.T. Goals®)[1]. In this chapter, we introduce students to a variation called "S.M.A.A.R.T.E.R. Goals," which stands for specific, measurable, achievable, ambitious, relevant, timely, everlasting, and rewarding goals. Students are also introduced to a variation of S.M.A.A.R.T.E.R. Goals that scaffolds the learning process and reduces the amount of planning for smaller, less complex goals called "Goal Bursts".

Setting goals provides students with clarity and direction, helping them identify priorities, establish a clear vision, and create a roadmap for their actions. Clear goals instill a sense of purpose and increase motivation. They foster resilience and adaptability in students, as setbacks are viewed as learning opportunities rather than failures. Students learn to embrace challenges, persist in the face of obstacles, and adjust strategies accordingly, promoting a growth mindset.

Progress monitoring complements goal setting by systematically tracking and assessing one's progress toward achieving set goals. It involves evaluating the steps taken, milestones achieved, and growth made in relation to desired outcomes. Through progress monitoring, students gain insights into their strengths, weaknesses, and areas for improvement. This feedback loop allows for adjustments to be made, ensuring that efforts remain focused and aligned with objectives. Regular progress monitoring and witnessing incremental success build confidence and fuel persistence.

Effective goal setting leads to improved time management and planning skills. Students learn to prioritize tasks, allocate resources appropriately, and organize their schedules. Progress monitoring acts as an evaluation tool, determining whether adjustments are needed to ensure goals are met within the desired timeframe. It also fosters self-awareness in students, helping them discover their learning styles, study habits, and areas where they need to invest more time and effort.

Goal setting and progress monitoring enhance academic performance, as students who set goals and monitor progress are more likely to stay focused, complete tasks, and achieve higher levels of success. These skills also encourage students to seek out additional resources, engage in effective study strategies, and take ownership of their learning. Students develop the ability to take charge of their education, identifying their educational needs, setting goals aligned with their aspirations, and tracking their progress independently. This autonomy prepares them for lifelong learning and empowers them to navigate future challenges.

Furthermore, goal setting and progress monitoring foster decision-making skills as students assess goals, track data, consider obstacles, and select effective strategies. These skills are essential for long-term planning and career readiness. Students learn to set long-term goals, break them down into manageable steps, and consistently monitor their progress toward achieving them.

1. S.M.A.R.T. Goals® is a registered trademark of Leadership Management® International, Inc.

Imagine the following fictional classroom scenario:

In Mrs. Johnson's eighth-grade classroom, a spirit of independence and self-direction fills the air. Students have fully embraced the power of goal setting and progress monitoring using the S.M.A.A.R.T.E.R. Goal Setting Process, taking complete ownership of their learning journey. Mrs. Johnson has fostered an environment that supports student self-direction, and the results are remarkable.

At the beginning of the school year, Mrs. Johnson introduced the S.M.A.A.R.T.E.R. Goal Setting Process to her students, and taught several of the mini-lessons described in this unit. She explained the importance of setting specific, measurable, achievable, ambitious, relevant, timely, everlasting, and rewarding goals. The students were intrigued by this approach and were excited to apply it to their own lives.

Armed with this knowledge and the permission to work on this independently, students embarked on a journey of self-improvement. Each student identified their personal strengths, weaknesses, and aspirations. They set ambitious yet attainable goals that stretched their abilities and motivated their pursuit of excellence. Some students aimed to improve their math skills, others focused on developing their writing abilities, and many even set goals that attempted to improve social interactions with their peers, personal responsibility, and their own leadership qualities!

With their S.M.A.A.R.T.E.R. goals in mind, the students created detailed action plans. They researched effective study strategies, sought advice from mentors, and explored available resources. They broke down their goals into smaller, manageable steps, mapping out a roadmap to success. Mrs. Johnson provided guidance and feedback and acted as a valuable resource, but the students were the driving force behind their own plans.

As the weeks went by, the classroom transformed into a hub of focused activity. Students took charge of their learning, whole-heartedly participating in all of the class work assigned by the teacher. They actively collaborated with all peers equally effectively, valuing the diverse perspectives and contributions of their classmates. The classroom buzzed with discussions, as students shared their progress and exchanged tips and strategies. They also sought out additional learning opportunities to extend their learning beyond the curriculum, demonstrating their enthusiasm for continuous growth.

Progress monitoring became a routine part of their academic lives. Students tracked their achievements and reflected on their growth. They celebrated milestones, no matter how small, and learned from setbacks with resilience and determination. Mrs. Johnson provided a supportive environment where mistakes were viewed as stepping stones toward improvement, fostering a growth mindset among her students.

The impact of student-led self-improvement was evident. Academic performance soared as students became more focused, organized, and self-motivated. They developed effective time management skills, allocating their resources wisely and balancing their commitments. The classroom became a vibrant space where students took ownership of their learning, supporting one another to reach new heights. Outside the classroom, the influence of student-led self-improvement extended into other aspects of their lives. The students applied goal setting to personal growth, extra-curricular pursuits, and even long-term career planning. They became adept decision-makers, weighing options, considering obstacles, and selecting strategies that aligned with their aspirations.

In this classroom, student-led self-improvement using the S.M.A.A.R.T.E.R. Goal Setting Process proved to be a powerful force. With a supportive environment and guidance from their teacher, the students embraced this comprehensive approach to goal setting and progress monitoring as essential tools for personal growth. Each student developed the skills and mindset necessary to navigate challenges, persist in the face of setbacks, and continuously strive for excellence. The impact of their self-directed efforts extended far beyond academics, preparing them for a future where they could confidently take charge of their own success.

Within this unit, you have been provided with tools and strategies to empower students in their academic growth. The lessons focus on breaking down tasks, creating plans for improvement, and engaging in self-assessment. Students learn to set goals, create action plans, monitor progress, and make adjustments. These lessons empower students to take ownership of their learning and become active participants in their own success.

As their teacher, you play a vital role in guiding your students through the goal setting and progress monitoring process. By implementing these lessons, you can foster a positive and growth-oriented learning environment, where students develop skills that benefit them throughout their lives.

INTRODUCTION
PLANNING
METACOGNITION
SYNTHESIS
REFLECTION
SELF-ASSESSMENT
GOAL SETTING
FEEDBACK

269

How should students organize their goals?
It's up to you, but here are some ideas and additional tips and suggestions

Goal Organization: As mentioned on page 2, there are seven steps in the Student-Led Self-Improvement Process (SLSI). All seven steps are taught to the students during each Instructional Spiral. One of those steps is Goal Setting (which includes Progress Monitoring). *Optimized Learning* teaches students to create two types of goals:

- S.M.A.A.R.T.E.R. Goals (explained in Unit 6 - page 280) and
- Goal Bursts (explained in Unit 6 - page 282)

If you have a moment, it might be a good idea to skip over to those two lessons right now, so you understand them before moving on.

Since students will be setting goals, progress monitoring and eventually achieving goals on a schedule that won't likely follow your Instructional Spiral schedule, it's a smart idea to have students keep their goals in a separate place than they keep their Learning Cycle packets and Student Handouts for each lesson. This allows flexibility in the duration of goals, which can range from a day to a week, month or even a year. By keeping goals separate from the Learning Cycle packets, the completion of one cycle does not automatically signal the end of a goal, and vice versa.

Please note that the specific Student Handouts for each goal setting mini-lesson will still be found within each learning cycle packet. These handouts are designed to improve goal setting skills in general, rather than being tied to specific goals. To ensure easy access to goals over time and while working on other subjects, students should keep their actual goal sheets separate. Here are a few different ideas for organizing this separation:

- Provide students with a dedicated folder or binder specifically for their goals.
- Use sticky notes, dividers or tabs within a binder to separate goals from Learning Cycle packets and Student Handouts.
- Teach students to keep their goal sheets in a designated location in the classroom.
- Utilize digital tools or apps that allow students to create and track their goals electronically.

By implementing any of these strategies, students will be able to effectively manage and track progress on their goals, while working on various subjects and learning cycles.

It is recommended that students have constant access to blank S.M.A.A.R.T.E.R. Goal sheets and Goal Burst sheets at all times throughout the school year. Keep these materials in one location that students can access, so they can grab the forms whenever they decide to create new goals. If using binders, I recommend hole-punching the forms yourself ahead of time.

Goal Setting sheets kept in binders

As students complete more and more goal setting mini-lessons, their skills will grow, your expectations will increase, and it all should lead to more meaningful goals, more detailed plans for achieving their goals, more specific evidence, and a stronger motivation to pursue independent goals without requiring adult support or permission.

As with everything in this program, the ultimate goal is to eventually eliminate the use of graphic organizers and have students implement the microskills independently without teacher support or reminders. Do your best toward the end of your time together to ween your students off of the goal setting sheets and help them transition to creating goals more informally, monitoring progress toward those goals, and acknowledging when a goal has been met.

Students are encouraged to set and work toward as many goals as they think they can handle, but students often need direction on choosing the right number for themselves. I recommend monitoring each student's workload and providing feedback. I've learned that the students who need the most help academically are not always the ones who can handle the most goals and vice-versa. Try to help students choose an appropriate number for themselves.

Students who struggle in a lot of areas should be encouraged to create goals on foundational skills that are needed on a regular basis or will be needed in the near future. Discourage them from setting goals on skills that will only be used once in a while or that are less important. Limit their goals to a number that they can manage. Some of my struggling 4th and 5th graders focused on goals that built up their math fact fluency, focused on their learning process, or involved asking the teacher for help.

Students who excel in a lot of areas should create goals that help them self-differentiate. If you see that they are bored during certain subjects or come in with lots of background knowledge on a unit of study, think about how YOU would differentiate for them and teach them to do that themselves. Some of my advanced 4th and 5th graders focused on goals that improved their leadership skills in class, got them to seek alternative answers to problems, asked them to expand on their explanations, and focused on areas where they might have been ahead of others but weak relative to themselves.

Although monitoring each students' goal setting workload can be a daunting task, guiding your students to make the best choices for THEM will likely lead to better independent decisions in the long run!

Unit 6 - Goal Setting

INTRODUCTION

PLANNING

METACOGNITION

SYNTHESIS

REFLECTION

SELF-ASSESSMENT

GOAL SETTING

FEEDBACK

If you've made changes to any of the slides from Optimized Learning and think that other educators might enjoy having access to them, please submit them here and they will be uploaded to the Google Drive so everyone can access them!

The QR Code and short link on the right will take you to a Google Form that will allow you to submit a link to a template that you create for your modified slide(s). The directions for creating a template are on the form and are very easy to do, so please don't think that this is outside your comfort zone!

If you have any notes for teachers (grade level each slide has been created for, reasons for making the change, etc.), please include that in the provided sections.

Thanks so much for making this a valuable tool for other educators!

Have you made changes to any slides?

bit.ly/492T23Y

Students with well-developed GOAL SETTING MicroSkills...

Set specific and measurable goals

Break down larger goals into smaller, manageable tasks

Create a plan with clear timelines and deadlines

Monitor their progress and make necessary adjustments to stay on track

Adjust their plans and strategies as needed

Seek feedback & guidance from others to refine their goals

Stay motivated and committed to their goals

Reflect on their goal-setting process and learn from their experiences

Take responsibility for their own progress and hold themselves accountable

Celebrate their successes and use setbacks as learning opportunities

Prioritize their goals based on importance and relevance

Monitor their own motivation and adjust strategies to stay motivated

Celebrate milestones and achievements along the way

Stay committed to their goals even when faced with challenges

Set challenging but realistic goals that push their limits

Use self-reflection to evaluate their goal-setting process and identify areas for improvement

Set short-term, medium-term, and long-term goals, prioritizing them based on importance or timeliness

Students with poorly-developed GOAL SETTING MicroSkills...

Set vague or unrealistic goals

Become overwhelmed by large, complex goals leading to a lack of progress

Lack a structured plan or fail to set deadlines

Neglect to monitor their progress or fail to make adjustments

Stick rigidly to ineffective plans and strategies

Avoid seeking feedback & rely solely on their own judgment

Lack motivation and easily give up on their goals

Neglect to reflect on their goal-setting process and miss opportunities for improvement

Blame external factors for lack of progress and avoid taking responsibility

Get discouraged by setbacks and view them as failures

Set multiple goals without prioritizing and work on less important goals before more important ones

Struggle to maintain motivation and give up easily

Fail to acknowledge progress or celebrate achievements

Give up easily when faced with obstacles or setbacks

Set goals that are too easy or unrealistic

Neglect to reflect on their goal-setting process and miss opportunities for growth

Get stuck only setting goals for the short- or long-term instead of maintaining a variety of goals

INTRODUCTION

PLANNING

METACOGNITION

SYNTHESIS

REFLECTION

SELF-ASSESSMENT

GOAL SETTING

FEEDBACK

bit.ly/3RbB74b

Evaluate GOAL SETTING MicroSkills to take pride in relative strengths and to set personalized goals for areas of weakness

Essential Question

How strong am I at each of these GOAL SETTING Skills?

Lesson Overview

In this lesson, students evaluate their perceived ability for each of the identified GOAL SETTING skills. These skills have been chosen from the lessons that follow in this unit. Although students are choosing a somewhat arbitrary number from 1-10, the self-assessment process requires them to (1) understand what the skill means, (2) determine their perceived ability for the skill, and (3) sort each skill into areas of weakness or strength (or in-between) so that they help others improve at the skill (for scores 7-10) or make the skill into a goal that they try to achieve (for scores 1-4). If a student scores a 5 or 6, they are asked to reassess themselves after the unit to determine if they would benefit from making it a goal or not.

Teacher Tips

- On the Student Handouts, it tells students to "highlight all the numbers up through your score." The reason I didn't just have them circle the number is so they can see "how full" their grade band is if they choose a high number, and "how empty" their grade band is if they choose a low number. If you don't think it's too important for your students, feel free to let them just circle their number.
- When doing a self-assessment like this, I like to teach my students about the importance of being honest with themselves. I remind them that self-assessment in our classroom don't affect your grades or the way I see them. Self-assessments help us focus in on what matters to us, rather than focusing in on everything and not spending enough time on the skills that we need to improve most. No one is a 10 on all of these skills and no one is a 1 on all of them, but there's a good chance that each of us is a 10 and a 1 on at least one skill in this self-assessment!

Big Idea

By evaluating our current level of achievement on the MicroSkills that will be taught in this unit, we gain a clearer understanding of our individual strengths and weaknesses. Additionally, by synthesizing each MicroSkill, we develop a stronger understanding of the MacroSkill that this unit focuses on, which is GOAL SETTING.

Discussion/Reflection Questions

- Which goal setting skills did you feel you were strongest at? Provide some evidence to support your self-assessment.
- Which goal setting skills did you feel you were weakest at? Explain why you feel that this is true.
- If you could set a goal to improve ONE of these skills, which one would you choose? Why did you choose that one? How do you plan to improve this skill? What will you do?

Student Tasks 〉 Transfer Goals

Student Tasks	Transfer Goals
Students assess themselves on various goal setting skills using a scale from 1 to 10.	Students become more self-aware of their abilities and areas in which they need to grow.
Students are asked several goal setting questions that require them to explain their self-assessments and to set a goal for one skill.	Students understand that having weaknesses is normal and that they should be improved through goal-setting.

INTRODUCTION

PLANNING

METACOGNITION

SYNTHESIS

REFLECTION

SELF-ASSESSMENT

GOAL SETTING

FEEDBACK

Instructional Poster(s)

- This lesson has ONE Instructional Poster.
- A variation of this Instructional Poster is used with the first lesson of each unit. It shows students how to use the 1-10 scale for assessing their current level of ability with each skill. Numbers 1-4 mean that they know they need to improve at this skill (and maybe create a goal for the skill), and numbers 7-10 mean they believe that they are capable of helping others improve this skill. (4-5 means they will reassess at the end of the unit - which will be up to you or the student to remember to do. It's not a lesson.)
- Tell students that the real value in this activity is discovering their relative strengths and weaknesses, so giving yourself a 10 for each skill is wasting everyone's time, as is repeating any other number. Finding the variation in each skill is the key, so give yourself scores of 1, 2, and 3 and give scores of 8, 9, and 10 as well!

Student Handouts

- This lesson has FOUR Student Handouts.
- DIRECTIONS: Look at the Goal Setting MicroSkills in each box below and on the following page(s). Determine a rating from 1-10 for yourself on each, and then circle it. For your lowest MicroSkill(s), create a S.M.A.A.R.T.E.R. Goal to address each weakness.
- If you have not taught the lesson on Goal Bursts, let students know that they can just make the skill a personal goal to improve, but nothing needs to be written out (unless they want a reminder to actually do it). Obviously, the more seriously they take things, the more likely they'll improve!

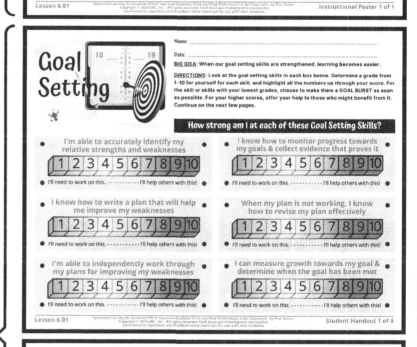

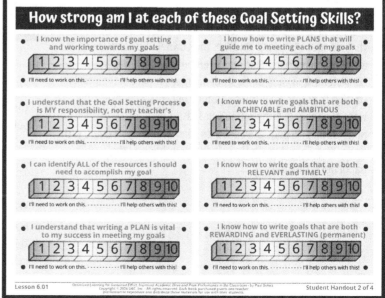

bit.ly/3uH8Af0

Learn to formulate achievable goals, break them down into actionable steps, and create a roadmap for success

6.02

Essential Question

What is Goal Setting?

Big Idea

Goal setting is the process of identifying relative weaknesses, writing a plan for improving those skills, working through the plan while monitoring progress, and revising the plan as needed. Some goals can be achieved quickly, while other goals may take months or years to complete, but the act of trying to improve is truly valuable.

Lesson Overview

In this lesson, students learn that "Goal Setting" is the process of identifying relative weaknesses, writing a plan for improving those skills, working through the plan while monitoring progress, and revising the plan as needed. Students or others can determine when a goal has been met, but any goal that is considered "complete" needs to be maintained by the student without reverting back to old habits.

Discussion/Reflection Questions

- Why is it important for us to spend time setting new goals and monitoring our progress on the others? What would happen if we didn't spend much time on it?
- What is one goal you would create today (not anything from the activity)? Why would you create this goal?
- How would you try to accomplish this goal? What would be a few steps in your plan? (We'll learn more about making a strong plan in a future lesson.)

Teacher Tips

- In our classroom, each student used a binder to keep all of their goal sheets in. You may want to consider how your students will manage their goal sheets.
- I gave my students 15-30 minutes every week to work on goal setting and progress monitoring. You might want to decide what your level of commitment will be when it comes to classtime dedicated to this. All I can say is that it was worth every second that we spent, because students took ownership of their deficits and worked hard to make improvements. Since it was a consistent time each week, students made it part of their daily routine to create goals on skills and concepts whenever they were challenged. Although this process is very rote & explicit, it mimics what responsible adults do whenever they struggle with something important to them (usually without all the paperwork, though!).

Student Tasks 〉 Transfer Goals

Student Tasks	Transfer Goals
Students learn about the steps in the Goal Setting Process.	Students own the goal setting process since all of the steps are completed by them and not their teacher.
Students complete a Basic Goal Setting organizer to think through the key steps in the goal setting process.	Students use this experience to more comfortably expand their knowledge during future lessons.

Instructional Poster(s)

- This lesson has THREE Instructional Posters.
- The first Instructional Poster for this lesson defines Goal Setting as "the process of identifying relative weaknesses, writing a plan for improving those skills, working through the plan while monitoring progress, and revising the plan as needed."
- It also explains the basic format of goal setting in our classroom:
  1. Identify relative weaknesses.
  2. Write a plan for improving those weaknesses.
  3. Work through the plan.
  4. Monitor your progress.
  5. Revise your plan, as needed.
  6. Do it all over again with a different skill.
- The second Instructional Poster is a blank generic Goal Setting form. It asks four questions and gives students sentence starters: (Discuss this with your students using a pretend goal of yours.)
  - What is something you'd like to improve? Write this as a goal statement.
  - Why is this important?
  - How will you try to reach this goal?
  - How will you know when you accomplished this goal?
- The third Instructional Posters is an exemplar for the second Student Handout.

Student Handouts

- This lesson has TWO Student Handouts.
- DIRECTIONS: Let's practice with a pretend goal. Imagine you want to get better at measuring the number of degrees in an angle using a protractor. Complete the Goal Setting steps below using this information and what has been given to you within the form.
- The first Student Handout provides students with an exemplar to model their answer on the next page after.
- DIRECTIONS: Now, choose a fairly simple goal that you can pretend to work toward. The purpose of this is to get practice brainstorming relative weaknesses, write a basic plan, pretend to monitor your progress, and decide to revise the goal or not.
- Have the students choose a goal (or choose one for them all to do). Have students work through the steps, writing each answer with as much detail as possible.

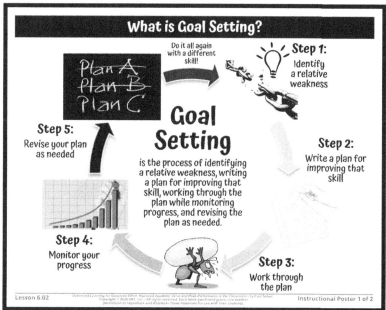

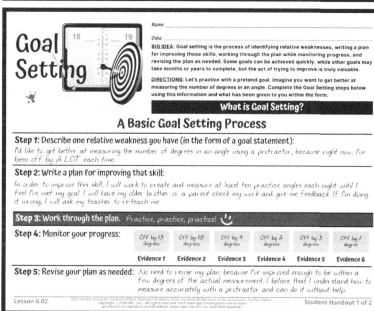

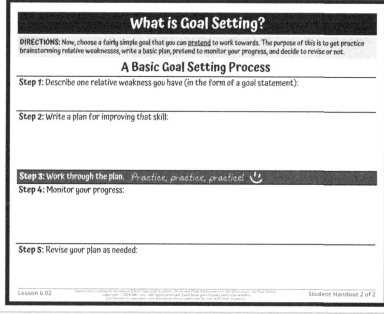

bit.ly/485jWb7

Discover how goal setting can ignite your inner flame, fuel your motivation, and help you achieve personal satisfaction

Essential Question

Why should we take time to set goals?

Lesson Overview

In this lesson, students discover and brainstorm the benefits of goal setting. They also learn why they are in charge of this process instead of their teacher. Students use this information to defend their teacher's use of class time for goal setting in a friendly letter.

Big Idea

There are many reasons why goal setting is worth the time and energy it takes. Some of these reasons are intrinsic and some extrinsic. Some are meant to avoid punishment or consequences, while others may be to earn rewards or praise. Regardless of the reason for working toward a goal, learning the goal setting process is a valuable life skill that can and should be used all throughout one's life.

Discussion/Reflection Questions

- Why is goal setting a worthwhile use of our time?
- What are two reasons why students are in charge of this process instead of the teacher?
- How might you try to convince your future teachers to provide time in class for student-led goal setting? What might you say to them, respectfully?

Teacher Tips

- If you haven't recently taught and practiced "friendly letter writing" or "business letter writing," I recommend that you don't assess students too harshly based on their writing skills. Instead, focus on the content of the letter and whether they convey the proper message or not. Feel free to use it as a pre-test of sorts if you'd like to use this assignment as a source of feedback to jump start a lesson or unit on letter writing, though!
- Some of the reasons why goal setting is NOT successful in some classrooms is because students don't do it consistently (once per week, or so), teachers don't have enough structure or appropriate expectations for the format of goals, or students aren't given assignments where they can identify areas of strength and weakness and then actually do something about improving their weaknesses. In order to have success, try hard not to fall into any of those categories.

Student Tasks 〉 Transfer Goals

Student Tasks	Transfer Goals
Students learn the benefits of goal setting.	Students know how valuable setting goals can be, so they put in a strong effort to get the most out of the process.
Students learn the reasons why they are in charge of the goal setting process instead of their teacher.	Students no longer rely on adults to tell them what they need to do to improve and take on that responsibility themselves.

INTRODUCTION

PLANNING

METACOGNITION

SYNTHESIS

REFLECTION

SELF-ASSESSMENT

GOAL SETTING

FEEDBACK

Instructional Poster(s)

- This lesson has ONE Instructional Poster.
- The Instructional Poster for this lesson lists 14 benefits of goal setting. You may need to explain each with some supporting information or examples from your classroom to help students understand each.
- How many additional benefits of goal setting can you and your students brainstorm?

Student Handouts

- This lesson has TWO Student Handouts.
- DIRECTIONS: Read through the notes on the next page and the Instructional Poster. With those in mind, defend your teacher's decision to use some class time on goal setting to an upset parent. Let them know why you believe goal setting is worth the class time and what you hope to gain from learning this skill.
- The first Student Handout asks students to write a letter to their teacher defending her use of class time for student-led goal setting. For students to be successful with this, they will need to identify several reasons why goal setting is a valuable use of time and state it cogently in a letter to their teacher.
- The second Student Handout gives four reasons why students are in charge of goal setting, rather than the teacher. Students will use these four reasons to help them write their letter to their teacher on the first Student Handout.
- Can you or your students add any additional reasons why students are in charge of goal setting, rather than the teacher?

Why should we take time to Set Goals?

Benefits of Goal Setting:

Goals that are properly planned help you reduce procrastination and meet deadlines

Goals help you focus on what's most important to you

Lofty Goals give you perspective and help you plan for the long-term

Goals help you use your time, energy and resources efficiently

Goals that are broken down into chunks help make complex tasks more manageable

Goals reduce stress when your focus is on following the plan that you set, rather than thoughts and ideas that pop up

Goals make you feel good, especially when you focus on improvement, rather than perfection

Goals that you believe in and want to attain help you stay motivated, even after setbacks

Goals help you get started - it is often hard to begin self-improvement without structure of some sort

Goals push you forward, rather than being comfortable in the present

Goals help you achieve results faster and stronger

Goals with mini deadlines keep you accountable to yourself and your timeline

Goals help you see the value of hard work and drive

Goals make dreams more realistic and attainable

What other benefits of Goal Setting can you think of?

Lesson 6.03 — Optimized Learning for Sustained Effort, Improved Academic Drive and Peak Performance in the Classroom - by Paul Solarz. Copyright © 2024 GBC, Inc. - All rights reserved. Each book purchased grants one teacher permission to reproduce and distribute these materials for use with their students. — Instructional Poster 1 of 1

Goal Setting

Dear Mrs. Cinderblock:

Name: _____

Date: _____

BIG IDEA: There are many reasons why goal setting is worth the time and energy it takes. Some of these reasons are intrinsic and some extrinsic. Some are meant to avoid punishment or consequences, while others may be to earn rewards or praise. Regardless of the reason for working towards a goal, learning the goal setting process is a valuable life skill that can and should be used all throughout one's life.

DIRECTIONS: Read through the notes on the next page and the Instructional Poster. With those in mind, defend your teacher's decision to use some class time on goal setting to an upset parent. Let them know why you believe goal setting is worth the class time and what you hope to gain from learning this skill.

Why should we take time to Set Goals?

_____

_____

_____

_____

_____

_____

_____

_____

Sincerely,

Lesson 6.03 — Optimized Learning for Sustained Effort, Improved Academic Drive and Peak Performance in the Classroom - by Paul Solarz. Copyright © 2024 GBC, Inc. - All rights reserved. Each book purchased grants one teacher permission to reproduce and distribute these materials for use with their students. — Student Handout 1 of 2

Why should we take time to Set Goals?

Reasons why YOU, the student, are in charge of this

To ensure that school is meaningful & valuable to YOU!

What do you think you'd be most proud of:
(1) Finally being able to do something that you never could do before, OR
(2) Taking notes during a lecture and answering questions on a worksheet? Goals help you focus on what's important to YOU!

Because YOU know what you need to work on better than anyone!

Your teacher is happy to make decisions for everyone in class on **what** they should learn, **when** they should learn it, and **how** they should go about learning it, but you're going to end up being bored or confused more often than you should if that's ALWAYS the case!

You're much more likely to invest your time & energy if you're in charge!

Everyone has to attend class and do their work, but if it's not interesting to you it can be hard to be motivated to do it well. But when you're working on goals that you know are important, you're more likely to invest time & energy into doing it well!

Who's going to be in charge of this in the future, if not you?

If your teacher or parents are always telling you what's most important and what you should be spending your time focusing on, you'll never learn how to do it yourself! The main purpose of education is learning to do things independently. Let's start now!

Lesson 6.03 — Optimized Learning for Sustained Effort, Improved Academic Drive and Peak Performance in the Classroom - by Paul Solarz. Copyright © 2024 GBC, Inc. - All rights reserved. Each book purchased grants one teacher permission to reproduce and distribute these materials for use with their students. — Student Handout 2 of 2

bit.ly/3GuazWX

Learn to craft goals that are specific, measurable, achievable, ambitious, relevant, timely, everlasting, and rewarding

Essential Question

How do I write a S.M.A.A.R.T.E.R. Goal?

Big Idea

Writing a S.M.A.A.R.T.E.R. Goal is one way to set a worthwhile goal, work toward it, achieve it, and maintain it. It is an acronym that stands for Specific, Measurable, Achievable, Ambitious, Relevant, Timely, Everlasting, and Rewarding. Follow the S.M.A.A.R.T.E.R. Goal process whenever you want to achieve a goal that can't be achieved immediately or with a simple change.

Lesson Overview

In this lesson, students learn about the *Optimized Learning* variation on S.M.A.R.T. Goals®[1] called S.M.A.A.R.T.E.R. Goals (with two A's). In addition, they learn about the importance of Progress Monitoring, which is a core component of this program. They learn what the S.M.A.A.R.T.E.R. acronym stands for and how to use the acronym to write goals that are specific, measurable, achievable, ambitious, relevant, timely, everlasting and rewarding. In addition, students consider what materials they may need in order to accomplish this goal, how to acquire these materials, and consider what steps might be in their plan to accomplish this goal. Future lessons will develop each of these skills further.

Discussion/Reflection Questions

- Why do you think there are so many steps in the S.M.A.A.R.T.E.R. Goal Setting Process? (Hint: It's not because we like to make life more challenging for you!) :)
- What is one goal that you would like to work on that you haven't already thought about? Why do you want or need to work on it?
- How will you use the S.M.A.A.R.T.E.R. Goal Setting Process to achieve that goal? What will you do on your own?

Teacher Tips

- This is a CORE Lesson and is taught within all lesson clusters. There are no pre-requisite or post-requisite lessons, but the next lesson on "Goal Bursts" is an excellent way to help students set more basic goals in a simpler, quicker manner, so it is highly recommended to be used in addition to this lesson (which has a much higher level of success for achieving goals due to the steps involved).
- The exemplar for this lesson is written using a skill that can span nearly all age levels (focusing & attending while reading), but it has been answered at a high, "exemplar level." I believe that exemplars should show students what they can strive for. If this is too complex for your age group, just be sure to explain what it means as you share it. and let your students know that they can have more age-appropriate answers on their goal sheets!
- In practice, it's often easier to have students complete Step 11 before Step 10. Sorry about that! :)

1. S.M.A.R.T. Goals® is a registered trademark of Leadership Management® International, Inc.

Student Tasks ⟩ Transfer Goals

Student Tasks	Transfer Goals
Students learn what the S.M.A.A.R.T.E.R. Goal Setting Process is and what the acronym stands for.	Students understand why each step is beneficial and see the value of the goal setting process.
Students create their first S.M.A.A.R.T.E.R. Goal and track their progress toward that goal.	Students can use the S.M.A.A.R.T.E.R. Goal Setting Process independently without support.

Instructional Poster(s)

- This lesson has ONE Instructional Poster.
- The Instructional Poster for this lesson transitions students from a basic way of setting goals and monitoring their progress to the S.M.A.A.R.T.E.R. Goal Setting Process, which is the core goal setting process used in this program. The S.M.A.A.R.T.E.R. acronym is explained and a few additional steps are included at the bottom. You may need to elaborate on a few terms so that your students understand what they mean (e.g. ambitious, relevant, etc.).

Student Handouts

- This lesson has FIVE Student Handouts.
- DIRECTIONS: Complete the organizer based on the directions provided in each section.
- The S.M.A.A.R.T.E.R. Goal Setting Process is started by completing steps 1-11 on the two Student Handouts from this lesson. Step 12 is to be completed over time as students collect evidence of growth toward their goal. An exemplar has been provided to help you explain to the students how they will need to complete this form independently.
- Ideally, it would be great if you can have these forms copied and available for students to complete whenever they have a goal they wish to develop. In our classroom, students kept these forms in a binder and we worked on them at the end of the day each Friday for 30 minutes. But I've also had students work on these during RtI Time (a.k.a. Tier 2 Time) while I worked with students in small groups. In order to provide time for each student to work on their goals in class, I created schedules for each student that told them when they should work on "Goal Setting & Progress Monitoring" in addition to other tasks.

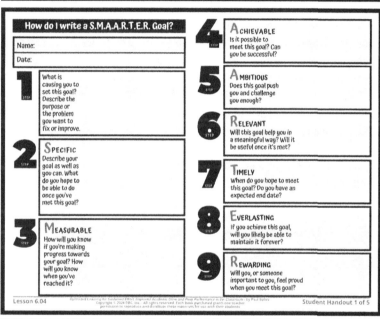

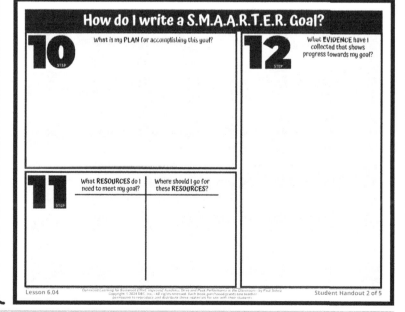

6.05

Utilize "Goal Bursts" to attain rapid improvement by targeting smaller skill deficits with laser-sharp concentration

bit.ly/3T9ebFh

QR Code links to: bit.ly/3T9ebFh

Essential Question

How do I write a Goal Burst?

Big Idea

Not everything we struggle with needs to become a S.M.A.A.R.T.E.R. Goal. Some issues that require a quick fix can become GOAL BURSTS instead! Goal Bursts are skill deficits that you try to address immediately while working on other things in class. Hopefully, you won't need to spend much more time on it than a period or two.

Lesson Overview

In this lesson, students about Goal Bursts, which are like mini-goals that don't require the same amount of preparation and internalizing that a S.M.A.A.R.T.E.R. Goal requires., but only works on goals that students can achieve quickly (like in a couple class periods, or within a few days). The Goal Burst Process works by identifying something that you know you can achieve if you put your mind to it and focus on it for a short period of time. When the student wants to work on this Goal Burst, they integrate it into another activity in class, or schedule an immediate time to focus on achieving the goal. If done properly, the goal should be accomplished as quickly as it was set and the student should be able to move on to bigger and better things.

Discussion/Reflection Questions

- Why do we need to have both S.M.A.A.R.T.E.R. Goals AND Goal Bursts? Can't we have just one?
- What are some differences between S.M.A.A.R.T.E.R. Goals and Goal Bursts?
- How will you make Goal Bursts a habit of yours? How will you make sure that you address your needs quickly and independently?

Teacher Tips

- If you can, provide your students with some examples of when a Goal Burst might be a better choice than writing a S.M.A.A.R.T.E.R. Goal so they can envision when it will be most useful to them. Some examples have been provided on the next page. If you can think of any times where you have done something similar or wish you had used this method in your life, share it with the class. I've used it when meeting new people and trying to remember their names (using the strategy of repeating their names in my head), when writing portions of this book (I need to complete three lessons before doing something else), when cooking (I will have all of my ingredients ready before starting to cook to make sure I have everything), etc.
- Although this is encouraging multi-tasking (which is generally discouraged because it usually diminishes the quality of both tasks), it is a valuable way to address a goal embedded in an experience, rather than done in isolation.

Student Tasks 〉 Transfer Goals

Student Tasks	Transfer Goals
Students learn what Goal Bursts are, when to use them, and they even write one to work on.	Students internalize the process and use it in their daily lives (without needing to fill out the form).
Students learn five different types of Goal Bursts and brainstorm possible ideas that could fit within each category.	Students see that Goal Bursts have many uses and are really just ways to address important, short-term needs.

INTRODUCTION

PLANNING

METACOGNITION

SYNTHESIS

REFLECTION

SELF-ASSESSMENT

GOAL SETTING

FEEDBACK

Instructional Poster(s)

- This lesson has TWO Instructional Posters.
- The Instructional Poster for this lesson explains to students how to complete a Goal Burst, which is a short-term, intensely-focused goal that students need to achieve quickly.
- Goal Bursts can be minor or major, but it's something that a student will want to achieve ASAP. For example, a student might want to work on speaking loudly while working with peers, which can be accomplished by following a Goal Burst.
- Goal Bursts are often integrated into another activity by the students, so they can be mindful of this goal WHILE they are doing their math work, for example. They can remind themselves and those around them that they want to speak loudly so their peers can hear them.

Student Handouts

- This lesson has FOUR Student Handouts.
- DIRECTIONS: Read the notes below. Then, brainstorm some potential GOAL BURST subjects. Finally, write a real or pretend GOAL BURST on the next page (they're short!).
- The first Student Handout is informational and asks the students to brainstorm potential ideas for Goal Bursts. A few ideas from our classroom Include: writing your name on your paper before turning it in, adding on to others' conversations, politely disagreeing with others while adding support for your reasons, being mindful of capitalization, punctuation & spelling, remembering units on math answers, checking off directions as they are completed, etc.
- The second Student Handout is the Goal Burst form that students will always use when writing out a Goal Burst. It's simple to fill out, but needs to be done before & after working.

How do I write a Goal Burst?

Not everything that you struggle with needs to become a S.M.A.A.R.T.E.R. Goal. Some minor issues can become GOAL BURSTS instead! Goal Bursts are skill deficits that you try to address immediately while working on something else in class. The hope is that you won't need to spend much more time on it than a period or two.

These are the only steps in a Goal Burst:

BEFORE THE ACTIVITY:
- What GOAL BURST are you working on today?
- Why is this goal important enough to focus on today?

AFTER THE ACTIVITY:
- Describe how well you did on today's GOAL BURST. Explain it well. Describe any evidence of growth.

For example, if I'm having some trouble remembering that the dollar sign goes IN FRONT of the number and the cents sign goes BEHIND the number, I don't need to write a S.M.A.A.R.T.E.R. Goal for it because there likely won't be tons of opportunities to work on it after the few math lessons that focus on money problems. So I will make it a GOAL BURST and spend a lot of time and attention on making sure I do the dollar sign and cents sign correctly this week while we work on these problems.

Goal Setting

Name: _____
Date: _____

BIG IDEA: Not everything we struggle with needs to become a S.M.A.A.R.T.E.R. Goal. Some issues that require a quick fix can become GOAL BURSTS instead! Goal Bursts are skill deficits that you try to address immediately while working on other things in class. Hopefully, you won't need to spend much more time on it than a period or two.

DIRECTIONS: What examples can you think of that would have made high quality GOAL BURSTS recently? Brainstorm one for each type below. Then, create your first real GOAL BURST on the next page (they're quick!).

How do I write a Goal Burst?

Rehearsal	Need it NOW	Unlearn-Relearn	Intense Focus	Perfect Timing
You know WHAT you need to do and HOW you need to do it, but you haven't practiced it yet, so it hasn't become a habit yet. Rehearsal Goal Bursts let you practice (and refine) a skill until it becomes a habit.	You kept telling yourself that you will learn it eventually, and it just so happens that TODAY is "eventually"! Your teacher has given your class time to study in class for tomorrow's test. This is your chance to figure it all out!	You have always done something wrong and it is now a bad habit. You know what to do differently, but you need to break the old habit first and then create a new habit by practicing it correctly.	You've procrastinated or not given it much of your attention or effort, but now you want to really focus on it and get it done.	You've been wanting to work on a certain skill, but there weren't any situations that allowed it before today. This is your opportunity!
Create a Goal Burst that will allow you to rehearse over and over until it becomes natural to you:	Create a Goal Burst that will force you to focus on what matters, and to do it all by the end of the period:	Create a Goal Burst that will allow you to unlearn the incorrect way of doing things, and then relearn the correct way:	Set a Goal Burst that will allow you to intensely focus on your task. Consider using timers, rewards, consequences, or delayed gratification as tools to help you:	Create a Goal Burst that will allow you to practice this skill WHILE you work on what your teacher needs you to work on. Since this chance is a rare moment, use your time wisely & accomplish your goal:

How do I write a Goal Burst?

Goal Bursts

Here's how a GOAL BURST is created:
1. What is something that you want or need to improve? Maybe you've already written a SMAARTER Goal for it, maybe it's something new, or maybe it's something that can be corrected quickly without needing to write a SMAARTER Goal. Choose one now.
2. Ask your partner for this activity or your Success Partner to help you meet this goal or work towards this goal during this work period.
3. Do the same for your partner if they are working on a Goal Burst.
4. At the beginning of this activity AND at the end of this activity, complete this organizer.

BEFORE THE ACTIVITY:
- What GOAL BURST are you working on today?

- Why is this goal important enough to focus on today?

AFTER THE ACTIVITY:
- Describe how well you did on today's GOAL BURST. Explain it well. Describe any evidence of growth.

bit.ly/484CckX

Transform vague dreams into meaningful goals using the power of specificity by providing simple & focused details

Essential Question

How do I write my goal so it is SPECIFIC?

Lesson Overview

In this lesson, students learn how to improve their S.M.A.A.R.T.E.R. Goals to make them more SPECIFIC. Students learn a three step process where they start with the basic goal that they would have created naturally. Next, they add WHY they want to accomplish this goal (what purpose it serves). Finally, students "Tell Me More" by adding some more detail, WITHOUT increasing the complexity of the goal by adding additional components to fix or address. It is important to teach students that our goals need to focus on ONE improvement, rather than many (although their can be MANY results that come from improving this one area).

Big Idea

Any goal is better than no goal, but the BEST goals are SPECIFIC. By adding specific details to your goal, both you and others gain a clearer understanding of exactly what you hope to improve. Goals that aren't very specific make it harder to write your plan and monitor your progress because it's not clear what specifically you hope to do, and they make it hard on others who want to know how they can help you.

Discussion/Reflection Questions

- Why is it important to write S.M.A.A.R.T.E.R. Goals that are SPECIFIC, rather than GENERAL?
- What are the three steps you should follow to make your goals more specific?
- Why is it important to focus on only ONE area of improvement within each goal, rather than several areas? (Even though you can have MANY results that come from the improvement in that ONE area.)

Teacher Tips

- PREREQUISITE: Lesson 6.04
- It could be beneficial to have a list of poorly written goals to practice improving with your students. At the moment, the focus is on specificity, but future lessons will focus on other qualities of well-written goals. If you don't have any poorly written goals, consider taking your students' current goals and reversing the process to make them more general so your students can practice improving them!
- Exemplars have been provided for this lesson - you may want to share them with the class as a way to review the lesson and show how they can improve their goal statements with specific examples.

Student Tasks ⟩ Transfer Goals

Student Tasks	Transfer Goals
Students learn a three-step process for writing goals that are SPECIFIC, rather than GENERAL.	Students know exactly what they want to accomplish with their goals before they begin working on them.
Students transform several GENERAL goals into SPECIFIC goals using the three-step process.	Students understand the value of SPECIFIC goals and aim to create goals this way throughout life.

INTRODUCTION

PLANNING

METACOGNITION

SYNTHESIS

REFLECTION

SELF-ASSESSMENT

Instructional Poster(s)

- This lesson has ONE Instructional Poster.
- The Instructional Poster for this lesson teaches students how to write goals that are SPECIFIC, rather than general. It uses a three step process where you start with the basic goal that students would have created naturally. Next, they add WHY they want to accomplish this goal (what purpose it serves). Finally, students "Tell Me More" by adding some more detail, WITHOUT increasing the complexity of the goal by adding additional components to fix or address.
- Students will follow this model on the Student Handouts, and are encouraged to write their goals using this process. It will be up to you whether they continue doing so or not.

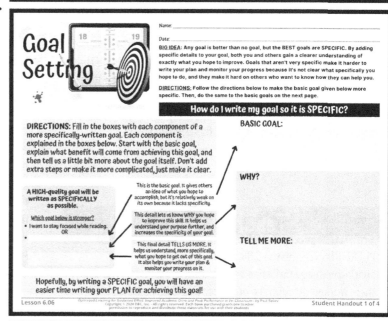

Student Handouts

- This lesson has FOUR Student Handouts.
- DIRECTIONS: Follow the directions below to learn WHY we want specific goals. Then, turn some BASIC goals into SPECIFIC goals on the next page.
- The first Student Handout just has the students copy the answer over from the left-hand box to the three boxes on the right. It's just a small scaffold to help them be successful on the second Student Handout.
- The second Student Handout asks students to write SPECIFIC goals for four different GENERAL goals that have been provided, using the process learned in today's lesson.
- A word or two is underlined in each GENERAL goal to show students that the way they word their goal can vary - they do not always have to start a specific way. This is to help them transfer this process to their daily life. Don't focus on the minutia - focus on the big picture of specific goals.

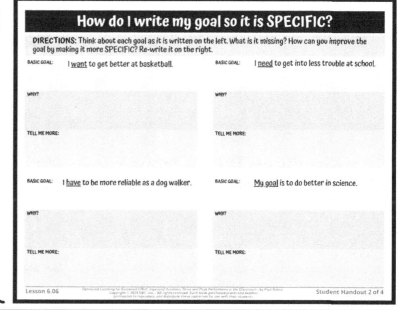

285

bit.ly/3TfZeRI

Identify your starting point and your desired destination, and measure your progress every step of the way

6.07

Essential Question

How do I MEASURE growth toward my goal?

Big Idea

In order to measure growth, we need to know where we are starting (our baseline) and where we want to get to (our learning target). When you're writing a goal, you should decide how you will determine if you're making growth.

Lesson Overview

In this lesson, students consider how they will measure growth toward their Learning Target for each goal that they've written. The main skill taught in this lesson is determining a unit of measure (and then deciding how much of that unit needs to improve in order to consider the goal achieved). But in order for students to do that, they need to know their baseline (current level of achievement) using the unit of measure they've chosen, and the plan they will use to reach their Learning Target. After all of that, it's simply a matter of progress monitoring until the goal has been achieved.

Discussion/Reflection Questions

- Why does the organizer say that the levels continue up and down the staircase? Isn't the baseline the bottom and the Learning Target the top?
- Why are you asked to identify your baseline and Learning Target as part of measuring growth toward your goal? What is the benefit?
- How will you measure growth for a goal that doesn't have a measurable unit? For example, "I want to become a more positive person, because people tell me I'm always so negative. I hope that by being more positive, I can be happier and become a better friend."

Teacher Tips

- PREREQUISITES: Lesson 5.04, Lesson 6.04, Lesson 6.06
- Sharing some quantitative and qualitative goals that you show them worked through the organizer would be beneficial for students to see. I recommend some that are specific to your class, but some of your own personal goals are also great to see so students transfer the skill outside of the classroom.

Student Tasks ⟩ Transfer Goals

Student Tasks	Transfer Goals
Students learn to identify the unit they will measure to determine growth toward a goal.	Students determine growth using objective methods, whenever possible.
Students use baseline data and a Learning Target to measure growth between each in order to determine when a goal has been achieved.	Students see learning as a point that moves between their starting point (baseline) and their desired ending point (Learning Target).

Instructional Poster(s)

- This lesson has ONE Instructional Poster.
- The Instructional Poster for this lesson focuses on the process of measuring GROWTH toward their goal. In order to get at the heart of measuring growth, students learn that they need to (1) identify their baseline (with data or self-assessment), (2) consider the plan they will follow to achieve this goal, (3) determine the unit of measure that will show growth (although not all goals have a unit and that's completely okay), and (4) determine a learning target that will signify success in achieving this goal. An exemplar has been provided to teach this process. It uses a measurable unit, but remember that not all goals need to have those.

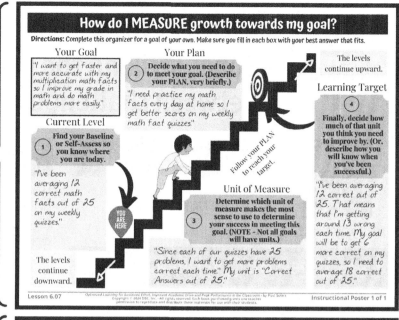

Student Handouts

- This lesson has TWO Student Handouts.
- DIRECTIONS: Read the important note in the box on the bottom-left of this page. Then, read each goal and determine your current level and the level you hope to get to in order to consider this goal met. Using the examples given, write appropriate answers for the six blanks below.
- The first Student Handout introduces the idea of qualitative goals that don't have a unit of measure (but it is not explained in detail yet). Students need to describe their current baseline (using data or self-assessment) and a Learning Target that needs to be reached in order to consider the goal achieved for four different goals.
- DIRECTIONS: Complete this organizer for a goal of your own. Make sure you fill in each box with your best answer that fits.
- The second Student Handout asks students to complete the organizer for a goal of their own. It is not something students should do forever, but is a good scaffold for now.

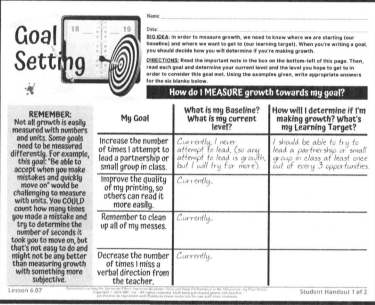

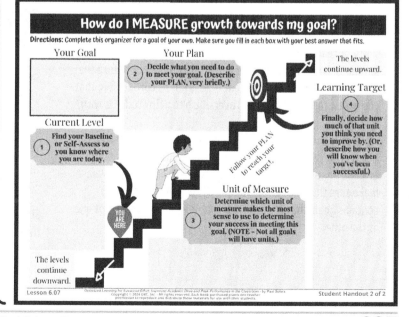

bit.ly/3Nim3At

Discover the goal setting "Goldilocks Zone" striking the perfect balance between challenge and confidence

Essential Question

Is this goal ACHIEVABLE?
Is it AMBITIOUS enough?

Big Idea

Creating goals that challenge us, but are possible can be a challenging task. It doesn't do us any good to write goals that are too easy to accomplish, because it's a waste of our time. It can be deflating to set goals that are impossible or improbable, and can make us frustrated with the process. Therefore, we need to be able to find the "Just Right" area between too easy and too hard. We can call it the "Goldilocks Zone."

Lesson Overview

In this lesson, students learn how to write goal statements that are not too easy and not too hard. We call this range the "Goldilocks Zone." We want goals that challenge us (ambitious goals), but when students write goals that are too challenging, it sets them up for failure and unnecessary struggle that they can't overcome. We want goals that are attainable, but when students write goals that are too easy, they achieve the goal quickly, without much effort, and rarely does their success translate into long-term improvement.

Discussion/Reflection Questions

- Why is a goal that is both achievable AND ambitious considered to be in the "Goldilocks Zone"?
- What might happen if you create a goal that is too EASY? How might it impact the goal setting process for you?
- What might happen if you create a goal that is too HARD? How might it impact the goal setting process for you?

Teacher Tips

- PREREQUISITES: Lesson 5.04, Lesson 6.04, Lesson 6.06, Lesson 6.07
- Students will need some baseline data OR they need to self-assess their current level of ability for the skills they're writing goals for. They might not understand how to do that yet, so you can either help them, pre-teach the concept of collecting baseline data, teach them how to self-assess these particular skills, or teach Lesson 6.07 first.
- Remind students to do the second Student Handout before the first one today. The first Student Handout is a reproducible that you may want to use over and over again to help students with this skill.
- Some students may think that they need to choose between being achievable and being ambitious because of the way the graphic organizer is set up on the first Student Handout. Please make sure that they understand that the Goldilocks Zone contains goals that are both achievable AND ambitious. Not one or the other.

Student Tasks 〉 Transfer Goals

Students learn that goals that are too EASY are not ambitious enough for our goal setting process.

Students write goals that challenge them, so they see value in setting goals and monitoring their progress toward them.

Students learn that goals that are too HARD are not achievable enough for our goal setting process.

Students write goals that they can actually attain, so they see how goal setting and progress monitoring can lead to success.

Instructional Poster(s)

- This lesson has ONE Instructional Poster.
- The Instructional Poster for this lesson shows students that their goals need to be BOTH achievable and ambitious, but not TOO achievable or TOO ambitious! Therefore, we have the "Goldilocks Zone" where the challenge level is "just right!"
- In my students' experience, finding the Goldilocks Zone is a really important step in creating a goal that is worth working on. Many students have grown frustrated over goals they created for themselves that were too hard, and similarly, many students wondered why they bothered to go through the S.M.A.A.R.T.E.R. Goal Process for easily attainable goals. Ensure that students take this step seriously, and help them fine tune their goal statements.

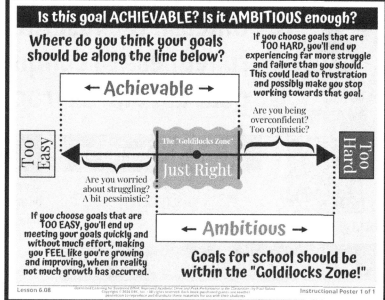

Student Handouts

- This lesson has TWO Student Handouts.
- DIRECTIONS: Re-write each goal from the left and right columns as one that is "Just Right" - not too easy and not too hard. Then, fill in all the blanks on the next page.
- The first Student Handout is the standard reproducible that students should use when fine tuning their goal to make it appropriately achievable and ambitious. Since this is their first time using it, they are asked to do the second Student Handout first to practice the skill with goals that have been provided.
- The second Student Handout has empty boxes that students need to fill in to show they understand when a goal is too easy, too hard, or just right. Ask your students to avoid the absurd and provide goals that are reasonable for the too easy and too hard sections. (Depending on their maturity, they may go straight to the absurd.)

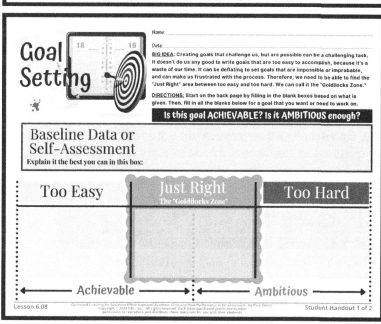

INTRODUCTION

PLANNING

METACOGNITION

SYNTHESIS

REFLECTION

SELF-ASSESSMENT

GOAL SETTING

FEEDBACK

bit.ly/3Rvms55

Unleash the laser focus of relevance and timeliness to conquer your overflowing goal list and skyrocket your success

Essential Question

Is this goal RELEVANT?
Is it TIMELY?

Big Idea

Since we're limited in the number of goals that we can actually work on at one time, it's important that we prioritize them. Relevance and Timeliness are two characteristics of a goal that can help us prioritize our goals effectively. When a goal is relevant, it matches our current needs and/or what we happen to be learning about. When it's timely, we're choosing to work on this goal at the most appropriate time.

Lesson Overview

In this lesson, students learn how to prioritize their goals based on relevance and timeliness. In a perfect world, we could work on ALL of the goals we set for ourselves at once, but the reality is that we only have enough time to dedicate to a few goals at a time. But how do we determine which goals to prioritize? We want to work on goals that will impact our lives in the most meaningful ways, so working on goals that are relevant and timely helps us accomplish that goal. If we work on a goal that isn't achieved until it is too late, we've wasted our time. If we work on a goal that turns out not to have much impact, then we've also wasted our time. Relevance and Timeliness help us avoid wasted time.

Discussion/Reflection Questions

- Why do we want to work on goals that are relevant and timely before working on other goals?
- What will you do when you have more goals than you can handle that are all relevant and timely?
- What is the most relevant and timely goal that you have right now? How is it relevant? How is it timely? How will you achieve this goal in time?

Teacher Tips

- PREREQUISITES: Lesson 5.04, Lesson 6.04, Lesson 6.06, Lesson 6.07, Lesson 6.08
- Students will benefit from having a small collection of goals that they can prioritize during this lesson. It is not required, but would make this lesson slightly more meaningful to them.
- Potential Answers to the first Student Handout:
  - Learn to divide fractions first, because the test is coming up in a week.
  - Learn how to write stories faster to get more done each Writing class period, because improving your academic work is arguably more important than the other goals.
  - Learn to distinguish between your right and left. You definitely need this, but it can come after the more timely goals.
  - Learn how to drive a bus last, because you are not likely to need this skill for awhile!

Student Tasks 〉 Transfer Goals

Students learn that relevance is an important factor when choosing which goals to prioritize.	Students write goals that are relevant to them, so when they actually achieve their goals, they reap the benefits.
Students learn that timeliness is an important factor when choosing which goals to prioritize.	Students write goals that are timely, so when they actually achieve their goals, they are done in time to reap the benefits.

Instructional Poster(s)

- This lesson has ONE Instructional Poster.
- The Instructional Poster for this lesson teaches students two important components of the S.M.A.A.R.T.E.R. Goal Setting Process: Relevance and Timeliness. Students are encouraged to prioritize goals that are relevant & timely over goals that lack relevance or timeliness.
- The calendar image reminds students that it's important to pay attention to deadlines when setting goals. How much time you have to achieve a goal before it becomes less useful is an important consideration. For example, if you have a month to write a paper and a week to prepare for a test, it's a good idea to work on the test first.

Student Handouts

- This lesson has TWO Student Handouts.
- DIRECTIONS: Read each goal below. Then answer each question with a Yes or a No. On the next page, answer each question using a real or pretend goal of your own.
- The first Student Handout gives students four fictional goals to evaluate based on their relevance and timeliness. Students will need to determine the importance of each goal and then prioritize them in order of importance. While there may be slight differences in students' answers, they should be based on similar logic. Refer to the Teacher Tips section on the previous page for potential answers. This activity is designed to help students practice evaluating and prioritizing goals in a structured and strategic way. Possible Answers: 4, 3, 2, 1
- DIRECTIONS: Choose a goal of your own to focus on. Answer each Yes/No question and explain your answers. If you answer "No" to any question, decide if it's okay to continue with this goal or if you need to revise your goal, switch goals, or do something else. YOU need to make this decision, because YOU are in charge of the goal setting process! These questions are designed to help you make these decisions!
- The second Student Handout is a reproducible worksheet that you can use repeatedly with your students to help them prioritize their goals. The worksheet guides students through a series of questions that prompt them to consider the relevance and timeliness of one of their current goals.

Is this goal RELEVANT? Is it TIMELY?

Since we are limited in the number of goals that we can actually work on at one time, it's important to prioritize them. Relevance & Timeliness are two characteristics that can help us prioritize our goals effectively. When a goal is relevant, it matches our current needs. When it's timely, we're choosing to work on this goal at the most appropriate time.

Relevant
- Will this goal help me with something I want or need right now?
- Does it connect with something I'm learning in class?
- Might I need this skill before learning other skills?

What else?

Timely
- Is this the right time to work on this goal?
- Is it worth the time I will need to spend on it?
- Can I complete this goal before it's no longer useful?

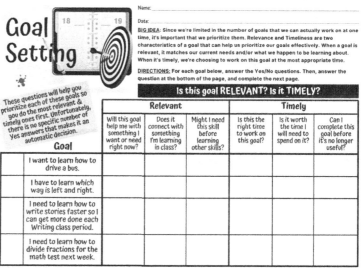

Goal Setting

Name:
Date:

BIG IDEA: Since we're limited in the number of goals that we can actually work on at one time, it's important that we prioritize them. Relevance and Timeliness are two characteristics of a goal that can help us prioritize our goals effectively. When a goal is relevant, it matches our current needs and/or what we happen to be learning about. When it's timely, we're choosing to work on this goal at the most appropriate time.

DIRECTIONS: For each goal below, answer the Yes/No questions. Then, answer the question at the bottom of the page, and complete the next page.

These questions will help you prioritize each of these goals so you do the most relevant & timely ones first. Unfortunately, there is no specific number of Yes answers that makes it an automatic decision.

Is this goal RELEVANT? Is it TIMELY?

Goal	Relevant			Timely		
	Will this goal help me with something I want or need right now?	Does it connect with something I'm learning in class?	Might I need this skill before learning other skills?	Is this the right time to work on this goal?	Is it worth the time I will need to spend on it?	Can I complete this goal before it's no longer useful?
I want to learn how to drive a bus.						
I have to learn which way is left and right.						
I need to learn how to write stories faster so I can get more done each Writing class period.						
I need to learn how to divide fractions for the math test next week.						

Which goal should you work on 1st, 2nd, 3rd & 4th? Write those numbers to the left of each goal above.

Is this goal RELEVANT? Is it TIMELY?

DIRECTIONS: Choose a goal of your own to focus on. Answer each Yes/No question and explain your answers. If you answer "No" to any question, decide if it's okay to continue with this goal or if you need to revise your goal, switch goals, or do something else. YOU need to make this decision, because YOU are in charge of the goal setting process! These questions are designed to help you make these decisions!

My Goal:

Relevant

Question	Explain:
Will this goal help me with something I want or need right now? Yes / No	Explain:
Does it connect with something I'm learning in class? Yes / No	Explain:
Might I need this skill before learning other skills? Yes / No	Explain:

Timely

Question	Explain:
Is this the right time to work on this goal? Yes / No	Explain:
Is it worth the time I will need to spend on it? Yes / No	Explain:
Can I complete this goal before it's no longer useful? Yes / No	Explain:

bit.ly/3Td3ce0

Learn to write rewarding and everlasting goals that maximize your long-term progress as well as your immediate needs

Essential Question

Is this goal likely to be REWARDING? EVERLASTING?

Big Idea

Since we're limited in the number of goals that we can actually work on at one time, it's important that we prioritize them. Goals that are "rewarding" and "everlasting" will usually take priority over goals that are not. A rewarding goal is one that will make us feel happy and proud when we achieve it. An everlasting goal is one that will make a permanent improvement to our skills or knowledge, so we won't need to work on it again in the future (unless it gets harder). By picking goals that are both rewarding and everlasting, we focus on goals that have the most long-term impact.

Lesson Overview

In this lesson, students learn how to assess the value of their goals, so they can prioritize which ones to pursue first. Students are taught to prioritize goals that are both "rewarding" and "everlasting" over goals that lack those qualities. A rewarding goal provides a sense of accomplishment and fulfillment when it is achieved, while an everlasting goal is one that will not need to be revisited in the future, as the knowledge or skill will be permanently retained. This approach allows students to use their goal setting time more effectively, by focusing on goals that will have the greatest impact on their growth.

Discussion/Reflection Questions

- Why is it important to prioritize goals that are rewarding?
- Why is it important to prioritize goals that are everlasting?
- How can you improve a goal that isn't likely to be very rewarding or everlasting? How can you revise it to make it a higher priority?

Teacher Tips

- PREREQUISITES: Lesson 5.04, Lesson 6.04, Lesson 6.06, Lesson 6.07, Lesson 6.08, Lesson 6.09
- Goals can be classified as either intrinsically rewarding or extrinsically rewarding. Intrinsically rewarding goals are pursued for their own inherent value or enjoyment, while extrinsically rewarding goals are pursued to achieve external rewards or recognition, such as pleasing others or receiving a reward. While truly intrinsic goals are not very common, it's important to find ways to make extrinsic goals more personally meaningful. When we can connect our extrinsic goals to our own values, interests, or aspirations, we are more likely to be motivated, engaged, and proud of our accomplishments. I suggest having a discussion with your students about how they can derive intrinsic value from pursuing goals that may have been encouraged by others or external factors. By finding ways to make these goals more personally meaningful, students can experience greater satisfaction and fulfillment in their pursuits.
- Most goals will increase in complexity over time, but it's important to distinguish between these scenarios and repeating the same goals without making any progress. For example, a goal to improve public speaking skills may start with basic techniques and progress to more advanced topics over time. In this case, the overarching goal remains the same, but the specific skills and strategies being developed become more advanced. However, simply repeating a goal without any progress or improvement is not effective goal setting.

Student Tasks 〉 Transfer Goals

Student Tasks	Transfer Goals
Students learn to prioritize goals that are likely to be intrinsically or extrinsically rewarding once met.	Students work on goals that they believe will be rewarding, or they find ways to make them intrinsically rewarding.
Students learn to prioritize goals that are likely to be everlasting once met.	Students work on goals that they believe will be everlasting, so they don't end up working on the same goals over and over.

Instructional Poster(s)

- This lesson has ONE Instructional Poster.
- The Instructional Poster for this lesson teaches students what "rewarding" and "everlasting" means in regard to the S.M.A.A.R.T.E.R. Goal acronym. Synonyms are given to help clarify each term, and the purpose is set for each as well.
- The purpose of this lesson is to use these two steps in the S.M.A.A.R.T.E.R. Goal Process to prioritize our goals, so we spend our immediate time on goals that will mean something to us and will last permanently. If we accomplish goals that have little benefit or only temporary effect, goal setting feels less beneficial.

Student Handouts

- This lesson has TWO Student Handouts.
- DIRECTIONS: For each goal below, answer the Yes/No questions and explain your answers. Answer the question at the bottom of the page. Then, complete the next page.
- The first Student Handout provides students with three sample goals and are asked to answer questions that hone in on whether the goal will be rewarding and everlasting or not. In addition, students are asked to explain their answers so they clearly understand their reasons for their answers.
  - Possible Answers: 3, 1, 2
- DIRECTIONS: Choose one of your own goals to focus on for this handout. Answer each Yes/No question & explain your answers. If you answer "No" to any question, decide if you should continue with this goal, or if you should revise your goal or switch goals. YOU need to make this decision, because YOU are in charge of the goal setting process! These questions are here to help you make these decisions.
- The second Student Handout is a reproducible that can be used over and over, because students use this handout to determine whether their goal will be rewarding and everlasting or not. Their explanations are important to prevent them from just answering "Yes" for each question, and because it helps students choose to work on the most valuable goals that they can set for themselves.

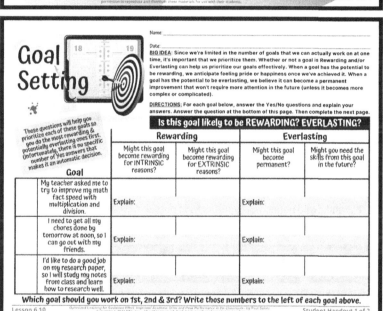

bit.ly/3t91sYz

Ensure immediate access to resources by identifying and gathering them before embarking on a new S.M.A.A.R.T.E.R. Goal

Essential Question

What RESOURCES will I need to accomplish this goal?

Big Idea

It's a common mistake to set a goal without considering the resources that may be needed to achieve it. If we take time at the beginning to consider the resources we will need, we can ensure that we are prepared and ready to work toward the goal.

Lesson Overview

In this lesson, students will learn about the importance of identifying the supplies they will need to work toward their S.M.A.A.R.T.E.R. Goals, and determining where to obtain each of these supplies. While not all goals will require supplies, it's a crucial step that is often overlooked. Failure to consider the necessary supplies can derail a goal before it even begins. When a goal requires specific supplies that are difficult to obtain, students should factor in additional time and effort to acquire them before committing too much time to the goal. In some cases, the lack of access to certain supplies may force students to revise or even abandon their goal altogether. By learning how to identify and acquire the necessary supplies, students can set themselves up for success and avoid unnecessary setbacks in pursuit of their goals.

Discussion/Reflection Questions

- Why is it important to consider the supplies we might need BEFORE beginning to work on a goal?
- What are the steps you can take if you need supplies that you don't have?
- Describe ONE idea for a goal that will require you to gather some supplies outside of what you have handy.

Teacher Tips

- PREREQUISITES: Lesson 5.04, Lesson 6.04, Lesson 6.06, Lesson 6.07, Lesson 6.08, Lesson 6.09, Lesson 6.10
- It's important to try to help your students acquire any supplies they need to accomplish meaningful goals, so please offer the use of classroom supplies or even personal supplies if you see the value in your students' goals. Assuming that they can gather the supplies from home or that a parent can go out and buy them is a slippery slope that brings equity into the equation. I always tried to provide everything my students needed (within reason) and let them know that if they wanted something expensive or different than what I had, that they would need to get that themselves by a certain date. If they couldn't have it in class by that date, they wouldn't be able to work on that goal, as written.
- You may want to change the sample S.M.A.A.R.T.E.R. Goals provided on the second Students Handout for this lesson if they are too easy or too difficult for your students. You might also need to explain what those goals mean and the types of supplies students are likely to need in order to address them.

Student Tasks 〉 Transfer Goals

Students learn to identify the supplies that they might need when working on a new S.M.A.A.R.T.E.R. Goal BEFORE starting on it.	Students consider supply needs before undertaking a new goal, leading to deeper visualization of the goal setting process.
Students learn to revise or abandon goals that require supplies that are not easily accessible or affordable.	Students don't waste their time creating and working on goals that can't be met due to lack of access to supplies.

- This lesson has ONE Instructional Poster.
- The Instructional Poster for this lesson teaches students to identify the supplies they will need in order to achieve the goal they are about to set. If a goal requires supplies that are difficult to obtain, they may need to revise their goal so it needs only simple supplies, or take additional steps in order to gather the supplies they will need to achieve their goal.
- I've had students take on goals that required supplies that were difficult to gather and it completely derailed their goal. You don't want your students wasting any time on a goal that isn't likely to pan out!

Student Handouts

- This lesson has TWO Student Handouts.
- DIRECTIONS: Complete the next page first. It includes two goals that require identifying the necessary supplies and where you can find them. Then, do the same thing below, but with a goal of your own (instead of one that is provided for you).
- Students should complete the second handout first. This provides them with two practice goals that they can brainstorm what supplies will be needed and where they could go to get those supplies. When finished, they can do one of their own goals on the first Student Handout which can be re-used as often as necessary.
- DIRECTIONS: Read each goal. Determine what resources and supplies you'll need to accomplish each goal AND where you can get them. If there are any resources that you think are close to impossible to get, write "Not Possible" in the column on the right and know that you will either need to revise the goal or drop it. This exercise will help you determine if a goal requires too many supplies or hard-to-find supplies.

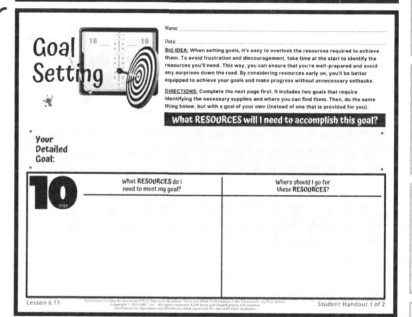

bit.ly/3Rjmyvw

Transform your goals from hopes, wishes and dreams to concrete action plans, paving the path to achievement

6.12

Essential Question

Do I have to write a PLAN for each of my goals?

Big Idea

Setting goals is important, but having a plan is what makes them happen! Without a plan, our goals are just like wishes that may never come true. With a good plan, we can break down our goals into smaller steps, track our progress, stay motivated, and achieve our goals. So remember to always make a plan for your goals and work hard toward making them a reality!

Lesson Overview

In this lesson, students learn why it's important to create a plan for each of their goals. Goals don't just happen by themselves - we need to work hard to achieve them! Simple goals require some planning and effort, while more challenging goals require even more time and work. By creating a plan, we can focus on what matters, stay motivated, and work toward achieving our goals step by step. So this lesson reminds students to always remember to make a plan for their goals, no matter how big or small they may be!

Discussion/Reflection Questions

- Why is it extremely important for us to create a plan for accomplishing our goals?
- What should we do when we don't know how to make a plan for our one our goals?
- How do you think your teacher became a teacher? What was their plan in order to accomplish their goal of becoming a teacher?

Teacher Tips

- Just like many of the previous lessons, this lesson focuses on a component of S.M.A.A.R.T.E.R. Goal Setting, but can be used using any goal setting process.
- Exemplars have been provided for both of the Student Handouts for this lesson.
- This lesson is just an introduction to writing plans for our goals and it is recommended that you also teach the next lesson (Lesson 6.13) in order to teach students the importance of being more specific with their plan, rather than allowing students to write very general, simple plans to try to achieve their goals. The more specific students are with their plan, the more likely they are to achieve their goals.

Student Tasks 〉 Transfer Goals

Student Tasks	Transfer Goals
Students learn that they need to devise a plan for all of their goals: big or small.	Students know what they plan to do while trying to accomplish a goal, rather than wasting time doing things that likely won't work.
Students infer what experts' plans were for accomplishing their goals and then create some simple plans for their own goals.	Students have a clearer understanding of the work that goes into accomplishing a goal and devote the proper time and energy to their goals.

Instructional Poster(s)

- This lesson has ONE Instructional Poster.
- The Instructional Poster for this lesson describes planning as a vital part of goal setting and compares a goal without a plan to a wish which, students may need to be reminded, don't often come true. Instead of wishing for goals to be accomplished, it's in our best interest to plan out the steps we can take to achieve our goals through hard work and attention to detail.
- This would be a good time to share some stories about people who persevered to get to the top of their field or who built their business up to what it is today. You can compare that to those who won the lottery or inherited money as opposed to following a detailed plan to accomplish their goals.

Student Handouts

- This lesson has FOUR Student Handouts.
- DIRECTIONS: Complete the chart below. Describe what you think goes into becoming a leader in each of their fields. On the next page, come up with three new goals (real or pretend) & write a plan to achieve each goal. Your plans can be simple right now, but as you work toward more complex goals, your plans need to become more detailed.
- The first Student Handout asks students to describe what experts in their field might have done to get to where they are today (a precursor to writing detailed plans).
- The second Student Handout provides students with some sample plans for ordinary goals and asks them to do the same for three goals of their own (real or pretend). Please remind students that these are basic right now, but that our goals will need to be much more detailed eventually.

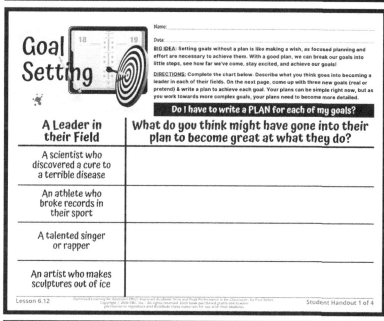

Do I have to write a PLAN for each of my goals?

It's easy to dream up LOFTY goals:
- I want to play in the NBA.
- I want to become a famous rapper.
- I want to make millions on YouTube.

But what some people don't understand is that "Goals don't just happen." You need to WORK on them. You need to have a PLAN. You need to WORK on your PLAN!

What kind of NBA star waited until he was 18 to start playing basketball? None of them! They all started playing at a relatively young age. They played nearly every day, against TOUGH competition, that involved LOSING a ton and getting schooled ALL THE TIME!

"A goal WITHOUT A PLAN is just a wish."
- Antoine de Saint-Exupéry

Lesson 6.12 — Instructional Poster 1 of 1

Goal Setting

Name:
Date:

BIG IDEA: Setting goals without a plan is like making a wish, as focused planning and effort are necessary to achieve them. With a good plan, we can break our goals into little steps, see how far we've come, stay excited, and achieve our goals!

DIRECTIONS: Complete the chart below. Describe what you think goes into becoming a leader in each of their fields. On the next page, come up with three new goals (real or pretend) & write a plan to achieve each goal. Your plans can be simple right now, but as you work towards more complex goals, your plans need to become more detailed.

Do I have to write a PLAN for each of my goals?

A Leader in their Field	What do you think might have gone into their plan to become great at what they do?
A scientist who discovered a cure to a terrible disease	
An athlete who broke records in their sport	
A talented singer or rapper	
An artist who makes sculptures out of ice	

Lesson 6.12 — Student Handout 1 of 4

Do I have to write a PLAN for each of my goals?

Goal	Goal without a Plan	Simple Plan	Goal WITH a Plan
Buy my first car without having to do monthly payments	(a wish)	Save $100 each week for the next year	A strong chance of success!
Play "Ode to Joy" on recorder in front of our music class	(a wish)	Practice my recorder for 20 minutes each night	A strong chance of success!
Be able to speak to locals when visiting Mexico	(a wish)	Spending 45 minutes each weeknight learning Spanish	A strong chance of success!
Be able to switch to a more physical position in football	(a wish)	Lift weights for 10 minutes a day, 4-5 days per week, for the next six months	A strong chance of success!
	(a wish)		A strong chance of success!
	(a wish)		A strong chance of success!
	(a wish)		A strong chance of success!

Lesson 6.12 — Student Handout 2 of 4

bit.ly/3R3An0Q

Learn the essential skill of crafting a "Good Plan" for every goal by incorporating seven essential elements

Essential Question

How can I write PLANS that help me achieve my goals?

Big Idea

Sometimes, we set goals but neglect to make a plan for accomplishing those goals. Without a plan, a goal is just a wish. Focused, well-thought-out plans help us achieve our goals.

Lesson Overview

In this lesson, students learn how to create a "Good Plan" for achieving their goals. They'll be introduced to a simple structure they can use to write their plan, with ideas for improving it as they become more confident. They'll also learn a strategy called "chunking", which involves breaking down the steps involved in achieving a goal into manageable parts. Students will be taught to describe each task in their plan, estimate how long it will take, and decide on the order in which they'll complete each step. By learning these skills, students can create effective plans to achieve their goals and stay motivated along the way.

Discussion/Reflection Questions

- Why do our plans need to be focused and well thought out, instead of generic and simple?
- What is chunking? What are chunks? (as they relate to the plans for our goals)
- How do we write a "Good Plan"?

Teacher Tips

- PREREQUISITE: Lesson: 6.12.
- There are two additional Student Handouts available for this lesson. One of them is an alternate organizer that doesn't break down the plan into chunks. This can be used right away if you'd rather have students write their plan BEFORE chunking it, or if you'd rather not have your students chunk their plan. The alternate organizer can also be used as a scaffold between the original organizer and not having the students use an organizer.
- The other additional Student Handout is a "Ten-Chunk Organizer" that students can write on when breaking their plan down. They DO NOT have to use all ten chunks - most plans do not have that many!

Student Tasks 〉 Transfer Goals

Student Tasks	Transfer Goals
Students learn about the components of a "Good Plan" and write one of their own.	Students don't just hope & wish to accomplish a goal. They create a plan that leads them to success.
Students learn how to break down their plan for meeting a goal into manageable "chunks."	Students don't get overwhelmed by complicated, challenging plans. They accomplish one small part at a time.

INTRODUCTION

PLANNING

METACOGNITION

SYNTHESIS

REFLECTION

SELF-ASSESSMENT

GOAL SETTING

FEEDBACK

Instructional Poster(s)

- This lesson has TWO Instructional Posters.
- The Instructional Poster for this lesson focuses on a quote about creating a plan that identifies each of the steps involved in accomplishing your goal. That quote helps introduce the concept of "chunking" that will be practiced during this lesson.
- Some goals have complex plans that can feel overwhelming to students, so they will be asked to break their plan apart into more manageable steps called chunks (or mini-goals). Students then put each chunk in the order that they want to accomplish them and estimate the time it should take them to achieve each chunk, for planning purposes.
- Students can break down their goals into as many chunks as they need. When they finish each chunk, they'll feel proud and accomplished, which will keep them motivated to keep going.

Student Handouts

- This lesson has THREE Student Handouts.
- DIRECTIONS: In order to successfully meet your goals, you need to create a strong plan for accomplishing each goal. Read the tips below. Then, take some time to brainstorm ideas for your plan and write your plan on the scroll on the next page. Once your plan is complete, be sure to follow it through or make adjustments to make it work!
- The first Student Handout contains step-by-step instructions for writing a good plan. It explains the basics and then offers ideas for improving their plans further.
- The second Student Handout helps students write a plan for achieving their goals and can be used as much as needed. For today's lesson, students will use the organizer to break down one of their current goals into six or fewer manageable steps, as discussed on the Instructional Poster. This process of "chunking" helps students break down a seemingly overwhelming plan into small, achievable steps that they can tackle one at a time. As they complete each step, they'll feel proud of their progress and stay motivated to keep going.

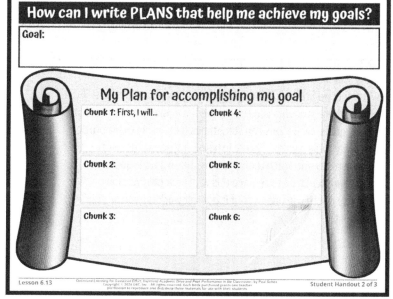

299

bit.ly/3RePp3Z

6.14 Take charge of your goals, deciding when, how, and how often to work on them, and which lessons to integrate goal work into

Planning 1
Meta-cognition 2
Synthesis 3
Reflection 4
Self Assessment 5
Goal Setting 6

Essential Question

How can I authentically work on improving my goals?

Big Idea

Since YOU are in charge of your goals (and not your teacher), YOU are the one who needs to decide WHEN there is a good time to focus on a goal and try not to let too much time pass without working on each goal. YOU are also the one who needs to decide HOW it is done.

Lesson Overview

In this lesson, students will learn about how they are expected to work on their goals in school. Some goals can be worked on while completing other assignments, such as improving participation during class discussions. Other goals may need to be worked on in isolation because they don't integrate well with other activities, like remembering to put all homework and study materials in their backpack before the end of the day. Students will also learn to keep track of the number of times they work on each of their goals to ensure that they practice regularly and make steady progress. By learning these strategies, students can effectively work on their goals and improve their chances of success.

Discussion/Reflection Questions

- Why is it important to record the times we work on our goals? How does it help us get better at goal setting?
- What is the difference between "Embedded Practice" & "Focused Practice"?
- How will you MAKE time for goal setting, practice and progress monitoring? How will you make this a habit that lasts longer than this school year?

Teacher Tips

- As the teacher, it's important to encourage students to work on their goals whenever there are natural opportunities to do so while working on other assignments. The goal setting process in this program relies on students having the freedom and expectation to work on their goals without needing constant guidance or permission from the teacher. By fostering a culture of independent goal-setting and self-directed learning, you can empower your students to take ownership of their growth and development and achieve greater success in and out of the classroom.
- The second Student Handout (and additional handout) is a "Goal Log" where students can record the times they work on each of their goals. While logs can sometimes feel like an extra burden, they can play a valuable role in helping students develop consistency and track their progress toward their goals. However, feel free to replace this with your own version or choose not to use one at all if it doesn't work for you or your students.

Student Tasks 〉 Transfer Goals

Student Tasks	Transfer Goals
Students learn how to use "Embedded Practice" and "Focused Practice" as strategies for working on their goals.	Students apply these strategies to their independent goal practice both in school and at home.
Students record the times that they worked on their goals to ensure that each goal is getting the time and attention it needs.	Students make working on their goals a daily habit that needs no reminders and happens naturally.

Instructional Poster(s)

- This lesson has TWO Instructional Posters.
- The first Instructional Poster for this lesson (Not Pictured) sets the purpose of the lesson and explains the best ways to authentically work on improving your goals in class. Goal Bursts are slightly different from S.M.A.A.R.T.E.R. Goals and so there are a few differences in how each are practiced.
- The second Instructional Poster for this lesson teaches students how to work on a goal WHILE working on another assignment in class. We call this "Embedded Practice" and it's one of the more authentic ways of working on our goals. The timing is important, though, and students need to learn how to ensure that they prioritize the completion of the academic assignment rather than the goal.

Student Handouts

- This lesson has THREE Student Handouts.
- DIRECTIONS: Read about "Embedded Practice" & "Focused Practice" below. Then, write an example of each based on the directions. On the next page, answer each question AFTER YOU'VE WORKED ON A GOAL as a way to monitor & assess your progress on it.
- The first Student Handout teaches students the difference between "Embedded Practice" and "Focused Practice" of their goals. Then, students are asked to write an example of each.
- DIRECTIONS: In order to make working on goals a GOOD HABIT, track how often you work on your goals below. Try not to go too long between practice sets. You might start slowly, but practice opportunities should increase as you begin to see the value of goal setting and prioritize it as a daily practice.
- The second Student Handout (and the additional handout) is a "Goal Log" where students will record the times that they worked on each of their goals. Feel free to replace this with your own version or a log for each goal. Or you may choose not to have one at all (to minimize the paperwork for students).

How can I authentically work on improving my goals?

Since YOU are in charge of your goals (and not your teacher), YOU are the one who needs to decide WHEN and HOW you're going to work on each goal. While your teacher will likely provide you with some time in class to organize and update your goal paperwork, most of the work towards improving your goals will need to be done during other activities, at home, or when you have a few minutes of class time that you can spare to focus on improving a goal. You need to decide when there is a good time to focus on a goal and try not to let too much time pass without working on each goal.

Goal Bursts	S.M.A.A.R.T.E.R. Goals
1 Usually Short-Term goals - Focus on these goals for a few minutes, a day or even an assignment or two! If you need more time, consider making it a S.M.A.A.R.T.E.R. Goal.	**1** Usually Long-Term goals - Often takes weeks or months to meet these goals.
2 Once you have several Goal Bursts to work on, it's a good idea to select one or two to focus on while completing other assignments in class. Match the goal to the activity, so you have an authentic opportunity to practice your goal!	**2** Depending on the types of S.M.A.A.R.T.E.R. Goals you have, you may or may not have one to focus on during each assignment or task. For example, "Doing math without a calculator" would be a hard goal to work on during a writing assignment!). Choose one if it works with the task.
3 If you're not finding any natural connections to address a Goal Burst, force a connection so you can address it and move on.	**3** If you're not finding any natural connections to address a S.M.A.A.R.T.E.R. Goal, set aside some time to work on the goal on its own.

Lesson 6.14 — Instructional Poster 1 of 2

Goal Setting

Name: _____
Date: _____

BIG IDEA: Since YOU are in charge of your goals (and not your teacher), YOU are the one who needs to decide WHEN there is a good time to focus on a goal and try not to let too much time pass without working on each goal. YOU are also the one who needs to decide HOW it is done.

DIRECTIONS: Read about "Embedded Practice" & "Focused Practice" below. Then, write an example of each based on the directions. On the next page, answer each question AFTER YOU'VE WORKED ON A GOAL as a way to monitor & assess your progress on it.

How can I authentically work on improving my goals?

Embedded Practice	Focused Practice
Your teacher has given you an assignment to work on in class and you know that this is a great opportunity to work on one of your goals WHILE you complete the assignment.	You want to improve a goal of yours, but there hasn't been a good time to embed it into another assignment, so you set aside 15 minutes to work on it today and tomorrow.
Share one possible example below using one of your goals and an assignment from class:	Share one possible example below using one of your goals and a realistic time when you could possibly do this in school:

Lesson 6.14 — Student Handout 1 of 3

How can I authentically work on improving my goals?

Directions: In order to make working on goals a GOOD HABIT, track how often you work on your goals below. Try not to go too long between practice sets. You might start slowly, but practice opportunities should increase as you begin to see the value of goal setting and prioritize it as a daily practice.

Date	Goal (shortened)	What you did	How it went
EXAMPLE: March 12th	Improving my printing	I completed two practice worksheets from my packet.	I did a good job. I highlighted the best in yellow + my worst in blue.

Lesson 6.14 — Student Handout 2 of 3

bit.ly/3uNnqRg

Monitor your progress, evaluate the effectiveness of your plan, and make necessary changes for maximum impact

Essential Question

How can I monitor & assess progress on my goals?

Big Idea

Since YOU are in charge of your goals (and not your teacher), it's important that you monitor and assess your progress on your goals to determine if you are improving or not. If you are NOT improving, it's up to you to revise your plan to make it more effective. If you are making progress, continue with your plan and determine when you believe that you have met your goal and that it will be everlasting.

Lesson Overview

In this lesson, students learn about the importance of monitoring and assessing progress toward their goals. This is a vital component of the Student-Led Self-Improvement Process, but it's not something that comes naturally to students who have only experienced traditional schooling. By teaching students how to take ownership of their goals and providing daily opportunities to assess their progress, we can help them develop into lifelong learners who take an active role in their own growth and development. Instead of trying to hide their weaknesses, students will feel empowered to be open about them with others and work toward addressing them through the plans they've created and implemented.

Discussion/Reflection Questions

- Why is it important to keep track of your scores or self-assessments on your goals (the first Student Handout)?
- What is the difference between goals that are PROGRESSING and goals that are REGRESSING? (It was taught on the Instructional Poster.)
- How many scores or self-assessments do you think you will need to collect for one of the goals you are currently working on before you can decide if you've made enough progress?

Teacher Tips

- Providing students with multiple copies of the Student Handouts for this lesson can be helpful, as they can use the Data Collection form (Student Handout 1) for each goal they're actively working on and the self-assessment form (Student Handout 2) each time they work on one of their goals in class. These handouts serve as scaffolds to support students as they become more independent with goal setting, but they shouldn't be used any longer than necessary.
- When students know that their teacher will be reading and providing feedback on their organizers and forms, they're more likely to complete them to the best of their ability. Therefore, it's highly recommended that you find a way to regularly talk with each of your students about their goals and progress, and to review the paperwork they've completed. This level of feedback is especially important at the beginning of the Student-Led Self-Improvement Process, as students are still developing their skills and confidence. As they become stronger and more independent, the need for regular feedback may decrease, but it's still important to check in periodically to ensure that they're on track and making progress toward their goals.

Student Tasks 〉 Transfer Goals

Student Tasks	Transfer Goals
Students collect assessment data over time on a goal of theirs before determining if their plan is working or if it needs revision.	Students understand that a plan isn't working if their data doesn't show growth, and revise their plan when that's the case.
Students formally reflect and assess themselves after working on one of their goals in order to deepen their understanding of goal setting and progress monitoring.	Students understand the importance of working on their goals in order to see progress.

Optimized Learning: 180 mini-lessons that transform today's students into confident, capable & collaborative, self-directed learners

Instructional Poster(s)

- This lesson has ONE Instructional Poster.
- The Instructional Poster for this lesson teaches students what it means to "Monitor their Progress" (to regularly reflect on whether a plan is working or if it needs to be revised.) and "Assess their Progress" on their goals (to use tests or other assessment tools to measure growth from their baseline). Students are also taught that if there aren't any appropriate assessment tools for this particular goal, they should use self-assessment.
- It also sets the purpose for the lesson, and it shows what to do when progress is being made (keep going until you meet your goal) AND when it is not (revise your plan to fix what isn't working. Then, try again).

Student Handouts

- This lesson has THREE Student Handouts.
- DIRECTIONS: As you assess your progress on each of your goals, fill out a "Score Chart" like the one below. For this assignment, you might not have enough data for any of your goals, so if that's the case, use fictional data for one of your goals below.
- The first Student Handout is a record of the scores or self-assessments they've collected while working on ONE of their goals. Five entries are provided, but students need to be encouraged to add more or use fewer if that's what is most appropriate for their goal. A new sheet should be used for additional goals.
- The second Student Handout is a Self-Assessment of their time spent working on a goal. It asks them to summarize what they did to try to improve their goal, how well they think they did on it, any evidence that supports their self-assessment, what else needs to be done to achieve this goal, and what their next steps will be.

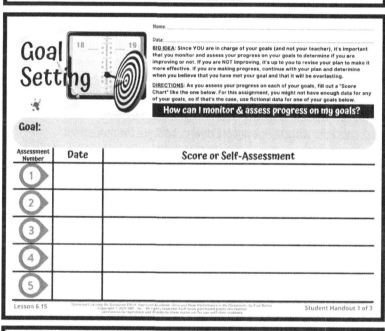

6.16

Collect evidence of your growth every step of the way, building a clear and accurate record of your achievements

bit.ly/3uERrCH

bit.ly/3uERrCH

Essential Question

How do I collect and organize my evidence of growth?

Big Idea

Don't wait until the last minute to collect evidence that shows you're getting better at a goal. Make sure you gather evidence as you go and keep it organized until you're ready to look at it. When it's time to see how much you've improved (or if you need to work harder), you'll have plenty of proof to help you.

Lesson Overview

In this lesson, students learn two methods for collecting and organizing their evidence of growth for their goals. They can choose between the Sticky Note Method or the Hierarchical Organizer. Both methods contain the same steps, but are carried out differently. The main reason to choose one method over another is whether or not your students will have immediate access to their goal sheets at all times throughout their school day. If they do, writing their evidence on the Hierarchical Organizer is easiest. If they don't, they can use sticky notes to write their evidence down, and store the notes until they are ready to transfer them to the Sticky Notes Organizer.

Discussion/Reflection Questions

- Why do you think you've been given two different methods for collecting and organizing the evidence for your goals?
- Which method do you think you will use the most? Why?
- What kind of Hierarchical Organizer did you create or would you create that you would find fun and engaging as you worked through the levels? Super Mario Brothers characters? Chicago Cubs players? Heavy Metal bands?

Teacher Tips

- The Sticky Note method is a great option, because they don't need to have their goals in front of them to record their evidence. They can put their completed sticky notes into an envelope, box, folder, or whatever system works best for your students, and then transfer them to the organizer when given time in class to work on this.

- It can be really motivating to let your students create their own Hierarchical Organizer for them to use. I created the pirate organizer because it connected with my book, "Learn Like a PIRATE" which motivated me to research the ranks of pirates.

- I asked my nephew to create one using Super Mario Brothers®[1] characters, and he came up with:
  - See the hierarchy to the right. >
  - Students should have fun trying to advance to the next level of their own hierarchy!

  - Level 10 - Superstar Mario®,
  - Level 9 - Bowser®,
  - Level 8 - Mario®,
  - Level 7 - Luigi®,
  - Level 6 - Princess Peach®,
  - Level 5 - Wario®,
  - Level 4 - Toadette®,
  - Level 3 - Toad®,
  - Level 2 - Hammer Bro®,
  - Level 1 - Koopa Troopa®, and
  - Level 0 - Goomba®.

1. All Nintendo characters and games mentioned above are registered trademarks owned by Nintendo.

Student Tasks 〉 Transfer Goals

Student Tasks	Transfer Goals
Students learn two systems for collecting and organizing the evidence of their growth toward a goal.	Students are motivated to use the organizational system they've chosen, because they chose what worked best for them.
Students choose one of the two methods to organize their evidence to determine when they've met their goal.	Students use one of the methods from this lesson or their own to help them determine when they've met a goal of theirs.

Instructional Poster(s)

- This lesson has TWO Instructional Poster.
- The instructional poster for this lesson outlines a hierarchical system that students will use to track their progress and determine when they have achieved their goals. The system involves various levels, with the example given using pirates to illustrate rankings from a stowaway at Level 0 to a captain at Level 10. Students will have the opportunity to create their own system using athletes or characters from a video game to motivate them to progress through the levels as they set and achieve goals.
- For each skill that students set a goal for, they will begin at Level 0, which requires no evidence, and they will progress through the levels by providing evidence of growth. While Level 10 represents the highest level, students are not required to reach this level for every skill. Instead, they can choose to end their goal at any level, as long as they follow the guidelines established in Lesson 6.19.

Student Handouts

- This lesson has FIVE Student Handouts.
- DIRECTIONS: Read through each method & example below for tracking progress on your goals. Choose one method for each of your goals (they don't all have to be the same method, however). Collect evidence of growth for each goal and record it in one of the organizers from this lesson.
- The first Student Handout teaches students two methods they can choose between for collecting & organizing their evidence of growth for a goal. They only need to choose one method, but can alternate if they'd like. Ensure that your students read through each exemplar.
- DIRECTIONS: Every time you have evidence of growth, write it on a sticky note and place it in a box below. Keep going until you believe that you've met your goal and can maintain it permanently.
- The second Student Handout is whichever organization tool they choose to use for their goal: either the sticky note organizer (two pages) or the Hierarchical Organizer (their own creation or the pirate version).

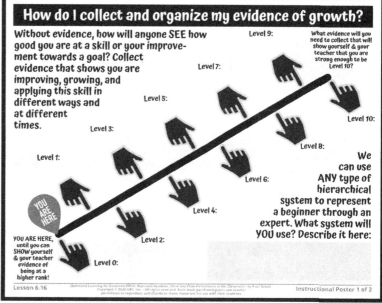

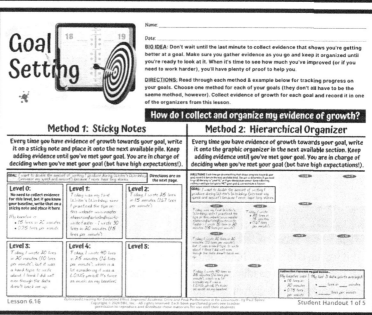

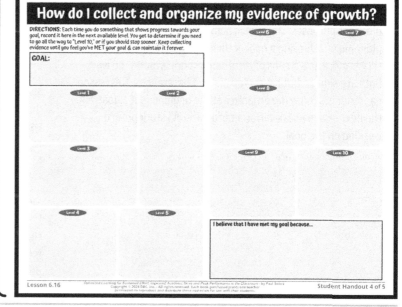

INTRODUCTION

PLANNING

METACOGNITION

SYNTHESIS

REFLECTION

SELF-ASSESSMENT

GOAL SETTING

FEEDBACK

bit.ly/3Rw5iTV

Create and utilize "Check-In Stations" (mini-deadlines) to ensure that you're "on track" to finish on time before it's too late

6.17

Essential Question

How can I use Check-In Stations to manage my time?

Lesson Overview

In this lesson, students explore the importance of setting a deadline for achieving a goal and implementing mini-deadlines, known as Check-In Stations, to track their progress along the way. Each station represents a milestone on their path toward their goal. By using these checkpoints, students ensure they stay on track and avoid reaching their deadline without significant progress. Furthermore, students learn the value of adjusting their goals if they find themselves falling behind or not making sufficient progress at any given point. Lastly, students discover the significance of thoughtful planning in achieving desired results.

Teacher Tips

- This lesson is best used at the beginning of a new goal, so students can set a deadline and create mini-deadlines to ensure a successful completion of their goal.
- You may want to explore the next lesson now, and determine if you want to teach both lessons, or just one of them. Both lessons utilize the idea of Check-In Stations, but they serve slightly different purposes. This lesson helps students with timely planning of achieving a goal of theirs, while the next lesson serves more as a means of recording progress along the way. Both are similar, but have a few distinct differences. This lesson has students using the organizer at the beginning of a goal, and the next lesson uses a different organizer AS students are working on the goal.

Big Idea

It's important to plan specific times to check on our progress while working toward a goal. This helps us make sure our methods are working and that we're actually making progress. By creating a deadline date, we end up using our time more wisely. A few times, between the start and finish dates, we should look at our progress and decide if we need to make any changes to the plan. This way, we can make sure we're on the right track!

Discussion/Reflection Questions

- How do you think checking on your progress at different times can help you with your goal? Why is it important to see how you're doing along the way?
- If you had checkpoints between the start and finish of your goal, what kinds of things could you look for to see if you're doing well? How could these check-ins help you change your plan if you need to?
- Think about why it's important to be flexible and willing to change your plan along the way. How might adjusting your plan make it easier for you to reach your goal?

Student Tasks ❯ Transfer Goals

Student Tasks	Transfer Goals
Students create a specific deadline for a goal of theirs and make a plan that helps them reach that goal on time.	Students set goals and attempt to complete them within a specific timeframe to maximize the benefits they can gain from those goals.
Students plan out three Check-In Stations to ensure that they are on track to meet their goal by their deadline.	Students regularly monitor their progress on goals to stay on track and ensure success by meeting deadlines.

INTRODUCTION
PLANNING
METACOGNITION
SYNTHESIS
REFLECTION
SELF-ASSESSMENT
GOAL SETTING
FEEDBACK

Instructional Poster(s)

- This lesson has TWO Instructional Posters.
- The first Instructional Poster for this lesson teaches students what Check-In Stations are in regards to goal setting, and it helps students see how these Check-In Stations can help them manage their time more effectively when used properly.
- An exemplar has been provided on the second Instructional Poster showing a non-academic goal: saving money for a big purchase.
- Please make sure that the students realize that the first answer: "I could wait until June 19th..." is NOT the correct answer and that this lesson helps them see how to avoid doing just that! The more responsible way to achieve this goal is to create a plan and monitor it along the way.

Student Handouts

- This lesson has TWO Student Handouts.
- DIRECTIONS: (1) Read the exemplar and the tips to the right. (2) On the next page, describe your baseline (current level of achievement or ability) with the goal you are working on achieving in Train Station 1 and add the date. (3) Enter the date when you hope to achieve this goal in Train Station 5. (4) Find three dates in between to check in and share progress toward your goal. (5) In each yellow box, describe how your skill is improving (or isn't). (6) Plan out your learning experiences so you meet the deadline(s) you have set.
- The first Student Handout shows students an exemplar for the next page & provides helpful tips for managing their time.
- DIRECTIONS: Starting at Check-In Station 1, DESCRIBE your current level of ability or achievement with the skill you're working on improving & add the date. Then, enter the date when you hope to achieve this goal in Check-In Station 5. Find three dates in between to check in and share progress toward your goal. Describe in each box how your skill is improving (or isn't).
- The second Student Handout can be used over and over to help students manage their time during the goal setting process.

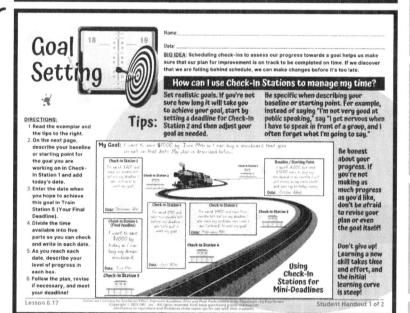

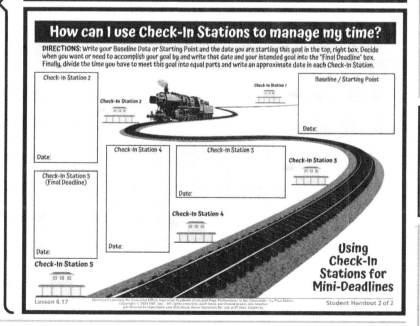

bit.ly/484K18X

Create and utilize "Check-In Stations" as strategic pit stops to assess progress and potentially make changes to your plan

Essential Question

How can I use Check-In Stations to track my progress?

Big Idea

Checking in to assess our progress toward a goal is really important to ensure that our plan for improvement is working and that we're making enough progress to achieve our goal on time. If we discover that our methods are NOT working, we can make changes to the plan before it's too late to do so.

Lesson Overview

In this lesson, students use Check-In Stations to monitor their actual progress toward their goal. At each Check-In Station, students record their accomplishments up to that point and determine if they are on track to achieve their goal by the deadline. Based on their progress assessment, students can choose to continue following their plan or make revisions to enhance their growth. (This lesson can be used WITH Lesson 6.17 or instead of Lesson 6.17, which also uses the concept of Check-In Stations.)

Discussion/Reflection Questions

- Why do you think it's important to have regular check-ins to see how you're doing with your goal? How can these check-ins help you know if your plan is working and if you're making progress?
- Imagine you're working on a goal and, during a check-in, you find out that you're not making as much progress as you hoped. How would you feel, and what would you do to change your plan? Why is it important to fix any problems as soon as possible?
- Think about the good things that can happen when you make changes to your plan based on check-in assessments. How can adjusting your strategies or approach make it easier for you to reach your goal?

Teacher Tips

- Unlike most lessons, students cannot complete the Student Handout immediately. They will need to use the Student Handout throughout the entire process of working on a goal. Once their goal has been achieved or the deadline that they set has passed, they can complete this Student Handout for you to review or give feedback on.
- This lesson is similar to the previous lesson and can be combined with it, taught instead of the previous lesson, or skipped if the previous lesson matches your students needs best. It's suggested to use both in combination: Lesson 6.17 is done BEFORE students start working on a goal and Lesson 6.18 (this lesson) is done WHILE students work on their goal, matching up the Check-In Station dates from each lesson. If you are following the Instructional Spirals, these will be completed in Spiral 6 and 7, respectively.
- The two additional Instructional Posters ease the transition between this lesson and the prior lesson (6.17). They don't take much time to discuss and aren't used again in the future.

Student Tasks ❭ Transfer Goals

Student Tasks	Transfer Goals
Students evaluate if they are making enough progress on their goal to finish by their deadline.	Students are aware of when they are falling behind as they try to accomplish their goals and do something to remedy it.
Students revise or adjust their goal if they feel they are not making enough progress on their goal to finish on time.	Students consider alternate approaches to achieving their goals whenever progress is too slow or ineffective.

INTRODUCTION

PLANNING

METACOGNITION

SYNTHESIS

REFLECTION

SELF-ASSESSMENT

GOAL SETTING

FEEDBACK

Instructional Poster(s)

- This lesson has TWO Instructional Posters.
- The Instructional Poster for this lesson introduces students to another purpose of Check-In Stations. In the previous lesson, students used Check-In Stations to plan mini-deadlines that help them ensure progress toward their goal. In this lesson, students use Check-In Stations to monitor their actual progress toward their goal. At each Check-In Station, students record their accomplishments up to that point and determine if they are on track to achieve their goal by the deadline. Based on their progress assessment, students can choose to continue following their plan or make revisions to enhance their growth.
- All of this is done by looking at the PAST, PRESENT, and FUTURE.

Student Handouts

- This lesson has TWO Student Handouts.
- DIRECTIONS: As you're working on a goal, take a moment to reflect and self-assess on your progress toward that goal by answering the questions at a Check-In Station below and on the next page. Adjust your plan as needed.
- The first Check-In Station asks: (1) What is my goal? (2) What is my Baseline or Starting Point? (3) What is my plan? and (4) What do I still need to do?
- Check-In Stations 2-4 ask students (1) What have I done since the previous Check-In Station? (2) What do I still need to do? AND (3) Do I feel that I am "on-track" or "falling behind"?
- Check-In Station 5 asks students (1) What have I done since the previous Check-In Station? (2) Have I accomplished my goal? What do I still need to do? When do I expect to meet my goal? AND (3) Do I feel that I am "on-track" or "falling behind"?

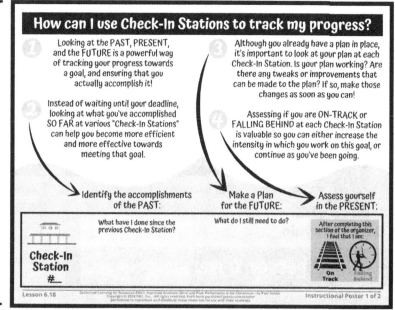

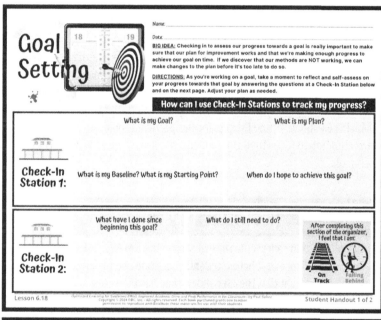

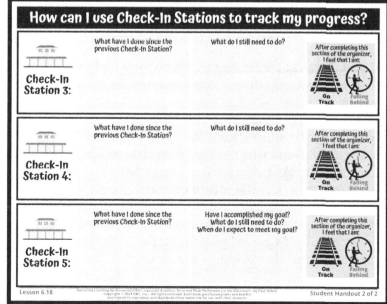

bit.ly/47x9bi6

Confidently declare victory with these final steps when you've conquered a goal and have evidence to support your claim

Essential Question

What do I do once I believe I've accomplished a goal?

Big Idea

Successful, independent learners are able to determine when they feel they've met their goals. They collect plenty of evidence to support their decision. They believe that they will be able to maintain the goal moving forward, and they feel proud of their accomplishment, because they know that it challenged them.

Lesson Overview

In this lesson, students determine if they have accomplished one of their goals, and if so, they fill out a Certificate of Achievement to congratulate them and (optionally) decide how they would like to be congratulated by their teacher (publicly, privately, or not at all). If at any point in time the student decides that they are not actually done with the goal, they can stop filling out the forms, resume working on the goal, and then return to the forms when they have actually achieved their goal. This is one way to mark the end of the S.M.A.A.R.T.E.R. Goal Setting Process for this particular goal, and allows students to focus their time and attention on some of their other goals.

Discussion / Reflection Questions

- Why do you think it's important to complete these forms before determining that a goal is complete?
- What did you learn from the exemplars in this lesson?
- How many goals do you think you will be able to accomplish this school year? Why that many?

Teacher Tips

- This mini-lesson represents the last step in the S.M.A.A.R.T.E.R. Goal Setting Process. It helps students feel pride and pleasure in completing a goal that they set and worked hard towards.
- This mini-lesson can be used even if your students are not using that specific process to create and track goals. (But don't stop teaching mini-lessons here - there are additional activities in this unit that can help students improve their goal setting abilities.)
- This lesson contains three exemplars that can be used to show students how to complete their Student Handouts completely and correctly.
- I really enjoyed having the "Goals Accomplished Board" in our classroom, and I think my students enjoyed it too. They were asked to place a completed sticky note in one of the sections on the board showing me which goal they accomplished and letting me know how they would like to be congratulated (publicly, privately, or not at all). Every time the board was filled up, we would have a celebration to acknowledge all of the students' who accomplished a goal and wanted it to be public . The private celebrations would happen while I walked around the classroom on other days.

Student Tasks 〉 Transfer Goals

Student Tasks	Transfer Goals
Students observe and analyze exemplars for each form to learn what is expected of them, and how to complete them properly.	Students complete each form properly, leading to a better application of each of the concepts embedded in each form.
Students complete three forms when they believe that they have achieved one of their goals.	Students naturally apply the concepts on the three forms to goals they are working on to determine if they are indeed done with one of their goals.

Instructional Poster(s)

- This lesson has TWO Instructional Posters.
- The Instructional Poster for this lesson walks students through the three Student Handouts for this lesson. These Student Handouts help students determine if they are indeed done with a goal of theirs and helps them celebrate that goal with a Certificate of Achievement (and optionally, a Goals Accomplished Board that students would add a sticky note to expressing their desire to celebrate publicly, privately, or not at all. See image included in this lesson). Once these handouts have been completed, the SLSI Process is considered complete for this particular goal (at least until they want to increase the level of challenge or, bite your tongue, if the student reverts back to old ways).

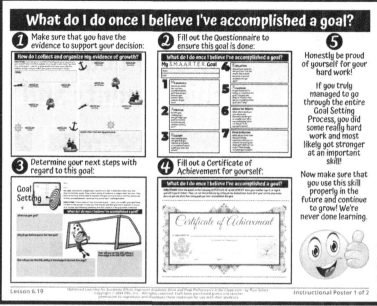

Student Handouts

- This lesson has SIX Student Handouts.
- DIRECTIONS: You've done it! You've scored a goal - I mean, you've MET your goal! Now it's time to celebrate! To help you find closure with this goal and to maintain a record of it, answer the following questions and then staple it to the goal sheet it matches.
- The first two Student Handout ask students to reflect on the goal that they believe they have accomplished. They answer the questions that make up the S.M.A.A.R.T.E.R. Goal Setting Process to ensure that they indeed are actually finished with this goal (at least until they want to increase the level of difficulty on it down the road).
- The third Student Handout is a Certificate of Achievement that they should complete to end their process and to keep as a record of their accomplishments. I highly recommend reading these from each student to ensure that they are completing the process correctly.
- The rest of the Student Handouts are exemplars showing students how to fill out each graphic organizer correctly.

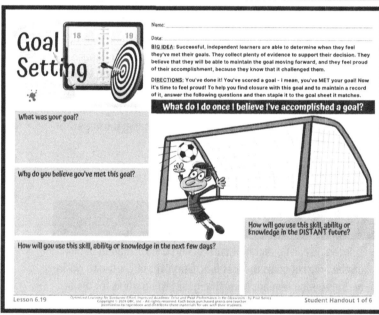

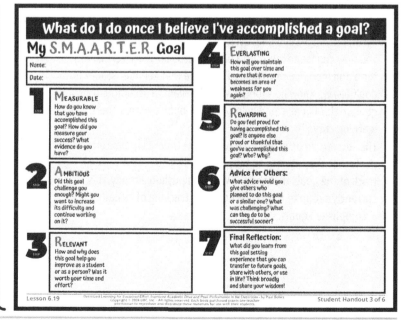

bit.ly/46AdTKC

Learn to blend challenging, moderate, and easy goals to enjoy both monumental achievements and fleeting triumphs

Essential Question

What kinds of goals should I be working on?

Lesson Overview

In this lesson, students discover the significance of creating goals that tackle both small and big challenges, as well as everything in between. Instead of solely concentrating on goals that can be quickly achieved or those that require extensive time and effort, students will learn the value of choosing a combination of goal types. Through the activity, they will engage in categorizing their goals based on the level of accomplishment each goal has on them. While the specific allocation of each goal is not overly important, the process of analyzing each goal and understanding the impact of its accomplishment is.

Teacher Tips

- This lesson can be taught when students are struggling to mix up the types of goals they set for themselves or choose to work on. This lesson reminds them that goal setting works for major AND minor accomplishments, as well as everything in between. By tracking their goals on this student handout, they will come to realize if they are always choosing the same level of accomplishment over and over.
- You may choose to mix it up a bit and focus on short-term, long-term and medium-term goals. I've found that younger students don't always know how long it will take them to accomplish a goal, so this tweak could help with that, but know that there is a learning curve.
- This lesson can be used as a way to help students brainstorm goals that they want to accomplish OR they can use it to keep track of the goals that they HAVE accomplished already. It is currently set up to mostly focus on the tracking of already-accomplished goals.

Big Idea

Over time, we sometimes get stuck doing the same things when setting goals. We might keep choosing similar goals or pick ones that don't make a big difference. But goal setting is actually about helping us achieve all sorts of amazing things! The trick is to find the perfect balance between big, medium, and small accomplishments. This way, we can reach for the stars while also celebrating the little victories along the way.

Discussion/Reflection Questions

- Why is it important that we dedicate time to focusing on all kinds of goals (ones that lead to major, minor AND medium accomplishments)?
- When setting goals, which level do you usually find yourself choosing? (Minor, Medium, Major)? Why do you think that is?
- How will you try to focus on goals in the other two levels? What will you do to ensure that you end up with some goals in all three levels?

Student Tasks ⟩ Transfer Goals

Student Tasks	Transfer Goals
Students learn about the importance of creating and working on goals that lead to both minor AND major accomplishments.	Students work on goals at all levels and see how they can accomplish all types concurrently.
Students categorize their own goals based on the level of accomplishment each goal led to.	Students are aware of the types of goals they set for themselves and work on goals at all levels.

Instructional Poster(s)

- This lesson has ONE Instructional Poster.
- The Instructional Poster for this lesson enters the mind of a student who is wondering what his teacher wants him to work on, regarding his goals. He wonders if he should work on minor goals, major goals, medium goals, or all of the above! Some goals will take a long time to complete, while others might be accomplished in a week, or so. Discuss the thoughts together with the class. During this discussion, advise students to choose some goals from each category, and to only work on as many as they can give the appropriate amount of attention to. Some goals might just require 10 minutes of attention per week, while others might need 30 minutes a day for a while. Students can work on both, but probably not two goals that each require 30 minutes per day of their time!

Student Handouts

- This lesson has THREE Student Handouts.
- DIRECTIONS: As you complete a goal, decide if it is a Major, Medium, or Minor Accomplishment and write it in the correct column on the next page. Keep this page available so you can share your accomplishments with anyone who would like to learn about them. Add more of these pages as you need them.
- The first Student Handout teaches students what Major, Minor and Medium Accomplishments are, and provides an example of each (more examples are available on the Exemplar). There is nothing they need to complete on this page.
- The second Student Handout asks students to keep a log of their "Accomplished Goals" by categorizing them into one of the three sections. For the lesson, you might want students to brainstorm goals that can go into each section (for practice). They can predict where their current goals will end up once accomplished, students can individually brainstorm potential goals, or you can brainstorm goals together as a class and categorize them appropriately.

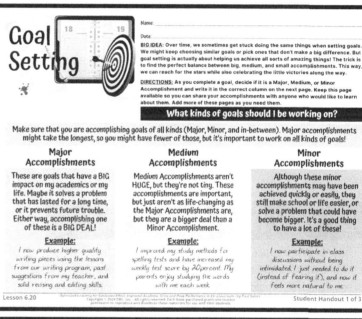

INTRODUCTION

PLANNING

METACOGNITION

SYNTHESIS

REFLECTION

SELF-ASSESSMENT

GOAL SETTING

FEEDBACK

bit.ly/47zmT3M

Ensure continual growth by brainstorming challenges from your past, present, and anticipated future to create new goals

Essential Question

How do I come up with new goals to work on?

Big Idea

We are always uncovering skills and abilities that we don't possess, but sometimes embarrassment or disappointment stops us from thinking clearly about how to address them. It's time to shift from our emotional brain to our rational brain! Whenever you come across something you're not good at, transform it into a S.M.A.A.R.T.E.R. Goal (or Goal Burst)!

Lesson Overview

In this lesson, students will discover that there are endless opportunities for new goals in our lives. Anything that we currently struggle with can serve as an excellent goal to work toward. Similarly, things that we struggled with in the past, which still hold importance, can be transformed into valuable goals, as well as things we anticipate struggling with in the near future. Through brainstorming their past, present, and future struggles, each student will identify numerous potential opportunities for setting new goals.

Discussion / Reflection Questions

- Why should we look to our past, present and future for new goal ideas?
- We don't actually achieve EVERY goal that we set for ourselves. So, how will you (how should you) handle setbacks and failures when it comes to achieving your goals?
- How can you stop yourself from overreacting when you feel frustrated, embarrassed, or disappointed in yourself for doing something poorly or incorrectly?

Teacher Tips

- This lesson would pair well with a Social-Emotional lesson on dealing with frustration, embarrassment or disappointment. From Simple Psychology: "The amygdala perceives a threat and triggers a fight-or-flight response before the cortical centers can fully assess the situation, essentially "hijacking" the rational response process. This can lead to impulsive reactions to perceived threats." Whenever we have negative feelings about something we are currently bad at, we need to think about it as an opportunity to write a goal for ourselves. We can't be great at everything! And the way we getter better at almost anything is by practicing it the right way over and over until it improves!
- There are additional questions that students can attempt to answer on the second Student Handout (that aren't on there), such as "What might happen if I DO accomplish this goal?" and any of the questions listed in the S.M.A.A.R.T.E.R. Goal Setting Process. Feel free to expand the lesson to include some of those.

Student Tasks 〉 Transfer Goals

Student Tasks	Transfer Goals
Students think about the various ways they might react when they discover that they are not good at a particular skill.	Students learn to view negative emotions like embarrassment and disappointment as opportunities to set goals.
Students consider skills they needed in the past, need in the present, and might need in the future to come up with new goals.	Students draw from a wealth of possibilities to create new goals to work on.

INTRODUCTION

PLANNING

METACOGNITION

SYNTHESIS

REFLECTION

SELF-ASSESSMENT

GOAL SETTING

FEEDBACK

Instructional Poster(s)

- This lesson has ONE Instructional Poster.
- The Instructional Poster for this lesson attempts to change students' thinking from a fixed mindset of "failure is bad" to a growth mindset of "failure means setting a goal." Confusion, frustration, struggle, failure, and every other word to describe the trouble we all have learning something new should trigger a response in everyone to (1) accept is as a limitation of ours and (2) to set a goal to try to improve it.
- Read through the Instructional Poster as a class and discuss why this is important and how it can be done in your classroom this year.

Student Handouts

- This lesson has FOUR Student Handouts.
- DIRECTIONS: Using the Past, Present, Future Chart below, brainstorm and list as many skills as you can in each column. Afterward, choose the four most important skills to carry over to the next page. As you do this, explore and uncover the potential negative consequences of not improving these skills, both for yourself and others.
- The first Student Handout asks students to brainstorm and list as many skills as they wish they had in the past (but didn't, which caused struggle), in the present (which are currently causing struggle), and in the future (which will likely cause struggle). They will then choose four of those skills (from any of the columns) to transfer to the next Student Handout.
- The second Student Handout asks students to explain why they need each goal and what might happen if they don't accomplish each goal. If they internalize the activity properly, they should discover the value of creating goals for each skill.
- The final two Student Handouts are exemplars.

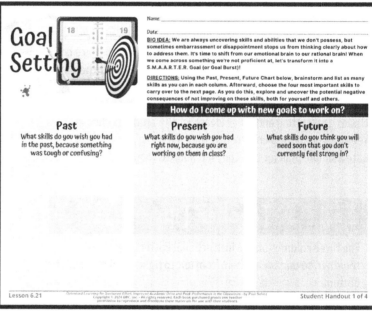

bit.ly/47u6ayW

Connect Self-Assessment to Goal Setting by regularly setting & working on goals that address our perceived weaknesses

Essential Question

Can I use self-assessment to create new goals?

Lesson Overview

In this lesson, students think about what they should do AFTER they self-assess. Whenever students decide that they are struggling with a skill or Success Criterion, they need to decide if they are going to write a S.M.A.A.R.T.E.R. Goal, a Goal Burst, or do something else about it. The important thing is not just accepting that they are bad at something without doing something about it. This lesson helps students brainstorm areas that they are weak in, reasons why they should want to improve, and things they can do to improve (which includes goal setting and other ideas). Finally, students choose three skills or Success Criteria that they will try to improve and create a simple plan for how they will address them.

Teacher Tips

- The three columns on the Instructional Poster do NOT go together, so don't read them from left to right. Read them top to bottom.
- Let the students know that they will be doing an entire unit on Goal Setting after this one, so goal setting for now looks very simplistic and possibly confusing, but it will become clearer soon.
- Reinforce the idea that we should always try to address areas of weakness from our self-assessments, and that ignoring those weaknesses is irresponsible. ONE way to do that is to set a goal and work on it, but there are other ways that can also be used, like asking a friend for help, looking it up, watching a YouTube video, etc.
- Be sure to remind students to work on the three goals on their Student Handouts over the next few weeks!

Big Idea

Periodically, it's important to take a few minutes to brainstorm areas where we feel we need to improve, and then make a plan for that improvement. If we can make this a weekly or every-other-week activity, we can individualize our learning most effectively, and prevent our little struggles from turning into overwhelming challenges.

Discussion/Reflection Questions

- Why are we talking about goal setting in the self-assessment unit? (There is a very important answer to this question.)
- What should we do whenever we discover a weakness of ours while self-assessing? What is our next step?
- How will you ensure that you continue to work on your three goals that you set for yourself today on the Student Handouts? How will you make sure we don't just forget about them after torday? (Remember, the main purpose of this program is to make you more independent and less-reliant on your teacher to do all of the thinking!)

Student Tasks 〉 Transfer Goals

Student Tasks	Transfer Goals
Students identify several areas of relative weakness based on recent self-assessments (and more).	Students connect self-assessment and goal setting, and use many different ways to attempt to address weaknesses.
Students write informal, basic goals to attempt to address three of these weaknesses.	Students know that the SLSI Process doesn't end with Self-Assessment, and attempt to address all of their weaknesses.

Instructional Poster(s)

- This lesson has ONE Instructional Poster.
- The Instructional Poster for this lesson helps guide students through the process of taking self-assessments into the goal setting process to create S.M.A.A.R.T.E.R. Goals, Goal Bursts, and more. (If you don't know what these are yet, check out the next chapter).
- Read though the first column all the way and discuss how these questions would be helpful to ask ourselves in order to create meaningful goals. Next, read through the second column and discuss how these are excellent reasons to WANT or NEED to create a goal. Finally, read through the third column and discuss how these are smart actions to take in these situations. Don't worry about explaining the types of goals right now - they will come soon enough.

Student Handouts

- This lesson has TWO Student Handouts.
- DIRECTIONS: Brainstorm several skills or Success Criteria that YOU believe you need to improve. These can come from feedback you've received, self-assessments, or recent experiences. They can be academic, social-emotional, behavioral, etc. but they must benefit you IN SCHOOL in some sort of way. Write these in the box below. Then, choose three skills to plan to improve within the chart below and on the next page.
- The Student Handouts for this lesson guide students to brainstorm reasons to set goals for improvement based on self-assessments. It connects the two steps in the SLSI Process (Self-Assessment and Goal Setting) and ensures that students see their cause & effect relationship and interrelatedness. This serves as a brief introduction to goal setting.

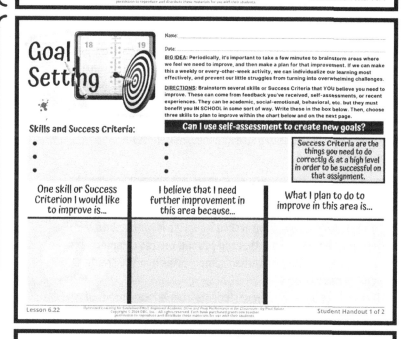

INTRODUCTION
PLANNING
METACOGNITION
SYNTHESIS
REFLECTION
SELF-ASSESSMENT
GOAL SETTING
FEEDBACK

Can I use self-assessment to create new goals?

Ways I can create a list of my weak skills & unmet Success Criteria	Reasons why I might want to improve a particular skill or Success Criterion	Things I can do to try to improve a particular skill or Success Criterion
• What feedback have I received recently?	• I KNOW that I don't understand it (I used metacognition to know this.)	• Write a SMAARTER Goal to intensely try to improve it.
• What is the most challenging skill or success criteria for me?	• Whenever it comes up in class, it makes me uncomfortable, frustrated, or embarrassed because it's difficult for me	• Focus on the weak skill or unmet Success Criterion through one or more GOAL BURSTS!
• What slows me down?	• New skills that we're learning are building on the skills that I'm struggling with & it's going to start snowballing soon	• Ask a peer for some help
• What makes me have to ask others for help the most?		• Ask my teacher to re-teach it to me or give me additional support
• What kind of mistakes do I make most often?	• It's causing me to do more poorly than I should be doing	• Spend time working on it and practicing it (at home or school)
• What skills prevent me from feeling successful?	• I WANT to get better at it!	• Look back at old work and try to improve it
• What else?	• It can help me get ahead, and I'm ready for a new challenge!	• What else?
	• What else?	

Lesson 6.22

Instructional Poster 1 of 1

Goal Setting

Name:

Date:

BIG IDEA: Periodically, it's important to take a few minutes to brainstorm areas where we feel we need to improve, and then make a plan for that improvement. If we can make this a weekly or every-other-week activity, we can individualize our learning most effectively, and prevent our little struggles from turning into overwhelming challenges.

DIRECTIONS: Brainstorm several skills or Success Criteria that YOU believe you need to improve. These can come from feedback you've received, self-assessments, or recent experiences. They can be academic, social-emotional, behavioral, etc. but they must benefit you IN SCHOOL in some sort of way. Write these in the box below. Then, choose three skills to plan to improve within the chart below and on the next page.

Skills and Success Criteria:

Can I use self-assessment to create new goals?

Success Criteria are the things you need to do correctly & at a high level in order to be successful on that assignment.

One skill or Success Criterion I would like to improve is...	I believe that I need further improvement in this area because...	What I plan to do to improve in this area is...

Lesson 6.22

Student Handout 1 of 2

Can I use self-assessment to create new goals?

One skill or Success Criterion I would like to improve is...	I believe that I need further improvement in this area because...	What I plan to do to improve in this area is...
One skill or Success Criterion I would like to improve is...	I believe that I need further improvement in this area because...	What I plan to do to improve in this area is...

Lesson 6.22

Student Handout 2 of 2

bit.ly/3SXeSBq

Prioritize your goals to ensure you tackle the most critical, timely, or personally meaningful ones right away

Essential Question

How do I prioritize which goals to focus on first?

Big Idea

By taking time to prioritize our goals, we can focus on what's most important first. We can also choose to allocate our time to those goals that are most timely or one of dozens of other reasons.

Lesson Overview

In this lesson, students are introduced to a method of prioritizing goals using sticky notes. They not only learn seven ways to prioritize their goals but are also encouraged to brainstorm additional ideas as a class. By applying these tips, students determine which of their goal ideas take priority, helping them make the most of their goal-setting efforts. The use of sticky notes throughout the year enables students to jot down goal ideas whenever they come to mind, without the need to immediately fill out a S.M.A.A.R.T.E.R. Goal form for every idea. This leads to a strengthened awareness for improvement.

Discussion/Reflection Questions

- Why should we prioritize our goals? Why not just work on all of them at the same time?
- Do you have sticky notes in your possession? If not, please get some now so you have them whenever you think of a goal idea.
- Which of the seven prioritization suggestions do you think you will use the most? How about second most? Third most?

Teacher Tips

- Students will need to have around 6 goal ideas to complete this lesson. If they don't have that and you still want to complete this lesson, you can practice with six sample goals that you create together as a class.
- Please don't discourage your students from writing dozens of sticky notes with goal ideas! They can never have too many of these! This encourages constant awareness of the need to improve and instills a stronger growth mindset in your students. If you feel that a student is going too far with goal ideas, limit the number of goals that they work on ACTIVELY, at least until the goal setting process becomes second nature to them. As this process becomes more innate, they can begin to tackle more and more goals at once.
- Most of my fifth graders would work on two or three goals ACTIVELY at a time, while a handful of them would work on a few more. It depended on the complexity of each goal and the time needed to address it effectively. Students were also given 30 minutes EVERY week to work on their goals AND they were encouraged to address them independently throughout each day, so since students knew they could work on several goals at once, it wasn't too difficult for them to accomplish.
- Make sure that goal creation and achieving goals doesn't become a competition to see who can do the most, because the quality of work ends up diminishing.

Student Tasks 〉 Transfer Goals

Student Tasks	Transfer Goals
Students learn a method for prioritizing their goal ideas using sticky notes.	Students use sticky notes to jot down goal ideas as they think of them leading to a higher quantity (& quality) of goals achieved.
Students learn seven ways they can use to prioritize their goals.	Students work on goals that meet certain criteria before other goals, leading to more goals being met and meeting them in a timely manner.

Instructional Poster(s)

- This lesson has ONE Instructional Poster.
- The Instructional Poster for this lesson teaches the students a method for prioritizing their goals using sticky notes, but more importantly, it teaches students seven ways they can use to prioritize their goals (and invites additional ideas).
- Although writing goal ideas on sticky notes is not a required step in the goal setting process, it is a great way to learn how to prioritize several goals to address what needs to be addressed before those that can wait. You can encourage students to continue this method throughout the year, or you can use it as a scaffold until students become more effective at prioritizing their goals.

Student Handouts

- This lesson has TWO Student Handouts.
- DIRECTIONS: Whenever you create a goal, write it on a sticky note & place it here. Once you've created six goals, transfer them to the next page. As you become more experienced with Goal Setting, you may end up having 12 or 18 goals at a time, but don't stretch yourself too thin! Focus on what matters most!
- DIRECTIONS: Put your goals in order using any method suggested below or a method of your own. Once you're done, it's important to put a great deal of effort and time into working on the first goal. but don't ignore the other goals! All of them need to be addressed to some degree!
- The Student Handouts for this lesson ask students to write their goals onto sticky notes, place them randomly on the first Student Handout, and then prioritize them on the second Student Handout.

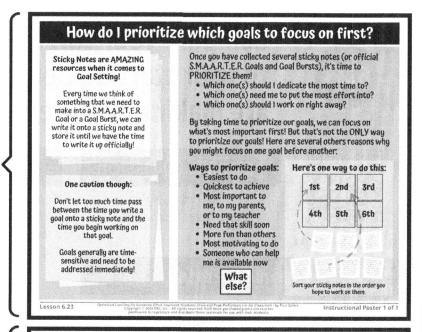

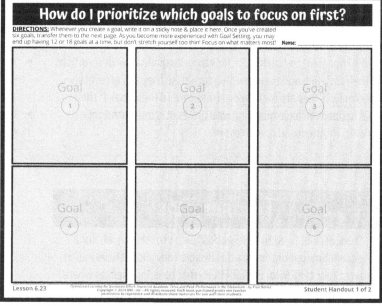

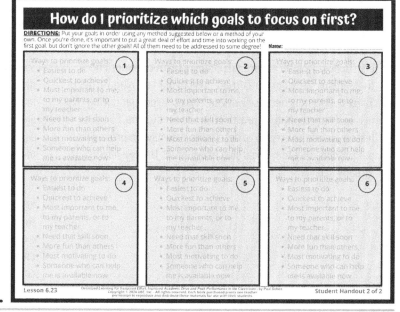

6.24

Compare your current level of achievement to your starting point to ensure that you are making sufficient progress

bit.ly/3SXYyAr

Essential Question

Am I improving?
What evidence supports that?

Big Idea

We can see how much we've improved by comparing where we are today to where we started. If we've improved a lot, it means our plan is working well. If we haven't improved much or at all, it means we might need to change our plan and try something different.

Lesson Overview

In this lesson, students learn how to determine if they are improving on their goal or not by looking at their baseline, their current level of achievement and the learning experiences that have led them to where they are today. Teachers are used to focusing on quantitative data, but most goals that students work on in school are qualitative, so it's important to teach them how to write qualitative descriptions of their baseline and their learning target, so they can accurately determine if they are making progress toward their goal. If their goal happens to have quantitative aspects, it is more straightforward for them and needs less practice.

Discussion/Reflection Questions

- Why should we take time to determine if we are making progress on our goal LONG BEFORE we determine that we've achieved it?
- What are some tips you can give others to help them write clear descriptions of their baseline, current level and learning target when numbers and data aren't involved?
- What will you do if you discover that your learning experiences have NOT led to improvement?

Teacher Tips

- Students will need to have worked on one of their goals for a decent amount of time for this lesson. They should have had at least four LEARNING EXPERIENCES that have led them to where they are today on their efforts to achieve this goal.
- The second Student Handout can be used multiple times to help students describe how various learning experiences have helped them grow and improve.
- Students might be confused by the second half of the Instructional Poster regarding planning learning experiences that help us get from our current level to our Learning Target or Success Criterion, because we aren't focusing on that during this lesson. That step will be practiced in the next lesson. For this lesson, we are just trying to determine if we have improved from our baseline due to the learning experiences that we have already had.

Student Tasks 〉 Transfer Goals

Students learn to describe their baseline, learning experiences and current level of achievement in measurable ways.	Students don't shy away from qualitative goals and address important needs that might otherwise be avoided when quantitative goals are prioritized.
Students determine if their learning experiences have led to enough improvement to continue with their plan.	Students are aware of their progress toward goals and understand when it's time to revise a goal or abandon it.

Instructional Poster(s)

- This lesson has ONE Instructional Poster.
- The Instructional Poster for this lesson walks students through the process of determining growth toward achieving a goal. Starting with their baseline that is generally identified at the beginning of a Learning Cycle, students look at the learning experiences that have led them to their CURRENT level of understanding. Students describe each LEARNING EXPERIENCE that they took part in to get them to where they are today. Spend extra time explaining these. (For now, students ignore the Learning Experiences that are still needed in order to help them reach their Learning Target, but it should be mentioned that there is still learning that needs to happen to get there.)
- FYI: Not all Baseline data is quantitative! Look at the examples on the Student Handout for some qualitative examples.

Student Handouts

- This lesson has TWO Student Handouts.
- DIRECTIONS: Read each example below. On the next page, choose one goal that you've worked on and improved. Write down where you started with that goal in the box for the BASELINE hexagon. Write where you are today in the box for the CURRENT LEVEL star. Write the LEARNING EXPERIENCES you completed in the boxes for each banner.
- The first Student Handout contains five examples showing the process of determining growth from a baseline to the Current Level. (Remind students that the next steps are determining what learning experiences are NEEDED in order to reach your Learning Target or Success Criteria but this will be practiced in the next lesson).
- The second Student Handout provides students with an opportunity to describe their learning process for one goal that have already worked on a bit (or they can create a fictional example with your permission). Make sure they try to list four separate learning experiences in the boxes even though the examples on the first Student Handout summarize multiple experiences.

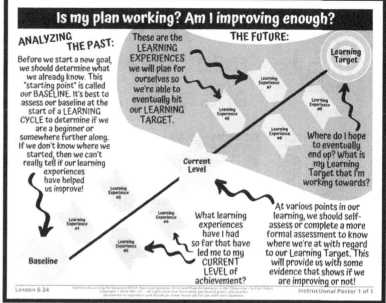

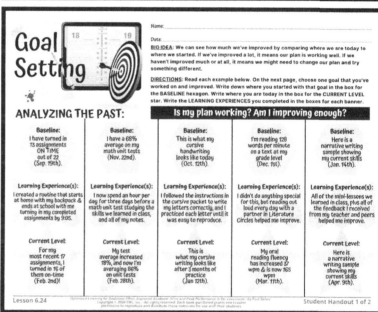

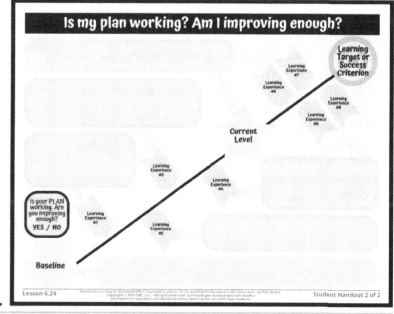

INTRODUCTION

PLANNING

METACOGNITION

SYNTHESIS

REFLECTION

SELF-ASSESSMENT

GOAL SETTING

FEEDBACK

bit.ly/3uI2VVY

Analyze your current level of achievement, clearly define your learning target, and make your next steps really count

Essential Question

What do I need to do in order to reach my target?

Big Idea

Determining our next steps in the learning process is an important part of becoming an independent learner. In order to do this, we need to understand our Current Level of achievement AND our Learning Target. Once we have that information, we can create a plan (or revise our old plan) for achieving our goal.

Lesson Overview

In this lesson, students learn how to determine their next steps in achieving a goal. This may be after a mid-point check-in to ensure that progress is being made, or this may be due to a need for revision of a goal due to a lack of progress. Regardless of the situation, students determine their next steps, aiming to reach their Learning Target. These steps could involve repeated practice of a single task to enhance skill proficiency or a combination of various Learning Experiences that pave the way to success. Ultimately, this lesson empowers students to map out a clear plan for achieving their specific goals.

Discussion/Reflection Questions

- Think about a goal you are currently working on. Reflect on your original plan for achieving that goal. Is it still effective, or does it need revision? Why? How do you know?
- Think about a goal you are currently working on where you feel the need to revise your plan. What are some specific next steps you can take to move closer to your learning target? How will these steps help you progress?
- Think about the resources and support available to you. How can you use these resources to help you take your next steps toward achieving your learning goal?

Teacher Tips

- The skills taught in this lesson serve two main purposes: (1) to act as a mid-point check-in for a goal that has taken awhile already, but is not yet met, and (2) for students who need to revise or rewrite their goal due to a lack of progress.
- This lesson is designed to be taught after students have dedicated time to working on at least one goal.
- Since everyone's goals require different Learning Experiences, specific tips cannot be taught within this lesson. The main reason this lesson has value, though, is because students need to be told to evaluate their progress on their goals, determine when plans need to be revised or replaced, and that goals don't just happen - they require planned learning experiences (that the students need to do themselves) and strong effort. This lesson and others helps them understand that it's their responsibility to make these decisions and that they are in charge of their learning journey.

Student Tasks 〉 Transfer Goals

Student Tasks	Transfer Goals
Students think about the effectiveness of their current plan for achieving a goal and decide if they should stay the course or revise.	Students constantly evaluate the effectiveness of their plans as they work on goals and change them whenever needed.
Students create a new and improved plan for getting themselves from their Current Level to their Learning Target.	Students create better plans as they learn what works and what doesn't while trying to achieve their goals.

Instructional Poster(s)

- This lesson has ONE Instructional Poster.
- The Instructional Poster for this lesson walks students through the process of determining their next steps toward hitting their Learning Target. Starting with their Current Level, students look at the remaining learning experiences that they need to plan in order to reach their Learning Target. Students describe each of these potential LEARNING EXPERIENCES in the order that they plan to complete them. Let students know that for some goals, they may need to plan in dozens of days of repeated practice of a single task to enhance skill proficiency (like with math facts or muscle memory), or plan a combination of various Learning Experiences that get them to their Learning Target (like improving writing with brainstorming sessions, revising time, peer editing, etc.).

Student Handouts

- This lesson has TWO Student Handouts.
- DIRECTIONS: Read each example below. On the next page, choose one goal that you'd like to work on. Write down where you are today in the box for the CURRENT LEVEL star. Write down where you hope to end up by your deadline in the box for the LEARNING TARGET. Finally, write down the LEARNING EXPERIENCES you plan to do in order to meet your LEARNING TARGET in the boxes for each banner.
- The first Student Handout is a series of five examples for students to see where a student notes their current level, the learning experiences they plan to complete, and the learning target that they hope to hit.
- The second Student Handout can be completed over and over. It helps students map out their plan for accomplishing their goal, taking them from their current level to their learning target. Each learning experience may be the same or different. Students may need to add more learning experiences or might use fewer. Either way, this is their plan for advancing from their current level to their learning target.

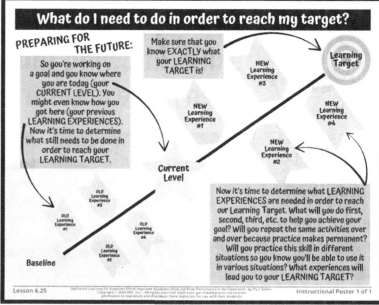

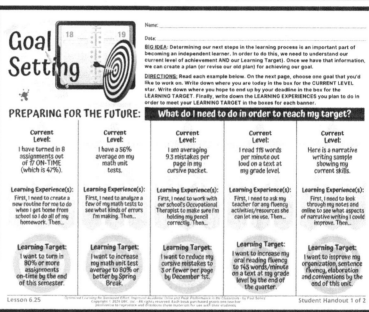

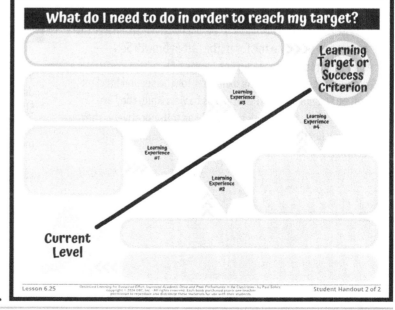

Sidebar tabs: INTRODUCTION · PLANNING · METACOGNITION · SYNTHESIS · REFLECTION · SELF-ASSESSMENT · GOAL SETTING · FEEDBACK

bit.ly/3RlboHB

Embrace working on less quantifiable skills, knowing those skills matter too, even if the measurement path is unique

Essential Question

How can I measure growth objectively and subjectively?

Big Idea

Measuring growth using objective (quantitative) data has been the way schools have preferred to determine growth and grades, but many of the goals that we set for ourselves don't work nicely within an objective system of measurement. Therefore, developing subjective (qualitative) measurement systems that track growth differently should get a lot of our attention during Goal-Setting.

Lesson Overview

In this lesson, students learn that both OBJECTIVELY and SUBJECTIVELY measured goals are accepted and encouraged, despite the fact that subjective goals don't have an easily measured system of growth. Since most skills that students want to improve are not easily quantifiable, students have historically avoided working on them in academic settings. But, these goals are extremely important and need to be worked on, even if it means being less accurate when measuring growth! Don't let the lack of accuracy deter your students from working on these important skills. Instead, encourage them to create their own systems of measurement and progress monitoring.

Discussion/Reflection Questions

- Why is it important to create an effective system of measuring for our SUBJECTIVELY measured goals?
- Why do you think the author of this program believes that students are likely to have more SUBJECTIVELY measured goals than OBJECTIVELY measured goals in school?
- Create a fake SUBJECTIVELY measured goal below. It can be for school or for home, but needs to be accurate and appropriate. You do NOT need to work on this goal!

Teacher Tips

- If students already have any goals that need to be measured SUBJECTIVELY, the second Student Handout for this lesson is designed to address those. If they don't, you may want to provide extra time for students to create a new S.M.A.A.R.T.E.R. Goal this is subjective, so they can go through the process of creating an effective system of measuring growth. If students are just beginning a new goal, they will not have an answer for the last two boxes on the form (the "After-Growth Self-Assessment" and "My plan going forward.")
- I would suggest leaving the exemplar for the second Student Handout displayed for the students to view while they are completing that page independently or collaboratively. They will likely need to see an example in order to complete it accurately.

Student Tasks 〉 Transfer Goals

Student Tasks	Transfer Goals
Students learn the difference between SUBJECTIVELY measured goals and OBJECTIVELY measured ones.	Students achieve goals that would have otherwise been off limits due to the fact that they are difficult to measure growth.
Students create a system of measuring growth for a SUBJECTIVELY measured goal of their own.	Students more accurately measure their growth toward SUBJECTIVELY measured goals due to practicing it and learning about its importance.

Instructional Poster(s)

- This lesson has THREE Instructional Posters.
- The first Instructional Poster for this lesson introduces the idea of Subjective and Objective Measurement by having students analyze examples of each WITHOUT knowing the purpose of the task. They are just asked to discover similarities and differences between each of the goals in the top section, then the bottom section. The most important part of the discussion is determining how the top four goals are different from the bottom four goals, and the answer is that the top goals are measured OBJECTIVELY and the bottom goals are measured SUBJECTIVELY.
- The second Instructional Poster is a Venn Diagram that describes the similarities and differences between OBJECTIVELY and SUBJECTIVELY measured goals. Notice that the facts align with both halves of the Venn Diagram, so you are encouraged to read them that way to the students.
- The third Instructional Poster is an exemplar for the second Student Handout.

Student Handouts

- This lesson has TWO Student Handouts.
- DIRECTIONS: Read each goal below and circle whether it is an example of an Objective or Subjective goal. Then, complete the self-assessment on the next page using a scoring system of your own creation for a Subjective goal that you have worked on.
- The first Student Handout asks students to read through each goal and determine if it is OBJECTIVELY measured or SUBJECTIVELY measured.
- The answers are as follows (from left to right, top to bottom): O, O, S, S, O, O
- It's in your best interest to go over these answers together as a class since knowing this information is what will ensure that students write goals that are measured with the best system possible and that goals that might otherwise have been passed on due to their difficult nature of measuring growth, are still addressed.
- The second Student Handout asks students to create their own SUBJECTIVE system of measurement for a goal of theirs. This can be used over and over.

INTRODUCTION
PLANNING
METACOGNITION
SYNTHESIS
REFLECTION
SELF-ASSESSMENT
GOAL SETTING
FEEDBACK

How can I measure growth objectively & subjectively?

What do you notice about each of these GOALS that past students have set for themselves, and the measurements they've used to determine their growth? In what ways are they similar and different?

In the past two weeks, I've turned in 14 out of 20 assignments on time. I want to improve that to at least 18 out of the next 20.	On my last three social studies tests, I have a 47% average. I want my next three tests to average 75% or above.	By the end of April, I want to improve my oral reading fluency from 112 words per minute to 145 words per minute or more.	Over the past two weeks, I've only participated in one class discussion. My goal is to participate in at least five class discussions in the next two weeks.

How about these? How are these similar and different? Most importantly, how are all four of these goals different from the four goals listed above?

I want my writing pieces to be organized into paragraphs better, so by December 12th, I want to make a significant improvement.	When I work with a partner, I usually accept whatever they say, even if I disagree. I want to be politely assertive the next three times I have the opportunity.	I have a tendency to overreact to my peers when they say something I don't agree with. I want to fix that by the end of the quarter.	The notes I take in class are terrible. I will research note-taking skills and implement those ideas within the next two weeks. My notes need to be better by then.

Lesson 6.26

Instructional Poster 1 of 3

Goal Setting

Name: _____

Date: _____

BIG IDEA: Measuring growth using objective (quantitative) data has been the way schools have preferred to determine growth and grades, but many of the goals that we set for ourselves don't work nicely within an objective system of measurement. Therefore, developing subjective (qualitative) measurement systems that track growth differently should get a lot of our attention during Goal-Setting.

DIRECTIONS: Read each goal below and circle whether it is an example of an Objective or Subjective goal. Then, complete the self-assessment on the next page using a scoring system of your own creation for a Subjective goal that you have worked on.

How can I measure growth objectively & subjectively?

I started at: A 63% average test score on my science tests.	**I started at:** Nine points out of 15 on my weekly vocabulary assessment.	**I started at:** A basic level of understanding the elements on the Periodic Table.
I am now at: A 65% average test score on my science tests.	**I am now at:** Fourteen points out of 15 on my weekly vocabulary assessment.	**I am now at:** An intermediate level of understanding the elements.
Therefore, I have made SOME growth, but not enough to consider my efforts successful, so I need to change my plan.	**Therefore,** I have made STRONG growth and should continue with my current plan for improvement or consider my goal accomplished.	**Therefore,** I made SOME growth. My evidence is that I can now identify 22 elements based on their abbreviations. I need to increase the intensity of my plan.
Objective or Subjective?	**Objective or Subjective?**	**Objective or Subjective?**
I started at: A 6 out of 10 on my personal rating system for paying attention when the teacher is talking.	**I started at:** F&P Reading Level H	**CHALLENGE QUESTION:**
I am now at: A 9 out of 10.	**I am now at:** F&P Reading Level M	**I started at:** Level A in swimming (my swim coach calls it "Apples").
Therefore, I made STRONG growth. My evidence is that I haven't missed any directions or had to ask what we're doing in weeks. I will continue my plan.	**Therefore,** I made STRONG growth. My evidence is that we are only expected to increase our reading level by a few letters each school year, and I've already increased it five levels and still have two months of school left!	**I am now at:** Level C in swimming (my swim coach calls it "Cherries").
		Therefore, I made SOME growth, and I think my plan has worked, so I will continue my plan until I get to Level E.
Objective or Subjective?	**Objective or Subjective?**	**Objective or Subjective?**

Lesson 6.26

Student Handout 1 of 2

How can I measure growth objectively & subjectively?

Success Criteria are the things you need to do correctly and at a high level in order to be successful on that skill, assignment or goal.	Baseline Self-Assessment:	After Growth Self-Assessment:

What do you want to accomplish? What is your Success Criteria? I want...

because...

Since this is a SUBJECTIVE skill, I created the following way to measure my improvement:

As of today, I believe that...

↓	←→	↑	↑↑↑
I might have gotten worse at this skill since the last time I self-assessed.	I don't believe I've improved at this skill since the last time I self-assessed.	I believe that I've improved this skill A LITTLE since last time I self-assessed.	I believe that I've improved this skill A LOT since the last time I self-assessed.

My plan going forward:

Lesson 6.26

Student Handout 2 of 2

bit.ly/3Rik4P5

Avoid common goal-setting pitfalls, ensuring your journey is paved with impactful achievements, not wasted time

Essential Question

What are some goal setting mistakes I should try to avoid?

Big Idea

The Goal Setting Process is an extremely valuable one, but can feel like a huge waste of time when done ineffectively. Avoid the most common mistakes and you should be able to reap the benefits.

Lesson Overview

In this lesson, students will engage in critical thinking by reflecting on and discussing potential mistakes they may encounter during the Goal Setting Process. By collectively brainstorming and utilizing the suggestions provided on the Instructional Poster, students will enhance their awareness of common pitfalls and develop strategies to prevent them. While making mistakes is a natural part of the learning process, being well-prepared for familiar pitfalls can empower students to better navigate unforeseen challenges.

Discussion/Reflection Questions

- Why is it important to consider some of the more common mistakes that people make while goal setting?
- Which mistake from the Student Handout or from your class discussion do you think will be toughest for you to avoid? How do you think you will overcome it?
- Which mistake from the Student Handout or from your class discussion do you think will be easiest for you to avoid? How do you think you can help others avoid it?

Teacher Tips

- If students have been goal setting for a while, asking them to share some goal setting mistakes they've made throughout the process not only provides great tips and ideas to the rest of the class but also improves students' willingness to be vulnerable and not afraid to look inexperienced or make mistakes. By openly discussing their past errors, students create a supportive and non-judgmental classroom environment that encourages learning from one another's experiences. This cultivates a growth mindset where students understand that making mistakes is a natural part of the learning process and helps them build resilience and confidence in their ability to set and achieve goals.
- In order to get the best use of the second Student Handout, I recommend having the students do something with their self-assessments. Maybe they could write one Goal Burst to address a potential mistake or you could have a class discussion where students share their thoughts about their answers.

Student Tasks ⟩ Transfer Goals

Student Tasks	Transfer Goals
Students discover several common mistakes people make during the Goal Setting Process.	Students have increased awareness of potential mistakes and are better equipped to do something about them.
Students assess themselves on all of the potential mistakes to discover which ones they may need to do something about.	Students pay deeper attention to the potential mistakes they think might trip them up, helping to avoid them.

Instructional Poster(s)

- This lesson has ONE Instructional Poster.
- The Instructional Poster for this lesson is a collection of "Goal Setting Mistakes" to avoid. You can start the lesson by teaching this poster like most lessons begin, OR you can ask the students to brainstorm potential Goal Setting Mistakes to avoid before they see these. (You may need to share a few to get them started.)
- Many of the "Goal Setting Mistakes" that are listed are based on the steps in the S.M.A.A.R.T.E.R. Goal Setting Process. Others have been from past students' experiences.
- If you do choose to read through the tips first, be sure to ask the "What else?" question so students have a chance to brainstorm some ideas too.

Student Handouts

- This lesson has TWO Student Handouts.
- DIRECTIONS: Add as many "Goal Setting mistakes to try to avoid" in the bubbles below. You can add your own or any that other students in class brainstormed. When you run out of new ideas, write in some that you need to focus on from the instructional poster. Then, on the next page, place a check mark in the each of the correct columns for you.
- The first Student Handout asks students to write some "Goal Setting Mistakes to Avoid" for themselves. You can choose to have them brainstorm their own, have them use some from the Instructional Poster , or a combination of both.
- The second Student Handout asks students to assess themselves on each "Goal Setting Mistake to Avoid." They can create a goal for any of the mistakes they know they are bad at, if they'd like!

What are some goal setting mistakes I should try to avoid?

Goal Setting Mistake	This one has a chance to give me some trouble!	I'm not too worried about this one	Goal Setting Mistake	This one has a chance to give me some trouble!	I'm not too worried about this one
Avoiding subjectively measured goals since they're harder to measure			Trying to do it all alone - make sure you include helpful peers and adults on your journey		
Not having a plan for achieving your goal (or having a weak plan)			Not asking for help when you aren't sure how to achieve your goal		
Setting goals that aren't clear or specific			Not using the correct resources to help you meet your goal		
Not having a deadline or missing your deadline			Not giving Goal Setting enough of your time and attention		
Making your goal too easy or too hard to achieve			Getting frustrated when you don't make strong progress or even decline		
Not breaking down your goal into manageable chunks			Not taking Goal Setting seriously, or not believing in its value		
Not keeping track of potential goal ideas as they come up			Choosing goals that aren't meaningful to you (or important)		

bit.ly/3T4qvGU

Embrace obstacles & setbacks as integral parts of your adventure, as they build resilience with every hurdle you overcome

Essential Question

How much time might I need to achieve my goal?

Lesson Overview

In this lesson, students consider how long it might take them to achieve their goal, and they discover the importance of being prepared for unexpected challenges along the way. It's rare for our journey from Point A to Point B to be a straight line. Instead, it often includes unexpected twists and turns caused by obstacles and setbacks that we couldn't have predicted. As a result, students learn to allocate extra time for achieving their goals, understanding that it may take longer than initially anticipated. Rather than feeling frustrated, embarrassed, or disappointed, they learn that encountering bumps on the road is a normal part of the process, and everyone faces similar challenges.

Teacher Tips

- I suggest having a class discussion about how much time students think it may take them to achieve different goals. For instance, Student A wants to increase their reading fluency from 160 words per minute to 200 words per minute using fluency strategies they found online. They might estimate it will take 15 minutes of practice each day for two weeks, while others may think it could require twice as much time. The actual answers matter less than the discussion itself, as it prompts students to consider HOW they will improve their goals, HOW OFTEN they should work on them, and HOW LONG they might need to dedicate to each goal. (These are addressed in the first Student Handout.) Accurately estimating time is an important executive function skill that is often overlooked in school and at home.

Big Idea

Working on our goals is like going on an adventure with lots of surprises! The path we take is not always a straight line from Point A to Point B. Sometimes, things can get a bit tricky. But when we learn to expect challenges and build in some extra time to accomplish our goals, we handle each setback calmly and meet our goals on time.

Discussion / Reflection Questions

- Can you think of a time when you faced challenges while trying to get better at something? How did you handle those challenges?
- Have you ever felt like giving up when things got difficult while learning a new skill? What helped you keep going?
- Tell me about a time when you struggled to improve your skills. How did you feel when you finally succeeded?

Student Tasks 〉 Transfer Goals

Student Tasks	Transfer Goals
Students consider how obstacles that may come up while working on a goal can cause them to miss deadlines.	Students plan in extra time to complete their goals, allowing for setbacks along the way.
Students estimate the time it will take them to achieve their goals.	Students' improved time management skills enable them to make more precise estimates for both their goals and other tasks.

Instructional Poster(s)

- This lesson has ONE Instructional Poster.
- The Instructional Poster for this lesson tries to show students that our goals aren't usually accomplished by following a straight line from our Baseline to our Learning Target. There are usually obstacles, setbacks and bumps in the road that slow us down and potentially prevent us from being successful.
- The poster takes students on a journey from Point A to Point B, but the path there meanders along the way and ends up taking a lot longer than expected to achieve their goal. This simulates the reality of most journeys to a final destination. It can't easily be prevented, so instead of letting it get us frustrated and feel like we failed, let's prepare for obstacles and tackle them head on!

Student Handouts

- This lesson has THREE Student Handouts.
- DIRECTIONS: Consider the questions on the left side of this page (you don't need to write any of your answers). Then, choose a new goal that you'd like to complete. Use that goal to complete the organizer below. Then, complete the next page.
- DIRECTIONS: Think of a time when you were trying to do something, but obstacles kept getting in your way. It doesn't have to be goal-related - any task that you were trying to complete but you had at least four setbacks or obstacles that slowed your progress.
- The first Student Handout poses three questions that the students should consider before continuing on with the lesson. The rest of the page is a graphic organizer that should be used to help them estimate the time it should take them to achieve a new goal of theirs.
- The second Student Handout asks students to tell a story through a graphic organizer about a time when they tried to accomplish something, but obstacles kept getting in the way. But ultimately, they were able to accomplish their task. If students can't think of a real story, consider letting them make something up.
- The third Student Handout is an exemplar.

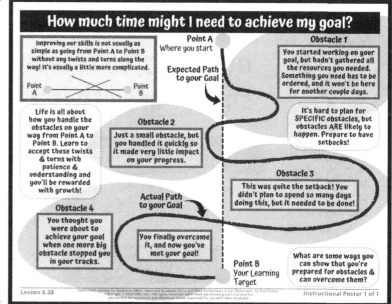

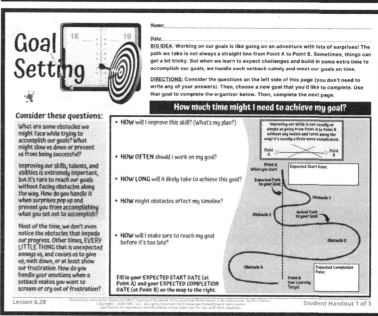

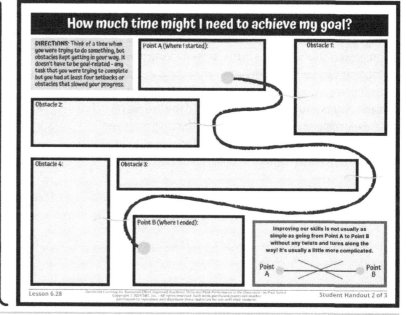

bit.ly/3sTJPfg

Progress can look different for new and old skills, so celebrate every step, big or small - growth is a journey, not a race

Essential Question

What impact do new and old skills have on my growth?

Big Idea

Growth is often faster with new skills since there is a lot of room for improvement. Growth in older, more secure skills can be slower since there is less room for improvement. Therefore, we should not get discouraged when progress is slower in our older, more secure skills. If you keep practicing regularly, even small improvements can add up to big things in the long run. Embrace each journey, stay motivated, and celebrate every little step of progress. Every bit of improvement counts and can make a real difference!

Lesson Overview

In this lesson, students explore the concept of growth in skills, specifically focusing on the differences between new and already established skills. They discover that growth for new skills may start slowly as they gain background knowledge, but eventually speeds up as they tackle the basics. On the other hand, students who aim to improve already strong skills may not experience as much noticeable growth because they've already learned the fundamentals and are now tackling more complex aspects. They recognize that there's less room for growth compared to beginners. As a whole class, students analyze line graphs to discover these concepts and engage in discussions about how new and old skills impact individual growth.

Discussion/Reflection Questions

- Can you think of a new skill you recently learned? Was it a bit slow at first as you gained background knowledge and then fast afterwards as you learned all the basics?
- Reflect on a skill that you've been practicing for a long time. Have you noticed that progress is slower now compared to when you first started? Why do you think this is?
- How do you feel when progress is slower in skills you already know well? Do you ever get discouraged?

Teacher Tips

- The three Instructional Posters for this lesson will take longer to work through than most lessons. You can either allow for additional time to get to everything, or you can use the Answer Keys to speed things along. Answer Keys (or exemplars) are also included for the Student Handouts.
- Although this is not a core lesson, its benefits are significant. . By engaging in this lesson, students who often feel frustrated when progress is slow will gain a better understanding of why that happens. Similarly, students who tend to compare themselves to their peers and become upset by their slower progress will also gain insights into the reasons behind it. If you believe your class already comprehends the importance of setting goals and monitoring progress, and they are comfortable with slower progress, you may consider skipping this lesson.

Student Tasks ⟩ Transfer Goals

Student Tasks	Transfer Goals
Students explore how new skills initially progress slowly while acquiring background knowledge, but then experience rapid growth as the basics are mastered.	Students know to expect this pattern of growth for new skills and understand that acquiring background knowledge takes extra time.
Students explore how older, more secure skills experience slower and less overall growth due to having less room for improvement.	Students know to expect this pattern of growth for older, more secure skills and understand that growth may be limited and slow.

Instructional Poster(s)

- This lesson has FIVE Instructional Posters.
- The first three Instructional Posters for this lesson take students through several line plots that show growth (or lack of growth) on a goal that students have set for themselves. To keep things consistent, the goal focuses on improving an assessment that they take each week that always has ten questions. Please make sure you let your students know that goals do NOT have to be assessed with a test like this - it is just an example!
- The first Instructional Poster focuses on three students who are beginners at the skill (starting with a Baseline of zero correct). The second poster has three students who are experienced, but not experts. The third poster compares all six students to each other. There are a LOT of questions that go with each poster!
- Instructional Posters 4-5 are an Answer Key for the teacher - you don't likely need to display these for the students - they are for your own reference.

Student Handouts

- This lesson has FOUR Student Handouts.
- DIRECTIONS: Start by choosing a timeframe to focus on (the past week, month, year or some other timeframe. Write that into the box to the right. Then, choose three skills that you've just begun to learn about within that timeframe, and three skills that you feel that you've strengthened during that timeframe to put into the circles associated with TALL TREES and SEEDLINGS.
- The first Student Handout is for students to brainstorm three beginning skills and three skills that they feel they are strong in.
- DIRECTIONS: Complete the handout by circling the correct answers and writing your answers in each box.
- The second Student Handout helps students synthesize what they learned in this lesson. If they are struggling with the concepts in this lesson, you can complete this together as a class.
- The remaining Student Handouts are exemplars.

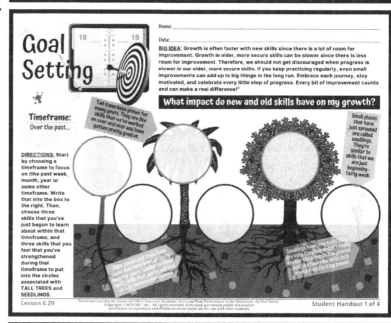

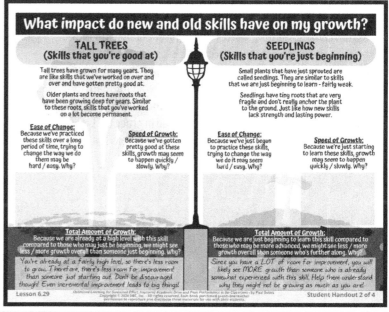

bit.ly/3GolYaF

Clearly define the skills and abilities needed to "Level up" in your chosen area, giving you challenges to try to tackle

Essential Question

How can I "Level Up"?

Big Idea

We don't want our growth to be too subjective, so it's a good idea to identify what someone needs to be able to do in order to "Level Up" and demonstrate growth. Although it can be easy to distinguish between a beginner and an expert, it can be harder to distinguish between the levels that lie in between. Identifying those differences can help focus your efforts and recognize your improving abilities.

Lesson Overview

In this lesson, students explore the connection between video games and goal setting, recognizing that both involve advancing levels to achieve success. Similar to video game designers determining tasks for players to progress from level to level, students need to identify the abilities required to move to the next level of the skill they are working on improving through the goal setting process. The practice that students get from this lesson will help them "chunk" their goals into more manageable pieces in order to accomplish complex goals that may have otherwise been overwhelming, increasing their chances of success.

Discussion/Reflection Questions

- Why do you think video games use levels to break down big challenges like the ones you might face at the highest level? How does this help you in your learning and enjoyment of the game?
- How does it feel when you accomplish a small milestone or level of achievement while learning a new skill? Why is it important to celebrate these small successes?
- Can you think of a time when you faced a difficult challenge while learning a new skill? How did you break it down into smaller steps to make it more manageable?

Teacher Tips

- Remind students that "Expert" does not mean that growth is complete. A ten-year old who is an expert at soccer can't necessarily beat an adult like David Beckham at soccer. Even experts continue to improve their skills. (Learning doesn't have a ceiling - we can always improve!)
- In order to increase the motivation of your students who don't always connect well with academic or sports examples in these lessons, you may want to have a quick discussion about some current video games that use levels to advance through the game. Remind them to discuss games that are appropriate for their age and appropriate for school. Have them describe some examples of what needs to be accomplished in order to "Level Up" in each game. See if they can draw an connections between the video game and a goal of theirs.

Student Tasks ⟩ Transfer Goals

Student Tasks	Transfer Goals
Students brainstorm things that have levels to see that just like floors in a building represent different heights, levels of a skill represent increasing ability.	Students understand that skills develop progressively and require incremental steps to achieve higher levels of proficiency.
Students break down the abilities one would need to become an "expert" at a specific skill of theirs into five levels.	Students are able to "chunk" a complex goal into five manageable levels that ultimately help them become an expert.

INTRODUCTION

PLANNING

METACOGNITION

SYNTHESIS

REFLECTION

SELF-ASSESSMENT

GOAL SETTING

FEEDBACK

Instructional Poster(s)

- This lesson has TWO Instructional Posters.
- The first Instructional Poster for this lesson connects the big ideas from this lesson and the previous lesson by showing how growth often occurs for a new skill.
- The second Instructional Poster for this lesson breaks down the skill of "Actively participating while working with others" into five levels. It shows students how they can do the same for a skill of their own on the second Student Handout. Point out how each level builds on the prior level(s), so the skills are cumulative (e.g. you can't jump from Level 2 to Level 4 without acquiring the skills of Level 3).

Student Handouts

- This lesson has THREE Student Handouts.
- DIRECTIONS: Answer the questions below with as many bulleted items as you can think of (some examples have been provided). Then, complete the next page.
- The first Student Handout asks students to brainstorm things that have levels (like wedding cakes), things that have levels AND each level represents improvement (like the belts in martial arts), skills they are good at, and skills they would like to improve.
- DIRECTIONS: Everyone is an EXPERT at something. What are you an expert at? What can experts do that others can't? How did you become an expert? Describe the abilities someone would have as they improved over five levels from Novice to Expert.
- The second Student Handout asks students to describe the five levels of a skill they have mastered. Please remind students that each level builds on the prior level(s), so the skills are cumulative.
- The third Student Handout is an exemplar.

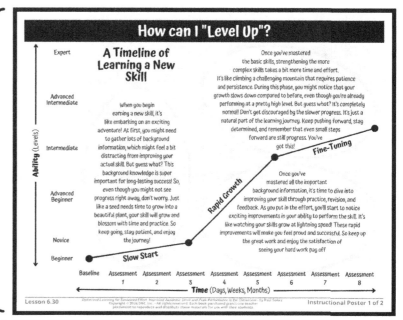

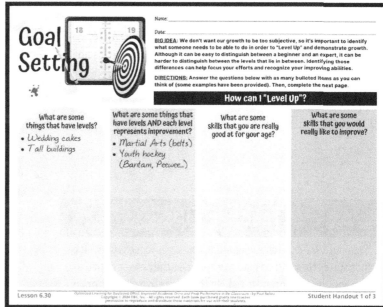

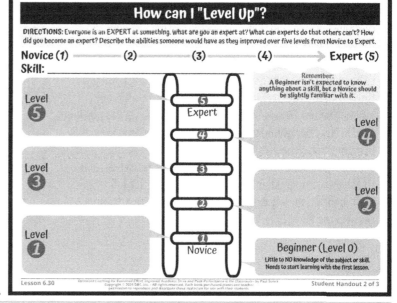

bit.ly/3GmOutm

Success Partners keep each other on track, motivate with encouragement, and offer each other support without judgment

Essential Question

What are Success Partners?

Lesson Overview

In this lesson, students learn about "Success Partners." Success Partners are semi-permanent partners who mutually support each other through the goal setting and progress monitoring process. Partners are responsible for providing reminders, motivation, assistance, support, etc. If you as the teacher provide time for goal setting and progress monitoring during class, Success Partners sit together but work individually while also being there for their partner as it is needed.

Teacher Tips

- You might want to have your students sign a Success Contract that states they will be kind to whomever they are assigned as a partner, they will promise to help them improve on their goals, and they will ask for their partner's help doing the same. Some students in some classes will mistreat students who are lower on the social ladder or someone who they don't have a good relationship with, and that will ruin the system for them and possibly others in class.
- If you haven't already done so, teach your students to learn how to be mature enough to care about everyone in class, not just those they are friends with or know well. I use a classroom meeting called, "Marble Theory," where I try to level the playing field in class by helping everyone see each other as equals. They learn how to ask each other for help, even if historically, someone has done more poorly in class than themselves, and they begin to understand that most of what we think of as intelligence is merely exposure, effort, and practice. (from: Learn Like a PIRATE)

Big Idea

While some of us prefer working independently, many find value in having companions on our journey. Improving multiple goals within a short period of time can feel overwhelming, but with the support of a Success Partner, it becomes more achievable. A Success Partner is someone who reminds you of your goals, practices with you, and helps you assess progress on your goals, making the process less daunting and more enjoyable.

Discussion/Reflection Questions

- Who is someone in class who would make a good Success Partner? What qualities do they have that likely make them a quality Success Parter?
- Imagine your Success Partner reminding you about a goal you want to achieve. How do you think it would feel? How might it help you stay focused and motivated?
- If you become Success Partners with someone in your class, how do you think you can practice and support each other in reaching your goals? What ideas do you have for assessing your progress on each of your goals together?

Student Tasks 〉 Transfer Goals

Student Tasks	Transfer Goals
Students learn about the responsibilities of a Success Partner.	Students know what they are expected to do for their partner and also know what they can go to their partner for,
Students brainstorm additional responsibilities of a Success Partner.	Students use their deep understanding of Success Partners to maximize their benefits in the goal setting process.

INTRODUCTION

PLANNING

METACOGNITION

SYNTHESIS

REFLECTION

SELF-ASSESSMENT

GOAL SETTING

FEEDBACK

Instructional Poster(s)

- This lesson has ONE Instructional Poster.
- The Instructional Poster for this lesson introduces the concept of "Success Partners." Success Partners are semi-permanent partners who mutually support each other through the goal setting process. Partners are responsible for providing reminders, motivation, assistance, support, etc. If you as the teacher provide time for goal setting and progress monitoring during class, Success Partners sit together but work individually while also being there for their partner as it is needed.
- There are six responsibilities listed on this Instructional Poster, and students will be asked to brainstorm six more on their Student Handouts.

Student Handouts

- This lesson has TWO Student Handouts.
- DIRECTIONS: Having a Success Partner is like having a personal coach. Yours will know everything about you & your goals, they'll know all of your plans for meeting each goal, and they'll be close by to give you advice on meeting those goals. You'll also be THEIR Success Partner! Read the bulleted information below and then fill out the piece of notebook paper.
- The first Student Handout asks students to think about potential matches for Success Partners using the information provided.
- DIRECTIONS: Below are six things Success Partners do. Come up with six more (draw pictures and use words to explain each).
- The Student Handout asks students to come up with six more responsibilities that Success Partners share. This will help them internalize their responsibilities and fulfill them.

What are Success Partners?

What are Success Partners?

Success Partners are two or more people who agree to help each other grow and improve without judgment or emotion.

They share RESPONSIBILITY for their partner's successes AND failures. Therefore, when their partner fails at a goal they've set, they've also failed.

Remember, failure is not a bad thing if you learn from it and find a way to grow! It's a Success Partner's job to turn a recent failure into a "Success Story."

The best way to do that is to work WITH your partner to find ways for them to improve AND your Success Partner needs to do the same for you!

Success Partners spend a lot of time talking with each other about their goals.	Success Partners discuss each other's goal plans and help them stay on schedule.	Success Partners check in with each other everyday and remind each other of their goals.
Success Partners help each other monitor progress, help each other practice, etc.	Success Partners collaborate with each other & benefit from each others' strengths.	Success Partners make sure that their partner is successful in meeting goals.

Lesson 6.31 — Optimized Learning for Sustained Effort: Improved Academic Drive and Peak Performance in the Classroom - by Paul Solarz — Instructional Poster 1 of 1

 Goal Setting

Name: _____

Date: _____

BIG IDEA: While some of us prefer working independently, many find value in having companions on our journey. Improving multiple goals within a short period of time can feel overwhelming, but with the support of a Success Partner, it becomes more achievable. A Success Partner is someone who reminds you of your goals, practices with you, and helps you assess progress on your goals, making the process less daunting and more enjoyable.

DIRECTIONS: Having a Success Partner is like having a personal coach. Yours will know everything about you & your goals, they'll know all of your plans for meeting each goal, and they'll be close by to give you advice on meeting those goals. You'll also be THEIR Success Partner! Read the bulleted information below and then fill out the piece of notebook paper.

I think that the following students in our class would make excellent Success Partner choices for me:

What are Success Partners?

Give your teacher valuable input on some strong Success Partners

- Choosing a quality Success Partner for each student in a classroom can be challenging for a teacher. Letting students choose their own partners can also present challenges.
- Therefore, your teacher would like to get your input, but they will be responsible for making the final decision, because they want to set you up for success. You need to graciously accept the Success Partner you are given because a lot of thought will have gone into the decision.

Considerations for YOU:
- You DO want to suggest people who are your friends, because you are more likely to WANT to check in with each other on a daily basis, BUT you don't want to suggest friends who might be more of a distraction than a help. Think carefully!

I understand that I might not get any of my choices above, but thanks for letting me give my input!

Lesson 6.31 — Optimized Learning for Sustained Effort: Improved Academic Drive and Peak Performance in the Classroom - by Paul Solarz — Student Handout 1 of 2

What are Success Partners?

DIRECTIONS: Having a Success Partner is like having a personal coach. Yours will know everything about you & your goals, they'll know all of your plans for meeting each goal, and they'll be close by to give you advice on meeting those goals. You'll also be THEIR Success Partner! Below are six things Success Partners do. Come up with six more (draw pictures and use words to explain each).

Success Partners spend a lot of time talking with each other about their goals.	Success Partners discuss each other's goal plans and help them stay on schedule.	Success Partners check in with each other everyday and remind each other of their goals.	Success Partners help each other monitor progress, help each other practice, etc.	Success Partners collaborate with each other & benefit from each others' strengths.	Success Partners make sure that their partner is successful in meeting goals.
7	8	9	10	11	12

Lesson 6.31 — Optimized Learning for Sustained Effort: Improved Academic Drive and Peak Performance in the Classroom - by Paul Solarz — Student Handout 2 of 2

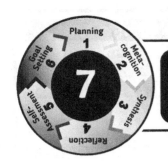

Feedback

Download the Slides for this Unit:

bit.ly/41Pd8g5

> "It takes humility to seek feedback.
> It takes wisdom to understand it, analyze it
> and appropriately act on it."
> — Stephen Covey

Feedback plays a vital role in student learning and growth in an Optimized Learning Classroom. It serves as a powerful tool that allows students to gain valuable insights into their work from diverse perspectives. Receiving feedback from their peers exposes students to different viewpoints and ways of thinking, which broadens their understanding of their own work. This exposure to varying perspectives helps students identify areas for improvement they may not have considered on their own.

In addition, feedback promotes self-reflection and self-assessment. When students receive feedback, they become more self-aware of their abilities and areas in which they need to grow. This self-awareness is crucial for personal growth and is also necessary for fostering a growth mindset, as students come to understand that having weaknesses is normal and that they can be improved through goal-setting and hard work.

Feedback fosters a collaborative and supportive learning environment. When students engage in the process of giving and receiving feedback, they actively participate in constructive discussions and share their knowledge and expertise with their peers. This collaborative exchange of ideas and perspectives not only strengthens their understanding of the subject matter but also promotes critical thinking skills. Students learn to articulate their thoughts and provide constructive criticism, while also learning to accept and incorporate feedback from others. This collaborative process builds a sense of community among students, creating a classroom of learners who help each other grow academically. The supportive learning environ-ment nurtures a culture of mutual respect and encourages students to take risks, learn from their mistakes, and embrace continuous improvement. Additionally, The iterative process of receiving and incorporating peer feedback enables students to continuously refine their work and strive for excellence.

Throughout the entire "Student-Led Self-Improvement Process," students are expected to actively seek feedback from others and provide feedback to others as a means of continuously improving their skills. Feedback is more than just determining if someone's work is "good enough." It involves a deliberate effort to pinpoint areas where peers can improve their performance and requires the feedback provider to give high-quality instruction to help them progress independently.

Feedback can take various forms, ranging from seeking clarification on directions to assisting peers in solving complex math problems. It often intertwines with offering support to others, meaning that providing feedback is often a multi-step process that doesn't end with identifying areas their peer can improve but continues through the teaching stage.

Feedback without support is often wasted. Let's consider an example that shows this: Student A provides feedback to Student B on their completed writing assignment by mentioning that Student B frequently switches verb tenses throughout their story, which can confuse readers. Student B appreciates the feedback but turns in the assignment anyway because they have no idea how to fix the verb tense issue in their story!

Feedback should not end after identifying a peer's weak areas! The feedback provider should now demonstrate to the author HOW to make those changes in their work. They don't have to do everything for them, but they should assist until the student grasps their next steps and is unlikely to repeat the same mistake in the future. Students of all ages can follow this process for skills they are competent in. Kindergarteners can teach their peers tasks appropriate for their level, while adults can guide their peers in tasks suitable for their own level. This feedback process simply needs to be taught, encouraged, reinforced, and praised. My fourth and fifth-grade students quickly grasped this concept, thanks to a few students taking the lead, and others following shortly after.

So, why incorporate so much peer-to-peer feedback? Over the past 20 years, I often referred to our classroom as "An Improvement-Focused Classroom" and jokingly stated that the only way we could all improve every day is if I cloned myself so I could work with every student with all of their struggles. When they finally processed what I was talking about, I would say, "But alas, science hasn't come along far enough to clone myself, so I guess I'm going to need all of YOUR help with this!"

I would proceed by setting expectations about providing feedback, emphasizing the importance of offering respectful and polite feedback while also seeking feedback from others. I would let them know that unlike their previous teachers who may have told them to "mind their own business" and "worry about yourself," our class would be different. I expected everyone to mind EVERYONE'S business and care about their own growth AND the growth of others! The important caveat being that we wouldn't use these powers to snitch on one another or get others in trouble. Instead, we would harness our abilities to help everyone improve in every possible skill area!

Occasionally, we had setbacks where students would engage in snitching, competing, or bragging, but a gentle reminder about maintaining positive friendships and using our "powers" of minding others' business for good, not evil was usually all anyone ever needed. Occasional whole-class reminders often did the trick to prevent setbacks. Luckily, almost every student was eager to make this approach work, perhaps due to its novelty or the strong relationships we built throughout the year. As a result, 99% of student-to-student interactions were positive, and the remaining 1% were usually easily handled.

A teacher can't do it all by themself. It's only natural to ask the students to help support everything that's going on; therefore, students should be empowered to help their peers grow and improve every day, all day (with only a few exceptions).

Imagine that you are observing the following classroom where the students are spread out, with assigned random partners working on an assignment that the teacher has given them: Students turn to nearby peers to ask questions that help them know exactly what's required of them, how to find the proper resources, etc. Some students finish early but understand the value of feedback, so they find nearby

partnerships who are also finished or close to it and ask them to provide some feedback on specific components of their work. The peer stops what they're doing to oblige, and moments later resumes the work they were doing prior. Meanwhile, the fast finisher now has something meaningful to try to improve in their work and is quickly refocused and actively learning.

Another student begins to struggle on their assignment, and instead of raising their hand for their teacher to support them, they see that you are working with a small group of students and know that it's important to ask several peers first. Since they were working collaboratively with their partner, they already know that they can't help with this, so they move on to another nearby student. That one provides the help they need, and the student is able to quickly resume their work.

A partnership in the corner appears off-task, but after a little eavesdropping, you discover that they are quite excitedly sharing their work with each other in the hopes that their partner can provide feedback to help them improve. Not all feedback is quiet! You get back to work with the small group you are working with at the center table. Students in your small group are so used to this that they don't bat an eye at the distraction because they are completely capable of keeping the learning going without needing the teacher.

You take a look at one of your students who often struggles to participate in group work and doesn't always use their time wisely. You wonder if they're letting their partner do all of the work. Surprisingly, you see them working collaboratively, each of them discovering that they have a great deal of skill they can teach each other to help them complete this assignment. A simple glance at their shared Google Doc on your laptop shows they're making excellent progress on their assignment.

These are the types of moments I experienced with my students repeatedly over the years. I often had to say to myself, "Assume the best, but verify." If I had students out of my line of vision, I physically got up and checked on them often. If I had students who weren't always successful when allowed to work without the teacher nearby, I made a rule that they always needed to be within my sights! But the only way these students were going to get better at these skills was by consistently giving them opportunities to succeed or fail. Even the failures were great opportunities to improve. I just needed to make time to discuss what they did wrong with them and help them see what they should have done instead. My students didn't like to disappoint me, so they tried their best to make improvements!

INTRODUCTION

PLANNING

METACOGNITION

SYNTHESIS

REFLECTION

SELF-ASSESSMENT

GOAL SETTING

FEEDBACK

Unit 7 - Feedback

43 Mini-Lessons

INTRODUCTION

PLANNING

METACOGNITION

SYNTHESIS

REFLECTION

SELF-ASSESSMENT

GOAL SETTING

FEEDBACK

Have you made changes to any slides?

If you've made changes to any of the slides from Optimized Learning and think that other educators might enjoy having access to them, please submit them here and they will be uploaded to the Google Drive so everyone can access them!

The QR Code and short link on the right will take you to a Google Form that will allow you to submit a link to a template that you create for your modified slide(s). The directions for creating a template are on the form and are very easy to do, so please don't think that this is outside your comfort zone!

If you have any notes for teachers (grade level each slide has been created for, reasons for making the change, etc.), please include that in the provided sections.

Thanks so much for making this a valuable tool for other educators!

bit.ly/492T23Y

Students with well-developed FEEDBACK MicroSkills...	Students with poorly-developed FEEDBACK MicroSkills...
Select specific portions of their work to ask for feedback on	Ask for feedback on the entire assignment, overwhelming the peer
Actively listen to feedback without becoming defensive	React defensively to feedback and resist accepting or considering it
Ask clarifying questions to ensure a clear understanding of the feedback	Fail to seek clarification and misunderstand the feedback received
Use feedback to identify areas for improvement and set goals	Disregard feedback and fail to set goals for improvement
Apply feedback to revise and improve their work	Neglect to make revisions based on feedback received
Express gratitude and appreciation for the feedback received	Disregard or dismiss the feedback without expressing appreciation
Analyze patterns and trends in feedback to identify areas of strength and weakness	Fail to identify patterns in feedback and miss opportunities for growth
Actively engage in dialogue with peers or teachers to clarify feedback	Avoid discussing feedback and miss opportunities for clarification
Apply feedback to future assignments or tasks	Fail to apply feedback to future work and repeat the same mistakes
Seek feedback early in the process to make timely adjustments	Delay seeking feedback and miss opportunities for timely adjustments
Use feedback to challenge themselves and strive for continuous improvement	Resist feedback and remain complacent with their current level of performance
Seek feedback from individuals with different perspectives and expertise	Limit feedback to a narrow group of individuals without diverse perspectives
Seek opportunities to provide constructive feedback to others	Avoid providing feedback to others or provide unhelpful feedback
Provide specific and actionable feedback to guide improvement	Offer vague or general feedback without clear suggestions for improvement
Offer constructive criticism in a respectful and supportive manner	Provide negative or harsh criticism without considering the impact on the recipient
Tailor their feedback to the needs and preferences of the recipient	Provide feedback without considering the individual needs or preferences of the recipient
Provide examples or specific evidence to support their feedback	Provide feedback without offering any examples or evidence to back it up
Offer guidance for improvement without taking over	Take over peers' work instead of guiding their learning
Return to feedback providers after making the suggested changes to see if there's anything else they can do	Assume that feedback ends after they are given feedback
Close their feedback loop by applying feedback suggestions to new situations	Leave their feedback loops open and don't transfer specific feedback to new situations

INTRODUCTION
PLANNING
METACOGNITION
SYNTHESIS
REFLECTION
SELF-ASSESSMENT
GOAL SETTING
FEEDBACK

341

bit.ly/46I2Xul

Evaluate FEEDBACK MicroSkills to take pride in relative strengths and to set personalized goals for areas of weakness

Essential Question

How strong am I at each of these FEEDBACK skills?

Big Idea

By evaluating our current level of achievement on the MicroSkills that will be taught in this unit, we gain a clearer understanding of our individual strengths and weaknesses. Additionally, by synthesizing each MicroSkill, we develop a stronger understanding of the MacroSkill that this unit focuses on, which is FEEDBACK.

Lesson Overview

In this lesson, students evaluate their perceived ability for each of the identified FEEDBACK skills. These skills have been chosen from the lessons that follow in this unit. Although students are choosing a somewhat arbitrary number from 1-10, the self-assessment process requires them to (1) understand what the skill means, (2) determine their perceived ability for the skill, and (3) sort each skill into areas of weakness or strength (or in-between) so that they help others improve at the skill (for scores 7-10) or make the skill into a goal that they try to achieve (for scores 1-4). If a student scores a 5 or 6, they are asked to reassess themselves after the unit to determine if they would benefit from making it a goal or not.

Discussion/Reflection Questions

- Which feedback skills did you feel you were strongest at? Provide some evidence to support your self-assessment.
- Which feedback skills did you feel you were weakest at? Explain why you feel that this is true.
- If you could set a goal to improve ONE of these skills, which one would you choose? Why did you choose that one? How do you plan to improve this skill? What will you do?

Teacher Tips

- On the Student Handouts, it tells students to "highlight all the numbers up through your score." The reason I didn't just have them circle the number is so they can see "how full" their grade band is if they choose a high number, and "how empty" their grade band is if they choose a low number. If you don't think it's too important for your students, feel free to let them just circle their number.
- When doing a self-assessment like this, I like to teach my students about the importance of being honest with themselves. I remind them that self-assessment in our classroom don't affect your grades or the way I see them. Self-assessments help us focus in on what matters to us, rather than focusing in on everything and not spending enough time on the skills that we need to improve most. No one is a 10 on all of these skills and no one is a 1 on all of them, but there's a good chance that each of us is a 10 and a 1 on at least one skill in this self-assessment!

Student Tasks 〉 Transfer Goals

Students assess themselves on various feedback skills using a scale from 1 to 10.	Students become more self-aware of their abilities and areas in which they need to grow.
Students are asked several feedback questions that require them to explain their self-assessments and to set a goal for one skill.	Students understand that having weaknesses is normal and that they should be improved through goal-setting.

Instructional Poster(s)

- This lesson has ONE Instructional Poster.
- A variation of this Instructional Poster is used with the first lesson of each unit. It shows students how to use the 1-10 scale for assessing their current level of ability with each skill. Numbers 1-4 mean that they know they need to improve at this skill (and maybe create a goal for the skill), and numbers 7-10 mean they believe that they are capable of helping others improve this skill. (4-5 means they will reassess at the end of the unit - which will be up to you or the student to remember to do. It's not a lesson.)
- Tell students that the real value in this activity is discovering their relative strengths and weaknesses, so giving yourself a 10 for each skill is wasting everyone's time, as is repeating any other number. Finding the variation in each skill is the key, so give yourself scores of 1, 2, and 3 and give scores of 8, 9, and 10 as well!

Student Handouts

- This lesson has FIVE Student Handouts.
- DIRECTIONS: Look at the Feedback MicroSkills in each box below and on the following page(s). Determine a rating from 1-10 for yourself on each, and then circle it. For your lowest MicroSkill(s), create a S.M.A.A.R.T.E.R. Goal to address each weakness.
- If you have not taught the lesson on Goal Bursts, let students know that they can just make the skill a personal goal to improve, but nothing needs to be written out (unless they want a reminder to actually do it). Obviously, the more seriously they take things, the more likely they'll improve!

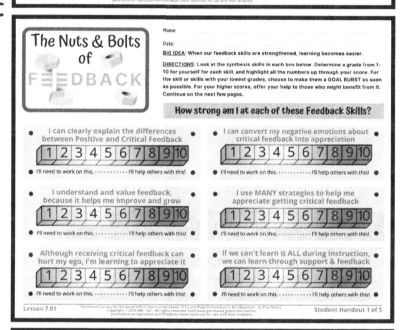

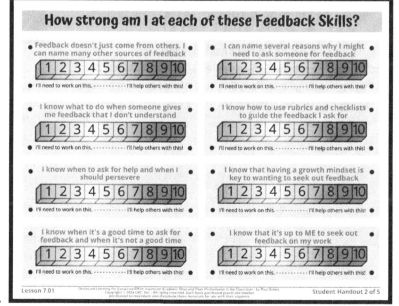

bit.ly/46PwVNb

Learn that critical feedback, while often challenging to receive, is essential for personal and academic growth

Essential Question

What is Positive Feedback?
What is Critical Feedback?

Big Idea

While Positive Feedback reinforces what we are doing and makes us feel good about our progress, Critical or Constructive Feedback actually helps us improve and grow. It tells us what we can be doing better, corrects misunderstandings, and refocuses us on what's most important. Although it often points out what is wrong, it should be welcomed, since its purpose is to help us improve.

Lesson Overview

In this lesson, students explore the distinction between Positive (Complimentary) Feedback and Critical (Constructive) Feedback. They discover that while both types are valuable, critical feedback specifically aims to assist the recipient in improving and growing. When providing critical feedback, it is advisable to begin with positive feedback to alleviate any potential tension and convey that the forthcoming critical feedback is not intended to be competitive or an attack on their abilities. Instead, it is intended to foster growth and development.

Discussion/Reflection Questions

- How does Positive (Complimentary) Feedback make you feel? Why is it important to receive positive feedback?
- What is the purpose of Critical (Constructive) Feedback? How does it differ from Positive Feedback?
- Why is it important to welcome and appreciate Critical Feedback, even though it may point out what's wrong?
- Can you think of a time when you received Critical or Constructive Feedback? How did it help you improve or grow?
- How can you use both Positive Feedback and Critical or Constructive Feedback to develop your skills and reach your goals? Provide an example.

Teacher Tips

- This lesson can be done quickly with older students. Just be sure to focus on the important notes such as starting with Positive Feedback before giving Critical Feedback whenever possible and that Critical Feedback should never be competitive or mean - it's entire purpose is to help their peers grow and improve.
- You may want to teach your students what a Frayer Model is since they will be used during this lesson. A Frayer Model typically contains four quadrants that are labeled: characteristics, definition, examples, and non-examples. But there are alternate versions that may include a drawn picture, facts, essential characteristics or non-essential characteristics.

Student Tasks 〉 Transfer Goals

Student Tasks	Transfer Goals
Students learn the difference between positive and critical feedback and the value of each.	Students value receiving feedback, regardless of its nature, as they understand it reflects the giver's intention to be helpful.
Students discover that providing positive feedback before sharing critical feedback can enhance the recipient's response to it.	Students are able to accept and deliver critical feedback without negative emotions from either party.

Instructional Poster(s)

- This lesson has FIVE Instructional Posters.
- The first Instructional Poster for this lesson introduces students to the two main types of feedback, both of which need to be used in the SLSI Process (often at the same time). Complimentary Feedback (or more simply, "Positive Feedback") is a great way to start a feedback session with a peer. It helps the person getting the feedback lower their guard and react less defensively if Constructive Feedback is coming next. Constructive Feedback (or "Critical Feedback") helps the person receiving the feedback improve their skills and grow in ability. It's purpose is to help them improve, not to make them feel badly.
- The final four posters are modified Frayer Models of Positive & Critical Feedback to help students further understand the distinctions between each. The four categories for each are (1) Your Definition, (2) Characteristics, (3) Examples, and (4) Non-Examples. You only need to show your students two posters (one Critical Feedback and one Positive Feedback). Pick which ones suit your needs best.

Student Handouts

- This lesson has TWO Student Handouts.
- DIRECTIONS: Using the information from the Instructional Posters, create a short conversation between two peers giving Positive Feedback and giving Critical Feedback. Also, write the purpose of each type of feedback in the boxes immediately to the right. On the next page, use the information from each Frayer Model to describe what's the same and what's different between Positive Feedback and Critical Feedback, and what they both share.
- The first Student Handout asks students to create a new conversation between peers that shows Positive Feedback and another that shows Critical Feedback.
- The second Student Handout asks students to identify the differences between Positive and Critical Feedback, as well as the similarities, and write them into a modified T-Chart, set up similar to a Venn Diagram. Separating lines have been provided in an attempt to help students see that when listing differences, they should identify components that are shared (e.g. hot and cold, night and day).

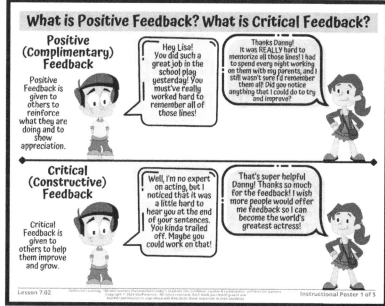

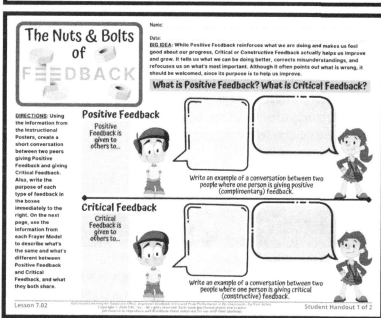

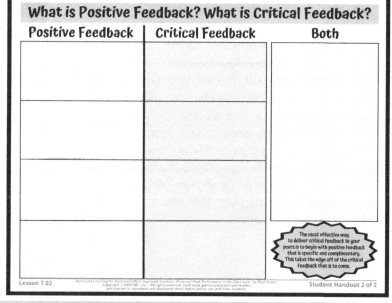

7.03

bit.ly/3ReDseu

Break through the initial hesitation of providing critical feedback and transform yourself into a catalyst for others' growth

Essential Question

Why should we take time to give and ask for feedback?

Big Idea

Feedback is important because it helps us grow and get better at what we do. When others give us feedback, it's like they're offering us their help and support. Feedback shows us what we're doing well and how we can improve. By listening to feedback and using it to learn and grow, we become better at the things we need to do!

Lesson Overview

In this lesson, students delve into the concept of providing critical feedback to their peers, even if it feels uncomfortable initially. They explore the incredible benefits that critical feedback brings for personal and academic growth and improvement. Throughout the process, students gradually discover that giving feedback becomes easier, more natural, and less awkward with practice. In addition, they engage in reflection, identifying three specific instances when they initially struggled with a skill but experienced improvement after receiving valuable feedback.

Discussion/Reflection Questions

- Think of a time when someone gave you feedback that helped you improve in a specific area? How did that feedback make you feel, and what actions did you take as a result?
- Reflect on a recent project or assignment you completed. How would feedback from others have helped improve it?
- Think about a skill you feel you need to improve. How will you seek feedback from others to improve your abilities in that area? Who will you ask? What will you say?
- How does it feel to help others? Isn't it worth it to get through the awkwardness and uncertainty of providing critical feedback since the payoff for both people is so valuable?

Teacher Tips

- Sharing examples from your own life of times where you struggled with something at first, but received feedback and ended up improving would be valuable for this lesson. Students need to see that you, the expert in the room, also receive and invite critical feedback in order to improve. It also shows your students that you consider yourself a work-in-progress like all lifelong learners, helping them improve their growth mindset and interest in improvement.
- The discussion about the awkwardness that students feel when giving their peers feedback is essential in this lesson. Even if they've given their peers feedback for many years, it can be awkward any time they are in a new classroom with new classmates. Be understanding of this and allow time for students to get to know their peers before expecting them to give each other critical feedback. This is another reason why daily, randomly assigned partnerships are vital to an improvement-focused classroom. Help them build strong relationships with each other!

Student Tasks 〉 Transfer Goals

Student Tasks	Transfer Goals
Students acknowledge the many benefits of feedback, and discuss why it's important to get past any discomfort from providing it to their peers.	Students ignore the discomfort that may come from providing their peers with critical feedback because they know its benefits.
Students reflect on three experiences where they see how critical feedback helped them improve a skill or concept.	Students have a solid understanding of the value of feedback, which leads them to giving and receiving feedback more often.

Instructional Poster(s)

- This lesson has TWO Instructional Posters.
- The first Instructional Poster show students a conversation between two students who are expressing their concerns about having to give their peers critical feedback. This is a normal concern for just about everyone who is asked to provide others with critical feedback! This provides an excellent context for sharing the benefits of all kinds of feedback, which lends credence to why it's worth the awkward feelings it may produce at first. Ensure them that those feelings will go away once they've accepted this as part of their learning process.
- The second Instructional Poster is a chart with eight benefits of feedback and it encourages further ideas from the students.

Student Handouts

- This lesson has TWO Student Handouts.
- DIRECTIONS: Read the chart below that shows what someone was like before they asked for help or used resources for feedback. Then, notice how feedback helped them improve their skills. Fill out the chart on the next page with three experiences of your own. Be sure to mix up the kinds of skills you share.
- The first Student Handout has two examples of what the students are being asked to do on the next page. It shows how a fictional student performed BEFORE feedback, and then how they performed AFTER feedback (showing improved skills).
- On the second Student Handout, students share three actual (or made up) experiences that shows how feedback helped them improve their skills. They need to include what the feedback addressed and be sure that the connection is made clear.

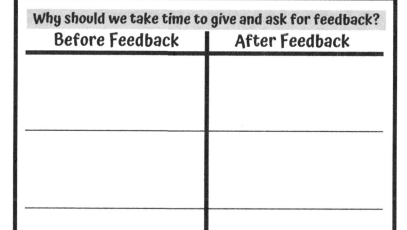

INTRODUCTION
PLANNING
METACOGNITION
SYNTHESIS
REFLECTION
SELF-ASSESSMENT
GOAL SETTING
FEEDBACK

bit.ly/46UD9eU

Embrace critical feedback as the gift it's intended to be and use it as a stepping stone for growth

Essential Question

How do you feel when people give you feedback?

Big Idea

It's not always easy to receive critical feedback. Sometimes, it can feel like someone is being mean or trying to show they're better than you. But you know what? People who give us feedback are actually trying to help us get better at what we do! Once we understand that they want us to improve, it becomes easier to accept their feedback and learn from it.

Lesson Overview

In this lesson, students discuss their current feelings about receiving critical feedback from others. Students learn reasons why they should begin to appreciate critical feedback as a valuable tool for growth. By embracing feedback, each student becomes a valuable contributor to the classroom. The more students embrace feedback, the sooner you as the teacher can gain additional teachers in the classroom! Each student possesses the ability to provide feedback that has the potential to help others improve, and they should be empowered to do so. As teachers, we can't do it all ourselves. By fostering a culture of feedback and collaboration, we create a supportive learning environment where everyone's contributions are valued.

Discussion/Reflection Questions

- How did learning about the importance of critical feedback change your thoughts on receiving feedback?
- Can you think of a time when someone's feedback felt mean or made you feel bad? How might understanding their intention behind the feedback have made a difference?
- What are some ways you can handle your initial feelings when you receive feedback that is meant to help you improve?

Teacher Tips

- Every student enters our classroom having had different experiences. Some of our students may struggle with perfectionism. Some may have received incorrect feedback from their peers in the past leading to mistakes. Some might have been teased for not being smart while receiving feedback from a peer. Every experience each student has had over time gets synthesized and results in their current perspective on feedback. It's our responsibility to create a learning environment where these issues no longer exist or are no longer a problem. How will you respond to students who accepted feedback which led to more mistakes on their work? How will you respond to a student who is teasing another student because they can't do what they're expected to do? How will you help a student overcome perfectionist tendencies so they can learn to appreciate critical feedback instead of dread it? These are all important considerations when creating an improvement-focused classroom where students help each other grow and improve!

Student Tasks 〉 Transfer Goals

Student Tasks	Transfer Goals
Students discuss how they feel when receiving critical feedback from others.	Students embrace critical feedback as a positive experience that is meant to help them improve.
Students discover the value of critical feedback and demonstrate that understanding through a Problem-Solution Cartoon.	Students understand the connection between critical feedback and improvement and seek out feedback to grow.

INTRODUCTION
PLANNING
METACOGNITION
SYNTHESIS
REFLECTION
SELF-ASSESSMENT
GOAL SETTING
FEEDBACK

Instructional Poster(s)

- This lesson has TWO Instructional Posters.
- The Instructional Poster for this lesson shows a typical conversation between two students. One student doesn't like getting critical feedback because he doesn't understand its purpose, value, and why others are giving him the feedback. The girl already sees those things and has learned to appreciate critical feedback that helps her grow.
- Discuss, as a class, how everyone feels about RECEIVING critical feedback from their teacher or their peers.
- The second Instructional Poster, walks you through two class discussions that are very important in order to get to the heart of why some students struggle to accept critical feedback. Discuss each question and try to tell students that you will be trying to create a classroom environment where everyone helps everyone grow and improve and feedback is appreciated.

Student Handouts

- This lesson has TWO Student Handouts.
- DIRECTIONS: Read the scenario below that shows a Problem-Solution Cartoon. Critical feedback SOLVED the PROBLEM of inaccurate target shooting. On the next page, create your own Problem-Solution Cartoon where feedback leads to improvement.
- The first Student Handout provides students with an example of a "Problem-Solution Cartoon" where someone is struggling in archery and someone offers to give them help.
- Students are asked to create their own Problem-Solution Cartoon showing how feedback can help them improve a skill on the second Student Handout. They begin by planning out the scenario by explaining the problem (can't hit the target with my arrows) and explaining the solution that feedback was able to address (I can now hit the target). Then, they draw the cartoon in a similar way as the example on the first Student Handout, complete with dialogue bubbles.

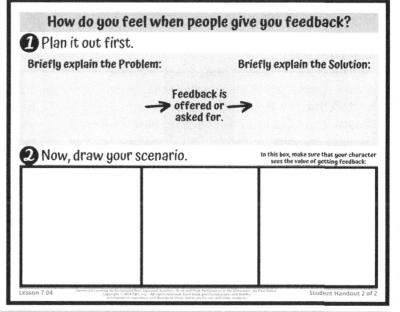

bit.ly/3t7JB4e

Embrace the emotional rollercoaster that comes with receiving critical feedback to become a growth-minded learner

Essential Question

How can I learn to APPRECIATE Critical Feedback?

Lesson Overview

In this lesson, students identify common emotions that we feel when we are given critical feedback (many of which are negative). Students also brainstorm positive emotions they WANT to feel when they receive critical feedback from someone who is trying to help them grow and improve. Using these emotions, students complete sentence starters that help them process that it is natural to feel these negative emotions, but that it is our responsibility to learn to see critical feedback in a positive light and react with appreciation for the time someone spent trying to help us grow.

Teacher Tips

- This lesson connects well with the prior lesson (Lesson 7.04) and also the next two lessons (Lessons 7.06 and 7.07), and all of them can easily be combined if you think your students only need 1-3 lessons to learn how to appreciate critical feedback from their peers and their teacher. I've chosen to separate them out because this is one of the toughest parts of feedback for most students and the additional lessons seem to help students develop this skill.
- For the first Student Handout, here are some additional emotions people may feel when they are getting critical feedback that are unhelpful: Defensiveness, Anger, Disappointment, Embarrassment, Discouragement, Resentment, Insecurity, Discomfort, Overwhelm, Guilt, and Sadness. Feel free to discuss some of the subtleties of each of these emotions with the class.
- Here are some helpful emotions we can train ourselves to feel when receiving critical feedback: Open-mindedness, Accountability, Humility, Adaptability, Resilience, Motivation, Self-compassion, and Patience.

Big Idea

Feedback is emotional. It's easy to become defensive when others correct you or give you advice, but know that feedback is someone's intention of helping you improve, grow, or learn new information. It's not a personal attack and shouldn't cause you to get upset. Try hard not to show any negative emotions that might come with being corrected or evaluated, and appreciate the message for what it's worth. It's your responsibility to respond to feedback calmly, logically and with appreciation.

Discussion/Reflection Questions

- Think about a time when you tried to help someone and they didn't show any appreciation. How did this make you feel? Do you see how this question connects with today's lesson?
- What can you do to remind yourself that feedback is meant to help you and not to make you feel bad? How can you keep a positive attitude when receiving corrections or evaluations?
- How can you develop a mindset that sees feedback as an opportunity to grow and learn? What are some ways you can value and appreciate the feedback you receive?

Student Tasks 〉 Transfer Goals

Student Tasks	Transfer Goals
Students identify common emotions that we feel when we are given critical feedback.	Students understand the value of expressing positive emotions to those who are trying to help us.
Students brainstorm positive emotions they WANT to feel when they receive critical feedback from someone who is trying to help them grow.	Students stay calm, reframe negative emotions, and maintain a positive mindset when receiving critical feedback.

Instructional Poster(s)

- This lesson has ONE Instructional Poster.
- The Instructional Poster for this lesson shows a short conversation between two students about the value of appreciating critical feedback from others. Use this conversation as a discussion starter to go BEYOND accepting critical feedback and instead, asking for it, welcoming it, and appreciating it. This lesson help students get to the point of appreciating feedback, while the next lesson shows them how to do so.

Student Handouts

- This lesson has TWO Student Handouts.
- DIRECTIONS: Read through the chart below. Add at least three more emotions to each side.
- DIRECTIONS: Complete the following sentence starters by choosing one of the "Unhelpful Emotions" from the previous page to create a scenario where you are given critical feedback and now feel that emotion.
- DIRECTIONS: Complete the following sentence starters by choosing one of the "Helpful Emotions" from the previous page to create a scenario where you are given critical feedback and now hope to feel that emotion.
- DIRECTIONS: Create two guidelines or tips for responding to feedback in a calm and appreciative manner. Try to create effective guidelines or tips that other students don't come up with - Think Creatively!
- This final section asks students to think creatively to come up with unique guidelines, tips or suggestions for responding to critical feedback in a calm & appreciative manner. Ideas:
  - Take a deep breath
  - Reflect before responding
  - Embrace a growth mindset
  - Remind yourself why they're giving you feedback

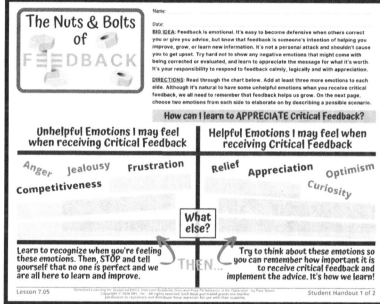

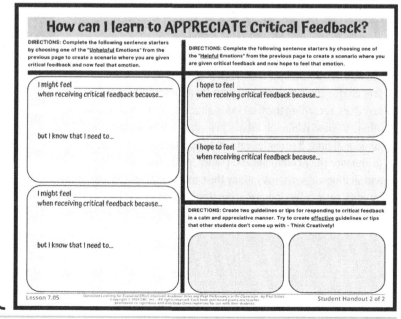

351

bit.ly/46LLLUW

Demonstrate sincere appreciation for critical feedback, recognizing the time and effort of those who are helping you grow

Essential Question

How should I show appreciation for Critical Feedback?

Lesson Overview

In this lesson, students explore the significance of responding to critical feedback in a calm and logical manner, rather than reacting defensively and emotionally. It's important to understand that impulsive responses often disregard the feedback giver's intention. They usually stem from emotions like embarrassment, frustration, or a desire for perfection. Regardless of how the feedback is delivered, if it is intended to help us grow, it's crucial for us to appreciate the time and effort the feedback giver has invested and reflect on how their feedback can contribute to our improvement.

Teacher Tips

- This lesson is similar to the prior two lessons and the next lesson. All of these lessons can be combined if your students already understand how to show appreciation for feedback, no matter the person giving it to them or the way it's delivered. I've found that this skill can be tough for students, so it's been broken down into very specific lessons that address it in several ways.
- If you're interested in exploring alternatives to paper and pencil activities, I would suggest encouraging students to mentally prepare for conversations and then engage in role-playing exercises, recording them on video and sharing them online for others to view. While this interactive approach might require additional time, it provides valuable opportunities for students to enhance their communication skills. In addition, role-playing and sharing videos helps solidify the concept in students' minds for long-term retention and understanding.

Big Idea

Feedback and feelings go hand in hand. Sometimes, when people correct us or give us advice, we might feel defensive or upset. But remember, feedback is meant to help us get better, learn, and grow. It's not about attacking us personally or making us feel bad. So, let's try our best not to let negative emotions take over when we are corrected or evaluated. Instead, let's appreciate the message and respond calmly, using our thinking skills and showing gratitude for the helpful feedback we receive.

Discussion/Reflection Questions

- Think about a time when you felt upset when receiving feedback.
  - How do you think those feelings affected your ability to learn from it?
  - How could staying calm and open-minded have helped you use the feedback more effectively?
  - What can you do next time to handle those feelings better?
- Why is it important to say thank you and appreciate feedback? How do you think showing gratitude can make feedback conversations better?

Student Tasks 〉 Transfer Goals

Student Tasks	Transfer Goals
Students explore the importance of responding to critical feedback without getting defensive or emotional.	Students use their skills of resilience and adaptability to embrace constructive criticism as an opportunity for personal growth.
Students understand the value of responding to critical feedback in a calm, logical manner while expressing appreciation for the feedback received.	Students transfer their ability to express appreciation for critical feedback to other contexts and increase their drive for personal improvement.

Instructional Poster(s)

- This lesson has ONE Instructional Poster.
- The Instructional Poster for this lesson focuses on how a student might respond to feedback they were given. One response is defensive and emotional. The goal for students is to avoid these kinds of responses. The other response is calm and logical. Students need to aim for this kind of response.
- If you have the time, you may find it beneficial to role play interactions like this one as a class. Rather than partner students up to do this, you might consider doing a whole class brainstorm of potential critical feedback students might receive from their peers, jotting the ideas down as they are mentioned. Then, ask for both types of potential responses and allow volunteers to perform the "right way" and the "wrong way" for each scenario in front of the class.!

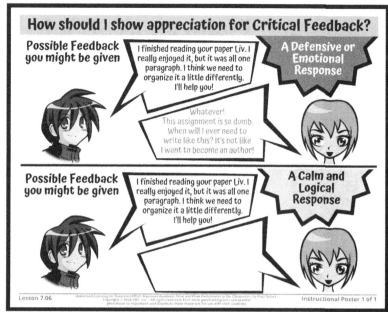

Student Handouts

- This lesson has TWO Student Handouts.
- DIRECTIONS: Complete the chart below according to the column headers (and just like the Instructional Poster). On the back side, come up with three of your own examples of feedback and examples of the right way and the wrong way to respond.
- The first Student Handout guides students through the process of filling out the chart using scaffolds that release responsibility to the students one step at a time.
- On the second Student Handout, students need to come up with:
  - possible feedback they might be given on a task or assignment,
  - a defensive/emotional response that shows how NOT to react, and
  - a calm/logical response that shows how they SHOULD act.

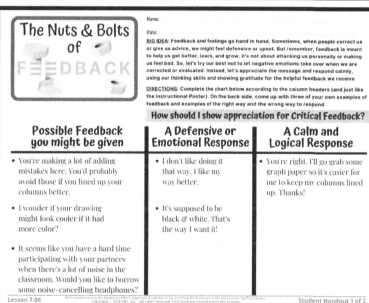

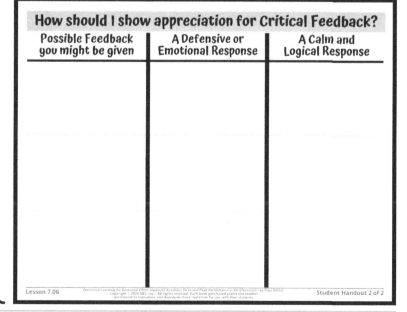

bit.ly/481HRZ5

Equip yourself with a toolbox of strategies to navigate the emotional landscape of feedback with gratitude

7.07

Essential Question

What if I still can't handle getting critical feedback?

Lesson Overview

In this lesson, students explore multiple strategies for effectively handling critical feedback in a positive manner while demonstrating appreciation for the feedback giver's time and effort. Through individual reflection, students evaluate each strategy's potential for success and articulate their reasoning for choosing to use or not use a particular strategy. As a culminating activity, students create a short, personalized plan to assist themselves or others when facing challenges in handling critical feedback.

Teacher Tips

- This lesson is similar to the prior three lessons. All of these lessons can be combined if your students already understand how to show appreciation for feedback, no matter the person giving it to them or the way it's delivered. I've found that this skill can be tough for students, so it's been broken down into very specific lessons that address it in several ways.
- Alternatively, consider teaching the three prior lessons as planned, and keep this lesson reserved for future use if and when it becomes relevant. This lesson specifically addresses a unique problem that arises occasionally among students, which may not be applicable every year.

Big Idea

Getting feedback can sometimes make us feel emotional. Depending on how we understand others' intentions and how mature we are, we might react strongly or let our feelings take over. That's why it's important to have a toolbox of strategies to handle feedback in a positive and appreciative way. Using the right strategy for each situation can help us respond well to feedback and make the most of it.

Discussion/Reflection Questions

- How do you think having a toolbox of strategies for handling critical feedback can benefit you?
- How does your age (maturity level) affect how you react to critical feedback? Do you think being older or more experienced can make a difference in how you handle feedback? Why?
- What steps can you take to become more mature in handling critical feedback in a positive manner? What can you do to become better at handling feedback in a positive way?

Student Tasks 〉 Transfer Goals

Student Tasks	Transfer Goals
Students learn several strategies for handling critical feedback in a positive way.	Students use one or more of these strategies the next time they discover they are struggling with critical feedback.
Students create a plan for handling critical feedback in a positive way in the future.	Students use this plan themselves or help others use it when struggling to receive critical feedback.

INTRODUCTION

PLANNING

METACOGNITION

SYNTHESIS

REFLECTION

SELF-ASSESSMENT

GOAL SETTING

FEEDBACK

Instructional Poster(s)

- This lesson has ONE Instructional Poster.
- The Instructional Poster walks the students through a few specific strategies for handling critical feedback in a positive way. There are examples of preparing yourself for critical feedback, identifying what you're feeling when listening to critical feedback, using Positive Self-Talk and Emergency Strategies students can use if nothing else seems to be working.
- Add some of your own strategies to the list and also consider seeing if the students have any ideas that have worked for them in the past.

What if I still can't handle getting critical feedback?

Use Positive Self-Talk
- "If I want to get better at this, I can do it!"
- "No one is calling me stupid. They're just sharing their opinion."
- "I've given others feedback before, and I didn't mean it a bad way."
- "I am good. I am safe. I've got this."
- "They're just trying to help me grow."
- "No one is perfect. Not even me!!!"

Emergency Strategies
- Count to ten before you say anything. Try to calm down and avoid responding emotionally.
- Identify your feelings and remind yourself why feedback helps us improve.
- Use Positive Self-Talk to remind yourself why you are receiving feedback, and that you need to respond calmly, logically, and with appreciation.
- If you need a few seconds to calm down, politely excuse yourself from the conversation and walk away. Use a strategy that works for you and come back to the conversation as quickly as you can.

Prepare Yourself for Feedback
- If you know you're about to receive some feedback, use some of the following strategies proactively (before you need them)!
- Whenever possible, ask for feedback a day or two after you create whatever it is that you're seeking feedback on. Time helps you become less emotional.
- You are new at receiving feedback and your peer is new at giving it. Cut each other some slack and focus on the information in the feedback, not the delivery. Avoid allowing your emotions to ruin a good thing!

Identify what you're feeling
- "I feel like I look dumb. I need to remember that feedback is emotional, but it's only meant to help me improve."
- "I'm annoyed that they think they know more than me, but I need to remember that our class is not a competition. We're all here to help each other."

Lesson 7.07 — Optimized Learning for Sustained Effort, Improved Academic Drive and Peak Performance in the Classroom - by Paul Solarz — Copyright © 2024 OEC, Inc. - All rights reserved. Each book purchased grants one teacher permission to reproduce and distribute these materials for use with their students — Instructional Poster 1 of 1

Student Handouts

- This lesson has TWO Student Handouts.
- DIRECTIONS: Place an X in one column for each strategy below. Try to put an X in each column at least once. Be ready to defned your answers. On the next page, make a plan to use some of them next time you feel like you won't handle accepting feedback well.
- The first Student Handout asks students to read each strategy for handling critical feedback and reflect on whether they think they will ever use it or not. They are asked to put an X in each column at least once AND they are asked to be ready to defend their answers.
- On the second Student Handout, students are asked to describe the reason they chose one strategy to use in the future and one strategy they never want to use in the future. Then they are asked to write a PLAN for them or someone else to follow the next time they need to show better appreciation for someone providing them with critical feedback.

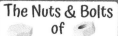

The Nuts & Bolts of FEEDBACK

Name:

Date:

BIG IDEA: Getting feedback can sometimes make us feel emotional. Depending on how we understand others' intentions and how mature we are, we might react strongly or let our feelings take over. That's why it's important to have a toolbox of strategies to handle feedback in a positive and appreciative way. Using the right strategy for each situation can help us respond well to feedback and make the most of it.

DIRECTIONS: Place an X in one column for each strategy below. Try to put an X in each column at least once. Be ready to defend your answers. On the next page, make a plan to use some of them next time you feel like you won't handle accepting feedback well.

What if I still can't handle getting critical feedback?

This is one that I will try for sure	I might try this, but I'm not sure	I don't think I'll try this one	Strategies for Handling Critical Feedback
			When receiving critical feedback, take a deep breath, think about trying to stay calm, and respond with appreciation.
			While listening to the feedback giver's words, write down the important parts of the feedback. Writing can pause your emotions.
			Remind yourself that feedback is meant to help you improve. It's not about being perfect, but about growing and learning.
			Ask sincere, non-defensive questions to understand the feedback better. It shows that you care, want to learn more & calms you down.
			Instead of focusing on the criticism (the past), think about ways to improve what you're doing (the future).
			Know that the feedback is about your work or your actions, not about who you are as a person. Don't let it feel like a personal attack.
			Remind yourself that nobody is perfect. Embrace feedback as a chance to learn and become the best version of yourself.
			Counting slowly from one to ten can give you a moment to collect your thoughts and regain composure before responding.

Lesson 7.07 — Optimized Learning for Sustained Effort, Improved Academic Drive and Peak Performance in the Classroom - by Paul Solarz — Copyright © 2024 OEC, Inc. - All rights reserved. Each book purchased grants one teacher permission to reproduce and distribute these materials for use with their students — Student Handout 1 of 2

What if I still can't handle getting critical feedback?

Describe ONE strategy from the previous page that you plan to try the next time you're not handling critical feedback well. Why did you choose that one and why do you think it will be effective for you?

Describe ONE strategy from the previous page that you DON'T plan to use in the future. Why did you choose that one and why don't you think it will be effective for you?

Write a PLAN for you or someone else to follow the next time they need to show better appreciation for someone providing them with critical feedback.

Lesson 7.07 — Optimized Learning for Sustained Effort, Improved Academic Drive and Peak Performance in the Classroom - by Paul Solarz — Copyright © 2024 OEC, Inc. - All rights reserved. Each book purchased grants one teacher permission to reproduce and distribute these materials for use with their students — Student Handout 2 of 2

bit.ly/3t9NZzF

7.08

Venture beyond your usual sources and discover a universe of feedback, embracing insights from every dimension of life

Essential Question

What are some OTHER sources of feedback?

Lesson Overview

In this lesson, students explore sources of feedback that they might never have considered. The obvious sources of feedback include their teachers, parents and peers, but they might not have thought about how checklists, rubrics, grades and even self-assessments can be valuable sources of feedback. Digging a little deeper, students explore how artificial intelligence, the internet, and websites like YouTube can provide them with amazing feedback. Finally, students explore more "outside the box" sources of feedback like how a mirror gives feedback on facial expressions or how a baby gives feedback on what it needs at that moment. The sky's the limit for students brainstorming creative sources of feedback!

Teacher Tips

- This lesson takes less time to complete than most.
- Here are 30 sources of feedback that you can discuss with your students:
  - Teachers,
  - Parents,
  - Peers,
  - Coaches,
  - Mentors,
  - Experts,
  - Dictionaries,
  - YouTube videos,
  - Podcasts,
  - Online tutorials,
  - Online forums,
  - Self-assessment,
  - Reflection,
  - Checklists,
  - Rubrics,
  - Grades,
  - Answer keys,
  - Role-playing,
  - Surveys,
  - Questionnaires,
  - Report cards,
  - Experiments,
  - Simulations,
  - Hands-on activities,
  - Artificial Intelligence,
  - Assessment tools,
  - Automated feedback from tech tools
  - Personal experiences,
  - Trial-and-error results,
  - Feedback from emotions & feelings...

Big Idea

We usually think of feedback as coming from teachers, adults, or friends, but guess what? Feedback can come from so many other places too! Imagine using an answer key or a dictionary to check if we got something right. YouTube videos and podcasts can teach us new things and help us improve our skills and knowledge. In school, we can get feedback through checklists, rubrics, grades, and even by doing our own self-assessments! Did you know that our own emotions can also give us feedback? They tell us how we feel about something even before we think about it! So, try to think of critical feedback as advice that could lead to positive growth if you take action on it!

Discussion/Reflection Questions

- Which sources of feedback mentioned in the lesson were new to you? How do you think these sources can help you improve your learning?
- Now that you've discovered different sources of feedback, why do you think it's important to get feedback from many places?
- How do you think considering feedback from different sources can make you learn and grow even more? Can you give an example?

Student Tasks 〉 Transfer Goals

Student Tasks	Transfer Goals
Students learn to consider feedback from a multitude of sources, rather than limiting themselves to traditional sources.	Students seek feedback from a variety of non-traditional sources including checklists, rubrics, grades, self-assessments, etc.
Students identify several sources of feedback that they may never have considered and learn to use them as such.	Students consider various feedback sources to gain a more complete under-standing of their growth and areas for improvement.

Instructional Poster(s)

- This lesson has ONE Instructional Poster.
- The Instructional Poster for this lesson is a Graffiti Board of sources of feedback. Go over each with the class and explain how each can be used as a source of feedback. (They will need to know this for their Student Handouts.) Most importantly, see if students can come up with any additional sources of feedback - especially those outside the box! It is great when students can see how feedback comes from so many different possible sources!
- One outside the box example is a mirror if you want feedback on how you look when you pose for a picture or give a speech. Another one is how a baby gives you feedback when you're holding it. They cry if you're not doing what they want or need. They smile when you are! There are 30 more sources of feedback listed in the Teacher Tips section on the previous page.

Student Handouts

- This lesson has TWO Student Handouts.
- DIRECTIONS: Explain how you can get valuable feedback from each source below. If your class brainstormed any new sources of feedback, you can explain those instead by writing them in and crossing out the original source.
- Both Student Handouts ask students to explain how they can get valuable feedback from each of the sources listed. Answers will vary, but try to ensure that each student understands how each source of feedback can be used to their advantage when trying to improve a skill or knowledge. Sample Answers:
  - A grade on a test: Grades can show me what I understand and don't understand.
  - A YouTube video: Can show me how to do something better or what I'm doing wrong.
  - AI: Can correct my work & provide support.
  - Parents/Siblings: Complaints mean that I should fix the problem.
  - Peers/Classmates: Since they know what I know, they can help me make revisions.
  - Teachers: Constant tips for improving.
  - Rubric/Checklist: Compare my work to the expectations on a rubric or checklist.
  - Self-Assessment: After work is done, I can determine how well I met expectations.
  - Answer Key: See which answers are right and which are wrong.

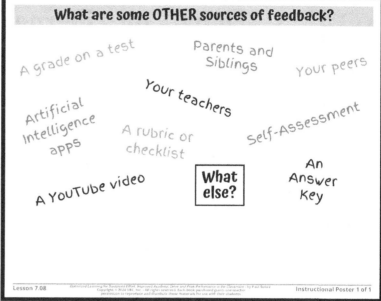

What are some OTHER sources of feedback?

A grade on a test · Parents and Siblings · Your peers · Your teachers · Artificial Intelligence apps · A rubric or checklist · Self-Assessment · A YouTube video · What else? · An Answer Key

Lesson 7.08 — Instructional Poster 1 of 1

The Nuts & Bolts of FEEDBACK

Name:

Date:

BIG IDEA: We usually think of feedback as coming from teachers, adults, or friends, but guess what? Feedback can come from so many other places too! Imagine using an answer key or a dictionary to check if we got something right. YouTube videos and podcasts can teach us new things and help us improve our skills and knowledge. In school, we can get feedback through checklists, rubrics, grades, and even by doing our own self-assessments! Did you know that our own emotions can also give us feedback? They tell us how we feel about something even before we think about it! So, try to think of critical feedback as advice that could lead to positive growth if you take action on it!

DIRECTIONS: Explain how you can get valuable feedback from each source below. If your class brainstormed any new sources of feedback, you can explain those instead by writing them in and crossing out the original source.

What are some OTHER sources of feedback?

Feedback Source	Explain how you can get valuable feedback from each source
A grade on a test	
A YouTube video	
Artifical Intelligence Apps like ChatGPT	

Lesson 7.08 — Student Handout 1 of 2

What are some OTHER sources of feedback?

Feedback Source	Explain how you can get valuable feedback from each source
Parents or Siblings	
Your peers (classmates)	
Your teachers	
A rubric or checklist	
Self-Assessment	
An Answer Key	

Lesson 7.08 — Student Handout 2 of 2

bit.ly/47FAvuu

Embark on a journey of feedback excellence by identifying essential principles for delivering meaningful & impactful guidance

7.09

Essential Question

What are some tips for giving others feedback?

Lesson Overview

In this lesson, students will brainstorm and create their own tips for giving effective feedback using carefully selected words as idea generators. Instead of providing pre-determined tips, the focus is on encouraging students to think critically and generate their own valuable ideas based on essential words. While the outcome may vary as students create their unique tips, the discussion will lead to valuable insights. Many of these tips will be revisited and reinforced in future lessons to further enhance their understanding.

Teacher Tips

- There are many possibilities for student responses for each set of words provided in this lesson. Here are a few possibilities to help get the discussion started:
  - Emotions: Recognize and consider the emotions of the person receiving feedback. Be mindful of how feedback may impact their feelings and deliver it in a supportive and empathetic manner.
  - Attention: When giving feedback, give your full attention to the person receiving it. Listen actively, observe their work carefully, and provide focused feedback that addresses specific aspects.
  - Accuracy: Ensure that your feedback is accurate and based on objective observations. Avoid making assumptions and provide feedback that is factual and relevant to the task or learning goal.
  - Timeliness: Provide feedback promptly to maximize its impact. Waiting too long may diminish its effectiveness, so aim to deliver feedback in a timely manner.

Big Idea

When we give others feedback, it's important to realize that even though WE completely understand what we are explaining to our peer, there's a good chance that THEY don't completely understand what we're talking about. Therefore, it's our responsibility to consider as many of these tips as possible whenever we give feedback to others.

Discussion/Reflection Questions

- Which words from this lesson made you think the most about giving helpful feedback? Why did these words stand out?
- Out of the tips you created, which ones do you think are the most important or interesting? Can you explain why they are valuable when giving feedback to someone?
- Did anything surprise you or give you new ideas while you were discussing and creating your tips? How did those new thoughts help you understand feedback even better?
- How will the tips you made in this lesson make a difference when you give feedback in the future? How can you use and improve those tips to become even better at helping others?

Student Tasks 〉 Transfer Goals

Student Tasks	Transfer Goals
Students creatively use carefully selected words to generate helpful tips for giving feedback.	Students transfer their creativity to other tasks that require thinking outside the box.
Students brainstorm four of their own words and use these idea generating words to write helpful feedback tips.	Students independently generate ideas, solve problems, and make informed decisions in new situations.

Instructional Poster(s)

- This lesson has ONE Instructional Poster.
- The Instructional Poster asks students to use the eight words and phrases in each circle to inspire a conversation that answers the question: "What feedback tips can you come up with, using these words as inspiration?" Don't worry too much about what my intentions were in including each, just see if the students can come up with good suggestions for giving feedback effectively using these words as a starting point.
- If you have time, consider having students assess themselves on each tip that was brainstormed during the discussion. What are they already pretty strong at, and what could they work on improving?

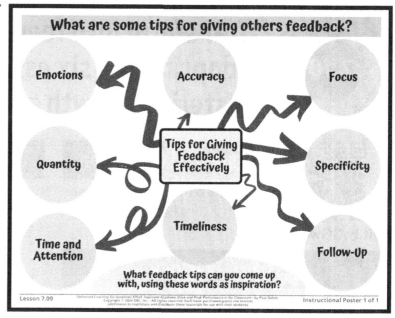

Student Handouts

- This lesson has TWO Student Handouts.
- DIRECTIONS: What feedback tips can you come up with, using these words as inspiration? Write your answers in the blanks. You need to write four new words into the blanks on the next page.
- The Student Handouts contain the eight words and phrases from the Instructional Poster and two new words (importance and varied or different).
- At the bottom of the second Student Handout are four boxes for students to write their own words or phrases into the green circles and write tips using those words as inspiration.
- Here are some possible words that students might consider using on the second Student Handout: empathy, clarity, relevant, specific, supportive, individualized, constructive, engaging, encouraging, consistent...

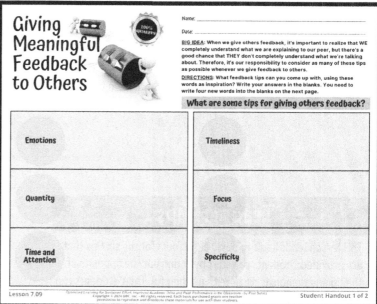

Transform into feedback champions by adopting the six essential principles for fostering growth and development

7.10

bit.ly/3Gw48T3

Essential Question

How good am I at implementing these feedback tips?

Lesson Overview

In this lesson, students learn about six helpful tips for giving feedback to others. They talk about what each tip means and why it's important. If teachers want to expand the lesson, they can have students act out each tip and also act out what happens when they don't follow each tip. Then, students rank the tips from easiest to hardest and choose two tips they want to get better at. Finally, they think about times in the past when they would have liked to use these tips while giving or receiving feedback.

Big Idea

When we give others feedback, it's important to remember the following tips:

- Give your peer a voice
- Watch your speed
- Simplify your directions
- Check for understanding
- Use visuals and examples
- Let your peer speak

Discussion/Reflection Questions

- How do you think using these six feedback tips can improve the way you communicate with others?
- Can you think of a time when someone gave you feedback and used any of these tips? How did it make you feel?
- Imagine you are giving feedback to a friend who is feeling down. Which tip would you use to make sure your feedback is supportive and encouraging?

Teacher Tips

- This lesson lends itself to doing act-it-outs for the six tips that are provided. Students can start by acting out the opposite of the tip and demonstrate how it's not helpful. Then, students can do the act-it-out over again but this time implement the suggested tip. They can end by reflecting on the differences in each act-it-out.
- If you feel there are any other foundational feedback tips you want your students to understand, add them in to this lesson. Feel free to remove any that you don't agree with as well.
- If you've already taught your students how to create S.M.A.A.R.T.E.R. Goals, you may want to have students create a goal for their one or two weakest skills (out of the six). If so, they can skip the second Student Handout.

Student Tasks 〉 Transfer Goals

| Students rank the six tips from easiest to hardest and choose two tips they want to get better at. | Students actively apply the six tips in various situations, both in and outside of the classroom. |

| Students think about times in the past when they would have liked to use these tips while giving or receiving feedback. | Students use their improved self-awareness to give feedback more constructively using the six tips. |

Instructional Poster(s)

- This lesson has ONE Instructional Poster.
- The Instructional Poster contains six important tips for students to consider when giving peers feedback. Discuss what each of these mean, why they are important, and ways students may have done this in the past.
- If students have any additional details for any of these tips, please encourage them to share them with the group.

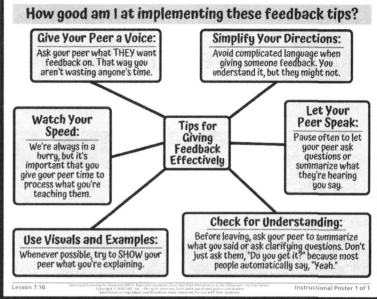

Student Handouts

- This lesson has THREE Student Handouts.
- DIRECTIONS for the first Student Handout: Carefully reflect on how strong you are at performing each of the following skills while giving others feedback. If you haven't had much experience giving feedback, think about what will likely come easiest to you and what will likely be hardest. Draw a line from the "1" to your strongest or easiest skill. Draw a line from the "2" to your next strongest or easiest, etc. The "6" should be connected with your weakest or most difficult skill. A faint line has been drawn as an example.
- DIRECTIONS for the second Student Handout: Look back at the last page, and re-copy your 5th and 6th best skills in the boxes below (these are your two weakest skills). Then, write a plan for improving your ability with each skill. Use the sentence starters provided to help. Finally, write at least one additional skill that was not mentioned in the original list of six for "Giving Feedback Effectively" in the box at the bottom of the page.
- The third Student Handout asks students to consider recent assignments or experiences where they could have applied each of these tips. If they can't come up with one, they can create a fictional experience.

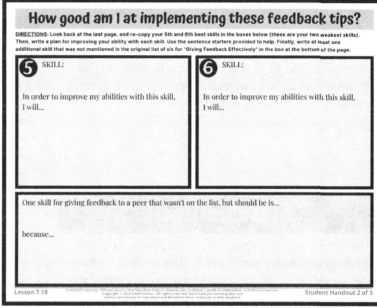

7.11

bit.ly/418sifX

Provide tailored and actionable guidance to ensure that your peers receive the specific feedback they need to excel

Essential Question

Why should I give feedback that is SPECIFIC?

Lesson Overview

In this lesson, students explore the distinction between general and specific feedback. They discover that specific feedback is more valuable as it directly addresses the recipient's needs. One of the great advantages of one-to-one feedback among students is its customization to the individual. General feedback is acceptable in situations where specific feedback may not be feasible. As a final step, students discuss how they intend to incorporate this concept into future feedback and goal-setting experiences.

Big Idea

Giving specific feedback helps your peers understand exactly what they did well and what they can do better. It's like giving them a detailed treasure map that shows them the exact steps to succeed. When you give specific feedback, you're like a helpful guide, showing them the clear path to improvement and making their journey even more awesome!

Discussion/Reflection Questions

- How would you explain the difference between general feedback and specific feedback in your own words?
- Why is specific feedback preferred over general feedback whenever possible?
- How do you plan to apply the concept of specific feedback in future feedback-giving experiences? What steps will you take to ensure your feedback is tailored to your peer's needs?
- Think of a time when you received specific feedback that made a significant impact on your learning or performance. How did it help you improve?

Teacher Tips

- The Student Handouts attempt to connect the idea of specific feedback with writing specific GOALS. Make sure that students understand the connection without confusing goal setting with giving feedback.
- Consider sharing these tips with your students: Specific feedback is better than general feedback because:
  - it gives clear guidance and actionable steps for improvement, preventing ambiguity and confusion.
  - it allows the recipient to understand their strengths and weaknesses in detail, enabling them to make targeted adjustments and achieve better results.
  - it provides concrete examples and specific observations, making it easier for the recipient to visualize and understand the areas they need to focus on.
  - it fosters a deeper level of self-awareness and personal growth, encouraging their peers to reflect on their performance and take ownership of their development.
  - it builds trust and credibility between the giver and receiver, demonstrating that the feedback is thoughtful, considerate, and tailored to the unique needs of their peer.

Student Tasks 〉 Transfer Goals

Student Tasks	Transfer Goals
Students learn why it is better to provide our peers with specific feedback over general feedback, when possible.	Students internalize the importance of providing specific feedback and integrate it into their interactions with peers.
Students analyze eight different goals to determine which goals are specific and which are general.	Students identify examples in their life that are too general and work to make them more specific.

INTRODUCTION
PLANNING
METACOGNITION
SYNTHESIS
REFLECTION
SELF-ASSESSMENT
GOAL SETTING

Instructional Poster(s)

- This lesson has ONE Instructional Poster.
- The Instructional Poster for this lesson explains the difference between giving specific feedback and general feedback. BOTH can be valuable, but specific feedback is usually preferred as it applies to the receiver's needs directly. As teachers, we often provide general feedback to the whole class, but one of the main benefits of one-to-one feedback between students is that it can be tailored to the individual receiving the feedback. This is the type of feedback we want our students to give.
- Please make sure that students understand everything on the slide.
- Ask students if they can come up with anything additional to add to each quadrant that would be helpful for others to consider. Discuss each idea.

Student Handouts

- This lesson has TWO Student Handouts.
- DIRECTIONS: Complete the boxes below following the directions provided. Then, do the same on the next page.
- The first Student Handout asks students to summarize the idea of "Specific Feedback vs, General Feedback." They are also asked to describe how they might use this idea in class.
- DIRECTIONS: Read "Goal 1" and "Goal 2." Circle the one you think will lead to the most improvement, based on how it's written. Do the same for all four rows. Then, answer the four questions on the right and below.
- The second Student Handout asks students to analyze two different goals (one that is written with specificity and one that is general). They are asked which goal is better and why they think that is true.

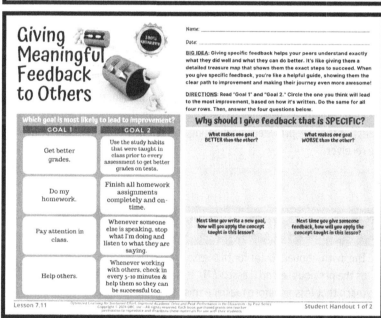

bit.ly/418REdG

Embrace the power of immediacy, harnessing the momentum of timely feedback to support your peers' growth

Essential Question

Why should I give feedback that is IMMEDIATE?

Big Idea

Giving feedback right away helps us learn and improve faster. It's important to understand that when we receive feedback right after we do something, it can make a big difference in how well we understand it and how quickly we can make changes. We learn that immediate feedback is like getting help right when we need it, and it can help us do better in school, learn new skills, and become even better versions of ourselves.

Lesson Overview

In this lesson, students explore the distinction between immediate and delayed feedback. They discover that immediate feedback is more valuable since it addresses the recipient's needs in real time, rather than after the fact. One of the great advantages of one-to-one feedback among students is its ability to be timely. Delayed feedback is acceptable in situations when immediate feedback may not be feasible. As a final step, students describe the benefits of immediate feedback over delayed feedback in four different scenarios that are provided, highlighting how it positively impacts the receiver.

Discussion/Reflection Questions

- Think about a time when you received immediate feedback. How did it help you improve or understand something better right away?
- Can you think of a specific example where immediate feedback would be beneficial in a classroom activity, like solving a math problem or giving a presentation? How would it make a positive impact?
- How can you use the concept of immediate feedback in your everyday life, outside of the classroom? How might it help you grow and improve in different areas?

Teacher Tips

- The Instructional Poster for this lesson follows the same format as the previous lesson (Lesson 7.11). It is somewhat beneficial to teach that lesson before teaching this lesson, although not necessarily a prerequisite.
- Consider sharing these tips with your students: Immediate feedback is better than delayed feedback because:
  - It helps us correct mistakes right away, so we can learn and improve faster.
  - It gives us a clear understanding of what we did well and what we need to work on immediately.
  - It allows us to make adjustments in real time, helping us avoid repeating errors or developing bad habits.
  - It keeps us motivated and engaged by providing timely recognition and guidance.
  - It prevents misunderstandings from lingering and becoming harder to address, ensuring we stay on the right track toward success.

Student Tasks 〉 Transfer Goals

Student Tasks	Transfer Goals
Students learn why it is better to provide our peers with immediate feedback over delayed feedback, when possible.	Students internalize the importance of providing immediate feedback and make a serious effort to provide it to their peers.
Students predict how delayed feedback could impact the receiver in a negative way and describe how immediate feedback would be more beneficial.	Students internalize the importance of providing immediate feedback and make a serious effort to provide it to their peers.

INTRODUCTION

PLANNING

METACOGNITION

SYNTHESIS

REFLECTION

SELF-ASSESSMENT

GOAL SETTING

FEEDBACK

Instructional Poster(s)

- This lesson has ONE Instructional Poster.
- The Instructional Poster for this lesson explains the difference between giving immediate feedback and delayed feedback. BOTH can be valuable, but immediate feedback is usually preferred as it helps the receiver see what they can do differently WHILE they are practicing, instead of afterwards. This timeliness ensures that the need is high, the desire to learn the information is high, and the opportunity to practice it correctly is available. As teachers, we often provide delayed feedback to individual students because it is difficult to provide meaningful personalized feedback to all students in real-time, but we all wish we could give meaningful immediate feedback to our students!
- Please make sure that students understand everything on the slide.
- Ask students if they can come up with anything additional to add to each quadrant that would be helpful for others to consider. Discuss each idea.

Student Handouts

- This lesson has TWO Student Handouts.
- DIRECTIONS: Answer the two questions on this page. Then, on the next page, fill in the chart with complete answers for each scenario.
- The first Student Handout asks students to summarize the idea of "Immediate Feedback vs. Delayed Feedback." They are also asked to describe how they might use this idea in class.
- The second Student Handout provides the students with four scenarios and asks them to describe what might happen if feedback is NOT given immediately and what the benefit is to giving immediate feedback in this situation.

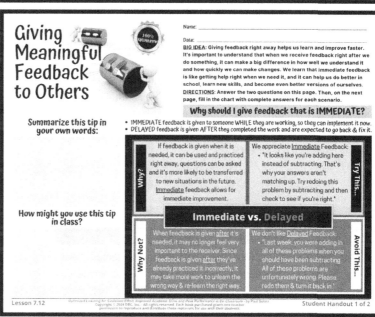

Why should I give feedback that is IMMEDIATE?

Scenario	What might happen if feedback isn't given right away?	What would be the benefit of giving feedback immediately?
You are playing an instrument and practicing the song incorrectly. It sounds okay to you, but you've never heard the "right" way to play it.		
This is your first year playing baseball. When you swing the bat, your hands are reversed. Your swing is all messed up, but no one is correcting you.		
You're in charge of baking cookies for your weekly club meeting. You read the recipe wrong and put baking soda in instead of baking powder & the cookies taste weird.		
You are doing a packet full of 2-digit times 2-digit multiplication problems, but you never learned how to put a zero in the ones place when multiplying tens.		

bit.ly/3R5BWvc

Tailor your feedback to the unique needs of your peer in order to elevate its impact and fuel their development

Essential Question

Why should I give feedback that is PERSONALIZED?

Big Idea

When we give feedback to others, tailoring it to their needs can have a greater impact on their growth and improvement. By providing personalized feedback to others, we discover their specific, individual needs and help them reach their full potential. Giving generic, universal feedback may not be as effective because it doesn't address their specific needs and areas to work on.

Lesson Overview

In this lesson, students explore the distinction between personalized and universal feedback. They discover that personalized feedback is more valuable since it addresses the recipient's specific current needs, rather than generic feedback that might benefit others, but not this receiver at this time. One of the great advantages of one-to-one feedback among students is its ability to be personalized. Universal feedback is acceptable in situations where personalized feedback may not be feasible. As a final step, students consider four scenarios and attempt to provide personalized feedback for each.

Discussion/Reflection Questions

- Think about a time when someone gave you personalized feedback. How did it make you feel? How did it help you improve in that specific situation?
- Imagine a situation where personalized feedback may not be possible. How might that affect your learning or progress? What challenges could arise?
- Think of a specific example where personalized feedback would be beneficial, like in a group project or learning a new skill. How would personalized feedback help you or your classmates improve in a way that fits your individual needs?

Teacher Tips

- The Instructional Poster for this lesson follows the same format as the two previous lessons (Lesson 7.11 - 7.12). It is somewhat beneficial to teach those lessons before teaching this lesson, although they are not prerequisites.
- Consider sharing these tips with your students: Personalized feedback is better than universal feedback because:
  - It shows that we care about each person's individual strengths and weakness, making the feedback more helpful and meaningful.
  - It gives specific advice that is just right for each person, helping them understand how to get even better in a way that matches their needs.
  - It makes learning more fun and enjoyable because we know that our progress is noticed and celebrated, creating a positive and supportive environment.
  - It gives us personalized tips and tricks to overcome challenges and keep getting better, so we can achieve our goals and reach new heights.

Student Tasks 〉 Transfer Goals

Student Tasks	Transfer Goals
Students learn why it is better to provide our peers with personalized feedback over universal feedback, when possible.	Students internalize the importance of providing personalized feedback and make a serious effort to provide it to their peers.
Students practice giving personalized feedback on paper in four fictional scenarios.	Students improve their abilities to provide personalized feedback to their peers in different academic situations.

Instructional Poster(s)

- This lesson has ONE Instructional Poster.
- The Instructional Poster for this lesson explains the difference between giving personalized feedback and universal feedback. BOTH can be valuable, but personalized feedback is usually preferred as it targets the specific needs of the receiver. As teachers, we often provide universal feedback to our students because it is difficult to provide meaningful personalized feedback to all students in real-time, but we all wish we could give personalized feedback to everyone, all the time!
- Please make sure that students understand everything on the slide.
- Ask students if they can come up with anything additional to add to each quadrant that would be helpful for others to consider. Discuss each idea.

Student Handouts

- This lesson has TWO Student Handouts.
- DIRECTIONS: Answer the two questions on this page. Then, on the next page, fill in all four boxes with complete answers for each scenario.
- The first Student Handout asks students to summarize the idea of "Personalized Feedback vs, Universal Feedback." They are also asked to describe how they might use this idea in class.
- The second Student Handout gives students four different scenarios and they are asked to explain what they would do in each situation or how they can make universal feedback more personalized.
- If students have any stories that are similar to these that they want to share with the class during the class discussion, it may be valuable to see how personalized feedback helped them improve.

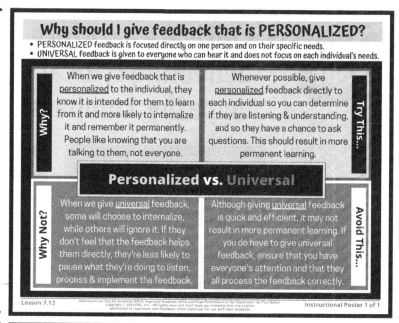

bit.ly/41a5zjy

Cultivate a culture of kindness by delivering critical feedback to peers with empathy, compassion and understanding

Essential Question

How can I make sure that my feedback is KIND?

Big Idea

Learn how to give feedback kindly so your peer never feels dumb or inadequate. It is YOUR responsibility to help them see your feedback as something positive. You can use feedback starters or structures to ensure a kind delivery.

Lesson Overview

In this lesson, students learn about the importance of delivering critical feedback in a kind way, and learn several strategies for doing so. Students start by learning 15 sentence starters that can help prepare a peer for receiving critical feedback, so their immediate reaction isn't negative. Students are also asked to create four new sentence starters that might work in certain situations. Then, students learn a feedback structure called, "I like, I wonder, Next Steps..." which starts with specific, positive feedback before questioning something in their work and suggesting the next steps the peer should take. Students also brainstorm four additional things they can do to ensure kindness when giving peers critical feedback.

Discussion/Reflection Questions

- How do you think the sentence starters will help you prepare a peer for receiving critical feedback without making them feel bad?
- Reflect on a time when someone gave you critical feedback in a kind way. How did it make you feel? How did it encourage you to make improvements without feeling discouraged?
- Think of a time when you think using one of those sentence starters would have been helpful in delivering critical feedback to a peer (or when a peer delivered critical feedback to you)?

Teacher Tips

- Although you may wonder if your students are too old or too advanced to benefit from this lesson, but I've found that there are often one or two students at every grade level that have never been explicitly taught this skill, never been corrected when delivering feedback in a mean way, or haven't yet made the connection between their own personal experiences receiving critical feedback in a mean way and their current experiences giving others critical feedback. This lesson provides that opportunity. If students struggle with this concept in practice in the classroom, you can remind them of the importance of this lesson.
- Since the examples provided on the Instructional Poster use the Feedback Starters to give critical feedback in WRITING, you may want to consider sharing some examples that would work with your subject area or the subject students are learning about in your class at this time. The more you connect these lessons to your own class, they easier it will be for them to transfer the skills.

Student Tasks 〉 Transfer Goals

Student Tasks	Transfer Goals
Students learn fifteen Feedback Starters that help deliver critical feedback in a kind way.	Students use Feedback Starters naturally whenever giving peers critical feedback in order to ensure it is delivered kindly.
Students learn a feedback structure called, "I like, I wonder, Next Steps..." that help them deliver critical feedback in a kind way.	Students use this feedback structure (or variations of it) naturally whenever giving peers critical feedback in order to ensure it is delivered kindly.

INTRODUCTION

PLANNING

METACOGNITION

SYNTHESIS

REFLECTION

SELF-ASSESSMENT

GOAL SETTING

FEEDBACK

Instructional Poster(s)

- This lesson has ONE Instructional Poster.
- The Instructional Poster for this lesson teaches students about the importance of giving feedback that is constructive AND kind! There is definitely an art to giving feedback in a way that allows their peer to feel appreciative for the suggestions, instead of embarrassed, defensive or frustrated. One way to ensure that our feedback is delivered in a kind manner is to use feedback starters/structures.
- Most of the feedback starters that students will use on the Student Handouts are on this Instructional Poster using examples from writing. Feel free to discuss examples from other subjects.

Student Handouts

- This lesson has TWO Student Handouts.
- DIRECTIONS: Start by reading through the Feedback Starters below. Which ones can you imagine yourself using? Add your own in the box at the right. Then, complete the next page.
- The first Student Handout provides students with 15 feedback starters they can use when giving peers critical feedback. They are asked to create four more of their own.
- DIRECTIONS: Read through the "I like, I wonder, Next Steps" example below, and create your own "I like, I wonder, Next Steps" example. Then, add some of your own ideas to the box on the right. Share your ideas with your peers so we all learn to give and accept feedback happily and with respect. Finally, be sure to use these ideas when giving critical feedback!
- The second Student Handout teaches students a feedback structure called, "I like, I wonder, Next Steps…" They also brainstorm four additional things they can do to ensure kindness when giving peers critical feedback.

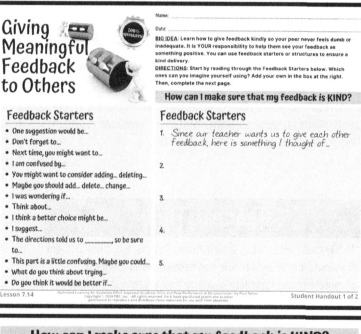

bit.ly/483yyIe

Embrace the nuances of feedback delivery by considering factors like your approach, tone, timing, intentions, and cultural norms

Essential Question

What factors should I consider when giving feedback?

Big Idea

Considering all of these factors when giving others feedback demonstrates empathy, respect, and a genuine desire to support your peer's growth. It increases the chances of the feedback being well-received, understood, and acted upon, leading to a more beneficial feedback experience.

Lesson Overview

In this lesson, students learn several factors that need to be considered when giving others feedback (especially critical feedback). If these factors are not taken into account, the receiver of the feedback is less likely to listen to it carefully, take it seriously, and implement it. Since the goal of giving others feedback is to help them improve, it's important to do the best we can to deliver the feedback in the most effective way. In this lesson, students come up with a plan for addressing each factor when that factor is difficult to address. Sentence starters have been provided to help students form meaningful responses.

Discussion/Reflection Questions

- Why is it important to listen carefully to the person's perspective before giving feedback? (It's important to listen because...)
- What are some ways I can make sure my feedback is relevant to the person's needs? (I can make my feedback relevant by...)
- How can I communicate my good intentions when giving feedback to someone? (I can show my good intentions by...)

Teacher Tips

- This lesson contains two Instructional Posters and three Student Handouts. Because of this, it may take students longer to complete than a typical lesson, and it might take the teacher slightly longer to introduce. Adjust your plans accordingly.
- If you'd prefer to only assign two of the Student Handouts, the directions are worded so that you can choose two pages to assign without the students being confused. In my mind, the real value of the lesson is in reading each factor, processing what they mean, and then thinking about how they can ensure they implement it in their plans for giving feedback to their peers. The written portion is less important, so if you'd like to choose one page to complete together as a class, you can simply assign the other two for students to work on independently (or collaboratively with a randomly assigned peer, which is my preference).

Student Tasks 〉 Transfer Goals

Students learn that there are factors that need to be considered when giving feedback to others.	Students will empathize with others when giving feedback, adapting to their specific needs.
Students learn 16 specific factors that help the person receiving feedback be more receptive to hearing it and implementing it.	Students consider each factor when giving feedback demonstrating empathy, promoting sensitivity & strengthening relationships with peers.

Instructional Poster(s)

- This lesson has TWO Instructional Posters.
- The Instructional Posters (two) for this lesson describe 16 factors that we should consider when giving our peers feedback. By taking these factors into account, it makes it easier on the receiver to listen to the feedback, handle any criticism that may come with it, and then implement the feedback on their own.
- Spend a little time discussing what each factor means and how they can improve each factor in your classroom. On the Student Handouts, students will describe how they can overcome certain challenges related to each factor.
- Ask students if they can think of any more factors that should be considered. This is not meant to be an exhaustive list. Feel free to add your own as well!

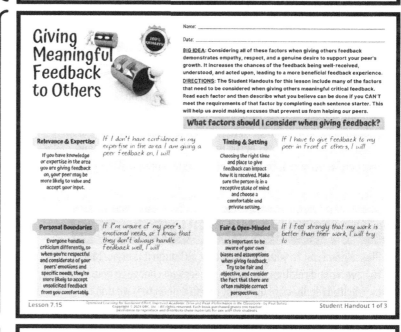

Student Handouts

- This lesson has THREE Student Handouts.
- DIRECTIONS: The Student Handouts for this lesson include many of the factors that need to be considered when giving others meaningful critical feedback. Read each factor and then describe what you believe can be done if you CAN'T meet the requirements of that factor by completing each sentence starter. This will help us avoid making excuses that prevent us from helping our peers.
- Ask students to complete each section on all three Student Handouts with complete ideas that clearly explain what they would do in that situation. Hopefully, this exercise will help students become more aware of each factor and overcome some of the factors that otherwise might have gotten in the way of giving others meaningful feedback.

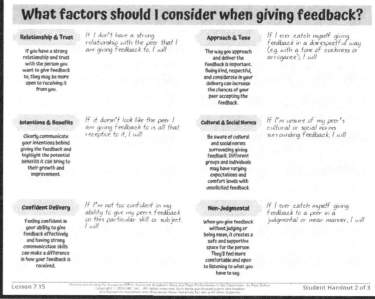

bit.ly/481HgXl

Proactively seek opportunities to provide peers with unsolicited feedback that supports them on their learning journey

7.16

Essential Question

How do I offer feedback if they didn't ask for it?

Big Idea

Giving unsolicited feedback to our peers can begin with a simple question like "Would you mind if I gave you some feedback to help you improve?" When done respectfully, unsolicited feedback helps to creates a classroom community where everyone supports each other's growth, and rapid improvement becomes the rule rather than the exception for all students.

Lesson Overview

In this lesson, students discuss several questions regarding giving their peers unsolicited feedback as a whole class. They learn that giving others unsolicited feedback is generally considered to be off-limits, but in an improvement-focused classroom, it can be done assuming the students have a good relationship and that the offer for feedback is introduced slowly, through a question like "What can I give you feedback on?" or "What are you working on and how can I help?" Students are given several fictional scenarios to come up with questions that are appropriate for that instance. Once students learn that this process is part of the learning in this classroom, it no longer feels weird and becomes a fantastic element of learning.

Discussion/Reflection Questions

- Why is it important to have a good relationship with someone before giving them feedback? What problems might you run into if you give a peer unsolicited feedback and you have a strained relationship?
- How can we approach our peers with unsolicited feedback in a friendly and helpful way?
- Why are we encouraged to give feedback to our peers without them asking for it? What positive outcomes can occur when everyone learns to give and receive feedback without negative emotions?

Teacher Tips

- Please point out to your students that although it is important to have a good relationship with the peers we choose to give unsolicited feedback to, BUT that doesn't mean that we don't give unsolicited feedback to everyone else. It means that you work on improving your relationship with each of those peers so you can quickly get to the point where they appreciate unsolicited feedback from you because they know you have their best interests in mind. This is true for all tips given in this book. We never make excuses - we work to improve the situation so we can collaborate with everyone in class, not just a select few!
- Don't consider the second Instructional Poster a true Answer Key. It's merely sample answers that might be true for you and your students. If these are not true for you, think about what answers you believe to be true and discuss those with your students.

Student Tasks 〉 Transfer Goals

Student Tasks	Transfer Goals
Students consider the relationship they have with their peer before offering unsolicited feedback.	Students assess the nature of their relationship with their peer and tailor their feedback approach accordingly.
Students prepare an opening question to break the ice before offering unsolicited feedback.	Students determine which opening question would most likely prepare their peer to receive and implement feedback.

Instructional Poster(s)

- This lesson has THREE Instructional Posters.
- The first Instructional Poster for this lesson asks several questions that students should reflect on in preparation for this lesson. An "Answer Key" has been provided, but the answers are simple & subjective (this is the second Instructional Poster).
- The third Instructional Poster gives students eleven possible questions they can use to "break the ice" before offering unsolicited feedback.
- Most teachers don't encourage their students to give unsolicited feedback to their peers, because it has traditionally caused problems. However, this is essential to a classroom that believes in improvement and growth, because the teacher can't possibly provide each student with enough personalized, specific, immediate feedback to help them grow at a fast pace, but when the students are taught to give meaningful feedback to each other in effective ways, growth becomes exponential and everyone starts helping everyone grow! The upcoming lessons will help your students refine this skill.

Student Handouts

- This lesson has TWO Student Handouts.
- DIRECTIONS: Start by reading through the chart below. Try to get an idea of the types of situations you might have to give feedback to someone who hasn't asked for it, the different relationships you have with each student in your classes and the questions you might ask to break the ice. Then, complete the chart on the next page with your best answers.
- The two Student Handouts ask students to fill in the empty boxes following this format: (1) When might you offer feedback without first being asked? (2) How well do you know and get along with this student? and (3) What question will you ask to try to encourage them to be open to your feedback?

How do I offer feedback if they didn't ask for it?

Should I ever offer unsolicited feedback (a.k.a. feedback they didn't ask for)? If so, when?

When would I not want to receive unsolicited feedback? Why?

Is there anyone I shouldn't offer unsolicited feedback to?

How do I offer feedback if they didn't ask for it?

What might happen if I DON'T offer my feedback?

How can I make it easier on others to give me unsolicited feedback?

What happens if my feedback is NOT well-received?

Giving Meaningful Feedback to Others

Name: _____

Date: _____

BIG IDEA: Giving unsolicited feedback to our peers can begin with a simple question like "Would you mind if I gave you some feedback to help you improve?" When done respectfully, unsolicited feedback helps to creates a classroom community where everyone supports each other's growth, and rapid improvement becomes the rule rather than the exception for all students.

DIRECTIONS: Start by reading through the chart below. Try to get an idea of the types of situations you might have to give feedback to someone who hasn't asked for it, the different relationships you have with each student in your classes and the questions you might ask to break the ice. Then, complete the chart on the next page with your best answers.

How do I offer feedback if they didn't ask for it?

When might you offer feedback without first being asked?	How well do you know & get along with this student?	What question will you ask to try to encourage them to be open to your feedback?
I've been assigned to this student by my teacher and we are being asked to work together on helping each other improve our writing.	I've only seen this student around school, but never worked with them before. He seems nice, though.	"Looks like you're pretty far along in your writing. What kind of feedback might you be looking for? I'd love to try my best to help!"
Our teacher has asked us to give feedback to the students who are sitting at our table. We're all working on our own projects & they're all different.	This student sits next to me in class and we've been in class together many times before, but we're not really friends (nor are we enemies).	"Mrs. Cluckbaum wants us to give each other feedback on our projects. I'm building a scale model of our school. What are you working on?"

How do I offer feedback if they didn't ask for it?

When might you offer feedback without first being asked?	How well do you know & get along with this student?	What question will you ask to try to encourage them to be open to your feedback?
	I've known her for many years and we're really close friends. I don't want to give her any negative feedback because I don't want her to get angry with me!	
	He and I have had trouble getting along since 2nd grade. I avoid him and he avoids me. I have no idea how I'm going to be able to give him feedback!	
My math teacher has assigned us partners to work with while we're practicing our problems from this lesson. My partner is solving them the wrong way and getting the wrong answers.		

Sidebar tabs: INTRODUCTION, PLANNING, METACOGNITION, SYNTHESIS, REFLECTION, SELF-ASSESSMENT, GOAL SETTING, FEEDBACK

bit.ly/3T9fFzl

Actively engage your peer in the feedback process, ensuring they understand and effectively apply the guidance provided

7.17

Essential Question

How do I make sure they understood my feedback?

Big Idea

Ensure that the person you are giving feedback to completely understands the feedback you've given them before moving on to other things. Don't think of giving feedback as a task you just check off a To Do List. Understand that it is your responsibility to help them grow and improve. We all share responsibility for helping each other grow!

Lesson Overview

In this lesson, students are introduced to four strategies aimed at ensuring their peers grasp and effectively apply the feedback provided. Without verifying comprehension, there is a significant risk that peers may struggle to fully comprehend and integrate the feedback into their work. However, by actively practicing the feedback together, encouraging questions even if initially none seem apparent, requesting a summary of the information conveyed, and offering support as peers review their work, we can greatly enhance the likelihood that our feedback is comprehended accurately and implemented successfully.

Discussion/Reflection Questions

- Can I think of a time when I received feedback and didn't understand it well? How can I avoid that happening to my friends by using the strategies we learned?
- How can I make sure my friends feel supported and encouraged when we work together on their feedback?
- Can I think of a fun way to summarize the feedback I gave to my friend? Maybe through a drawing or a short skit?
- How can I celebrate and recognize my friends' progress when they successfully implement the feedback I give them?

Teacher Tips

- This is a reminder to have students avoid questions that elicit an automatic response like:
  - "Do you understand?"
  - "Do you get it?"
  - "Does this make sense?"
  - "Sound good?"
- Students are asked to come up with one more strategy to check for understanding after giving a peer feedback. If you need any suggestions, here are a few:
  - Ask the peer to share examples of how they plan to incorporate the feedback.
  - Ask the peer to share their first implementation of the feedback for you to review and assess.
  - Gradually release responsibility to the peer by doing one example first, then slowly withdrawing support.
  - Have a reflective conversation with the peer, discussing their perception of the feedback, any concerns they have, and their plan for implementing the feedback.

Student Tasks 〉 Transfer Goals

Student Tasks	Transfer Goals
Students learn to check for understanding after giving a peer feedback to ensure it's understood and implemented correctly.	Students give their peers feedback and then check for understanding before moving on.
Students learn four strategies they can use to check for understanding after giving a peer feedback.	Students implement one or more of the strategies to check for understanding after giving a peer feedback.

Instructional Poster(s)

- This lesson has ONE Instructional Poster.
- The Instructional Poster for this lesson talks about how we struggle to multi-task. Giving 100% of our attention to two or more things at once is nearly impossible, so transferring this concept to giving others feedback means that we need to ensure that we have their undivided attention AND that we are giving them our undivided attention. Then, we need to follow that up with a check for understanding and potentially a little help implementing the feedback.
- Students are warned about questions that elicit automatic responses like, "Do you get it?" Yeah. "Do you understand?" Yeah. ("How was school today?" Fine.)

Student Handouts

- This lesson has TWO Student Handouts.
- DIRECTIONS: Read through the steps on this page ensuring your peer understands the feedback you are giving them. Then, complete the next page by following the directions in each column heading.
- The first Student Handout shows students the steps for ensuring your partner understands the feedback you've given them and provides options for how to check for understanding.
- The second Student Handout asks students to explain why each strategy to check for understanding can be effective, and why asking questions that elicit automatic responses are not effective.
- Finally, students describe one more strategy that they come up with to check for understanding. Be sure to evaluate each students' ideas here to determine if they are likely to work or not. Provide students with feedback on these answers.

How do I make sure they understood my feedback?

Think about all the times you've been in class and the teacher announces some direction to the whole class. You are only partially paying attention, but really your mind is still thinking about whatever you're working on. Two minutes later, you have no idea what your teacher said. I bet you're thankful that he or she didn't "Check for Understanding" with you, because you had no idea!

This is normal. Our brains don't switch gears that quickly or that easily. Our brains can't really multi-task. If we try to do two things at once, one of the tasks suffers. Therefore, we almost always choose to give something like 10% of our attention to the announcement, and 90% of our attention to our work!

When we give others feedback, it's important to make sure they are paying attention to our feedback with no distractions. When we're done giving that feedback, we need to check to see if they understood it by asking questions, having them summarize it for us, or having them show it to us. The one thing we should never do is ask, "Do you understand?" Because we all know that the only answer anyone ever gives to that question is, "Uh huh." (Otherwise, we have to listen to it all over again. And who wants to do that?) :-)

There are other forms of that question we need to avoid as well, such as, "Do you get it?" or "Does this make sense?" or "Sound good?" or anything else that's similar! "Okay?" (NO! That's another version of "Do you understand?")

Check for Understanding

Giving Meaningful Feedback to Others

Name: _____

Date: _____

BIG IDEA: Ensure that the person you are giving feedback to completely understands the feedback you've given them before moving on to other things. Don't think of giving feedback as a task you just check off a To Do List. Understand that it is your responsibility to help them grow and improve. We all share responsibility for helping each other grow!

DIRECTIONS: Read through the "Steps for ensuring your partner understands the feedback you've given them." Then, complete the next page by following the directions in each column heading.

How do I make sure they understood my feedback?

Steps for ensuring your partner understands the feedback you've given them

Not an Option:
Whatever you do, don't ask, "Do you get it?" or "Do you understand?" Everyone's initial reaction to that question is, "Yep!" even when they're confused!

1 Explain your feedback well and encourage them to ask Clarifying Questions as you explain.

2 Check for understanding.

Option 1:
Practice implementing the feedback WITH your peer. Help them at first, then see if they can do it without help. Try not to leave until they've got it!

Option 2:
Ask them to ask you a question, even if they don't think they have one. This might make it easier for them to ask you a question without feeling dumb.

Option 3:
Ask them to summarize what it is that you just taught them. Ask THEM clarifying questions as they explain to ensure they understand everything well.

Option 4:
Sit with them as they go through some of their work, looking for ways to improve their process based on your feedback. Give support if they need it.

How do I make sure they understood my feedback?

Ways to check for understanding	Explain why this is or is not a good strategy	Ways to check for understanding	Explain why this is or is not a good strategy
Practice implementing the feedback WITH your peer. Help them at first, then see if they can do it without help. Try not to leave until they've got it!		Sit with them as they go through some of their work, looking for ways to improve their process based on your feedback. Give support if they need it.	
Ask them to ask you a question, even if they don't think they have one. This might make it easier for them to ask you a question without feeling dumb.		Whatever you do, don't ask, "Do you get it?" or "Do you understand?" Everyone's initial reaction to that question is, "Yep!" even when they're confused!	
Ask them to summarize what it is that you just taught them. Ask THEM clarifying questions as they explain to ensure they understand everything well.		Describe one more good strategy to check if a peer understands the feedback you've given them:	

INTRODUCTION | PLANNING | METACOGNITION | SYNTHESIS | REFLECTION | SELF-ASSESSMENT | GOAL SETTING | **FEEDBACK**

bit.ly/48oh0qv

Set a positive tone for feedback exchanges by sharing genuine compliments before introducing constructive suggestions

7.18

Essential Question

How can a compliment help me give critical feedback?

Lesson Overview

In this lesson, students learn an important way to give feedback to their peers. They discover that it's helpful to start with a specific compliment about their peer's work before sharing any criticisms. This approach sets a positive tone of improvement and support instead of competition and teasing. Students are more likely to accept feedback from someone who wants to help and is kind and respectful. It can be tough to accept feedback from a peer who doesn't show interest in complimenting their work or doesn't respect them. To practice this skill, students write two specific compliments for fictional peers before giving them some helpful feedback to help them grow and improve.

Teacher Tips

- This lesson pairs well with the next lesson (Lesson 7.19). They both focus on feedback delivery methods. This lesson focuses on giving compliments to the person receiving feedback in order to help set the tone for a helpful interaction and try to prevent the receiver from becoming defensive or upset. If you are following the Instructional Spirals that are suggested in the Introduction chapter, you will have already taught Lesson 7.19 during the last Instructional Spiral.
- If the math problem on the second Student Handout is too difficult for your students, use it as an example to do together as a class. If your students are the right age to work on that type of problem, use it as an authentic opportunity to introduce the idea of long multiplication to the class!
- Most students are not naturals at giving people compliments. Be patient with them, but remind them to be specific and detailed with their compliments so they serve the purpose they are intended to serve (to set the tone of improvement, not competition).

Big Idea

Before giving constructive feedback, it's often beneficial to begin with a compliment. Find ways to point out strong parts of your peer's work in addition to giving them critical feedback. Sometimes it can be hard to find things to compliment on others' work because it's not up to the quality that you're used to, but it's even more important that you give high-quality compliments to students who are struggling on their work, because they may have more anxiety accepting your feedback.

Discussion/Reflection Questions

- Think about a time when someone gave you feedback and started with a compliment. How did it make you feel? Did it make you more open to listening and making improvements?
- Think of a time when you gave feedback to someone without starting with a compliment. How do you think starting with a compliment could have made your feedback better?
- Imagine giving feedback to a peer who is not as strong as you at the current skill you're both working on. Why is it important to begin with a compliment before sharing a criticism?

Student Tasks 〉 Transfer Goals

Student Tasks	Transfer Goals
Students learn about the importance of giving a specific compliment before sharing critical feedback.	Students prefer to give critical feedback to peers once they've made it clear that their purpose is to help, not show off.
Students practice giving compliments to fictional peers before providing critical feedback on their work.	Students apply the skill of giving a specific compliment to a peer before giving critical feedback in order to show kindness & reduce competitiveness.

Instructional Poster(s)

- This lesson has ONE Instructional Poster.
- The Instructional Poster for this lesson explains to students the importance of attaching specific compliments to any constructive feedback they give to their peers.
- It goes on to say that getting to know the person you are giving feedback to is important, so you know how important compliments are to them, and if they will trust the feedback you are giving them.
- Discuss how strong relationships can help the feedback process, BUT that even with weaker relationships, feedback should still be given and accepted. We can't use poor relationships as an excuse not to accept helpful feedback from certain peers in our class. Everyone needs to learn from everyone!

Student Handouts

- This lesson has TWO Student Handouts.
- DIRECTIONS: Read through the following compliments and the helpful feedback that goes along with them. Then complete the next page.
- Notice how each compliment sets up the critical feedback that is to come. It shouldn't feel like you're tricking the person you are giving critical feedback to. It should just feel like you are strengthening your relation-ship before addressing what appears to be a weakness in your work.
- DIRECTIONS: A peer in your classroom has come to you seeking feedback on their work. Do your best to answer their question, BUT equally important, give them a meaningful compliment about their work that builds them up. Your responses should be several sentences long.
- Remind students that the compliment should come BEFORE the critical feedback in order to set the tone.

How can a compliment help me give critical feedback?

Before giving constructive feedback, it's often beneficial to begin with a compliment. Find ways to point out strong parts of your peer's work in addition to giving them critical feedback. Sometimes it can be hard to find things to compliment on others' work because it's not up to the quality that you're used to, but it's even more important that you give high-quality compliments to students who are struggling on their work, because they may have more anxiety accepting your feedback.

Some students don't want to hear compliments on their work and they would just prefer to hear the constructive feedback you have to offer. Some students normally would need a compliment, but have such a strong relationship with you that they know you're just trying to help them (not trying to feel superior). Take time to discover what each of your peers need from you to be most comfortable. Don't take it upon yourself to "teach them to handle constructive criticism" or to "toughen them up before the real world eats them up." They still have plenty of time to develop a thick skin. But for now, they need help improving their skills in our class!

Lesson 7.18 — Instructional Poster 1 of 1

Giving Meaningful Feedback to Others

Name: _____
Date: _____

BIG IDEA: Before giving constructive feedback, it's often beneficial to begin with a compliment. Find ways to point out strong parts of your peer's work in addition to giving them critical feedback. Sometimes it can be hard to find things to compliment on others' work because it's not up to the quality that you're used to, but it's even more important that you give high-quality compliments to students who are struggling on their work, because they may have more anxiety accepting your feedback.

DIRECTIONS: Read through the following compliments and the helpful feedback that goes along with them. Then complete the next page.

How can a compliment help me give critical feedback?

"Wow! How did you get so good at sculpting? It's clear that you've worked hard at this! I especially like the curves you've put into this. What are your thoughts about including small carvings on this side to represent feathers?"

"Your swing has improved a ton! Don't worry if you don't hit the ball just yet. If you keep swinging like this, you'll start hitting the ball in no time! Our next step is to work on our eye-hand coordination. As the ball is being pitched..."

"I remember at the beginning of the year when you and I both only wrote like a sentence or two in a class period. Now we're both writing a ton more! I think I can help you with paragraphing if you could help me with spelling. Deal?"

"I honestly think the best way to improve your grades on tests is to improve your memory and study skills. I could never do well on a social studies test if I didn't read through my notes, make flash cards and have a friend quiz me. Let's start by..."

Lesson 7.18 — Student Handout 1 of 2

How can a compliment help me give critical feedback?

DIRECTIONS: A peer in your classroom has texted you seeking feedback on their work. Do your best to answer their question, BUT equally important, give them a meaningful compliment about their work that builds them up. Your responses should be several sentences long.

Lesson 7.18 — Student Handout 2 of 2

INTRODUCTION · PLANNING · METACOGNITION · SYNTHESIS · REFLECTION · SELF-ASSESSMENT · GOAL SETTING · FEEDBACK

bit.ly/41d4PKC

Nurture a supportive feedback culture by incorporating these three strategies into your critical feedback conversations

7.19

Essential Question

What are some formal strategies for giving feedback?

Lesson Overview

In this lesson, students learn three strategies for giving their peers feedback (especially critical feedback). The first is called a Compliment Sandwich where the critical feedback is delivered between two specific compliments about their peer's work. The second is called "Just in CASE Feedback" and involves giving a compliment, asking a question, suggesting something specific to help them improve, and ensuring that the feedback was received accurately. The final strategy is called "RISE and Shine Feedback," which is an adaptation of the RISE Model™[1] created by Emily Wray and is being used with permission. RISE and Shine Feedback has four steps: (1) Reflect, (2) Inquire, (3) Suggest, and (4) Elevate. All four steps are delivered to their peer with patience and kindness (the "Shine" component).

Teacher Tips

- PREREQUISITE: Lesson 7.18.
- The three strategies taught in this lesson have been "leveled" to show you, the teacher, that each strategy builds on the previous, and to offer differentiation opportunities for you. If your students need a challenge, you might choose to suggest that they complete all three strategies on their Student Handout, or that they choose two of the three to complete. If your students are younger or new to this concept, you might suggest that they choose one feedback strategy to complete for now or you might choose to focus solely on the Level 1 strategy exclusively.
- Decide if your students will be completing the Student Handouts for real situations in class where they give their peers feedback, or if they will need to create fictional examples - the directions allow for either.
- Since there are three strategies, you need to decide if students need three separate feedback experiences or if they can do the same experience multiple times.

1. © 2011 by Emily Wray - www.risemodel.com

Big Idea

Giving constructive or critical feedback to your peers can be tough sometimes. You don't want to upset a friend. You don't necessarily feel like you're any better than they are. And you worry that you might actually suggest things that are wrong or make suggestions that are worse than what they already have! Because of that, there are several strategies you can use to make giving constructive feedback easier.

Discussion/Reflection Questions

- How do you usually feel when you have to give constructive feedback to a peer? What are some specific worries or concerns that come to mind in those situations?
- Why is it important to find ways to make giving constructive feedback easier? How can it benefit both you and your peer?
- What are some strategies you learned in this lesson that can help make giving constructive feedback easier?
- Imagine giving constructive feedback to a peer in the future. How might you apply the strategies you learned to make the experience more positive and supportive for both of you?

Student Tasks 〉 Transfer Goals

Student Tasks	Transfer Goals
Students learn three specific strategies for giving their peers feedback.	Students have the tools to give their peers feedback (especially critical feedback) and use these tools whenever needed.
Students apply the three strategies in real or fictional situations to learn the pros and cons of each, and to become more confident delivering feedback.	Students deliver feedback to peers confidently (especially critical feedback) and with kindness & patience.

Instructional Poster(s)

- This lesson has ONE Instructional Poster.
- The Instructional Poster for this lesson teaches students three formal strategies for giving their peers critical feedback.
  - The first strategy is called a "Compliment Sandwich" because the critical feedback is sandwiched between two compliments.
  - The second strategy is called "Just in CASE Feedback" in which "C.A.S.E." is an acronym explained on the poster. Here, students check for understanding "just in case" their peer didn't understand everything.
  - Finally, the third strategy is called RISE and Shine Feedback. RISE is an acronym explained on the poster, and "shine" refers to the positive nature in which students should give each other feedback. "RISE and Shine Feedback" is an adaptation of the RISE Model™ created by Emily Wray, and is being used with permission. Learn more at - www.risemodel.com.

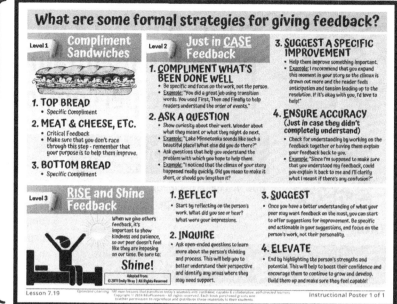

Student Handouts

- This lesson has TWO Student Handouts.
- DIRECTIONS: Using the three feedback strategies you learned from the Instructional Poster, complete each section below and on the next page for a real or fictional situation where you need to give someone feedback.
- Read through the Teacher Tips on the previous page for important considerations for this lesson.
- If the space is too small for your students to write everything in, feel free to ask them to complete this on a separate piece of paper (or online) and attach it to the assignment.
- If your students are comfortable recording themselves, have your students act out the three strategies on video instead of having to write them all.

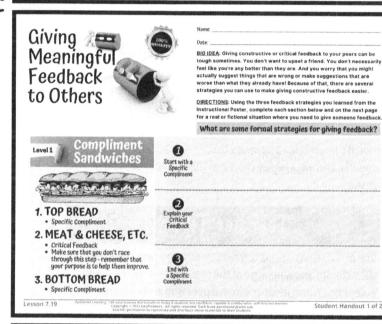

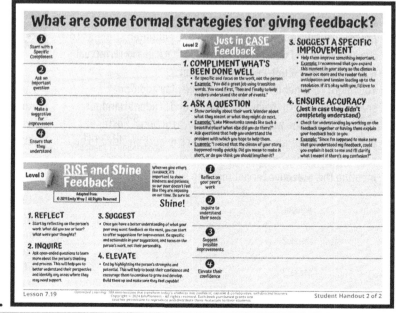

bit.ly/3uJwnLr

Focus feedback on the work instead of the person to maintain positive relationships & avoid the perception of personal attacks

Essential Question

How do I focus my feedback on the work, not the person?

Lesson Overview

In this lesson, students will first listen to examples of feedback that puts too much emphasis on the person rather than their work. They will understand how this type of feedback can strain relationships and learn to shift their focus toward providing feedback on the work instead. The concept is reinforced through the Student Handouts, which explore why personal-focused feedback can cause trouble and provide examples to illustrate this. Students will then imagine themselves in their peer's shoes to empathize with how it might feel to receive critical feedback. As students take on the role of an advisor, it's important to be aware that if feedback is delivered improperly, there is a higher chance of the recipient becoming defensive.

Teacher Tips

- One of the main reasons teachers avoid using peer feedback in their classrooms is because of the challenges associated with accepting critical feedback from a peer who is not highly respected. By focusing their feedback on the work instead of the person, students will have more success delivering feedback of a constructive nature than they would if they focused on the person. Therefore, this lesson attempts to enlighten students to the importance of delivering critical feedback in a kind, factual way instead of a blunt, opinionated manner.
- You might consider having students role play additional scenarios similar to the ones on the second Student Handout. This could be done while teaching the Instructional Poster or you might have students record their act-it-outs on video to be saved in an online portfolio. The video can act as evidence of meeting this objective (or not meeting it).

Big Idea

Compliments and Critical Feedback are both extremely important, but it's also important that you make sure your feedback compliments the WORK and not the PERSON. Your job is to help them improve the quality of their work, not the quality of their character or personality (so don't evaluate and share aspects of their personality, character, behaviors, etc. - that can be too personal and can lead to animosity between you both). The only exception is if they come to you asking for help on a personality or behavior issue.

Discussion/Reflection Questions

- How is focusing on the work instead of the person a better approach for giving feedback?
- How might it affect your relationship with a peer who gives you critical feedback that focuses too strongly on you rather than your work?
- How does understanding this concept help you become a better feedback giver?

Student Tasks 〉 Transfer Goals

Student Tasks	Transfer Goals
Students practice giving others' feedback that focuses on the work rather than the person.	Students give others feedback that doesn't make them feel defensive, making it easier for them to accept and implement.
Students put themselves in their peer's shoes and imagine what it might feel like when critical feedback is focused on them instead of their work.	Students have empathy when delivering feedback and strive to maintain strong relationships with those they are helping.

INTRODUCTION

PLANNING

METACOGNITION

SYNTHESIS

REFLECTION

SELF-ASSESSMENT

GOAL SETTING

FEEDBACK

Instructional Poster(s)

- This lesson has ONE Instructional Poster.
- The Instructional Poster for this lesson shows students examples of giving someone feedback that focuses on the person (which isn't recommended if you want students to accept critical feedback from their peers), an explanation of why that style of feedback isn't preferred, and then goes on to show an example of feedback that focuses on the work. While this may sound like political correctness or trying to avoid hurting the feelings of someone who is overly sensitive, it's actually an important consideration for students since critical feedback usually comes from the teacher, not their peers. In order to maintain strong relationships, we need to try to do everything in our power to avoid experiences that weaken those relationships.
- Try to brainstorm some more examples together as a class.

Student Handouts

- This lesson has TWO Student Handouts.
- DIRECTIONS: Read through the feedback examples below. Then, read and follow the directions on the next page.
- DIRECTIONS: A peer in your classroom has come to you seeking feedback on their work. Do your best to answer their question and give a meaningful compliment. Make sure your compliment AND critical feedback focus on the work and NOT the person. Each response should be several sentences long.
- The first Student Handout gives a few reasons & examples of why focusing feedback on the person instead of the work can cause trouble with peers.
- The second Student Handout asks students to apply what they've learned using two fictional scenarios.

How do I focus my feedback on the work, not the person?

Feedback that focuses on the PERSON	Feedback that focuses on the WORK
• "You are such an amazing writer! It seems to come so easily to you. I wish I had your talent!" 　• Although this is very kind to say to someone, it doesn't take into account how hard they might have worked to improve their skills. It's best to focus your feedback on the specific aspects of their writing.	• "This writing is filled with really strong ideas like _____ and _____! I'd love to learn how you came up with so many great ideas!"
• "You're not getting a lot of these math problems right, but this math is hard. You just might not be ready to 'get it' yet. Don't worry about it now. Maybe it'll be easier next year." 　• Even if this might be true, to some people, this can sound like, "You're not smart enough to learn this right now. Wait until you're smarter." Your job is to focus on helping them learn it the best they can and don't assume they won't be able to do so.	• "Finding equivalent fractions can be really hard at first. What helped me understand them was multiplying by the same number on top and on bottom..."
• "You've got a lot of spelling mistakes in this paper. Spelling is hard, and not everyone is good at it. I'd recommend you use Spell Check when you type your stories." 　• This is a good solution to the problem, but it doesn't demonstrate a GROWTH MINDSET. If this student works hard at improving this skill, it will likely improve. Try not to discourage their efforts, just help them make the necessary edits and any tips you can think of that might help.	• "It seems like you might be having some trouble with word endings -sion and -tion. One tip that I use is: If the ending is pronounced like CONFUSION, then it's usually spelled -sion. If the ending is pronounced like STATION, then it's usually spelled -tion."

Giving Meaningful Feedback to Others

Name: _____

Date: _____

BIG IDEA: Compliments and Critical Feedback are both extremely important, but it's also important that you make sure your feedback compliments the WORK and not the PERSON. Your job is to help them improve the quality of their work, not the quality of their character or personality (so don't evaluate and share aspects of their personality, character, behaviors, etc. - that can be too personal and can lead to animosity between you both). The only exception is if they come to you asking for help on a personality or behavior issue.

DIRECTIONS: Read through the Feedback examples below. Then, read and follow the directions on the next page.

Why Feedback that focuses on the PERSON can cause trouble	How do I focus my feedback on the work, not the person? Example
When we focus our critical feedback on the person, it allows them to take it "personally!" This brings emotions into it. We want to separate emotions from the feedback process.	"You're still not getting it. Let me show you how to do it again." This can be interpreted as being called stupid by the feedback giver.
When we give compliments that are focused on the talent or abilities a person has, it can take away from the hard work they put in to becoming so talented.	"You're so lucky that you can draw like that!" This can be annoying to hear when you know how hard it was to build those skills. It didn't just come naturally! It took lots of hard work, but others might be seeing it as a gift that you were born with.
Complimenting the person can also build an expectation in the receiver that they always need to demonstrate that level of ability.	"You're so smart!" may cause the person to become extremely uncomfortable when they make a mistake or have a wrong answer because they learn to think of their intelligence as their defining characteristic.

How do I focus my feedback on the work, not the person?

DIRECTIONS: A peer in your classroom has come to you seeking feedback on their work. Do your best to answer their question and give a meaningful compliment. Make sure your compliment AND critical feedback focus on the work and NOT the person. Each response should be several sentences long.

❶

"I finished my "Color By Number" turtle. What do you think?"

❷

"I think I'm done with my Science Fair slideshow. Can you tell me if there's anything I can do to improve these slides?"

bit.ly/3RvmUAc

Welcome feedback requests from peers as valuable opportunities to share your insights & contribute to their learning journey

Essential Question

How do I show tact when being asked for feedback?

Lesson Overview

In this lesson, students learn that it's natural to have impulsive thoughts that are not very tactful, but that it's not okay to share those thoughts verbally or non-verbally (gestures, sighs, frowns, etc.). They learn that it's important to review their internal dialogue quickly before impulsively reacting to the request from their peer. Once they've formulated a kind response, they can express their thoughts. It's crucial to emphasize that providing feedback often requires pausing their own work, as it plays a vital role in the learning process. However, you may also address situations where compromises or delayed feedback might be necessary to meet immediate needs in the best possible way.

Teacher Tips

- If you are fully-implementing the SLSI Process, students should be encouraged to give feedback or provide help nearly every time someone asks them to do so. If students are asking the same student constantly, have a quick chat with the class about the importance of asking everyone, not just the same people. Although this lesson teaches students about how to politely delay giving feedback or avoid giving help, this should not be used too often.
- This lesson integrates well with Social-Emotional Learning, so feel free to combine lesson objectives to accomplish both at once.

Big Idea

It's important for all of us to make time to provide feedback to others. We should never make others feel like their needs are less important than ours. Sometimes, it may be a little inconvenient to stop what you're doing to help someone else, but it's still worth trying to find some time for it. Before you speak or act, take a moment to think about how your words and actions might unintentionally make them feel like a burden. Everyone should feel valued and supported in our classroom.

Discussion/Reflection Questions

- Why is it important to pause and review your internal dialogue before responding to someone asking for feedback?
- How can non-verbal cues, such as gestures, sighs, or frowns, affect the way others perceive your thoughts or feedback?
- In what ways can providing feedback to others help both the giver and the receiver? Can you think of any examples of this?
- Imagine that you just asked for feedback from a peer and you noticed their non-verbal cues (such as gestures, sighs, or frowns) expressing their impulsive thoughts. How might those cues make you feel? Elaborate on this (tell me more).

Student Tasks 〉 Transfer Goals

Student Tasks	Transfer Goals
Students brainstorm correct and incorrect ways to tell someone that you don't have time to give them feedback right now.	Students apply problem-solving skills to find alternative solutions or suggestions when they can't give a peer feedback immediately.
Students imagine impulsive, negative thoughts entering their minds when being asked to give feedback and they re-phrase their words to show tact.	Students use empathy to ensure tactful communication, improving their self-awareness skills.

Instructional Poster(s)

- This lesson has ONE Instructional Poster.
- The Instructional Poster for this lesson demonstrates how our impulses don't always lead to tactful interactions with others. But when we take a moment to silently observe our impulses before speaking, we can often identify the problem with our thoughts and change the wording to show more tact. Discuss the poster with the class and see if any of your students have ever been in a similar situation before where they had to fight their initial thoughts in order to show more kindness and tact.
- If you have time, see if students can create their own act-it-outs with a scenario of their own, or with the one provided on the Instructional Poster. Remind them to keep everything school-appropriate!

Student Handouts

- This lesson has TWO Student Handouts.
- DIRECTIONS: Read the examples below in each box. Then, try to add three more (serious and school appropriate) responses next to each bullet provided.
- Possible answers for the left column might be some form of: Ignoring or dismissing their peer, Being sarcastic or mocking, Blaming others, Lying or giving misleading reasons.
- Possible answers for the right column might be some form of: Being too busy, Also being confused on that topic, or Not feeling well.
- DIRECTIONS: Your name is Hazel in each of these simulations. Read what your friend Charlotte asks you to do for them. Then, write what you might immediately think (but don't say) in the Internal Dialogue bubble. Finally, write what you DO say in the speech box. Be tactful!
- The first scenario should end with an acceptance to help or some sort of polite compromise (After I finish with...), etc.
- The second scenario should end with an acceptance to help or some sort of polite compromise (Could you also help me study my flash cards too?).

How do I show tact when being asked for feedback?

Impulse Control is an extremely important skill that is worth trying to improve throughout life. Your immediate reaction to others can make or break relationships, jobs, friendships, and so much more. Whether you blurt out the first thing that comes into your head, roll your eyes, make faces in disgust, or something else, these immediate reactions aren't usually accepted well by others. It would probably be better if you tried your best to think through your reactions, before letting them out!

Your friend Charlotte came to you with a question. Your immediate thoughts are not tactful. See how this plays out.

Internal Dialogue (You're allowed to think it, but it's not okay to say it)

"Oh man! I'm never going to finish my work on time if I help Charlotte. But then again, if I was stuck and someone didn't help me, that would really stink, so I think I can spare a few minutes to help her. It wouldn't be fair for me to be finished with my work and her to have nine problems left!"

"Hi Hazel – Is there any chance you can help me understand Problem #18? My partner and I are both stuck on it."

"Of course! That one was hard for me too, but I think I figured it out. Why don't you bring your partner over here and we'll work on it together!"

What you say out loud

Lesson 7.21 — Instructional Poster 1 of 1

Giving Meaningful Feedback to Others

Name: _____
Date: _____

BIG IDEA: Understand the importance of devoting quality time to offer others feedback that helps them grow. In order for our classroom to be successful, we all have to ask for feedback and provide time for giving others feedback. We should not make others feel like they're a burden. Sometimes, it's a bit inconvenient to pause what you're doing to help someone else, but you still should do it. In that case, use some internal dialogue before responding to the peer asking for feedback.

DIRECTIONS: Read the examples below in each box. Then, try to add three more (serious and school appropriate) responses next to each bullet provided.

How do I show tact when being asked for feedback?

WRONG ways to tell someone you can't help them

- "Sorry. I can't help you."
- "I don't have time right now to help you."
- "Can't give you feedback - too busy."
- "Everyone's asking me questions. Go ask someone else."
- "I have no idea how to do that."
- "Why do you always ask me?" Ask someone else!
- "I'm helping Kristen - I can't help everyone!"

RIGHT ways to tell someone you can't help them

- "I'm sorry, but Brandon asked me the same question and I honestly don't know how to help with that one."
- "I would really love to help you, but I'm worried I won't finish mine on time. Could you check in with someone else this time? I'm sorry!"
- "I'm not on that problem yet, but I think Yasmine was helping someone on it. Maybe check with her?"

Lesson 7.21 — Student Handout 1 of 2

How do I show tact when being asked for feedback?

DIRECTIONS: Your name is Hazel in each of these simulations. Read what your friend Charlotte asks you to do for them. Then, write what you might immediately think (but don't say) in the Internal Dialogue bubble. Finally, write what you DO say in the speech box. Be tactful!

Internal Dialogue (Think it, don't say it)

What you say out loud

"Hi Hazel - Can you record me dating my act-it-out? I can't just set my computer to record because it'll be moving all around."

Internal Dialogue (Think it, don't say it)

What you say out loud

"Hi Hazel - Can you help me review my note cards for the social studies test tomorrow? There are still a few that I don't understand."

Lesson 7.21 — Student Handout 2 of 2

bit.ly/47LTTGd

Improve the quality of the feedback you give others by following the three valuable tips taught in this lesson

Essential Question

What are some final tips on giving feedback to others?

Lesson Overview

In this lesson, students will learn a valuable strategy to provide feedback on the most crucial aspects of their peers' work. This will help them develop the ability to identify and prioritize the most significant areas for improvement. Students will also learn the importance of explaining the "why" behind the feedback and offer guidance on "how" to do it properly themself. Lastly, students will discover that giving feedback benefits both the receiver and the giver by enhancing understanding and retention. They'll drive this point home by reflecting on past experiences to see how feedback has positively influenced their own skill development and retention of knowledge.

Teacher Tips

- Younger students might not have as many experiences to draw from in order to complete the Student Handouts in this lesson, so it is advised to either have them use fictional (but realistic) scenarios instead of real-life experiences, or to do these pages together as a class (filling out the handouts or not.)
- You might want to display a poster with the four questions from the Instructional Poster for students to consider when trying to choose what to give feedback on. You can modify the questions or add additional ones as well. Many times, it's important to ask the receiver of the feedback what they want the giver to focus on, but sometimes the feedback that needs to be given the most is not obvious to the receiver.

Big Idea

Three Big Ideas:

1. GIVING feedback helps you learn even more than RECEIVING feedback! Students who teach what they've learned remember & understand more than those who spend the same time studying.
2. Giving feedback to a peer that doesn't result in meaningful improvements is not time well-spent, so choose WHAT you give them feedback on wisely, and
3. Feedback isn't just identifying what's "right or wrong" or what's "good or bad." Feedback needs to explain WHY it's not good enough and help the receiver understand HOW to make it better.

Discussion/Reflection Questions

- Imagine you're going to teach a friend about something you just learned. How do you think teaching them will help you remember and understand the topic better?
- Pretend you're giving feedback to a friend on a story they wrote. How will you make sure your feedback helps them improve? How will you decide what to give feedback on?
- You just got your project back from your teacher and it has a "C" or a 75% written on it but nothing else. Is this helpful or would you like more information? What do you wish your teacher could tell you?

Student Tasks ⟩ Transfer Goals

Student Tasks	Transfer Goals
Students learn to ask themselves four questions that help them hone in on what's best to give their peer feedback on.	Students will make wise decisions when giving their peers feedback so the time spent is efficient and valuable.
Students learn not to just grade their peer's work. They also need to explain WHY something is not good enough and HOW to make it better.	Students explain the reasons why something is not satisfactory and offer specific guidance on how it can be improved.

Instructional Poster(s)

- This lesson has ONE Instructional Poster.
- The Instructional Poster for this lesson goes over two final tips students can use when giving feedback to others. Since it's often hard for students to choose the best feedback to give, they are given a guide to think through. There are four potential priorities when it comes to choosing the most important feedback to give first: (1) What the teacher needs to see in this assignment, (2) a past skill that is still not mastered, (3) a grade level skill that is not yet mastered, and (4) a skill that is repeatedly done incorrectly.
- The second tip is to always try to teach your peer WHY something is wrong and HOW to fix it, so they don't come to rely on their peers forever. ("Give a man a fish...")

Student Handouts

- This lesson has TWO Student Handouts.
- DIRECTIONS: In the large, empty rectangles, write about a time when you either gave someone feedback that helped you remember or understand it better OR when you had to teach someone how to do something and it helped you become better at that skill or knowledge. Finally, answer the Yes/No question that follows the rectangle.
- The first Student Handout asks students to think of three times when they gave someone feedback or received feedback from someone else and reflect on whether it helped them remember that feedback well (giving others feedback helps recall).
- DIRECTIONS: Fill in each circle on this page with your answers.
- The second Student Handout asks students to brainstorm eight final tips on giving others feedback that haven't been mentioned in these lessons.

What are some final tips on giving feedback to others?

Know how to focus in on critical (constructive) feedback that helps your peer improve THE MOST. Don't focus on one small mistake in their work when there are more important areas in which to give them feedback.

When giving peers critical feedback, think about what you say to them in this order:

1 What is it that our teacher wants us to do on this assignment or task? Did my peer do that, and did they do it well?

2 What is it that our teacher has taught us in the past that my peer is still not doing correctly? Can I help them learn this?

3 What is it that students in this grade level should be able to do, that my peer is not able to do? Can I help them learn this?

4 What is this peer doing wrong repeatedly that I can help them improve or fix?

The goal is to teach your peer WHY something is wrong and HOW to fix the error so they don't keep making the same mistake in the future. The goal is NOT just to identify and fix mistakes for them.

Example 1:
It looks like you're forgetting to carry the one in these problems. The way you're doing it means that 4 times 3 is 2, but when we carry the one, that means that 4 times 3 is 12. This one ends up making a big difference in the problem! After you do problem 7, you can check it against my answer to see if you've got it!

Example 2:
Just a reminder that patriots were the Americans who wanted to break away from the British, and the loyalists were the Americans who wanted to stay loyal to the King of England. Do we have it backwards in our script?

Instructional Poster 1 of 1

Giving Meaningful Feedback to Others

Giving other people feedback ends up helping the GIVER as well as the RECEIVER! Any time you teach something to someone, it makes the skill or understanding more permanent!

Name: _____
Date: _____

BIG IDEA: Giving others feedback doesn't just help the recipients, it also helps the givers! Studies show that giving feedback helps you learn even more than receiving feedback! In addition, students who spend time teaching what they've learned go on to show better understanding and knowledge retention than students who simply spend the same time studying. Do yourself a favor: give someone some meaningful feedback!

DIRECTIONS: In the large, empty rectangles, write about a time when you either gave someone feedback that helped you remember or understand it better OR when you had to teach someone how to do something and it helped you become better at that skill or knowledge. Finally, answer the Yes/No question that follows the rectangle.

What are some final tips on giving feedback to others?

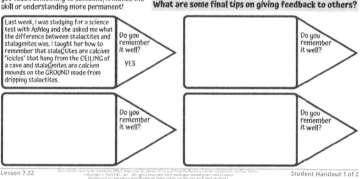

Last week, I was studying for a science test with Ashley and she asked me what the difference between stalactites and stalagmites was. I taught her how to remember that stalaCtites are calcium "icicles" that hang from the CEILING of a cave and stalaGmites are calcium mounds on the GROUND made from dripping stalactites.

Do you remember it well? YES

Do you remember it well?

Do you remember it well?

Do you remember it well?

Student Handout 1 of 2

What are some final tips on giving feedback to others?

What final tips, tricks, ideas, observations, etc. should be added into our "Giving Feedback to Others" curriculum?

What has worked well for you?
What hasn't worked well for you?

What was hard at first, but you discovered a way to make it easier?

What feedback idea have you heard about that you might like to try some time? What feedback technique would you like to invent & try out?

What do you wish others knew about giving feedback to their peers?

Fill in each circle on this page with your answers.

Student Handout 2 of 2

7.23

Decide when to persist independently, when to seek peer assistance, and when to consult the teacher for guidance

bit.ly/3RbDJiv

Essential Question

When do I ask for help?
When should I persevere?

Lesson Overview

In this lesson, students learn that there are usually three strategies they should choose between when they are confused or challenged. These strategies include persevering, asking a peer, or asking the teacher. Through a class discussion, students learn some guidelines for when to use each strategy AND they brainstorm some examples that would prompt students to use each strategy in their classroom.

Teacher Tips

- There are five sections in the Feedback Unit. This lesson begins the "Seeking feedback from others" section.
- You might want to consider displaying a poster of the Guidelines students come up with on their Student Handout that the class agrees to. You can refer them to the poster whenever students come to you for something you'd rather they ask a peer or persevere. This act will help them build collaboration skills and problem-solving skills. By the end of the year, students will likely only come to the teacher with questions that involve unclear directions or permission to do something. The rest will be solved independently or collaboratively.
- You may want to mention that asking a parent, older sibling, neighbor or someone else who is capable of helping can be a strategy students use at home.

Big Idea

I'm confused. What do I do? I know that it's important to persevere and struggle sometimes, because that's how we learn. But I also know that I'm supposed to ask for help when I need it. So when do I keep trying on my own and when do I ask others for help? After all, there are times to persevere, times to ask a peer, and times to bend the teacher's ear!

Discussion/Reflection Questions

- Think about a time when you used one of the three strategies taught in class. Reflect on your decision and consider if it was the most effective strategy in that situation.
- Reflect on the importance of balancing perseverance with seeking help. Why is it valuable to try and figure things out on your own before asking for assistance? How does this help with your learning and growth?
- Imagine that a classmate has come to you for help, but it was for a task that they needed to persevere on, rather than ask a peer for help. What do you do? Remember to be tactful!

Student Tasks ⟩ Transfer Goals

Student Tasks	Transfer Goals
Students learn three strategies they should use when they are confused or challenged.	Students no longer rely on asking the teacher for help on everything or melting down when confused.
Students develop guidelines to follow for when to choose each strategy and brainstorm examples of each.	Students use each strategy appropriately in class and in life so they are appropriately challenged, yet get help when warranted.

INTRODUCTION

PLANNING

METACOGNITION

SYNTHESIS

REFLECTION

SELF-ASSESSMENT

GOAL SETTING

FEEDBACK

Instructional Poster(s)

- This lesson has ONE Instructional Poster.
- The Instructional Poster for this lesson shows students that there are at least three things they can do when they are confused or challenged. They can persevere and keep trying to figure it out, they can ask a peer for help, or they can ask the teacher. The trick is figuring out which one to do when. That's what this lesson is all about. If you have any additional strategies students should consider, now is the time to introduce them.
- You don't need to expand on each strategy too far, because students will be expanding on them on their Student Handouts. Please just make sure they understand your expectations.

Student Handouts

- This lesson has TWO Student Handouts.
- DIRECTIONS: Read through each of the SITUATIONS in each column below. Then, add more SITUATIONS in each box that fit the column. Do the same for the GUIDELINES on the next page.
- The first Student Handout asks students to brainstorm examples of times students should persevere, ask a peer, or bend their teacher's ear. These should be specific to their classroom. You might need to give them examples if it's early in the year.
- The second Student Handout asks students to brainstorm guidelines to follow regarding when to persevere, ask a peer, or bend their teacher's ear. These should be specific to their classroom. You might need to help them get started if it's early in the year.

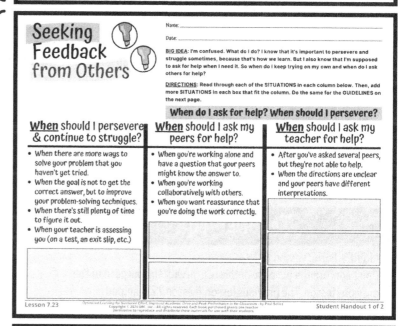

Seek input at appropriate times, ensuring that both the provider and receiver can fully engage in the feedback process

7.24

bit.ly/3sYAMtA

bit.ly/3sYAMtA

Essential Question

What are some good & bad times to ask for feedback?

Big Idea

There are good times to ask a peer for feedback and there are bad times.! Therefore, it's important to identify situations when you MIGHT consider asking someone for feedback and situations when you MIGHT NOT want to ask for feedback. Sometimes, it's just a matter of waiting a few minutes!

Lesson Overview

In this lesson, students analyze different scenarios to determine if they would be good times to ask for feedback or if they would be bad times to do so. Some of the situations can be argued either way, so it's the reasoning behind their answer that matters most. Next, students create their own scenarios, two of which are good times to ask a peer for feedback and two of which are bad times, explaining why they believe that to be true for each. There are times in a school day that lend themselves well to asking peers for feedback and times that don't. Students need to learn how to distinguish between both. They learn to do so in this lesson.

Discussion/Reflection Questions

- How can you tell if it's an appropriate moment to ask a peer for feedback during a class activity? What signs or clues would you look for to know if it's the right moment? If it doesn't seem like the right time, how would you adjust your approach?
- Imagine you're working on something in class, and you're not sure if it's the right time to ask a friend for feedback. What can you do to figure out if it's a good moment? What strategies or tricks can you use to make that decision? How will you balance your need for feedback with what's happening in the classroom and the task you're working on?

Teacher Tips

- PREREQUISITE: Lesson 7.23
- Don't confuse the purpose of this lesson with the purpose of the previous lesson. The previous lesson (Lesson 7.23) helped students identify when they should persevere, ask a peer for help/feedback, or ask a teacher for help/feedback. This lesson assumes that the student believes the situation requires them to ask a peer for help/feedback, but now they need to consider other factors before asking that peer for help/feedback. This lesson explores those other factors.
- Suggested answers for the Instructional Poster:
  - 1 - You might want to write a bit more before asking for feedback unless you worry you might be doing something wrong.
  - 2 - Since you've been assigned a partner, they are probably there to give feedback, so ask away!
  - 3 - Not a good time.
  - 4 - Great time to ask for feedback to be sure you've done it correctly.
  - 5 - Assuming it's a good time for the peer and your teacher, it's a good time to ask for some help.
  - 6 - Not a good reason to ask a peer for feedback. You're taking time away from them so you can get a break.

Student Tasks ⟩ Transfer Goals

Student Tasks	Transfer Goals
Students analyze different scenarios to determine if they would be good times to ask for feedback or if they would be bad times to do so.	Students have a clearer understanding of appropriate and inappropriate times to ask peers for feedback.
Students create their own good and bad time scenarios, explaining why they believe that to be true for each.	Students use this technique when considering asking a peer for feedback to determine if it's an appropriate time to do so.

Instructional Poster(s)

- This lesson has ONE Instructional Poster.
- The Instructional Poster for this lesson helps students identify when it's a good time to ask their peers for feedback and when it's a bad time to ask. This will help them understand that they can't go asking a peer for help when it interrupts instruction or during times when silence is required, etc. You will need to help guide students through each scenario so they know what is expected in your classroom. Every teacher is different, so try to prepare ahead of time for these situations. For the record, my students were allowed to ask for feedback on everything except an assessment, but they were asked not to interrupt direct instruction to do so. They could ask a peer just about any other time, though. I never prioritized formative assessment over another opportunity to learn.

Student Handouts

- This lesson has TWO Student Handouts.
- DIRECTIONS: Read each bubble below. Think about whether it is an appropriate time to ask for feedback, or if it wouldn't be the best time to ask for feedback. Then, answer the question in the bubble wand below it. Finally, create your own on the next page.
- The first Student Handout gives students two scenarios that are good times to ask a peer for feedback and two scenarios that are bad times to ask a peer for feedback. They are asked to explain why this is true for each.
- The second Student Handout asks the students to come up with two new scenarios that are good times to ask a peer for feedback and two more scenarios that are bad times to ask a peer for feedback and explain why for each.

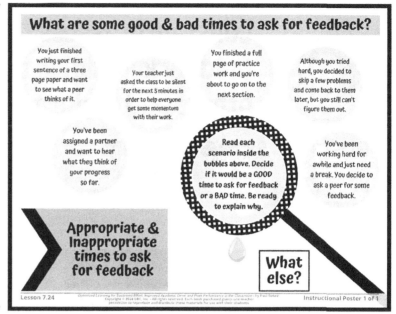

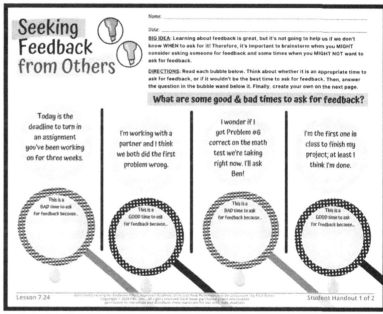

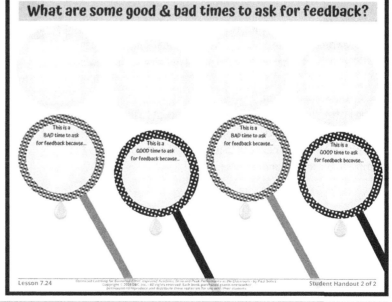

bit.ly/3NhBKbf

Constantly assess the quality of the feedback you give others and receive from others and make adjustments, as needed

Essential Question

What are some reasons feedback might not be helpful?

Big Idea

Feedback isn't automatically valuable. For example, if you always ask for feedback on the same thing, you miss out on so many opportunities to grow other skills! But if we focus on giving and asking for feedback that is valuable, it will ultimately have a bigger impact on everyone's learning.

Lesson Overview

In this lesson, students learn about situations where feedback they receive may not be helpful. They understand what factors can affect the quality of feedback and how to consider those factors when giving feedback to others. They learn to avoid situations that make feedback less useful and improve their own feedback by thinking about what the receiver needs. Then, students look at new situations and explain why the feedback given in those situations is often not helpful. Finally, students reflect on and write about times when they received unhelpful feedback or set goals for themselves to give better feedback in the future.

Discussion/Reflection Questions

- Reflect on your own experiences of receiving unhelpful feedback.
  - What made one situation's feedback less helpful?
    - How did it affect your learning and growth?
    - How could the feedback have been improved to make it more valuable?
  - What do a lot of those experiences of receiving unhelpful feedback have in common?
  - How can you apply what you've learned in this lesson to avoid giving unhelpful feedback to others in the future?

Teacher Tips

- This lesson is a prerequisite for the next lesson (Lesson 7.26) which focuses on what students can do to ensure that they get the best feedback possible.
  - For older students: You may want to combine this lesson with the next lesson if you have the time to teach them together.
  - For younger students: You may want to teach this lesson on a Friday and the next lesson on a Monday (or any longer stretch of time) because it lends itself nicely to reviewing and revisiting the first lesson's important concepts during the second lesson.
- The Instructional Poster and Student Handouts use a diamond metaphor to symbolize something valuable. However, in this lesson, we explore feedback that may not be very helpful, so we refer to these diamonds as "imitations."

Student Tasks 〉 Transfer Goals

Student Tasks	Transfer Goals
Students learn about situations where feedback they receive may not be helpful.	Students' increased awareness of the value of their feedback is heightened, resulting in more effort and care when providing it to others.
Students explain why the feedback given in specific situations is often not helpful and reflect on past situations involving unhelpful feedback.	Students avoid situations where giving or receiving feedback might result in a waste of time for both parties.

Instructional Poster(s)

- This lesson has ONE Instructional Poster.
- The Instructional Poster for this lesson gives eight examples of how some feedback is NOT valuable to the receiver. These are all areas that we need to be aware of so we can avoid giving (and asking for) feedback that doesn't end up valuable to the receiver. Take a little time to go over each "imitation diamond" on the Instructional Poster. See if you or your students can brainstorm any additional ideas to add to the discussion.
- This is a great opportunity to discuss potential solutions to the ideas on the Instructional Poster and those generated in class. Students might make incorrect assumptions about how to solve each of these, but you have the chance to correct those.

Student Handouts

- This lesson has TWO Student Handouts.
- DIRECTIONS: Read the reasons why feedback might not be valuable to you in the imitation diamonds below. Then, explain why that is true on the lines (like the Instructional Poster).
- Encourage students to "Tell Me More" so their answers aren't bare bones.
- DIRECTIONS: Read each bullet on the right. Then, choose one for each index card below to complete according to the column header. Finally, draw a line connecting your card to the bullet.
- If your students are young, they might need to explain "how this type of unhelpful feedback could happen this year in school if we're not aware of it" but if your students are older, they might be able to describe actual instances when they received feedback that wasn't helpful to them in the past. Either way is fine - you can even allow them to "invent" fictional scenarios that sound real!

What are some reasons feedback might not be helpful?

Feedback might not be VALUABLE to you if...

...it's not about the specific thing you're trying to improve. It might be about something different or not related to what you're doing right now.

... it comes from someone who lacks the confidence to give you their true thoughts or opinions. Maybe they're unsure of it themselves or maybe they don't know much about the topic.

...it's confusing or incomplete. If the feedback isn't clear or leaves a lot of important details out, it's hard to know what to do with it.

...the feedback only points out problems without telling you how to fix them, it's not very helpful. Valuable feedback should give you ideas, suggestions and examples on how to get better.

...it's influenced by someone's personal opinions or biases. This means that the feedback you get might not be completely focused on the facts, but more about what someone likes or dislikes.

...it's given in a way that feels mean or attacks your confidence. This kind of feedback doesn't help you improve because you get emotional instead of focusing on the content of the feedback.

...you don't trust the person giving it. If you don't believe they have good intentions or if they've been unreliable in the past, it can be hard to accept their feedback.

...it's given at the wrong time or in a situation where it doesn't make sense. Getting feedback that doesn't match what you're working on or when you're not ready for it can be confusing.

Seeking Feedback from Others

Name: _____
Date: _____

BIG IDEA: Feedback isn't automatically valuable. For example, if you always ask for feedback on the same thing, you miss out on so many opportunities to grow other skills! But if we focus on giving and asking for feedback that is valuable, it will ultimately have a bigger impact on everyone's learning.

DIRECTIONS: Read the reasons why feedback might not be valuable to you in the imitation diamonds below. Then, explain why that is true on the lines (like the Instructional Poster).

What are some reasons feedback might not be helpful?

Feedback might not be VALUABLE to you if... it's given to you too fast or if too much information is given to you all at once.

Feedback might not be VALUABLE to you if... it's too general and doesn't give you specific information about what you did well or need to improve.

Feedback might not be VALUABLE to you if... it's too advanced or complicated for your age or level of understanding.

Why?

Why?

Why?

What are some reasons feedback might not be helpful?

DIRECTIONS: Read each bullet on the right. Then, choose one for each index card below to complete according to the column header. Finally, draw a line connecting your card to the bullet.

Examples from your life OR How this could happen in school this year if we're not aware of it

Feedback might NOT be valuable to you if...

...it's not about the specific thing you're trying to improve. It might be about something different or not related to what you're doing right now.

... it comes from someone who lacks the confidence to give you their true thoughts or opinions. Maybe they're unsure of it themselves or maybe they don't know much about the topic.

...it's confusing or incomplete. If the feedback isn't clear or leaves a lot of important details out, it's hard to know what to do with it.

...it's influenced by someone's personal opinions or biases. This means that the feedback you get might not be completely focused on the facts, but more about what someone likes or dislikes.

...it's given in a way that feels mean or attacks your confidence. This kind of feedback doesn't help you improve because you get emotional instead of focusing on the content of the feedback.

...the feedback only points out problems without telling you how to fix them, it's not very helpful. Valuable feedback should give you ideas, suggestions and examples on how to get better.

...it's given at the wrong time or in a situation where it doesn't make sense. Getting feedback that doesn't match what you're working on or when you're not ready for it can be confusing.

bit.ly/3uOgIdS

Optimize the benefits of peer feedback by implementing techniques that promote impactful feedback exchanges

Essential Question

What should I do to get the most valuable feedback?

Lesson Overview

In this lesson, students explore and talk about some helpful tips for asking others for meaningful feedback. These tips help ensure that the feedback they receive from others is valuable and a worthwhile use of time for everyone involved. Students then share a personal example of when they've used each tip recently, or set a goal to use them soon, and write about that goal. By doing this, the feedback exchange between students should become more helpful and effective.

Teacher Tips

- PREREQUISITE: Lesson 7.26
  - For older students: You may choose to combine this lesson with the previous lesson if you have the time to teach them together.
  - For younger students: You may want to teach these two lessons straddling a weekend (or any longer stretch of time) because this lesson lends itself nicely to reviewing and revisiting the first lesson's important concepts.
- Asking for feedback and asking for help often go hand in hand. When students give each other feedback, it's important to also offer help in putting that feedback into action. So, don't worry if your discussions seem centered around students asking each other for help. In a supportive and collaborative classroom, it's vital to see students asking their peers for help and providing help in return.

Big Idea

Sometimes, the easiest or most obvious feedback we give to our peers may not be the most helpful. Let's say a student has trouble with spelling. They might receive lots of feedback on their spelling mistakes in their writing, but they might also need feedback on how to organize their ideas or form better sentences. To get the most valuable feedback from others, we need to follow a few helpful tips, just like that one!

Discussion/Reflection Questions

- Which tip for getting valuable feedback did you like the most? Why? How do you think following that tip can make the feedback you receive even better?
- Picture yourself asking a classmate for feedback on something you're working on. How can you follow the tips we learned today to make sure you get valuable feedback?
- Imagine you're giving feedback to a friend on their project. How can you use the tips we learned to make your feedback really helpful?

Student Tasks 〉 Transfer Goals

Student Tasks	Transfer Goals
Students explore and talk about some helpful tips for asking others for meaningful feedback.	Students' increased awareness of the tips presented in class enhances the quality of the feedback they seek and provide.
Students share a personal example of when they've used each tip recently, or set a goal to use them soon.	Students give each other more helpful and effective feedback because of the goals they've set.

Instructional Poster(s)

- This lesson has ONE Instructional Poster.
- The Instructional Poster is a Warning List of seven things students should do (and not do) when it comes tor asking for feedback. (Each tip starts with a "Don't" and ends with what they should do.) Highlight verbally (or visually) what students SHOULD do since that's what directly answers the essential question of the lesson. (They didn't make sense without the "don'ts".)
- As a class, come up with some of your own Do's and Don'ts for getting the most valuable feedback from others.

Student Handouts

- This lesson has TWO Student Handouts.
- DIRECTIONS: Read the feedback suggestions in the symbols below. Then, give a specific example of when you've implemented each tip in the recent past, or make a specific goal to do so soon and explain that goal in the space provided. Do the same on the next page.
- The first Student Handout and the second one have the same directions, but focus on different tips.
    - For younger students: You might choose to do the first handout together as a class to set the tone for what you expect and then allow students to complete the second student handout without teacher support. If they don't meet your expectations, you can ask them to analyze how the first handout and second handout differ with regards to their work, and then have them revise.
    - For older students: You might choose to do one of them together to set the tone for your expectations, but then have students complete the rest independently or with a partner.

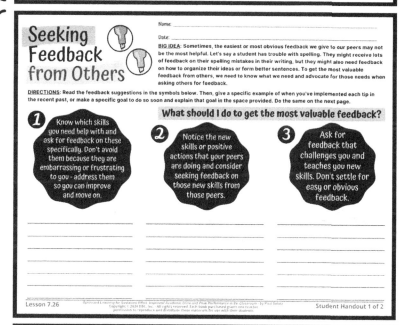

INTRODUCTION
PLANNING
METACOGNITION
SYNTHESIS
REFLECTION
SELF-ASSESSMENT
GOAL SETTING
FEEDBACK

bit.ly/3GudhvB

Communicate your preferred "level of feedback" to ensure that the feedback you receive can be successfully utilized

Essential Question

What "level of feedback" do I need?

Lesson Overview

In this lesson, students learn to evaluate the situation they find themselves in when asking someone for feedback on their work. They consider important factors like how much time they have and what specific area of their work they want to improve. By understanding their specific needs for each assignment, they can save time and effort for themselves and their peers. They also discover the value of setting clear boundaries, like focusing on a particular section, to avoid wasting time on unnecessary feedback. By being mindful of their goals and communicating effectively, students can make the feedback process more efficient and beneficial for everyone involved.

Teacher Tips

- One suggestion is to apply the four levels of feedback to a specific assignment or subject. Set up fairly explicit descriptions of each level and have students practice asking for feedback at each of the levels over time. Just be sure to teach them how to apply this concept to other assignments and subjects so they transfer the skill.
- This lesson is all about teaching students to:
  - Reflect on their needs, goals, and limitations before seeking feedback, to better understand what specific areas they want to improve and the level of feedback they require.
  - Prioritize what feedback would be most beneficial for the situation and set boundaries for those providing the feedback to ensure that time is saved and attention is given to the most pressing issues.
  - Use effective communication so what they are thinking is clearly passed on to their peer.

Big Idea

In order to get the best feedback from others, make it easy on them by giving them the "level of feedback" you want to receive. You are more likely to use the feedback they give you if it fits within your timeframe and willingness to make changes. It also saves them the frustration of having to guess just how much feedback you want. Finally, don't feel like you need them to give you feedback on the entire assignment. Consider using the "levels of feedback" on just a section of your work.

Discussion/Reflection Questions

- Think about a time when you asked someone for feedback on your work, but you didn't receive the type of feedback that you needed most. How could you have better explained your needs beforehand to make sure the feedback you got was the feedback you needed?
- Imagine that you have a big project due tomorrow and JUST received a TON of feedback on the things you could fix to improve it. You know you have a busy evening ahead. How might this make you feel? How could you have prevented this? What will you do at this point?

Student Tasks 〉 Transfer Goals

Student Tasks	Transfer Goals
Students learn to be aware of their timeframe for implementing feedback and to prioritize areas that need feedback the most.	Students apply time management and prioritization skills to important areas of their life.
Students learn about the four levels of feedback and how to use them to ensure that the feedback provided is most useful.	Students apply the four levels of feedback to effectively request feedback in various situations.

Instructional Poster(s)

- This lesson has ONE Instructional Poster.
- The Instructional Poster for this lesson teaches students a method for asking for just the right amount of feedback for their situation. Sometimes, you want every bit of feedback you can get so you can fix everything and end up with a near-perfect end product (e.g. a book editor or a product design team). Sometimes, you just want to know if there's anything that HAS to be fixed, because time is of the essence. And there are two levels described in between those extremes.
- Dialogue examples have been provided to help students "hear" what it sounds like to ask for each level of feedback from a peer.

Student Handouts

- This lesson has TWO Student Handouts.
- DIRECTIONS: Read through the poster on the right. Imagine an assignment and a timeframe when you might ask someone for feedback at each level, and write your answers in each column on the next page. Follow the directions in each column header to make sure you complete the page correctly. An example has been provided.
- The first Student Handout just gives students the Big Idea, Directions, and a description of the four levels of feedback.
- The second Student Handout is where students write example assignments, timeframes and quotes that show how they might ask a peer for feedback in class at each level of feedback.
- Encourage students to use real examples from your class where each level of feedback might have been needed.

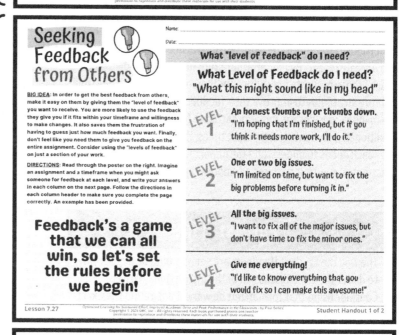

What "level of feedback" do I need?

What Level of Feedback do I need? "What this might sound like in my head"		"Ways you might ask others for this level of feedback"
LEVEL 1	An honest thumbs up or thumbs down. "I'm hoping that I'm finished, but if you think it needs more work, I'll do it."	• "Did I do this right?" • "What do you think about my drawing?" • "Do you think I did enough?"
LEVEL 2	One or two big issues. "I'm limited on time, but want to fix the big problems before turning it in."	• "Is there anything I should do to this before I turn it in?" • "Would you change anything on this?"
LEVEL 3	All the big issues. "I want to fix all of the major issues, but don't have time to fix the minor ones."	• "Is there any way you could look this over and let me know what I NEED to fix? I'm turning it in tomorrow."
LEVEL 4	Give me everything! "I'd like to know everything that you would fix so I can make this awesome!"	• "I'm entering the Writing contest and want this to be amazing. Is there any way you can help me make it great?"

Lesson 7.27 · Instructional Poster 1 of 1

Seeking Feedback from Others

Name: _____
Date: _____

BIG IDEA: In order to get the best feedback from others, make it easy on them by giving them the "level of feedback" you want to receive. You are more likely to use the feedback they give you if it fits within your timeframe and willingness to make changes. It also saves them the frustration of having to guess just how much feedback you want. Finally, don't feel like you need them to give you feedback on the entire assignment. Consider using the "levels of feedback" on just a section of your work.

DIRECTIONS: Read through the poster on the right. Imagine an assignment and a timeframe when you might ask someone for feedback at each level, and write your answers in each column on the next page. Follow the directions in each column header to make sure you complete the page correctly. An example has been provided.

Feedback's a game that we can all win, so let's set the rules before we begin!

What "level of feedback" do I need?

What Level of Feedback do I need? "What this might sound like in my head"

LEVEL 1	An honest thumbs up or thumbs down. "I'm hoping that I'm finished, but if you think it needs more work, I'll do it."
LEVEL 2	One or two big issues. "I'm limited on time, but want to fix the big problems before turning it in."
LEVEL 3	All the big issues. "I want to fix all of the major issues, but don't have time to fix the minor ones."
LEVEL 4	Give me everything! "I'd like to know everything that you would fix so I can make this awesome!"

Lesson 7.27 · Student Handout 1 of 2

What "level of feedback" do I need?

Assignment or Skill	Timeframe to make changes	Feedback Level	A quote that shows how you will ask for feedback
A piece of artwork that focuses on shading.	I have the weekend to make changes.	2	"Could you help me improve two or three of my biggest problems?"
		1	Ask for Level 1 Feedback:
		2	Ask for Level 2 Feedback:
		3	Ask for Level 3 Feedback:
		4	Ask for Level 4 Feedback:

Lesson 7.27 · Student Handout 2 of 2

bit.ly/3R7A5pP

Minimize the burden on those you request feedback from by being concise, focused, and considerate of their time and resources

Essential Question

How can I make it easy on others to give me feedback?

Big Idea

In order to get the best feedback from others, make it easy on them by:

- limiting what you ask them to read through or look at,
- highlighting the most important sections for them to look at,
- having them check the hardest problems first,
- referring to the part of the rubric or directions you need help improving, etc.

If your peer gets overwhelmed, feels annoyed, or feels like you're asking too much, then they aren't likely to take it all that seriously, resulting in poor feedback.

Lesson Overview

In this lesson, students engage in a brainstorming activity to identify situations that may lead to frustration when receiving a peer's request for feedback. Sample scenarios include where the timeframe is too short, the workload is overwhelming, expectations are unrealistic, etc. By empathizing, students gain an understanding of why these requests may appear bothersome to others. They then explore strategies to improve their feedback requests, making them more considerate and approachable for their peers. Additionally, students learn that at times, the peer being asked for feedback needs to understand the importance of supporting their classmates, even if it requires a temporary pause in their own work.

Discussion/Reflection Questions

- Why is it important to understand how others might feel when you ask for feedback? How does thinking about their perspective help you receive stronger feedback?
- Imagine that you're nervous to ask a friend for feedback because you think it might be too overwhelming or complicated for them. How can you make it easier for them to help you? (Chunk it? Simplify it? Make it fun for them?)

Teacher Tips

- The way the Student Handouts are set up would be a great way to direct the class discussion of the Instructional Poster. Consider using that format, but be wary of answering the exact same questions that are on the handout.
- As a conclusion to this lesson, please tell your students that no matter what, we all need to control our emotions when it comes to asking for feedback and giving others feedback. We can't be too worried to ask or too annoyed to take time for others. We need to understand that we are a collaborative team, working hard to help everyone grow and improve. If emotions get too involved, it will only hinder that. So if you want to help your peer improve their request for feedback or the way they deliver the feedback to you, ask them if you can calmly and factually give them a suggestion to help them improve. (Feedback on their feedback.)

Student Tasks 〉 Transfer Goals

Student Tasks	Transfer Goals
Students brainstorm and analyze ways peers might ask for feedback that may end up annoying the feedback provider.	Students are aware of potential negative aspects of the feedback process and can respond, rather than react to each.
Students explore solutions to each problem brainstormed earlier to ensure that the feedback process continues to work effectively.	Students anticipate potential annoyances in the feedback process but use strategies to address each to avoid conflict.

Instructional Poster(s)

- This lesson has ONE Instructional Poster.
- The Instructional Poster for this lesson initiates a classroom discussion that provides a collection of issues that need to be addressed before they become problems. As the teacher, you need to guide the discussion to help your students decide how to solve each problem. Is this something that needs to be fixed by the student asking for feedback or the student being asked for feedback? Both?
- For example: "Sometimes they need it quickly and I can't get them their feedback that soon." A possible solution to this is that everyone needs to try be mindful of time when asking others for feedback. If someone is truly in a bind, helping them out occasionally by setting aside your own work is a kind consideration.

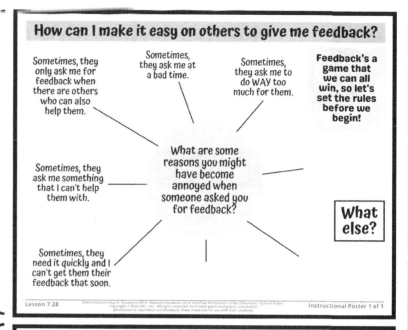

Student Handouts

- This lesson has TWO Student Handouts.
- DIRECTIONS: Read through the sample situation below. Use that as a guideline to complete the chart on the next page. I've already done some of it for you, so make sure your answers match what is already entered.
- The first Student Handout is a completed example of what students will be doing on the next page. Encourage your students to use quotation marks around the peer's reaction to their unrealistic request for feedback AND quotes around their better way to ask for feedback. This will help them see it as a conversation between peers.
- Consider extending this Student Handout by using some of the brainstormed ideas from the Instructional Poster in the first column and having students come up with answers for all four of the other columns.

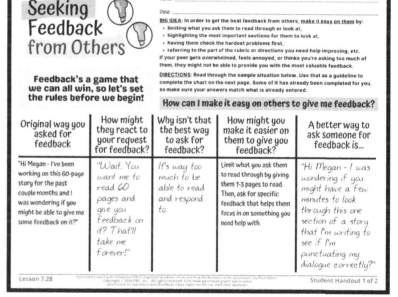

INTRODUCTION
PLANNING
METACOGNITION
SYNTHESIS
REFLECTION
SELF-ASSESSMENT
GOAL SETTING
FEEDBACK

bit.ly/3Rd2sTj

Embrace the spirit of continuous learning and growth mindset by actively soliciting critical feedback on your work

Essential Question

How can I show a strong desire to seek out feedback?

Big Idea

Show a strong desire to seek out feedback on your work. Don't assume your work is perfect or that there are no peers who are qualified to help. Even grizzled, old veterans of their craft learn new things when they open their minds to it. Surely, YOU can still learn something new!

Lesson Overview

In this lesson, students learn to make their desire for critical feedback on their work apparent to all by performing certain actions. These actions are normally avoided by students who worry about receiving feedback or dread having to make improvements to their work. By regularly performing these actions, it is made clear to the teacher and everyone else that this student is interested in improving their skills and abilities in the classroom. This is essentially the foundational skill needed to be a self-directed learner! Without performing the types of actions explained in this lesson, a student likely continues to rely on others for direction and motivation.

Discussion/Reflection Questions

- Why is it important to be open and obvious to everyone in class that you are asking someone for feedback on your work? Why shouldn't you do so in secret?
- How could you encourage your classmates to become better at asking for feedback on their work? What could you do to ease their worries?
- Imagine you are someone who avoids asking for feedback because you believe your work is already perfect. How can you change that mindset and be more open to suggestions that might make your work even better?

Teacher Tips

- Teach your students the importance of this lesson when it comes to self-direction (being self-directed)! Most students prefer the idea that they are in charge of their actions, rather than admitting that their teacher controls everything that they do! Use this preference to remind them that self-direction involves doing what is expected of them in school without needing to be told to do it. (Self-direction is not choosing to do whatever they want, regardless of what is expected of them. That just leads to consequences which are teacher-directed. Power struggles end up hurting the student in the end, whether it's through immediate consequences like detentions, failing grades, summer school, etc. Self-direction is doing what is expected of you without needing reminders or guidance.)

Student Tasks 〉 Transfer Goals

Student Tasks	Transfer Goals
Students learn that self-directed students are those that seek out feedback in order to improve their skills.	Students rely less on others to think for them and make decisions for them. They are self-directed learners.
Students learn to make their desire for critical feedback on their work apparent to all by performing certain actions.	Students perform these actions innately, without thinking, because it becomes natural for them to want to improve.

Instructional Poster(s)

- This lesson has ONE Instructional Poster.
- The Instructional Poster for this lesson goes over nine student behaviors that demonstrate a sincere desire to receive feedback on their work. The bullets should be discussed in order as they are a bit chronological when it comes to implementation.
- In the center is an image of one way NOT to show a strong desire for feedback and that's to pester everyone in class by asking them for generic feedback simply as a means of doing it to say it's done! Although this may inspire your students to go around the classroom doing this (sorry!), it's kind of a fun way to show students the right and wrong way to ask others for feedback! Consider letting everyone do this action for 30 seconds! But then discuss the right ways to ask for feedback afterwards!

Student Handouts

- This lesson has TWO Student Handouts.
- DIRECTIONS: Start by completing the BACK side of this page. Then, come back to the front and read the column headers and the example answers. Finally, complete this chart with recent examples and strong plans.
- The second Student Handout should be completed first. It is more like a traditional worksheet in that it is not reflective or personal, but a fictional scenario with questions. For younger students, you may want to complete this together, but older students will likely be okay on their own or with an assigned, random partner.
- The first Student Handout asks students to write out how they might show a sincere interest in getting feedback on three specific skills or assignments from class. You may want to choose these assignments for them but have them complete the rest.

How can I show a strong desire to seek out feedback?

Ways that I can show a strong desire to receive feedback on my work

- Set a goal for yourself to ask for more constructive feedback on your work and then monitor your progress on that goal.
- Seek feedback often from your teacher or peers by asking them to look at your work and give suggestions.
- Be open to suggestions and listen with a positive attitude when people give you ideas for making your work better.
- Really listen when someone is giving you feedback and ask questions if you need more help understanding.
- After receiving feedback, ask follow up questions like having them explain things more, giving examples, or showing different ways to solve a problem.

Whatever you do, don't do it like this:

Can you give me feedback? (repeated)

- Take some time to reflect - think about the feedback you received and how it can make your work stronger.
- Use the feedback you received to actually make improvements in your work, like fixing mistakes, adding details, or trying new ideas.
- Show gratitude to those taking the time to give you feedback and let them know you appreciate their help.
- Offer feedback to your classmates or friends on their work, sharing your ideas and suggestions to support their learning too.

Lesson 7.29 — Instructional Poster 1 of 1

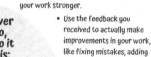

Seeking Feedback from Others

Name: _____
Date: _____

BIG IDEA: Show a strong desire to seek out feedback on your work. Don't assume your work is perfect or that there are no peers who are qualified to help. Even grizzled, old veterans of their craft learn new things when they open their minds to it. Surely, YOU can still learn something new!

DIRECTIONS: Start by completing the BACK side of this page. Then, come back to the front and read the column headers and the example answers. Finally, complete this chart with recent examples and strong plans.

How can I show a strong desire to seek out feedback?

Assignment or Skill	Evidence that shows I'm seeking feedback	My plan for seeking out MORE feedback
Making my printing neater	I asked my teacher if she could help me improve my printing, and she gave me a packet that really helps!	After I complete the packet she gave me, I will ask her for feedback on how well I improved.

Lesson 7.29 — Student Handout 1 of 2

How can I show a strong desire to seek out feedback?

Mrs. Cluckbaum has been teaching middle school English THE SAME WAY for 35 years. Making the switch from a chalkboard to a whiteboard nearly caused her to retire! Although she's very kind, her students don't really enjoy her class.

1 Mrs. Cluckbaum probably thinks that she knows how to teach her subject really well, and probably believes that she doesn't really need to change her ways. But what she might not realize is that...

2 List at least three ways Mrs. Cluckbaum could show a desire to improve. What could she do to learn new teaching methods? Who could she talk with to improve her teaching skills for her students?

3 What are some things that Mrs. Cluckbaum probably doesn't do in her classroom? What are some things she could do that would make her students enjoy learning in her class more?

4 Why does Mrs. Cluckbaum even need to change? What if she doesn't seek feedback on her teaching methods or doesn't try to learn the best ways to teach students today? Why should we care?

Lesson 7.29 — Student Handout 2 of 2

bit.ly/41eUduS

Actively seek feedback from all classmates, recognizing the valuable contributions each individual can make

7.30

Planning 1
Goal Setting 6
Meta-cognition 2
Synthesis 3
Reflection 4
Self-Assessment 5

Essential Question

How do I get better at asking EVERYONE for feedback?

Big Idea

Every peer in class has valuable talents that you need to discover. Seek feedback from EVERYONE and give everyone a chance to show you what they know. You might be surprised!

Lesson Overview

In this lesson, students learn the importance of asking everyone in class for help or feedback instead of assuming that some students wouldn't be as good as others. Building a successful classroom community requires trust and confidence in one another, which is strengthened when viewing everyone as equals. To achieve this goal, students participate in a classroom discussion to address concerns about this concept collectively, without naming names. Students are taught to consider proximity as a key factor in seeking help or feedback, but also considering factors like if the nearest person is too busy to help or if they've already been asked and don't know how to help.

Discussion/Reflection Questions

- How did your understanding of your peers' talents change after learning about asking everyone for help or feedback?
- Can you think of a time when you thought someone couldn't help you? What might have happened if you gave them a chance?
- Why is it important to trust and believe in each other in the classroom? How does treating everyone equally when asking for help or feedback make our class community stronger?
- What are some factors you plan to consider when asking a peer for help or feedback besides proximity (distance)?

Teacher Tips

- This lesson naturally connects with Lesson 1.05 and students should be reminded of the earlier lesson while discussing this lesson. Although there is overlap in concepts, this lesson focuses on the application of "Marble Theory," while Lesson 1.05 tries to level the playing field for students with regards to intelligence through the idea of "Marble Theory."
- Be sure to remind your students that we do not name names or give hints that allow others to figure out who we are talking about when sharing stories or past circumstances that involve others.
- The map on the first Student Handout will not actually represent your classroom. It doesn't need to represent your classroom. It just provides a context for students to think about proximity as it relates to the peers they should go to for help or feedback after their own partner.

Student Tasks 〉 Transfer Goals

Student Tasks	Transfer Goals
Students learn the importance of asking everyone in class for help or feedback instead of assuming that some students wouldn't be as good as others.	Students see the importance of asking a nearby peer for help or feedback over others and do so automatically on their own.
Students participate in a classroom discussion to address concerns about the idea of asking everyone in class for help or feedback.	Students' concerns have been addressed and no longer have apprehension about asking others for feedback or help.

Instructional Poster(s)

- This lesson has ONE Instructional Poster.
- The Instructional Poster for this lesson focuses the whole class discussion on reasons why some students avoid certain students in class when asking for help or feedback. By the end of this lesson, every student is expected to view every peer as a potential resource. Through this discussion, try to discuss the realities, the misconceptions, and the reasons why choosing kind over comfort is needed in a collaborative, improvement-focused classroom like our own. Add points like these:
  - "If all of us always go to the same person for help or feedback, they'll never get any of their own work done!"
  - "If no one ever asks you for help or feedback, you might believe that you aren't capable of helping! That won't help your effort and self-esteem!"

Student Handouts

- This lesson has TWO Student Handouts.
- DIRECTIONS: Look at the classroom map below. Pretend that your teacher has taught today's math lesson and has assigned you a random partner to work with on the practice problems from the lesson. You are expected to work together with your partner and not split up the work. You are Student #5. Read all of the questions on the next page before answering any. Some later questions will help you on the previous questions. While answering the questions, remember the BIG IDEA of the lesson.
- The first Student Handout teaches students about the importance of considering proximity when going to a peer for help or feedback.
- The second Student Handout tries to address many of the other considerations.

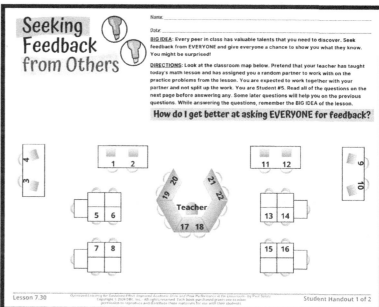

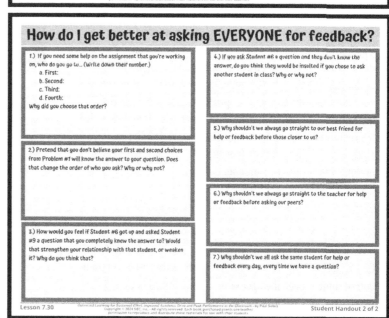

7.31

bit.ly/3ReB5s6

Treat all classmates with kindness and respect, regardless of personal biases, past experiences or preconceived notions

Essential Question

Why is it not enough to just tolerate others?

Lesson Overview

In this lesson, students watch a TED Talk by Julia Galef in order to think deeply about flexible & inflexible thinking and about how we tolerate others along a continuum. Through the video, the Student Handout questions and the discussion, students are expected to see their peers in a new way. They learn to set aside differences, ignore social status, and find ways to appreciate everyone they work, leading to stronger collaboration and a kinder classroom community.

Teacher Tips

- This lesson will take twice as long as most lessons do. Feel free to teach it over two periods, or if possible, provide a double period for this lesson. If your students are used to flipped learning, you can assign them the video to watch at home, which would allow you to accomplish the rest in a normal period.
- There are three Student Handouts for this lesson (instead of the usual two). The second Student Handout is optional - it can be used as a comprehension check to see if your students understood the video. You might even choose to integrate the questions into a web tool that proposes questions for the students to answer while they watch the video (like EdPuzzle). It's recommended that younger students watch the video in class with teacher support (because it's not an easy video to understand completely independently).

Galef, J. (TEDxPSU • 2016, February). Julia Galef: Why you think you're right -- even if you're wrong. www.ted.com/talks/julia_galef_why_you_think_you_re_right_even_if_you_re_wrong

Big Idea

Process intently (by listening or reading carefully) to EVERYONE who offers you feedback, no matter how you feel about the person giving you feedback. Avoid letting negative memories or emotions cloud your judgment. Sometimes, history with a peer, stereotypes, or social standing can cause you to dismiss feedback from some peers, but be more mature than that. Do better than "tolerate others." Treat everyone with respect, appreciation, and kindness.

Discussion/Reflection Questions

- Reflect on the video. How did it make you think differently about how we should treat others and appreciate their ideas? How can being open-minded and kind to others help YOU grow as a person?
- Remember a time when you didn't get along with someone because they were different from you or had a different social status. How did that affect your teamwork? How can you change your mindset to see the value in everyone and work together better?
- Imagine a classroom where everyone listens carefully to each other and treats everyone with kindness. How would that make learning more enjoyable? What can YOU do to create a classroom like that, where everyone's ideas are respected?

Student Tasks 〉 Transfer Goals

Student Tasks	Transfer Goals
Students learn the difference between having a Soldier Mindset and a Scout Mindset.	Students are more flexible in their thinking, especially when it comes to relationships with others.
Students learn about the Tolerance Continuum and try hard to treat everyone with unconditional appreciation.	Students form stronger relationships with their peers, forgive & forget past problems, and work collaboratively with everyone.

Instructional Poster(s)

- This lesson has ONE Instructional Poster.
- The Instructional Poster should NOT be shown until after the video is watched (see Student Handout #1). Here is the TEDx page: bit.ly/3U7Cnll and if you want to provide access to the video for the students, here is the YouTube link: bit.ly/3kvxKUC
- The image on the left side of the Instructional Poster describes the ideas within the video about Soldier vs. Scout Mindset. The image on the right takes those concepts and applies them in a context of "flexible vs. inflexible thinking." Finally, the idea of flexible thinking is expanded to include the level in which we tolerate others in our lives. Interpret & discuss the poster together as a class.

Student Handouts

- This lesson has THREE Student Handouts.
- DIRECTIONS:
  1. Start by watching the TEDx Talk by Julia Galef about "Scout Mindset" here: https://bit.ly/3kvxKUC - Learn the difference between having a Scout Mindset and having a Soldier Mindset.
  2. Then, read through "The Tolerance Continuum." Try to understand the differences (improvements) as you go up the line from Intolerance to Unconditional Appreciation.
  3. Finally, complete all of the upcoming questions as thoroughly and as correctly as you can.
- The first Student Handout is mostly directions for the teacher to watch the video. It also has the Big Idea and the directions for the students.
- The second Student Handout is optional - it has comprehension questions for understanding the video.
- The third Student Handout is the most important one - it has the students interpret and apply what they've learned from the lesson.

Galef, J. (TEDxPSU • 2016, February). Julia Galef: Why you think you're right -- even if you're wrong. www.ted.com/talks/julia_galef_why_you_think_you_re_right_even_if_you_re_wrong

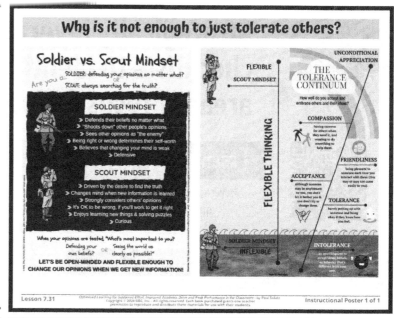

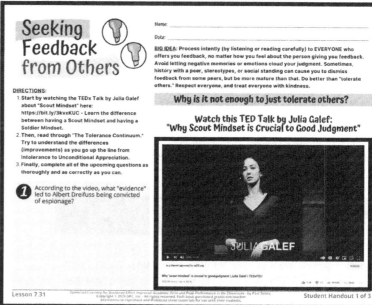

INTRODUCTION

PLANNING

METACOGNITION

SYNTHESIS

REFLECTION

SELF-ASSESSMENT

GOAL SETTING

FEEDBACK

bit.ly/4ac3BDE

Strategically leverage rubrics and checklists to identify the most critical areas of focus for peer feedback

Essential Question

How can rubrics and checklists guide my feedback?

Lesson Overview

In this lesson, students learn how to utilize rubrics and checklists as guides to determine the feedback they should seek from their peers. They're taught that rubrics and checklists encompass the most crucial aspects of an assignment, typically including grading criteria. As part of this process, students identify the types of questions they should ask their peers based on the criteria outlined in the rubrics and checklists and prioritize them. Additionally, students are given a sample assignment where the teacher has not provided a rubric or checklist. Students are asked to imagine the criteria that would be included on a rubric or checklist for this assignment, and determine what feedback they should request from their peers.

Teacher Tips

- Since every classroom is different and every grading system varies, you will want to consider how this lesson relates to your own system. Should you have a class discussion about how this lesson may be slightly different than the way your classroom works? Should you modify the materials to match your system? Should your students complete this lesson as-is because it is still valuable as they proceed to higher grade levels? These are some considerations you might want to address before teaching this lesson.
- This lesson focuses in on traditional rubrics, but the next lesson focuses on Single-Point Rubrics. Single-Point Rubrics are a type of assessment tool that focuses on providing feedback to students based on specific criteria or learning objectives. Unlike traditional rubrics that describe multiple levels of performance, single-point rubrics have only one set of descriptors that describe the targeted achievement level or expectations for the assignment. *

Big Idea

The type of feedback we need often depends on several factors. Have we been given a rubric, checklist, or set of guidelines for the assignment? Do we know what's expected even if the teacher didn't say it directly? Are WE deciding what's most important, or did the teacher tell us what to focus on? These are some of the questions that help us figure out what kind of feedback we need from our peers.

Discussion/Reflection Questions

- How can rubrics, checklists, or guidelines help us determine the type of feedback we need from our peers?
- What are some examples of grading criteria that are often included in rubrics and checklists?
- Why is it important to prioritize the questions we ask our peers based on the outlined criteria?
- How can we adapt our feedback-seeking approach when a rubric or checklist is not provided by the teacher?

Student Tasks ❯ Transfer Goals

Student Tasks	Transfer Goals
Students learn how to utilize rubrics and checklists as guides to determine the feedback they should seek from their peers.	Students use their time wisely when seeking feedback from others by prioritizing the most important criteria first.
Students are asked to imagine the criteria that would be included on a rubric or checklist for an assignment where one isn't provided.	Students create their own criteria for success in assignments where a rubric or checklist has not been provided.

INTRODUCTION

PLANNING

METACOGNITION

SYNTHESIS

REFLECTION

SELF-ASSESSMENT

GOAL SETTING

FEEDBACK

Instructional Poster(s)

- This lesson has ONE Instructional Poster.
- The Instructional Poster for this lesson is short and sweet because there are four Student Handouts for this lesson (instead of the usual two).
- Read through the Instructional Poster with the class and set the purpose for the lesson. Then, go over the first Student Handout together so students know what to do independently or with an assigned, random partner. Then, give them enough time to complete the work!

How can rubrics and checklists guide my feedback?

If you've been given guidelines or expectations for your assignment like a:

Rubric or Checklist

Make sure you use them when asking for feedback or giving others feedback!

If you have NOT been given specific guidelines or expectations for your assignment:

Think about what your teacher is assessing, and what has been taught in recent weeks when asking for or giving feedback.

Student Handouts

- This lesson has FOUR Student Handouts.
- DIRECTIONS: Your teacher has provided you with a set of pretend assignments or tasks below and on the next several pages. Read through each one carefully and think about the kind of feedback you would ask your peers for IF you were asked to complete each task. Your goal is to determine the most important feedback you would want from your peers to ensure that you do the task as well as you possibly could. You do NOT actually have to complete each assignment or task! :) The first one has been done for you.
- The first Student Handout contains the Big Idea, Directions and a sample problem that has already been completed. Go over this with your students if you can.
- The next three Student Handouts provide examples of assignments with rubrics and checklists that students need to use when asking their peers for feedback. Feedback requests should relate to the criteria given for each assignment. Younger students might only be expected to ask for one piece of feedback, while older students can request several.

Seeking Feedback from Others

BIG IDEA: The type of feedback we need often depends on several factors. Have we been given a rubric, checklist, or set of guidelines for the assignment? Do we know what's expected even if the teacher didn't say it directly? Are WE deciding what's most important, or did the teacher tell us what to focus on? These are some of the questions that help us figure out what kind of feedback we need from our peers.

How can rubrics and checklists guide my feedback?

DIRECTIONS: Your teacher has provided you with a set of pretend assignments or tasks below and on the next several pages. Read through each one carefully and think about the kind of feedback you would ask your peers for IF you were asked to complete each task. Your goal is to determine the most important feedback you would want from your peers to ensure that you do the task as well as you possibly could. You do NOT actually have to complete each assignment or task! :) The first one has been done for you.

Directions for the assignment or task with a Rubric or Checklist	Imagine what your product will look like	The most important feedback I should ask for is...
DIRECTIONS: Solve a math word problem and follow all of the steps on the "Math Extended Response Checklist" below. Your final answer should be in paragraph form. **Math Extended Response Checklist** • Calculate everything correctly. • Answer the question correctly. • Show all of your work (diagrams/pictures are OK too). • Label your answer. • Explain what you did and why you did it for every step.	Imagine that your answer looks something like this (but with real math work and a real written answer):	The most important feedback for me would be: 1. Did I do everything that was asked of me on the checklist? 2. Did I do my math correctly and show all my work? 3. Did I explain "what I did" and "why I did" for every step of the problem?

How can rubrics and checklists guide my feedback?

Directions for the assignment or task with a Rubric or Checklist	Imagine what your product will look like.	The most important feedback I should ask for is...
DIRECTIONS: Revise your written "Public Service Announcement" (PSA) using the Six Traits of Writing checklist on the right.		
DIRECTIONS: Create a display board for your Science Fair Project using the following criteria. Science Fair Display Board Grading Criteria Display (30 points) Title is neat and/or creative and easy to read _____/3 Title catches your attention _____/2 Below the title are interesting/important artifacts _____/2 Side panels contains important pages from report _____/10 Creativity and color were used extensively _____/3 The report and other artifacts are on the table _____/10		

bit.ly/3sXfa0F

Harness the simplicity and effectiveness of Single-Point Rubrics to provide clear, concise, and actionable feedback to peers

7.33

Essential Question

How can Single-Point Rubrics help me with feedback?

Lesson Overview

In this lesson, students learn about Single-Point Rubrics and how they help with feedback. Because the Success Criteria are so explicitly spelled out in a Single-Point Rubric, students are easily able to identify if their peers (or themselves) have met all of the expectations. In addition, students should be able to identify areas where expectations are not fully met or where expectations have been exceeded. By explaining those areas where a student's work is above or below expectations, students give constructive feedback to help improve their work and positive feedback to acknowledge exceeded expectations.

Teacher Tips

- Single-Point Rubrics are a type of assessment tool that focuses on providing feedback to students based on specific criteria or learning objectives. Unlike traditional rubrics that describe multiple levels of performance, single-point rubrics have only one set of descriptors that describe the targeted achievement level or expectations for the assignment. In a single-point rubric, the criteria for success are clearly defined in the form of specific descriptors or statements. The rubric typically includes space for feedback or comments to be provided by the teacher, highlighting strengths and areas for improvement. The feedback is tailored to the individual student's performance, allowing for personalized and constructive feedback. Single-point rubrics promote a more holistic approach to assessment by emphasizing the quality of work and providing clear guidance for improvement. They also encourage self-reflection and self-assessment, as students can compare their work against the defined criteria and assess their own progress. *

Big Idea

Single Point Rubrics are a convenient and effective way to give others feedback when you can't be face-to-face. Unlike traditional rubrics, Single-Point Rubrics have only one level of success. Single-Point Rubrics usually have a space for others to give you comments to improve your work (so you can go back and make revisions) or to describe how you exceeded expectations (to feel proud of yourself)!

Discussion/Reflection Questions

- How can Single-Point Rubrics be a helpful tool for giving feedback when you can't be face-to-face with someone?
- What makes Single-Point Rubrics different from traditional rubrics? What are the Pros and Cons of each?
- Why is it important to identify areas where expectations are not fully met or where expectations have been exceeded?
- How can providing constructive feedback using Single-Point Rubrics help someone improve their work, and why is it important to acknowledge when expectations have been exceeded with positive feedback?

Student Tasks 〉 Transfer Goals

Student Tasks	Transfer Goals
Students learn about Single-Point Rubrics and how they help with feedback.	Students are able to use Single-Point Rubrics as a tool for giving their peers meaningful feedback on their work.
Students explain how a peer's work needs improvement and how it exceeds expectations based on Success Criteria on a Single-Point Rubric.	Students focus their feedback on the important Success Criteria identified on the rubric instead of focusing on less-important skills.

INTRODUCTION
PLANNING
METACOGNITION
SYNTHESIS
REFLECTION
SELF-ASSESSMENT
GOAL SETTING
FEEDBACK

Instructional Poster(s)

- This lesson has ONE Instructional Poster.
- The Instructional Poster for this lesson shows a filled-out Single-Point Rubric. This particular version shows the Success Criteria in the first column and asks the the student to complete the center column as a Self-Assessment (explaining how they met each Success Criteria). A peer or teacher has completed the other two columns (how they didn't meet the Success Criteria and how they went above & beyond the Success Criteria).
- Please explain to your students that Single-Point Rubrics can come in many formats, so they need to be flexible in their thinking when they look different or have different directions. This is simply one version.

Student Handouts

- This lesson has TWO Student Handouts.
- DIRECTIONS: Read the directions and guidelines for giving or receiving feedback using a Single-Point Rubric below. Understand that not all Single-Point Rubrics look alike, so your rubric may be set up differently in class - Be flexible with your thinking so you can complete them correctly! Then, on the next page, complete a Single-Point Rubric for a completed or in-progress assignment of your own.
- The first Student Handout describes the guidelines, rules and directions for completing a Single-Point Rubric of this design.
- The second Student Handout asks students to identify two Success Criteria (you can add more pages if you want more Success Criteria) and has them Self-Assess their work according to each criterion. Then, students need to find a peer who can give them feedback and fill in the other two columns. It is possible that some boxes may end up blank.

How can Single-Point Rubrics help me with feedback?
Single-Point Rubric

Success Criteria	Needs Improvement (Feedback from others)	How did I meet each Success Criteria?	Above & Beyond (Feedback from others)
Keep track of what you eat for one week. List at least 20 different elements that you leave eaten based on Nutrition Labels. Do not include any compounds or mixtures. Only include elements that are found individually on the Periodic Table.	In the future, try not to copy and paste information from the internet whenever possible. See if you can put it into your own words so that it demonstrates understanding, not just completion. Thanks! ☺	I found and listed at least 20 different elements in food that I eat by reading Nutrition Labels on the food in my home. I did not list any compounds or mixtures, just pure elements that can be found on the Periodic Table.	I'm so glad to read that you allowed yourself some flexibility in your schedule to let life happen, but didn't miss any deadlines! It was also very wise of you to research online when you hit a dead-end and to ask your uncle to help you verify the accuracy of your answers on the Periodic Table! I'm very impressed by your skills!
Choose ten elements and describe how each of those elements are needed by the human body. Be sure to include at least one interesting fact for each element.	Although not required, I would love to read about how the three additional elements you researched. Which three were they and what made them less interesting to include in your assignment. Again - it's not required, just something I'd love to hear about from you!	For 10 of those elements, I researched and wrote about how that element is needed in our bodies. I also added at least one interesting fact for each element.	The ten elements that you chose to write about were excellent choices - all are very common elements in food, some occurring naturally and some being added during manufacturing. I appreciate you going above and beyond to learn about three additional elements and it's great to read that you chose the most interesting ones to include in your assignment! Great work!

Lesson 7.33 — Optimized Learning for Sustained Effort, Improved Academic Drive and Peak Performance in the Classroom - by Paul Solarz — Copyright © 2024 OBC, Inc - All rights reserved. Each book purchased grants one teacher permission to reproduce and distribute these materials for use with their students — Instructional Poster 1 of 1

Seeking Feedback from Others

Name: _____
Date: _____

BIG IDEA: Single Point Rubrics are a convenient and effective way to give others feedback when you can't be face-to-face. Unlike traditional rubrics, Single-Point Rubrics have only one level of success. Single-Point Rubrics usually have a space for others to give you comments to improve your work (so you can go back and make revisions) or to describe how you exceeded expectations (to feel proud of yourself!).

How can Single-Point Rubrics help me with feedback?

DIRECTIONS: Read the directions and guidelines for giving or receiving feedback using a Single-Point Rubric below. Understand that not all Single-Point Rubrics look alike, so your rubric may be set up differently in class - Be flexible with your thinking so you can complete them correctly! Then, on the next page, complete a Single-Point Rubric for a completed or in-progress assignment of your own.

Success Criteria	Needs Improvement (Feedback from others)	How did I meet each Success Criteria?	Above & Beyond (Feedback from others)
This will usually be given by your teacher, but you should also be able to explain many of these Success Criteria on your own - that shows that you know WHY you are doing this assignment and HOW you should ensure it is done correctly.	No one is perfect, so there are always areas where we can improve. When giving others feedback, try to focus on the most important areas for your peer to improve. When receiving this feedback, try to remember that we all have areas that we can improve - don't take it personally.	Make sure that all of your comments focus entirely on THIS Success Criterion. Be careful that you don't just give generic feedback on the entire assignment or task!	Not everyone exceeds expectations on every assignment or task. Sometimes, it can be hard to find comments for this section, but do your best! We appreciate when people notice us going above and beyond! If you don't receive any feedback in this area, don't get frustrated. Instead, try to identify an area that you could have exceeded expectations and try to do so in the future.

Lesson 7.33 — Optimized Learning for Sustained Effort, Improved Academic Drive and Peak Performance in the Classroom - by Paul Solarz — Copyright © 2024 OBC, Inc - All rights reserved. Each book purchased grants one teacher permission to reproduce and distribute these materials for use with their students — Student Handout 1 of 2

How can Single-Point Rubrics help me with feedback?
Single-Point Rubric

Success Criteria	Needs Improvement (Feedback from others)	How did I meet each Success Criteria?	Above & Beyond (Feedback from others)

Lesson 7.33 — Optimized Learning for Sustained Effort, Improved Academic Drive and Peak Performance in the Classroom - by Paul Solarz — Copyright © 2024 OBC, Inc - All rights reserved. Each book purchased grants one teacher permission to reproduce and distribute these materials for use with their students — Student Handout 2 of 2

bit.ly/4a7eN4g

Embrace the power of a Growth Mindset to transform critical feedback into positive fuel for improvement

7.34

Planning 1 · Meta-cognition 2 · Synthesis 3 · Reflection 4 · Self Assessment 5 · Goal Setting 6

Essential Question

How can a Growth Mindset help me improve my skills?

Lesson Overview

In this lesson, students read some Fixed Mindset statements and some Growth Mindset statements and see how the two vary from each other. Next, students read about how Growth Mindset means to keep an open mind to learning new things, accept it when you might not be ready to learn a skill, and keep a positive outlook when you struggle. They compare their struggles to the struggles of a baby trying to walk and they see that we aren't always ready to learn a new skill at the same time as everyone else, so patience is needed. Finally, students assess themselves on a few feedback skills that are taught within this unit. They then try to explain how they plan to improve the skills that they are weakest in by showing a Growth Mindset.

Teacher Tips

- This is the first of two Growth Mindset lessons in this unit. The next lesson is called, "How does Growth Mindset work in the brain?" and it is a scientific look at Growth Mindset that is appropriate for most ages (younger students would need some support). Teaching these lessons together is a good idea, but not required.
- This lesson is simply an introduction to Growth Mindset or a supplemental lesson for Growth Mindset that connects well to accepting feedback from others in order to improve our skills. I highly recommend adding other Growth Mindset components to this lesson or to teach around the same time as this lesson because this concept strongly supports everything students are asked to do within this program.
- Be sure to hammer home the idea that a strong Growth Mindset is needed in order to accept critical feedback from others to improve our skills.

Big Idea

A strong Growth Mindset is needed in order to accept critical feedback from others to improve our skills. Having a growth mindset means believing you can always learn and improve, no matter what. It helps you handle life's ups and downs with strength and flexibility. You see problems as chances to learn, instead of obstacles blocking your way. This gives you the power to try new things, take educated risks and keep pushing yourself as you try to reach your full potential. With a growth mindset, your current skills are just the starting point, not the limit.

Discussion/Reflection Questions

- How does believing that you can always learn and improve affect how you view critical feedback from others? How can a growth mindset help you keep a positive attitude and stay strong when receiving constructive criticism?
- How can having a positive mindset about growth help you use feedback to keep getting better?
- Why is it that people with a growth mindset are able to avoid getting defensive or embarrassed when receiving critical feedback?

Student Tasks 〉 Transfer Goals

Student Tasks	Transfer Goals
Students compare and contrast Fixed Mindset and Growth Mindset statements to strengthen their understanding of each concept.	Students know that they can always learn in the future, despite any struggles they've had in the past.
Students explain how they plan to improve the feedback skills they are weakest in by showing a Growth Mindset.	Students embrace a Growth Mindset so they can accept critical feedback from others to improve their skills.

Instructional Poster(s)

- This lesson has ONE Instructional Poster.
- The Instructional Poster for this lesson shares some students' thoughts when being told they're going to work on a unit about Peer Feedback. Their reactions might show a Fixed Mindset (where they think they know all they need to know or don't keep an open mind to new reasons why Peer Feedback might be effective). Or their reactions could show a Growth Mindset (where they see the potential value in the upcoming work and keep an open mind to learning new strategies to make Peer Feedback effective).
- As a class, try to come up with more responses that students might have. Encourage your students to follow up their examples with, "This show a (Fixed or Growth) Mindset because…"

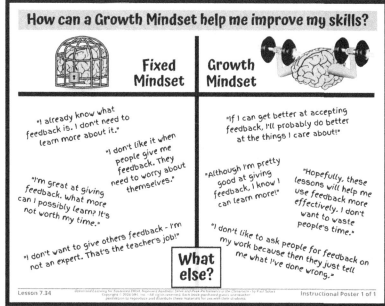

Student Handouts

- This lesson has TWO Student Handouts.
- DIRECTIONS: Read through the lesson below in order. Think about your answers to Steps 2 and 5 before moving on to the back of this page. If you need more information on Growth Mindset (or its opposite, called Fixed Mindset), take some time to research that now online.
- The first Student Handout teaches students about Growth Mindset (in case this is a new concept to them). If you do this side together as a class, students can discuss Step #5.
- DIRECTIONS: Assess yourself on the eight feedback skills below. Fill in the bars to show how full your cup is currently. Then, answer the questions at the bottom of the page.
- The second Student Handout leads students to using their Growth Mindset to try to improve their feedback skills through the remaining lessons in this unit.

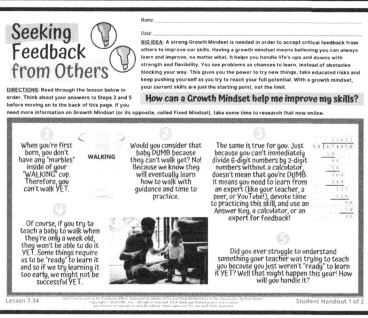

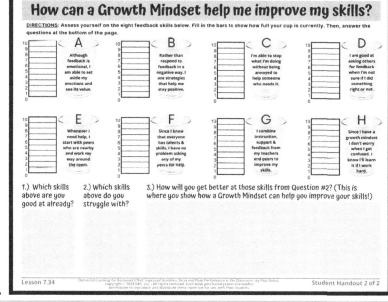

INTRODUCTION
PLANNING
METACOGNITION
SYNTHESIS
REFLECTION
SELF-ASSESSMENT
GOAL SETTING
FEEDBACK

409

7.35

Build intricate brain networks every time we learn and strengthen them through continuous practice and repetition

bit.ly/47N99CM

bit.ly/47N99CM

Essential Question

How does "Practice Make Permanent" (not perfect)?

Big Idea

It's easy to fall into bad habits. Maybe you get lazy and stop brushing your teeth before bed for a few days. Before you realize it, you've completely forgotten that step in your bedtime routine. The same is true in school. If you complete your work quickly and don't ask for feedback on it, you can slide into some bad habits. Be sure to remind yourself about the power of a Growth Mindset, as consistently seeking feedback and striving to improve your skills through collaboration will help protect you from losing those hard-earned abilities over time.

Lesson Overview

In this lesson, students discover how learning is "coded" in our brain, showing a neuron with its axon, dendrites and nucleus connecting with another neuron to transmit electrical impulses to facilitate memory storage and information retrieval. Since this is a complicated concept, it is made easier with graphics and a metaphor of a jungle that is explained by the teacher. Students then reflect on some possible bad habits that they might find themselves getting into at school or at home that might affect their learning and are asked to brainstorm some possible negative consequences that could arise from this bad habit, and write a simple plan to try to improve each bad habit.

Discussion/Reflection Questions

- Can you describe the connection between "asking others for feedback on your work in order to constantly improve" and "how learning is 'coded' in our brain"? Why are these two ideas in the same lesson?
- What are some bad habits you or others can occasionally fall into in your school or home environment that could impact your learning (e.g. rushing through assignments, not seeking feedback, avoiding challenges, etc.)? What are some ways to break those habits and get back to a positive routine?

Teacher Tips

- This lesson is appropriate for most fifth grade classrooms and up as-is. If you'd like to present it to younger students, just do so by letting your students know that they will not be required to memorize any of the vocabulary, but should just try to grasp the concept of how it all works. Younger students should also probably skip the third Student Handout since explaining this concept in their own words might prove to be overly difficult.
- There's not a lot of room on the Student Handouts to really explain everything, so you might have your students write their answers on sticky notes that they attach to their papers or if doing this electronically, use a font size smaller than usual. Maintaining high expectations for detailed answers is always recommended and the space provided makes that a bit challenging for this lesson. ("Tell me more!")

Student Tasks ⟩ Transfer Goals

Student Tasks	Transfer Goals
Students learn to do everything possible to learn new information and skills, including seeking out critical feedback on their work to help them improve & grow.	Students apply the concept of seeking critical feedback and utilizing it for learning new information and skills, as well as personal growth.
Students reflect on bad habits that could affect their learning, brainstorm negative consequences of those habits, and write plans to try to improve each bad habit.	Students apply this reflective process to bad habits beyond the context of learning, and develop plans for improvement in various aspects of life.

Instructional Poster(s)

- This lesson has FIVE Instructional Posters.
- The Instructional Posters (there are four of them) for this lesson teaches the science of learning. It tells the story of how brain cells (neurons) form strong connections in order to send messages effectively. Because this is a challenging subject, it is simplified and graphics are provided to discuss the basic concepts. A metaphor is also provided of a dense jungle that takes time to navigate, just like learning often takes time to strengthen.
- Feel free to connect any science content to this lesson as you see fit. This would work well in a unit studying the nervous system or one on scientific processes.

Student Handouts

- This lesson has TWO Student Handouts.
- DIRECTIONS: Read through the potential bad habits, potential negative consequences of those bad habits, and our plans to improve for addressing those bad habits below. Use the example to help you complete the others. Do the same on the next page.
- The first two Student Handouts for this lesson ask students to reflect on some possible bad habits that they might find themselves getting into at school or at home that might affect their learning. Students are asked to brainstorm some possible negative consequences that could arise from this bad habit, and write a simple plan to try to improve.
- DIRECTIONS: How would you answer the Essential Question above when talking with a parent?
- There is one additional Student Handout where students explain how practice makes permanent based on what they learned during this lesson.

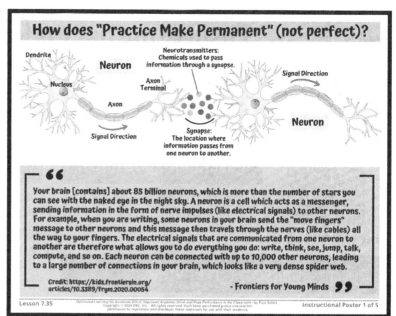

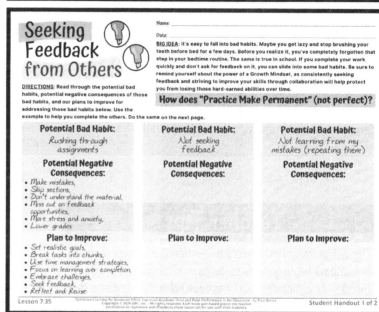

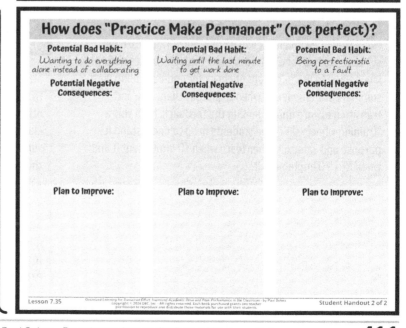

INTRODUCTION
PLANNING
METACOGNITION
SYNTHESIS
REFLECTION
SELF-ASSESSMENT
GOAL SETTING
FEEDBACK

bit.ly/48316BB

Ensure mutual understanding of feedback by asking the feedback provider clarifying questions or summarizing what you heard

Essential Question

What do I do immediately after receiving feedback?

Big Idea

When you're getting feedback face-to-face from a peer or a teacher (for example), be sure to ask clarifying questions to ensure that you completely understand what they're suggesting OR if you feel that you understand it well and don't have any questions, summarize what you heard and allow them to correct or improve your summary.

Lesson Overview

In this lesson, students learn how to respond effectively to oral feedback from others by either asking questions to better understand points they are unsure about or summarizing what they think they heard and give the feedback provider a chance to correct or clarify. This skill is not something students need to do every time they receive feedback, but it's encouraged for a while until they become proficient at using it whenever necessary. Students practice writing questions and summaries for different feedback examples to become confident in applying this skill beyond this lesson.

Discussion/Reflection Questions

- Why is it important to ask clarifying questions when receiving feedback face-to-face?
- How can asking clarifying questions help ensure that you fully understand the feedback being given?
- What are the benefits of summarizing the feedback you receive and allowing the provider to correct or improve your summary?
- In what situations might you choose to ask clarifying questions instead of summarizing, and vice versa?

Teacher Tips

- The Instructional Poster and Student Handouts have examples of feedback being given to students in a Compliment Sandwich format. The critical feedback has been bolded so students know what portion they should focus their clarifying questions or summary on.
- Although students will not likely follow this lesson's objective every time they receive feedback, it is encouraged to have students do this for a period of time until it becomes natural to know when to ask questions or check for understanding via a summary statement and when to just say thank you and transition toward implementing the feedback. I call this a "training wheels skill" and students need to understand its purpose and value and then learn when TO implement it and when NOT TO implement it.

Student Tasks 〉 Transfer Goals

Student Tasks	Transfer Goals
Students learn to respond to oral feedback from others by either asking clarifying questions or summarizing what they think they heard.	Students implement feedback correctly, rather than allowing misunderstandings to make feedback unhelpful or even detrimental.
Students practice writing questions and summaries for different feedback examples.	Students become confident in applying this skill beyond this lesson and do so independently.

Instructional Poster(s)

- This lesson has ONE Instructional Poster.
- The Instructional Poster for this lesson describes what students should do immediately after receiving oral feedback from others. They should ask clarifying questions about the points that they weren't completely clear on, or they should summarize what they think they heard and give the feedback provider a chance to correct or add more detail.
- Sentence starters have been provided, but students do not have to use them if they naturally think of questions to ask while listening to feedback.
- An example is given that shows feedback received, some possible questions a student could ask to clarify the feedback and a potential summary of what they think they've heard.

Student Handouts

- This lesson has TWO Student Handouts.
- DIRECTIONS: Start by reading the example on the instructional poster. Follow the same format below and on the next page for three new situations that you create. Describe some feedback you might receive from a peer or your teacher in the boxes on the left. Then fill in the other open boxes according to the headers. (Complete all of the empty sections, but ignore the sections that have been darkened out.)
- Student Handouts: Just like on the Instructional Poster, students are given feedback from a peer or teacher and asked to write clarifying questions, a summary of what they think the feedback provider said, or both. Feedback has been written in a Compliment Sandwich format but students are not required to add the compliments when they get to the final problem and have to create their own feedback situation.

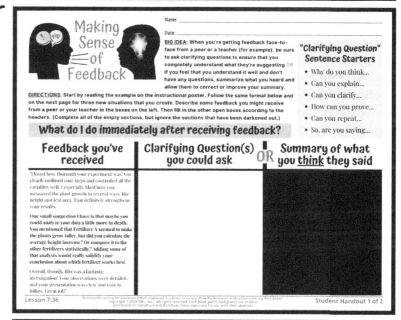

INTRODUCTION

PLANNING

METACOGNITION

SYNTHESIS

REFLECTION

SELF-ASSESSMENT

GOAL SETTING

FEEDBACK

7.37

bit.ly/47LLvGT

If feedback is incorrect or unhelpful, politely express gratitude and ask another peer, adding context to improve its value

Essential Question

How do I respond to feedback I disagree with?

Lesson Overview

In this lesson, students learn about the process they should use when receiving feedback from others to ensure the accuracy and quality of the feedback they accept. If they receive feedback from a peer that is incorrect or lacks value, they are encouraged to express gratitude and seek additional feedback from another peer. During each successive feedback request, students are taught to provide specific details that might enhance the precision and helpfulness of the feedback received. Through practice scenarios, students evaluate the correctness and value of feedback, ask clarifying questions or summarize what they heard, and express gratitude to the peer for their input.

Teacher Tips

- Students with a Fixed Mindset are much more likely to LOVE this lesson than students with a Growth Mindset, because it gives Fixed Mindset students (and strangely enough, perfectionists) permission to disregard critical feedback from others on the grounds that it does not help them improve their work. Therefore, this lesson is extremely optional and should only be used if needed. I never needed this lesson in my classroom because students would discreetly use this strategy on their own anyway, but because we never said that it was okay to do, students were careful not to ever let their peers know that they were ignoring their feedback or that they didn't agree with the feedback they had been given. If you can silently support this happening naturally in your classroom, you can skip this lesson. The way I've tried to stop this lesson from becoming the start of trouble is by adding that the student needs to seek out MORE feedback whenever they don't agree with the feedback they've been given. This should discourage students from evaluating all feedback as worthless.

Big Idea

Weigh the value of the feedback you receive, but if you don't feel that the feedback you received is correct, or an improvement, don't ever dismiss a peer's suggestion in person. Take time to evaluate their feedback after they've left and if you still don't feel that it's valuable feedback, ask someone else for feedback, but be sure to provide them with some extra background knowledge to help them hone in on what it is that you need.

Discussion/Reflection Questions

- Why is it important to listen to what your peers say, even if you don't agree or find it helpful at first?
- How can taking some time to think about the feedback after your peer has left help you decide if it's useful or not?
- What are the good things about asking someone else for feedback if you feel the first feedback wasn't right or helpful?
- How can providing extra background knowledge when seeking feedback from someone else help them understand your specific needs?

Student Tasks 〉 Transfer Goals

Student Tasks	Transfer Goals
Students learn about the process they should use when receiving feedback from others to ensure the accuracy and quality of the feedback.	Students react to poor-quality feedback kindly and seek out higher quality feedback without embarrassing anyone.
Students evaluate the correctness and value of fictional feedback and determine what they will say and do afterwards.	Students improve how they evaluate the feedback they receive and maintain strong relationships with peers who provide feedback.

Instructional Poster(s)

- This lesson has ONE Instructional Poster.
- The Instructional Poster for this lesson describes the process that students should use when receiving feedback from others to ensure that they don't blindly accept incorrect feedback. If the feedback they receive from a peer is incorrect or not valuable, they need to thank their peer and move on to another peer for more feedback. They should be sure to add specific details to their feedback request though, to ensure a higher quality of feedback during this second attempt.
- The most important point of this poster is to ensure that students never make their peers feel badly about giving feedback that isn't useful.

Student Handouts

- This lesson has TWO Student Handouts.
- DIRECTIONS: Start by reading through the two steps to weighing the value of feedback below. Then, read the examples in the chart below and on the next page. Fill in the remaining boxes with examples of your own. Try to be creative and use new subjects or situations (unlike me who chose to use one of the same ones as before)!
- Student Handouts: Students are asked to weigh the feedback they received from a peer in order to determine if it's correct and valuable or not. Either way, students are expected to ask clarifying questions or summarize what they heard and thank the peer for their feedback. If the feedback is not valuable, students are then asked to seek additional feedback from a different peer, while providing more information to ensure the feedback is more valuable this second time around.

How do I respond to feedback I disagree with?

1 Once you've been given feedback and have made sure that you completely understand it, it's time to evaluate whether or not it is beneficial. Most of the time, the feedback we get is an improvement over what we had originally (even if it's not always the most important feedback we really needed). But occasionally, the feedback we get is inaccurate or doesn't actually result in an improvement to our work.

Not all feedback is correct or beneficial, but how we accept that feedback is still VERY important!

Feedback you've received → Weigh the value of that feedback.

If it's valuable, use it and thank the person who gave it to you.

If it's NOT valuable, thank the person who gave it to you and seek out more feedback.

2 If you're sure that this feedback is inaccurate or does not actually improve your work, you can choose to seek feedback from someone else. But it's absolutely vital that you don't make the person who gave you the feedback feel badly about it. So, always thank them for the feedback (like you should do with everyone who gives you feedback) and seek out more feedback from someone else.

Making Sense of Feedback

Name: _____

Date: _____

BIG IDEA: Weigh the value of the feedback you receive, but if you don't feel that the feedback you received is correct, or an improvement, don't ever dismiss a peer's suggestion in person. Take time to evaluate their feedback after they've left and if you still don't feel that it's valuable feedback, ask someone else for feedback, but be sure to provide them with some extra background knowledge to help them hone in on what it is that you need.

DIRECTIONS: Start by reading through the two steps to weighing the value of feedback below. Then, read the examples in the chart below and on the next page. Fill in the remaining boxes with examples of your own. Try to be creative and use new subjects or situations (unlike me who chose to use one of the same ones as before)!

Feedback you've received → Weigh the value of that feedback.

If it's valuable, use it and thank the person who gave it to you.

If it's NOT valuable, thank the person who gave it to you and seek out more feedback.

How do I respond to feedback I disagree with?

1 Once you've been given feedback and have made sure that you completely understand it, it's time to evaluate whether or not it is beneficial. Most of the time, the feedback we get is an improvement over what we had originally (even if it's not always the most important feedback we really needed). But occasionally, the feedback we get is inaccurate or doesn't actually result in an improvement to our work.

2 If you're sure that this feedback is inaccurate or does not actually improve your work, you can choose to seek feedback from someone else. But it's absolutely vital that you don't make the person who gave you the feedback feel badly about it. So, always thank them for the feedback (like you should do with everyone who gives you feedback) and seek out more feedback from someone else.

Feedback you've just received	Weigh the value of the feedback	What you will SAY	What you will DO
FACE-TO-FACE FEEDBACK: "You might want to use less dialogue, because it sounded more like a play than an argumentative essay."	It WAS valuable feedback, although it could have been worded more kindly.	**FACE-TO-FACE RESPONSE:** "Thank you for reading my essay and for the suggestion. That should really improve my essay!"	Make the changes to my essay and ask a different peer for feedback on the most recent changes.

How do I respond to feedback I disagree with?

Feedback you've just received	Weigh the value of the feedback	What you will SAY	What you will DO
WRITTEN FEEDBACK: "All of the colors you're using are very dark. You might want to consider lightening things up in the sky or down here."	It was NOT valuable feedback because I am trying to create a mood of sadness and dark colors help me do that.	**WRITTEN RESPONSE:** "Thanks for the feedback on my artwork. I'll definitely think about what you suggested."	Ask another peer for feedback, but begin by telling them the mood that I am trying to create.
	It was NOT valuable feedback because...		

INTRODUCTION · PLANNING · METACOGNITION · SYNTHESIS · REFLECTION · SELF-ASSESSMENT · GOAL SETTING · FEEDBACK

bit.ly/3R5zZyS

Maximize learning impact with a feedback log to record, track, and implement the abundance of feedback you receive

7.38

Essential Question

How can I keep track of all the feedback I receive?

Big Idea

In an improvement-focused classroom, everyone gets tons of feedback on their work everyday. It can be nearly impossible to keep track of it all and ensure that all feedback is used whenever it's needed. Keeping a "Feedback Log" will help ensure that all of your accurate feedback has been applied and will continue to be applied in the future.

Lesson Overview

In this lesson, students learn an important strategy for remembering and using feedback in an improvement-focused classroom. It can be challenging to remember all the helpful feedback we receive, but a Feedback Log can help. By jotting down the feedback received and tracking its application, we ensure that every feedback loop is closed. We start by examining a sample log entry and observing how someone recorded and utilized their feedback. Then, students get to practice using the log by entering a fictional piece of feedback for a different scenario. Finally, students enter recent feedback they've received in real life, recording it in the log along with how they've utilized this feedback (or plan to).

Discussion/Reflection Questions

- Why is it important to keep track of the feedback you receive in an improvement-focused classroom?
- How can a Feedback Log help you remember and utilize the feedback you receive?
- What are the benefits of closing the feedback loop by applying the feedback you receive?
- What are some good things about looking back at your previous feedback entries in the Feedback Log? How might this help you become better at what you do?

Teacher Tips

- This lesson pairs well with Lesson 7.39 on Feedback Loops. If you choose to teach these lessons back-to-back, I recommend starting with Lesson 7.39 and finishing with this one (go in reverse order).
- Feedback Logs can be used throughout the year or as long as you feel that your students need to track their feedback. Since they have tremendous value in ensuring a closed feedback loop, it's a valuable use of time for older students who can fill it out in minutes. With younger students, you might want to weigh the costs vs. the benefits.
- The example provided on the first Student Handout is purposely challenging (students younger than fifth grade won't likely understand it). That's done on purpose so they can see how complicated feedback is recorded and utilized on a Feedback Log. An easier example might have left students with questions about what to do with more complicated feedback.

Student Tasks 〉 Transfer Goals

Student Tasks	Transfer Goals
Students learn an important strategy for remembering and using feedback (Feedback Logs).	Students understand the value of the feedback they receive and want to make sure to apply it to new situations over time.
Students enter recent feedback they've received in real life, recording it in the log along with how they've utilized this feedback (or plan to).	Students use their Feedback Logs to refer back to old feedback, track progress and avoid repeating past mistakes.

Instructional Poster(s)

- This lesson has ONE Instructional Poster.
- The Instructional Poster for this lesson teaches students that it can be hard to remember all of the feedback we receive in an improvement-focused classroom. Instead of allowing ourselves to forget valuable feedback, we should jot it down in a Feedback Log and keep track of how we used it. This ensures that the feedback loop is closed (more information on the Feedback Loop in Lesson 7.39).
- The idea of a Feedback Log is not new, but does serve a very important purpose in a classroom that relies on feedback for student growth. Have your students create Feedback Logs any way that you see fit (use these Student Handouts OR have students create a notebook OR...).

Student Handouts

- This lesson has TWO Student Handouts.
- DIRECTIONS: Every time you receive quality feedback, briefly describe it below or on the following page(s). Once you've used the feedback in a productive way, jot it down in the right-side column so you have evidence of your growth through feedback. Draw a line to separate each feedback note so they don't all blend together.
- The first Student Handout teaches students how to properly complete the Feedback Log by looking at an example and then completing one using the example as a guide.
- The second Student Handout can be reproduced as many times as needed for students to log their actual feedback for their records. For this assignment, they are asked to record some of the feedback they've received in real life to show the teacher that they know how to fill out this form.

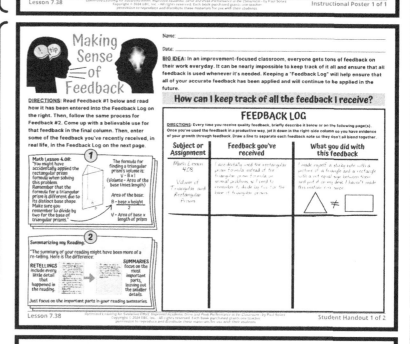

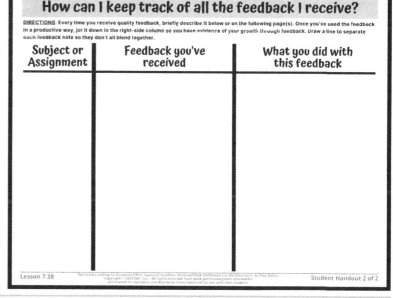

7.39

Ensure that your efforts to seek & interpret feedback translate into meaningful improvement by closing feedback loops

bit.ly/41cMqxr

Essential Question

What does it mean to "close my feedback loop"?

Big Idea

Imagine going through all of the work of asking someone for feedback, interpreting it and asking clarifying question, and then evaluating it only to stop there and never use the feedback on your work or in your life! Well, that's what happens when you forget to close the feedback loop!

Lesson Overview

In this lesson, students learn the importance of applying feedback to their work and future situations to ensure its value is not wasted. It is crucial to "close the feedback loop" by completing all the necessary steps in the feedback process. Next, students analyze open feedback loops and consider the potential negative consequences if those feedback loops remain open. They also answer questions related to different scenarios involving open feedback loops. Finally, students complete a graphic organizer where they explain how they have successfully closed one of their own feedback loops.

Discussion/Reflection Questions

- Think of a time when you did NOT close a feedback loop? How do you think applying the feedback could have helped you?
- Imagine a pretend scenario where you received feedback but didn't apply it immediately. How might this have impacted you in a negative way?
- In your own experience, share an example of how you successfully closed a feedback loop (it doesn't have to be school-related). How did applying the feedback result in positive consequences or results?

Teacher Tips

- This lesson pairs well with Lesson 7.38 on Feedback Loops. If you choose to teach these lessons back-to-back, I recommend starting with this lesson and then finishing with Lesson 7.39 (go in reverse order).
- Steps 6 and 7 of the Feedback Loop can be challenging to "close" within the school setting. These steps involve applying the skills to new situations, often outside the classroom, and continuously monitoring their impact. While completing these steps entirely in school may not be easy, it doesn't mean we should avoid teaching this lesson. Instead, it's important to have a conversation with students about the value of feedback. Emphasize that feedback is most valuable when it can be applied beyond a single assignment. The best feedback helps students succeed long after its initial use and serves as a foundation for developing broader skills.

Student Tasks > Transfer Goals

Student Tasks	Transfer Goals
Students learn the importance of applying feedback to their work and future situations to ensure its value is not wasted.	Students utilize feedback both immediately and as needed in the future. Feedback is not wasted.
Students explain, on a graphic organizer, how they have successfully closed one of their own feedback loops.	Students understand how the seven steps of a Feedback Loop are vital to enjoying the benefits of accurate feedback.

- This lesson has TWO Instructional Posters.
- The Instructional Poster for this lesson teaches students that it's important to APPLY our feedback to our work and future situations.
- The first Instructional Poster teaches this concept to the students and gives two examples of "open feedback loops" that need to be closed.
- The second Instructional Poster explains all of the steps in a Feedback Loop (the students should know the first four steps if they've completed the earlier feedback lessons). Otherwise, we soon forget the feedback we've been given.

Student Handouts

- This lesson has THREE Student Handouts.
- DIRECTIONS: Answer each question below and on the next page. Use the "Feedback Loop" diagram to help you answer each question. Then, be sure to transfer the idea of this lesson to your life and close all of those feedback loops!
- The first Student Handout's Possible Answers: (Question 1) You might not grow as much, Your skills might get rusty, You might miss out on new things, Your creativity might get stuck, You might get discouraged. (Question 2) Doesn't fit with your current needs, You might make unnecessary changes to your work, You might not learn from the feedback, You might not make an informed decision about the feedback, You might miss out on opportunities to really improve your work.
- The second Student Handout's Possible Answers: (Question 1) Steps 3 & 4 - Understand and clarify the feedback, then Evaluate it. (Question 2) Step 1 - Ask for feedback on it. (Question 3) They mean I should go back to step 4 and re-evaluate my feedback. (Question 4) They mean that I should finish the remaining steps in the Feedback Loop.
- The third Student Handout is for students to show evidence of completing one Feedback Loop. This can be used over and over again, as needed.

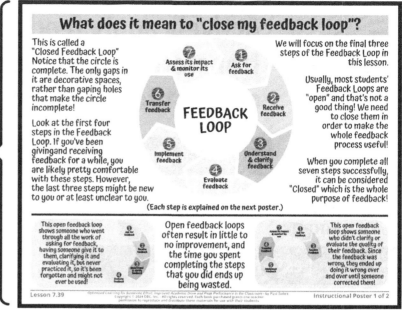

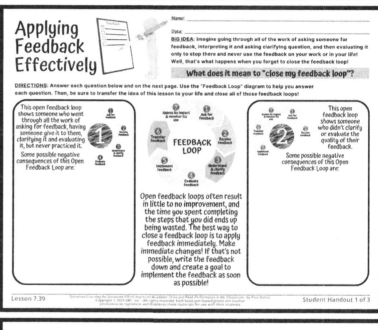

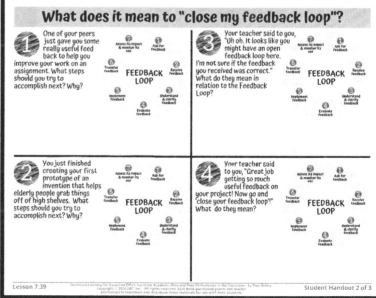

bit.ly/3NfRFH8

Actively apply feedback to your work, transforming it from mere words into a catalyst for continuous improvement

Essential Question

How do I get the most out of the feedback I receive?

Big Idea

Accurate feedback should never be wasted. When we receive accurate feedback, we have a responsibility to apply it to our work. It's not enough to simply acknowledge the feedback; we must actively incorporate it into our process. Failing to apply accurate feedback is like having a solution to a problem right in front of you but choosing to ignore it. The feedback is there to help us and it's our responsibility to embrace that guidance.

Lesson Overview

In this lesson, students develop the crucial skill of applying feedback effectively and permanently. They learn that acting on feedback promptly minimizes the risk of forgetting details or misinterpreting its meaning. This immediacy is vital for ensuring that the feedback translates into lasting change. If old habits resurface, the feedback hasn't achieved its full intended purpose. To solidify their understanding of applying feedback across contexts, students complete a "Feedback-Application" graphic organizer. This activity begins with fictional scenarios and progresses to personal examples, encouraging them to articulate how they've incorporated feedback into new situations as evidence of successful transfer.

Discussion/Reflection Questions

- What are some potential consequences of failing to use accurate feedback? Why is it important to take action on the feedback we receive?
- What are the benefits of acting quickly on feedback and avoiding delays in using it? How does this help us remember the details and understand the feedback better?
- Why is it important for feedback to be remembered and used permanently?
- What should you do if you discover that old habits have returned, despite having been given accurate feedback on it?

Teacher Tips

- The focus of this lesson and the remaining lessons in this unit are on applying the feedback we receive to new situations both in and out of the classroom for the foreseeable future. This doesn't mean that students can improve upon the feedback they've received or even change their mind about the feedback they receive. It just means that accurate feedback is really only valuable if it leads to actual permanent improvement, not temporary adjustments. There are many analogies you can share with your students about how an athlete uses feedback to improve and when he or she reverts back to old ways, a coach would likely need to provide "reminder feedback" (for lack of a better term). But the goal of the feedback that every coach gives their athletes is to use it independently moving forward. An athlete who requires constant feedback to help manage adjustments is not likely to make it very far in their sport.

Student Tasks	Transfer Goals
Students learn that acting on feedback promptly minimizes the risk of forgetting details or misinterpreting its meaning.	Students translate accurate feedback into permanent improvement with minimal misinterpretation.
Students explain how they've applied accurate feedback to new situations as evidence of successful transfer.	Students try hard to transfer all accurate feedback to new situations in order to ensure that feedback leads to permanent improvement.

INTRODUCTION
PLANNING
METACOGNITION
SYNTHESIS
REFLECTION
SELF-ASSESSMENT
GOAL SETTING
FEEDBACK

Instructional Poster(s)

- This lesson has ONE Instructional Poster.
- The Instructional Poster for this lesson starts with a quote that attempts to explain that feedback needs to be used, otherwise it's wasted time, effort and a valuable growth opportunity. Note that it was generated by Artificial Intelligence, as was the image that accompanies it.
- This lesson teaches students to use accurate feedback IMMEDIATELY and PERMANENTLY.
  - The sooner we act on feedback, the less likely we are to forget details or misinterpret its meaning.
  - To truly benefit from feedback, we need to make sure that it lasts. Avoid slipping back into old habits and ensure lasting improvements.

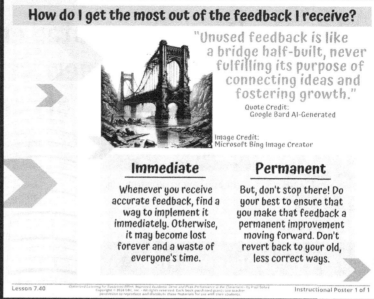

How do I get the most out of the feedback I receive?

"Unused feedback is like a bridge half-built, never fulfilling its purpose of connecting ideas and fostering growth."

Quote Credit:
Google Bard AI-Generated

Image Credit:
Microsoft Bing Image Creator

Immediate

Whenever you receive accurate feedback, find a way to implement it immediately. Otherwise, it may become lost forever and a waste of everyone's time.

Permanent

But, don't stop there! Do your best to ensure that you make that feedback a permanent improvement moving forward. Don't revert back to your old, less correct ways.

Lesson 7.40 — Instructional Poster 1 of 1

Student Handouts

- This lesson has TWO Student Handouts.
- DIRECTIONS: Start by reading through the two examples below. Then, mimic the process on the next page.
- The first Student Handout provides an example that students will need to emulate on the second page. It explains two fictional examples of feedback that they could have received and evidence of how they could have applied their feedback to a new situation.
- The second Student Handout provides students with some information and they need to fill in the rest. The final problem asks students to use feedback that they actually received and describe how they actually applied that feedback to a new situation.

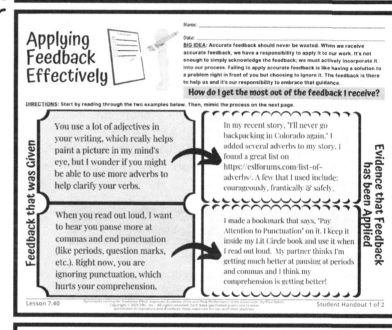

Applying Feedback Effectively

Name: _____
Date: _____

BIG IDEA: Accurate feedback should never be wasted. When we receive accurate feedback, we have a responsibility to apply it to our work. It's not enough to simply acknowledge the feedback; we must actively incorporate it into our process. Failing to apply accurate feedback is like having a solution to a problem right in front of you but choosing to ignore it. The feedback is there to help us and it's our responsibility to embrace that guidance.

How do I get the most out of the feedback I receive?

DIRECTIONS: Start by reading through the two examples below. Then, mimic the process on the next page.

Feedback that was Given:

You use a lot of adjectives in your writing, which really helps paint a picture in my mind's eye, but I wonder if you might be able to use more adverbs to help clarify your verbs.

When you read out loud, I want to hear you pause more at commas and end punctuation (like periods, question marks, etc.). Right now, you are ignoring punctuation, which hurts your comprehension.

Evidence that Feedback has been Applied:

In my recent story, "I'll never go backpacking in Colorado again," I added several adverbs to my story. I found a great list on https://eslforums.com/list-of-adverbs/. A few that I used include: courageously, frantically & safely.

I made a bookmark that says, "Pay Attention to Punctuation" on it. I keep it inside my Lit Circle book and use it when I read out loud. My partner thinks I'm getting much better at pausing at periods and commas and I think my comprehension is getting better!

Lesson 7.40 — Student Handout 1 of 2

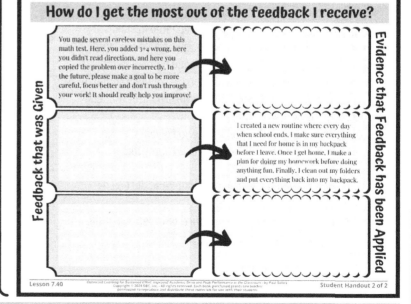

How do I get the most out of the feedback I receive?

Feedback that was Given:

You made several careless mistakes on this math test. Here, you added 3+4 wrong, here you didn't read directions, and here you copied the problem over incorrectly. In the future, please make a goal to be more careful, focus better and don't rush through your work! It should really help you improve!

Evidence that Feedback has been Applied:

I created a new routine where every day when school ends, I make sure everything that I need for home is in my backpack before I leave. Once I get home, I make a plan for doing my homework before doing anything fun. Finally, I clean out my folders and put everything back into my backpack.

Lesson 7.40 — Student Handout 2 of 2

bit.ly/3Re2kD4

Prevent repeated errors by applying feedback to new situations, enhancing the prospects of continuous growth

Essential Question

How do I avoid repeating mistakes?

Big Idea

Do your best to not repeat errors that you've already received feedback on. We know that it can take some time to improve your skills, but the goal should always be to transfer your feedback to any new situations that may apply. When you do repeat an error, create a S.M.A.A.R.T.E.R. Goal to try to prevent it from happening again.

Lesson Overview

In this lesson, students reflect on the importance of preventing repeated mistakes. While acknowledging that mastering complex skills requires multiple learning experiences, the lesson emphasizes addressing careless mistakes and simple errors that students understand but neglect to fix. This helps avoid situations where repeated feedback on the same issue becomes tedious and frustrating for feedback providers. Students learn to identify skills in which they continue to make mistakes despite having received feedback, and are taught to develop actionable S.M.A.A.R.T.E.R. Goals to address them. They do this through fictional examples, because it may take time for students to identify areas for personal improvement.

Discussion/Reflection Questions

- Why is it important to make an effort to avoid repeating errors that you have already received feedback on?
- What is the purpose of creating S.M.A.A.R.T.E.R. Goals when you repeat an error? How can a S.M.A.A.R.T.E.R. Goal help prevent repeated mistakes?
- Why is it important to address careless mistakes and simple errors that you understand but neglect to fix when they seem so minor or insignificant?
- How will you create a S.M.A.A.R.T.E.R. Goal that addresses a repeated mistake? Share how you hope to fix this problem.

Teacher Tips

- While explaining the Instructional Poster:
  - Go over the first Student Handout with your students so you can discuss the information together. This will help them complete the second Student Handout more successfully and more meaningfully.
  - Discuss the importance of your students creating S.M.A.A.R.T.E.R. Goals for their own repeated mistakes. If you don't think that your students will be able to identify a repeated mistake today, skip that page for now. But if you think they will be able to identify one, have them complete the third Student Handout, which is an organizer that goes through these steps:
    - What accurate feedback were you given?
    - How many times did you correctly apply this feedback? Explain each.
    - How did you repeat this mistake? What did you do wrong?
    - What did you do to prevent further repetition of the mistake (I made a S.M.A.A.R.T.E.R. Goal)

Student Tasks ⟩ Transfer Goals

Student Tasks	Transfer Goals
Students reflect on the importance of preventing repeated mistakes.	Students appreciate the importance of avoiding repeated mistakes, especially as it may affect those providing them with feedback.
Students identify skills in which they continue to make mistakes despite feedback, and develop S.M.A.A.R.T.E.R. Goals to address them.	Students use their increased awareness of repeated mistakes to actively address them so they don't require additional feedback over time.

INTRODUCTION

PLANNING

METACOGNITION

SYNTHESIS

REFLECTION

SELF-ASSESSMENT

GOAL SETTING

FEEDBACK

Instructional Poster(s)

- This lesson has ONE Instructional Poster.
- The Instructional Poster for this lesson focuses on the importance of not repeating your mistakes. While this instructional poster emphasizes the importance of learning from mistakes, it doesn't imply that students should grasp everything immediately. Multiple learning opportunities are still encouraged, especially for challenging skills. The focus is on avoiding careless mistakes and simple errors that students understand how to fix but may neglect if they seem unimportant.
- Another key aspect is recognizing that everyone struggles with certain concepts or skills. Students should internally acknowledge these struggles and actively work around them to minimize their impact. This might involve using readily available tools, like Spell Check for spelling challenges or ChatGPT for converting passive voice to active voice. By acknowledging and proactively addressing their weaknesses, students can effectively compensate for them.

Student Handouts

- This lesson has THREE Student Handouts.
- DIRECTIONS: Read Scenarios #1 and #2 and the sentences below each. Notice how they each lead to creating S.M.A.A.R.T.E.R. Goals? On the next page, read through the scenarios and complete the empty boxes with possible examples.
- The Student Handouts for this lesson helps students understand that whenever mistakes are repeated, they should create a S.M.A.A.R.T.E.R. Goal (or a Goal Burst if it's a quick fix) to address them, so they don't persistently recur in the future. This further strengthens the recursive process of "Student-Led Self-Improvement."

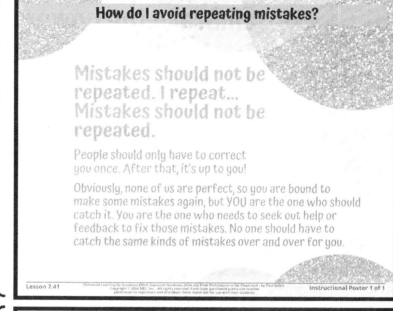

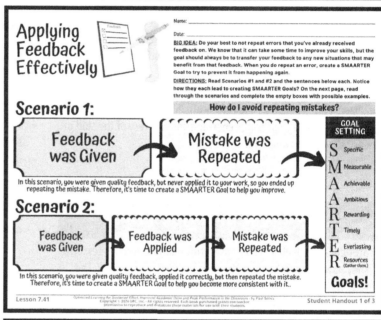

bit.ly/47HnzV9

Embrace the power of cumulative feedback by synthesizing insights from all feedback sources to drive improvement

Essential Question

How do I synthesize my feedback effectively?

Big Idea

New feedback needs to build on old feedback. Be sure to combine feedback from your self-assessments, reflections, observations, and feedback from your peers, teachers and others to synthesize the information. Then, use it to demonstrate new understanding (and hopefully permanent growth).

Lesson Overview

In this lesson, students explore the significance of merging accurate feedback received on a specific topic with their existing knowledge to develop a deeper understanding of the skill or subject under review. They are reminded to recognize that feedback can come in various forms and should consider information learned from diverse sources. To reinforce this concept, students engage in an activity where they complete a "Synthesizing Feedback" graphic organizer, showcasing how they integrate different feedback sources to enhance their comprehension and mastery of the skill or concept they aim to improve.

Discussion/Reflection Questions

- Why is it important to synthesize all of the different sources of feedback you've received? Why not just consider the most recent one or the easiest one to follow?
- What are the benefits of gathering feedback from multiple sources? What are the drawbacks?
- Describe the importance of self-assessment and reflection as valuable sources of feedback. How can these two skills help you improve your understanding of a skill or understanding?
- How does the skill of synthesizing feedback help you continuously improve and demonstrate new understanding?

Teacher Tips

- Students will likely have an easier time completing this lesson if they have already learned about the skill of synthesizing. The lessons in Unit 3 focus on this skill.
- The example used on the first Student Handout is not an academic example. You may wish to offer some educational examples for students to consider before completing their Student Handouts.
- Remember - Here are several excellent sources of feedback that students don't always consider: Teachers, Parents, Peers, Coaches, Mentors, Experts, Dictionaries, YouTube videos, Podcasts, Online tutorials, Online forums, Self-assessments, Reflections, Checklists, Rubrics, Grades, Answer keys, Role-playing, Hands-on activities, Artificial Intelligence, Assessment tools, Automated feedback from tech tools, Personal experiences, Trial-and-error results, Feedback from emotions & feelings, Surveys, Questionnaires, Report cards, Experiments, Simulations, etc.

Student Tasks 〉 Transfer Goals

Student Tasks	Transfer Goals
Students synthesize multiple alternative and traditional sources of feedback to enhance their comprehension and mastery of a skill or concept.	Students' increased awareness of alternative sources of feedback provides numerous additional opportunities to learn and grow.
Students merge accurate feedback with their existing knowledge of a skill or subject to develop a stronger and deeper understanding.	Students synthesize the countless sources of feedback that are all around them to facilitate a deeper understanding of skills and topics.

Instructional Poster(s)

- This lesson has ONE Instructional Poster.
- The Instructional Poster for this lesson ties Synthesis and Feedback together. Students are taught that they need to combine all of the accurate feedback that they receive with all of the accurate prior knowledge that they have to create a new, deeper understanding of the skill or subject that is the focus of their feedback. They are reminded that feedback is not always something someone tells you or writes to you, but that it's important to consider all information passed on to you in different ways.
- During your discussion, describe this process of synthesizing what they already know with what they are being "told" through feedback.

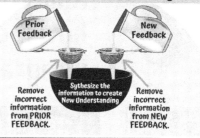

How do I synthesize my feedback effectively?

New feedback needs to build on old feedback. Be sure to combine feedback from your self-assessments, reflections, observations, and feedback from your peers, teachers and others to synthesize the information. Then, use it to demonstrate new understanding (and hopefully permanent growth).

Prior Feedback → New Feedback → Synthesize the information to create New Understanding

Remove incorrect information from PRIOR FEEDBACK.

Remove incorrect information from NEW FEEDBACK.

Feedback comes in all shapes and sizes, from unexpected sources, and at unimagined times.

Feedback helps you make improvements in everything you do. Feedback lets you know when you messed up and when you were successful.

When we take time to combine old feedback with new feedback, we SYNTHESIZE our learning and end up doing the best job we know how to do.

Feedback is not always face to face with a teacher or a peer. It's not always written down on a piece of paper.

Feedback isn't just for improving your schoolwork or musical abilities. It's not always to become a better athlete or friend.

Student Handouts

- This lesson has TWO Student Handouts.
- DIRECTIONS: Read through the four sources of feedback you received on your pancake-making ability below. Try to put them together in order to create a deeper understanding of pancake-making, and then read an example of what your synthesis could sound like in the middle of the page. Repeat this process with your own example of something you've received feedback on In multiple ways on the next page.
- The first Student Handout shows an example of how students can combine feedback from multiple sources with their prior knowledge in order to synthesize it all and create a new, stronger understanding.
- The second Student Handout asks students to mimic the process shown on the first handout by using a topic of their own choosing (doesn't have to be educational) to demonstrate their ability to synthesize feedback.

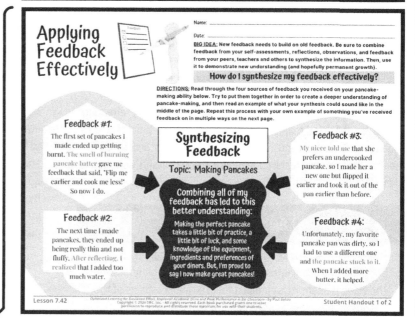

Applying Feedback Effectively

Name: _____
Date: _____

BIG IDEA: New feedback needs to build on old feedback. Be sure to combine feedback from your self-assessments, reflections, observations, and feedback from your peers, teachers and others to synthesize the information. Then, use it to demonstrate new understanding (and hopefully permanent growth).

How do I synthesize my feedback effectively?

DIRECTIONS: Read through the four sources of feedback you received on your pancake-making ability below. Try to put them together in order to create a deeper understanding of pancake-making, and then read an example of what your synthesis could sound like in the middle of the page. Repeat this process with your own example of something you've received feedback on in multiple ways on the next page.

Synthesizing Feedback
Topic: Making Pancakes

Feedback #1:
The first set of pancakes I made ended up getting burnt. The smell of burning pancake batter gave me feedback that said, "Flip me earlier and cook me less!" So now I do.

Feedback #2:
The next time I made pancakes, they ended up being really thin and not fluffy. After reflecting, I realized that I added too much water.

Feedback #3:
My niece told me that she prefers an undercooked pancake, so I made her a new one but flipped it earlier and took it out of the pan earlier than before.

Feedback #4:
Unfortunately, my favorite pancake pan was dirty, so I had to use a different one and the pancake stuck to it. When I added more butter, it helped.

Combining all of my feedback has led to this better understanding:
Making the perfect pancake takes a little bit of practice, a little bit of luck, and some knowledge of the equipment, ingredients and preferences of your diners. But, I'm proud to say I now make great pancakes!

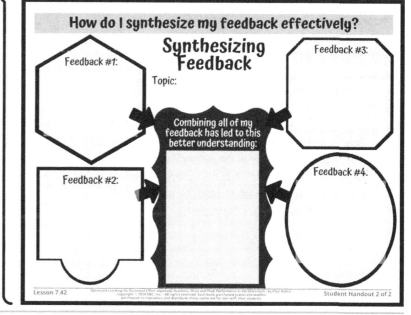

How do I synthesize my feedback effectively?

Synthesizing Feedback
Topic:

Feedback #1:

Feedback #2:

Feedback #3:

Feedback #4:

Combining all of my feedback has led to this better understanding:

bit.ly/4a6vSv8

Analyze the feedback you receive, reflect on how it can benefit you & purposely integrate it into your work and new contexts

7.43

bit.ly/4a6vSv8

Essential Question

How much can I grow if I seek out follow-up feedback?

Lesson Overview

In this lesson, students watch a video called "Austin's Butterfly" to witness the power of feedback, growth mindset, observing like a scientist and perseverance on enhancing students' skills (drawing a butterfly, in this example). Students then analyze how the details from the video are explained on the organizer they will complete later in the lesson. This organizer focuses on (1) identifying the problem, (2) documenting multiple sources or follow-ups of feedback, (3) evidence of their current skill level, and (4) reflecting on how feedback led to improvement. Additionally, students engage in a brainstorming activity, recalling four instances from their past where they received feedback and successfully applied it to make improvements.

Teacher Tips

- This lesson starts by showing the class a video called, "Austin's Butterfly." (It's 6 minutes long.) Here is the link: bit.ly/3uPJHOQ
- The video is a fantastic culmination of so many aspects of the lessons in this book. It shows how students as young as kindergarten can give their peers meaningful, actionable, accurate feedback with empathy and kindness. It talks about perseverance and creating multiple drafts to improve skills incrementally. But the main focus for this lesson is on how a first grade student named Austin, incorporated feedback to improve his drawing of a butterfly exponentially over a short period of time.
- The end of the video comes fast, so I would add the following:
  - Don't let perfectionism overshadow improvements.
  - Although the final color of the picture did not look the same as the original, Austin could have revised his colors further if it was important. Instead, the focus was on improving the drawing of the butterfly.

Big Idea

Receiving feedback and putting it into action can lead to growth and improvement. But have you ever thought about how much more you could improve by applying feedback to your work and then seeking MORE feedback? Each additional follow-up has the potential to exponentially boost your skills, especially if you get feedback from someone who is highly skilled and can provide advanced guidance!

Discussion/Reflection Questions

- Describe how the video, "Austin's Butterfly," exemplifies the power of feedback. What feedback tips did it provide?
- How can you apply the lessons learned from the video to your own skill development? What can you take away from this video to help improve your own skills (not related to drawing butterflies)?
- Why is it important to seek out feedback incrementally (step--by-step) over time? What are some risks of getting too much feedback all at once? What might happen if you only get one piece of feedback and stop there?

Student Tasks 〉 Transfer Goals

Student Tasks	Transfer Goals
Students watch a video called "Austin's Butterfly" to witness the power of "follow-up feedback" on enhancing students' skills.	Students don't stop after receiving feedback once for an important task. They make adjustments and then seek out more feedback.
Students complete an organizer that shows how multiple feedback follow-ups led to dramatic improvement of a skill.	Students appreciate how their skills improve at a greater pace and to a higher degree when feedback is followed up with additional feedback.

Instructional Poster(s)

- This lesson has ONE Instructional Poster.
- The Instructional Poster for this lesson teaches students to notice how they use feedback in their work and through reflection, describe how that feedback helped them improve a skill or understanding.
- The example provided comes from a great video called "Austin's Butterfly." It shows how time and feedback combine to work wonders on students' ability to improve a skill. Whether you show the video or not, it has been used to complete the graphic organizer on this lesson's Instructional Poster. Students will need to know how to do this for a feedback example of their own on the Student Handouts.

Student Handouts

- This lesson has TWO Student Handouts.
- DIRECTIONS: Think about a skill you recently improved or assignment you recently completed where you received multiple bits of feedback to help you grow. Explain the feedback on the left and how you used that feedback to improve on the right. Each "evidence of improvement" might focus on a different aspect of that assignment or skill OR it might focus on one specific aspect of that assignment or skill that got better and better!
- Some students may benefit from viewing a whole-class example.
- DIRECTIONS: Use the SYNTHESIZING Process below to show how you used multiple bits of feedback to improve a skill or assignment. Remember: there are many sources of feedback (e.g. tests, coaches, facial expressions...). Feedback doesn't have to come from someone helping you directly! Make sure that your evidence supports your explanation of improvement at the bottom of the page.

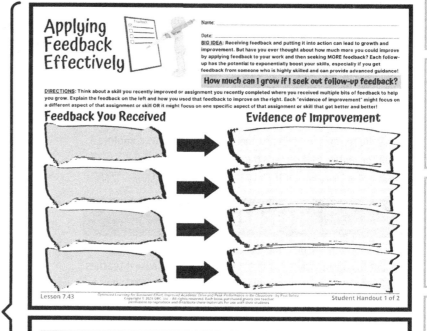

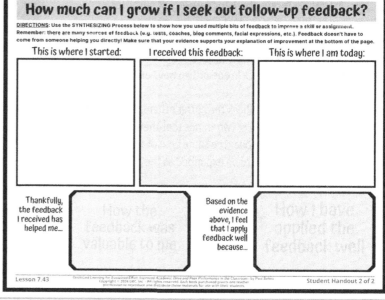

bit.ly/3GxbzcM

Explore novel reasons for seeking feedback, practice giving feedback with kindness, and document feedback interactions

Essential Question

What feedback did I use?
What did I give?

Lesson Overview

In this lesson, students discuss some of the reasons why someone in class might ask their peers for feedback. Students already know most of the typical reasons, but consider additional reasons to ask for feedback in order to increase their desire to seek out feedback from others. Students also learn the difference between meddling in other people's business and offering feedback that helps their peers grow. When students are young, they often want to "catch" their peers doing things wrong both to make themselves look good and to make their peers look bad - this is obviously unkind. They learn valid reasons for helping others. Finally, students complete a graphic organizer that records the details of each feedback interaction with a peer for their Learning Cycle packet.

Teacher Tips

- Although this lesson is the last lesson in the book, you might want to consider teaching it early in the year, because it teaches a few foundational microskills that are needed all year long:
  - Keep track of the feedback you receive from others in order to ensure it gets transferred to new situations.
  - Ask others for feedback for a variety of purposes.
  - Give KIND feedback that helps your peers grow.
- Encourage students to mix up the reasons why they asked for feedback from others so no one gets into a rut. Some students only think about feedback in one or two ways and can't seem to see it more broadly.
- Do the same for the feedback they offer others. Most young students will choose one or two things that they are confident with, and will give every peer the same type of feedback. This is okay to begin but needs to be expanded as they strengthen their feedback skills.

Big Idea

Getting into the habit of asking others for feedback every time you work on something that is new to you is a good idea. Feedback will help ensure that you are understanding things correctly and can help clear up any misunderstandings. In addition, you should offer feedback to others in an attempt to help them in the same way that others help you!

Discussion/Reflection Questions

- Describe how the video, "Austin's Butterfly," exemplifies the power of feedback. What feedback tips did it provide?
- How can you apply the lessons learned from the video to your own skill development? What can you take away from this video to help improve your own skills (not related to drawing butterflies)?
- Why is it important to seek out feedback incrementally (step--by-step) over time? What are some risks of getting too much feedback all at once? What might happen if you only get one piece of feedback and stop there?

Student Tasks ⟩ Transfer Goals

Student Tasks	Transfer Goals
Students learn new reasons why students might ask each other for feedback.	Students gain a stronger understanding of the situations they can receive feedback from others to improve their work.
Students record the feedback they received and gave to others in order to be accountable and ensure transfer.	Students collect feedback experiences and make efforts to transfer the feedback they received to new situations.

Instructional Poster(s)

- This lesson has ONE Instructional Poster.
- The Instructional Poster for this lesson focuses on the reasons why someone might ask for feedback and the difference between meddling in other people's business and offering feedback that helps their peers grow.
- In addition to those listed on the Instructional Poster, some other reasons why students may ask each other for feedback include:
  - Gain a fresh perspective on their work.
  - Ensure clarity and understandability of their work.
  - Enhance the overall quality of their work.
  - Receive suggestions for alternative approaches or solutions.
  - Identify any errors or mistakes that might have been overlooked.
  - Exchange knowledge and expertise in specific subject areas.
  - Gain insights into different perspectives and viewpoints.
  - Evaluate strengths and weaknesses in their work.
  - Identify gaps in their understanding.

Student Handouts

- This lesson has THREE Student Handouts.
- DIRECTIONS: Read through the guidelines on this page in order to complete the next page correctly.
- Use Student Handout 1 to teach students how to complete Student Handout 2 correctly. If you'd like to, share Student Handout 3 with your students - it's an exemplar.
- Student Handout 2 is the final page in the standard Learning Cycle Packet, so students will be completing this graphic organizer quite often.

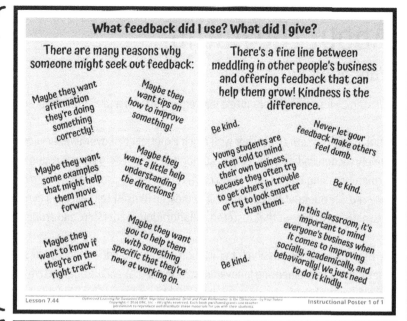

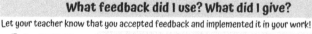

About the Author
Paul Solarz

Written by ChatGPT (after quite a few regenerations) and a few details added:

Paul Solarz is a retired teacher with a rich experience of over twenty years in education. He is widely recognized as an esteemed author and a pioneer in transforming classrooms through his groundbreaking book, *Learn Like a PIRATE: Empowering your students to collaborate, lead, and succeed.* Throughout his career, Paul dedicated himself to creating a dynamic and engaging learning environment that fostered collaboration, leadership, and student empowerment.

With an unwavering passion for education and a deep understanding of student needs, Paul revolutionized traditional teaching methods by implementing innovative strategies that encouraged active participation and critical thinking. He recognized the significance of student autonomy and sought to empower his students to take ownership of their learning journeys.

Paul's book, *Learn Like a PIRATE,* quickly became a renowned resource for educators seeking to transform their classrooms into vibrant, student-centered communities. In the book, he shared practical techniques and strategies for implementing a student-led learning approach that emphasized collaboration, inquiry-based learning, and creativity. Through concepts such as Peer Collaboration, Improvement-Focused Learning, Student Responsibility, Active Learning, Twenty-First-Century Skills, and Empowerment, Paul provided teachers with a roadmap to inspire and motivate their students.

Throughout his teaching career, Paul embraced the principles of student agency, creating a classroom environment where students felt valued, respected, and empowered. He encouraged them to set goals, take risks, and develop their leadership skills. By fostering a culture of collaboration and shared responsibility, he nurtured a sense of community and teamwork among his students.

Paul has garnered widespread recognition and celebration for his unwavering commitment to excellence in education. His innovative teaching practices were acknowledged in 2014 when he received the esteemed Illinois Teacher of the Year award from the Illinois Digital Educators Alliance. The following year, Paul's dedication to teaching earned him a place as a Top 50 Global Teacher Prize finalist, a distinction often likened to the Nobel Prize of Teaching, granted by the Varkey GEMS Institute in Dubai, UAE. In 2017, he was honored as a Top 50 Qudwa Fellow at the Qudwa Teaching for Tomorrow Conference in Abu Dhabi, UAE, in acknowledgment of his exceptional contributions to the field of education. Further confirming his commitment to educational excellence, Paul was bestowed with the prestigious Teacher of Excellence award by the Van Andel Institute of Education in 2020.

Even after his retirement from teaching, Paul continues to make a lasting impact on the field of education. He actively shares his knowledge and experiences through workshops, presentations, social media, and professional development sessions, inspiring educators worldwide to transform their teaching practices by embracing student-centered approaches. His book, *Learn Like a PIRATE,* remains a valuable resource for educators seeking to create dynamic and engaging classrooms that empower students to become active participants in their own education. His legacy as an innovative educator and advocate for student empowerment continues to inspire and shape the future of education.

When not spending time with his family, Paul can be found exploring his ancestry and genetics, embarking on daily walks where he enjoys identifying mushrooms and other wonders of nature, and enthusiastically cheering on his favorite Chicago sports teams.

Contact & Connect:
- E-mail: OptimizedLearningBook@gmail.com
- Twitter (X): @PaulSolarz
- Facebook: @solarzpaul
- Instagram: @psolarz
- Threads: @psolarz
- Snapchat: @paulhere138
- Bluesky: @paulsolarz
- Mastodon: @paulsolarz
- Ancestry.com & MyHeritage.com

58000467R00247